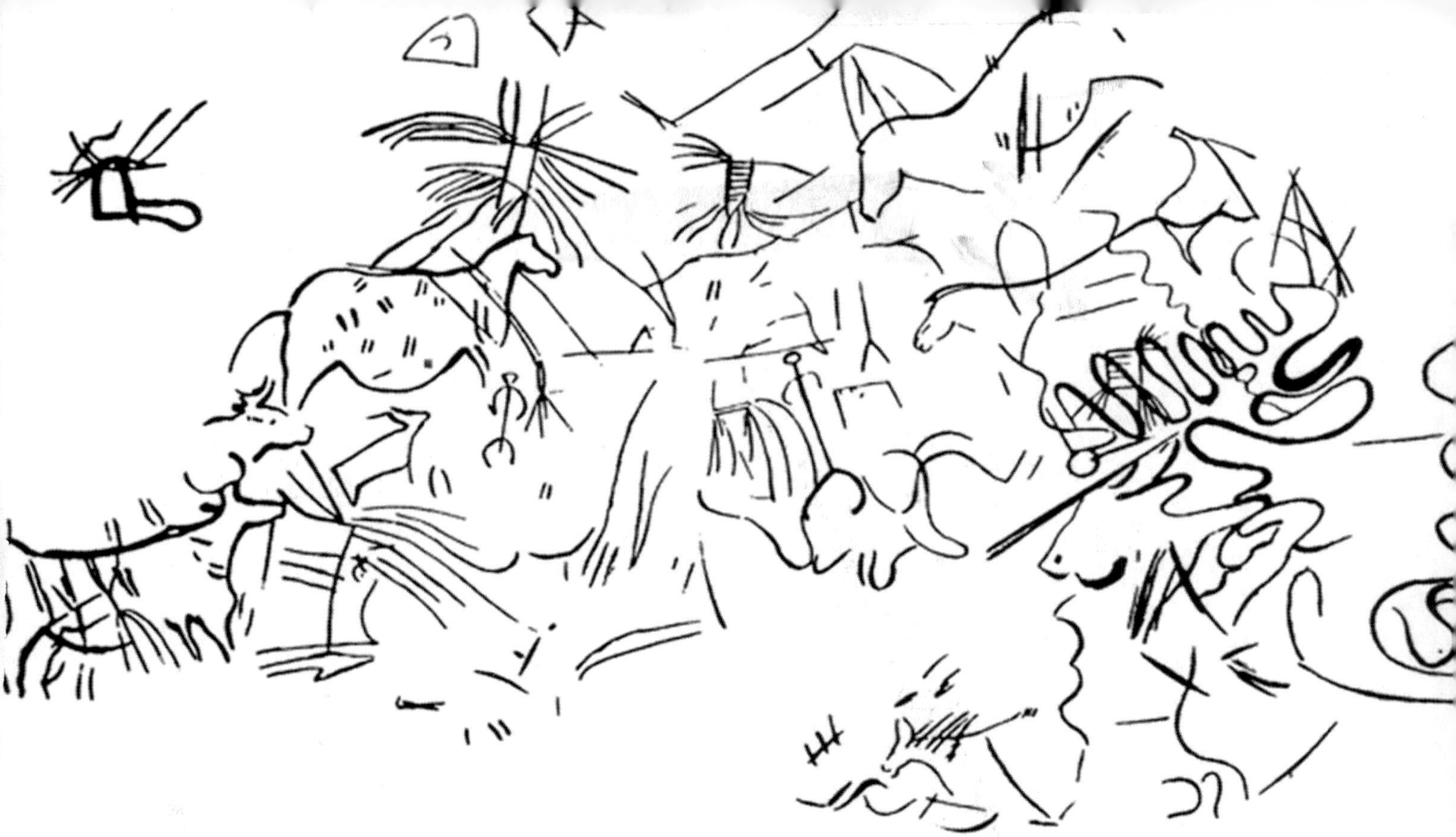

Rock Art Studies

I

Concept, Methodology, Context,
Documentation and Conservation

IGNCA Rock Art Series – 10

Rock Art Studies

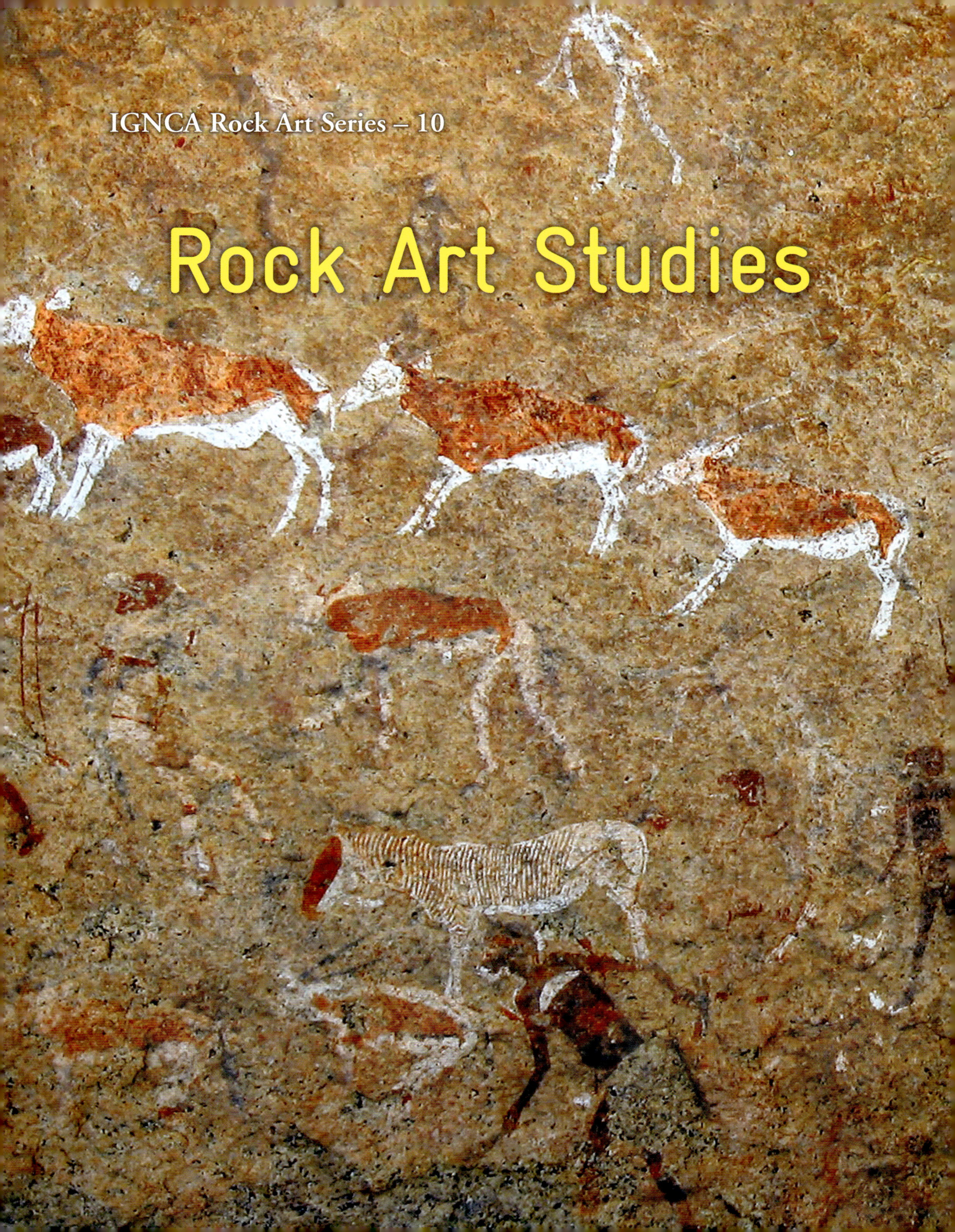

I

Concept, Methodology, Context, Documentation and Conservation

Edited by

Bansi Lal Malla

Indira Gandhi National Centre for the Arts
New Delhi

Aryan Books International
New Delhi

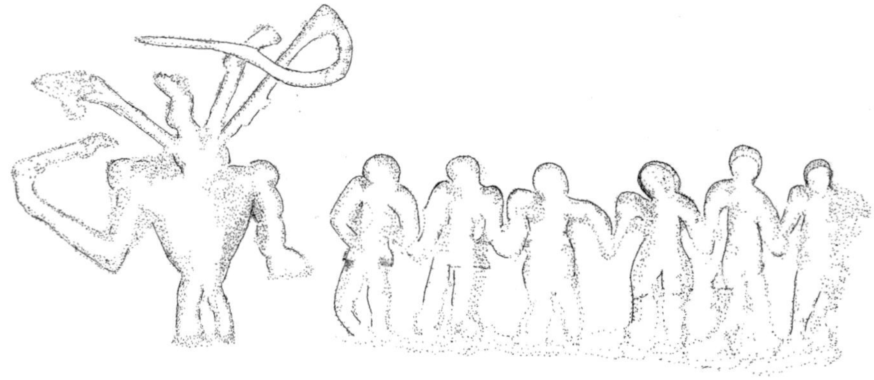

ROCK ART STUDIES-I
Concept, Methodology, Context, Documentation and Conservation

ISBN: 978-81-7305-491-4 (Vol. I)
978-81-7305-493-8 (Set)

First Published in **2014** by:

Indira Gandhi National Centre for the Arts
Central Vista Mess, Janpath, New Delhi - 110 001 (India)

and

Aryan Books International
Pooja Apartments, 4B, Ansari Road, New Delhi-110 002 (India)
Tel.: 23287589, 23255799; Fax: 91-11-23270385
E-mail: aryanbooks@gmail.com
www.aryanbooks.co.in

Designed and Printed by
ABI Prints & Publishing Co., New Delhi.

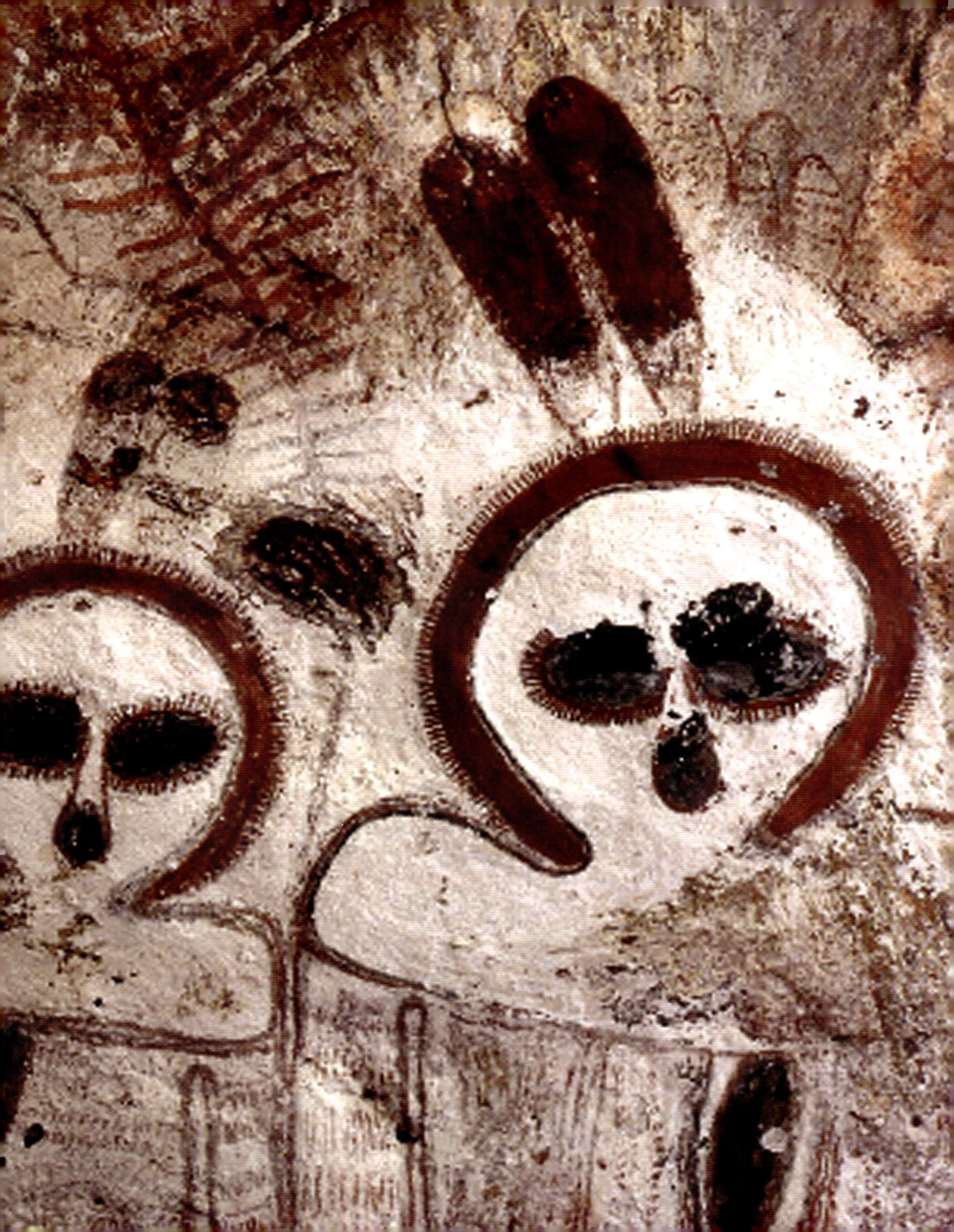

Foreword

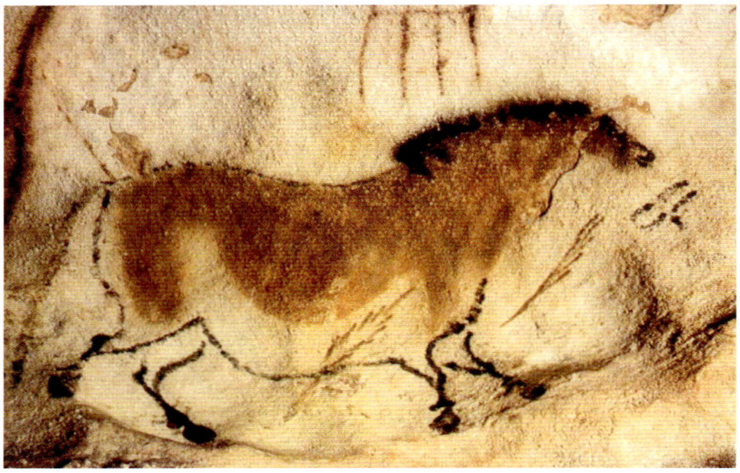

Human creativity is as ancient as human history itself. The first stirrings of our inherent inventiveness perhaps manifested itself through the form of rock art. As the written word had not yet been conceived, the urge to articulate, document and preserve ideas and events found expression through pictorial representation.

To celebrate what is undeniably one of the earliest forms of art, the Indira Gandhi National Centre for the Arts (IGNCA) organised an International Conference on Rock Art, comprising of special lectures, artists workshops and exhibitions. This global event, with the participation of renowned scholars from all over the world was held at New Delhi from 6th December, 2012 to 23rd January, 2013. The event attracted immense professional interest and was academically very rewarding. We are happy and proud that IGNCA is one of the few institutions in India to have undertaken substantial and significant interdisciplinary documentation and research studies in the field of rock art.

It is also a matter of great satisfaction and a happy coincidence that the International Conference on Rock Art marked the beginning of the year-long Silver Jubilee celebrations of IGNCA and would conclude with the release of this compilation of the conference proceedings in two volumes titled *Rock Art Studies*. These comprehensive and beautifully illustrated volumes will be the 10th and 11th publications under the rock art series. *Rock Art Studies, Volume–I* covers subjects relating to the content, context, methodology, conservation and management of rock art. *Rock Art Studies, Volume–II* is mainly based upon the most important aspect of rock art studies, i.e. the interpretation of rock art. I am confident that the present volumes would go a long way in enriching the knowledge of rock art and generating better understanding of this subject, apart from advocating it as a subject of interdisciplinary research.

I congratulate Dr. Bansi Lal Malla, the editor and his team of young scholars for their commendable efforts in bringing out these two volumes. I trust that these publications will achieve the objective of enhancing and promoting rock art studies at national and international levels.

(Dipali Khanna)
Member Secretary, IGNCA

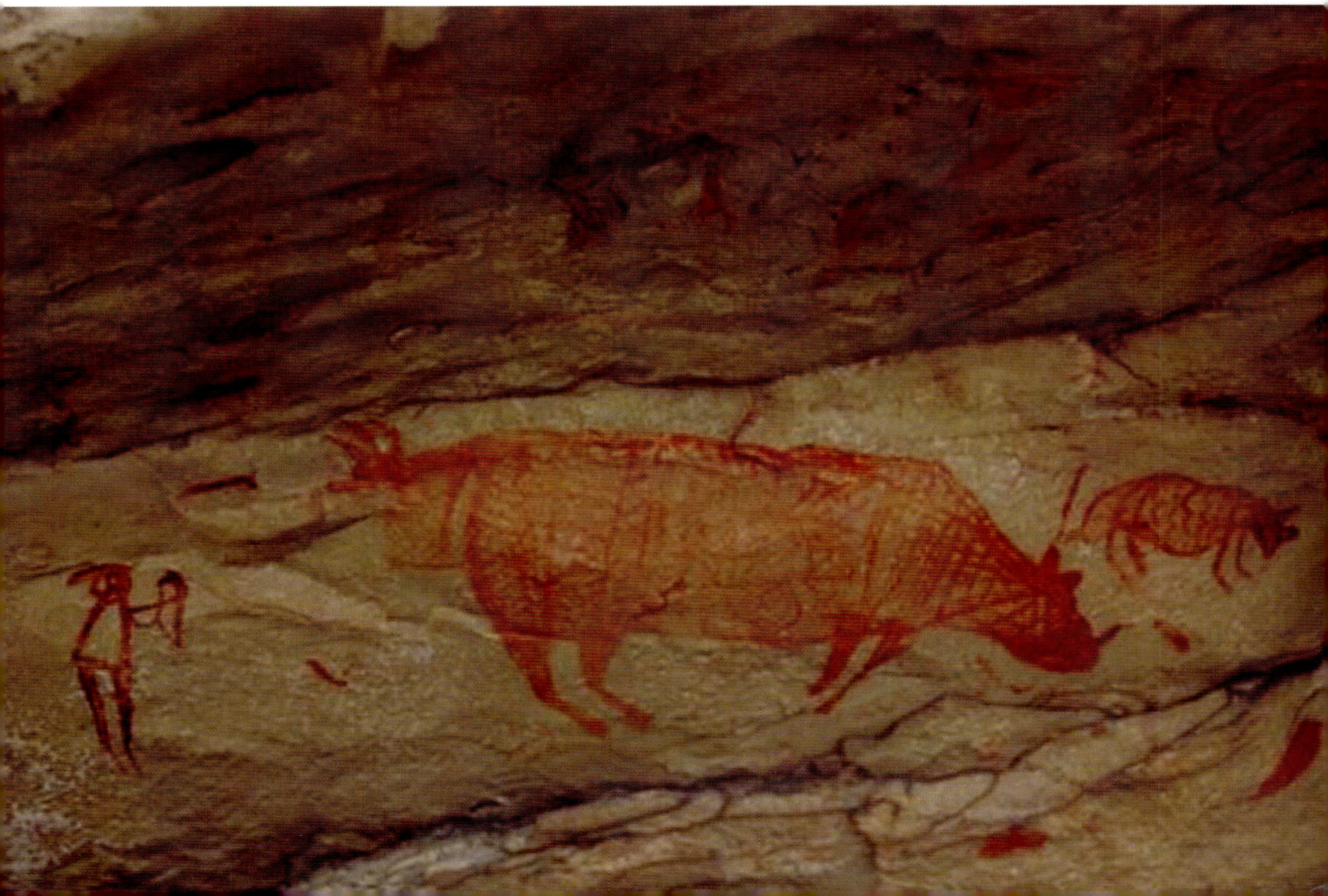

Contents

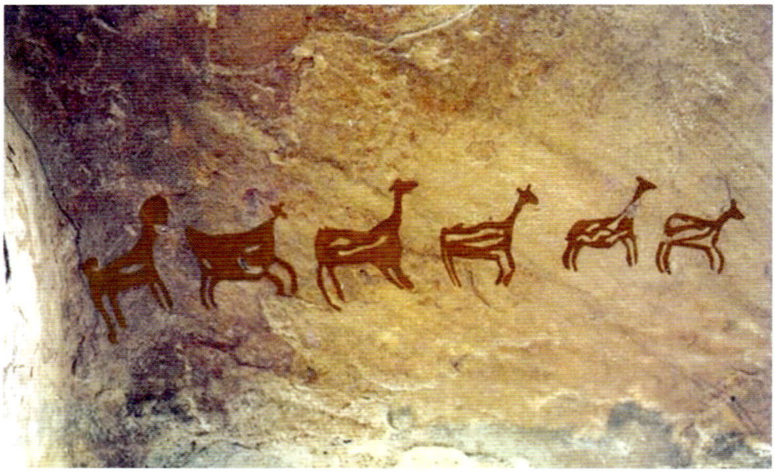

Acknowledgements

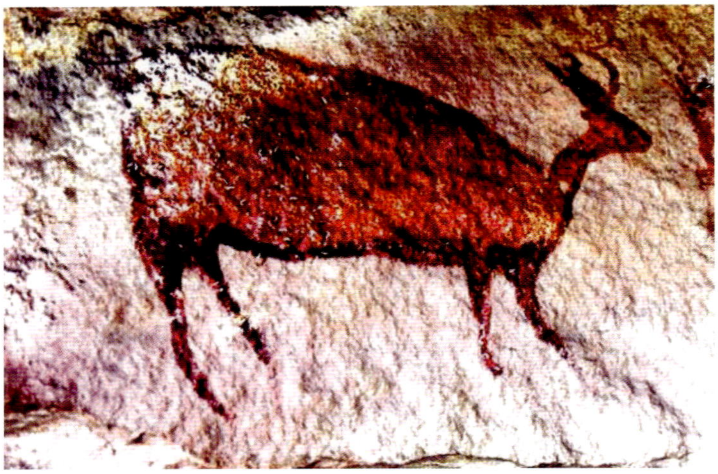

At the outset, I would like to take this opportunity to thank all those members of the Indira Gandhi National Centre for the Arts (IGNCA) family who made the international event on Rock Art (6th December, 2012- 23rd January, 2013) a grand success. All the members of the Rock Art Unit and Event Advisory Committee deserve a special mention for their contributions in making different components of this international event i.e. conference, exhibition, workshop, special lectures and field trip most-rewarding and professionally produced. As a proud privilege, we take this opportunity to put on record our sense of appreciation and gratitude towards Dr. (Mrs.) Kapila Vatsyayan, Member, IGNCA Trust, without whose guidance and encouragement, it may have been impossible to produce such an academically rewarding conference. The proceedings of this conference have been brought out in two beautifully illustrated volumes.

We are grateful to Shri Chinmaya R. Gharekhan, President, IGNCA Trust, who always encourages IGNCA scholars for bringing out publications. Mrs. Dipali Khanna, Member Secretary and Shri V.B. Pyarelal, Former Joint Secretary deserves our special gratitude for their guidance, co-operation and encouragements. The present publications could see the light of the day within record time because only of the great interest taken by our Member Secretary. Our thanks are also due to Dr. Jayanta Kumar Ray, Director (Adm.), Shri S.C. Gahlaut, FA & CAO, Shri Jayanta Chatterjee, Dy. FA & Sr. AO and Dr. A. Kaul, Chief Editor for their support in bringing out these publications.

In the different stages of its publication—right from compilation to proof reading—the scholars of the Rock Art Unit, Dr. Jyoti Tokas, Dr. Ranbeer Singh, Ms. Shalini Tripathi and Shri Rahas Mohenty contributed in one way or other. The dedication and hardwork of Dr. Jyoti Tokas, in particular, deserves special mention and appreciation.

I am also indebted to the contributors of this volume, distinguished scholars who chaired various sessions and to the participants for the lively and meaningful exchange of thoughts.

Finally, I owe my sincere thanks to Shri Vikas Arya, the quality conscious publisher, for gladly undertaking the publication work and for bringing out these volumes within a short time.

Editor

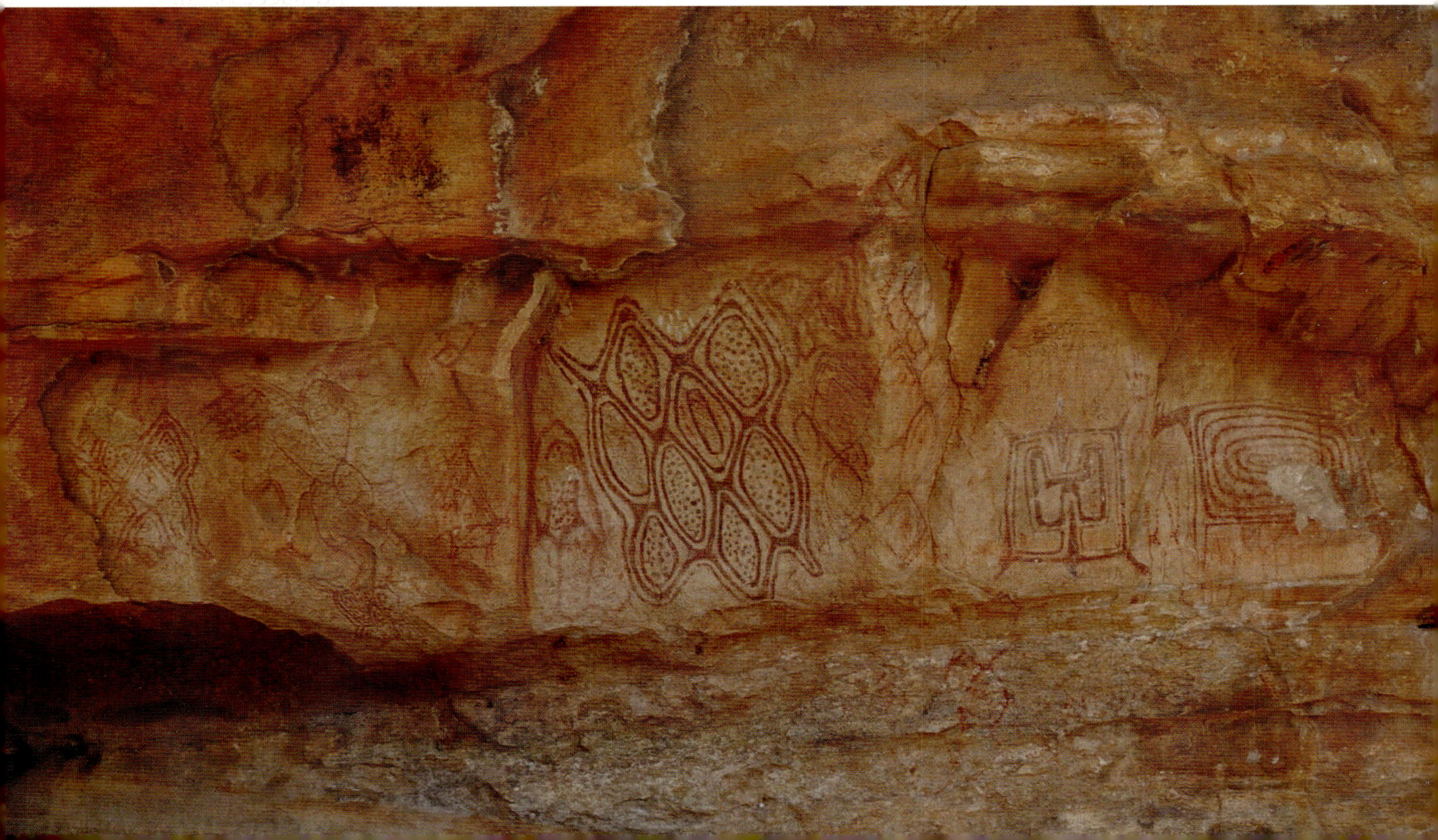

List of Illustrations

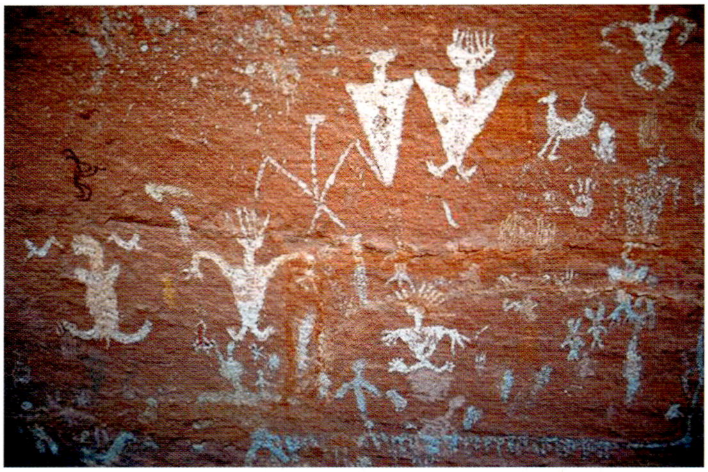

MAPS

FIGURES

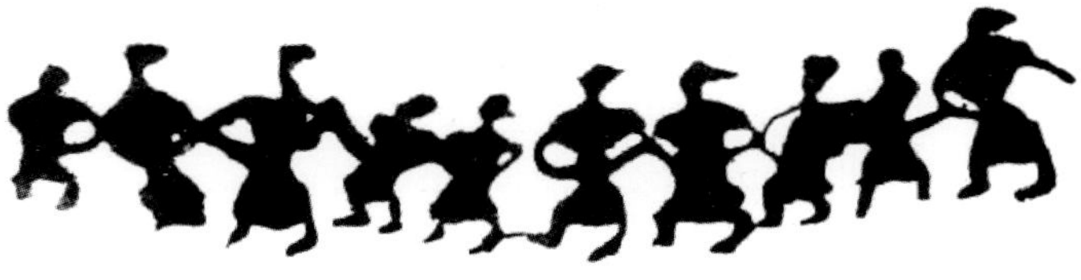

Introduction

Bansi Lal Malla

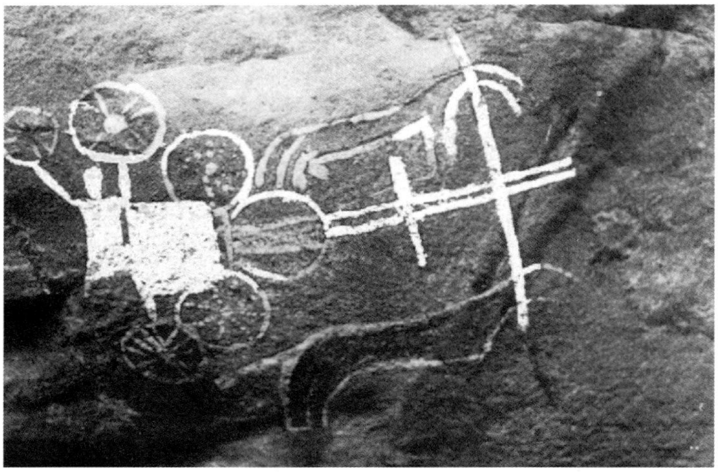

The present volumes—*Rock Art Studies, Volumes I & II*—are outcome of the International Conference on Rock Art held under the auspices of the Indira Gandhi National Centre for the Arts (IGNCA), New Delhi from 6–13 December 2012. IGNCA's year-long silver jubilee celebrations began with this event. It coincided with an impressive and well received rock art exhibition (6 December 2012 to 23 January 2013) and an exhibition of rock art books (6-12 December 2012), special lectures (7–11 December 2012) by renowned international scholars, artists' workshops (6–12 December 2012), and a field trip (12–13 December 2012) to the Bundi rock art site. These events highlighted the importance of rock art in archaeological, ethnological, and lifestyle studies. The event was inaugurated by the Hon'ble Vice President of India, Professor M. Hamid Ansari on 6 December 2012. Internationally renowned scholar Dr. (Mrs.) Kapila Vatsyayan, Founder Trustee, IGNCA gave a talk on 'Rock Art Studies: IGNCA's Experience' on the occasion, which set the foundation for further deliberations. Another reputed scholar, Professor Robert G. Bednarik gave an overview on 'The World of Rock Art'. Shri Chinmaya R. Gharekhan, President, the IGNCA Trust chaired the session. Many dignitaries like ambassadors, renowned scholars, and heads of institutes graced the occasion. Around 75 experts on rock art from all over the world participated in the conference and shared their experiences and researches on rock art. It was a well conceived and fruitful event, the second of its kind organized by IGNCA. The first Global Rock Art Conference was organized by IGNCA in 1993. These events have left an indelible impression on the minds of the participants, both for the quantity and quality of the exchanges and debates, and for the beauty of the various ceremonies and displays.

The present event, according to Professor Robert G. Bednarik, Founding Convener and Editor of the International Federation of Rock Art Organizations (IFRAO), "has added to the achievements of the IGNCA in the sphere of rock art promotion, which were already considerable, and it is self-evident that this creates the conditions under which rock art protection is most likely to flourish". Another internationally reputed scholar, Professor Lawrence Loendrof said that "from the inaugural function to the valedictory session, the conference was the best organized and managed international rock art event I have ever attended. All in all, it was a most-rewarding and professionally produced conference".

Some of the important recommendations made at the end of the conference include: (a) that all states should take active action in promoting rock art research and education at all levels; (b) research outcomes of rock art studies must be a tool for promoting cultural education and policy; (c) while carrying out research and documentation on rock art, ethics of documentation, magnitude and significance of the site, its sanctity, and the values, customs, and beliefs of the surrounding communities associated with the site should be taken into consideration; (d) standard guidelines and methodologies to carry out holistic research and documentation of rock art should be formulated. While formulating these, regional variations may also be taken into account; (e) there is an urge for protection, preservation, and conservation of many rock art sites so a separate policy for their protection and preservation has to be developed; (f) to achieve this, collaboration and coordination between major stakeholders/governments and community participation is strongly recommended; (g) there is a need to establish a Centre for Advance Rock Art Studies. National institutions like IGNCA are strongly recommended to establish this. Through this centre, a central digital data bank on world rock art and advance study of rock art may be developed. Research in the most updated methods of chronology, interpretation, and decoding of rock art will also be done by this centre; (h) it was highly recommended that the ongoing national project of creating a central repository for digitally archiving rock art and other forms of allied art traditions along with study and documentation at IGNCA should be strengthened and extended. Recognizing the genuine concern of these scholars, IGNCA recently established an independent unit for rock art studies.

Rock art is one of our greatest surviving art treasures. It possesses a large body of evidence of human artistic, cognitive, and cultural beginnings. The intrinsic efficacy of rock art lies in its universality of appeal and to sustain it in a manner in which all can discern it. Until the recent past, the content of rock art was much commented on as an indicator of the stage of development of the authors of rock art. But for quite some time now attempts have been made by many scholars to explore the possibility of the proximity of rock art with the art of many living communities in the world such as indigenous people, aboriginals, tribals, and nomads. India is fortunate in possessing one of the three largest concentrations of this world heritage, the other two being Australia and South Africa, where rock art is still a living tradition. Therefore, it was a proud privilege for IGNCA to host such an international event of academic merit with an urge to analyse where we stand in the global context especially in terms of rock art studies.

Keeping in mind the rich concentration of rock art in India along with a vibrant living art tradition practiced by several communities across the country, the conference focused on initiating a dialogue between the academia and practicing artists, both from rural and urban areas. The conference was conceived with special attention to interdisciplinary research involving allied disciplines like anthropology, geology, art history etc. that can open new horizons in the study of rock art. The deliberations in the conference sessions were mainly around the themes: Concept and Methodology; Forms Content Context; Interpreting Rock Art; and Documentation and Conservation. The conference was thus divided into different themes, each over-lapping, with an interface and inter-locking with other themes.

It would be worthwhile to mention here that IGNCA has conceived a major academic programme which relates to exploring artistic manifestations emanating from man's primary sense perceptions. Rock art forms a crucial component of this. A detailed account of the conceptual framework and objectives of this project are dealt at length in Chapter 19 by the editor. A huge data base has been compiled in the process of documentation and study related to rock art and its allied subjects since its inception.

IGNCA has, so far, produced nine well received publications under the **IGNCA Rock Art Series**, viz., *Rock Art in the Old World* (ed. Michel Lorblanchet), *Deer in Rock Art of India and Europe* (eds G. Camuri, A. Fossati, Y. Mathpal), *Rock Art in Kumaon Himalaya* (Yashodhar Mathpal), *Rock Art in Kerala* (Yashodhar Mathpal), *Conservation of Rock Art* (ed. B. L. Malla), *Global Rock Art* (eds B.L. Malla and V.H. Sonawane), *Rock Art of Andhra Pradesh: A New Synthesis* (N. Chandramouli, General editor B.L. Malla), *The World of Rock Art: An Overview of Five Continents* (ed. B.L. Malla), and *Rock Art: A Catalogue* (ed. S.S. Biswas). Besides these publications, a brochure in the International Conference on Rock Art 2012 titled *Understanding Rock Art in Context* (ed. B. L. Malla) and a set of postcards on Indian rock art have been published. Also, a CD ROM on 'Rock Art of India' and three DVDs on rock art of Jharkhand, rock art of Ladakh (J&K), and pan-Indian rock art have also been brought out. We have great pleasure now in bringing out the tenth and eleventh publications in this series.

The proceedings of the conference have been published in two volumes. These two volumes contain selected articles representing rock art from all over the world. In the first volume, papers related to concept, methodology, context, documentation, and conservation are included. In the second volume papers related to the interpretation of rock art are included. Some of the papers were read in the absence of the scholars who wrote them on our request; a few selected special lectures which were organized as a part of the circulatory rock art exhibition in different parts of India after the main event have also been included in these volumes to add to the content and quality of their academic input.

The first paper in Volume I, 'Structure of Art, Structure of Mind' by Emmanuel Anati proposes a structure of the elementary dynamics of the human cognitive system.

S. C. Malik in his paper 'Rock Art: A Universal Creative Act' rightly recommends that rock art qua art has to be seen as an aesthetic and creative activity and it requires an integral and holistic approach to the study of rock art.

N. Chandramouli's paper, 'The Concept of Style in Archaeology and its Application to Rock Art Analysis: A Case Study of the Rock Art of Peninsular India' initiates a 'stylistic' study of the rock art of peninsular India in the light of the pros and cons of the application of this concept.

''A Mark in the Way: Schematic Rock Art and Communication Routes' by Hipólito Collado Giraldo and José Julio García Arranz proposes a functional interpretative model for schematic rock art by studying the relation between communication routes and places chosen.

'Prehistoric-Kalimantan Rock Art as a Visual Study' by Pindi Setiawan describes the methodology for classifying Kalimantan rock art as a visual-language study: how to separate images by the way in which they have been drawn and spread on the walls and are connected with the (cultural) environment.

Somnath Chakraverty and Ruman Banerjee's paper, 'Constructed Landscape in Rock Art: Selection of Visual Space, Arrangement Pattern and Its Symbolic Significance' attempts to delineate the selection criterion, if any, for the space for display of art work, both in rock shelters and the location of the rock canvas in an isolated eco-geographical niche to define a boundary between utilitarian and symbolic space within the given cultural and natural setting.

Zhu Lifeng's paper 'The State of Chinese Rock Art' talks of the sites and subject matter of rock art in China and how they have a close inter-relation with its national culture. Chinese rock art is endowed with precious research value.

The paper 'Dominant Motivational, Thematic and Stylistic Traits in the Rock Art of Eastern India with Special Reference to Southern Bihar and Adjoining Jharkhand' by Awadh Kishore Prasad points towards the prevalence of different motivational, thematic, and stylistic traits in rock art in eastern India.

Patrick Paillet's paper 'Men and Cultures at the End of the Late Ice Age in the North of Perigord: Continuities and Ruptures' highlights how the transformations incarnated in artistic registers testify to the diversity of the Palaeolithic and Epi-palaeolithic trajectories.

Dwipen Bezbaruah in his paper 'Megalithic Monuments and the Context of Rock Art in North-East India' gives the origin and antiquity of the rock art tradition in North East India on the basis of secondary evidence and primary data collected by him.

'Pagoda-Shaped Depictions in Tibetan Rock Art' by Zhang Yasha proposes that those who executed the rock art belonged to the Qiang ethnic tribe, who migrated westwards during 2500-1000 B.P. and made a living by taming horses and hunting wild yaks. Their stories, as demonstrated in rock art, relate to the epic of Gesar.

Tashi Ldawa in his paper 'Spatial Attributes of Petroglyphs of Ladakh' reports only those art forms that are considered exotic, incongruous, and are primarily of the pre-Buddhist period. It is generally believed that the exotic petroglyphs which are mainly found on the trade routes existed from prehistoric times.

K. Rajan's paper 'Rock Art and Its Cultural Context: Recent Evidences in Tamil Nadu' gives a detailed account of the geographical distribution, socio-cultural contexts, themes, and chronological evolution of this rock art form in Tamil Nadu.

B. R. Mani and Shankar Sharma's paper 'Rock Art of Kaimur and its Authors: New Evidences' highlights various aspects of rock art including the subject matter of paintings and engravings belonging to Mesolithic and Chalcolithic periods reported in the recent exploration conducted by the authors in the region on the border of Uttar Pradesh and Bihar.

Zulfiqar Ali Kalhoro's paper 'Petroglyphs in Seeta valley, Sindh' interprets the rock carvings of Seeta valley, which is noted for Indus period petroglyphs, where one finds the most interesting petroglyphs of a horned deity with dancers.

Nandini Bhattacharya Sahu and Prabhas Sahu in their paper 'Decorated Rock Shelters of Gavilgarh Hills, District Betul, Madhya Pradesh' report about 18 decorated rock shelters in the ortho-quartzite formations of the Gavilgarh hills, a member of the Satpura range. These shelters contain pictographs and petroglyphs on their walls and ceilings. Seven groups of rock shelters, in different localities over the sprawling hills and cliffs have been identified with a rich variety of pictographs, sometimes superimposed on the engravings, mostly in burnt sienna in red hue and seldom in white.

J. N. Pal in his paper 'Prehistoric Rock Art in Vindhyas in Uttar Pradesh and Adjoining Areas, North Central India' gives a synthesis of the life and activities of prehistoric man right from the emergence of man in the middle Gangetic plain and the adjoining Vindhyan plateau to the south of the Gangetic plain.

R. K. Varma in the paper 'Rock Art in North Vindhyan region' highlights the importance of the rock art sites of the northern Vindhyan region, especially those located in undivided Mirzapur in Uttar Pradesh in Central India.

The paper 'Inventory of Indian Rock Art: A Multidisciplinary Approach' by B.L. Malla describes IGNCA's project for the survey, documentation, and study of Indian rock art sites with a holistic perspective. It also talks about the methodology adopted for the documentation, which is being done with scientific means in collaboration with local experts and institutions in the areas/zones concerned.

R. C. Agrawal in his paper 'Conservation of Rock Art Sites: Problems and Issues' discusses various aspects of the discipline including the protection of rock shelters and their ecosystems which are an essential aspect of preservation of rock art sites across the world.

In their paper 'An Analysis of the Evaluation and Diagnosis of Environmental Impacts of Rock Art sites of the Guaniguanico Mountain Range', Racso Ferníndez Ortega, Dany Morales Valdés, Dialvys Rodríguez Herníndez and Hilario Carmenate Rodríguez define, enumerate, and characterize the various actions and impacts that affect the state of conservation of this important Cuban heritage.

Devananda Beura in his paper 'Geological Aspects and Management of Rock Art with special Reference to Conservation' recommends that while preserving rock art, the natural settings of the rock surface containing the art, structural elements, composition, texture, and matrix of the rock and geological hazards like earthquakes and land use patterns should be kept in mind.

The paper 'Study and Conservation of Rock Art Sites in Andhra Pradesh: A Botanical Perspective' by M. Raghu Ram provides evidence about the material used for the drawings/paintings and proposes that the painting material was prepared by crushing flowers and fruits.

The articles included in this volume highlight the immense potential that rock art possesses in unraveling the mysteries of the past. The data and the interpretations put forward in this volume by various scholars are comprehensive and analytical. Most of their views are appropriate and hold good promise in terms of recent trends in rock art research and documentation. Some of the contributions give us an insight into the universality of rock art, chronology, physical preservation, conservation of rock art sites, conservation of the geological and environmental atmosphere of some rock sites, management systems, documentation, and making an inventory of rock art sites.

The main focus of the present publication is on recent developments in rock art research, documentation, and preservation. As rock art is an intricate and complex domain covering material and cognitive aspects of culture, a multidisciplinary approach is advocated to decode and understand it in all its dimensions. The role of scholars from different disciplines for the scientific study, documentation, and research in rock art has been highlighted in the volume. The second volume *Rock Art Studies, Volume–II*, covers papers on interpreting rock art.

This illustrated volume aims to boost and promote rock art research. It will not only interest scholars but also the public at large. It is also an important step in the journey of exploring together, globally, the source of creative energies and modes of expression of our ancestors. It will certainly contribute to rectify and enhance our vision of rock art.

Lastly, we would like to record that the views expressed by the scholars in their papers may not be taken as those of the editor or the Centre (IGNCA).

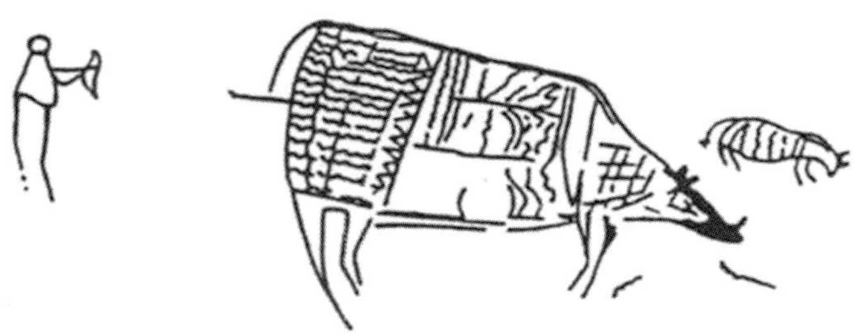

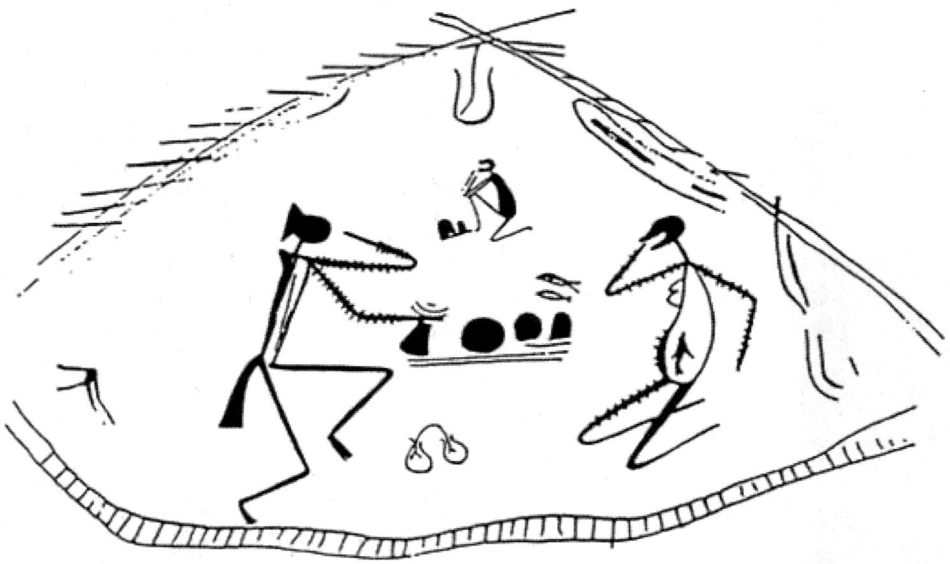

1

Structure of Art, Structure of Mind

Emmanuel Anati and Ariela Fradkin

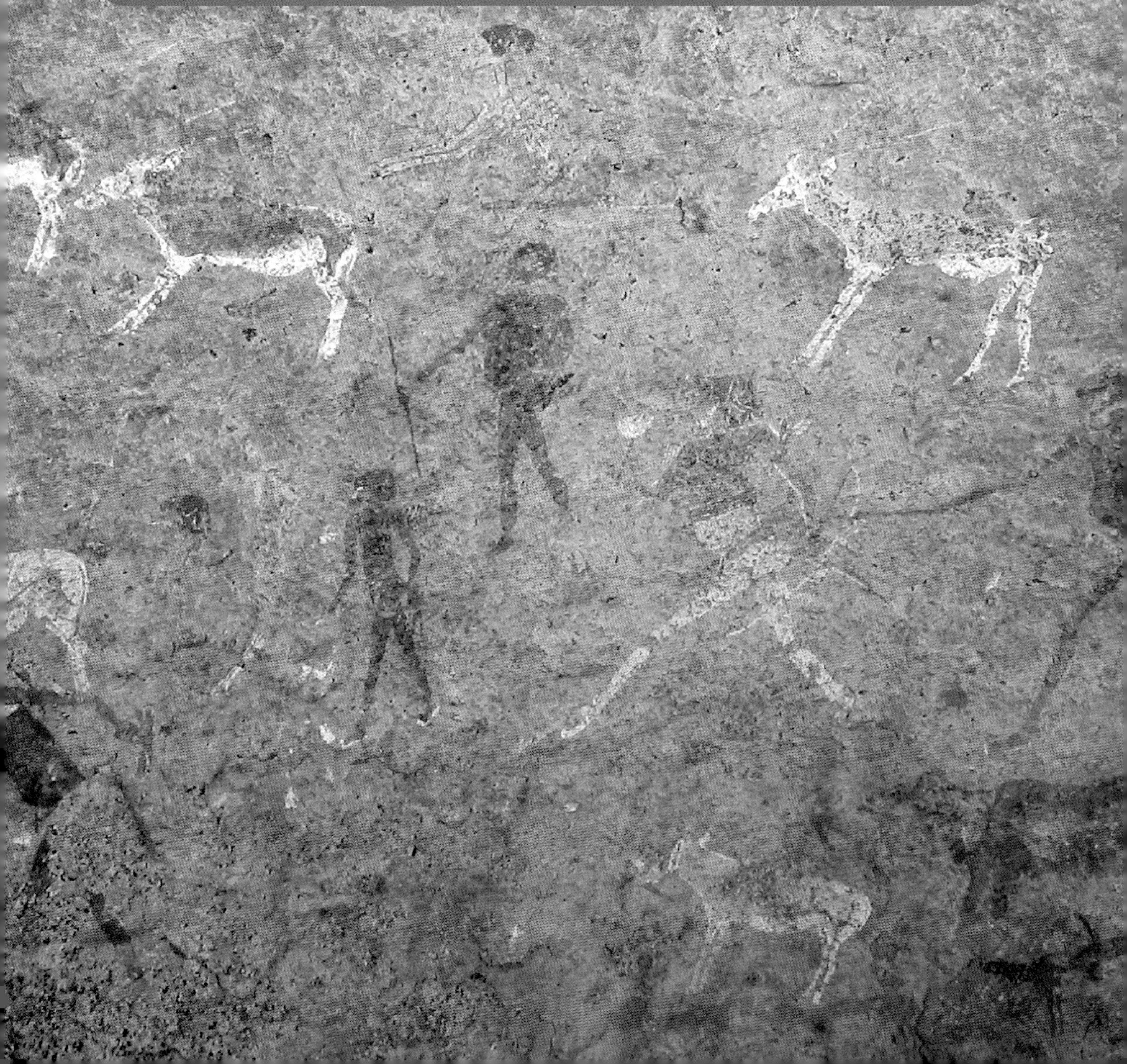

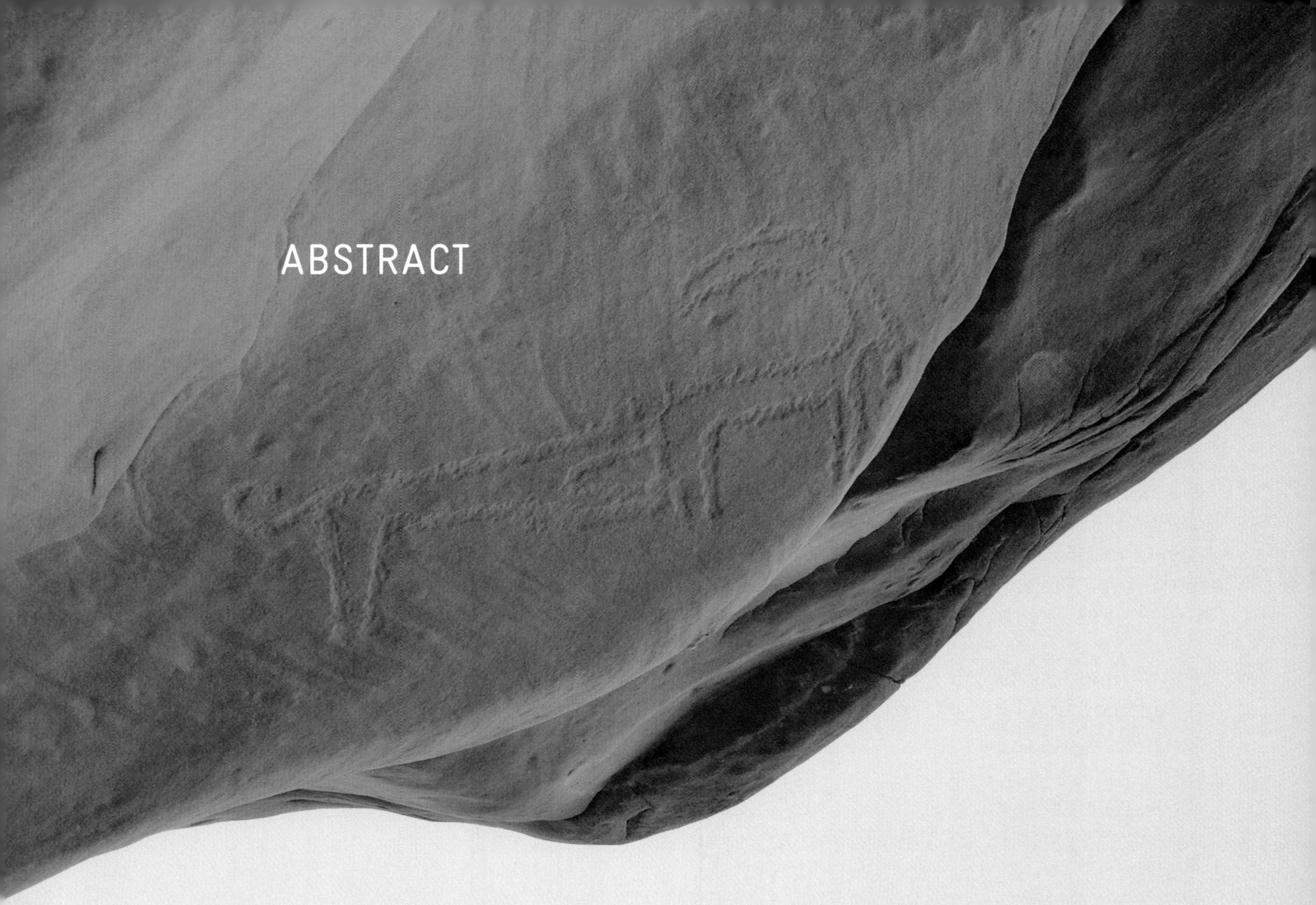

ABSTRACT

Using a comparative method on rock and mobiliary art of hunting-gathering populations from over 80 countries, Professor Anati defines basic 'grammatical structures' recurring in the earliest artistic expressions of humankind. A high percentage of the art of hunters from five continents reveals three major concerns: sex, food and territory. Three different grammatical categories of signs interplay in prehistoric art to formulate the content and meaning of the assemblages: pictograms, ideograms and psychograms. The structure of the earliest art reveals a consistent grammatical and syntactical system of elementary pictographic writing. Figurative art appears to have been born as a method of communication and memorisation, which follows the basic rules of writing. The sequences, associations and combinations of graphemes enable the establishing of a recurring system of an elementary cognitive process. By presenting the analysis of specific examples and their repetitive characters, Professor Anati's paper proposes a structure of the elementary dynamics of the human cognitive system.

THE CONTEXT

For over 2 million years, the hunting way of life shaped humanity and has left profound marks on the intellectual nature of the species. The fundamental process of association and the 'logic' of the human mind came into existence and developed throughout the periods during which the species acquired its basic behavioural patterns. These millennia were characterised by hunting bands, which shared activities and refined communication; teamwork enhanced socialisation.

This way of life reached a high level of perfection and efficiency over the last 200,000 years with the appearance of our direct forefathers, the *Homo sapiens.* They acquired developed technological skills and mental abilities; they were capable of producing precise and efficient implements and were responsible for creating an ideology whose matrix is still present at the core of modern conceptual thought. Our ancestors developed the capacity for synthesis and abstraction which, among other things, led them to produce art. Visual art as a common pattern is documented only in the last 50,000 years or in the last 1 per cent of the age of humankind.

As far as we know, artistic manifestations are exclusive to the human species. Graphic art has multiple functions including communication, memorisation, interpretation, commemoration and self-expression. Art is the mirror of the mind and constitutes a precious record of man's conceptual and psychological matrix. Graphic art is a cultural pattern, just like writing, dancing or singing. It implies specific abilities of synthesis, abstraction, mental association and logic.

A few cases of early graphic expressions are recorded in various parts of the world. The predecessors of figurative graphic art, which have reached us, are of various kinds, such as markings on stones and bones, giving harmonious shapes to stone implements and collecting objects of natural shapes or colours that attracted the human mind. Abstract markings are known from Africa, dating back to around 75,000 years to the Blombos Cave (South Africa). At Kununarra (Australia) or at Bacho Kiro (Europe), or in Bulgaria and at Tata (Hungary), they may be as old.

According to current debate, these finds may have been produced by Neanderthaloid people in Europe or by *Proto-sapiens* or archaic *Homo sapiens* elsewhere. The collection of natural shapes is documented from excavations and surface finds in layers of both *sapiens* and *pre-sapiens* humans in Africa, the Middle East and Europe.

According to our present knowledge, as a cultural pattern figurative art including images seems to be first documented as a production of *Homo sapiens.* The evidence concerns finds executed on durable materials. Art objects in wood, animal skins or other organic supports, which may have counted as a large majority of art production, have not survived.

Populations whose livelihood was based on hunting and gathering are today almost extinct and are confined to the most inhospitable parts of the planet, such as the deserts of Australia and of southern Africa, the Congo Basin, the tropical forests of the Amazon River, South-east Asia, the Arctic tundra of Lapland, Siberia, Alaska and the great Canadian north. They have been pushed to marginal areas and although they occupy territories which constitute more than 20 per cent of the earth's surface, they are less than 1 per cent of the world's population. Only 500 years ago, when America became known to Europeans, 70 per cent of the earth's surface was populated by hunting people, who then may have accounted for more than 20 per cent of the world's population. At the end of the Pleistocene, some 12,000 years ago, the entire world population pursued this means of subsistence, which was gradually replaced by economies based on food production. Since then, other ways of life have developed and patterns of visual art have become broadly differentiated.

Tribal societies around the world have the common habit of producing art, in particular rock art, that is, paintings and engravings on rock surfaces. It is recorded in thousands of zones distributed over 100 countries. It is a widespread way of expression and of communication. Over 45 million prehistoric images from about 70,000 sites are known today. Over 70 per cent of all known rock art was produced by hunting and gathering societies, while less than 30 per cent was the work of pastoralists and agriculturists.

Rock art is the product of pre-literate societies. It constitutes the most relevant record we possess of human history before the invention of what was officially recognised as writing.

Almost all prehistoric art focuses on three basic themes: sex, food and territory. These themes, expressed directly or indirectly, realistically or metaphorically, display the focus of interest of the human mind. Humans' main concerns do not seem to have changed much down the ages, as these remain the dominant themes faced by literate societies in their visual arts and in literature, dance and music. From the earliest historical documentation, they appear to be a source of inspiration for ideology and religion, and the main causes of war. Similarly, they are the main causes of conflict among other species.

Broad comparative studies are possible when pertinent documentation is available. Cataloguing and making inventories of rock art have been predominantly the work of students and amateurs, occasionally supported by universities and museums; basic research on decoding has been the private endeavour of a few scholars. It is only in the last few years that some governments have become aware of the importance of this documentation as an immense cultural and historical heritage and they are now embarking on finalised research. But rock art is the major archive of 50,000 years of human adventures and it is time that a major international project is conceived to unite all the efforts into a world database and decoded.

Mobiliary art, three-dimensional figurines, plaquettes and decorated objects have, on the other hand, received different treatment. Once discovered they are usually acquired by museums or collectors and inventories are produced that assess the properties and estimate their values. A single world inventory would be of significant value in the sector of mobiliary art also. However, both in terms of the size of existing documentation and of world distribution, rock art appears to be a global phenomenon, which constitutes more than 90 per cent of the known prehistoric art. It is found in all continents and has remained *in situ* where early man produced it. Nevertheless, it has not yet received appropriate academic attention and enjoys still less public awareness and valorisation.

CULTURAL PATTERNS

Comparative studies provide evidence of the presence of constant patterns in the production of art in five continents. They appear to be primarily derivative of the mental conditioning reflecting social and economic habits. Certain elements of style and content have been shown to be constant at a global level. Five categories of rock art have been defined according to subject matter, syntax and style (Anati 2002).

Early Hunters: This was the art practised by bands of big-game hunters who did not use bows and arrows. They usually hunted with spears and other throwing implements. Teamwork and in-depth observations of animal characters are reflected in the style. Animal depictions form the main theme. The syntax consists chiefly of logical sequences and metaphorical associations, combining signs, 'ideograms', figures and 'pictograms' with expressions of feelings and 'psychograms', while realistic anecdotal scenes are rare. The animal is the main subject. Ideograms may have the functions of verbs or of adjectives. (Fig. 1.1) Anthropomorphic figures are not common and often represent anthropo-zoomorphic beings likely to belong to the realm of myth.

In the past, hunters and gatherers were considered together as a single category. However, recent studies show consistent stylistic and conceptual differences in the art expressions between early hunters of big game, the late hunters of small and medium-sized game and food collectors. They have different concerns, different ways of observation, different lifestyles and different models of social interplay, and their art shows differences in visual output, styles, patterns of syntax and subject matter.

Early Gatherers: Here, the graphic expression is of people whose main economy was based on collecting wild fruits, leaves, tubers and other edible vegetables. Several such groups probably collected snails and other small animals, but they may have had a prevailing vegetarian diet. Animal depictions are not current features. Gatherers have anthropomorphic images as the main subject. They rely on individual activities and this is reflected in their visual expressions. The syntax is characterised by simple scenes of an allegoric nature depicting a surreal world. Human faces are often transfigured. The subject matter is mainly epic events concerning what appear to be supernatural anthropomorphic beings and the mysteries of communion between man and the forces of nature. Trends of monstrous and deformed human shapes reflect alterations in the state of consciousness. Some of this art seems to have been produced in a state of hallucination. Social events are important; music and dancing are often represented.

Late Hunters: This was the art practised by hunters who used bows and arrows. They usually operated alone or in small teams. Their visual art consists of realistic-dynamic anecdotal and descriptive scenes of the hunt. Social and economic happenings are represented. The human figure appears as the main protagonist. They tend to associate the hunt with sex and mythic beings are present in daily events. The animals depicted vary according to the area. Usually, they are caprines and cervines. Food, sex and territory are the themes of major concern. Both in North Africa and in the western region of Spain named Levante, human fights and warfare are common. In major areas of late hunter rock art in the Middle East and Central Asia, scenes of human fights are rare or non-existent. Hunting is by far the predominant theme.

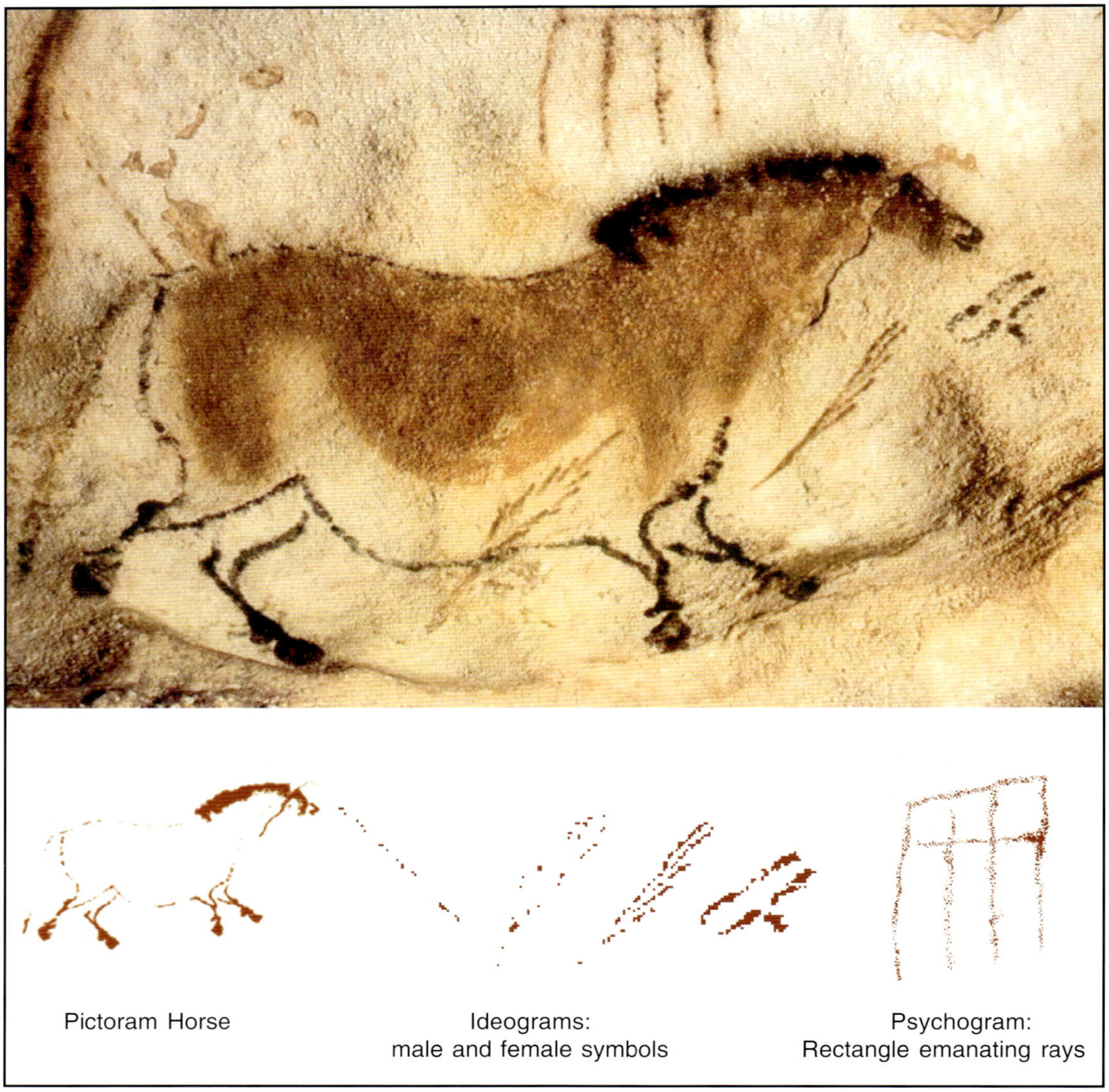

Fig. 1.1 Famous horse paintings of the Lascaux Cave, France.

Pastoralists and Herdsmen: This was the art practised by people whose primary economic activity is depicted as raising livestock with a focus on domestic animals and scenes of family life. Ethnic identity and wealth, in the form of livestock, are major issues. Human figures are given specific shapes and attributes, including hats, body decorations and associated ideograms, likely to define their social status and ethnic belonging. Tribal disputes are occasionally represented in an otherwise idyllic atmosphere.

Complex Economy: This was the art practised by non-urban, non-literate people with a diversified economy, including farming. The two main trends are: mythological and commemorative scenes and symbolic compositions made up of signs and patterns. Anthropomorphic divinities and/or supernatural beings are frequently represented. The complex economy group has a variety of styles, from the narrative scene to schematic compositions, with a range of themes much broader than the other categories. Like its economy, its art is characterised by diversity.

This classification, in general categories, is intentionally schematic. There are transitional phases and groups that display a mixture of characters, and there are also marked differences within each given category. Minor groups include the art of fishermen, of late food collectors and shell eaters. Considering the immensity of the material already recorded, there is a need to create a system for an effective cross-cultural comparative analysis based on thematic and stylistic elements in order to go beyond the limits of geographical boundaries.

It is noteworthy that conflicts and warfare are absent in the depictions of early hunters, sporadic in the art of pastoralists and late hunters and widespread in the art of complex economy groups.

As for distribution, the rock art of early hunters, early gatherers and late hunters exists wherever there is human presence, before the beginning of agriculture and the domestication of animals. These three categories are so far absent in Melanesia and Polynesia. Pastoralists are mainly concentrated in Africa and Asia. Complex economies and groups are almost absent in Australia, in southern Africa, in the southernmost part of South America and in several areas which are now deserts. They are mainly concentrated in Asia and Europe. Analyses of rock art are based on three principal criteria: grammar, syntax and style. Grammar is based on themes and typology; syntax relates to the associations, intentional sequences and scenes; and style considers the importance given to details and to schematisation and abstraction. Guidelines are certain ways of representing wild or domestic animals, the presence or absence of certain symbols which act as 'fossil guides', the emphasis on specific features, such as the stylisation of animal horns and of human genitals, and the degree of schematisation and synthesis of images.

The use of these criteria has led to the identification of a series of significant, recurrent elements. Such comparative studies suggest that living conditions, the economy and patterns of way of life influenced associative processes, behaviour, thought, ideology and, consequently, artistic manifestations. Visual art appears to be a synthesis of the human wit. An analysis of essential elements of rock art assemblages at the global level is leading to the determination of universal factors, identifying and distinguishing them from local factors, and provides a typological definition of art trends. This kind of analysis is particularly useful for defining the cultural significance of various patterns of rock art.

According to present data, the earliest known rock art expressions are located in Africa and Australia. It would be logical to consider that in between these two regions Asia too should have had such early manifestations, but so far there is no clear evidence of this. Known records of rock art start at a later date in Europe and in the Americas.

In all cases recorded so far in over 100 countries, figurative rock art is a product of *Homo sapiens*, a phenomenon of non-urban, non-literate societies. In all countries and in all the examined zones, there are areas of great concentration of rock art, which do not reflect an analogous concentration of people. It seems to be a universal pattern that rock art is scarce where the population is denser.

There appear to be many zones the world over where people purposefully went for artistic or other ritual and social activities connected to rock art. Like holy sites in recent societies, in most regions of the world and in most religions, such a pattern implies an attitude of reverence to 'holy' or particularly meaningful places of congregation at rock art sites. This trend has persisted ever since the earliest large-scale rock art manifestations.

TYPOLOGY AND GRAMMAR OF ART

The selection of subject matter is present as a factor of art analysis in every period, including in prehistoric art. Each human group in each period had a restricted repertory that differed in each case. Fighting scenes, for example, are the main subject matter in the Iron Age rock art of Europe, yet almost everywhere it is absent in Palaeolithic, Mesolithic and Neolithic art. Preferential subjects consistently appear even in modern artistic expressions. Greek and Roman classic sculptures, for example, focused on human rather than animal subjects. In different phases, female or male subjects were preferred. Weapons and tools are profusely represented in certain groups or periods of rock art but remain totally absent in others.

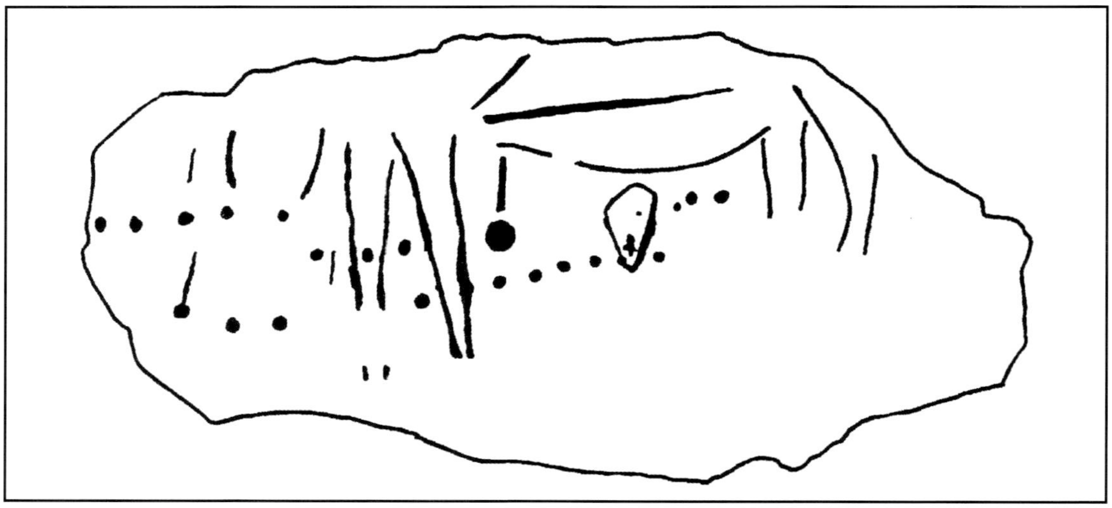

Fig. 1.2 Symbolic engravings La Ferrassie, Dordogna, France.

Note: The pictographic language of Early *Homo sapiens*, Symbolic engravings *ca.* 30,000 years old. The schematic outline of an animal is accompanied by a vulva and other recurring signs. The chart below illustrates the grammatical composition consisting of specific associations of points and of lines. (E. Anati, 1989, W00188).

Pittogramma	**Ideogrammi**				
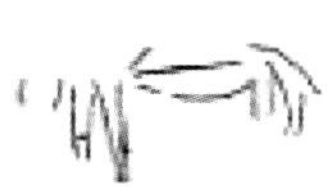		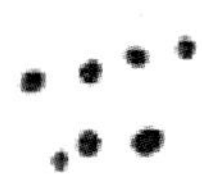	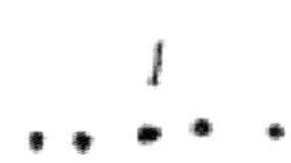	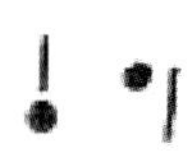	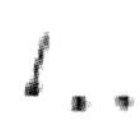
Schema di quadrupede	**Schema vulvare**	**Sequenza di punti**	**Associazione punto e linea**	**Coniugazione punto e linea**	**Accoppiamento punto-linea**

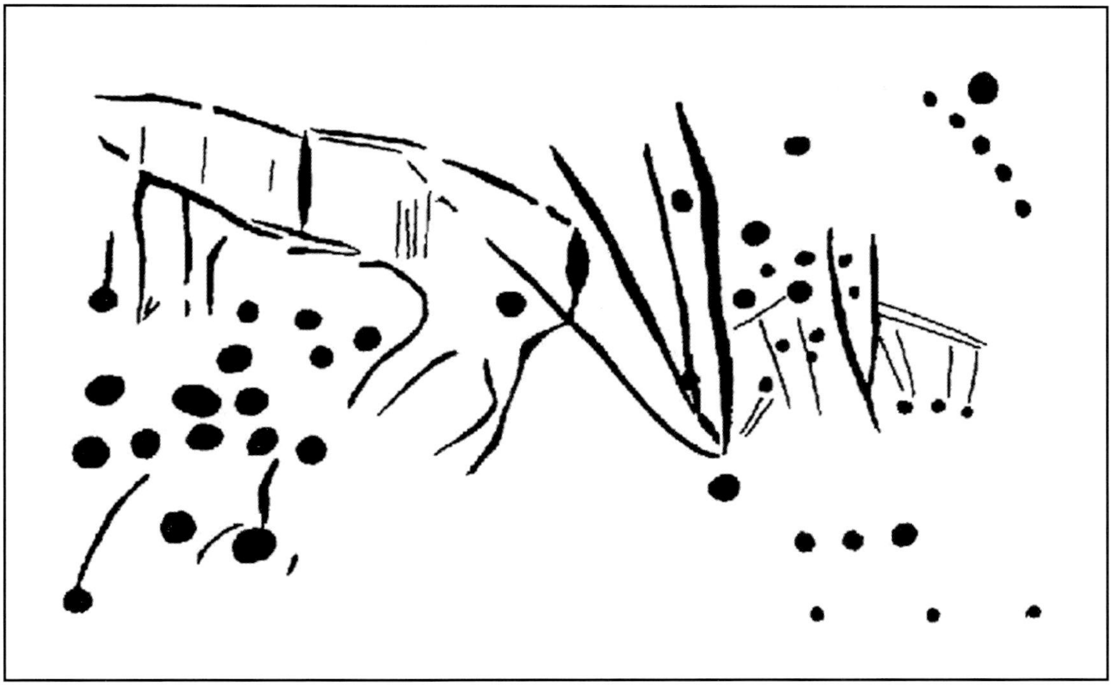

Note: Showing the same conceptual composition as that of the previous figure. Again here the outline of an animal is accompanied by a vulva and by the same kinds of associations of points and of lines. (E. Anati, 1989 W00189).

Fig. 1.3 Engraved surface in a rock shelter in the Murray River Valley, Australia.

Pittogramma	**Ideogrammi**			
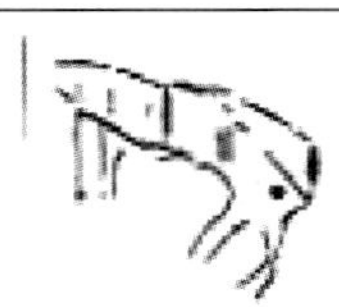	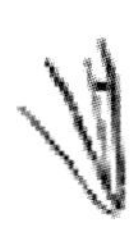	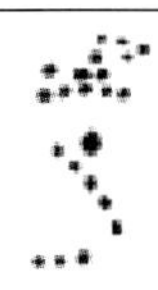	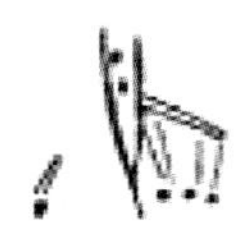	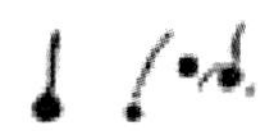
Schema di quadrupede	**Schema vulvare**	**Sequenza di Punti**	**Associazione punto e linea**	**Accoppiamento punto-linea**

All over the world, the subject matter in rock art tends to be restricted to five subjects: anthropomorphic; zoomorphic; objects and tools; structures and 'tectiforms'; and symbols or ideograms. Three types of signs are found grammatically different from each other: pictograms, ideograms and psychograms (Figs. 1.2 & 1.3). They recur globally not only in rock art but also in mobiliary art.

Pictograms (or *Mythograms*): These are representations of real or imaginary objects, animals or human beings. Pictograms are images whose shapes we may identify as anthropomorphic, zoomorphic, objects and tools, structures and tectiforms (Figs. 1.4 & 1.5). Only rarely do other themes occur, such as vegetation, landscape or realistic portraits, and only in specific contexts. The subject matter of prehistoric art appears to be globally restricted to these. Within each category the themes are even more limited.

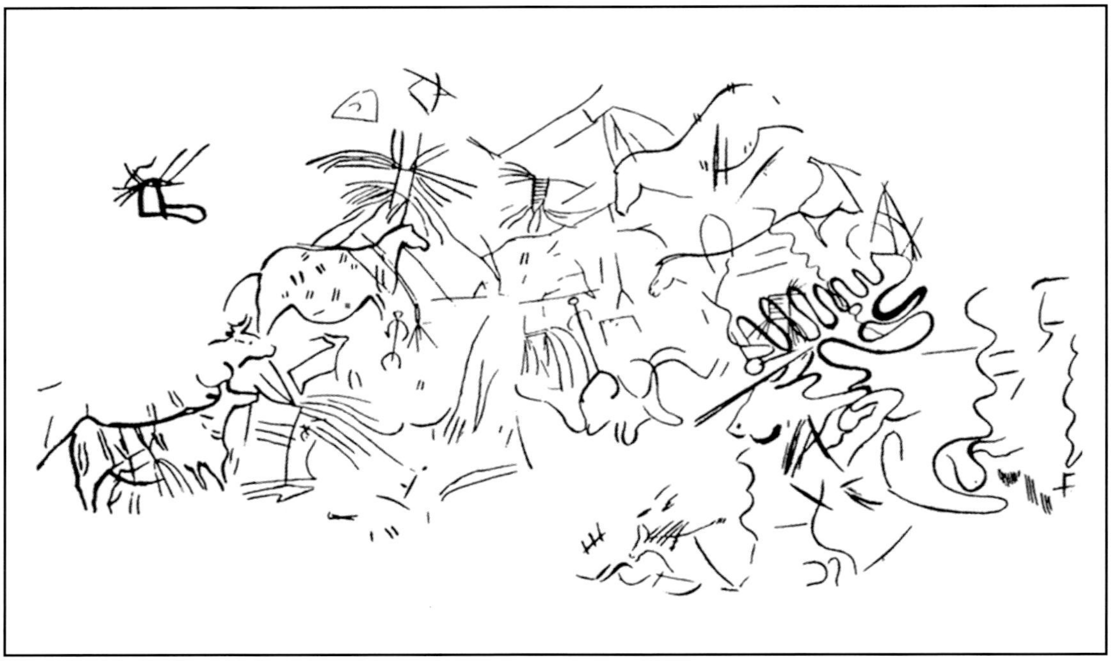

Fig. 1.4 A complex accumulation of parietal paintings in the cave of La Pileta, Spain.

Note: The panel is composed of several intentional associations of pictograms, ideograms and psychograms. One of the sequences is isolated in the following image. It appears as a readable pictographic script.

Ideograms: In prehistoric art, as well as in early ideographic writing, ideograms are repetitive signs or combinations of signs. Their recurrent nature and the particular relationship between them indicate that they were intended to convey conventional concepts.

Three main types of ideograms are: first, *anatomic,* reflecting real or symbolic functions or parts of the human body; second, *conceptual,* giving a conventional shape to ideas; and third, *numeric*, quantifying the real, the hypothetical or the imaginary. Such definitions do not necessarily imply their function. They reflect our way of seeing and classifying them. All together, there are just over 20 ideograms with a worldwide distribution. They may be classified as:

1. *Anatomic*: phallic, vulvas, hand and footprints.
2. *Conceptual*: disk, zig-zag, snake, branch, 'lips', 'T' shape, 'U' shape, 'H' shape, mouth shape, trident, half-ring, cup and ring, star, stick, triangle and square.
3. *Numeric*: groups of dots, of rings, of half-rings or lunates and of parallel lines.

Psychograms: These seem to represent neither objects nor symbols. Sometimes they may have the role of exclamation marks. They appear as a result of discharges of energy, to express feelings about pleasure and displeasure, love or hate, warning or fear, but could also express wishes or expectations. The choice of rock surface and its actual shape often fulfils the psychogram's role. In such cases, the location and nature of pictograms and ideograms appear to be related to the shape-psychogram, which was

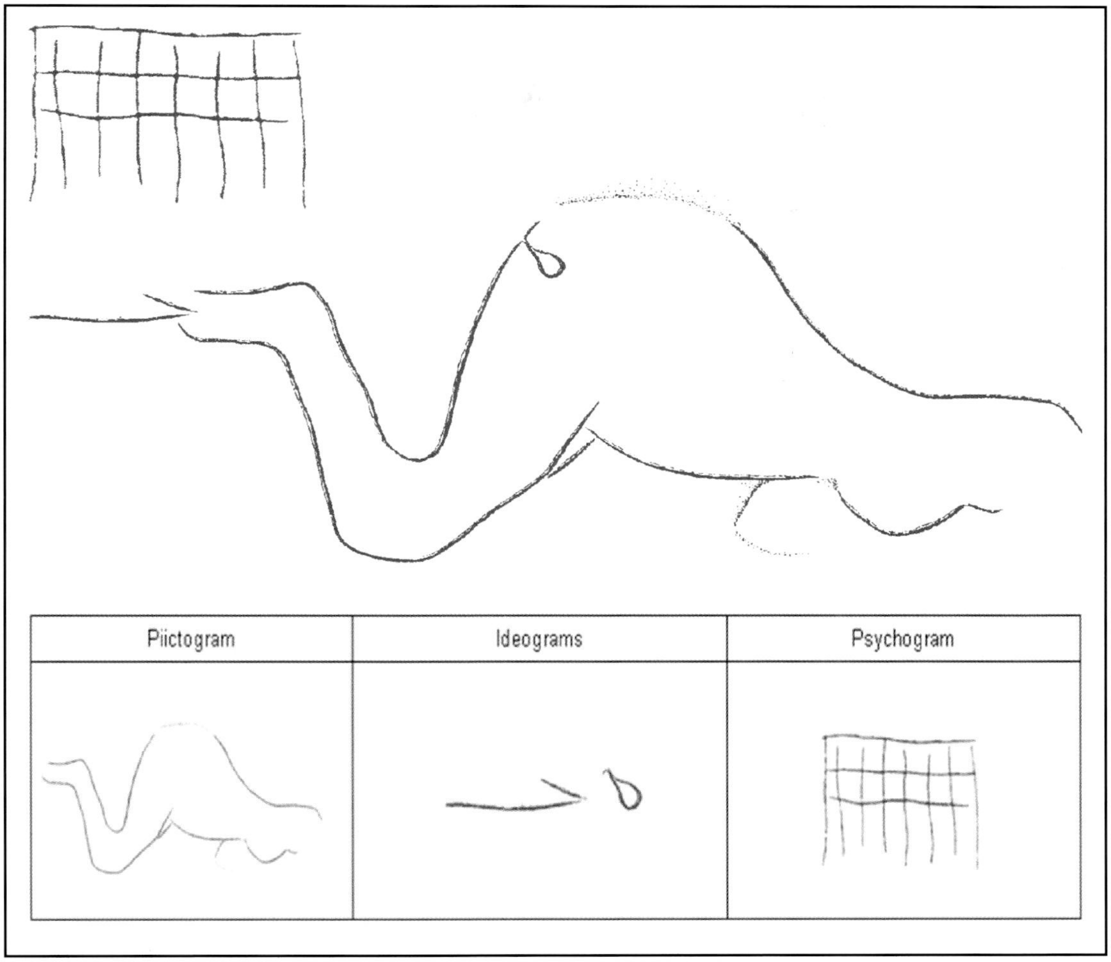

Note: Figure with indication of the vulva and an arrow reaching her foot. The pictogram is accompanied by male and female ideograms analogous to those of the previous figure. (Tracing by J. Gaussen 1964, W06797).

Fig. 1.5 Feminine figure, Gabillou, Sourzac, Dordogne, France.

selected to be depicted. Such interpretation of natural shapes is still widespread among Australian Aborigines.

The syntax of association between pictograms, ideograms and psychograms reflects the mental process of *Homo sapiens*. In present-day tribal societies, it is present in graphic arts as well as in diction and story-telling, in music (sound) and in dance (body motion).

The associative and metaphoric system has never ceased to be a basic means of expression. For Renaissance painters, the dove was undoubtedly a dove, but when Fra Angelico of Florence painted it in the Annunciation scene, in order to understand its meaning it is not enough to state that in a particular part of the painting there is a dove. When we know the theme that inspired the artist and when we are familiar with his methodological and conceptual equipment, the dove becomes an ideogram and takes on a metaphoric content and meaning as 'Holy Ghost'. For a non-Christian Bushman of the Kalahari Desert, the reading of this ideogram would be as improbable as reading some of the Palaeolithic ideograms would be for us, unless some reliable hints are gathered. The halo on the head of Mary is a psychogram meaning 'holy'. The same Bushman would again have some difficulties in understanding the meaning.

Similarly, other vernacular icons may not be explicit for everyone. The famous Picasso's dove is not merely a dove. The dove, considered to be a messenger, is carrying in its beak an olive branch, which in European Christian tradition means 'peace'. In this case, the dove is a pictogram, which is combined with the ideogram, the olive branch, that we may recognise as meaning 'peace' only if we are initiated. A thousand years hence, perhaps someone will ask what is meant by the ideogram near the beak of that strange pictogram that vaguely resembles a bird. For the Aranta tribesman of the Australian Central Desert, the reading of this message will be as difficult as it may be for us to understand some of the messages of his rock art.

Other examples could be cited, such as the eagle in Roman times or in the palaces of the Austro-Hungarian empire, or at the entrance of the White House in Washington. Yes, the bird represented does seem to be an eagle. Tests will prove this from the shape of the beak or from the wing span. But what does this eagle represent? Sometimes, when the pictogram is accompanied by four ideograms that nowadays we are able to read as SPQR, some inkling of the conceptual content of the figure will perhaps emerge. Since the four letters are a Roman ideogram, the initials of the Latin 'The Senate and the Peoples of Rome', it will become clear that the eagle represents the authority of Rome. But then eagle-like images appear in other periods and without the SPQR. What is the message behind a two-headed eagle on an Austrian coat of arms? What kind of totemic archetype is the eagle?

The information that can still be provided by surviving hunter-gatherers may constitute important support for the reconstruction of the cognitive processes of early art. Indeed, many hints are provided by present-day hunting clans. Humankind has now the last chance to gather such information. Otherwise it would be too late for the next generation.

Ideograms are signs that convey ideas in ancient writing and in many groups of rock paintings from the writer to the reader, from the painter to the real or imaginary beings to whom the message is addressed.

Psychograms are signs that convey sensations from the one who represents to the other who observes. The psychogram works at a subconscious level, as do certain archetypal signs that our conscious memory is no longer able to define. Psychograms do not seem to be intellectualisations; to us today they look like expressions of feelings, accents or exclamation marks.

In the art of early hunters, naturalistic portraits of people are rare, while naturalistic portraits of animals are common. In the rock art of all five continents in all categories, landscapes are extremely rare, as are images of plants, but they are common in a few specific cases. They are either completely absent or indicative of some particular characteristic if they do exist. Landscape, in the sense we conceive it, is present only in the art of groups with a complex economy. Figures of plants, leaves, roots or fruits are present in a circumscribed context. They seem to have been depicted primarily by food-gatherers.

In the past, gatherers and hunters were considered as a single category. In some cases we may identify groups showing mixed characters of both hunters and gatherers. However, recent studies have shown that there are marked differences in the grammar and syntax of art between groups with a prevailing carnivorous diet and those that have a prevailing vegetarian diet. The dynamic of daily actions have an impact on the cognitive system of a human being—that of hunters of big game is quite different from that of hunters of rabbits or of ducks, and both are different from that of shell or yam collectors.

In Tanzania, for example, the rock art sequence spans thousands of years, yet all the images of the vegetal world are concentrated in one phase, which may be related to the end of the Pleistocene or the beginning of the Holocene, in a period of 2,000–3,000 years between 14,000 and 8,000 years ago. It would appear to be a phase of gatherers rather than of hunters, even though it is considered to belong to a hunting and gathering period (Anati 1986). After this identification, analogous gatherers' styles and themes were recognised in the Kimberley region in north-west Australia, in the Tassili and other oases of central Sahara, in northern Mexico, in Texas and elsewhere. Similar patterns and typological categories are present in different parts of the world.

May we postulate that similar cognitive processes have led different people to similar visual outputs? Apparently, the structure of art reflects the structure of mind. These kinds of studies are relevant to psychologists and sociologists as well as to philosophers and anthropologists. No doubt, a perspective of 50,000 years may turn out to be useful in order to understand something more of the complex data processing that we perform in our brains.

RECURRING CHARACTERS

In each of the five categories of rock art, there are widespread paradigms. Some of them are rather obvious. Rock art is a world phenomenon practised by tribal groups on rock surfaces or on cave walls. It occurs in 160 countries in five continents. In the production of rock art, there are preferences for the type of place: cave, shelter or open air rock surface. There are preferences for the type of surface, be it horizontal, oblique or vertical, floor or ceiling. For each one of the five categories, there are choices made in the surface on which the painting or the engraving is done, and the chosen surfaces may have recurring characters of colour and form.

Technical preferential methods appear to have been used, whether for painting, engraving, graffiti, hammered pecking or for various types of relief. Certain elements are widely repeated and the phenomenon does not seem to reflect a process of acculturation or diffusion. In some cases, it may be the result of a given technological level, or lifestyle, or way of thinking or all these combined.

It may be postulated that even in the absence of direct communication between different populations, similar outputs were reached in places far apart. Such convergence is not necessarily the result of acculturation or any other type of external influence.

Certain aspects of the environment, economy, ideology, mood and social life do not enter into the artist's thematic range. Artists, hunters or otherwise, made precise choices of the themes they chose to represent; they did not paint or engrave just about anything. The definition of the subjects represented provides hints on the aims of visual art.

In all categories, there are themes of preference. For example, large representations of animals that may be life-size or larger, painted or engraved, are almost exclusive to early hunters. With pastoralists they are only to be found in certain zones that today are deserts, especially in Arabia and the Sahara, and then they are mainly concentrated in archaic phases of pastoralist art. It is likely that these people had an economy relying on both hunting and animal breeding. Their stylistic pattern is, however, quite different from that of early hunters. They are extremely rare in the rock art of complex economy groups. On the other hand, there are other phases in early and evolved hunters' art in which medium-sized or even miniature animal representations are found.

An interesting phenomenon has been noted: when large animals are prevalent, human figures are rare. Where the animals are smaller, the percentage of anthropomorphic figures is usually higher. However, hunters' art always tends to have animal images as the subject matter. Sometimes, humans have animal faces and other zoomorphic features.

The art of food collectors has anthropomorphic beings as the main subject matter. Life-size or larger images or anthropomorphic images are almost exclusively represented in the art of gatherers. In the rock art of northern Australia, Kimberley, Arnhem Land and the York Peninsula, in Australia, in Texas (Pecos River) and in northern Mexico (Baja California) and in America, large-sized anthropomorphic beings have been attributed to hunter-gatherer groups. However, they appear now to belong to gatherer rather than hunter societies.

In the art of early hunters, when there are associations, there are primary and secondary subjects. An initial choice concerns a dominant subject and then minor complementary themes are added. This may well be a reflection of the way of thinking (primary focus and secondary focus).

Repetitive elements, such as ideograms and pictograms accompany the dominant figure. It is currently stated that the animal is the most commonly represented figure in European Palaeolithic art and in early hunter art throughout the world. Animals are undoubtedly the main feature, subject or object of the graphic sentence. However, isolated animal figures are practically non-existent; they are almost always accompanied by ideograms. Animals may occupy a major space on the painted surface due to their size but symbols vary in quantity and they frequently exceed the number of animal figures with which they are associated.

As was brought to evidence by A. Laming (1962) and A. Leroi-Gourhan (1965), in the Palaeolithic art of Western Europe, there are frequent cases of animal figures of different species being associated with each other. There are two animal species, the bison and the horse, which are more frequently represented than others—one in front of or nearby the other. Their facing each other seems to imply something quite specific in the dialectic of associations. According to Leroi-Gourhan they could be symbols for a male and a female. In the Gobustan region of Azerbaijan, in a rich concentration of rock engravings, the main such association in early hunter animal figures concerns the ox and the horse, with types of compositions similar to those of the bison and horse in Western Europe.

In Tanzania, the early hunters' art contains representations of the elephant and giraffe which are associated in a similar way and play a similar role in terms of associations and quantitative proportions to other animals, like the horse and bison in Western Europe and the ox and horse in Gobustan. They are frequently associated and by far the most commonly represented animals (Anati 2000). In all the three areas, there are also other animal species represented in similar associations. There are also representations of animals of the same species facing each other.

Obviously, the repetitive depiction of two animals of the same species or of two different species facing each other is intentional; it is a statement illustrating some sort of intent or concept. It has been suggested that they may be totemic animals representing different clans facing each other, or that they may reflect a dual system of values symbolised by the animals or that they may constitute tribal or clan agreements on the selection of partners. The debate remains open and stimulates a healthy analysis.

In general terms, these are premises for yet another paradigm: the presence in the depiction of dominant animal species a dialectic, metaphorical relationship between them. Early hunters from different parts of the world seem to have had a rather similar way of reasoning.

In the rock engravings of late pre-literate Metal Age in Valcamonica (Italy), in Bohuslaan (Sweden) and in the Altai (central Asia), there are frequent fighting scenes where one fighter has an oval or round shield and the other a rectangular shield. Similar scenes appear in other corners of the world, such as in Mongolia and Kazakhstan. The shape of the shield is likely to indicate the ethnic or social identity of the fighter. Some of these fights in different areas represent images of both sexes: male facing female. They may be 'metaphorical' fights. Recurring characters appearing in different groups of rock art reveal similar systems of defining relevant identity details.

THE SYNTAX OF ART

A definition of the kind of syntax of art is determined by the presence or absence of various types of associations: the scene, the sequence, the assemblage and the abstract composition. They reflect different kinds of cognitive logic. Among early hunters the prevailing association is the sequence. Abstract compositions appear in the art of early hunters, and complex economy groups. Scenes are common in late hunters and in complex economy groups, and are rare or practically absent in most sites of the early hunters. However, many groups of all categories do not include scenes. The anecdotal descriptive scene illustrates an event, a specific moment. Early groups of art tend to represent concepts that go beyond specific events. Even their rare scenes seem to refer to recurring myths. A similar approach was still present in the art of hunting populations of a century ago, like the rock art of some Australian Aborigines of the Northern Territories and the York Peninsula, or the mobiliary art of the Inuit of the Canadian far north.

There are certain types of associations that resemble one another. An animal in the context of other associated figures does not necessarily reflect a naturalistic reality as our present-day thinking would assume; the animals are found repeatedly in similar relationships in accordance with rules that made sense for their makers but which do not correspond to the type of vision of our contemporary culture.

Large animals are placed on cave walls or on rock surfaces as if they were levitating or were suspended in mid-air. In most of the art of the early hunters, there is apparently no concept of a base or ground level. It has often been asked if they are meant to be spirits of animals or totemic images rather than the animals themselves. This trend is common in Europe as well as in Tanzania and Australia, for example.

Pastoral people and complex economy groups often represent scenes of daily life in their art. In the art of evolved hunters, scenes such as hunting scenes, scenes of war, dancing or other events, are common. Early gatherers produced allegoric and surrealistically simple scenes likely to illustrate mythic stories.

The association between animal and symbol recurs with analogies in all early hunting groups: the animal as the subject and the ideograms the symbol, as a type of logic and reasoning around it. In contrast with early hunters, for the early gatherers the main subject matter was not the animal but rather anthropomorphic images, often monstrous, likely to represent spirits or other supernatural beings. The presence of certain kinds of deformations in the faces and in the limbs appears to indicate states of hallucination. They reflect dreamy states of the mind.

With the evolved hunters, the main syntax is based on scenes and shows a specific approach to a temporal reality. The concern tends to focus on events of realistic daily life. As far as our way of thinking is concerned, the associations of evolved hunters are more narrative and naturalistic and less abstract than those of early hunters. Early hunters are more hermetic, with a high degree of symbolism and a metaphoric approach.

Early hunters also frequently display sequences of ideograms that appear as some sort of proto-writing. Symbols are engraved or painted in a row, appearing as a written message. Such proto-writing was still present, several millennia later, in the proto-literate periods in China, Mesopotamia, Egypt and Mexico; and it is still in use among recent hunting-gathering societies. The concept of writing, or marking readable messages through conventional graphemes, may go back, 50,000 years.

Changes in style and associations in art appear to illustrate changes in the cognitive processes which, in turn, reflect modifications in patterns of the associative system. This postulate may apply to all kinds of art, including dance and music, to all continents and all times (Anati 1999).

From an analysis of the thematic typology of the figures, marks and other graphemes, patterns emerge which constitute the grammar of prehistoric art, considering the images as words in sentences or in composite concepts. Isolated marks are as rare as isolated words in a conversation. In rock art, there are systems of associations referred to as syntax. They are sentences composed of groupings or sequences of graphemes just like in the spoken and written languages of today. Thus we may postulate the existence of logical archetypes. The art appears to be like the notebook of a self-psychoanalyst and contains some of the fundamental elements of man's cognitive dynamics.

Students who analyse isolated figures without considering them as part of associations will end up with a catalogue in which each figure is separated from the rest. It will be like reading separately each word in a sentence, without seeing the sentence as having a grammatical sense and syntax.

Over and above the specific characteristics found in the Spanish region of Levante, Valcamonica, Scandinavia, Tanzania, Madhya Pradesh or in the decorated Palaeolithic caves of France and Spain, types of languages are found which touch upon prototypes of a universal nature. Provincial characteristics also exist, which are referred to as vernacular. It is of course tempting to attribute a dialectal nature to all that we do not understand as language. However, it is increasingly clear that universal paradigms and archetypes occupy a large and relevant space in all art of all times.

CONSTANTS AND EXCEPTIONS IN PREHISTORIC ART

Sequences with certain constant features are widespread in different continents. The five categories—the early hunters, early gatherers, evolved hunters, animal rearers and complex economy groups—are present in the same chronological order, but not all of them are necessarily present everywhere. In Australia, no pastoralist-animal breeders' rock art has been noted so far. The Australian sequence is mainly composed of early hunters and early gatherers, and in a few rare areas in the north, evolved hunters. The complex economy category is represented in only a few very recent cases of post-contact art. Early gatherers' art in central Australia does not include scenes, although this type of syntax is present in the Kimberley in early gatherers' rock paintings.

In South Africa, the main figurative rock art zones comprise a sequence with little evidence of early hunters. Figurative paintings of early hunters appear further north, in Namibia, Zimbabwe and Tanzania, where early gatherers were also present. The greatest artistic activity of South Africa (probably the richest in rock art so far known in the world), emerges as the work of early evolved hunters from about 14,000 years ago, who maintained the same visual language with only minor modifications up until the present century. Previous graphic expressions were mostly non-figurative. Late pastoralists-animal breeders and complex economy groups also appear. Rock art is found among these patches of pastoralists and early farming populations, but in most of the territory, the evolved hunters' way of life persisted both before and after, until quite recently (Lewis-Williams 1983).

In Tanzania, there was a short parenthesis during the early hunter period in which fruits, leaves and flowers are represented. There are anthropomorphic figures including anthropomorphised plants and fruits, stylised animals considered to be totemic and mythic depictions rather than hunting prey. Such art appears to represent a culture whose economy was based on gathering. Analogous phenomena occur elsewhere. In central Sahara, a similar type of rock art seems to reflect a population whose lifestyle depended largely on gathering and who, most probably, made extensive use of drugs. As mentioned earlier, a similar trend is recognised in Baja California, Mexico and in the Pecos River and Seminole Canyon in Texas. This peculiar phenomenon is noticed in different parts of the world. At a certain point, carnivorous hunters turned into vegetarian food collectors. Why? What happened? In a few places this change took place in concomitance with warming and humidity in climatic conditions. As a theoretical hypothesis, climatic changes may have modified animal and vegetal resources of food. Another hypothesis suggests that certain diseases may have been caused by the use of meat in a wet-warm climate. Yet another hypothesis claims that dietary taboos or other religious rules may have been introduced to stop the killing of prey. The dynamics of pattern-changing may have a variety of motivations. Graphic output may provide some hints but it is not always explicit on motivation.

In Near Eastern deserts, the rock art shows sporadic examples related to a complex economy of food producers and agriculturists. In the Negev desert, there are even depictions of ploughs dating back about 2,000 years. This reflects a brief period of agriculture and complex economy performed by an exotic population, probably attempts at colonization by Roman or Byzantine soldiers in a period in which rain was more abundant. The stratigraphy of overlapping and superposition shows that both before and after this period, the makers of rock art were pastoralists. In itself the existence of a few drawings which indicate a complex economy does not always mean the beginning of a new era, but it may reveal some minor historical event.

CONCLUSIONS

Art is a means of expression and of communication. It reflects the language of its maker. The presence of animal couples from different species facing each other in a similar way, with a similar metaphoric approach in Tanzania, Azerbaijan and Western Europe represents a similar associative trend. But the animal species are not the same. In each area the metaphor used local animals. Obviously, the giraffe was in Tanzania and not in Europe. It is unlikely that we will find representations of llamas in Australia or of kangaroos in Argentina, but within the general framework we come upon animal subjects, associated in a similar way, with the same kind of values for different species, in different parts of the world. This example of the similarities existing between the constant association of the bison and horse in Palaeolithic Europe, of the ox and horse in Azerbaijan and the giraffe and elephant in the art of early hunters in Tanzania indicate a presence of a widespread pattern concerning the functioning of the cognitive process.

An essential piece of evidence lies in those ideograms that are found as constants the world over. Vulvas, phallic representations, cruciforms, stick-like, egg-like ideograms, cup marks, cup and ring marks, handprints, footprints and animal tracks are found in the Palaeolithic art of Europe as well as in hunter's art in Australia, South Africa and elsewhere. They are also found in the art of complex economy populations and are present in early ideographic scripts.

The art of early hunters and early gatherers appears to have more universal characters than other groups in terms of subject matter, types of association and stylistic trends. The art of evolved hunters has local features. The real 'Tower of Babel' came into being at the end of the hunting and gathering era. Such an event took place at different times in different parts of the world. The economy ceased to be that of hunters, but the spirit of man did not cancel the hunters' tradition. They remained hunters, in behaviour and instincts, from business to politics, to courting, to social relations, even when the economy turned to food production.

Art, like most other aspects of culture, became increasingly provincial and more conditioned by surrounding influences. However, on the whole, many common denominators persisted. The most obvious is the very fact of producing rock art at all and then, as we have seen, there are analogous typologies, choices of subjects and types of associations. The rules of grammar and syntax are global. Choices of subject matter are global because the human brain functioned everywhere in the same way. To be added to these base elements are styles, embellishments and the different means of expression used by various tribes. The most essential difference seems to reside in the seasoning rather than in the substance.

A world database is becoming available and is increasingly contributing to gathering a worldview on the patterns of art and their context. It allows us to assemble an archive on 50,000 years of human intellectual adventures.

Homo sapiens throughout the world are considered to be of one origin. A primordial tribe with one language and one ideology may well be the source of the entire modern humankind. Variations, both in language and in art, took place later. In different regions they reached through their diasporas and developed local dialects that became languages, which further developed dialects and so forth. The early evidence of this process is in visual art, which preserves glimpses of such human adventures.

Prehistoric art, in particular rock art, appears to be a paramount source for reconstructing the intellectual history of *Homo sapiens*. The structure of the mind is reflected in the structure of art. An analysis of rock art is like providing a source for the study of both—the early history of mankind and the development of the human mind.

REFERENCES

Anati, E. (1976), *Evolution and Style in Camunian Rock Art*. Capo di Ponte: Edizioni del Centro.

—— (1979), *L'art rupestre du Neguev et du Sinai*. Paris: L'Equerre.

—— (1981), 'The Origins of Art', *Museum* 33-34: 200-210.

—— (1983), *Gli elementi fondamentali della cultura*. Milano: Jaca Book.

—— (1984), 'The State of Research in Rock Art, a World Report Presented to UNESCO', *BCSP* 21: 13-56.

—— (1986), 'The Rock Art of Tanzania and the East African Sequence', *BCSP* 23: 15-68.

—— (1989), *Le origini dell'arte e della concettualità*. Milano: Jaca Book.

—— (1998), 'The Writing on the Wall. 40,000 Years of *Homo intellectualis*', *The Unesco Courier*, April: 10-16.

—— (1999), 'The Art of Beginnings', *Diogenes* 47–1: 5-16.

—— (1999), 'Grafismo e semiotica nell'arte preistorica e tribale', *BCSP* 30-31: 11-32.

—— (2000), 'Struttura dell'arte', in E. Anati (ed.), *40.000 anni di arte contemporanea*. Capo di Ponte: Edizioni del Centro, pp. 17-22.

—— (2003), *Aux Origines de l'art*. Paris: Fayard.
—— (2004), 'Memoria e oblio: Considerazioni di un archeologo', in M. Tartari (ed.), *Memoria ed oblio*. Bollettino dell'Istituto Italiano di Micropsiconalisi, n. 33-34-35, pp. 43-54.
—— (2004), 'Rock Art and Early Civilisations of China', in Xie Yujie (ed.), *Da Mai Di Rock Arts*. Shanghai: Shanghai Chinese Classics Publishing House, pp. 7-13.
—— (2005), 'La percezione di se stesso e l'immagine antropomorfa nella pareistoria', in E. Levis (ed.), *Le strutture corporee della vita*. Venezia: Cafoscarina, pp. 47-69.
—— (2005), 'A Search for the Meaning of Prehistoric Art', in V.S. Vetrov, *Art and Ritual of Ice Age*. Lugansk, pp. 6-14.
—— (ed.) (2003), *40.000 ans d'art contemporain. Aux origines de l'Europe*. Capo di Ponte: Edizioni del Centro.
Beltran, A. (1988), 'L'art préhistorique Espagnol: nouveaux horizons et problemes. Etat de la question', *BCSP* 24: 13-44.
Bosinski, G. (1999), *Homo sapiens. L'histoire des chasseurs*. Paris: Errance.
Breuil, H. (1952), *Quatre cents siècles d'art parietal*. Montignac: Centre d'etudes et de documentation.
Chen, Zhao-Fu (1988), *Arte rupestre preistorica in Cina*. Milano: Jaca Book.
Clottes, Jean and David Lewis-Williams (2000), *Les chamanes de la préhistoire*. Paris: La maison des roches.
Grant, C. (1983), *The Rock Art of the North American Indians*. Cambridge: Cambridge University Press.
Heyd, T. and J. Clegg (eds.) (2005), *Aesthetics and Rock Art*. Aldershot: Ashgate.
Kozlowski, J.K. (1992), *Preistoria dell'arte orientale europea*. Milano: Jaca Book.
Laming, A. (1962), *La signification de l'art rupestre paléolithique*. Paris: Picard.
Leroi-Gourhan, A. (1965), *Préhistoire de l'art occidentale*. Paris: Mazenod.
—— (1982), *The Dawn of European Art*. Cambridge: Cambridge University Press.
Lewis-Williams, J.D. (1983), *The Rock Art of Southern Africa*. Cambridge: Cambridge University Press.
Lommel, A. (1970), 'Shamanism: The Beginning of Art', *Current Anthropology* 11–1: 39-48.
Luquet, G.H. (1926), *L'art et la Religion des Hommes Fossiles*. Paris: Masson.
Marshack, A. (1972), *The Roots of Civilisation*. New York: McGraw-Hill.
Picq, P. and Y. Coppens (eds.) (2001), *Aux Origines de l'Humanité*. Paris: Fayard.
Schobinger, J. and C.J. Gradin (1985), *L'arte rupestre delle Ande e della Patagonia*. Milano: Jaca Book.
Smits, L.A. (1988), 'Recording and Deciphering of Rock Paintings in Lesotho', *BCSP* 24: 93-99.

2

Rock Art: A Universal Creative Act

S.C. Malik

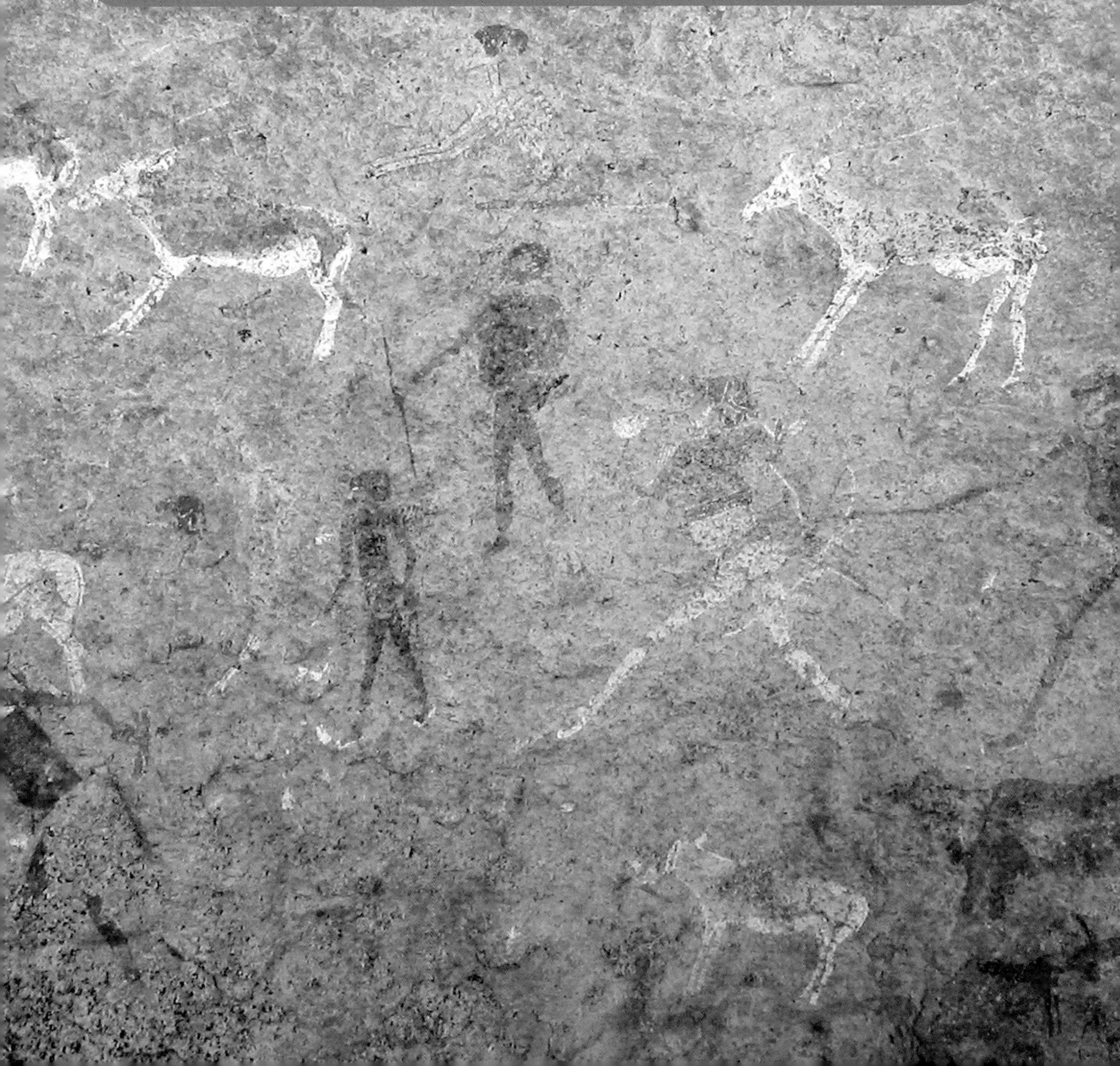

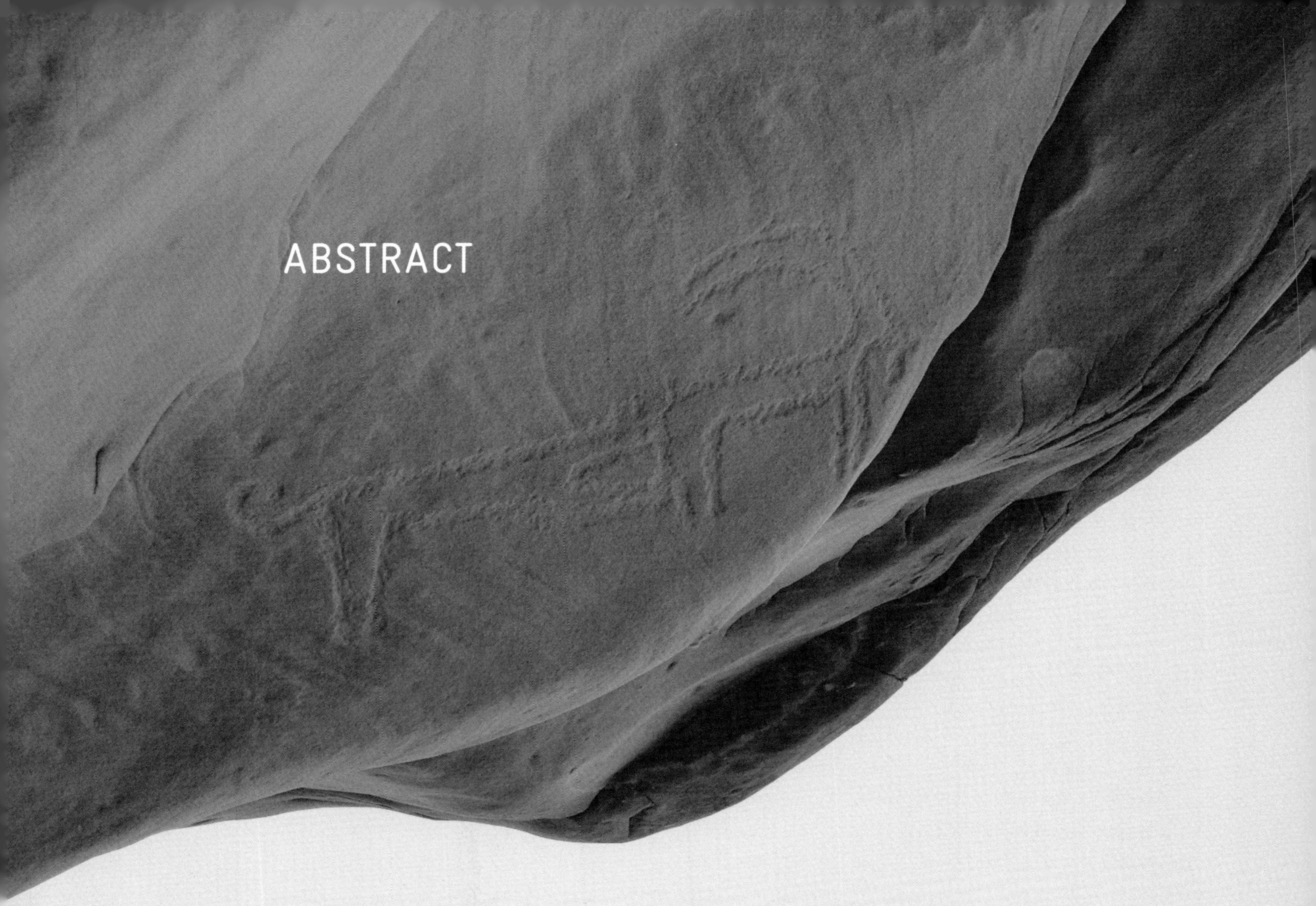

ABSTRACT

Studies on rock art require a healthy questioning of theoretical frameworks that have until now formed an unquestioned base for study. S.C. Malik's paper looks at some stylistic and chronological issues, comparative ethnographic data for interpretation, the constraints of individual and collective cultural subjectivity (Euro-centrism both in rock art and archaeological studies, which were attempted to be duplicated in non-European cultural zones), studying local, live indigenous traditions and to see rock art as a common cultural heritage of humankind.

Thinking along these lines, rock art research may provide crucial insights into many contemporary, long-standing dilemmas. This involves re-examining the concepts and definitions of art as such, irrespective of the definitions given by modern man. Thus, rock art qua art has to be seen as an aesthetic and creative activity and it requires an integral and holistic approach to study rock art.

INTRODUCTION

Rock art research is a well-established discipline in many parts of the world. Lately, there has been healthy questioning of theoretical frameworks and there is a great deal of interest in comparative ethnographic data for interpreting rock art. There is awareness about the constraints involved in reconstructing the past, especially an archaeologist's own point of view. Subjectivity here does not merely refer to an individual, it also points to cultural biases, say Euro-centrism, formulated within certain 'evolutionary' schemes beginning with the Palaeolithic along with the classificatory chronological concepts. There was little success when these sequences were applied in non-European zones. It also led to an almost total neglect of studying indigenous traditions, which have their own models appropriate to local spatio-temporal distributions. The aim of this paper is to indicate that rock art may be viewed within the framework of an overarching artistic-creative act, which runs as a common thread through various cultural communities. For instance, is it not possible to understand rock art by approaching it from a cosmogenic-universal act that is linked to local expressions irrespective of time and place? May it then not provide crucial insights into many contemporary human issues confronting modern man? Rock art thus also needs to be visualised as a universal phenomenon, in the sense of being a common cultural heritage of humankind as such. Of course, nations do claim it to be so but in terms of their cultural and political identity, or in search of man's common identity. However, this approach transcends regional identities.

In rock art studies, the word 'art' itself has a limited concept, as it is governed by various cultural connotations, often monolithic definitions, rather than by other sensibilities and freedom of expression that may be common to all humankind. The modern notion of art as mere aesthetic beauty for its own sake is a limited way of seeing artistic creations. Other cultural, especially non-industrial, communities locate art within many other aspects of life ranging from a sacredness of the world order to the supernatural or the noumenal dimension. This is why ethnology, myths and beliefs provide important alternate ways of viewing rock art, of course supplemented with archaeological records. Hence, it is important to enquire into unexamined assumptions which have governed the study of archaeology, culture and history in this subcontinent. In doing so, we may be able to formulate holistic approaches to the knowledge of the past. To illustrate, it is 'normal' to locate events within apast-present-future framework. This movement of time is considered external to the body-brain mechanism and it is seldom noted that the external-internal movement is not only closely linked but it is in fact one movement. It is split because of the socio-cultural system, within symbolic semiotic languaging terms that make up the framework of most human societies. In this way rock art may be viewed within the Indian setting where exist tremendous variations of cultural configurations, along with a multitude of variables. If the goal is to search for meaning behind rock art, we have to move beyond the mechanistic, analytical and evolutionary approaches to the direction of intuitive-aesthetic, beyond pseudo-religious explanations. This may allow the decoding of the total symbolic system, within the framework of the universal nature of art (Malik 1995).

ROCK ART QUA ART

There is growing realisation that any philosophy and explanation of art without an account and understanding of an aesthetic experience is inadequate and lifeless. The theory of an expression of this directedness of consciousness upon an object is quite different from the universe of discourse that is given shape by artistic experience and expression. Experience is definitely the primal source, common to all human communities. Art experience is an exudation of consciousness from the privacy of the inner, and cannot therefore be treated merely as a thing. The language of art moves beyond conceptual, semantic and syntactic constraints, to cognise reality in silence. Art experience, thus, both for the creator and the spectator, is dialogic in all its pre-linguistic, linguistic and trans-linguistic aspects (Biswas 1995). In this sense, art signifies a continuity of reality through different spatial and temporal levels. The images of poetry, painting, sculpture and architecture, music, dance and all other arts constitute such items of knowledge. The questions which arise from such an approach are:

1. What is one's relation with works of art?
2. What is the nature of the creative process?
3. What is the relation between man as an artist and his creations?
4. How is the meaning of art determined?
5. How is the ontological status of art determined? (Biswas 1995)

Viewed within this general framework, the approach provides a common platform on which all art stands. There is sense of indeterminacy in experiencing a work of art, and there is an absence of 'fact' of the kind which is commonplace in the modern world. The appearances of things are abstracted from their material existence and transformed into visions, forms and images in art. For example, a picture is made with pigments on a rock surface, but the painting that emerges is not 'pigment on canvas'. It expresses its own space and a particular relationship between the human and the world. In short, a work of art has a continuous existence and identity, and like a human being it is a 'no-thing', a non-factual order of being. The modern world is driven by fact-ridden realities, beset with dichotomies and hierarchies which become irreconciliable. It is only when one understands this basic holistic vision which gives rise to a non-utilitarian attitude to man and his creative work, that any meaningful insight of rock art research becomes possible. Thus, rock art qua art, as an artistic activity, is intrinsically an act of creativity. This is a departure from frameworks, such as conflict-confrontation binary opposites (sacred-secular, high-low, literate-non-literate, urban-rural or tribal, traditional-modern), structural-functional, uni-multilinear evolutionary models and so on. The integral way suggests principles of complementarity, pluralism, concurrency, coexistence, polyvalence and synergy, to view works of art. It is to focus on dynamic interrelationships, as distinct from de-contextualisation of artistic manifestations and expressions. This does not mean that any evolutionary processes for archaeological records as such are to be discarded altogether. The linear progressive movements may be seen as sub-sets of larger categories, especially at a time when the written word and thought had not become so specialised and when man was in touch with nature and the cosmos with highly sensitised senses.

Experience-experiencing played a central role. The expression of manifestation was through non-verbal images and symbols, artistic or otherwise. This viewpoint allows one to recognise fuzzy areas, twilight zones. These in short are perennial common core principles that are equally valid for all cultures albeit they are articulated in many different ways. While the natural and social environment does shape artistic expression, herein may also lay the cause of creativity, as there is no linear one-to-one logical connection of explanation of this order of artistic expression. Its source probably lies not in the phenomenal but in the nominal dimension. Art in this sense is both a participatory and universal activity, which is unique at the same time that it is timeless since it springs from a still interiority, a silence that is a form of contemplation. Art in this sense is a manifestation of the unspoken word, authentic in experience that invokes, evokes and provokes the viewer. It is an expression of the totality of life experience, even when connected to rituals, fairs, worship, beliefs and festivals—a very wide spectrum indeed. There are thus different orders of experience, different levels of functional attributes, and formal values and so on of art as such. While all this is valid for art as such, it is equally valid for rock art.

Several questions may arise in the context of viewing art in alternate ways. For instance:

a. What methodologies are to be evolved to avoid dichotomies and binary opposites?
b. In the holistic vision how is one to divide and sub-divide? For purposes of classification and analysis, can one eschew the analytical methodology?
c. How is one to define art, taking into account religious, technological and environmental parameters?
d. How is one to relate to other cultures, to language and non-language texts, of translating non-verbal phenomena?
e. Is it possible to address different levels at the same time?
f. Is it not possible to take into account the non-European or Indian view of culture, in applying it to rock art, as an organising principle in general? If so, what may be the key categories and definitions in the true sense, as the rubric of discourse?

To answer any of these questions, we need to adopt an approach that is different from a modern or any nationalistic viewpoint. Rock art may be viewed in a variety of ways, as history, psychology, religion, utilitarian-functional and graphic representational motifs of some underlying 'material' aspects of social and cultural life and subsistence patterns. Most of all, to see rock art as the main system to this notion of a sacred cosmic order from whence arises the creative urge that is common to all humanity. This is the silent common-communion-language of humankind, of an integral vision which is mystic, mysterious, divine and supernatural. This approach is beyond the questions of what, when, where and why without excluding any of them. It has the advantage that its dynamic and flexible framework of reference expresses different kinds of inherent cultural continuities in terms of myths, dream-times and other motifs which are common to the human species. It is like common geometrical patterns, stylised lines and so on, which arise from the basic rhythm of sound and light, of dance and music. This is the holistic vision of simultaneity that can be understood as part of the experiential level when one lives in touch with the sacred dimension. Modern man with his shrunken outlook is surprised that such 'primitive' people could produce art. The message of art is perennial and authentic because it arises from something 'non-material', in the spirit, and gives moral and spiritual values to one's life.

To illustrate, one can take a hint from living Indian traditions which still continue to exist in the so-called 'folk' and 'tribal' cultures that have local 'oral' histories in a non-historical way. Rock art designs may be seen as psychological symbols and signs, as *mandalas* that arise out of a common universal collective consciousness. For example, simple lines do not just reflect simplicity but are representations of an extreme sophistication; they are not untrained 'naturalism'. Such patterns are made in pre- and post-meditation states by children of various cultural groups (Kandinsky 1977; Saraswati et al. 1994). Art is the mother of all emotions as it unites all our senses; sound, sight, touch and smell are all interwoven with each other. Colours trigger off emotional states. As we all know, red provokes anger, blue is for peace, green is for jealousy. Paintings are thus symphonies of not only colours but also those of sound, taste, smell and feelings of warmth, coldness, lightness and darkness. In other words, a painting has a grammar which may be deciphered, horizontally and vertically and so on. These are expressed as:

1. Musical movement
2. Pictorial movement of melodic principles
3. Physical movement
4. Spiritual movement of triangles, circles, etc.
5. Mysterious and secret manifestations of the unknown

Again, traditional art as opposed to the modern is extensive and informal and, generally Speaking, it also has certain qualities:

1. It is formal—it involves intensive laborious formality.
2. It is repetitive and calls for concentration.
3. It has an element of faith and obedience.
4. There is respect and reverence.

Like music, painting is a combination of compositions, which may be melodic and simple, or symphonic and complex (Kandinsky 1977).

SUMMARY AND CONCLUSION

Rock art studies require healthy questioning of theoretical frameworks that have until now formed the unquestioned basis for its study. This paper looked at one of these issues with regard to approaches. The main approaches are stylistic and chronological studies, comparative ethnographic data in terms of interpretation, the constraints of individual and collective cultural subjectivity (for example, Euro-centrism in archaeology and rock art studies which were then attempted to be duplicated in non-European cultural zones) and studying local (indigenous) live cultural traditions, to see rock art as a common cultural heritage of humankind (for example, to see it as an overarching universal creative act built internally within the *Homo sapiens*). Thinking along these lines, can't rock art research provide crucial insights into many of the current dilemmas that humankind is facing? For this, concepts and definitions of art need to be looked at from many other viewpoints than the modern man's ideas of art which mainly look at aesthetic beauty for its own sake, maybe even as something functional but which certainly does not see it for its sacred context which most earlier societies linked it to, to the world at large and the cosmos or a cosmic vision. Thus, rock art qua art, as an artistic activity, is intrinsically an act of creativity. This understanding requires an integral and holistic approach. Creativity is timeless in this sense as it is always present as intelligence, which is inherent in the human species in a non-evolutionary sense. In this way it is also non-hierarchical as it exists in all human societies, both of the past and the present.

Some of the other issues and approaches discussed in this paper include:

1. Concepts and terms, for example, is it more accurate to say call it palaeo-art, rather than rock art since Petroglyphs also have to be included in this stream? Is the approach qualitative or only quantitative?
2. New and old methodologies, for example, stylistic approaches which are often subjective or mere opinions and notions arising from present-day ideas about art. Is there a system for such studies? Are these text-free interpretations of the distant past, especially when there is overlapping? These pictorial images are after all texts about economics, sustenance, technology, cultural myths, astronomy or night sky, and about the socio-cultural context which one can deduce from fragmentary inferential evidence?
3. How reliable is an ethnographic analogy, say, in seeking parallels? Are these interpretations evolutionary when chronologies are concerned, and even if so, do these archaeological records reflect an evolutionary sequence for art also? What is the function of art? Is it singular, multiple and/or holistic?
4. What are the concepts behind these studies, say, is one following the Newtonian 19th century approaches? Such other epistemological issues need to be taken into account, since science is itself subjective in many ways.
5. What is an ethnographic record? Is it correct to give interpretative explanations from information about motifs?
6. What are the broad anthropological perspectives? What should the rock art tradition be defined as?
7. How are we to understand cognitive symbolic representations? Are these religious?
8. What is our notion of indigenous people? Is it static like it is about 'prehistoric' people? Were those people less intelligent than us, especially when one calls them 'primitive' from our techno-economic viewpoint, ignoring the fact that human intelligence is the same everywhere and beyond time? Did these groups not have better extra-sensory perceptions of other dimensions which we have lost in the midst of our so-called 'progress' and onslaught of industrial urbanisation? The results of wars and famines indicate that we are more primitive than early man.

Finally, India has the third largest concentration of rock art. Of the over one million motifs, animals are the most frequent; humans come next, and symbols and designs third. Various pigments such as haematite and other oxides of iron were used to provide colours in red, yellow, orange or brown and also black and deep purple obtained from oxides of magnesium. For instance, 21 colours were counted in Bhimbetka ranging from ochre, raw sienna, ashy white, creamy white, vermillion, scarlet, light red, burnt amber, crimson, dark crimson, chocolate, emerald green to black and purple. Most of these compounds are available in surface deposits at a close distance from the paintings. All these facts are well known and need not be repeated.

A million years ago, *Homo sapiens* emerged from various ancestries, but there is no evidence that intelligence evolved from the 'primitive' to the modern, in art at least, if not in its expression, perhaps in technology, language and economics. Creative impulse is non-hierarchical and non-linear; it is a manifestation and movement of archetypes of invisible realities. Academics are out of touch with this cosmic dynamism and this area of the sacred. Today humankind has lost touch with some internal truths wherein lie the seeds of the future. Is it really possible to understand art and rock art within this nightmare of materialism and the despair of unbelief that divides life into various unrelated processes (Malik 1989)?

REFERENCES

Biswas, Goutam (1995), *Art as Dialogue—Essays in Phenomenology of Aesthetic Experience*. New Delhi: IGNCA.

Kandinsky, Wassily (1977), *Concerning the Spiritual in Art*. London: Dover.

Malik, S.C. (1989), *Modern Civilisation—A Crisis of Fragmentation*. New Delhi: Abhinav Publications.

——. (1995), *Reconceptualising the Sciences and Humanities—An Integral Approach*. New Delhi: Nehru Memorial Museum and Library and Manohar.

3

The Concept of Style in Archaeology and Rock Art: A Case Study of the Rock Art of Peninsular India

N. Chandramouli

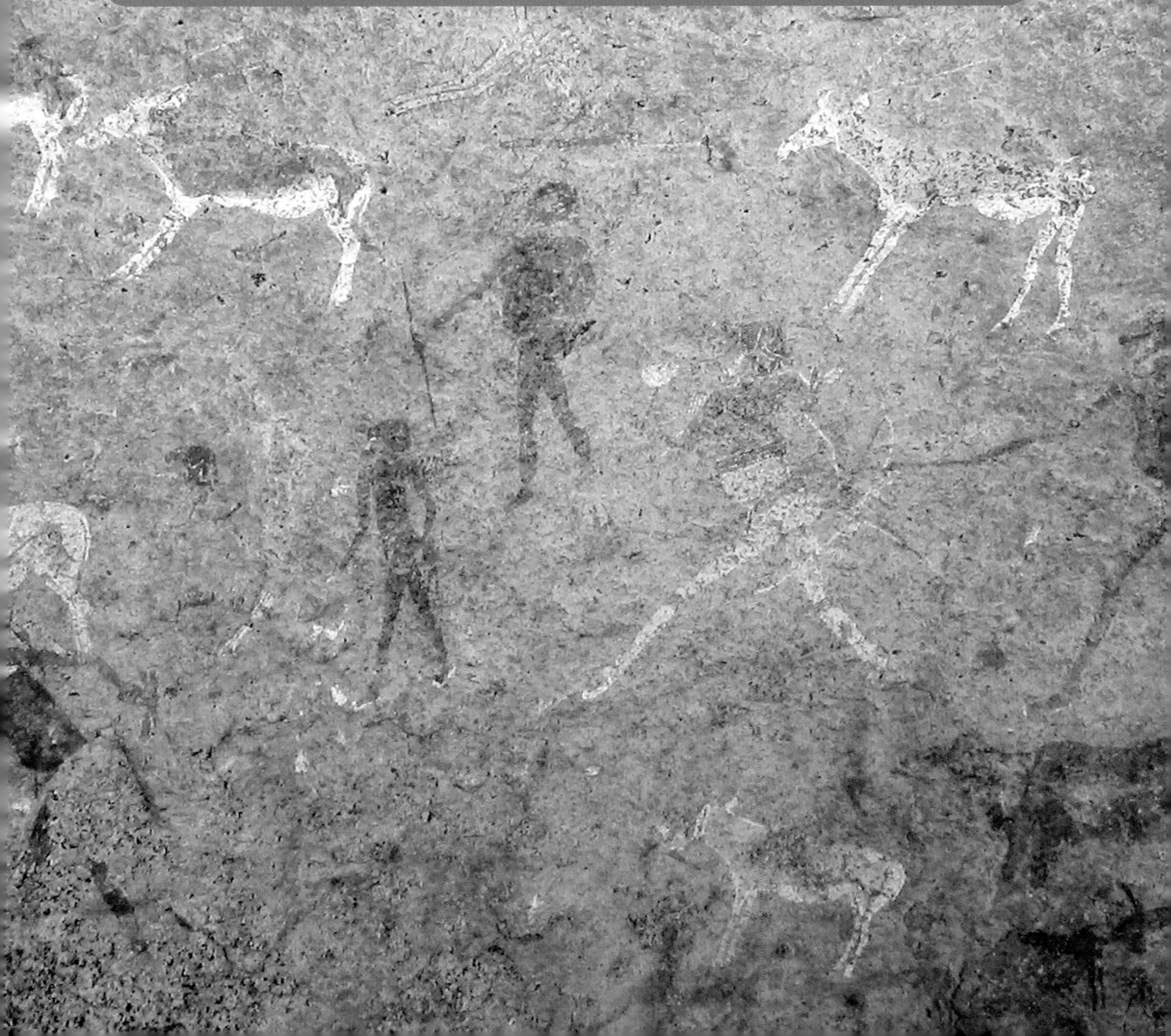

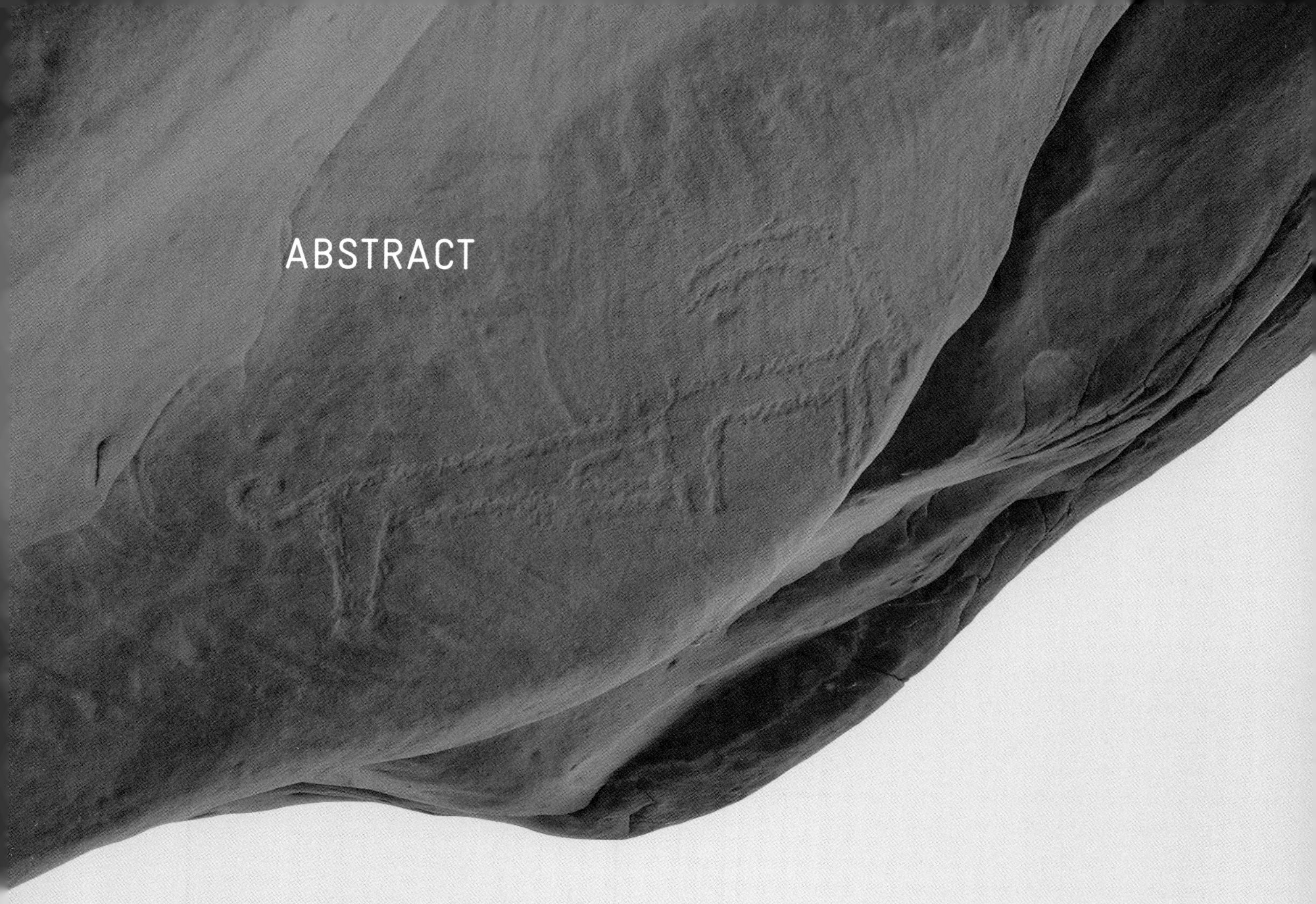

ABSTRACT

Style, defined as 'a way of doing', in theoretical archaeology was originally used to identify and segregate the 'types' in lithic material categories. It soon evolved into a major conceptual tool to analyse a variety of archaeological material, among which rock art is the most unique as it is the earliest 'speaking' material manifestation of the prehistoric past. Rock art has been classified and interpreted by scholars taking into consideration a variety of parameters, such as its context, superimpositions and 'style'. Although criticised by rock art scholars of the school of the 'post-stylistic era' as an exercise of misinterpretation, these studies provided early breakthroughs in making some sense out of the seemingly myriad forms of depictions in some equally mysterious contexts. Dr. Chandramouli's paper discusses the evolution of the concept of 'style' in archaeological and anthropological studies to understand how it came to be utilised in the analysis of rock art as well. It also evaluates the post-stylistic phase of archaeological research, which criticised the subjective interpretations of the stylistic categories, primarily on the basis of sophisticated scientific methods, particularly radiometric dating methods. The paper initiates a 'stylistic' study of the rock art of peninsular India in the light of the pros and cons of the application of this concept.

I

'Without style we have nothing to talk about; no problem to solve'

— Davis 1990:23

'Style is an archaeological construct which is impossible to define scientifically'

— Bednarik 1995a:877

These two statements by an art historian and a rock art specialist respectively portray the rapidly changing perceptions of the scholarly world in the last decade of the 20th century on the application of the concept of 'style' in rock art studies. On the one hand, it was considered to be an essential analytical tool, and on the other it was condemned as a premise scientifically untestable.

The concept of style is said to be the central feature of 20th century modernist thought that encompassed the entire gamut of human cultural life—art, architecture, paintings and even personal adornments (see Conkey 1990 for a review of the historical growth of the concept). Archaeology derived the concept of style from a facet of this modernist thought: *visualist ideology*, which emphasised that knowledge can be described, compared, classified and generalised and that the ways of knowing are visually rooted. Archaeologists are always concerned with identifying and interpreting similarities and differences (homogeneity and heterogeneity) among artefacts of the human past. In this task, 'style' came as a handy, readymade tool. It was during the 'culture history' phase (Trigger 1989:150-55), which dominated historical as well as archaeological studies throughout the 20th century (up to the 1960s and even beyond), that archaeological records themselves came to be 'described' primarily in terms of 'style'. In an effort at making sense out of prehistoric material, archaeologists inferred 'style' as 'some sort of formal statement of the particular ways in which different artefacts are similar or different to each other' (Davis 1986:124). Stylistic types (Kreigger 1944) are used to identify homologous similarities for the reconstruction of 'culture history', which is mainly concerned with the chronological context of different cultures. The purpose of 'style' here is to describe the cultures in a spatio-temporal context. During this period, stylistic types became representatives of Stone Age cultures: Aurignacian, Soultrean, Gravettian, Magdalenian, etc.

The culture history paradigm received a major shock with the introduction of alternate methods and theories by New Archaeology. 'The normative concept of culture was replaced by the systemic and the descriptive chronicling by the study of cultural processes. The kinds of 'styles' that the New Archaeologists described were oriented towards recording analogous similarities, rather than homologous similarities' (Conkey 1989: 123). For them 'style' was the 'formal variability (among the artefacts) that relates to the social contexts of manufacture and use rather than related to function' (Binford 1965:218). Here 'style' was thought to be rooted in the social context and the artefacts were thought to be outputs of cultural and behavioural systems and sub-systems. Wobst (1977: 321) widened the scope of 'style' when he defined it as 'formal variability that is related to the participation of artefacts in the processes of information exchange and about the maintenance of cultural boundaries'. The idea that cultural products contain coded information for target populations is one of the features of the Binfordian programmatics. Similar ideas were also expressed by Plog (1978), when he identified the prominent role of 'style' in social processes, social exchanges and interactions. Sackett (1977, 1990) added a new dimension to the ongoing debate on 'style' when he defined it as 'the passive aspect of material culture that speaks to us about such things as social groupings and ethnic geography'. According to him, the passive aspect of 'style' (termed *isochrestic style*) is the 'outsider's view', that is, our (researchers') view of 'style' in artefacts. The 'active aspect' of style (termed *iconological style*) is what the makers of the artefacts had in mind when they made, used, reused, modified and discarded them, signifying the 'insider's view'. 'Iconological style' is thought to be embedded in such attributes of artefacts that are aimed at a target population, and that are to be read by us.

Bednarik (2003: 515) put forth a similar argument when he said that 'style as an attribute does not exist independent of the original producer and consumer'. He, however, cautions that 'without direct ethnographic access the archaeologist's ability to correctly judge the stylistic variables may be severely limited. It is in any case not amenable to refutation, which render propositions about style unfalsifiable and thus nonscientific'.

Sifting through a plethora of definitions and conceptual elaborations on 'style', Weissner (1990:107) came out with a working concept: "style is a form of non-verbal communication through doing something in a certain way that communicates information about relative identity". 'Style' is considered to be an indicator of social processes, social boundaries, information transmission, ethnic geography and so on. 'Style', instead of signifying formal variations in the artefact typology, now took over the role of identifying and explaining the social dynamics in the manufacture, usage, discarding and continuation of the artefacts of both physical and visual forms. All the above analyses and descriptions of 'style' are focused on material examples, such as pottery, stone tools and other artefacts of archaeological and ethnographic context (Conkey 1980, 1987; Weissner 1983).

II

Among non-verbal evidences of the prehistoric past, which are rooted in contemporary social structures and belief systems, rock art occupies the most important position. "Art involves a culturally standardised system of visual representations that functions as a mechanism for ordering experience and segmenting it into manageable categories" (Conkey 1978: 63). It is in prehistoric art, both mobilary and parietal, that 'style' is thought to be prominently embedded and which can be visualised.

The definition of 'style' proposed by art historian Schapiro was the most influential one in its application to rock art analyses. According to Schapiro (1953: 287), 'style' is, above all, a system of forms with a quality and meaningful expression through which the personality of the artist and the broad outlook of a group are visible. This suggests that 'style' is a form of group expression that is generally used to fix and to communicate religious, social and moral values.

Rock art studies were under tremendous influence of the 'stylistic chronological paradigm' of Breuil and Leroi-Gourhan (whose period is called the 'stylistic era') until the 1990s. Abbe Breuil established the theoretical conception of 'unilinear progression' of Palaeolithic art and advocated a four-phased progressive evolution from simple to complex and refined. At the end of his career, Breuil suggested that Palaeolithic art had progressed through two periods: the Aurignacian-Perigordian and the Soultrean-Magdalenian cycles. Leroi-Gourhan (1968) criticised Breuil's 'cyclical chronology' and suggested that Palaeolithic art followed a 'coherent evolutionary curve' through five 'styles' corresponding to different epochs: the pre-figurative period (Chatelperronian); Styles I and II (primitive period) of Aurignacian and the Gravettian stage and the beginning of the Soultrean; Style III (Archaic period) analogous to the end of Soultrean and the early Magdalenian period; Old Style IV corresponding to the Magdalenian period; and Recent Style V corresponding to the end of the Magdalenian period. He established the notion that prehistoric art evolved in a 'single ascending curve' that spanned the entire upper Palaeolithic. This stylistic chronological method together with the 'Eurocentric origin of rock art' theory was accepted by a majority of the archaeologists until the last decade of the 20th century (Moro Abadia and Manuel 2008:542).

Lorblanchet (1990:20) announced the dawn of a 'post-stylistic era' in rock art studies in view of the 'revolutionary' changes brought about by scientific (radiometric) dating methods in the chronological assessment of rock art data, which was hitherto being done through a 'stylistic classification'. This heralded a long debate on the pros and cons of stylistic as well as scientific dating of rock art (for example, Bednarik 1995a, 1995b, 2001, 2003, 2007; Clottes 1993; Lorblanchet and Bahn 1993; Moro Abadia and Manuel 2007; Pettitt and Bahn 2003). The end result of the long debate was the total rejection of the unilinear evolution of Palaeolithic art from simple to complex. The consistency of AMS radiocarbon dates in the case of the Chauvet cave in southern France, led to the acceptance of the Aurignacian date for a majority of the rock art, thereby, disproving its unilinear evolution. At the same time, the dawn of the 'post-stylistic era' did not necessarily mean the death of 'style' as told by the very proponents of the post-stylistic era (Lorblanchet and Bahn 1993: vii).

The more recent work of Abadia and Manuel (2007: 115) looked at the definition of 'style' in rock art studies from the chronological, formal and thematic perspectives. According to them, firstly, the concept of 'style' implies a specific way of doing something in a specific time, implying the chronological value of 'style'. Secondly, 'style' is usually defined by a limited number of subjects. Thirdly, 'style' generally refers to a characteristic manner of representing images. Thus, style may broadly be defined as 'chronological, formal and a thematic coincidence in the way images are represented'. In this definition, 'style' means and includes the subject matter of rock art, the nature of its depiction and its chronological context.

III

In rock art literature in India also, the term 'style' is encountered frequently. It is necessary to look at these 'style types' of rock art and see how Indian scholars viewed and applied them in their analyses of rock art. As in the other parts of the world, stylistic types or categories in the Indian context are also aimed at answering the spatio-temporal questions

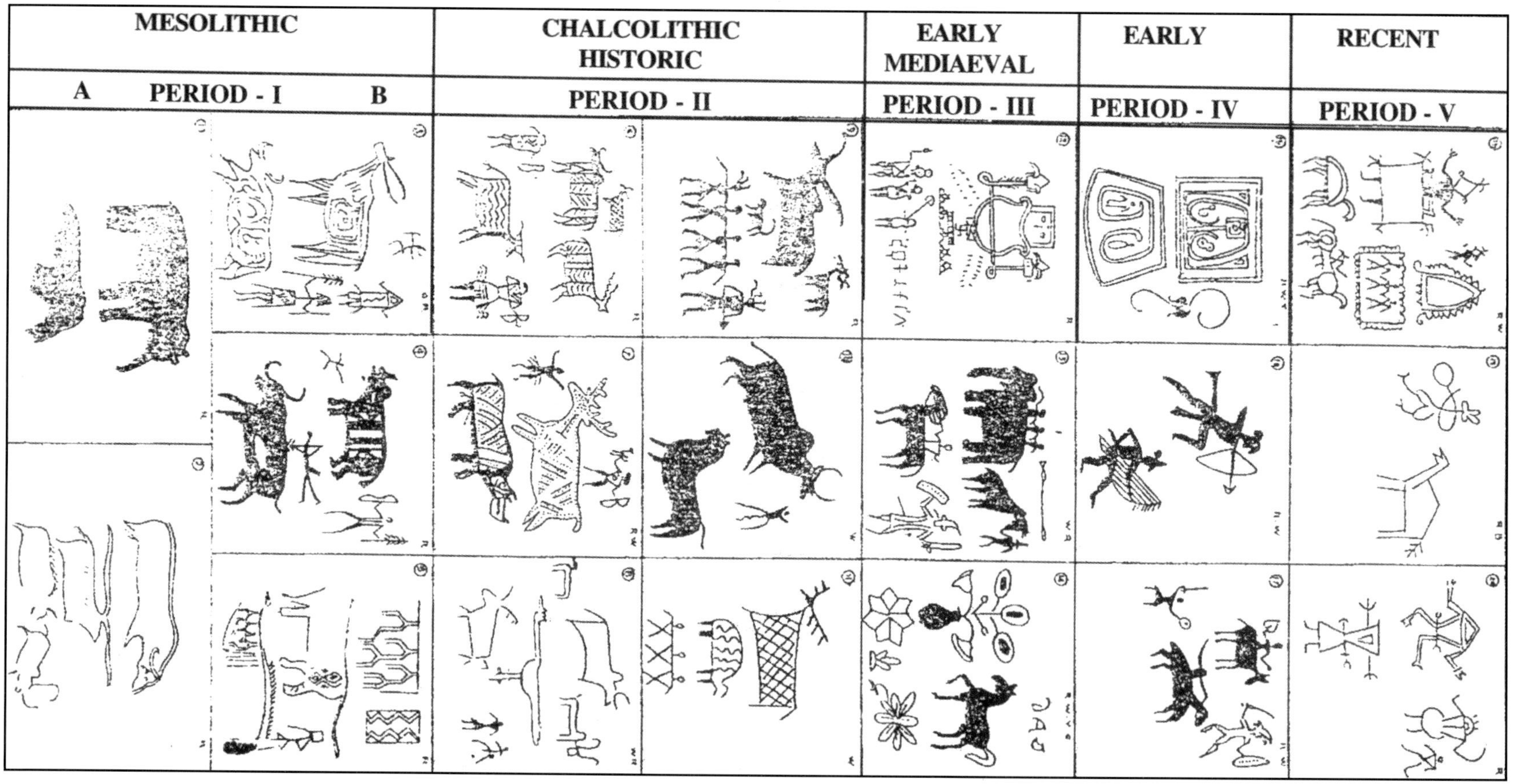

Fig. 3.1 Indian rock art style chart of Dr. V.S. Wakankar.

of archaeological cultures. However, in view of the absence or non-identification of sub-regional or geographical variations in lithic assemblages in either the upper Palaeolithic or the Mesolithic as has been done in the context of western Europe or elsewhere, where such regional variations are markedly distinct and hence given 'cultural identities', a theoretical debate over the concept of 'style' could not be initiated in India. However, as done in the context of European upper Palaeolithic, in India also, efforts were made by the early scholars to correlate the rock art phases with the excavated material remains in the rock shelters to build up a relative chronological sequence. But the scholars used the term 'style' as per their own individual perception and understanding. Wakankar (2005: 282-86) and Wakankar and Brooks (1976) were the first to adopt the word 'style' and they identified 20 'styles' in five periods (phases) of Indian rock art on the basis of colour schemes and superimpositions (Fig. 3.1).

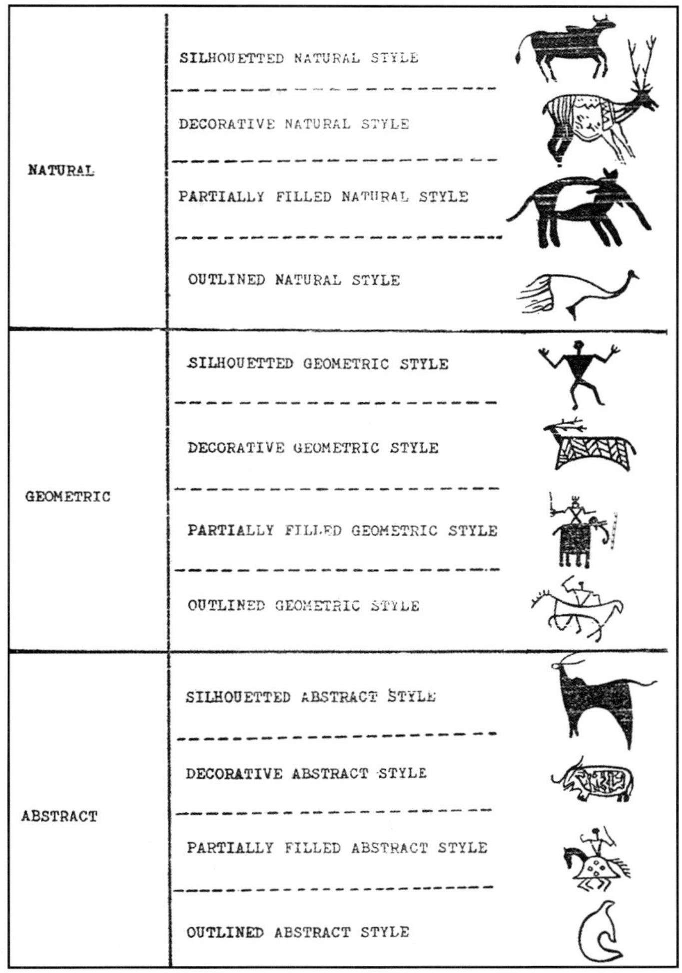

Fig. 3.2 Bhimbetka rock art style chart of Dr. Yashodhar Mathpal.

The 'style' classification is aimed to delineate the types of depictions so far as the physical appearance of the themes of rock art such as 'S' shape bodied human figures, silhouettes and X-rays in the paintings of the prehistoric period are concerned (Periods I & II). Each period is further sub-divided into categories A, B and C on the basis of styles predominantly showing variation in drawing techniques. Period I is dated to the Mesolithic and Period II to the Chalcolithic. Rock art depictions ascribed to historical times on the basis of dynastic appellations, such as Mauryan, Sunga and Gupta periods (Period 3a, 3b and 3c), were identified with separate 'style types' (Styles 11-16). Obviously, 'style' in this analysis was to place the rock art phases on a temporal scale, albeit on relative grounds. Wakankar also substantiated these style types or periods on the basis of superimpositions, colour schemes and state of preservation besides thematic changes.

Similarly, Mathpal (1984) (Fig. 3.2) identified 'style' from 'several ways of executing figures' in the rock paintings in Bhimbetka. In this micro-level study, 12 'styles' were identified on the fundamental idea of three approaches: 1. Representational or Natural Approach; 2. Geometric Approach; and 3. Abstract Approach. Each 'approach' is divided into four groups on the basis of the extent of colour infilling (Fig. 3.2). He states that the present system of stylisation is convenient for 'describing' rock art. Thus, in Mathpal's study, 'style' is visualised to describe rock art themes as also to classify and assign them to different chronological phases. Similarly, Neumayer (1983: 9) was quite explicit about his concept of 'style' when he propounded the 'chronology of styles' in his *culture-chronology method.*

Although Indian scholars mention style in their studies of rock art in India, they have not explained what they mean by 'style'. Wakankar's stylistic classification appears to have been influenced by that of Leroi Gourhan. However, in the absence of contextual excavated material remains as in the case of the European upper Palaeolithic as also due to the open air context of Indian rock art, Wakankar adopted a more native approach to the classification, study and analysis of rock art. From the various descriptions of style it appears that it has been taken to indicate the physical appearance of rock art themes or the technique of depiction. The Indian concept of 'style' thus has the following features:

a. Identification of the subject matter of the rock paintings.
b. Their forms in terms of their visual appearance.
c. Classification of phases on the basis of colour schemes, superimpositions and state of preservation.

The application of 'style' to the other aspects of rock art such as cultural exchanges and information transmission were not attempted. With this brief background of the concept of 'style' in Indian rock art research let us look at the rock art corpus of peninsular India.

IV

To analyse the rock art of peninsular India also from a stylistic viewpoint, attributes such as themes, forms and physical appearance should be taken into consideration. Regarding the criticism on the application of a stylistic analysis in the study of rock art, it must be emphasised that in view of the very expensive scientific dating procedures which are a luxury for rock art researchers in this part of the world, a stylistic analysis used with necessary care, and corroborated by archaeological material is the most plausible way of making rock art research meaningful.

A correlation between lithic and material assemblages of the prehistoric and historical past and rock art depictions is necessary to make sense of the superimposed mass of the rock art depictions. In comparison to the rock art of central India, rock art of peninsular India reveals certain peculiar features in terms of the nature of the rock art sites, flora and fauna, density of rock art representations as also the concomitant archaeological material. Allowing for the absence of comprehensive recording of rock art depictions in Peninsular India, the analogous similarities both in terms of the availability of archaeological evidence and rock art depictions should be taken into account in attempting a tentative inter-site stylistic analysis. Besides this, contextual chronological issues of archaeological cultures should also be taken into consideration as done by Wakankar and Mathpal. Thus, in this present attempt, the definition of *style* is taken as '*a chronological, formal and thematic coincidence in the way the images are represented*'.

The peninsular part of the Indian subcontinent displays an array of divergent physical features (rock formations, drainage, soil profiles, flora and fauna). These in turn reflect the availability of human occupational evidence belonging to various phases of the prehistoric and historical past. Before going into the study of rock art proper a general survey of the archaeological context of different cultures will not be out of place. On the basis of the density and analogous typo-technological similarities in archaeological occurrences in Peninsular India, two broad geographical divisions can be made: the Andhra-Karnataka zone and the Kerala-Tamil Nadu zone.

In the archaeological context of the Andhra-Karnataka region all the phases of prehistoric and proto-historic (Palaeolithic, Mesolithic, Neolithic-Chalcolithic and Iron Age) cultures are represented almost uniformly in the entire region including the densely forested plateau regions, river valleys, stream banks and so on, indicating a continuous prehistoric occupation of the region and also a gradual increase in settlements/population. The granite regions of Karnataka-Andhra contain the richest evidence of early agro-pastoral communities in India, which besides the archaeological data, contain rock art which could offer some interesting clues for understanding the evolutionary stages of the Mesolithic-Neolithic interface. Recent publications (David Raju 1985, 1990; Ravi Korisettar et al. 2002; I.K. Sarma 2003; Venkata Subbaiah 1992, 2007 for example) listed out more than 500 sites in these two regions making them as one of the most prolific areas of Neolithic evidences. These sites included as many as 70 'ash mounds' another interesting phenomena of the agro-pastoral context of the Neolithic culture in peninsular India (Zeunar1959; Paddayya 2002; Chandramouli 2012a).

In contrast to this, the Kerala-Tamil Nadu region revealed limited and stray occurrences of prehistoric (Palaeolithic, Mesolithic and Neolithic) periods that too concentrated in the northern parts of the Tamil Nadu region. Palaeolithic and Neolithic occurrences in the Kerala region are too sporadic. The emergence of Megalithic/Iron Age marks the beginning of the thorough colonization of the entire peninsular India, indicating the evolutionary transition of prehistoric societies into organised states of the early historical period almost uniformly all over the region (Chandramouli 2010-11, 2012b). Of all the Prehistoric material evidences, in the Kerala-Tamil Nadu region, Iron Age (Megalithic) evidence is the most prolific in the archaeological context. Similar to the archaeological context, rock art data also displays regional peculiarities in Peninsular India. At the present state of our knowledge, there are 38 rock art sites in the Andhra region (Chandramouli 2003, 2010-11), nearly 100 in Karnataka (Sundara 2006), more than 90 in Tamil Nadu (Rajan 2008) and 29 rock art sites in Kerala (Kurien 2010-11; Mathpal 1998).

Andhra-Karnataka Zone

This zone has as many as 138 rock art sites distributed in three geological formations-limestone/sand stone, granite/gneiss and shale. Rock art sites located in each of the geological formations display certain uniform features as well as striking differences in themes, in the density of rock art and in the contextual availability of archaeological material as also in the floristic and faunal compositions.

The rock art corpus of peninsular India contains both pictographic and petroglyphic content, the latter confined to the granite-gneiss zone of the black-cotton soil profiles, having the concomitant archaeological context of agro-pastoral cultures. The petroglyphic content continues to appear in subsequent cultural phases as well and extends right into medieval times. Pictographic content in the earliest of the rock art series contain a variety of subject matter, the majority of which comprise animals, both wild animals and domesticated ones, in an equal variety of forms and sizes. Other painting series include depictions of advanced cultural milieus such as caparisoned horses and elephants ridden by warriors with swords, lances and shields. Yet another painting series contains painted inscriptions of Brahmi, Kannada and Telugu scripts, religious symbols and personages datable to the historical period. In the same series are found multi-chrome frescoes depicting epic stories and deified figures in life-size proportions occurring in a couple of sites in Andhra – Karnataka region (in Warangal and Bellary districts respectively). The thematic content of these multi-chrome frescoes in relation to the other on site archaeological evidences helps us to date them to the medieval period.

Rock Art Stratigraphy

Classification of rock art series is attempted through an 'internal analysis' of Rock art. None of the painting series depict extinct animals and as such the Palaeolithic age of peninsular Indian rock art should be kept aside until convincing evidence is recorded (Chandramouli 2010-11). In rock art stratigraphy, the earliest painting series contain wild animals in a variety of styles. All of them can be seen even today in the surroundings of the rock art

Fig. 3.3 Deer figures in thick outline (Mesolithic Phase 1) Sangaronipalli, Andhra Pradesh.

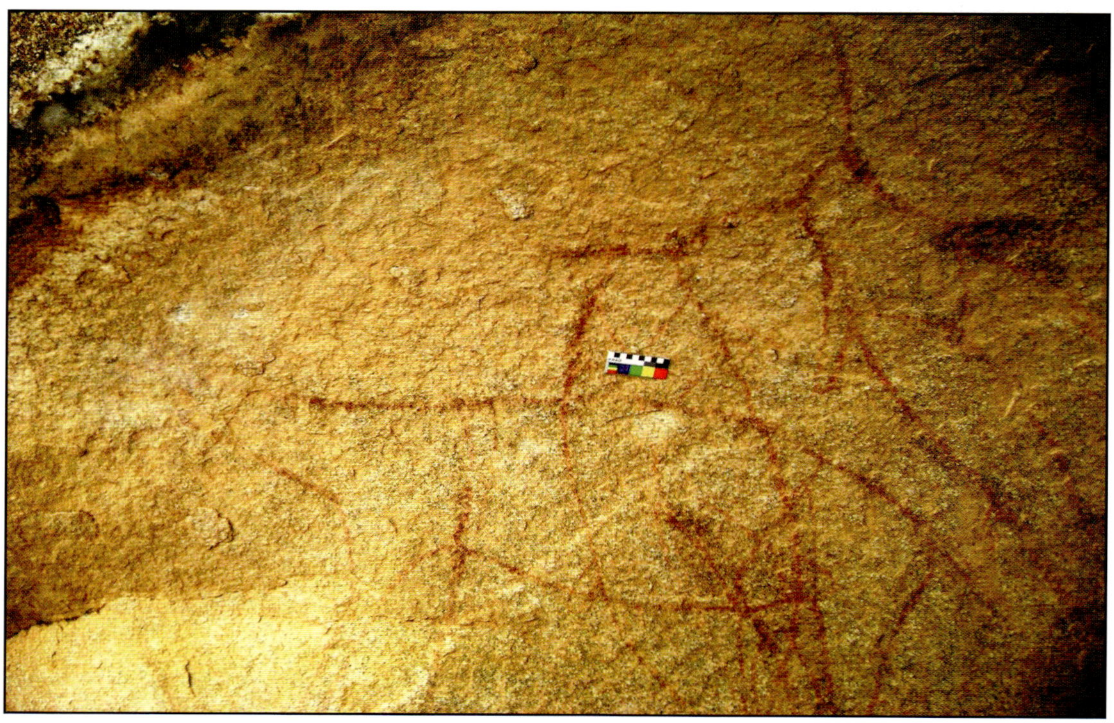

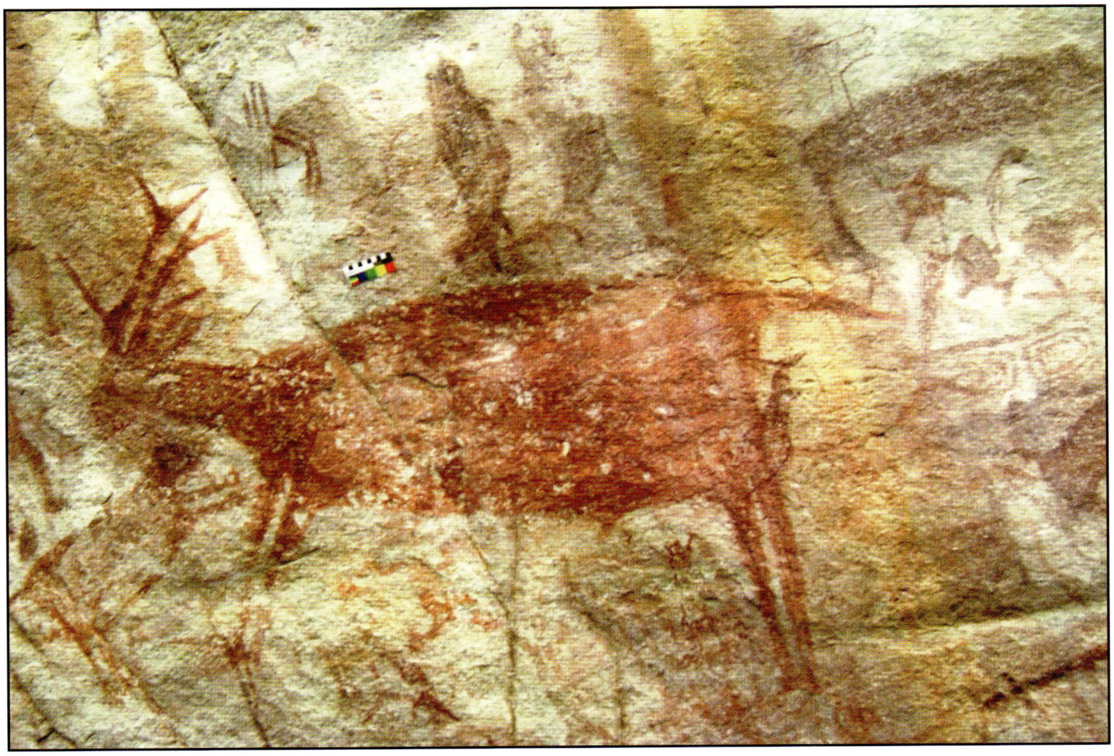

Fig. 3.4 An antler in flat-wash (Mesolithic Phase 1) Pandavulagutta, Andhra Pradesh.

sites indicating the Holocene antiquity of such rock paintings. The rock art of this phase predominantly contains representations of wild animal species such as deer, along with other animals like stag, antler, wild ox, tiger, dog, tortoise, rabbit, fox, hyena, mongoose, porcupine and langur; anthropomorphs; human figures; masked human figures (sorcerers?); geometric drawings and hand prints and drawings. A single colour scheme (red ochre) is followed in all the sites in this series. None of the animal representations in this series of rock art contain domesticated animals. The petroglyphic art is found in this series of rock art. Although no hunting scenes are depicted in the entire rock art of Peninsular India (except one site in Karnataka) the occurrence of wild game animals indicates their hunting-gathering cultural milieu. The important sites in this series are Chintakunta, Dappalle, the Kethavaram-Pulicherla complex, Sanganonipalli, Pandavula Gutta in Andhra Pradesh and Aihole, Ramadurga, Badami, Hosa-mahakuta and Kutakankeri in Karnataka. Rock art depictions of this series from all the sites number around 400 painted figures. Animal depictions of the early art within this series are few in number and these are large-sized (between 1 and 1.5 metres in length) such as deer (Figs. 3.3 & 3.4) and Rabbit (Fig. 3.5) done in thick outline/flat wash style. From the state of preservation the animal representations of the phase 1 of the First Series paintings are faintly visible and located invariably on the higher reaches of rock shelters at a height of 3-5 m above the floor level.

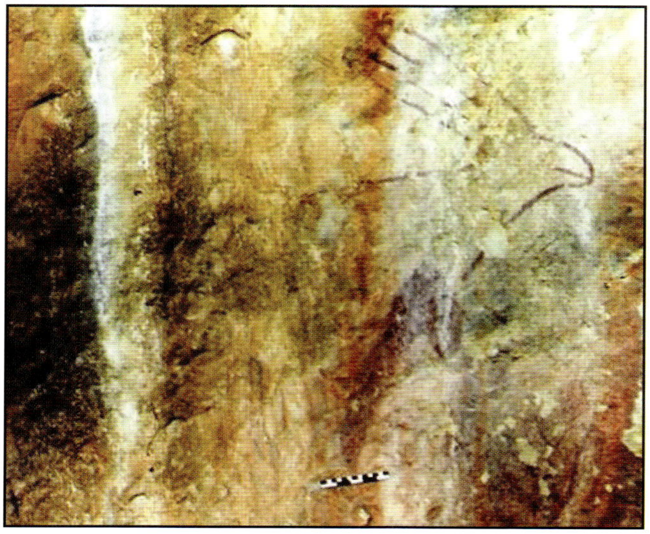

Fig. 3.5 A Rabbit in thick outline (Mesolithic-Phase1) Chintakunta, Andhra Pradesh.

Phase 2 within the First Series of rock paintings is represented by fresh looking ones in the same colour scheme depicting the same wild animal species—deer in a majority besides other animals, human/ anthropomorphic figures, geometric drawings, handprints and drawings. The paintings of this sub-phase are smaller in size ranging between 30-35 cm and are fresh in condition. Some of them are superimposed over faintly visible ones of the early series. A majority of them are done in flat wash although paintings in outline are not altogether absent. Thematic variety is very conspicuous in the second sub-phase of red ochre paintings which include besides the deer species (Fig. 3.6), antlers, a wild ox, langurs, tiger, dog, porcupine, tortoise, fish, mongoose, rabbit, human and anthropomorphic figures, masked human (Fig. 3.7), handprints and drawings. In the Rock art of peninsular India, masked human figures (sorcerer?) occur only at the Kethavaram-Pulicherla complex in the Andhra region.

The rock art of the First Series of paintings includes very interesting depictions of hunters found at sites like Ramadurga, Badami, Hosa-mahakuta and Kutakankeri in the Karnataka region. These were paintings done in red ochre (Sundara 2006: Figures 2-5, 7 and 9) which are stylistically and thematically similar to the early representations of central Indian rock art. The hunters are represented in a dynamic movement of body posture with elaborate head dresses (Fig. 3.8).

With regard to the availability of contextual archaeological material in the surface context in rock art sites, only microlithic tools are found

Left: **Fig. 3.6** A pair of deer figures in flat wash (Mesolithic Phase 2) Kethavaram, Andhra Pradesh.

Right: **Fig. 3.7** Masked human figure (Mesolithic Phase 2), Kethavaram, Andhra Pradesh.

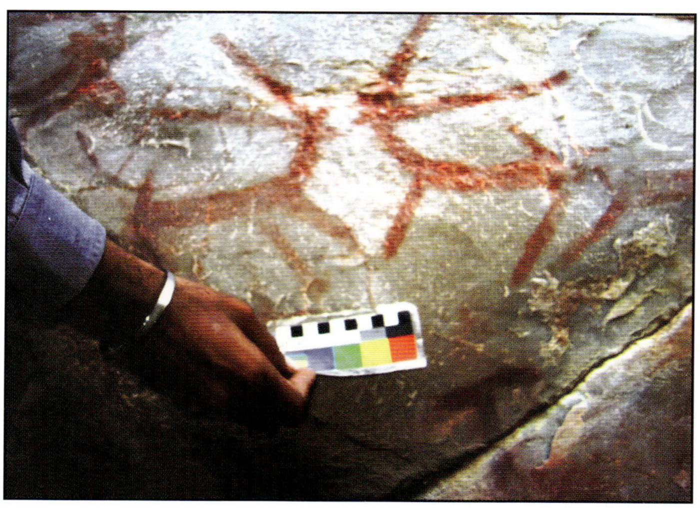

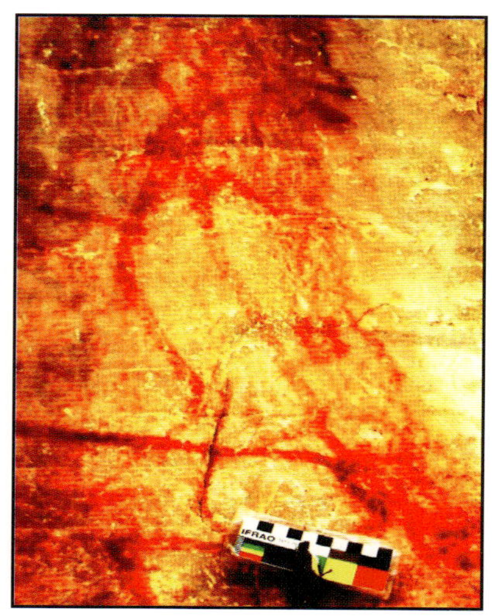

along with a few scatters of upper Palaeolithic material at some of the sites. As such the two phases of the first painting series can be dated to the Mesolithic period. Sporadic occurrence of lithic material indicates that the rock art sites were occupied only seasonally due to the non-availability of perennial water sources as also the lack of a substantial green cover. The seasonality of the occupation of the sites also gets reflected in the limited number of painted figures at all the sites (Chandramouli 1988b). To sum up, Mesolithic rock art in the Andhra-Karnataka zone is characterised by the occurrence of wild animals primarily of the deer species. The general thematic emphasis of rock art depictions is animistic and they are depicted naturally as compared to other representations, particularly of human figures. The depiction of stylised hunters with elongated bodies and elaborate head-dresses holding microlithic-tipped arrows are found in a couple of sites in the Karnataka region. Similar interesting masked human figures (sorcerer?) are found exclusively in the rock art site of Kethavaram in Andhra region. The most conspicuous feature of the early rock art of this zone is the total absence of hunting scenes.

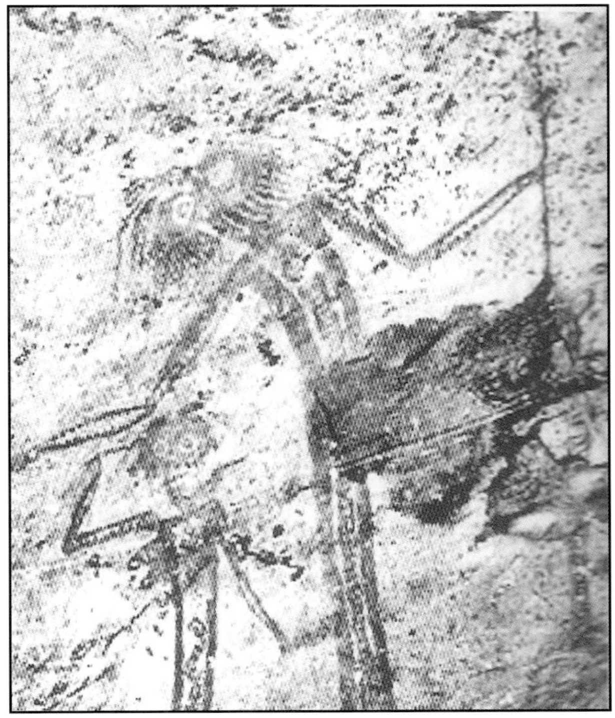

Fig. 3.8 Hunters with peculiar head-dress (Mesolithic), Bellary region, Karnataka.

The Second Series of rock art in the Andhra-Karnataka zone is interesting on three counts:

1. A change in the thematic content.
2. The appearance of the petroglyphic form of art.
3. Concentration of art in the granite-gneiss zone characterised by black cotton soil profiles.

The Second Series of rock art is identified on the basis of occurrence of domesticated animals (predominantly humped bulls) depicting the incipient agro-pastoral economy of its authors. These are characteristic traits of Neolithic rock art in entire Peninsular India. Besides the rock paintings, humped bulls are also found in petroglyphic art (peckings, bruisings and engravings) which make their appearance from this phase onwards. Besides red ochre which is the only colour scheme utilised in the rock art of the Mesolithic period, the use of white colour is also noticed in rock art depictions from the paintings of the Second Series onwards. The appearance of humped cattle does not indicate the absence of wild game animals, which continue to appear in this series of art also in both of its forms: petroglyphic and pictographic. However, the naturalism of the Mesolithic phase disappears in Neolithic art particularly in the depiction of wild game animals.

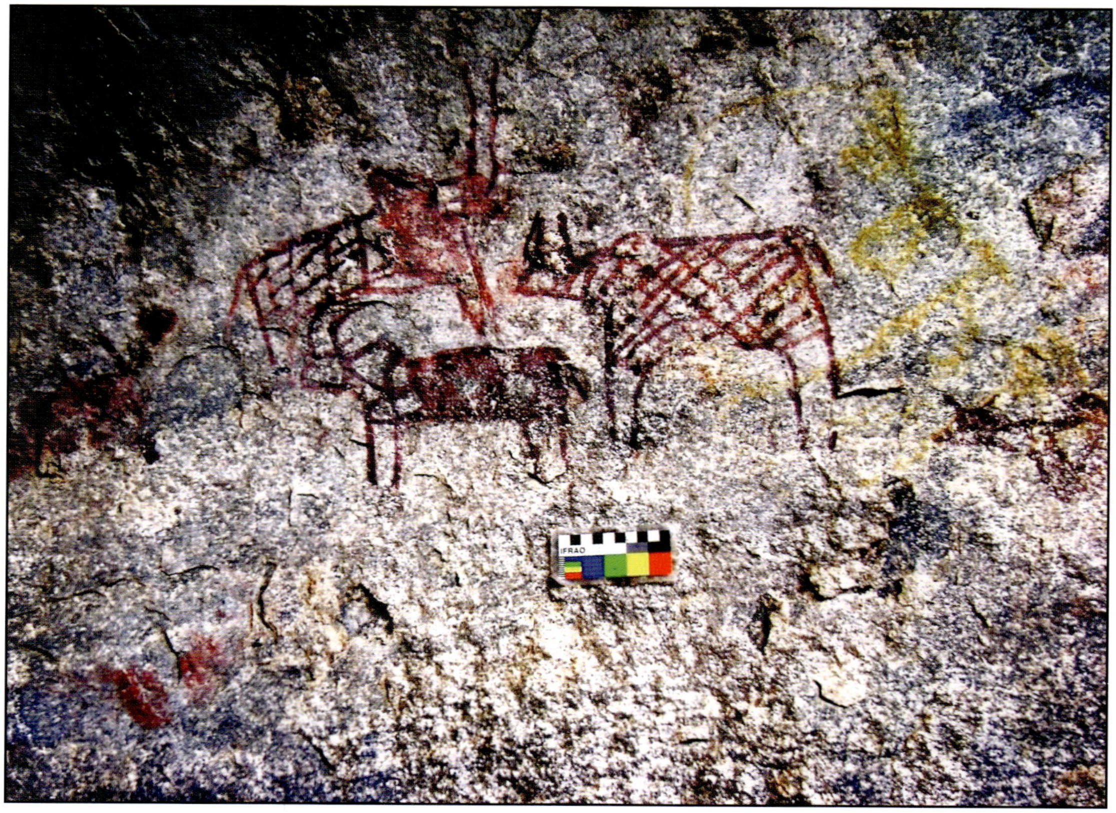

Fig. 3.9 Humped bulls in outline (Neolithic Phase 1), Budagavi, Andhra Pradesh.

Humped cattle in turn are now depicted naturally. Many interesting variations can be noticed in the depiction of the humped bulls on an inter-site comparison.

The painted humped bull figures at Budagavi (Chandramouli 1991) in Andhra Pradesh are in outline with slender body, low hump, straight horns and the body portion filled with straight, wavy and intersecting lines. At the nearby site Velpumadugu, Rami Reddy (1971) identified a pair of bruisings of humped bulls which are having straight horns. According to him, the bruisings of Velpumadugu are different in stylistic depiction from the Karnataka examples where the humped bulls are always shown with long and curved horns facing each other in a fighting mood. The paintings of humped bull at Budagavi and the bruisings of humped bull at Velpumadugu appear to depict the wild ox (*Bos Nomadicus*) with its low hump and straight horns, and as such represent the early Neolithic cultural horizon (Fig. 3.9).

It is identified that the bruisings of Velpumadugu, are the representations of the long-horned (acutifrons or longifrons). Allchin and Allchin (1974) and Clason (1977) have suggested that the acutifrons type, which typical of peninsular India in modern times could be representing an indigenous breed domesticated local wild populations. The paintings of humped cattle at Budagavi also seem to be the depictions of the same species of wild cattle population. These two cases of the humped cattle depictions seem to be the earliest of all the Neolithic rock art depictions of this species (Chandramouli

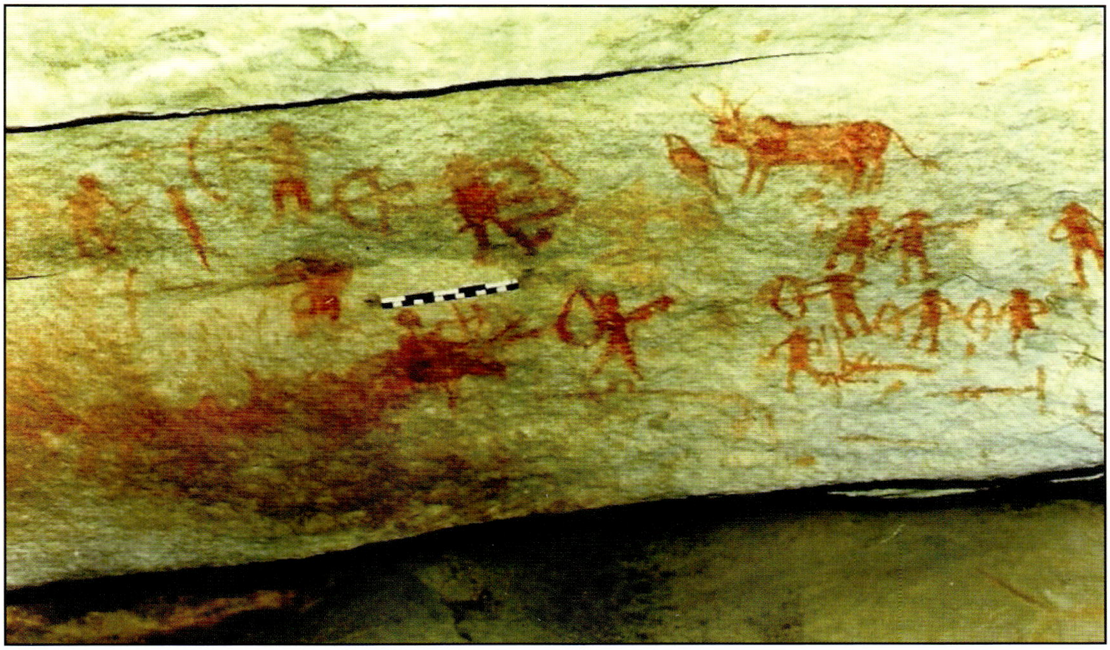

Fig. 3.10 Humped bulls & human figures with bow & arrow (Neolithic Phase 2), Chintakunta, Andhra Pradesh.

1991, 1994, 2003) in the Andhra region. This proposition seems to be correct in view of the proximity of these sites to the nuclear zone of the Karnataka Neolithic (Paddayya 2011) where the Neolithic phase I is represented in many of the sites. Those sites in other regional variants contain rock art depictions of the humped bulls which are stylistically different from those of the first phase as the Budagavi paintings and Velpumadugu bruisings (Chandramouli 2012a).

The depiction of human figures with bows and arrows in red ochre found in association with humped bull paintings in Chintakunta rock art site in the Andhra region (Fig. 3.10) seems to go well with the Neolithic phase and this may indicate the continuation of the hunting-gathering way of economic activity. On open air boulders and rock shelters around the well-known Neolithic-ash mound sites of Utnur, Tekkalakota, Kurugodu, Piklihal,Sanganakallu, Kupgal, Brahmagiri, Chitradurga, Adoni, Naidupalli, Sivaru-Venkatapur, Budagavi sites, engravings and peckings of humped bulls are reported in large numbers (Allchin 1960, 1963; Allchin & Allchin 1974, 1995; Keshav 2006). The depiction of humped bulls in pairs facing each other in a fighting mood is found in the petroglyphic art of the Karnataka region which can be identified as a characteristic feature of Neolithic art of the granite-gneiss region of Peninsular India.

One striking feature of agro-pastoral art is the gradual transition from naturalistic representations towards schematic/abstract representations. The transitionary stages of the Neolithic-Chalcolithic identified in excavated archaeological context are difficult to identify in rock art depictions. However, humped bulls with elongated and curved bodies with an erect penis (Fig. 3.11), found characteristically in Chalcolithic rock art of central India as also in pottery paintings found in a couple of sites in the Andhra region, such as

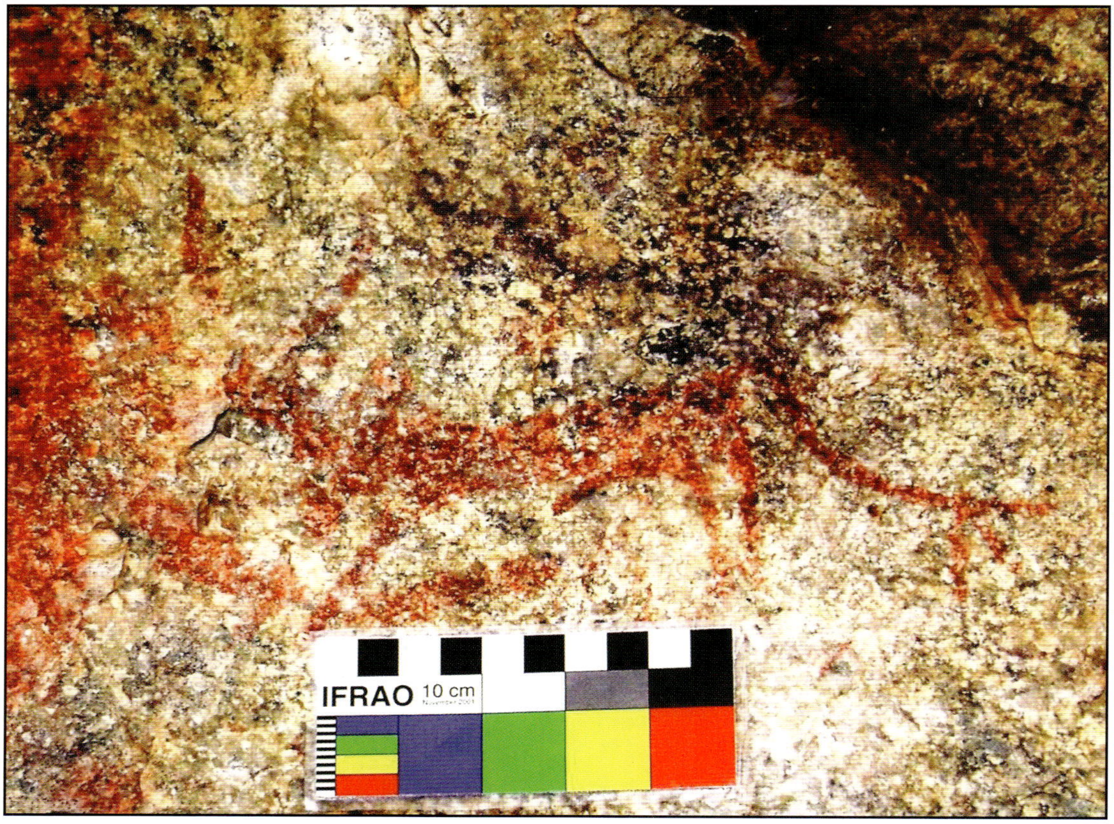

Fig. 3.11 Humped bull (Neolithic-Chalcolithic Phase 2), Sivaru Venkatapur, Andhra Pradesh.

Sivaru -Venkatapur, may be identified as belonging to the transitionary Neolithic-Chalcolithic stage (Fig. 3.11).

One interesting feature noticed in rock paintings series dated to the Mesolithic period at Kethavaram is the occurrence of a pair of humped bulls (Fig. 3.12), a characteristic trait of the Neolithic art of peninsular India. This region is part of the regional variant 7 of Paddayya's (2011) classification of south Indian Neolithic. However, we do not get any material remains of the Neolithic phase within the site or in its vicinity within a radius of 15 sq km (Chandramouli 1986, 1987, 1988a, 1988b, 1989). Keeping in view the non-availability of material remains of the Neolithic phase within the Kethavaram rock art site, we can postulate that the appearance of humped bulls in rock paintings of the Mesolithic period can be due to cultural or material contacts between the Mesolithic and Neolithic people. This hypothesis gains strength if we see the stylistic rendering of deer figures in a fighting mood at the same place. The depiction of humped bulls in a fighting posture facing each other is a characteristic feature of Neolithic art in Karnataka, both in paintings and in petroglyphs. Mesolithic artists of Kethavaram depicted deer figures in a fighting posture, a feature which in all probability was the result of cultural interaction. These rock art depictions indicate that Kethavaram could be a seasonal aggregation site for hunting-gathering and agro-pastoral cultures. Such cultural interactions between different prehistoric groups must have existed in this region right from upper Palaeolithic times (Murthy 1981, 1985a,

1985b, 1989, 1994, 2012). In the light of this discussion, the need for a critical appraisal of the upper Palaeolithic-Mesolithic and Mesolithic-Neolithic interfaces in archaeological as well as in the context of the rock art of Peninsular India is called for to understand the processes of domestication of plants and animals (Fig. 3.12).

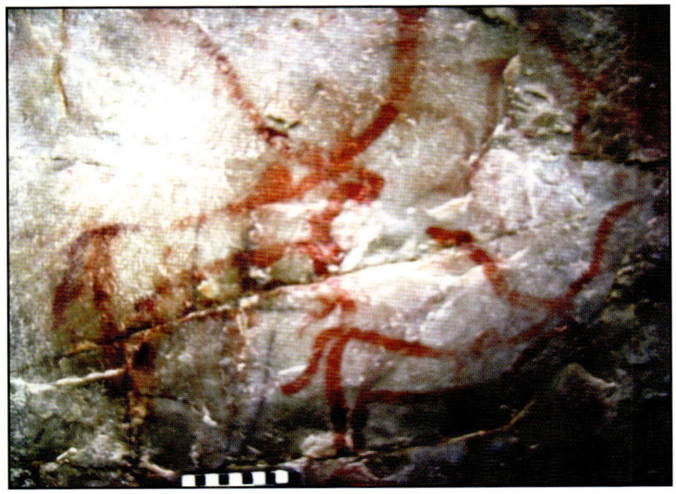

Fig. 3.12 Humped bulls (Mesolithic Phase 2), Kethavaram, Andhra Pradesh.

The next series of rock art stratigraphy, in view of its occurrence either on funerary monuments or in their proximity, can be ascribed to the Iron Age, which is coterminous with the Megalithic culture signifying the emergence of organised societies. The concomitant shift in the representational priority from the animal world to that of the symbolic is very prominent in rock art representations of the period. Further, in the rock art of this series the pictographic content gradually gives way to petroglyphic content. One particular symbol, the *circle-with-a-trident* appears to be the hallmark of Megalithic art of the Andhra sub-region where it occurs in a variety of shapes, forms and sizes close to burial sites or on the slabs/boulders of the burial monuments such as orthostats and boulders of the stone circles. The cultic nature of this symbol is indicated in one instance in which

Fig. 3.13 Circle-with-a trident symbol (Megalithic/Iron Age), Naidupalli, Andhra Pradesh.

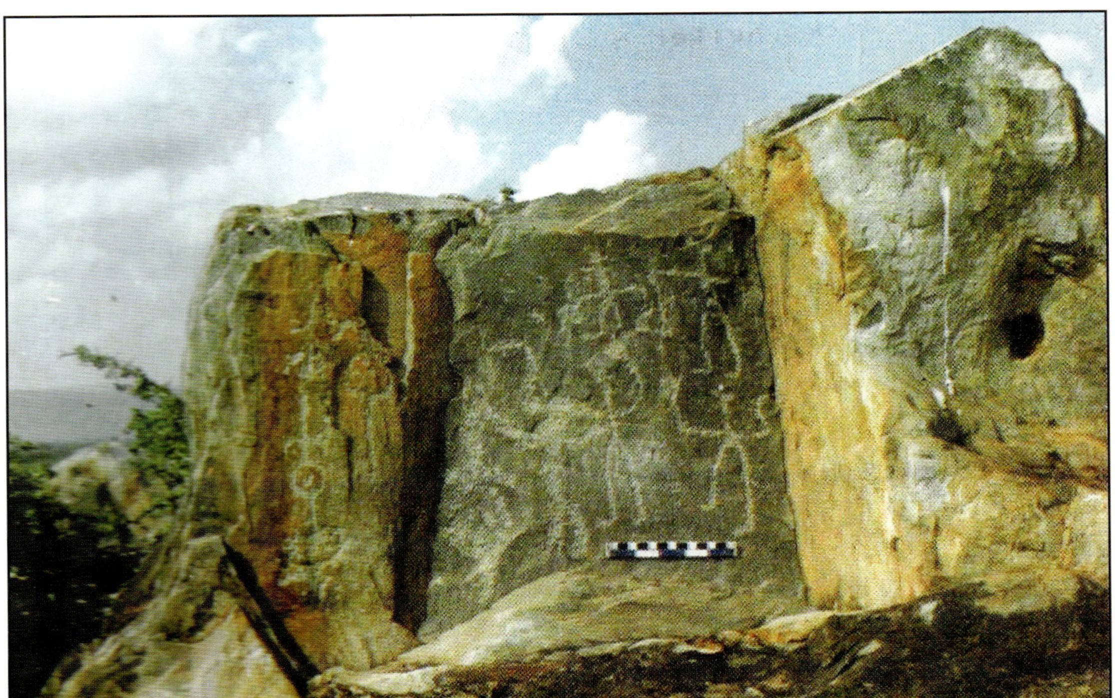

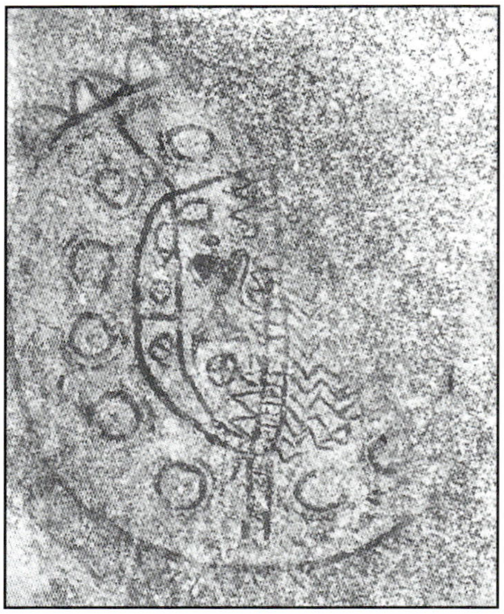

several schematic ithyphallic humans are shown in a dancing/praying posture in front of this symbol (Chandramouli 1995) (Fig. 3.13). Animal representations in Megalithic art wherever they occur are so abstract and schematic that the identification of the species represented is difficult. In the Chick-Rampura region of Karnataka, Megalithic art also contains very unique representations of Megalithic burials (stone circles) in a schematic manner in rock paintings (Sundara 1992) (Fig. 3.14).

During Early historical and medieval times, the rock shelters were inhabited by wandering ascetics from different faiths and these are also indicated by the presence of paintings and engravings of religious symbols such as swastika, and religious personages such as Jaina Tirthankaras; painted inscriptions in Brahmi as at Kethavaram (Fig. 3.15), Kannada and Telugu scripts and multi-chrome frescoes depicting scenes from the Epic *Mahabharata* as at Pandavula Gutta in the Andhra region (Fig. 3.16) and in Manvi in the Karnataka region (Sundara 2006: Figs. 18 & 19).

Fig. 3.14 Painting of a Megalithic (Stone Circle) Burial, Chick-Rampura, Karnataka.

Kerala-Tamil Nadu Zone

Rock art of the Kerala-Tamil Nadu zone portrays totally different features. Nearly 120 sites are reported in this region. Rock art datable

Fig. 3.15 Brahmi label inscription (Early Historical), Kethavaram, Andhra Pradesh.

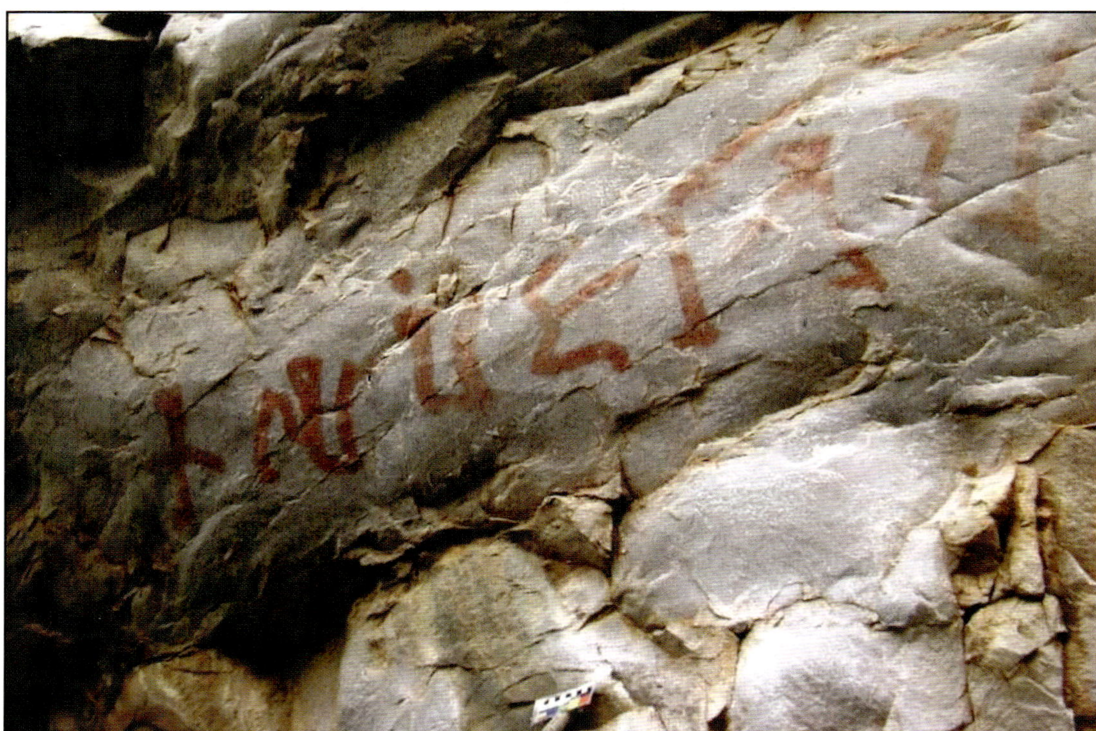

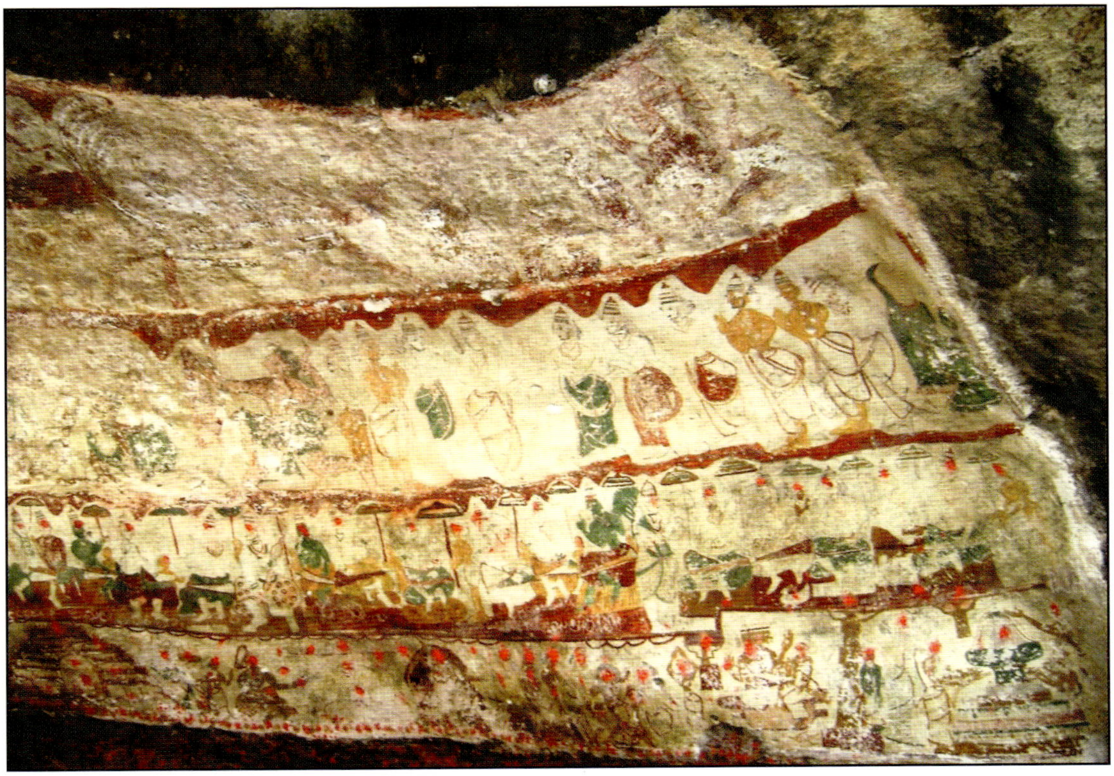

Fig. 3.16 Frescoes of epic *Mahabharata* (Medieval Period), Pandavulagutta, Andhra Pradesh.

to the Mesolithic and Neolithic periods, is not identifiable in this region. It was the rock art of Kerala region which attracted the attention of geologists of the colonial era pioneered by Fawcett (1901). Mathpal (1998) and Kurien's (2010-11) work brought knowledge of rock art in Kerala up to date. The bulk of the rock art in Kerala consists of petroglyphic content as in the Edakal cave, while two sites contain paintings in red and white. Although Mathpal dates some of the rock art of Kerala to the Neolithic period in view of the total absence of any habitation evidence of the Neolithic period in the region, such a proposition remains questionable. In such a situation, the entire corpus of the Kerala region located in the high altitude regions can be dated to Megalithic and succeeding historical phases only (Fig. 3.17).

None of the rock art sites in the Kerala-Tamilnadu zone have the rock art depictions portraying either hunting-gathering or agro-pastoral cultural milieu as noticed in other parts of the country. Although at a couple of sites, red ochre paintings are noticed superimposed by the paintings of white colour, nothing can be said about the thematic content of the red ochre paintings as they are just patches of painting only. In the case of Alambadi rock art site (Sridhar 2005:21) although a cow is depicted in red ochre, stylistically it is very different from the rest of the bovine paintings in the Andhra-Karnataka region and as such may be dated to a later period. Similarly, the beak-headed human figures in the red ochre rock paintings of Kilvalai and Alambadi also seem to be of a late age, possibly Megalithic. In the Tamil Nadu region a majority of the painted motifs are in

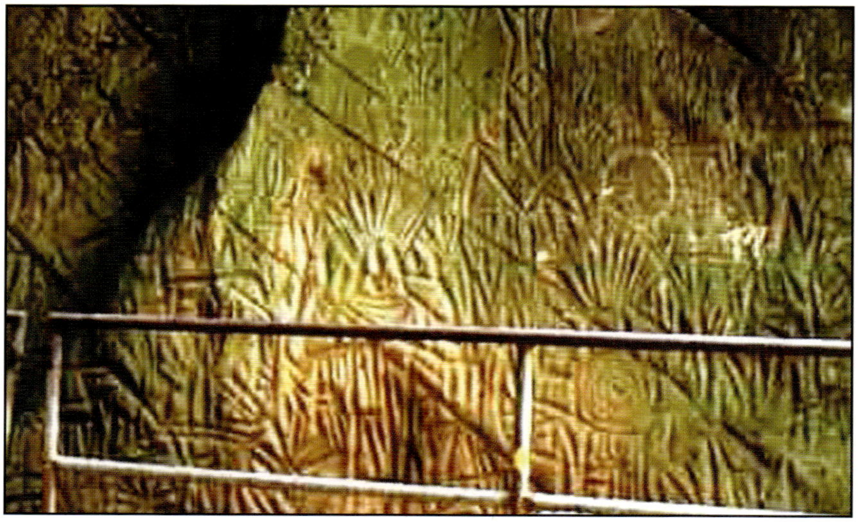

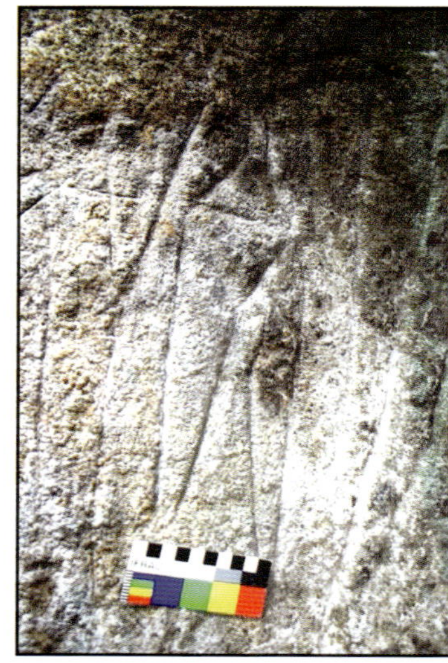

Left: **Fig. 3.17** Engravings from Edakal Cave (Megalithic/Iron Age), Kerala.

Right: **Fig. 3.18** Engravings of Perumukkal (Megalithic/Iron Age), Tamil Nadu.

Fig. 3.19 Painting of a Wild Ox/ *Bos Gaurus* (Mesolithic Phase 2), Pandavulagutta, Andhra Pradesh.

white colour and depict schematic representations of humans with perfect triangular-shaped bodies, animals and schematic drawings. The cultural content of the paintings indicates their Iron Age/historical antiquity. Some of them which are extremely fresh in condition could be of recent times done by the pastoral communities or shepherds.

Rock art of the Tamil Nadu region as documented sources indicate (Rajan 2008) is concentrated in the northern parts of the region and all of it is associated with or located close to Megalithic burial monuments.

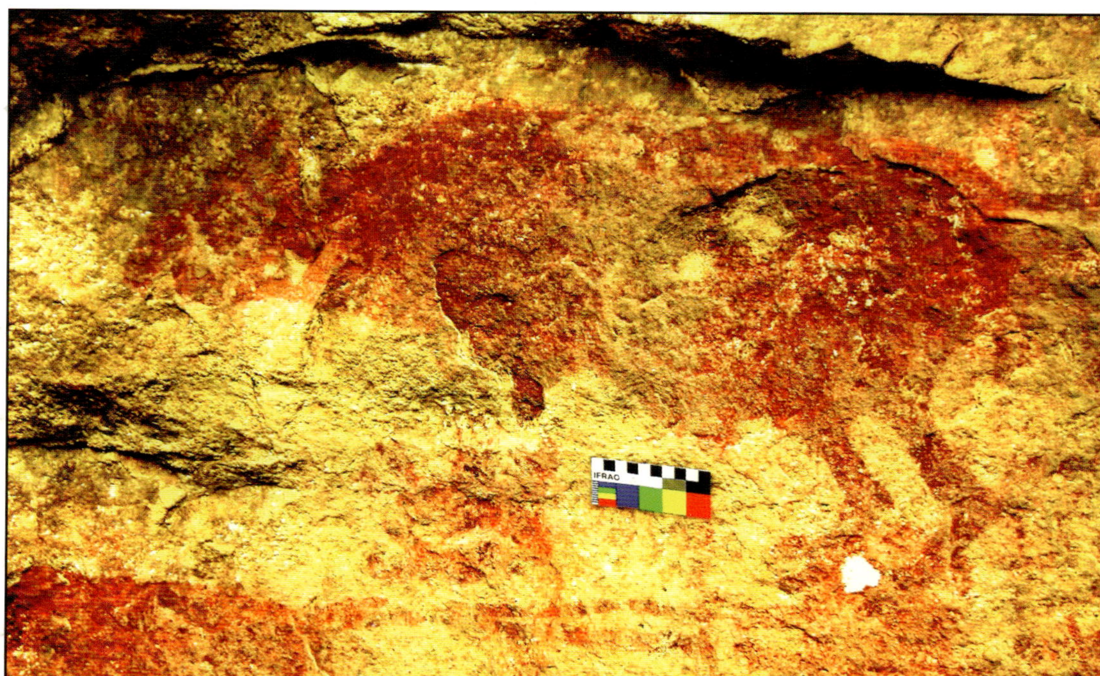

Recently discovered sites are located in the high altitude regions of the Nilgiri mountain ranges and in the Western Ghat areas bordering Kerala. The rock art of Tamil Nadu has paintings in red and white which depict schematic animals, human figures and some geometric symbols, most of which have either faded or are fragmentary. The paintings in red colour which are few in number are faded to such an extent that nothing can be made out from the fragmentary patches of red pigment. On the basis of superimpositions white paintings antedate red ones. White paintings are in a majority and depict horse-like animals mounted by human figures which indicate the historical antiquity of the paintings.Petroglyphic art is confined to only one site: Perumukkal in Villupuram district (Fig. 3.18) in Tamil Nadu (Rajan 1996).

The thematic content of the Perumukkal rock art contains schematic engravings of human/anthropomorphic figures similar to those found in the Edakal rock art site in Kerala, which is nearly 700 km away (Figs. 3.17 & 3.18).

A bulk of the recorded prehistoric evidence in the Tamil Nadu region as discussed before belongs to the Iron Age/Megalithic period. Since there are few dates available for Megalithic sites in Tamil Nadu and since Megalithism continued well into the early historical and medieval periods, nothing can be said about the dates of the paintings except that the paintings and engravings depict a metal using cultural environment of horse riding warriors probably belonging to the Megalithic period which extends between 1000 BCE–1000 CE in Peninsular India.

V

In the case of the Andhra-Karnataka region, contextual archaeological evidence in rock shelters or in their vicinity in the form of microlithic stone tool scatters are not extensive as in the case of rock art representations; these are few in number at almost all the sites in the region. These archaeological and rock art occurrences are directly in relation to the seasonality of occupation of the sites. In both these regions, the earliest rock art is datable to the Mesolithic period. One prominent feature of the rock art of this period is thematic and stylistic heterogeneity. Almost all the game animals are portrayed naturally. This was replaced by thematic as well as stylistic homogeneity of rock art themes with the onset of the agro-pastoral cultures of the Neolithic. This can be visualised even in the material manifestations in the archaeological context. Petroglyphic art makes its appearance during this phase the significance of which is yet to be investigated. However, within the paintings of the Neolithic period sub-phases can be delineated on stylistic grounds. The painted humped bull figures at Budagavi (Fig. 3.9) in Andhra Pradesh are in outline with slender bodies, low humps, straight horns and the body portions filled with straight, wavy and intersecting lines (Chandramouli 1991). At the nearby site of Velpumadugu, Rami Reddy (1971, 1976 and 1978) identified a pair of bruisings of humped bulls with straight horns. According to him, the bruisings of Velpumadugu are different in stylistic depiction from the Karnataka examples where the humped bulls are always shown with long and curved horns facing each other in a fighting mood. The paintings of humped bulls at Budagavi and the bruisings of humped bulls at Velpumadugu appear to depict the wild ox (*Bos Nomadicus*) with its low hump and straight horns, and as such represent the early Neolithic cultural horizon prior to the domestication of the wild ox.

The identification of wild ox (*Bos Nomadicus*) in Neolithic art of the south-western part of Andhra displays another dimension of the domestication of plants and animals in southern Indian Neolithic. This region, which is part of the 'nuclear zone' of the south Indian Neolithic, displays the same stylistic features as noticed in the petroglyphic examples of Karnataka. Biological records from the excavated Neolithic sites in the region contain evidence of this animal. Its existence during the preceding Mesolithic phase is however not established. The *Bos Nomadicus* paintings in the rock art of Budagavi and in the petroglyphs of a nearby site at Velpumadugu indicate that in the 'nuclear zone' of the Neolithic period of southern India, this animal seems to have been domesticated by Neolithic folk. The depiction of *Bos Indicus* in the rock paintings at Budagavi may be taken as indicative of the co-existence of both wild and domesticated cattle during the early Neolithic of this region. Another interesting theme noticed in the Mesolithic paintings at a site in the Andhra region is the depiction of wild ox (*Bos gaurus*) (Fig. 3.19).This animal is no more seen in any part of Peninsular India today but seems to be a native species during the early Holocene times (Chandramouli 2012a). The depiction of humped bull figures with long and slender bodies and in a sexually aroused condition appear to be of a late phase within Neolithic rock art as evidenced at the Sivaru Venkatapur rock art site. The Chalcolithic bull depictions of the Vindhyan series as well as the pottery paintings display the same stylistic features.

The entire Peninsular India comes under the Megalithic cultural ambit and barring minor variations, the rock art also displays uniform features so far as the thematic content and colour schemes are concerned (Chandramouli 2012b). The thematic content includes schematic animals, horses and horse and elephant riding humans with bows and arrows, swords and shields, abstract symbols and geometric drawings. The petroglyphic content of the rock art which takes precedence over the pictographic content also contains the same thematic content. However, in the sub-region of Andhra a particular symbol 'Circle-with-a-trident' seems to be the hallmark of Megalithic symbolism, as it occurs on the orthostats of Megalithic burials, on boulders in stone circle burial monuments, or in the vicinity of Megalithic/early historic habitation sites. The cultic nature of this symbol is attested by one composition which depicts five ithyphallic humans, whose heads are shown with a small horizontal stroke in a dancing posture in front of this symbol (Fig. 3.13).

VI

Keeping aside contextual differences and concomitant analytical variations in research, the concept of style had the same spatio-temporal utility both in Europe and in India. Constrained by contemporary research limitations, Brueil's unilinear progression of

Palaeolithic art as well as Gourhan's 'coherent evolutionary curve' of rock art are aimed at answering the 'what and when' of rock art. These two facets of the 'culture history paradigm' led to the creation of stylistic chronologies. With the arrival of refined theories and methods of New Archaeology, rock art studies along with archaeological researches took a new direction from the normative to the systematic and from descriptive chronicling to the study of cultural processes. Such analytical studies were further strengthened by radiometric dating methods which sounded the death knell for stylistic chronologies of rock art and heralded the post-stylistic era in rock art research. AMS dating of Chauvet cave in France shook the foundations of the stylistic chronology paradigm and destroyed Brueil and Gourhan's age-old theories along with the Eurocentric origin theories of Palaeolithic art.

As enunciated above, in tune with the Brueil-Gourhan's stylistic cultures of rock art, researchers in India utilised the concept of style to identify, classify and date the rock art phases by correlating them with contextual archeological cultures. However, the concept of style as discussed in this paper in the analysis of the rock art of peninsular India tries to give it a proper perspective. In addition to its traditional utility in terms of spatio-temporal dynamics, its discussion also proves to be useful as an interpretative tool in the archeological context of rock art. The inter-site and intra-site comparative studies, as discussed above, have proved the utility of the concept of style in making generalizations about the spacio-temporal dimensions of rock art, corroborated by contextual surface archaeological material. The stylistic study of the peninsular Indian rock art has also proved that prehistoric aggregation sites, social boundaries and processes of information transmission can also be fruitfully analysed. Research is an ongoing process and future researches may change the stylistic chronological paradigm in India also, but as of now 'style' is useful to make some sense out of the depictions to reconstruct the 'what', 'when' and 'why' of the prehistoric rock art.

The European Palaeolithic art, which is unique in terms of the thematic and stylistic diversity, context and chronology, continues to be so due to the intensive and extensive studies, researches and debates. The stylistic chronology as also the radiometric dating methods has not made such an impact on the rock art researches as it did in the case of the European Palaeolithic art. The post-stylistic era of the rock art research, as discussed above, need not mean the end of the stylistic chronologies. This is more so in the case of India where inherent limitations, particularly in the application of radiometric dating methods, make the stylistic classification and analysis, the only fruitful way to study rock art. The subjective definitions and categories of rock art can be sorted out if they are applied judiciously and logically.

To sum up, style, though debunked and ridiculed as a highly individualistic premise and an unscientific archaeological construct, should be considered as a useful concept to study and analyse rock art. Stylistic categories, although based on individual perceptions, can be verified and corroborated in inter-site and intra-site comparative analyses as done in this paper; they are thus testable too.

REFERENCES

Allchin, F.R. (1960), *Piklihal Excavations.* A.P. Govt. Archaeological series. No. 1, Hyderabad.

—— (1963), *Neolithic Cattle Keepers of South India: A Study of Deccan Ash Mounds*. Cambridge: Cambridge University Press.

Allchin, F.R. and B. Allchin (1974), 'Some New Thoughts on Indian Cattle', *South Asian Archaeology:* 24-32.

Allchin, B. and F.R. Allchin (1995), 'Rock Art of North Karnataka', *Bulletin of the Deccan College Research Institute* 54-55: 313-38.

Bednarik, R.G. (1995a), 'The Coa Petroglyphs: An Obituary to the Stylistic Dating of Palaeolithic Rock Art', *Antiquity* 69 (266): 877-83.

—— (1995b), 'The Age of the Coa Valley Petroglyphs in Portugal', *Rock Art Research* 12 (2): 86-103.

—— (2001), *Rock art Science: The Scientific Study of Palaeoart.* Belgium: Brepols Publishers.

—— (2003), 'A Major Change in the Archaeological Paradigm', *Anthropos* 98 (2): 511-20.

—— (2007), 'Antiquity and Authorship of the Chauvet Rock Art', *Rock Art Research* 24: 21-34.

Binford, L.R. (1965), 'Archaeological Systematics and the Study of Cultural Process', *American Antiquity* 28: 217-25.

Chandramouli, N. (1986), 'A Study of the Painted Rock Shelters and Microlithic Culture at Ketavaram, Kurnool District, Andhra Pradesh', M. Phil Dissertation. University of Hyderabad.

—— (1987), 'An Analytical Study of Rock Paintings at Ketavaram, Kurnool District', Proceedings of the AP History Congress XI Session, Nagaram, Guntur, pp. 28-36.

—— (1988a), 'An Attempt Towards the Interpretation of Rock Paintings at Ketavaram, Kurnool District', *Puratattva* 18: 72-78.

—— (1988b), 'The Microlithic Industry at Ketavaram, Kurnool District', Proceedings of the A.P. History Congress XII Session, Anakapalli, pp. 27-31.

—— (1989), 'Method and Theory in Rock Art—Some Hypotheses', *Itihas* XV(1): 1-16.

—— (1991), 'Rock art of Budagavi, Anantapur District, A.P.', *Man and Environment* XVII (2): 71-80.

—— (1994), 'Rock Art of Andhra Pradesh', *Purakala* V(1-2): 41-56.

—— (1995), 'Petroglyphs from Naidupalli, Andhra Pradesh', *Purakala* VI(1-2): 29-34.

—— (2003), 'Rock Art of Andhra Pradesh', in M.L.K. Murthy (ed.), *Prehistory & Proto History of Andhra Pradesh,* Vol. I (Comprehensive History of Andhra Pradesh Series). Hyderabad: Orient Longman, pp. 148-73.

—— (2010-11), 'Archaeology of Rock Art in Peninsular India', *Purakala* 20-21: 43-72.

—— (2012a), 'Beginning of Cattle Domestication in Andhra Region: Perspectives of Rock Art and Archaeology', *Purakala* 22: 47-60.

—— (2012b), 'The Megalithic-Early Historical Interface in Andhra: Some Observations', Proceedings of the Andhra Pradesh History Congress 32nd Session, pp. 5-10.

Clason, A.T. (1977), 'Wild and Domestic Animals in Prehistoric and Early Historic India', *Eastern Anthropologist* 30: 135-41.

Clottes, Jean (1993), 'Post-Stylistic', in *Rock Art Studies: The Post-Stylistic Era or Where Do We Go from Here?* (papers presented at Symposium A of the 2nd AURA Congress, Cairns 1992). London: Oxbow Books, pp. 19-26.

Conkey, M.W. (1978), 'Style and Information in Cultural Evolution: Toward a Predictive Model for the Palaeolithic', in C.L. Redman (ed.), *Social Archaeology: Beyond Subsistence and Dating*. New York: Academic Press, pp. 61-85.

—— (1980), 'Context, Structure and Efficacy in Palaeolithic Art and Design', in M.C. Foster and S.H. Brandes (eds.), *Symbol as Sense.* New York: Academic Press, pp. 225-48.

—— (1987), 'New Approaches in Search of Meaning: A Review of Research in Palaeolithic "Art"', *Journal of Field Archaeology* 14: 413-30.

—— (1989), 'The Use of Diversity in Stylistic Analysis', in G.T. Jones and R. Leonard (eds.), *Quantifying Diversity in Archaeology.* Cambridge: Cambridge University Press, pp. 121-32.

—— (1990), 'Experimenting with Style in Archaeology: Some Historical and Theoretical Aspects', in M.W. Conkey and Christine Hastorff (eds.), *The Uses of Style in Archaeology.* Cambridge: Cambridge University Press, pp. 5-17.

David Raju, B. (1985), Neolithic Cultures of the Central Coast of Andhra Pradesh, South India, Ph.D. thesis, Nagarjuna University.

—— (1990), The Settlement and Subsistence Pattern of the Neolithic Culture of the Lower Krishna Valley. *Man and Environment* 15(2): 45-51.

Davis, Whitney (1986), 'Comments on Nathalie Franklin "Stochastic vs Emblemic: An Archaeologically Useful Method for the Analysis of Style in Australian Rock Art"', *Rock Art Research* 3(2): 124-25.

—— (1990), 'Style and History in Art History', in Margaret W. Conkey and Christine A. Hastorff (eds.), *The Uses of Style in Archaeology.* Cambridge: Cambridge University Press, pp. 18-31.

Fawcett, F. (1901), 'Notes on the Rock Carvings in the Edakal Cave, Wynaad', *The Indian Antiquary* 30: 409-21.

Keshav, K.S.B. (2006), Megalithic Sites in Medak District with Special Reference to Sivaru Venkatapur Village. *Proceedings of the A.P. History Congress.* 30th Session. Siddipet, pp. 50-53.

Kreigger, Alex D. (1944), 'The Typological Concept', *American Antiquity* 9(3): 271-88.

Kurien, Benny (2010-11), 'Rock Art in East Anamalai Valley', *Purakala* 20-21: 73-86.

Leroi-Gourhan, Andre (1968), *The Art of Prehistoric Man in Western Europe.* London: Thames and Hudson.

Lorblanchet, M. (1990), 'The Archaeological Significance of the Results of Pigment Analyses in the Quercy Caves', *Rock Art Research* 7(1): 19-20.

Lorblanchet, M and Paul G. Bahn (1993), 'Rock Art Studies: The Post-Stylistic Era or Where Do We Go from Here?' (Papers presented at Symposium A of the 2nd AURA Congress, Cairns 1992). London: Oxbow Books.

Mathpal, Y. (1984), *Prehistoric Rock Paintings of Central India.* New Delhi: Abhinav.

—— (1998), Rock *Art of Kerala.* New Delhi: Aryan Books International & IGNCA.

Moro Abadia, O. and Manuel R. Gonzalez Morales (2007), 'Thinking about "Style" in the "Post-Stylistic Era": Reconstructing the Stylistic Context of Chauvet', *Oxford Journal of Archaeology* 26(2): 109-25.

—— (2008), 'Palaeolithic Art Studies at the Beginning of Twenty-First Century: A Loss of Innocence', *Journal of Anthropological Research* 64(4): 529-52.

Murty, M.L.K. (1981), 'Hunter-Gatherer Ecosystems and Archaeological Patterns of Subsistence Behaviour on the South-East Coast of India: An Ethnographic Model', *World Archaeology* 13(1): 47-58.

—— (1985a), 'The Use of Plant Goods by Some Hunter-Gatherer Communities in Andhra Pradesh', in V.N. Misra and Peter Bellwood (eds.), *Recent Advances in Indo-Pacific Prehistory.* Delhi: Oxford & IBH, pp. 329-36.

—— (1985b), 'Ethnoarchaeology of Kurnool Caves, South India', *World Archaeology* 17(2): 192-205.

—— (1989), 'Pre-Iron Age Agricultural Settlements in South India: An Ecological Perspective', *Man and Environment* 14(1): 65-81.

—— (1994), 'Forest Peoples and Historical Traditions in the Eastern Ghats, South India', in Bridget Allchin (ed.), *Living Traditions: Studies in the Ethno Archaeology of South Asia.* New Delhi: Oxford and IBH Publishing House, pp. 205-18.

—— (2012). 'Prehistoric Research in India: Concepts and Methods', in N. Chandramouli (ed.), *Twilight of the Past: Probing Indian History & Archaeology*. New Delhi: Aryan Books International, pp. 1-23.

Neumayer, E. (1983), *Prehistoric Indian Rock Paintings*. New Delhi: Oxford.

Paddayya, K. (2002), 'The Problem of Ash Mounds of Southern Deccan in the Light of Recent Research', in K. Paddayya (ed.), *Recent Studies in Indian Archaeology* (ICHR Monograph Series 6). New Delhi: Munshiram Manoharlal, pp. 81-111.

—— (2011), 'New Perspectives in the Investigation of Early Agro-Pastoral Cultures of India', *Man and Environment* 36(2): 1-19.

Pettitt, P. and P. Bahn (2003), 'Current Problems in Dating Palaeolithic Cave Art: Cardamom and Chauvet', *Antiquity* 75(295): 134-41.

Plog, Stephen (1978), 'Social Interaction and Stylistic Similarity: A Reanalysis', in Michael B. Schiffer (ed.), *Advances in Archaeological Method and Theory*, Vol. I. New York: Academic Press, pp. 143-82.

Rajan, K. (1996), 'Petroglyphs of Perumukkal, Tamil Nadu', *Purakala* 7(1-2): 3-10.

—— (2008), 'Rock Art in South India: A Status Report', *Purakala* 18: 5-23.

Rami Reddy, V. (1971), 'Rock Paintings and Bruisings in Andhra Pradesh', *The Eastern Anthropologist* XXIV(3): 289-94.

—— (1976), *The Prehistoric and Proto Historic Cultures of Paiavoy, Kurnool District, South India*. Hyderabad: Government of Andhra Pradesh.

—— (1978), *A Study of the Neolithic Culture of South Western Andhra Pradesh*, Archaeological Series 51. Hyderabad: Government of Andhra Pradesh.

Ravikorisettar, P.C. Venkatasubbaiah and Dorian Q. Fuller (2002), 'Bramhagiri and Beyond: The Archaeology of the Southern Neolithic', in S. Settar and Ravikorisettar (ed.), *Indian Archaeology in Retrospect, Volume I, Pre History: Archaeology of South Asia*. New Delhi: Manohar & ICHR, pp. 151-238.

Sackett, J.R. (1977), 'The Meaning of Style in Archaeology: A General Model', *American Antiquity* 42: 369-80.

—— (1990), 'Style and Ethnicity in Archaeology: The Case for Isochresticism', in Margaret W. Conkey and Christine A. Hastorff (eds.), *The Uses of Style in Archaeology*. Cambridge: Cambridge University Press, pp. 19-32.

Sarma, I.K. (2003), 'Neolithic-Chalcolithic Cultures of Andhra Pradesh', in M.L.K. Murthy (ed.), *Pre and Proto Historic Andhra Pradesh (upto 500 BC)*. Hyderabad: Orient Longman, pp. 88-106.

Schapiro, M. (1953), 'Style', in A.L. Kroeber (ed.), *Anthropology Today: An Encyclopedic Inventory*. Chicago. University of Chicago Press.

Sridhar,T.S. (ed.). (2005), *Rock Art of Tamilnadu*. Chennai: Department of Archaeology.

Sundara, A. (1992), *Prehistoric Rock Art of Karnataka* (*Karnatakada Pragaitihasika Kalada Kale*: in Kannada). Dharwad: Lalit Kala Academy.

—— (2006), 'Karnataka Rock Art: Some Distinctive Aspects', *Purakala* 16: 35-51.

Trigger, Bruce B. (1989), *A History of Archaeological Thought*. Cambridge: Cambridge University Press.

Venkata Subbaiah, P.C. (1992), Prehistoric and Protohistorical Cultures of the Central Pennar Basin, Cuddapah District. Unpublished Ph.D. thesis. Deccan College, Pune.

—— (2007), *South Indian Neolithic Culture: Pennar Basin, Andhra Pradesh*. New Delhi: Bharatiya Kala Prakashan.

Wakankar, V.S. and R.R.R. Brooks (1976), *Stone Age Painting in India*. Bombay: D.B. Taraporewala and Sons.

Wakankar, V.S. (2005) (reprint), *Painted Rock Shelters of India*. Bhopal: Directorate of Archaeology & Museums.

Weissner, P. (1983), 'Style and Social Information in Kalahari San Projectile Points', *Journal of Anthropological Archaeology* 3: 190-234.

—— (1990), 'Is There A Unity of "style"?', in M.W. Conkey and Christine Hastorff (eds.), *The Uses of Style in Archaeology*. Cambridge: Cambridge University Press, pp. 105-12.

Wobst, M.M. (1977), 'Stylistic Behaviour and Information Exchange', in C.E. Cleland (ed.), *For the Director: Research Essays in Honour of James. B. Griffin*. Michigan: University of Michigan, pp. 317-42.

Zeunar, F.E. (1959), 'On the Origin of Cinder Mounds of the Bellary District', *Bulletin of the Institute of Archaeology* 1: 37-44.

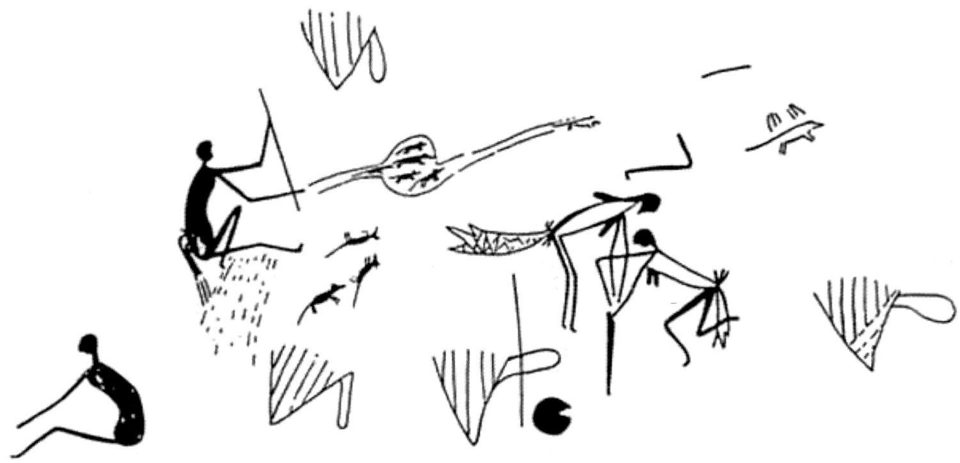

4

A Mark in the Way: Schematic Rock Art and Communication Routes

Hipólito Collado Giraldo and José Julio García Arranz

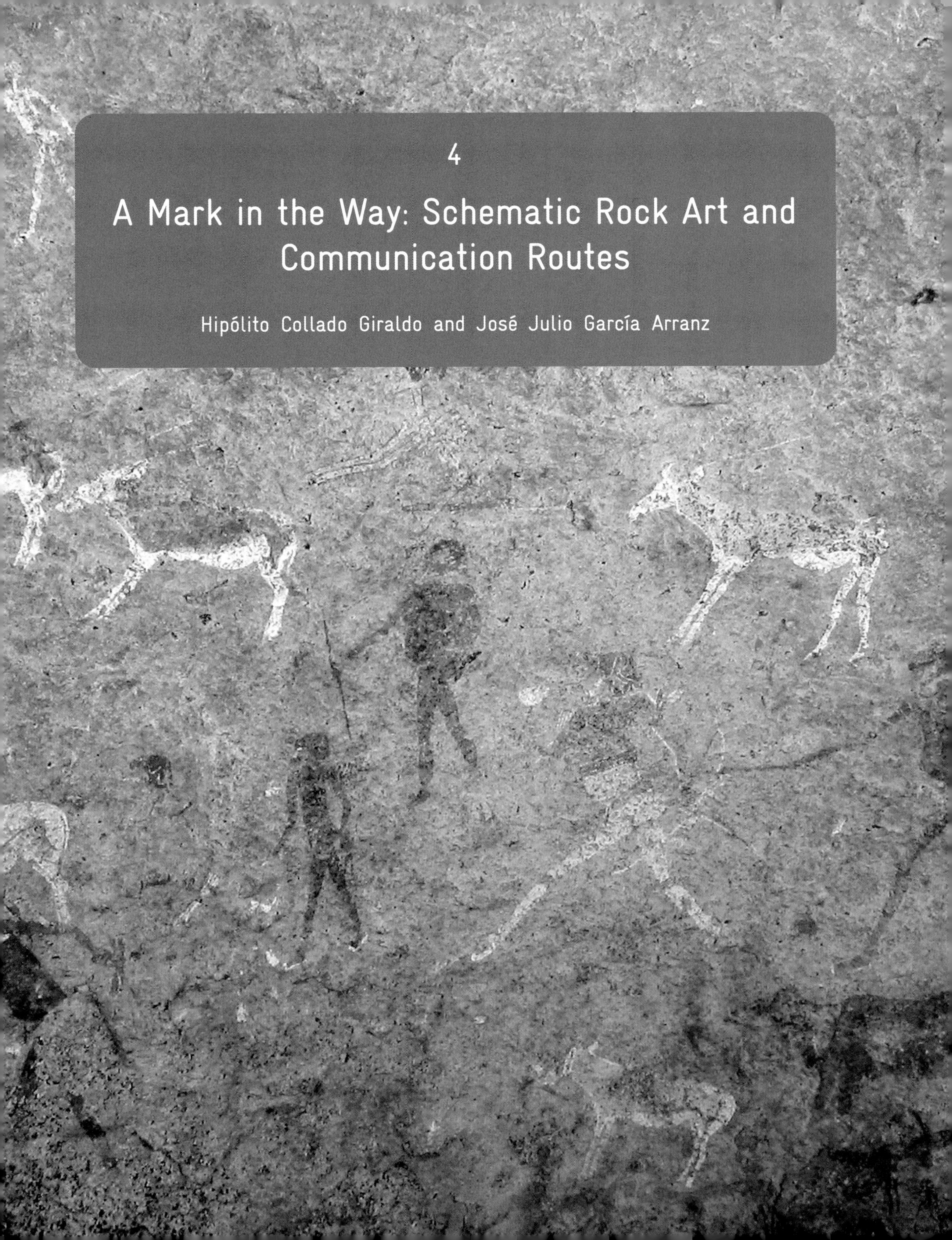

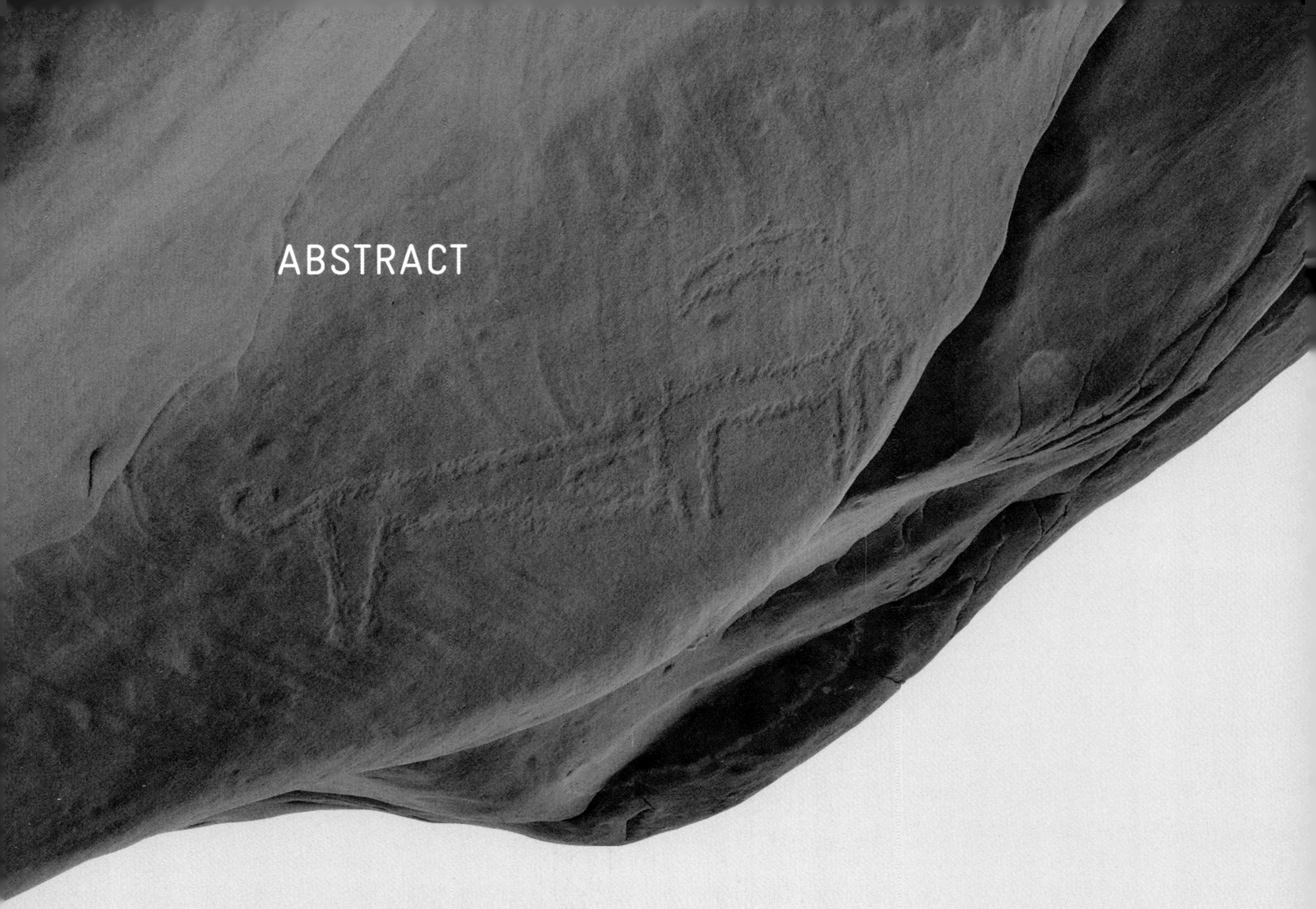

ABSTRACT

Schematic rock art appears in the Iberian Peninsula throughout the 6th millennium BP*. It is the cultural expression of human communities with a Neolithic lifestyle that has been interpreted from diverse points of view like religious, semiology and social. The present paper proposes a functional interpretative model for schematic rock art by studying the relation between communication routes and places chosen. Shelters and rock surfaces in open air are laid out along prehistoric ways. They contain different symbols (painted or engraved) that are analysed in this paper.*

HERE THERE IS SOMETHING THAT DOES NOT WORK...

More than 20 years ago, during our first moments as young researchers, we started taking into consideration the study of schematic rock art. We took as authentic dogmas the 'clues' or the instructions from excellent researchers like D. Alfonso Caballero Klink and Magdalena Ortiz Macías to localise the sheltered places with painted rock art (Caballero 1983: 513; Ortiz 1998: 242):

— Smooth walls with reddish and yellowish tones, occupied with live lichens in contrast to the greyish tone of the rocks.
— Overhang crags, almost individualised, in the mountain range.
— Smooth walls where reddish tones stood out.
— Holes or big cavities that can be seen perfectly from a distance.

With these indications, locating sheltered places or other types of places with rock art seemed to be easy and uncomplicated as compared to those from the vegetation in the mountain, which was the chosen place earlier for locating rock art. However, we had to live with many disappointments when we arrived at the sheltered places. According to our definitions, these sites should have had rock art but we did not find any trace of rock paintings or engravings here.

But, while the years passed and our research progressed, we found many places with schematic rock art. They were sheltered places, cavities or projections in small dimensions in the rock with slightly projected cornices that had nothing or almost nothing in common with the ideal place defined by these researchers.

It was clear that the reason why these places were selected for paintings was different from choosing an outstanding place.

The shelters, in the same mountain range line, were sometimes grouped in zones with the paintings located in more or less protected places and big spaces between them that did not have any graphic content, although these were big shelters.

On certain occasions, the rock art sites of varied typologies with different numbers of panels provided an important diversity of figures. These were followed along the mountain range without an apparent criterion that could help us understand the reason for the layout.

Finally, in isolated and outstanding hills also appeared painting shelters, painted in an individualised way or in groups with two shelters maximum.

In view of the results that our prospecting work provided, it was evident that we were facing different situations that, according to our hypothesis, answered to only one motivation: locating appropriate resources in the territory through symbolisation, either exerting control in their communication routes or the strategic enclaves associated with them (mountain passes, hills, fords, etc.), or depicting iconographic elements in association with the basic resources for group subsistence (sources of water, hunt, places for harvest), or indicating those elements that exist in the territory and also intercede in economic development, or in their economic chain (mainly outcrops or concentrations of minerals and raw materials).

ESTABLISHING A MODEL AS AN ANALYSIS STRATEGY

Extremadura is a region situated in south-western Spain next to the Portugal frontier. We have been focusing on this region for more than 20 years to study schematic rock art. We today know of more than 500 places with prehistoric schematic paintings or engravings all over the territory (Collado 2009; García 1997). Along with the group of shelters documented in the Andalusia region, this is one of the most important concentrations of post-Palaeolithic rock art in the Iberian Peninsula.

A detailed study of these enclaves, especially those in which localised elements form an important diachronic sequence of figures, allows us to establish a first chronological classification for schematic rock art, which is organised in three stages (Collado 2006) whose basics characteristics are:

1st Stage: *Ancient schematic art:* identified with the first signs of this style, mainly symbolic, during its introduction in the Neolithic period.

2nd Stage: *Middle schematic art:* maintains the basis of iconography, joins new figurative repertoires and modifies the percentage of depictions in an important measure, giving an outstanding prominence to human and animal figures in contrast to the symbolism of the former stage. An important thematic complexity is also perceived in the scenography of the panels and also a new territorial distribution of the shelters that prioritise the location in relation to strategic places for the control of the territory and communication routes.

3th Stage: *Recent schematic art:* has maintained the thematic, scenographic and typology criteria of the middle stage, as also the tendency to locations in places with important strategic values. Only

Fig. 4.1 Linus rock art shelter, Monfragüe National Park (Cáceres, Spain).

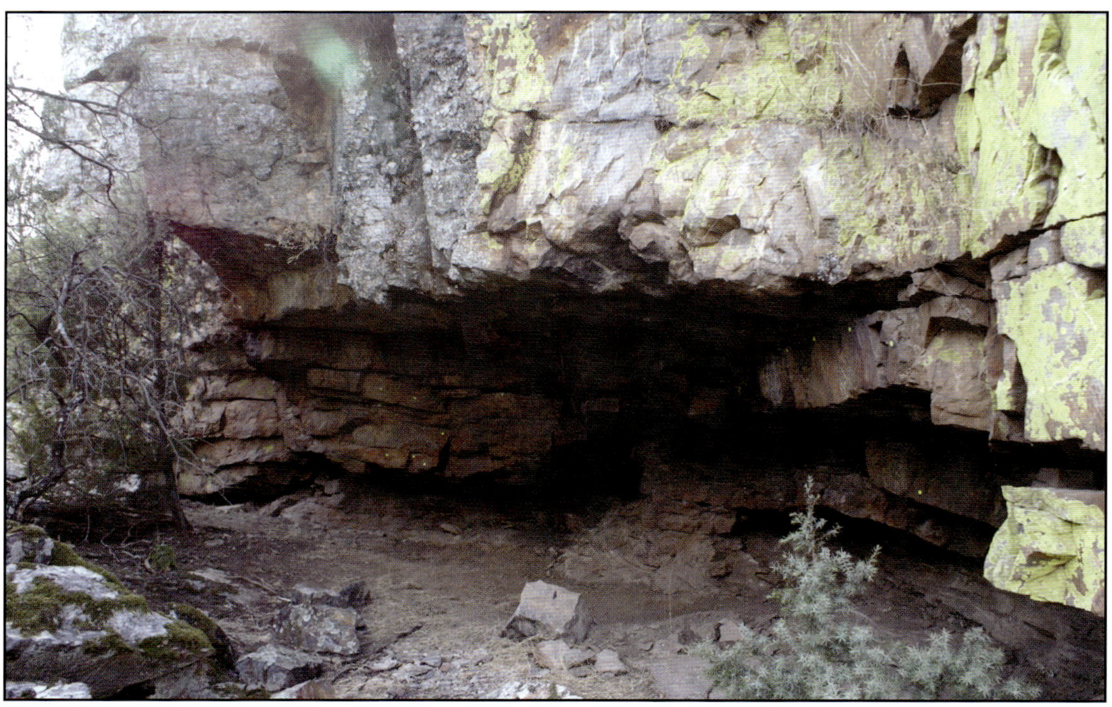

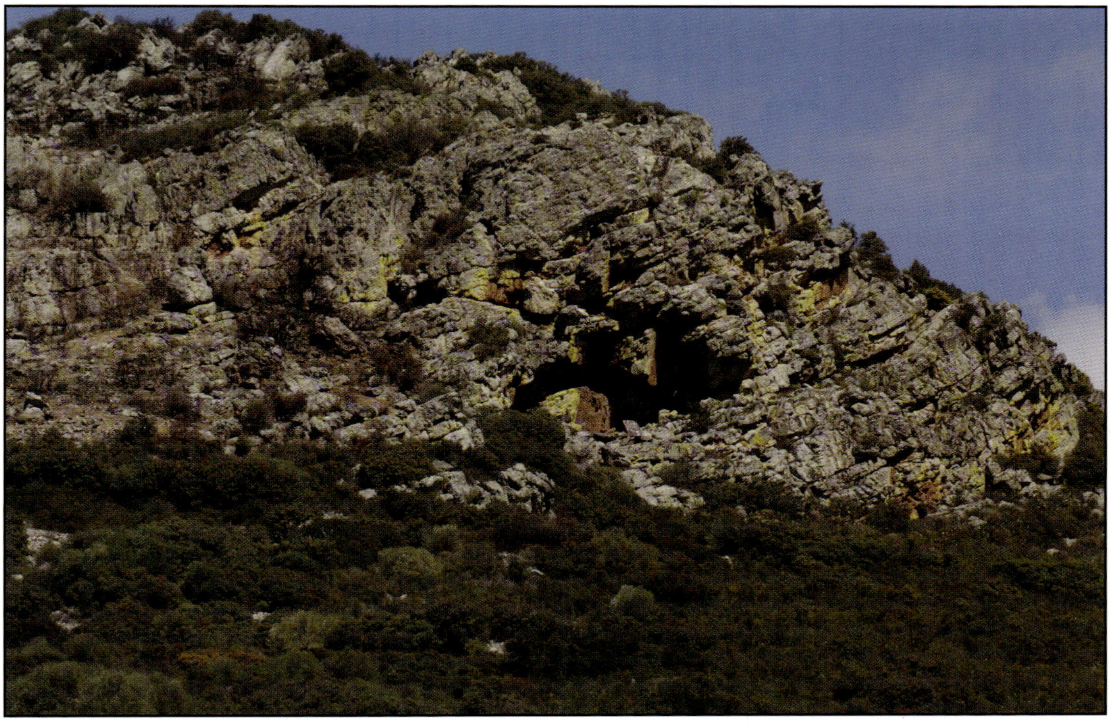

Fig. 4.2 Peñón Amarillo rock art shelter, Helechal (Badajoz, Spain).

the elements with an ethnographic character clearly related with the Bronze Age (weapons, horns head-dresses, chariots, etc.), allow us to ascribe certain motifs to this last stage.

Once we had established these first stages, it was necessary to analyse how the rock art of each stage interacted with the places where it had been represented. Therefore, this led us to establish a new classification as the first step of the analysis, strictly based on the morphological criteria of the enclaves in which schematic rock art appeared. In this way, five basic formats were established:

a) Big shelters, with depths and lengths that exceed 10 m, and an important height development. They are easily perceptible in the landscape and access to them usually does not present many difficulties (Fig. 4.1).
b) Shelters or hovels with a certain spaciousness and a variable depth, although not exceeding 10 m from the access zone, shaping environments that can be used easily as shelters for one or more people (Fig. 4.2).
c) Smooth walls slightly leaning and completely exposed to open air. Only a slight inclination permits the protection of motifs against the inclemency of the weather (Fig. 4.3).
d) Sites localised above big fallen blocks removed from quartzite outcrops, or in zones with granite outcrops that formed small protected areas from the inclemency of the weather (Fig. 4.4).
e) Small cavities or cracks of small dimensions, which most of the times are insufficient even to be used as a shelter for a man and always with access that compels one to

take a forced position in order to visualise the paintings (Fig. 4.5).

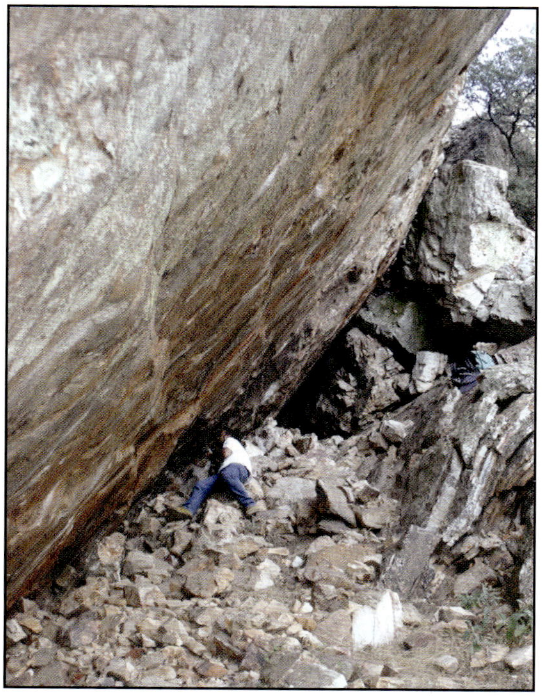

There also exists another criterion, very objective, for establishing a possible classification: the geological support used (granite, quartzite, slate, etc.). We did take this criterion into account during our analysis as it was not conclusive. In relation to this, it can be concluded that without forming a distinction of the chronological stage, the authors of rock art exploited without any obvious selection criteria those geological supports that were localised in their territorial action fields.

From here, it was necessary to compare the viability of our first hypothesis: the effective control that prehistoric societies exerted on territorial resources since Neolithic until the Bronze Age through rock art. In this line, we take as reference the post-processual approach applied to rock art interpretation, especially from the point of view of landscape archaeology. In this way, prehistoric rock art is considered another element of material culture (putting it on a level with a ceramic object or a lytic object). Schematic art, under this premise, is integrated in the cultural and socio-economic system that the social groups who occupied a certain territory along a certain period developed (Martinez 2002). In this cultural system, schematic rock art plays an outstanding

Fig. 4.3 Alía rock art shelter, Alía (Cáceres, Spain).

Fig. 4.4 Pradillo rock art shelter, Trujillo (Cáceres, Spain).

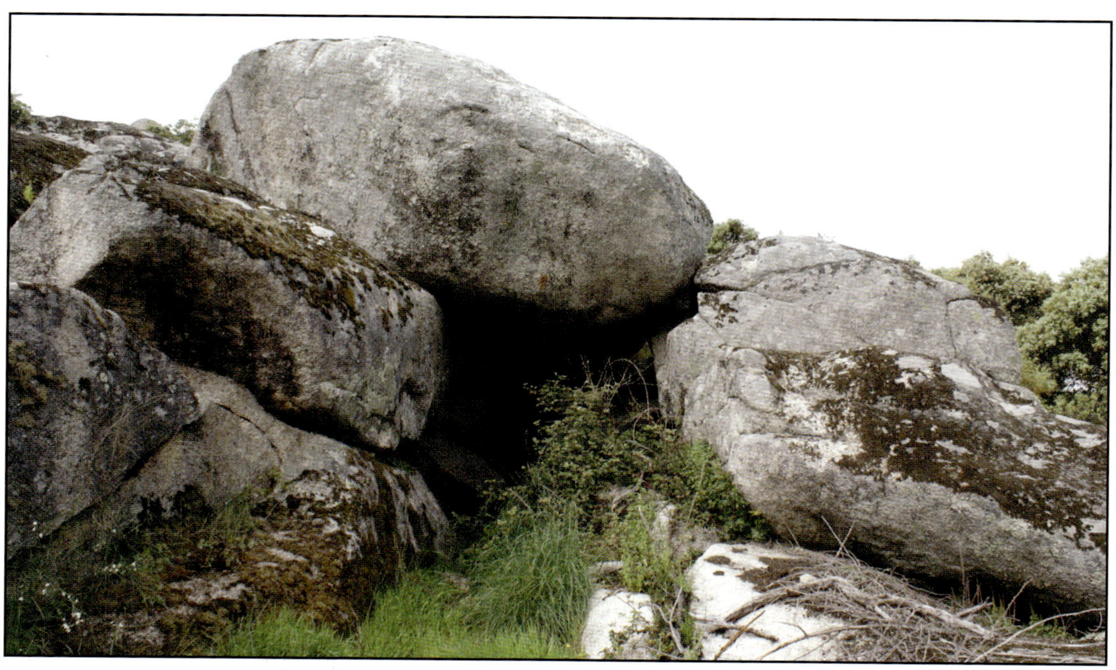

role in the context of interchange strategies and the control of the territory and its resources from its consideration as a communication system in which the figures depicted are part of a symbolic frame in a group of specific locations (shelters), whose meaning is different according to the chosen location and the audience to which the message is intended to be transmitted (Bradley 1997, 2002).

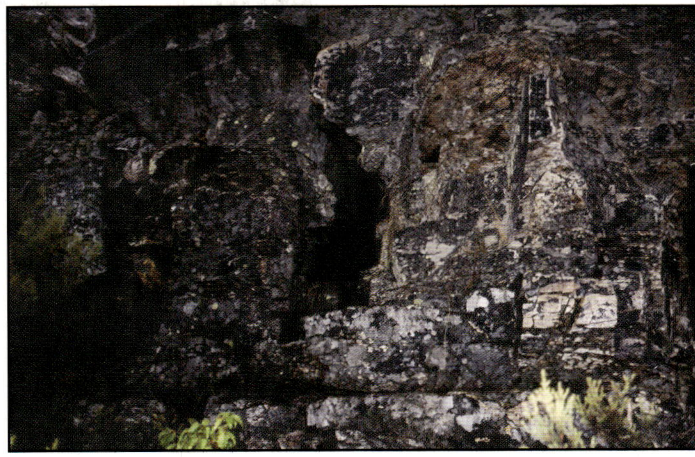

Fig. 4.5 Noe rock art shelter, Monfragüe National Park (Cáceres, Spain).

Without departing from this paradigmatic approach, and with the objective of studying in depth our proposal, we opted to continue with the line studied by Chippindale (2004). This author proposes a model in which technical aspects (strokes typology, pigments, etc.), stylistics (iconography, figurative compositions, panel distribution inside shelters) and geographical aspects (shelter typology, location of them and its relation with landscape) are inter-related in different stages.

This system allowed us to get through an interpretation with a strictly geographical basis. This interpretation was based in a conscious reiteration regarding the location of the shelters in certain geographical contexts with more or less strategic interests. In this interpretation, it was recognised that other constants related to the typology of the figures that appear in the shelters, the intensity and the diachronic limits in representations, the variability of techniques and pigments used and the location and visibility of the panels.

THE ENDORSEMENT OF THE HYPOTHESIS: THE CONTROL OF RESOURCES THROUGH SCHEMATIC ROCK ART

After the hypothesis had been posed and the analysis model had been established, what was needed was combining all those factors that we had considered before: the different chronological stages that we established in the development of schematic rock art, the different types of shelters and the different types of figures used in each case. The objective was to know when they appeared and how they developed the different figurative types, the places that they occupied in the panels, how they were combined with other figures, their compositions and visibility grades and, at the same time, how the panels with depictions interacted with the type of shelter where the location of the panel, its dimensions, orientation, preferential situation and type of relation with other palimpsests were taken into account. Finally, this information was connected to the geographical characteristics of the place where the shelter was located.

This led us to establish a new classification of the places where rock art appeared, which was based on their functionality.

1. Concentration Sites: Enclaves with a big identity that in relation to the morphology answers to an *a type* shelter of the last classification occupy an important place in

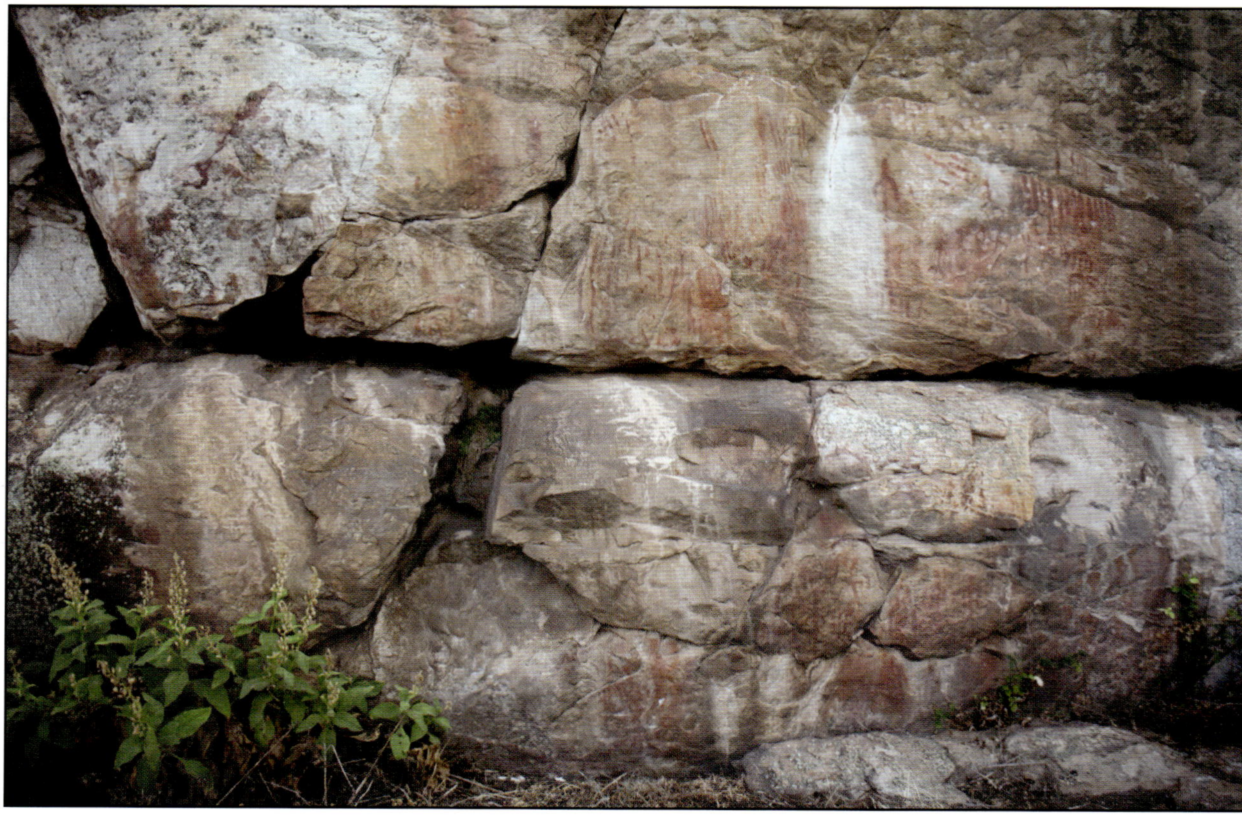

Fig. 4.6 Rock art in 'Concentration Sites'. Juanita rock art shelter. Oliva de Mérida (Badajoz, Spain).

the landscape, with outstanding visibility (from and towards the shelter), easy access and an important strategic value according to the dominant location in relation to passage zones, especially in fords, narrow passes and hills, in mountain regions or in access zones to the narrowed beds of the rivers that flow in a concrete place. On this site are localised an important number of figures depicted on panels, which are located in an indiscriminate way all over its range (ceiling, central panels, outside, rock cornices, etc.) at different heights and with different orientations. In these cases, a clear criterion of a tidy layout was not detected, but a reiterative desire through depicting as many graphemes as possible in order to record the use of the enclave. In this sense, the iconographic series is diverse. Human and animal depictions prevail, which are accompanied by a varied and important symbolic system. Superimpositions are very usual and these affirm a huge variety of techniques, pigments and style representations. All these reflect continuous use of the enclave through time (Fig. 4.6).

2. Indication Sites: Together with transit sites, these are the most numerous. Their size is variable within a level of spaces with a medium or a small magnitude and could fit perfectly with *type b, c and d* shelters of the last morphology stage. Generally appear at the base of the quartzite at the top of the mountain range, just in the use contact zone with the mountainside that precedes the rocky line. They

are visible from a short and medium distance, as the visual range from their access zone (sometimes vegetation, or the undergrowth in the area of woodland) limits the field of vision and the perception of the shelter. Its layout avoids proximity to transit zones or strategic spaces. The depictions are limited and reduced to a limited number of panels that generally do not have many figures and are located in not very visible places, although never with privacy criterion because you just have to move a step or access the shelter itself to realise the existence of motifs that are depicted inside. Technically, they are not very varied and it is usual to see figures made with regular strokes, usually thick, and with the same type of pigment, mainly red. Iconography is simple too; schematic motifs abound although with varied characters (circles, zigzag, angles, branch forms, rolling, dots, etc.) and human figures rarely appear. The lack of overlaps and the technique and stylistic regularity of representations invites us to consider a punctual use of these spaces, so it can be deduced that their presence in the territory can be linked with occasional or circumstantial control over some basic resources that were constantly located in the immediate surroundings of these shelters, especially in mountain zones: water sources, systematic hunt passes and even the very shelter (Fig. 4.7).

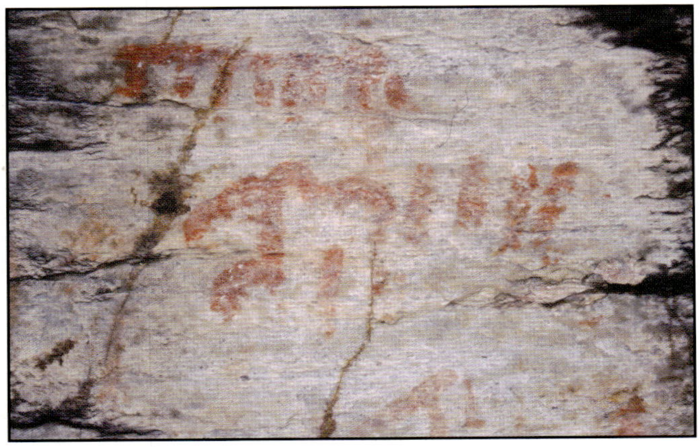

Fig. 4.7 Schematic rock art from 'Indication Sites'. Cuevas 3 rock art shelter, Hornachos (Badajoz, Spain).

3. Passage Shelters: These shelters are clearly related with dots or places linked to the passable character of a certain territory, either through the courses of rivers and streams, or next to mountain passes, fords or hills that permit communication through the mountain lines. Their sizes are varied, as are the visibility ranges but they usually abound in the middle and high ranges, especially in higher zones. However, this visibility range is reduced for those that are located in restricted areas at the end of gullies or in slotted river beds. Morphologically, they fit into the *b* and *c* shelter types, but with a clear predominance of the second over the first. Often, access to these shelters does not pose great difficulties, except in some cases where access is associated with places slotted in the valleys, where there are shelters that literally hang over the beds to which access is impossible without climbing equipment.

Technically there are not too many changes in relation with the previous group: very regular strokes, predominantly thick ones, although one notices an important presence of motifs made with a thin stroke (it was thin in indication shelters), as well as the use of only one type of pigment. Superimpositions are rare and the iconography is diverse, but in contrast with the previous group, some groups of motifs are systematically repeated, especially those with alignments of vertical

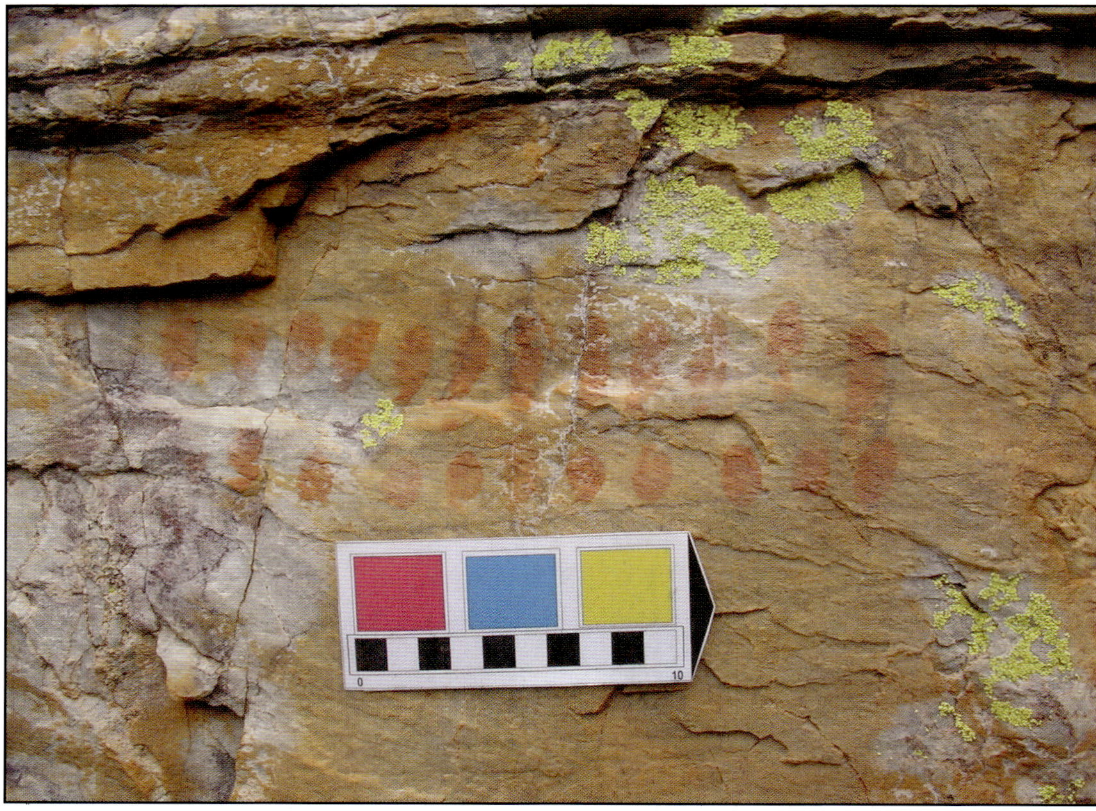

Fig. 4.8 Fingers in passage shelter, Sierra Grande rock art shelter, Hornachos (Badajoz, Spain).

bars. Depictions of anthropomorphic and zoomorphic motifs accompanying symbolic figurative paint are not strange. The compositional outlines are varied, from simple (alignments of vertical bars), to other more complex clearly structured and hierarchical ones used for the human figure. Also it was observed that some associative models are repeated in similar geographical enclaves. One with a sun-shaped or square-shaped motif (square or rectangular), with a zoomorphic comb-shaped figure is meaningful. This association is documented systematically in shelters associated with passable places, especially passes and hills. This was a pattern that from an interpretative criterion we put in relation with seasonal transit livestock (transhumance and local transhumance), especially if we consider the sun figure and the square-shaped motif in the sense of their meaning as a place to pen the livestock.

The topographic distribution of panels in this type of shelters has a distinctly public nature because they were used only in surfaces that were the most visible from the outside even from a notable distance. Therefore, the shelters are clearly linked with communication routes, authentic indicator signals in mountain passes or tracks associated with minor beds that permitted access to level zones with abundant grazing land which very adequate for seasonal settlements in ranching cabins during seasonal movements (Fig. 4.8).

4. Intimacy Sites: It is the smallest group and from a morphological point of view, their presence is reduced mainly to the shelters of type *b* and mainly to *e* of the preceding classification. Generally, they are not useful shelters because their size is very small and a person can hardly be inside them. Their visible ranges are always reduced and they can even go unnoticed in relation to the landscape around them or can be located in inaccessible areas. These sites are not used to contain a huge number of figures, and these are always located on panels situated in areas that are not very visible from inside, so anyone who wants to see them has to enter adopting forced positions. Technically, there is an important diversity, with figures filled with plain colour, indiscriminate use of strokes (thick and thin and even combinations of both) and the use of different types of pigments (black, red and white) even reaching the depiction of bichrome figures. The iconography is also singular; in this type of shelters rarely are there any depictions of animals and in addition to the usual depictions of anthropomorphic and schematic motifs (especially sun-shaped figures, bars and dots), there are some particular depictions which do not belong to any established typological classification. It is not easy to verify any clear typological association, neither a defined criteria of composition in the panels which usually have a small number of graphemes and where it is very difficult to appreciate the superimposed figures. From an interpretative point of view, we think that these shelters were used for very specific moments, sometimes used in an individualised way and with the aim that did not have any relation with everyday life but went to the field of rites and magic. They depict a place of contact between man and the supernatural world in which symbolic depictions should be an intrinsic part of the ritual (Fig. 4.9).

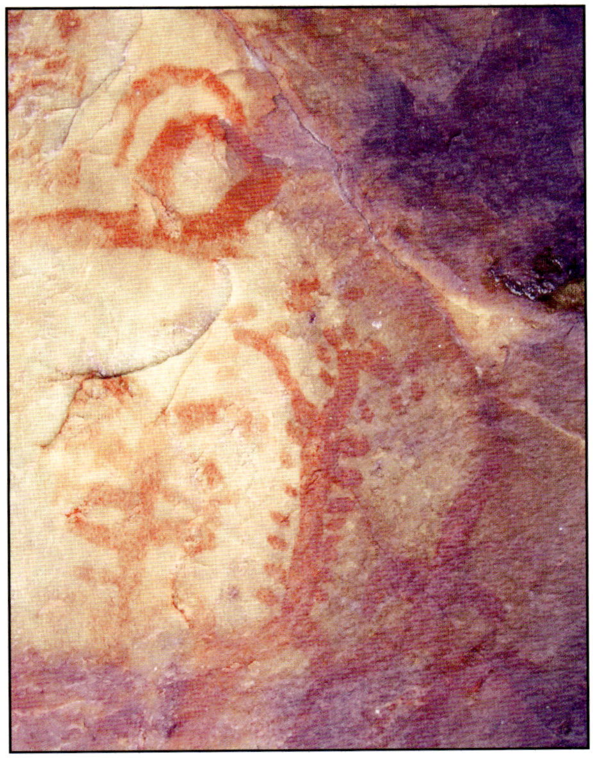

Fig. 4.9 Symbolic figures from Intimacy Site, El Límite rock art shelter, Monfragüe National Park (Cáceres, Spain).

DIACHRONIC EVOLUTION OF A SYMBOLIC LANDSCAPE

All these criteria show that the landscape of Neolithic rock art, or *ancient schematic art*, is a monotonous landscape. In the landscape, there are no reference elements that capture our attention; the shelter is not outstanding in a territory in which mountains, rivers, valleys and plains helped in raising resources for human groups who, although connoisseurs of agriculture and ranching, still depended heavily on hunting and harvest.

The rock art of this first stage uses a variety of pigments (red, black and white), but with a clear reiteration of the first one. Motifs have a preferential symbolic character with little presence of anthropomorphic and zoomorphic ones. The iconographical variety is also reduced and there are four most common types: bars, sun-shaped figures, circles and undulations. When there are anthropomorphic depictions, they adopt an arch-shaped format. Panels are small in size exploiting small superficial cracks in the rock that were useful for the depiction of motifs, without a standard location criterion (depth, lateral walls, roofs, etc.). Over these, there are a few graphemes, usually done with a thick stroke, with rarely any documented superimpositions.

Based on the previous theory, 'indication sites' are the typology clearly associated with the first stages of schematic rock art, without ruling out the shelters included under 'intimacy sites'. Both sites slot have the characteristics of their own rock art with an egalitarian social model that is reflected in the compositional outlines. In these outlines, the organisation into a hierarchy and complex scenes is not possible in a frame with a limited development and with few figures, most of the times with a strong symbolic content. It is not perceived as a social model in which the territory is taken as a place to control, because the only thing that the people wanted to achieve was the appropriation of basic resources for subsistence: mainly water and hunting. In this sense, the presence of shelters in the territory has a real naturalisation certificate. There is systematic association to motifs painted of water sources, springs or seasonal sources of water, as well as hunting grounds or small routes of animals in their movements to the water. The shelter is not visible from the landscape, but the landscape is visible from the shelter. It is necessary to approach it or even go inside to see that this space and the source or sources that are associated with it are linked at these first Neolithic groups through symbolic appropriation.

During the Copper Age, a progressive social complexity was produced that accompanied a different territorial dynamism. It was gone from a Neolithic territory that is immediate and is next to basic resources for subsistence that were had the most references, to a Chalcolithic territory that is large and complex in which it is necessary to exert control over the means of production in the framework of the diversification of principal and productive activities (agriculture, ranching and metallurgy). As a consequence, excess surplus was produced, that at the same time had an effect in the increase in exchange dynamics and a progressive asymmetry in inter-social relations (Hurtado 1995; Nocete 2001).

Middle schematic rock art corresponding to this cultural stage is not indifferent to this process, and in parallel with the dynamics of territorial control, the shelters are present in the territory taking up places with a clearly strategic character, dominating obligated places of passage for exchange routes (hills, mountain passes, courses of rivers, etc.) or exerting control over the areas with important resources, mainly metallurgical. The shelters gain in size and visibility, so the 'passage sites' and 'concentration sites' are localisation patterns that fix better in this new reality.

Panels gain in size and are localised in clearly visible places with special reiteration over the central areas on the back walls. The number of figures that appeared in them is multiplied and there are many compositions where there are depictions superimposed, showing a reiterative use of these spaces. We can begin to perceive them as real compositions, the most common of which are lineups with a horizontal tendency, although there are other, more complex ones also with vertical, triangular and circular characters. Nevertheless, the figurative typology is very homogeneous establishing the differentiation criteria in relation to the size and preferential position of the figure and not, as will happen in the last stage, the presence of prestige elements and ornaments give to the motif a special importance in relation to the rest of the figurative depictions.

Red pigments and thick strokes continue being clearly dominant. However, the typology scheme suffers an important change in the apparition percentage, such as the incorporation of anthropomorphics in an important percentage and also in a majority and zoomorphic figures with varied formats. These formats cover the most naturalistic to less detailed depictions. This does not mean that the figurative group has disappeared, particularly the symbolic group that was known in the previous stage but only the percentage of its appearances is much reduced in favour of the fundamental motif of this new stage: anthropomorphic depictions. All this is in tune with a process that characterises this chronological period and that some researchers have defined as the 'process of ideological anthropomorphising' (Enríquez 2000: 356). It is present not only in schematic rock art, but also in other ways of expression that are movable in character (anthropomorphic idols made of stones or bones), and that show a symbolic dynamism verified at the end of the second millennium through these expressive ways, geographically very extended, in which is perceived a process of '...self-affirmation of the leadership that makes to this figures to appear with elements of status and prestige' (Enríquez 2000: 356).

In the Bronze Age, the process of organisation into a hierarchy that had been developing through the previous stage intensified (Hurtado 1999), in the context of a new territorial reality that for Extremadura has been well defined by Pavón. It is characterised by the occupation of places with an outstanding grade of strategic meaning (Pavón 1998), but preceded by a first stage of transition in which its roots can be seen in Chalcolitic traditions, which are as artifactual and technological as they are territorial (in the sense of continuation in the pre-existing population occupations). All this happens in the middle of an outlook that, on a peninsular scale, puts us in view of very varied versions of a phenomenon of realignment of population, both socioeconomic and ideological (Rodríguez and Enríquez 2001: 77; Gálvez 2001).

Obviously, as happened in *middle schematic art*, the rock art of this stage, defined as *recent schematic art*, was also not indifferent to all the changes that were being produced at all the levels. However, in the sense of distribution, no other occupations appear, but in a systematic way, they used the shelters as they were being used in the previous stages ('transit sites' and 'concentration sites'), where the graphemes of this third stage were usually located overlapped with figures from the middle stage. Logically, the morphological, technical and compositional patterns from the previous stage were maintained, complicating the task of identifying the graphemes of this new phase. However, what is verified is a higher reiteration of the use of a thin stroke applied with one instrument that permits best attention to details in the execution of the figure and a tendency of darkest and densest tones in pigments (mainly red). All this is linked with the existence of the overlaps commented on earlier, especially to the presence of new figurative models whose main references are in peninsular iconographic groups, clearly ascribed to the Bronze Age, as concentric circles and spirals much repeated in the outdoor engraves of El Tajo, Galicia or the plateau Castellano-Leonesa whose chronology, according to their main researchers, seems to reach an important development throughout the Bronze Age (Costas and Novoa 1993: 34–71; Gómez Barrera 1992: 252; Varela 2001: 56), or the depictions of punctual objects as chariots (Collado, in press), weapons, horns, head-dresses and other ethnographic elements that seem to become widespread mainly from advance moments of the Bronze Age (Ruiz Gálvez 1995), and that help to single out *recent schematic art* from the precedent stages. Finally, the development of some stylistic concepts that would stand out and the ones that mainly affect anthropomorphic depictions that depict the head, the trunk and the upper extremities, with the fingers usually marked, with a frontal perspective and the rest of the figure in profile with the feet clearly individualised have also been recognised. A figurative scheme is detected in some shelters with rock art paintings, for example, the one in Crehuet, in Ceclavin (González Cordero 1999a) and that is systematically repeated in anthropomorphic depictions in engraves on the so-called warrior stele, with a chronology that refers to the end of Bronze Age (Domínguez, González and de Hoz 2005).

Recent schematic art ends the figurative sequence that we propose for Extremadura schematic rock art, closing an artistic and cultural cycle that had been in force for 4,000 years. However, it does not mean that rock art was interrupted in this moment, because Extremadura will know the introduction, with an unusual force, of a type of demonstration that constantly used engraves as a way of expression and is dated to the Iron Age. At the end we do not want to define the characteristics of this new artistic cycle, but we want to emphasise that with the end of the Bronze Age, there was also an end to another artistic cycle—schematic rock art—which started in the first moments of Neolithic with an indisputable personality that we have tried to reflect and sequence. Its end, from our point of view, happens with the beginning of the Iron Age, a new chronological and cultural framework that spans almost all of first millennium BCE and that was accompanied with a new way of understanding rock art, in which remarkable changes were perceived changes in all the orders: technical, stylistic, thematic, etc., which provoked a new artistic style with a personality, but not defined yet. In any case, this is different from the previous cycle of schematic rock art. Therefore, we think that in the context of rock art of producing societies, schematic rock art from the rock art of the Iron Age should be clearly separated because it answers to two different realities, and both should be studied and analysed independently.

REFERENCES

Bradley, R. (1997), *Rock Art and the Prehistory of Atlantic Europe: Signing the Land*. Routledge.

—— (2002), 'Access, Style and Imagery: The Audience for Prehistoric Rock Art in Atlantic Spain and Portugal 4000-2000 BC', *Oxford Journal of Archaeology* 21(3): 231-47.

Caballero Klink, A. (1983), 'La pintura rupestre esquemítica de la vertiente septentrional de Sierra Morena (provincia de Ciudad Real) y su contexto arqueológico', *Estudios y Monografías* 1 and 2 (9): 538.

Chippindale, C. (2004), 'From Millimetre up to Kilometre: A Framework of Space and of Scale for Reporting and Studying Rock Art in Its Landscape', in *The Figured Landscapes of Rock Art. Looking at Pictures in Place*. Cambridge University Press.

Collado, H. (2006), 'Arte rupestre en la cuenca del Guadiana: El conjunto de grabados del Molino Manzínez (Alconchel-Cheles)', *Memorias de Odiana-Estudos Arqueológicos do Alqueva* 4, Beja, EDIA.

—— (2009), 'Arte rupestre prehistórico en Extremadura: 1997-2006', in R. Balbín Behrmann (coordinator), *Arte prehistórico al aire libre en el sur de Europa*. Valladolid: Junta de Castilla y León, Consejería de Cultura y Turismo, pp. 287-322.

Costas, F.J. and P. Novoa (1993), 'Los grabados rupestres de Galicia', *Monografías del Museo Arqueolóxico e Histórico de A Coruña* 6: 291.

Dominguez, C., J.M. Gonzalez and J.M. y De Hoz, J. (2005), *Estelas decoradas del Museo Arqueológico Provincial de Badajoz. Siglos VIII-V a. C.* Consejería de Cultura. Badajoz, p. 54.

Enriquez, J.J. (2000), 'Nuevos ídolos antropomorfos calcolíticos de la Cuenca Media del Guadiana', *Spal* 9: 351-68.

Garcia, J.J. (1997), 'La pintura rupestre esquemítica en la provincia de Cíceres', *Extremadura Arqueológica* VII: 119-40.

Gomez Barrera, J.A. (1992), 'Manifestaciones de la facies esquemítica en el centro y norte de la Península Ibérica', *Espacio, Tiempo y Forma*, Serie I, Prehistoria y Arqueología, tomo V: 231-64.

Gonzalez Cordero, A. (1999), 'Datos para la contextualización del arte rupestre en la Alta Extremadura', *Zephyrus* 52: 191-220.

Hurtado, V. (1995), 'Interpretación de la dinímica cultural en la Cuenca Media del Guadiana (IV-II milenio a.n.e.)', *Extremadura Arqueológica* V: 53-81.

—— (1999), 'Los inicios de la complejización social y el Campaniforme en Extremadura', *Spal* 8: 47-83.

Martinez, J. (1998), 'Abrigos y accidentes geogríficos como categorías de anílisis en el paisaje de la pintura rupestre esquemítica. El sudeste como marco', *Arqueología Espacial* 19-20: 543-61.

—— (2002), 'Pintura rupestre esquemítica: el panel, espacio social', *Trabajos de Prehistoria* 59(1): 1-23.

Nocete, F. (2001), *Tercer milenio antes de nuestra era. Relaciones y contradicciones centro/periferia en el valle del Guadalquivir*. Barcelona: Bellaterra-Arqueología, p. 187.

Ortiz Macias, M. (1998), 'Pintura rupestre esquemítica al sur de la comarca de Mérida', *Serie Arqueológica* 17: 270.

Pavon, I. (1998), *El trínsito del II al I milenio a.C. en las cuencas de los ríos Tajo y Guadiana: la Edad del Bronce*, Cíceres: Servicio de publicaciones de la Universidad de Extremadura, p. 330.

Rodriguez, A. and J.J. Enriquez (2001), *Extremadura tartésica. Arqueología de un proceso periférico*, Barcelona: Bellaterra-Arqueología, p. 366.

Ruiz-Galvez, M. (ed.) (1995), *Ritos de paso y puntos de paso. La ría de Huelva en el Mundo del Bronce Final europeo*, Madrid: Complutum Extra 5: 250

Ruiz-Galvez, M.L. (coordinator) (2001), *La Edad del Bronce, Primera Edad de Oro de España?*. Barcelona: Crítica Arqueología, p. 352.

Santos, M. (1998), 'Los espacios del arte: el diseño del panel y la articulación del paisaje en el arte rupestre gallego', *Trabajos de Prehistoria* 55(2): 73-88.

Varela, M. (2001), 'Arte rupestre do vale do Tejo (Portugal). Antropomorfos (estilos, comportamientos, cronologías e interpretaçoes)', *Semiótica del arte prehistórico. Servicio de estudios valencianos. Serie Arqueológica* 18: 53-88.

5

Prehistoric Kalimantan Rock Art as a Visual Study

Pindi Setiawan

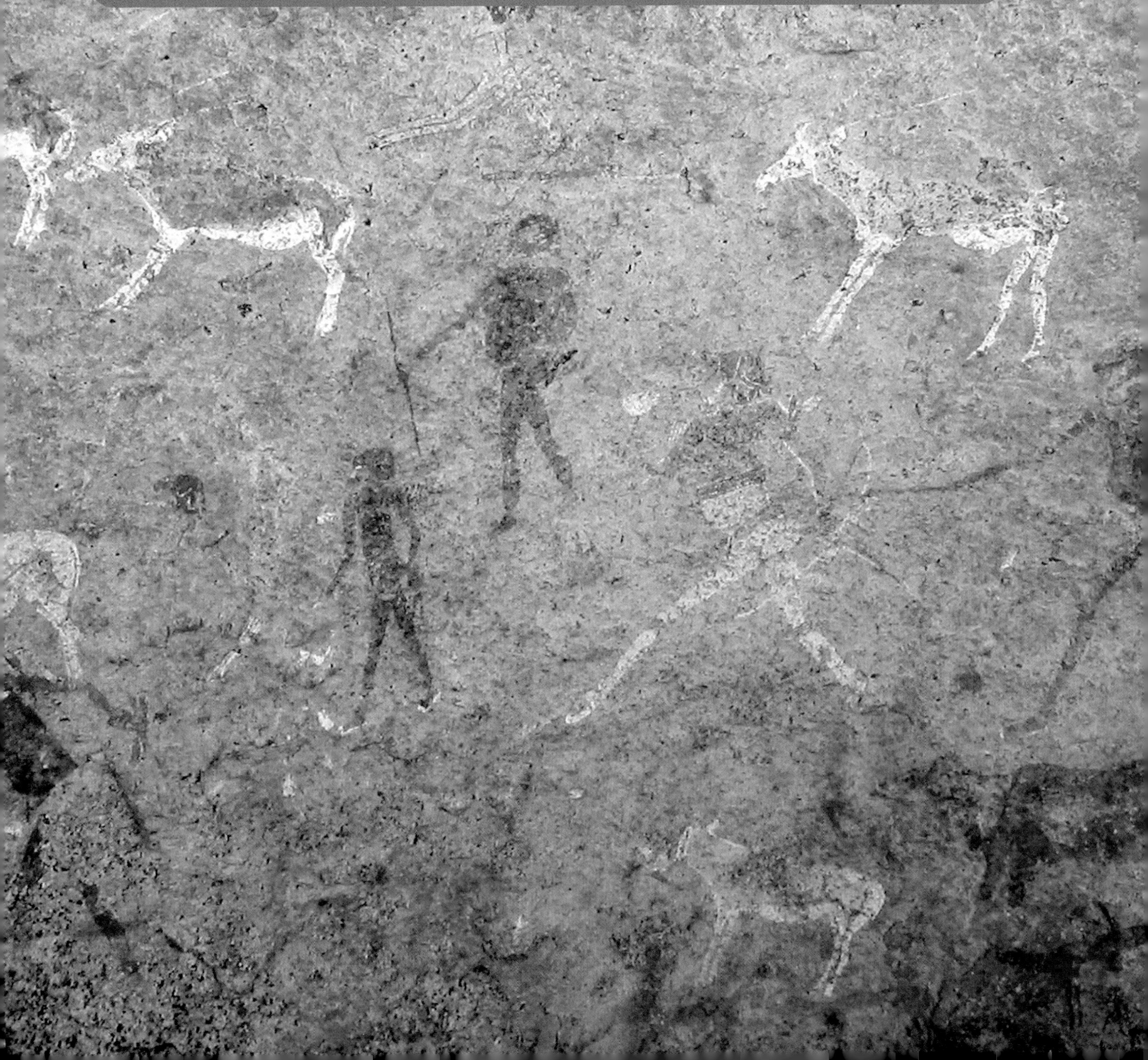

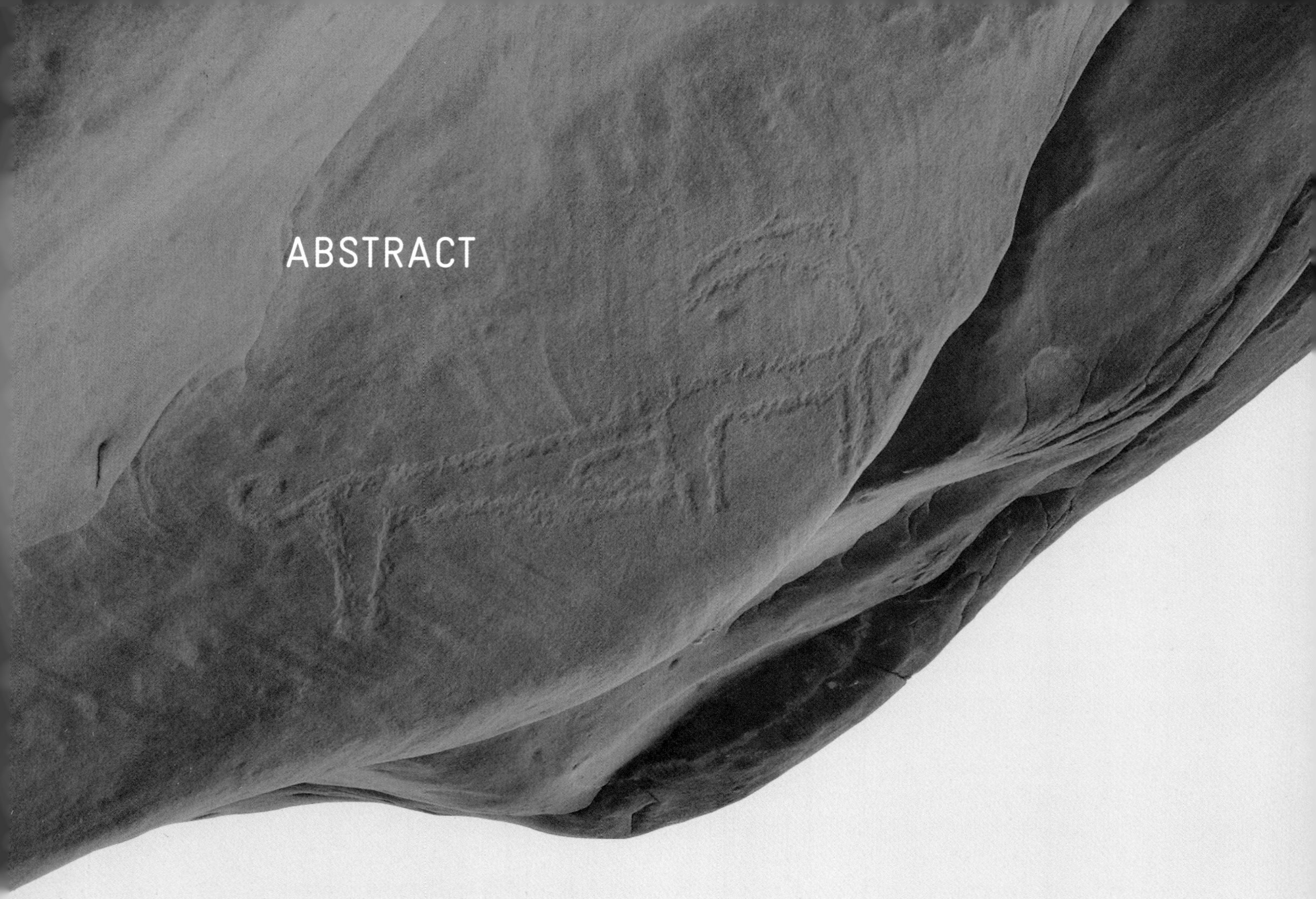

ABSTRACT

The rock art of prehistoric Kalimantan that is concentrated in the Marang mountains contains at least 25 caves with paintings from 10,000 years ago. These images were drawn by advance hunter-gatherers. This rock art has a large number of handprint motifs, and many of the Kalimantan handprints are decorated with dots, dashes and other patterns. The most interesting of these are hands linking with each other through curving lines or the row design. These images may depict the ties that bound individuals, families, territories or spirits to one another. The other images are of big mammals and gecko. Big mammals are deer (with antler), deer (without antler), bull, tapir, and (perhaps) dogs. The gecko appears to be an important image for prehistoric Kalimantan hunter-gatherer not because of the special way in which it is drawn but because of the large number of these drawings. The methodology for classifying Kalimantan rock art is a visual-language study: how to separate images by the way in which they have been drawn and spread on the walls and are connected with the (cultural) environment. The idea is to assume that rock art images have communication functions, and so each image should contain some information that should be collectively understood by a group.

INTRODUCTION

The world owes gratitude to the perseverance of Fage and Chazine who discoved the first red rock art site in Sangkulirang, East Kalimantan in 1994. After they found one site at 1994, they asked me to join their expedition in 1995 to help find other rock art sites. Year after year, we found at least 37 sites in the area, and in 2002, the author proposed to the National Research Centre of Archaeology to join the expedition. After 2002, the expedition became an official agenda of Indonesian archaeology (excavation and artefact analysis) with French collaboration. In 2008, the author started protecting the area with help from the local government and central authorities; and as a result this area will become a national heritage soon. Then at the beginning of 2011, the author went to survey new painted caves. In 2012, the author discovered two new sites, one in Kulat mountain and the other in Gergaji mountain. Hopefully, there are many more beautiful rock art sites which will be discovered in the future (Fig. 5.1).

THE ROCK ART SITE

Dating calculation (^{230}T/^{234}U disquilibrium technique) of this rock art is related to the dating of drapery formation, which 'grows' on the handprint images. The dating refers to 9,800–10,400 years (see Fage and Chazine 2001) and logically the handprint images under the drapery deposits are older. Another calculation used to chronicle C-14 art cave (Tengkorak cave) refers from 11750±50 to 5160±90 years ago. Thus, this prehistoric rock art of Borneo was created during a transition period from the end of Pleistocene to the beginning of Holocene, and the sea level slowly rose up to its present level. At the time of the creation of these images, Borneo Island was still a part of the east coast of Sundaland, and was dominated by savanna forests

Fig. 5.1 The geographical locations of the rock art sites.

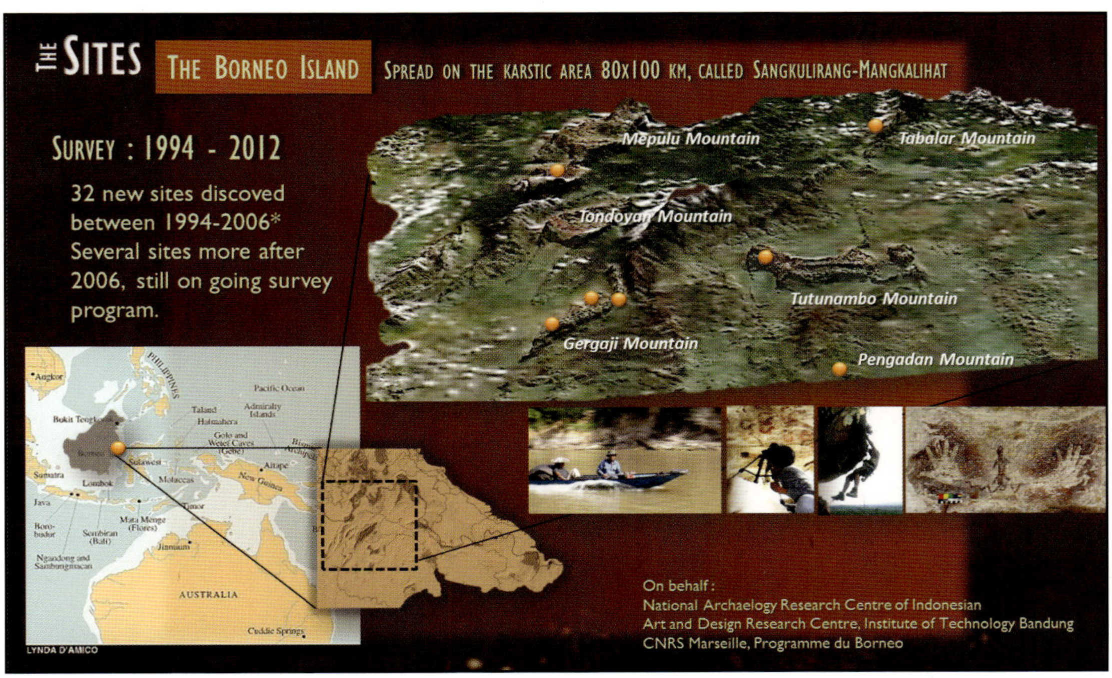

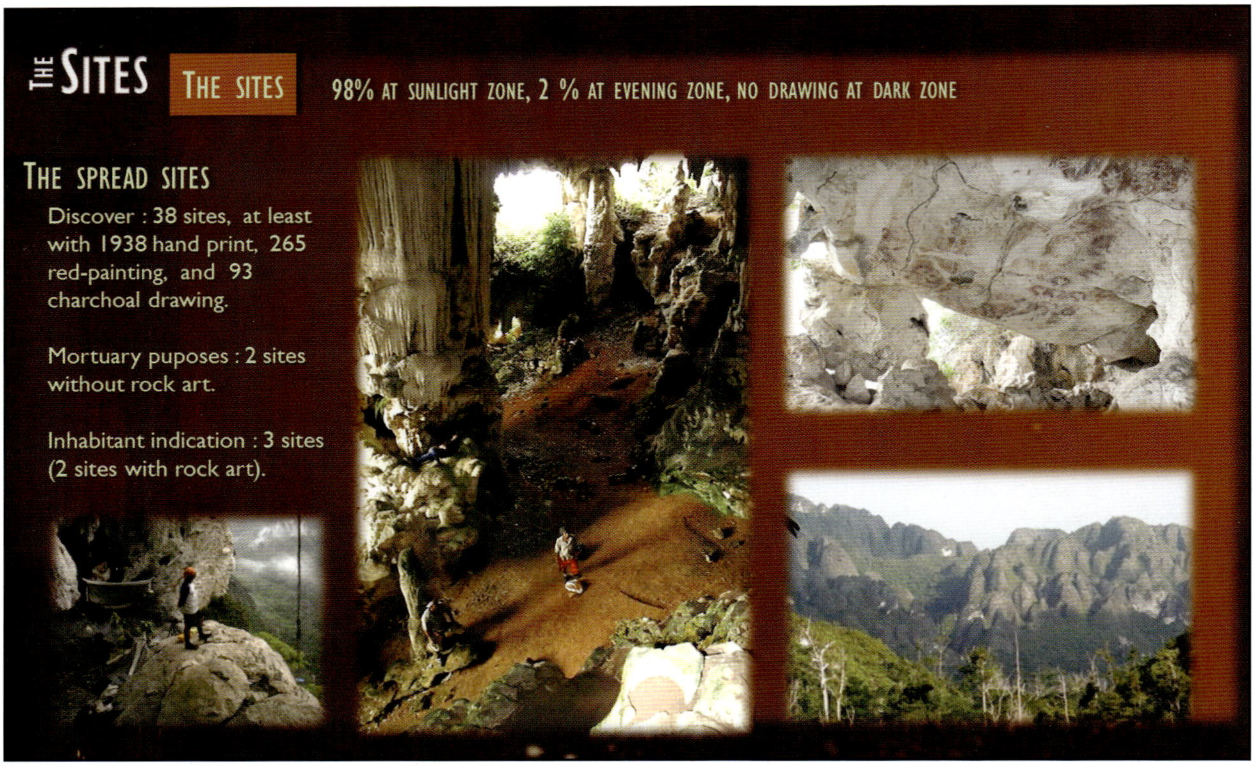

Fig. 5.2 The rock art sites.

and not tropical forests. These rock art sites are spread in the Karst region of Mangkalihat-Sangkulirang, but mostly appear on the west side in the region called Gergaji-Tutunambo-Kulat (GTK) Karst mountain. This sub-region is 73% in east Kutai district with 35 rock art sites, and 17% in Berau district with (at least) four rock art sites (Fig. 5.2).

Even in the western region (GTK) of Karst system, there are thousands of caves, but interestingly only those sites which face west or east have drawings. Rock art sites found on the flat floor covered by dry sand have nice panoramic views and the drawing panels have relatively flat and bright surfaces. These rock art galleries are either in the main chamber, tunnel or recess niches; and the drawing panels are located either on the vertical wall, ceiling or on pillars.

METHODOLOGY: VISUAL STUDY

Being a visual communication researcher, the author specialised in the visual communication system of non-literate people. Non-literate people need visual literacy to communicate their ideas, their fears or their knowledge. In this case, the author learned the communication system as a visual-literate.

In the world of visual-literates, everyone sharpens his sensitivity through the elements of forming a line, shape, colour, texture, dimension, light, and—on some installation works—also contain elements of motion and sound. The elements of communication 'forming' are interconnected into an expression of taste as unity, harmony,

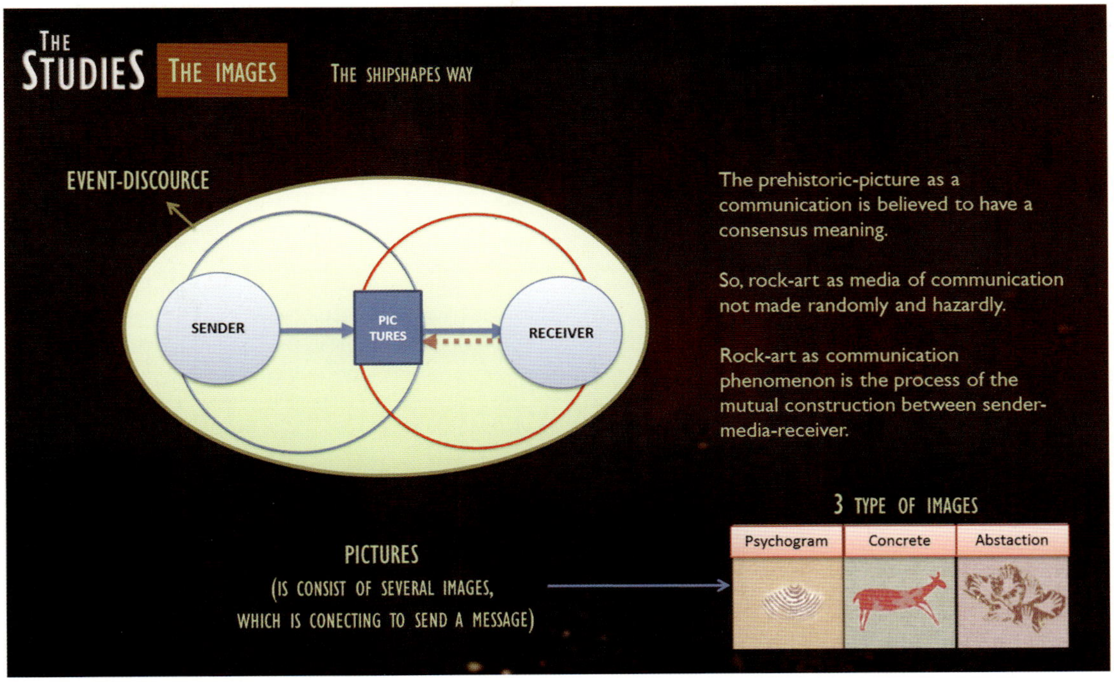

Fig. 5.3 The visual communication studies. The images are representative of the event discourse.

balance, repetition, proportion and accent-emphasis (see Dharsono 2003; The Liang Gie 1976; Tabrani 1991; Wheeler 1991). The elements and taste in the world of fine arts are created to convey a message as told to others. Therefore, in the world of visual communication, besides skills for creating an aesthetic message, skills are also required to convey that message effectively.

The visual message contains some information, the collective of which is one of the realisation of a group custom consensus (see Borosky 1994 and Strauss and Quinn 1997; also refer to Geertz's opinion and see Rohidi 2000) and the other is variations in an individual's thought interpretations (see Casson 1981 and Strauss and Quinn 1997; also refer to Goodenough's and Schneider's opinion and see Setiawan 2003). The message discloses its group distinction feature by itself or is an expression of self-identity. The messages on prehistoric rock art are believed to have a social function, so they have the characteristics of disclosing a group's distinctive features. It means that the message should be 'written' on the drawing and known implicitly by the community. The consequence is that the messages on rock art are a reflection of the collective information of the supporting community's knowledge. If rock art is self-expression and not for the community, the artist as a member of the community uses existing patterns so that his art is understood (see Magetsari 2001). That is why many experts are convinced that prehistoric rock art reflects a cognitive system of the community's life in that period (Fig. 5.3).

The main obstacle in understanding the message of historic art is that the supporting community is extinct and the traditions have been discontinued. In such a scenario, we need to study the archeological aspects of arts, the chronology of culture, reconstruction of the way of living, human activities and the features of environment in the past. In addition, studying the material used to draw, dating the pattern resemblance in informal or formal ways and forming an analogy of the resemblance of the pattern are also needed (see Chippindale 2000: 6-8 and Magetsari 2001).

However, rock art as a kind of visual message is worth studying from the visual-arts point of view. This reflects that rock art was not made randomly and haphazardly. According to the composition, the artist observed its design (the balance of the pictures and the media) attentively. Rock art can be studied through picture arrangement patterns, which show that the pictures were made with a careful (sacred) consideration to give them a certain meaning.

Rock art is better seen as a representation than as a writing discourse (Kechagia[1] 1995 in Ouzman 2000). According to Derida (1982), there is no relation between pictures made in prehistoric times and signs as we understand them at present. When the community of the rock art maker (artist) did not have writing tradition (had been non-literate), they communicated verbally and visually. Their equivalent in the present community is the verbal community (non-literate people), which have a tight relation between their verbal and non-verbal codes in communicating; this is often related to their supernatural mentality.

Rock art should be understood as a communication process, which means that the images consist of a visual code, a verbal code and a non-verbal code that inter-relate with each other. The problem that arises on the stage of visual communication is how to separate representations into sensory or mental ones. Therefore, there is a mechanism to differentiate between the visualisation and cognitive stages in visual communication.

VISUAL CLASSIFICATION

Rock art as a phenomenon of communcation is the process of the mutual construction between the sender-receiver-media (Fiske 1990; Sonesson 2006). So, rock art is an indirect medium of transferring information and because prehistoric society had not yet learned how to write, they used visual, auditory and maybe also aroma-taste-tactile healing. Unfortunately, only the visual phenomenon is left. But the visual phenomenon of rock art consists not only of rock art depiction but also site-imagery as a cultural (visual) landscape.

Cultural Landscape or Ecological Setting

Sites-imagery is collectively found as a complex in this area; it could be some cultural landscape of the past. The landscape is the Gergaji-Tutunambo-Kulat Karst tower mountain, which is 300–700 m above the river. Besides the landscape and geo-coordinates, the other site-imagery is spatial (cave, chamber, gallery, rooms and tunnels). The spatial aspect is carefully selected for the imagery. Even the shape of the cave is a natural formation. The prehistoric people brought a certain feeling that reshaped the spatial perception. They paid attention to perception effects of a specific condition (dark-bright, high-low, cool-warm). Also, prehistoric people were careful about the place for paintings;

clearly this was not determined randomly. The placing depended on the themes of the events that they needed to depict. After analysing 38 rock art sites in these three mountains, the orientation of site-imagery can be reflected as:

a. Level 1: The area closest to the river or under the forest canopy (understorey level). At this level, there are drawings of plain handprints, handprints with the entoptic motives, and handprints with special treatment of fingers. No gecko, mammals or anthropomorphic images are found at this level. Shelter and burial sites are also found at this level. All the images are on a vertical wall.
b. Level 2: The region at the centre of the cliff of tower Karst (above the forest canopy). Rock art sites are most commonly found at this level (74%). Here, there are depictions of hunting scenes, handprints, handprints with entroptic motives, handprints with zoomorphic images, and handprints with anthropomorphic images. Anthropomorphic images are depicted as the great shaman figure with a head-dress (59% of the appearances) and the great fauna (gecko, horned deer and magical beast) (66%). At this level, there are no burial or settlement sites. This level, which is approximately 50-100 m above from the valley is difficult to reach; 69% of the images here are on vertical walls and 31% are on the ceiling. The main theme is shamanic, except for special sites in Tutunambo mountain which contain images of hunting (Liang Sara cave) and images of gatherings (Payau cave). But, perhaps Liang Sara and Payau caves are integrated sites of the shamanic process.
c. Level 3: At this level, only six of the 38 sites have been found. Two sites appear to be an important venue for the prehistoric community of Kalimantan. Both are at the top of the ridge, have a spacious chamber and are tall; they have an abundant

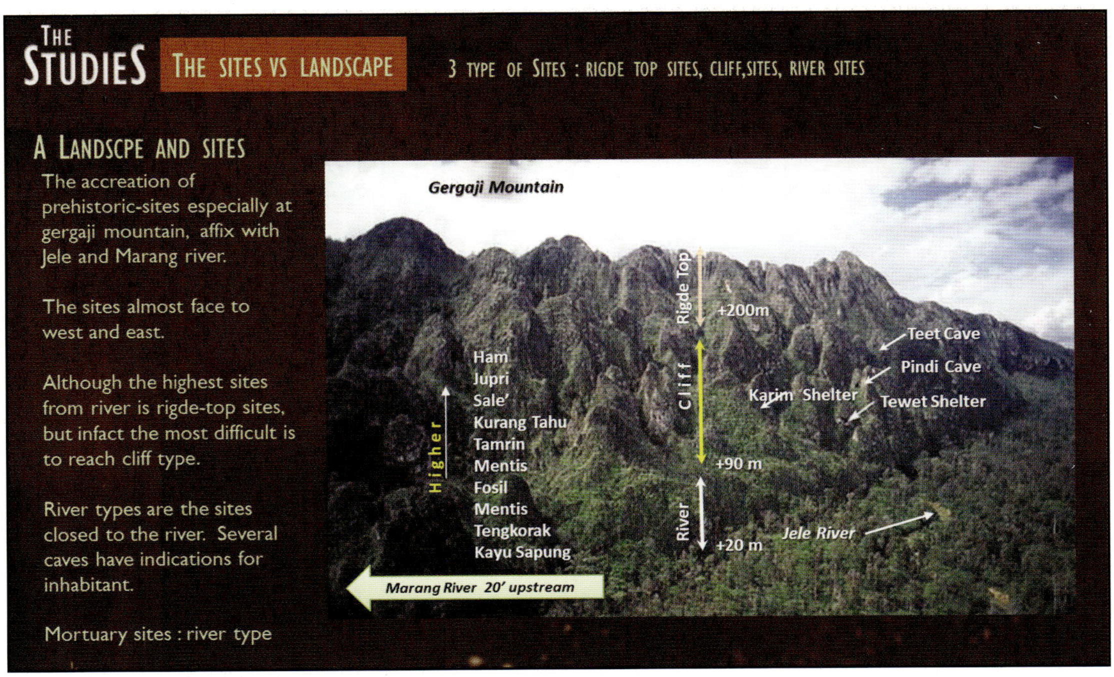

Fig. 5.4 The visual communication studies, the sites and their landscape anchor.

water source (from a dripping stone). Both these sites contributed 45% of all the images of prehistoric Kalimantan in this area. There are at least 492 images in Ham cave with 82% of them displayed on the wall and 18% on the ceiling. There are 253 images in Saleh cave with 40% of them on the wall and 60% on the ceiling. Rock art images are dominated by handprints, handprints with entroptic motives, handprints with zoomorphic images, and handprints with anthropomorphic images. The third level is approximately 200–450 m above the river front, but it is more easy to access than the 2nd level. There are no settlement or burial sites at this level.

Themes of Rock Art Depictions

Besides site-imagery as a cultural landscape, there is also rock art depiction. Roct art is depicted at two levels: image level and pictures level. According to Tabrani (2000), in visual communication, there are three types of images—pre-image, concrete image (replica of what the human eye sees) and delusion image (replica of what the human mind thinks, but still forms a 'thing'). Concrete image is revisualisation of something resembling the real thing, while delusion image is another visualisation that is linked to a certain mind. Pre-image is an entoptic stage of an image that is still floating in someone's conscious mind, and has not yet been separated into either a concrete image or a delusion image.

Concrete images are shown through zoomorphic, anthropomorphic, tools, leaf, and insects, which delusion images are shown as handprints, symbols of gods/goddesses, symbols of ancestors, symbols of fertility; a pre-image is entoptic like a single line, curve line, parallel line, geometric, chevron, divergence

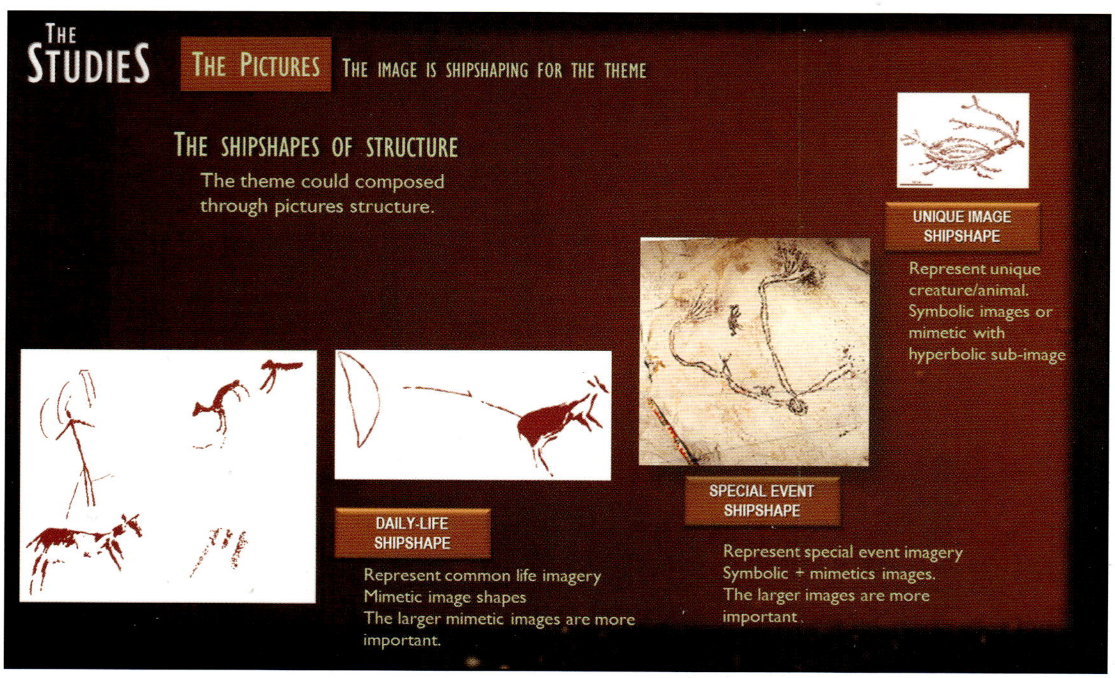

Fig. 5.5 The way of drawing ship shapes the message.

line and convergence line. In visual tabulation, of the 1,583 images found here[2], delusion-images of handprints were 76.8%. Concrete images were 8.9%, which were dominated by gecko, large mammals (deer, bull, pigs, tapirs) and anthropomorphs. Pre-images were very rare—only 4%—in all the observed images.

The images on top were painted with gradations of light red-brown to dark purple. There is no explanation about the meaning of using different gradations of red colour. It is to show an older image, or the image may have corroded, or a different process was used in making dye solutions of ochre. But, at least on the reused panel, frequently light red colour is seen under dark red-purple dye.

From visual communication perspective, the main function of a picture is, as a medium for sending a message, to transfer information. Consequently, a picture consists of a number of inter-related images, which aim to transfer a message. In fact, there are two types of pictures: single picture and series pictures. However, in prehistoric paintings (discovered until now), the depictions are mainly of single images. The depictions of stories through a series of images are not found in prehistoric paintings. For example, series pictures are relief, mural or wayang beber (scrolling puppets).

Kalimantan rock art features some concrete images and a few pre-images. In one rock art site, there is a painting of a hunting deer with bow and dart. All these are charateristics of advanced hunter-gatherer cultures (see Anati 1994). The pictures (and their inter-related images) are placed on the ceiling and walls, or on specific sites in order to bring out the four quadrants of events—ritual event, great shaman event, socio-economic event and great-fauna event. These four could collaborate with each other, for example a socio-ritual event (superimposed handprint panels); great shamanic and economic event (shaman with hunter scene panels); ritual-shamanic event (ritual event with the appearance of the great shaman); socio and great fauna (handprint with the appearance of the great fauna). Those 'tale-pictures' show that the real life of hunter-gatherers was not separate from their supernatural spirit.

The pictorial panels have two characteristics—panels drawn only once and panels that look painted many times. Panels which are drawn only once, feature zoomorphic and great shaman. Panels that are drawn many times were either continuously reused from event to event or from generation to generation. It can be concluded that the first panel demonstrates that a picture (a bulk of images) was more important than the drawing process, or that pictures and the process had the same importance. But, the second panels show that the drawing process was more important than the picture itself. On the second type, the images that are pale (orange-pink) are superimposed by images that are darker (red-purple).

'PREHISTORIC' VISUAL COMMUNICATION

Information on prehistoric pictures consists of four event quadrants. The paintings have a role as a preserver of past events, which are mutually understood by the artist, the paintings and his audience. The mutual understanding therefore needs to put the event, the artist, the picture and the audience in the same circumstance.

The same circumstance requires an 'anchoring' mechanism of overinformation as follows:

a. A mutual understanding of events, the events consist of four quadrants, each event can be joined together.
b. The existence of a guide as a messenger to advise or counsel audience through pictures, honouring together the drawing process (if it does not exist), both from the physical (real event) and mental (fictional event) perspective.
c. The appearence of a visual phenomenon, which is mutually understood, consists of site imagery and elements of rock art depiction. The visual phenomenon reflects the status of the symbolic, its ritual and practical utility and the mutual expression of visual aesthetics.
d. The occurrence of auditory senses that anchor a senses-hearing stimulate like the echo effect, the sequence of the narrative, the rhythm song and percussion, the mumble prayer, yell, outcry and even the sound of the wind. The occurence of smell gives an anchor to the aromatic sense as frankincense and incence. The dry and clean caves also give out a particular aroma. Also, maybe the occurence of tactile gives a certain anchor that stimulates a feeling of light-dark effect, warm-cool effect, flat effect, the effect of altitude and a panoramic effect. Of course, in addition to sensory effects, there should also be an effect of body movements, such as dancing, state of trance and meditating.

Fig. 5.6 The rock art paintings and way of observation.

Prehistoric paintings work as a communication process, which reflects mutual understanding between the narrative guide (artist,

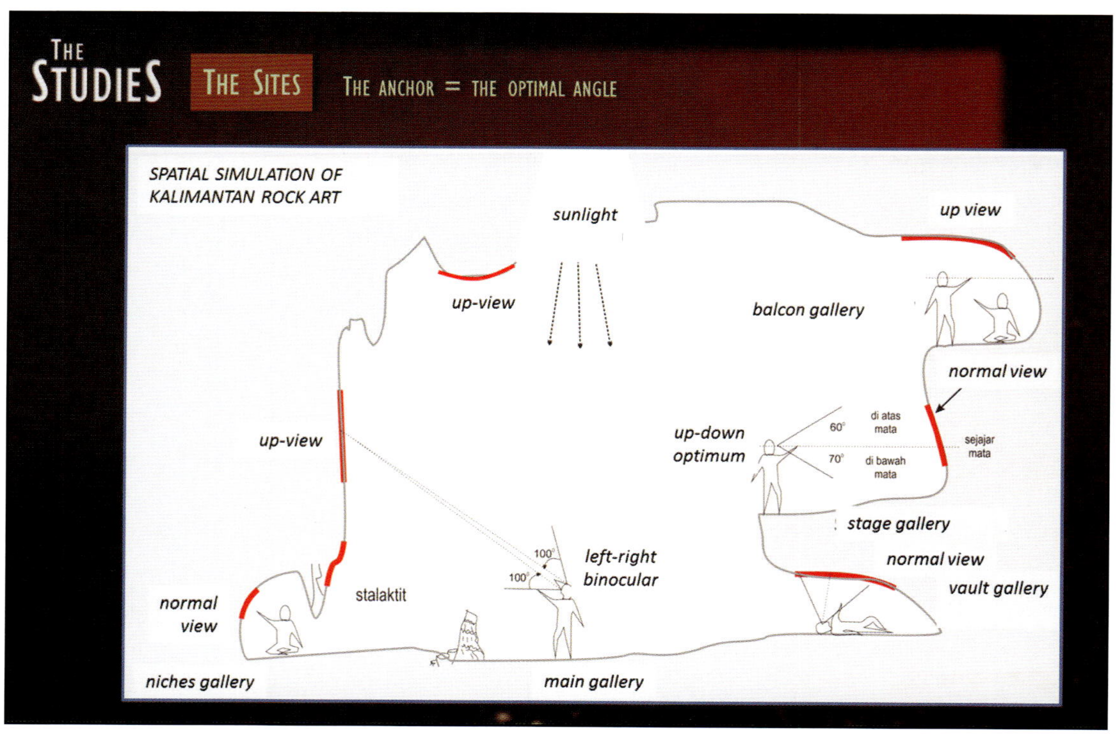

shaman) and his audience. Shared understanding is believed to occur because of a process of reciprocity; it is not single-way communication. Events in the painting are based on a communication process, but still need aesthetic 'engineering' to be understood.

On the part of the audience, the insights are not necessarily the same. The first understanding can occur by understanding the events experienced along with the drawing, or listening (fairy tales) to events as experienced by the person narrating them. Understanding both can be revealed by an understanding of the structure of the image. In this way the image is understood from its characteristics. Understanding of a metaphor can also be independent regardless of the drawing and image structure.

However, prehistoric visual communication requires an understanding of several anchors to 'seal' the gap of understanding. Distance understanding can occur due to differences in interests, differences in understanding the situation or differences in the way of looking at a particular event. Distance can occur between the narrative guide and his audience, as well as among the members of the audience (Fig. 5.6).

DISCUSSION

So the key is how the sender-receiver, through the media (rock art), could have a mutual understanding of the work. The process of communication in prehistoric paintings are interconnected to the quadrant of events. An event has a role to play, as fulfilling the need of what prehistotic people hoped, feared and knew. Those events then were 'woven' into pictures to make them mutually understood. Thus, the pictures not only served as a medium of communication, but also served other needs. Consequently, rock art

Fig. 5.7 3D site mapping, more digital and more convenient, to stimulate the visual anchor, the landscape perception.

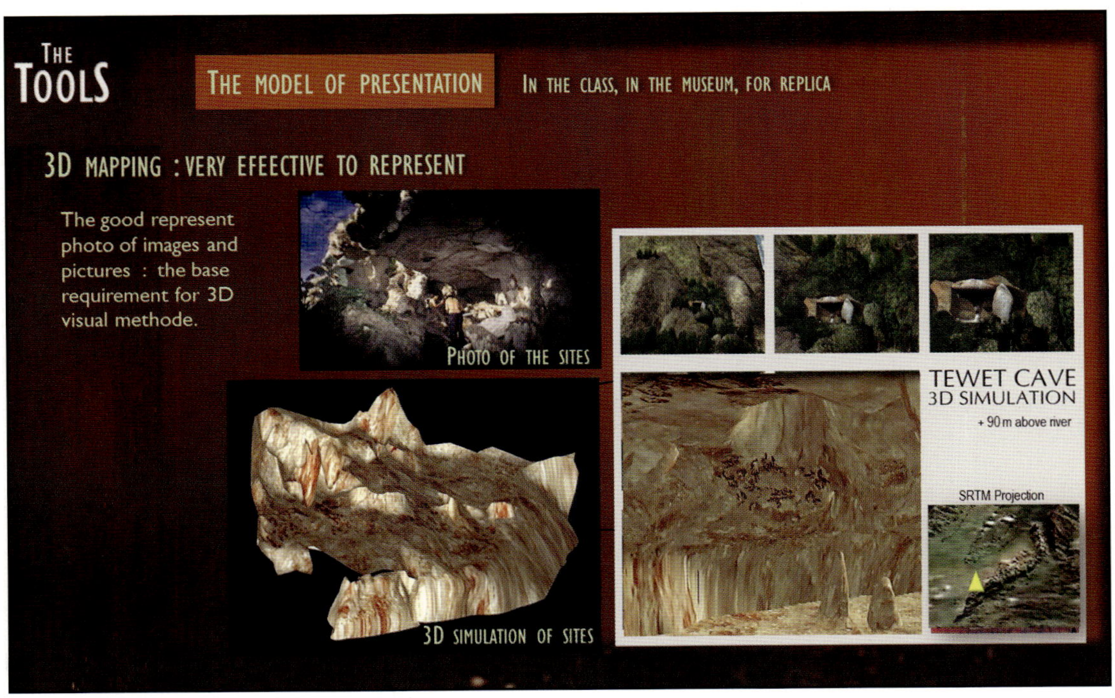

reseachers need to understand the event behind the pictures. This is a challenge, but we could take the help of ethno-archaeology or ethnographic methods.

The methodology of visual study is a multi-disiplinary approach to understanding rock art culture. This method not only enriches archaeological, psyco-analytical and ethnographic methods, but also tries to open wider the screen into the past, especially into rock art (non-literate) culture (Fig. 5.7).

NOTES

1. Kechagia is a 'visual phenomena' semiotic researcher. His writing on rock art research is titled 'The row and the circle: semiotic perspective of visual thinking' (1995). Tabrani is a fine arts researcher who invented and developed the science of non-western visual language.

REFERENCES

Anati, E. (1977), *Methods of Recording and Analysing Rock Engravings*. Camunian Studies, Volume 7, Edizioni Del Centro, Italy.

—— (1994), *World Rock Art: The Primordial Langage*. Studi Camuni-volume XII-3rd English Edition, 1994, Edizioni Del Centro, Italy.

Bednarik, R.G. (2002), Crisis in Palaeolithic Art Studies. AURA NET Australian Rock Art Research Association: Palaeoart epistemology, available at: http://mc2.vicnet.net.au/home/epistem/web/crisis.html (accessed on 15 May 2006).

—— (1998), The Lower and Middle Palaeolithic Origins of Semiotics, available at: http://me2.vicnet.net.au/home/epistem/web/lower.html (accessed on 4 October 2006).

Bellwood, Peter (2000), *Prasejarah Kepulauan Indo-Malaysia*. Jakarta: PT Gramedia Pustaka Utama.

Chaloupka, G. (1993), 'Journey in Time: The Longest Continuing Art Tradition, Reed, Australia', in Christopher Chippindale and P.S.C. Taçon (eds.), *The Archeology of Rock-Art*. Cambridge University Press.

Clottes, Jean (2003), *Le musée des roches: L'art rupestre dans le monde*. Paris: Seuil.

Clottes, Jean and David Lewis-William (1996), *Les Chamanes de la Préhistoire: Transe et magie dans les grottes ornées*. Paris: Seuil.

Dharsono (ed.) (2003), *Pengantar Estetika, Proyek Hibah Penulisan Buku*, P3M Dikti Diknas.

Djaldjoeni, N. (1984), *Geografi Kesejarahan II Indonesia*. Bandung: Penerbit Alumni.

Fiske, J. (1990), Cultural and Commucations Studies: Sebuah Pengantar Paling Konprehensif, Penerbit Jalasutra, Yogyakarta.

Henry, L. and J.M. Chazine (2001), L'art Pariétal de grotte de Kalimantan (Indonesié), Archéologie.

—— (2002), Rock Art of Kalimantan: 2002 Discoveries, Le Kalimanthrope.

Holt, Claire (1967), *Art in Indonesia, Continues and Change*. Ithaca: New York Cornel University Press.

Kasnowihardjo, H. Gunadi (2001), *Manajemen Sumber Daya Arkeologi*. Lembaga Penerbitan Universitas Hasanudin.

Lewis-William, D. and T. dan Dowson (1989), *Images of Power: Understanding Bushman Rock Art*. Johannesburg: Southern Book Publishers (Pvt.) Ltd.

—— (2002), *The Mind in the Cave*. London: Thames and Hudson.

Littlejohn, Stephen W. (1998), *Theories of Human Communication*.

Magetsari, N. (2001), Semiotik dalam Arkeologi, Meretas Ranah, Husen, Ida Sundari dan Hidayat, Rahayu (editor), Bentang, Yogyakarta, pp. 97-117.

Morwood, M.J. (2002), *Vision from the Past: The Archeology of Australian Rock Art*. NSW Australia: Allen & Unwin.

Ouzman, S. (2000), 'Towards A Mindscape of Landscape: Rock Art as Expression of World Understanding', Christopher Chippindale and P.S.C. Taçon (eds.), *The Archeology of Rock-Art*. Cambridge: University Press.

Patterson, C. (2007), 'Scientific Interpretation of Rock Art', in Chenna Reddy (ed.), *Exploring the Mind of Ancient Man (Festschrift to Robert G. Bednarik)*. New Delhi: Research India Press.

Sachari, Agus (2002), Estetika, Penerbit ITB, Bandung.

Setiawan, Pindi (1994), Gambar Cadas Dunwahan, Tinjauan awal isi-wimba berdasarkan posisi sebenarnya di cadas (undergraduate thesis), Fakultas Seni Rupa Institute of Technology Bandung, Bandung.

—— (1994), Metoda pendataan gambar cadas Indonesia. Paper for Pusat Penelitian Arkeologi Nasional, Jakarta.

—— (1998), *Pesan dari jaman yang hilang*. ITB, Bandung: Visual Language Research Group.

—— (1999), 'Gua-gua Prasejarah di Indonesia dan kendala pelestariannya', Workshop paper for Kawasan Kars, Jakarta, 29–30 September. Direktorat Jenderal Geologi dan Sumber Daya Mineral.

—— (2004), 'Kawasan kars Sangkulirang: Antropologi dan Arkeologi'. Research report on the Nature Conservancy, Samarinda.

—— (2010), Gambar Cadas Kutai Prasejarah: Kajian Pemenuhan Kebutuhan Terpadu dan Komunikasi Rupa (disertation), Sekolah Pascasarjana, Institute of Technology Bandung, Bandung.

Soedjono, R.P. (1981), Aspek-Aspek Arkeologi Indonesia: Tinjauan tentang pengkerangkaan prasejarah Indonesia, Proyek Penelitian Purbakala, Jakarta.

Sopandi, Ahmad Hasan (2004), *Lukisan gua di Malaysia*. Malaysia: Balai Seni Lukis Negara.

Tabrani, P. (1998), *Messages from Ancient Walls*. Bandung: Penerbit ITB.

—— (2005), *Bahasa Rupa*. Bandung: Penerbit ITB.

The Liang Gie (1977), *Filsafat Keindahan*. Yogyakarta: Pusat Belajar Ilmu Berguna.

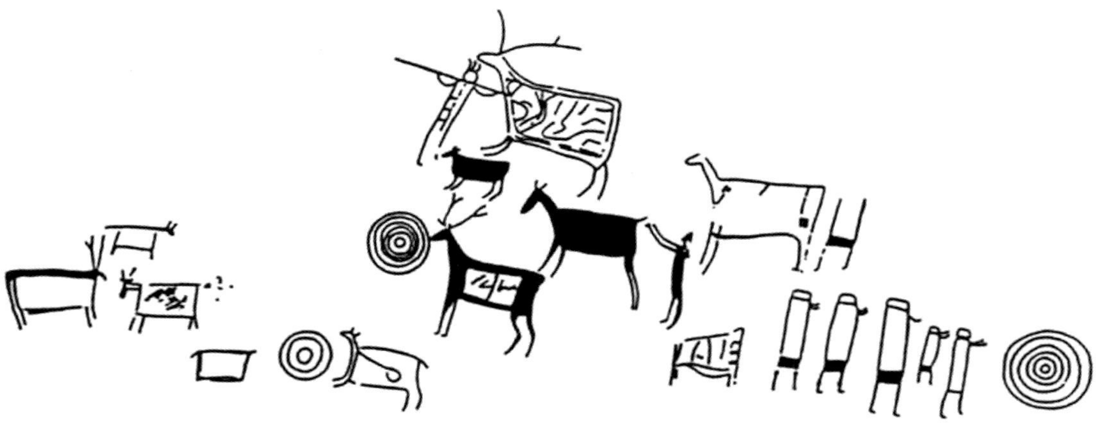

6

Constructed Landscape in Rock Art: Selection of Visual Space, Arrangement Pattern and Its Symbolic Significance

Somnath Chakraverty and Ruman Banerjee

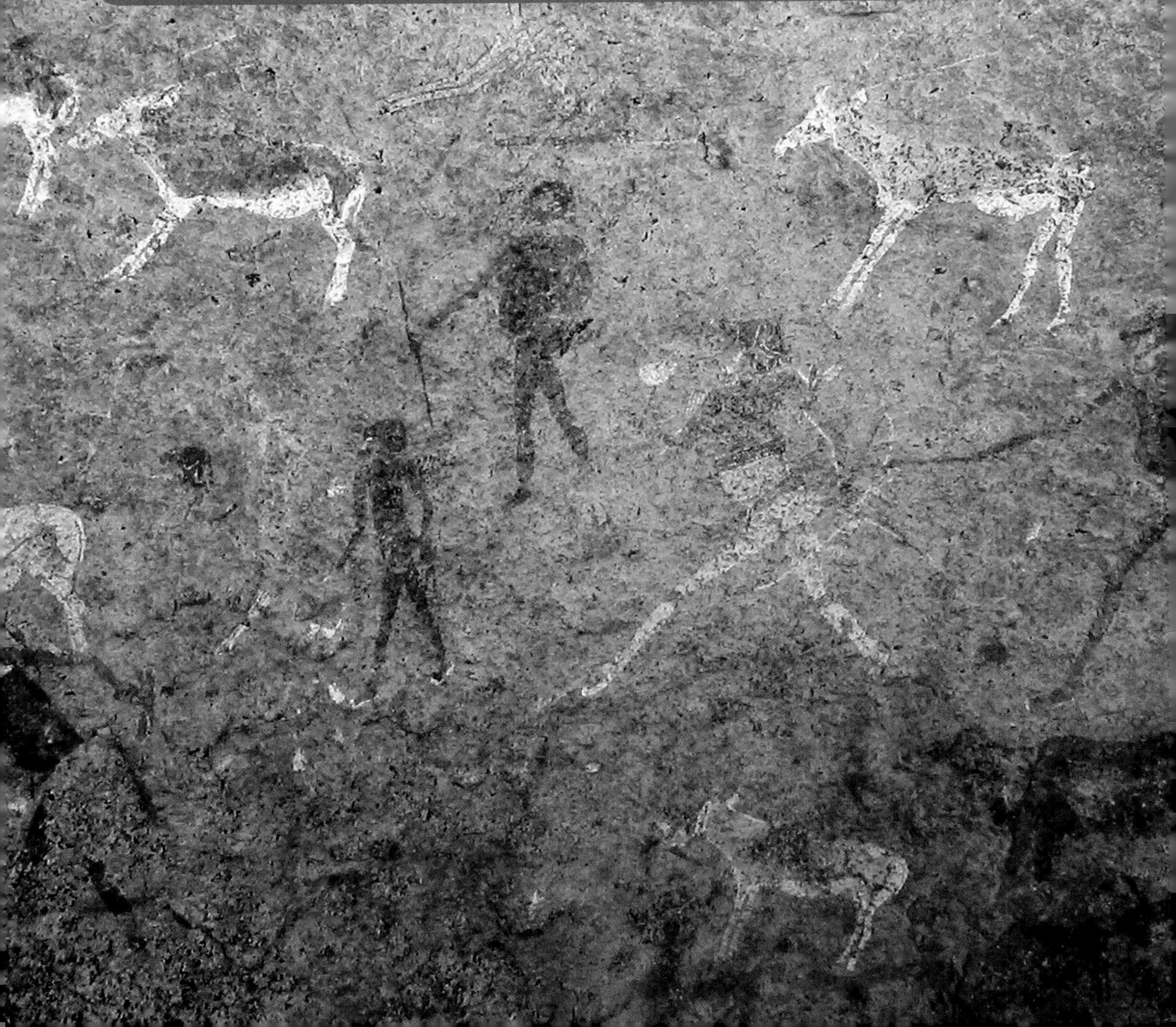

ABSTRACT

Central Indian rock art is viewed as an arrangement of icons which in its placement reflects its narrative significance and an attitude of its creators. Such designs had evolved on a synthetic landscape as an anti-landscape within the given natural setting to demarcate human activities. It reveals choices in terms of decision making and the selection of rocky canvas for the creation of art work. High elevations with steep slopes were not cost-effective for hunter-gatherers in terms of energy spent and foraging time and less attractive in terms of the availability of game and collectable food when compared to flat landscapes. Practically and cost-effectively, most of the painted rock shelters and caves should have been located at lower elevations; although data analysis from field work and GPS recordings suggest some contradictions in this paradigm. Somnath Chakraverty and Ruman Banerjee's paper attempts to delineate the selection criterion, if any, for the space for display of art work, both of rock shelters and the location of the rock canvas in an isolated eco-geographical niche to define a boundary between utilitarian and symbolic space within the given cultural and natural setting.

INTRODUCTION

Visual art in any form has some linkage with the setting for its display. Rock shelters and caves that contain manifestations of art are modifications of a natural habitat by either conscious or unconscious efforts. The unaltered landscape representing distinctive topography and geo-morphology of the region was repeatedly interrupted with periodic human interventions. Each period was marked by the presence of several groups and their activities and interactions with their surroundings, either permanently or temporarily altered the environment. Ultimately the contemporary galleries that are documented by rock art researchers are the cultural remains in successive periodic layers of such a manifold interaction.

Central Indian rock art is viewed as an arrangement of icons and their placement reflects its narrative significance and some attitude of its creators. Such designs evolved a synthetic landscape as an anti-landscape within the given natural setting to demarcate human activity. They reveal choice in terms of decision-making and selection of a rocky canvas for the creation of art work. This landscape was gradually created in successive periods by people ranging from foragers and hunters to pastorals and farmers. A general trend is estimated from the selection of the space for placing the motifs as a meaningful visual document where the spatial utilisation signifies appropriate societal functions.

High elevations with steep slopes were more costly for hunter-gatherers in terms of the energy that they had to spend and also the foraging time needed; they were also less attractive in terms of the availability of game and collectable food items when compared to flat landscapes. Practically and cost-effectively most of the painted rock shelters and caves should have been located at lower elevations; although data analysis from rigorous field-work and GPS recordings suggests some contradictions.

In this study an attempt is made to delineate the selection criteria, if any, for the spaces used for displaying and performing art work, both for the rock shelters and the location of the rock canvas in an isolated eco-geographical niche to define a boundary between utilitarian and symbolic space within the given cultural and natural setting.

The purpose or significance of creating rock art is still a debatable area and possibly such cultural elements like other aspects of culture vary both regionally and periodically. Thus, it is unlikely that any functional uniformity in the entire process that maintained its traditions can be identified. For a more analytical approach, rock art can best be viewed as evidence of an ethnic art tradition during the past. Conceptually, as also in actual situations, rock art and the indigenous folk art tradition are both manifestations of pre-literate societies. The mindset at both the levels, their basic pattern of beliefs and worldview are identical as revealed in global anthropological records. This theoretical framework and model supports the concept of a cultural continuum (Redfield 1965). In this paradigm, dynamics of culture are not ignored and the art tradition in its transforming cultural milieu becomes vibrant in historically accumulated experiences. In folk societies certain orthodox elements also survive for generations without much change.

The idea about the significance of the pattern of arrangement of art and the placement of art motifs in a particular location for fulfilling a certain purpose can be observed from examples of folk and tribal art that is still prevalent in pre-literate and pre-industrial societies (Chakraverty 2009). In such pre-urban settings, art motifs are usually inseparable from their life opportunities. Such artistic manifestations are mostly viewed by outsiders as aesthetically significant but to the indigenous communities, each element is connected to social customs, norms, and a wide range of practices. Sometimes the art motifs are an integral part of rituals and other such celebrations.

In folk societies, the placement and arrangement pattern of motifs indicates their specific functional roles. The present investigation and study is influenced by ethnographic evidence from tribal and folk societies which indicate that in pre-literate societies, variations in locations, use of space, and the arrangement patterns of motifs revealed their functional specifications.

For example, in West Bengal during various *vrata* or ritual performances by rural women, white paste made from rice flour is used for drawing *alpana* on the floors, doorways, and courtyards. This represents various designs, signs, and symbols to welcome deities and popularly such paintings include marks of the deities' feet. For such ritual functions the paintings are limited only to the floor and to certain other locations such as the entrance to doorways, courtyards, and within the cowshed. Therefore, for a particular ritual and purpose, a particular area of the household is painted. Similarly, the pattern of *rangoli* is common in certain parts of central and western India. In *rangoli*, various types of seeds in different colours and colour pigments are arranged on the floor by village womenfolk during rituals and festivities.

Among the Lanjhia Saoras, a tribal community living in the forest and hills of Koraput and Ganjam districts in Odisha, the practice of painting walls within the huts exists. Each painting is considered a secret seat of a particular deity. The shamans, in trance, illustrate icons in praise of their deities. Painted icons are considered a source of supernatural power and a means for curing diseases and also for getting relief from other misfortunes that the people experience in their daily lives. In each household elaborately painted walls contain a series of figures which are kept hidden within the dark parts. The painted walls are purposefully covered by hanging sheets, pots containing water, clothes, and other household utensils. The Saoras believe that any person from outside the family may cause severe harm by supernatural means if he or she can glance at the painted icon and identify the propitiating deity which protects the family. This example shows that painted icons are protected in dark, secret, and inaccessible places to prevent them from getting noticed by outsiders.

Santals, a numerically dominant tribal community in the Chotanagpur Plateau region decorate their households with floral designs and other motifs during annual festivities in winter after the harvest season. In Santal households, the outside walls are adorned with paintings and clay bas relief designs. Such decorations represent their joy and satisfaction after a successful harvest. Therefore, such visual expressions symbolise possession of wealth and happiness. In the case of death or any other disaster in a family, the household walls remain empty. Therefore, presence or absence of murals symbolises occurrence of prosperity or hardship in the tribal household.

Throughout India, including in its peninsular parts, votive figurines, mostly of horses and elephants are commonly placed as offerings under sacred groves in villages. Each location has a specific association and meaning related to particular images.

Among Gonds, Maria Gonds, and Murias of Chhattisgarh and Madhya Pradesh, carvings on wooden poles are frequent in youth dormitories. Similar wood carvings are also common in Juang tribal dormitories in Keonjhar district in Odisha. Such evidence of art is not represented in individual households and is only visible in dormitories. Such art is a conscious effort to illustrate visual narratives of traditional myths. It is meant for educating generations of youth who assemble in tribal dormitories.

Rituals for erecting memorial stones and carvings on wooden posts commemorating dead ancestors are mostly represented by figures like a man on horseback, group dancers, and other such figures. Such practices are common among Korkus and Bhils—tribal groups living in Madhya Pradesh and Rajasthan. Carved memorial pillars are placed under sacred groves; each grove is shared by a particular clan group of tribal descent.

In this study some of the representative rock art sites covering almost all parts of India are systematically investigated to locate the norms, practices, and principles behind the selection of the space for demonstrating rock art motifs. The final analysis is an attempt to retrieve and delineate a common factor or trend in the usage pattern generally followed in the sites.

The selected rock art sites and regions containing clusters of rock shelters, caves, and other forms of evidences are:

1. Panchmarhi, Mahadeo hills in Satpura region, Madhya Pradesh. Coordinates: 22° 272 103 N & 78° 262 493 E. Altitude of 905 (2970 feet) m above sea level.
2. Adamgarh, near Hoshangabad town, Narmada Valley, Madhya Pradesh. Coordinates: 22.75°N 77.72°E. *It has an average elevation of 278 m (912 feet)* above sea level.
3. Bhimbetka, Raisen district. Selection of 12 rock shelters from more than 300 rock shelters available in the Betwa source region, Madhya Pradesh. Coordinates: 22.55-22.56N 77.36-77.37E and 600 m above sea level.
4. Shyamla hills, near Bhopal, Madhya Pradesh. Coordinates: 23.2500° N, 77.4200° E. Average elevation: 523 m above sea level.
5. Chaturbhuj Nath Nala near Bhanpura, Madhya Pradesh. Coordinates: 24.52°N 75.73°E. It has an average elevation of 384 m (1,259 feet) above sea level.
6. Selected region in Rewa district, Madhya Pradesh. Coordinates: 24.53°N 81.3°E. Average elevation of 304 m (997 feet) above sea level.
7. Rock shelters in Badami region, Karnataka.Coordinates: 15°552 123 N 75°402 493 E. Average elevation of 586 m (1,923 feet) above sea level.
8. Pansaimal, South Goa. Coordinates: 15.563°N 73.818°E.
9. Edakkal Cave, Sultan's Battery, Wynnad district, Kerala. Coordinates: 11°372 28.813 N 76°142 8.883 E. Average elevation of 1,200 m above sea level.
10. Kotagiri sites, Nilgiri hills, Tamil Nadu. Coordinates: 11.43°N 76.88°E. Average elevation of 1,793 m (5,883 feet) above sea level.

11. Sundargarh district, Odisha. Coordinates: 22.116°N 84.016°E 243. Average elevation of 243 m (801 feet) above sea level.
12. Kaimur range, Bihar. Coordinates: 24°352 N 82°042 E. Average elevation of 100 m above sea level.
13. Jharkhand. Coordinates: 22°222 N 86°172 E. Average elevation of 103 m (338 feet) above sea level.
14. Purulia district, West Bengal. Coordinates: 23°072 233 N 86°392 113 E. Average elevation of 228 m (748 feet) above sea level.
15. Mirzapur, Uttar Pradesh. Coordinates: 25°152 N 82°582 E. Average elevation of 80 m (265 feet) above sea level.

Topographically, Panchmarhi in Mahadeo hills is a distinct and almost isolated hill station located 2,900 feet above the sea level. The area is surrounded by the Satpura mountain ranges. Exotic flora and wild fauna are abundant in this region. In this forest, rock art sites are distributed in several zones and each zone comprises clusters of painted rock art sites. Among the 1,953 motifs from all the sites 97.08 per cent are painted panels whereas engravings and painting on engravings are relatively few (2.87 and 0.05 per cent respectively) (Chakraverty 1999, 2003).

In Panchmarhi, paintings and engravings are present in the same context, sometimes overlapped by one on another layer. Contextually, both types coexist. Twenty rock shelters were randomly selected for the location analysis. The studied 20 rock shelters are distributed over 11 clusters located in separate areas within the entire zone. It was also observed that the selected rock shelters for art activities were placed in moderately well-accessible areas. The criterion of accessibility is not only on the basis of contemporary perceptions. Art activities existed during the past and the regional geomorphology and the concentration of forests in the earlier period has possibly undergone periodic changes.

In some of the painted rock shelters, the minimum space for a foot track approaching the shelter had collapsed and now the site is almost hanging over the canyon. Within the 20 rock shelters, 16 are located on relative plains at higher elevations. The minimum distance between the painted rock shelters is seen in Maradeo area in the north and in Bainganga river valley where the average distance is between 100 to 250 m. In a cluster of all such painted shelters, the periodic succession of rock art is uniform. Other associated archaeological material (Hunter 1936) in the form of microliths with gray ware found in all such shelters reveals the habitation in that area which was either seasonal or semi-permanent in nature.

Within the 20 different rock shelters, four are located on hill tops and are facing gorges and canyons whereas the remaining are within undulating plains close to seasonal and perennial hill streams. Other than the four small shelters, one on the bank of Bainganga river, a second one in the Maradeo region, and another two located in Nimbu Khud and Hanuman Mandir area, all the other painted rock shelters are medium to large in dimension, that is, they are moderately spacious.

In Narmada Valley in central India, rock art sites are mostly concentrated in the Vindhyas and in the Satpura region. Even within the same region, distribution of rock art sites along the Betwa source region is a unique backdrop for understanding the possible purpose of such activities. A chain of rock art sites extends from the Sagar region in the north-east of Bhopal to Shyamla hills near Bhopal Lake. Then the chain of sites extends in two parallel routes one of which goes further east and another moves towards south to Hoshangabad town and its nearby Adamgarh cliff located on the southern bank of river Narmada.

In the whole region the composition of rock art sites and their locations are similar. Sites were studied in Shyamla hills near Bhopal Lake at the northern extreme and at Kathotia Karad in the eastern part, Bineka and Bhimbetka in the middle part of the cluster and in Adamgarh at its southernmost limit.

In all these sites, some common features were identified which seem to be the basic selection criteria for rock art activities. In this entire area early human habitation continued at least from the final Pleistocene phase to later phases including successive cultural periods during Holocene. Archaeological studies (Hunter1936; Mathpal 1984; Wakankar and Brooks 1976; etc.) have confirmed the use of painted rock shelters and caves for habitation during Palaeolithic, Mesolithic, Chalcolithic and early Historic periods. An analysis of data on the location of art in rock shelters and caves reveal some basic and common features.

Mostly rock shelters with evidence of rock art are arranged in rows or in clusters. A majority of the rock shelters are relatively more spacious than other similar shelters which are abundant in the area. Such shelters without rock art are either located in relatively more inaccessible parts which are also less spacious. Such natural shelters without any trace of art either contain stiff walls with least curvatures; there is also the absence of any inclined walls on any side. Some basic requirements such as the presence of suitable covering or roof for protection from rain and wind and minimum space for household activities were essential considerations for selection of early habitation.

Size or dimensions of the images are proportionate to the length of the space available for their viewing. The greater the free space available for clear vision of the rock canvas from its anticipated distance by targeted viewers, bigger are the dimensions of the figure. A rational analysis of such behaviour reflected in this art leads to the conclusion that behind consciously or unconsciously, a norm was followed in rock art. Painters had targeted audiences or viewers in their mind; they also had a pre-fixed vision of the zone where it was possible to view the art.

It is important to mention here that in the entire region, particularly in the visual narration of episodes represented in a realistic form of art, rock art is mostly placed in the open visible parts of rock surfaces rather than within crevices or in less exposed darker zones inside the shelter. Again, within a stretch of a spacious wall, it is the central part or a most suitable canvas that was selected for display where no traces of a rough or uneven surface exist. Such avoidance is almost inherent in the rock art of the region. A rational observation on such a principle followed in rock art indicates that such galleries of rock art were meant for display and for possible free communication of ideas, experiences, and aspirations in a pre-literate community.

The trend of preserving art by its creators as well as their choice of a particular space for art activity reveals their intended usage pattern. They were possibly conscious about passing some information through a codified art form, which may even be transmitted to future generations. Such a view is also substantiated and supported by another set of data on a thematic analysis of rock art imagery (Chakraverty 1999; Mathpal 1984).

An average number of figures were placed at eye level. Although figures and compositions were also located at much higher levels—even on the ceilings. But incidence of placing figures on the top was encouraged when the huge empty wall of the rock shelter exceeded the average limit of 8-10 feet and the vertical space was more than 18 feet in height. Even in such locations, the distance and vacant space available in the open ground opposite the rock art gallery was an important consideration. In such a situation, space for viewing was a principal factor behind placing larger motifs on the upper level.

In some rock shelters paintings are also arranged at the lowest possible limit of the rock walls, sometimes even touching the floor. In some other sites some parts of the painted surface is embedded within the deposit on the floor. Such deposits were either because of natural causes or because of human activities. Layers of debris accumulated there and overlapped/covered some parts of the painted surface. Such occurrence may be a suitable source for chronologically determining the rock art. In some areas, paintings can also be seen on the top of the ceiling within a narrow space where such art activity could have only been possible either in a sitting or in a lying position on the rock floor. One pertinent question rises from such incidents: whether such art practices were an outcome of leisurely activity or otherwise. In such locations petroglyphs were not attempted as for engraving more space is needed for chiseling or hammering on the surface of the rock which is not available in such a narrow space between two solid blocks of rock.

In Pachmarhi, and also in the entire stretch in the Betwa source region, several rock shelters with suitable spaces were found vacant or with no traces of any painting or habitation. Such empty rock shelters are usually located far from the clusters with evidence of habitation. Therefore, it may be inferred that the groups responsible for creating rock art had a limited number of nomadic people who formed several small bands and habitations of the same group were evenly distributed in various locations within the same forest and mountainous setting during the same period. Such type of habitation was favourable for the sustenance of hunter-gatherers and foragers. In such communities, each band explored the area within its own territory; such evidential support is found from the distribution pattern of dwelling sites.

In identifying the shelters as dwelling sites, it may be mentioned here that at least in two rock shelters, one in Maradeo and the other in Mount Rosa, two different images indicate household activities under similar rock shelters. For interpreting pictorial evidence on the location of the habitation, a thematic analysis of the rock art imagery also has a significant facet to relate. The distribution pattern of the habitation in the form of rock shelters might have been suitable for food gathering activities and a number of rock art images in this region represent hunter-gatherers and their activities. But in art, a mention of a society that developed later and which experienced a battle or a feud is also distinctly visible in the same rock canvas. Therefore, it may be inferred that in this region, following the hunter-gatherers, pastorals dominated and thereafter during the later Historic phases human activities in rock shelters continued. Use of the rock shelters, at least for art activities continued uninterruptedly for generations. It is also significant that in the entire region (explored at least from the upper surface), rock shelters without any marks of rock art do not contain any artifacts or archaeologically significant deposits. This observation needs further verification by digging trial trenches. Association of the rock art and archaeological deposits may also reveal that successive generations and different cultural periods, used particular rock shelters repeatedly for both habitation and painting activities. Therefore, it may be predicted that in the Pachmarhi zone the rock art as depicted in the shelters was symbolic for attracting nomads from different periods for habitation, suitable sustenance, and living. In all painted rock shelters we find paintings superimposed on other layers and never in a single layer. Moreover, no incident of removing or repainting of rock surface is found. Possibly erasing of the earlier painted layer was taboo in the entire region and such a practice was common in several societies.

Rock art sites located in the western coastal region of South Goa, represent petroglyphs only. Carvings are arranged on lateritic bed rocks facing the water channel of a narrow hill stream. The exact locations of these are at Kajur, Pansaimol in Pirla village in Sanguem taluka and another site at Mauxi in Sattari taluka. In Pansaimal, Goa petroglyphs are distributed on lateritic bed rocks which cover a 5,000 square metres area on one bank of Kushabati river. Rock art is represented as carvings depicting symbols of the fertility cult, religious cosmology, zoomorphs such as Zebu bulls, deer, gaur, and scenes of mating animals, large animal hoofs, scenes of chasing animals, animals in pairs and in sitting postures, a bison with wound marks, X-ray figures of animals, dancing female figure, and a mother with her child. All the figures are depicted on the lateritic floor. A large figure of a pair of human feet directed towards the river bank, almost touches the water of Kushabati river and at its front a large symbolic figure of a labyrinth is visible. Such direction of the human feet possibly indicates the spot for bathing in Kushabati river and after the bath the feet are directed to enter the enclosure of a labyrinth for a possible ritual performance.

In several rock art sites located in Badami area of Karnataka, both petroglyphs and paintings coexist. Both wilds and domesticates are represented in the rock art of the region. Humped bulls and various types of stylised anthropomorphs, particularly hunting scenes and images signifying domestication of animals, are more frequent. In some rock art sites, early Kannada scripts and some form of Brahmi script are superimposed on earlier layers containing figurative art. An analysis of the data from five such rock art sites in Badami region shows that only spacious rock shelters and caves were selected for such activities. In one particular site, a natural cave which has a long tunnel inside like a dried water channel shows three wide natural holes on its ceiling. Such a natural formation was caused by early erosion activities. During the summer solstice, rays of the sun directly descend on a particular wall which is full of rock art images. The other wall on its opposite side which is equally wide, smooth, and spacious does not contain any evidence of rock art, either in the form of carvings or painting. The difference between the two walls is availability of more natural light on one wall where rock paintings and carvings are concentrated.

Therefore, light was the main reason for selecting one wall. In other sites in Badami area, each rock shelter indicates the presence of selected rock art all of which is located at a much higher level. Art is mostly placed within concave natural formations placed on the top level of rock shelters which can be viewed from a considerable distance, even from the downhill area. Such a perspective is almost identical to that prevalent in central India.

In the peninsular part of India, rock art sites like the Edakkal cave in Sultan's Battery, Wayanad district in Kerala has distinct features. There, hundreds of carved figures, signs, and symbols are depicted in a stretch on and around the walls of a dark cave. Carved figures are located from the floor level to an extent of about 8 feet from the base. The spacious cave is located on the top of a hill and during its discovery there were no definite entry or exit points for the cave chamber. In other words, the cave art site is solitarily located; possibly it was built in a remote and inaccessible part of a mountain range. Its isolation and the thematic content of its rock art, are only found in the single site within the entire region. This shows some signs of the cave becoming a shrine for ritual activities.

The Chotanagpur Plateau region in the eastern part of India, comprises some rock art sites within the administrative territories of Jharkhand and West Bengal. In Ghatsila, Subarnarekha river valley of Jharkhand, rock art sites are located in two different spots. Both the sites illustrate petroglyphs carved on huge gnessic bedrocks. Anthropomorphs, in crude form, along with other signs and symbols are also found depicted there. Similar anthropomorphs in a dancing pose with another erotic figure were discovered by the first author from a site near Kangsabati or Kasai river valley located in Purulia district in West Bengal. In both the areas, natural formations such as caves and rock shelters are rare and therefore bedrocks and boulders were the only option for rock art. Analysing the associated finds and symbolic significance of rock art imagery in the area, it is apparent that in the Chotanagpur Plateau, rock art was related to megalithic burial practices that are still prevalent among Mundas—tribal inhabitants of the area. Similar evidence of rock art is also evident from Ranchi and Hazaribagh districts in Jharkhand (Chakraverty 2003) and in Kaimur range in Bihar.

Mirzapur district in Uttar Pradesh, which is bordered by the districts of Sonbhadra in the south, Chandauli in the east, Banaras, Allahabad and Sant Ravidas Nagar in the north, and Rewa in the state Madhya Pradesh on the west reveals the presence of numerous painted rock art stations. Both from the perspective of archaeology and anthropology, Mirzapur district has been widely researched. During the British Raj, officers of the British East India Company took the first initiatives to study the archaeological remains of this region (Cockburn 1899). Gradually, after Independence Indian researchers also tried to

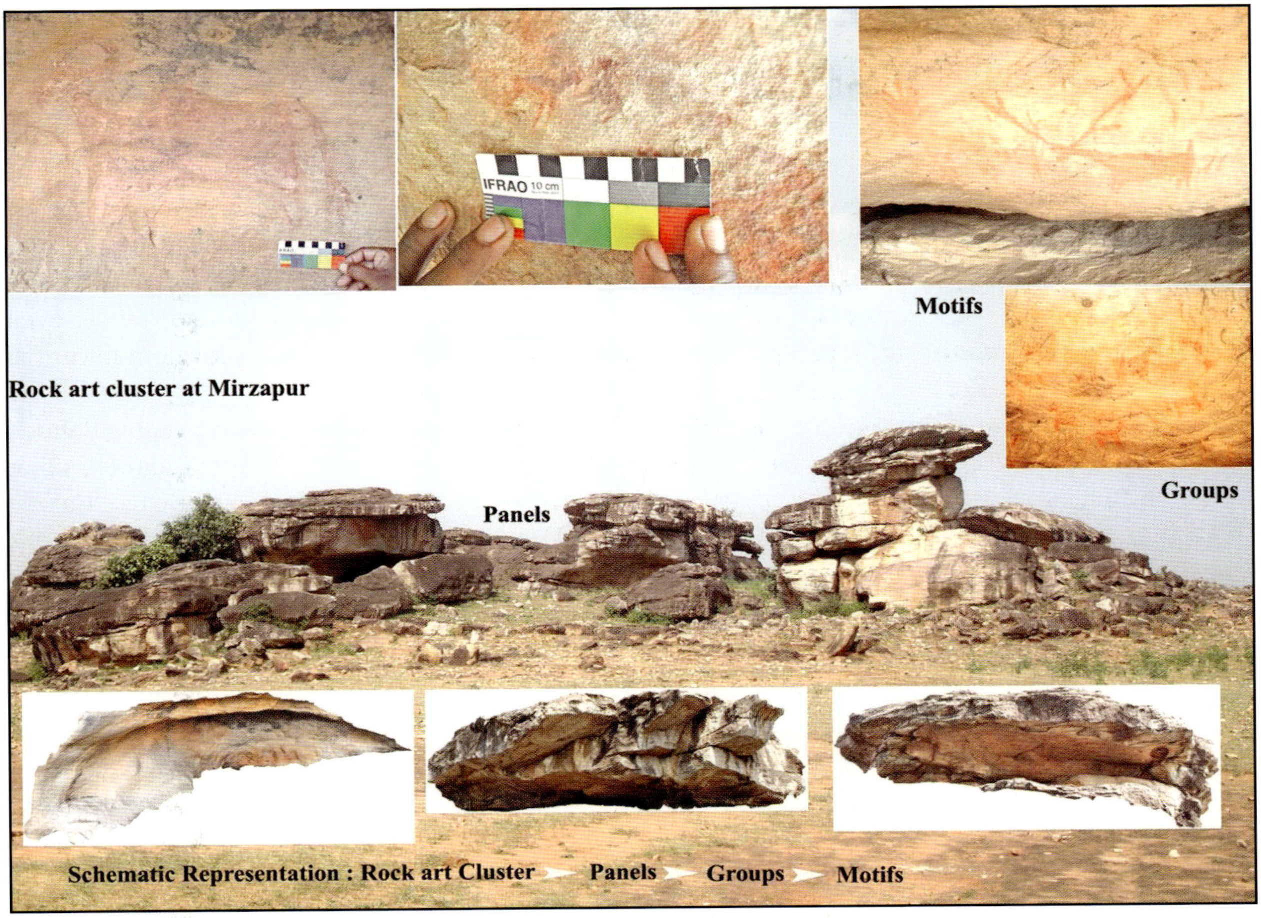

Fig. 6.1 Rock cluster at Mirzapur.

unravel the problems of regional archaeology and anthropology by discovering and documenting several painted rock shelters along with methodological excavations. A few skeletal remains from the painted rock shelters of Mirzapur have been dated to 14000-13000 BCE by means of radiocarbon dating (Varma 2012). New research on dating and mapping of rock art from this region is being carried out by other scientists and the future holds good promise.

Several new rock art sites have been discovered in recent years in Mirzapur, which has changed the present day scenario of rock art in central India. The paintings mostly depict hunting-gathering scenes with a predominance of extinct animals. In a few cases extant animals like a dog and a humped bull have been documented as well. The first layer of the painting in the rock shelters is made of Vindhyan sandstone and is naturalistic in nature. In some shelters the superimpositions help in identifying the occurrence of different phases and cultural periods when they are analysed chronostylistically and technostylistically. The area has a mixed variety, where very old paintings of hunting-gathering phases are superimposed by paintings of Chalcolithic and Metal ages, as deduced by the subject matter and/or themes. The early paintings are made of dark red pigments whereas the Chalcolithic and sometimes early Historic paintings are bichromatic in nature.

No association has been made as yet in terms of rock paintings and tribal domestic decorations in the villages. However, in some cases a few similarities have been observed, when geometric and symbolic designs from the rock art canvas can be compared to the local Kol, Gond, Agariya, Pahariya, and Korwa art. Overall the rock art of Mirzapur is Palaeolithic in nature with some late varieties, as opposed to the rock art of Pachmari in the Satpuras, where the nature of the art is distinctly late and resembles the tribal art of the same eco-geography.

Studying a cross-section of rock art sites in parts of India, a general trend can be deciphered about the selection criteria of space for early indigenous art activities. Barring a few exceptions, in most of the areas, rock art was motivated by the need to display it and to preserve visually narrated accounts on life activities, ideas, aspirations, and other symbolic messages transmitted by the pre-literate indigenous population. Thus, rock art was a medium for expressing ideas and accounts to strengthen the identity of the group and was a major guiding force for maintaining social norms and practices. During prehistoric times and thereafter rock art activities inspired and intimated pre-literate populations in the same way in which writing is doing this today. Rock art activity is still a living tradition among pre-literate communities in India. Developing a suitable methodology and a deeper insight for deciphering rock art may unveil unexplored areas of indigenous ethno-history in India.

REFERENCES

Anati, Emmanuel (1994), *World Rock Art - The Primordial Language*. Studi Camuni. 12. Italy.

Anderson, Richard I. (1979), *Art in Primitive Societies*. Englewood Cliffs: Prentice-Hall.

Archer, W. G. (1947), *The Vertical Man: A Study in Primitive Indian Sculpture*. London: George Allen and Unwin Ltd.

Boas, Franz (1955), *Primitive Art*. New York: Dover Publication.

Chakraverty, Somnath (1987), 'Tribal Murals of Chhotanagpur', *The India Magazine* 6(2): 20–27.

—— (1995a), 'Isco: Rock Art Site in Hazaribag', in R.K. Sharma and K.K. Tripathy (eds.), *Recent Perspectives on Prehistoric Art in India and Allied Subjects*. New Delhi: Aryan Books International, pp. 74-99.

—— (1995b), 'Rock Art and Ethnographic Data Retrieval in India', in Rabindra Nath Agrawal (ed.), *Rock Art vis-à-vis Ethnography*. Nagpur: Gupta Publishers.

—— (1999), 'Primeval Rock Art and Ethnographic Analogy in India', *Bollettino del Centro Camuno di Studi Preistorici* (31–32): 213–222.

—— (2003), *Rock Art Studies in India: A Historical Perspective*. Kolkata: The Asiatic Society.

—— (2004), 'Mystical Icons of Lanjhia Saoras: A Primordial Tribal Art Tradition of India', in *New Discoveries, New Interpretations, New Research Methods*. Brescia: Centro Camuno di Studi Preistorici, pp. 155-163.

—— (2009), 'Indigenous Tribal Art: Strategy for Conservation and Promotion', *Journal of Social Anthropology* 6(1-2): 87-102.

Cockburn, J. (1899), 'Art. V.—Cave Drawings in the Kaimūr Range, North-West Provinces', *Journal of the Royal Asiatic Society (New Series)* 31(01): 89–97.

Dalmia, Yashodhara (1988), *The Painted World of the Warlis: Art and Rituals of Warli Tribes of Maharastra*. New Delhi: Lalit Kala Akademi.

Das, A.K. (1979), *Tribal Art and Craft*. New Delhi: Agam Kala Prakashan.

—— (1992), 'North East India', in *Tribal India: Ancestors, Gods and Spirits*. Mumbai: Marg Publications, pp. 3-22.

Elwin, Varrier (1951), *The Tribal Art of Middle India: A Personal Record*. Mumbai: Oxford University Press.

—— (1955), *Religion of an Indian Tribe*. Mumbai: Oxford University Press.

—— (1959), *The Art of North-East Frontier of India*. Shillong: North-East Frontier Agency.

Fawcett, F. (1901), 'Notes on Rock Carving in the Edakal Cave, Wynaad', *The Indian Antiquary* 30: 409-421.

Firth, Raymond (1951), 'The Social Framework of Primitive Art', in R. Firth (ed.), *Elements of Social Organization*. London: Watts, pp. 155-182.

—— (1992), 'Art and Anthropology', in J. Coote and A. Shelton (eds), *Anthropology, Art and Aesthetics*. Oxford: Clarendon Press, pp. 15-39.

Fischer, J. L. (1961), 'Art Styles as Cultural Cognitive Maps', *American Anthropologist* 63: 79-93.

Ghosh, Asok K. and Somnath Chakraverty (1988–89), 'Genesis and Changes of Tribal Art—Examples from West Bengal', *Indian Museum Bulletin* 23 & 24: 136-141.

Ghosh, A.K. and Somnath Chakraverty (1995), 'Rock Arts of Eastern India and Their Bearing with Local Tribal Arts: A Cross-sectional Study on Continuity in India at the Dawn of History', in Asok Datta, Asok K. Ghosh and C. Margabandhu (eds.), *India At the Dawn of History*. Delhi: Agam Kala Prakashan.

Haselberger, H. (1961), 'Methods in Studying Ethnological Art', *Current Anthropology* 2: 341-384.

Hunter, G.R. (1936), 'Final Report on the Excavation in the Mahadeo Hills', *Nagpur University Journal* 2: 127-144

Jain, Jyotindra (1984), *Painted Myths of Creation: Art and Ritual of an Indian Tribe*. Delhi: Lalit Kala Akademi.

Layton, Robert (1991), *The Anthropology of Art*. Cambridge: Cambridge University Press.

Mathpal, Y.N. (1984), *Prehistoric Rock Paintings of Bhimbetka, Central India*. New Delhi: Abhinav Publications.

Mathpal, Yashodhar (1995), *Rock Art in Kumaon Himalaya*. New Delhi: Indira Gandhi National Centre for the Arts.

Mills, J.P. and J.H. Hutton (1929), 'Ancient Monoliths of North Cachar', *Journal of the Asiatic Society of Bengal* 25: 285-300.

Murdock, G.P. (1957), 'World Ethnographic Sample', *American Anthropologist* 59: 664-687.

Neumayer, E. (1983), *Prehistoric Indian Rock Paintings*. New Delhi: Oxford University Press.

—— (1993), *Lines on Stone—the Prehistoric Rock Art of India*. New Delhi: Manohar.

Pande, B.M. (1971), 'Neolithic Hunting Scene on a Stone Slab from Burzahom, Kashmir', *Asian Perspective* 14: 194-198

—— (1972), 'A Neolithic Tectiform from Burzahom, District Srinagar', *Journal of Indian Anthropological Society* 7: 175-177.

Pandey, S.K. (1993), *Indian Rock Art*. New Delhi: Aryan Books International.

Redfield, Robert (1956), *Peasant Society and Culture*. Chicago: University of Chicago Press.

Sundara, A. (1968), 'Rock Shelter, Hire Benakal Hills, Raichur', *Indian Archaeology 1967–68–A Review*, p. 67.

—— (2006), 'Karnataka Rock Art: Some Distinctive Aspects', *Purakala* 16: 35-49.

Verma, R.K. (2012), *Rock Art of Central India: North Vindhyan Region.* New Delhi: Aryan Books International.

Wakankar, V.S. and R.R.R. Brooks (1976), *Stone Age Paintings in India.* Mumbai: D.P. Taraporevala Sons & Co.

7

The State of Chinese Rock Art

Zhu Lifeng

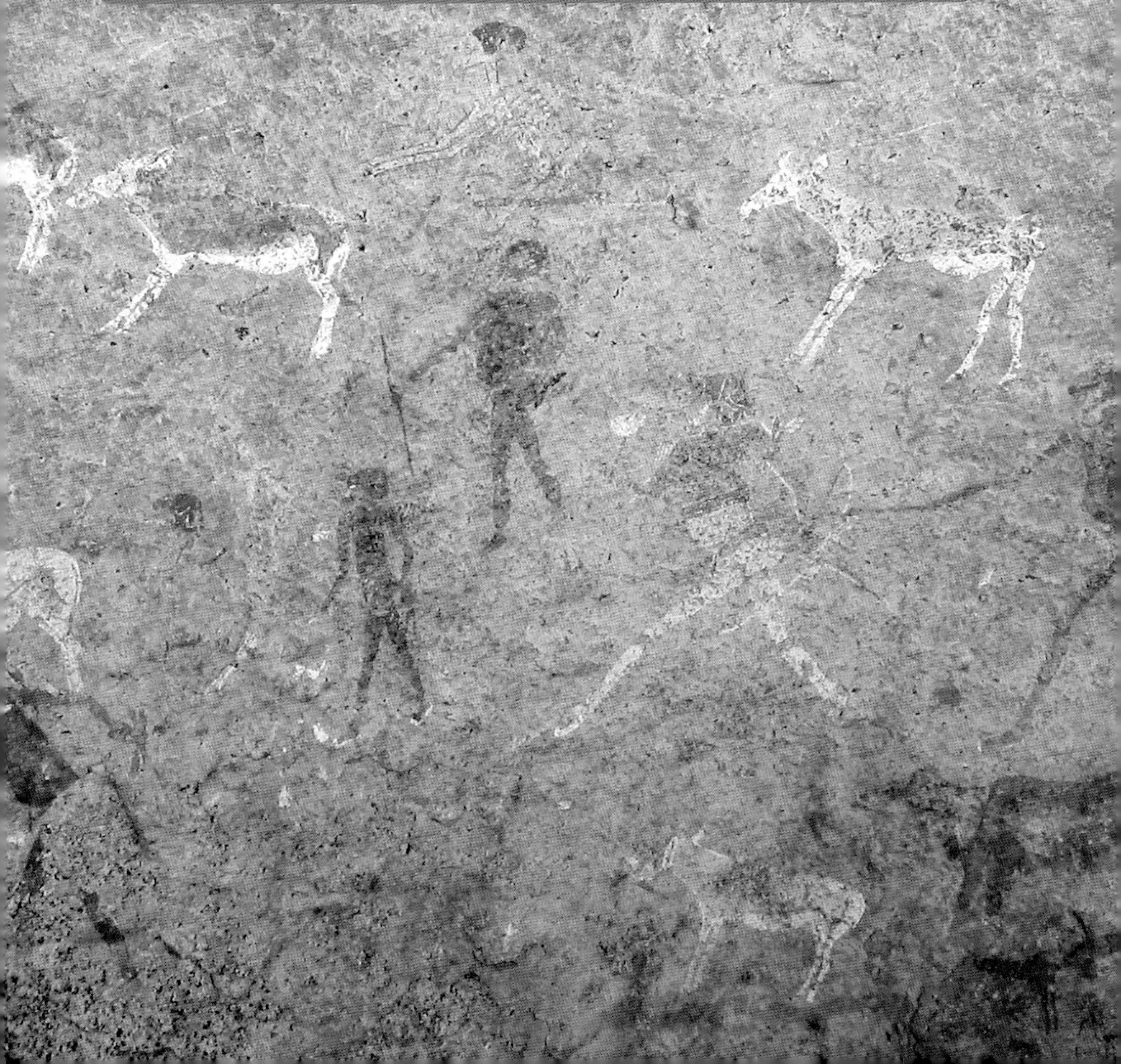

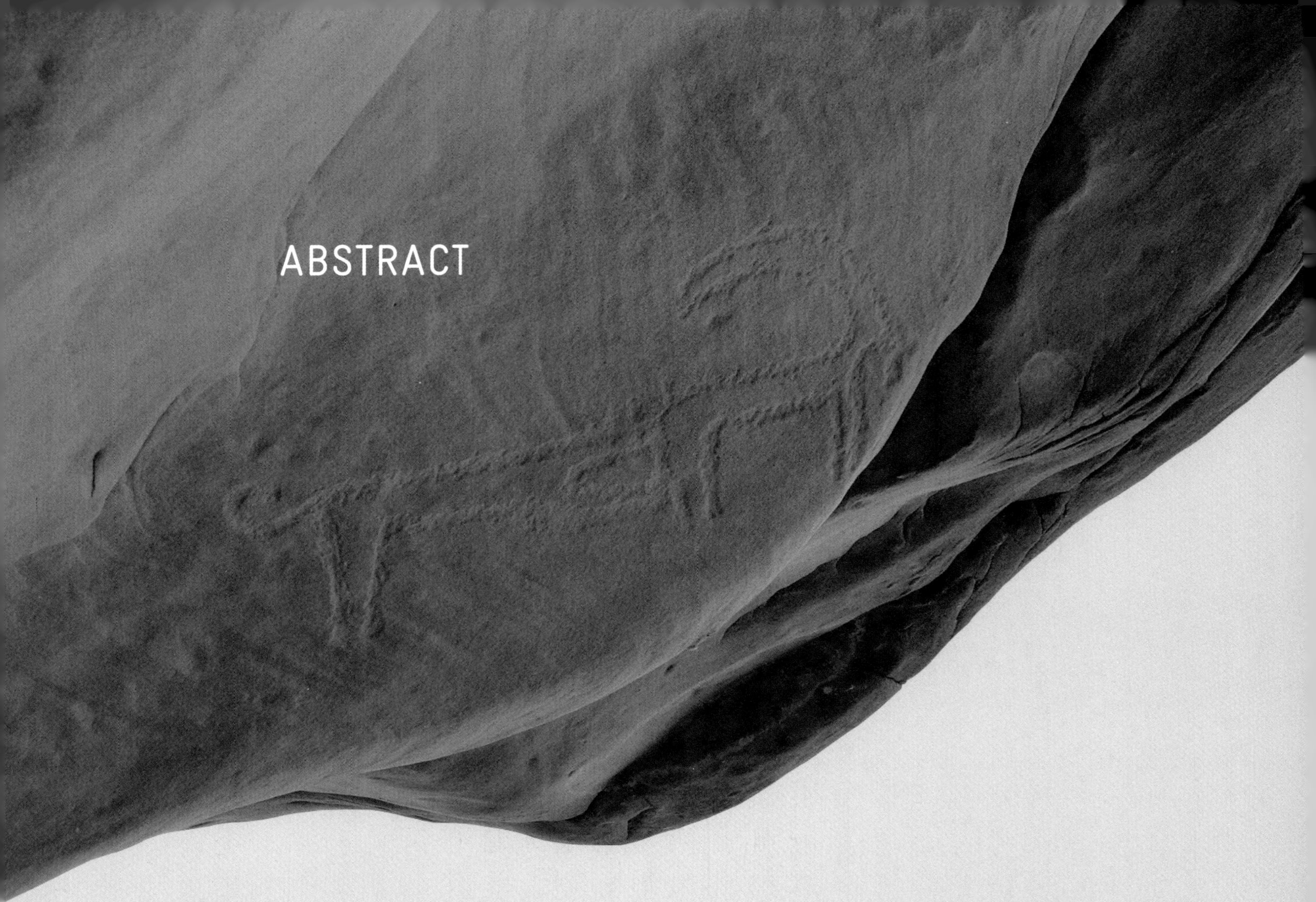

ABSTRACT

Remains of rock art are distributed throughout China. The sites and subject matter of rock art have a close interrelation with China's national culture. Chinese rock art is endowed with precious research value. In the 21st century, there have been new developments in the discoveries and scientific research of rock art through intensified efforts by the authorities, scholars and amateurs. These discoveries are of great significance among the cupules of central China's Henan, the hand stencils of southwest China, the masks of northeast China's Chifeng and those in Xinjiang, Yunan. These discoveries have brought about a new wave of scientific research, with investigations, documentation and protective areas of rock art being extended, the cultural industry developing with clear-end characteristics in some regions and new explorations of research obtaining certain breakthroughs in various fields, in particular archaeology, anthropology, art history, prehistoric philosophy, religious studies, iconography and symbolic signs.

China is one of the countries that boast the most abundant rock art resources in the world. According to the latest statistics collected by the Rock Art Research Association of China (RARAC) in 2012, rock art has been discovered in approximately 220 counties in 29 provinces and the total number of rock art sites has exceeded substantially, including more than 150,000 images (Map 7.1); and this number is still rising yearly. As prehistoric cultural heritage, rock art is spread all over ethnic regions in good quantity. Being a reason and wealth of early cultural messages it may be regarded as a treasure for studying Chinese cultural and ethnic history. After about a century's development, the study of Chinese rock art has made phenomenal progress.

However, since destruction, both natural and that caused by humans is becoming severe, the protection of rock art is a serious concern. This paper briefly reviews the discovery, research development and current research status of Chinese rock art, with special reference to its conservation and interpretation as well as the direction in which these should move.

THE DISCOVERY AND RESEARCH DEVELOPMENT OF CHINESE ROCK ART

China is the first country in the world to employ characters to record rock art. In ancient Chinese literature, earliest records about rock art can be traced back to the book *Hanfeizi* during the Warring States Period (c.3rd BCE), which was about 2,000 years ago. Later, over 20 sites of rock art nationwide, dating back to the northern *Wei* Dynasty about 1,500 years ago, were documented by Li Daoyuan's monograph *Shuijingzhu*. From the Song Dynasty onwards, ancient books and local records like *Taipingyulan, Taipingguangji, Yudijisheng, Xubowuzhi, Yiwenlu, Ningmingzhouzhi* and *Xinanxianzhi* were written on rock art discovered in various areas. Yet a formal research of Chinese rock art is supposed to have started from the beginning of the 20th century. Research of Chinese rock art during the pre-modern and modern period can be roughly divided into four stages:

The first stage is approximately from the beginning of the 20th century to the end of the 1970s, a stage of preliminary discovery and research. Chinese academia's attention to rock art started with Huang Zhongqin's investigation in the Hua'an region's Taixixianzitan's petroglyph in Fujian province in 1915 (Figs. 7.1 & 7.2). This investigation together with her 'Taixiguwen' published in the *Lingnan University Journal* in 1935 marked the beginning of Chinese rock art's research in pre-modern and modern times. Since then, some Chinese and foreign scholars have started discovering rock art in places including Xinjiang, Inner Mongolia, Guangxi, Hong Kong, Yunnan, Heilongjiang, Gansu and Sichuan; they have also published their reports. However, little attention was paid to these discoveries and in rudimentary records by specialists, with the result that scientific research of Chinese rock art advanced slowly.

The second stage starts from the 1980s and extends till the mid-1990s. Thanks to the launch of the Second National Cultural Relics Investigation of China, rock art in provinces like Inner Mongolia, Ningxia, Xinjiang, Gansu, Qinghai and Tibet was discovered on a large scale, which aroused an interest in investigating and studying rock

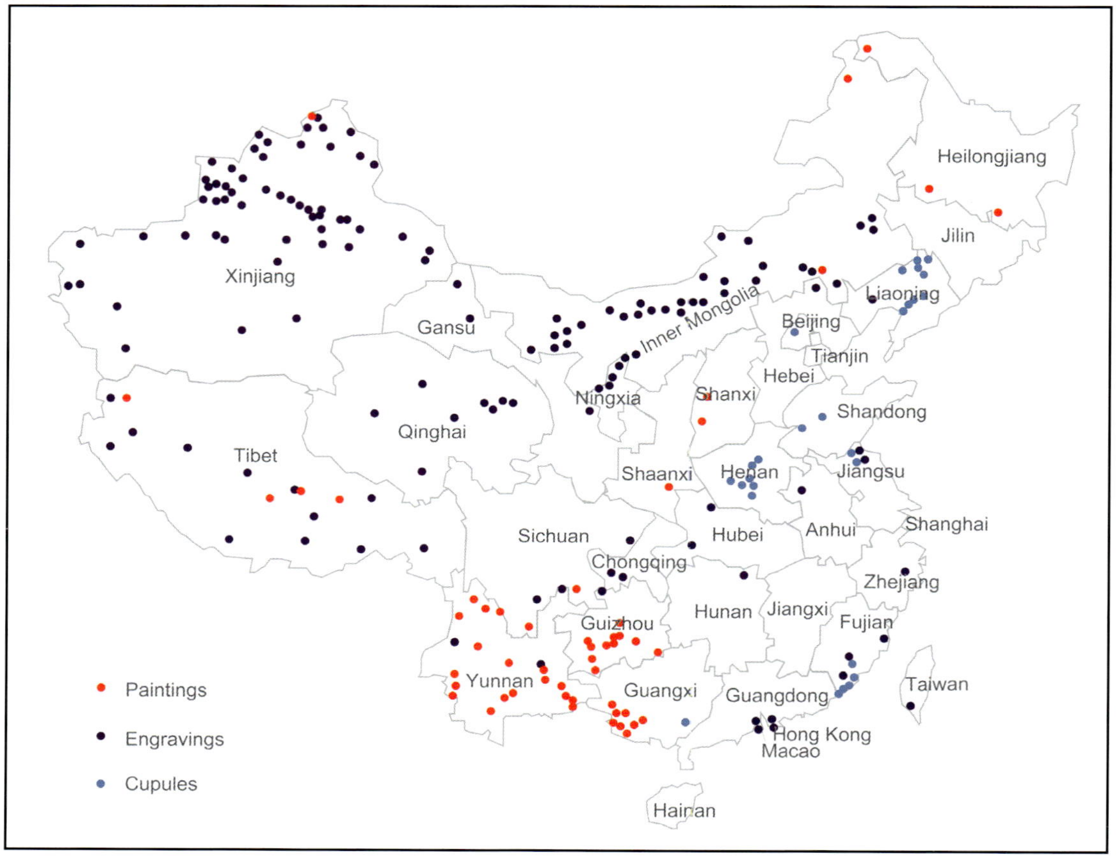

Map 7.1 Distribution of rock art in China.

art in the domain of archaeology and related fields (Figs. 7.3 & 7.4). Yet extensive discoveries of rock art in China could not draw enough attention from the world's academia. In the 'Distribution Map of World Rock Art', issued by the American journal *Archaeology* in 1983, China was left blank. It was not until Professor Chen Zhaofu's (the Minzu University of China or MUC) introduction that Chinese rock art became known to the outside world.

Left: **Fig. 7.1** 1st stage: 1915-1970s.

Right: **Fig. 7.2** 1st stage: 1915-1970s.

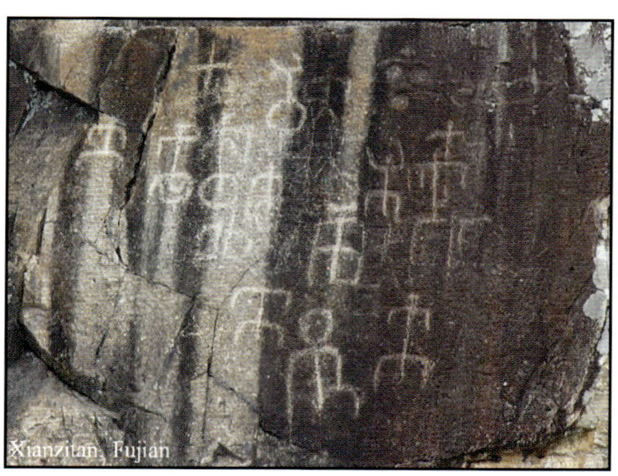

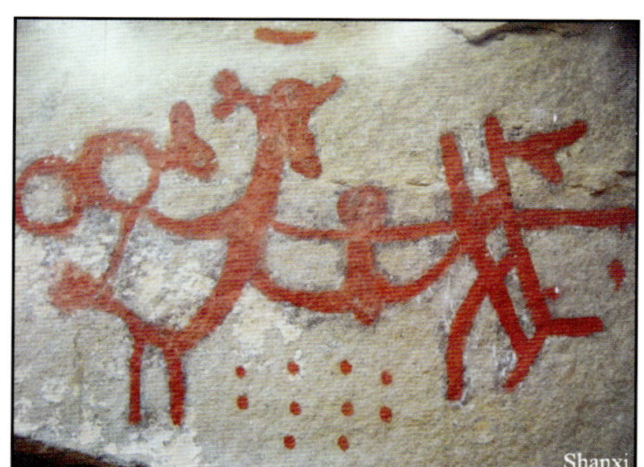

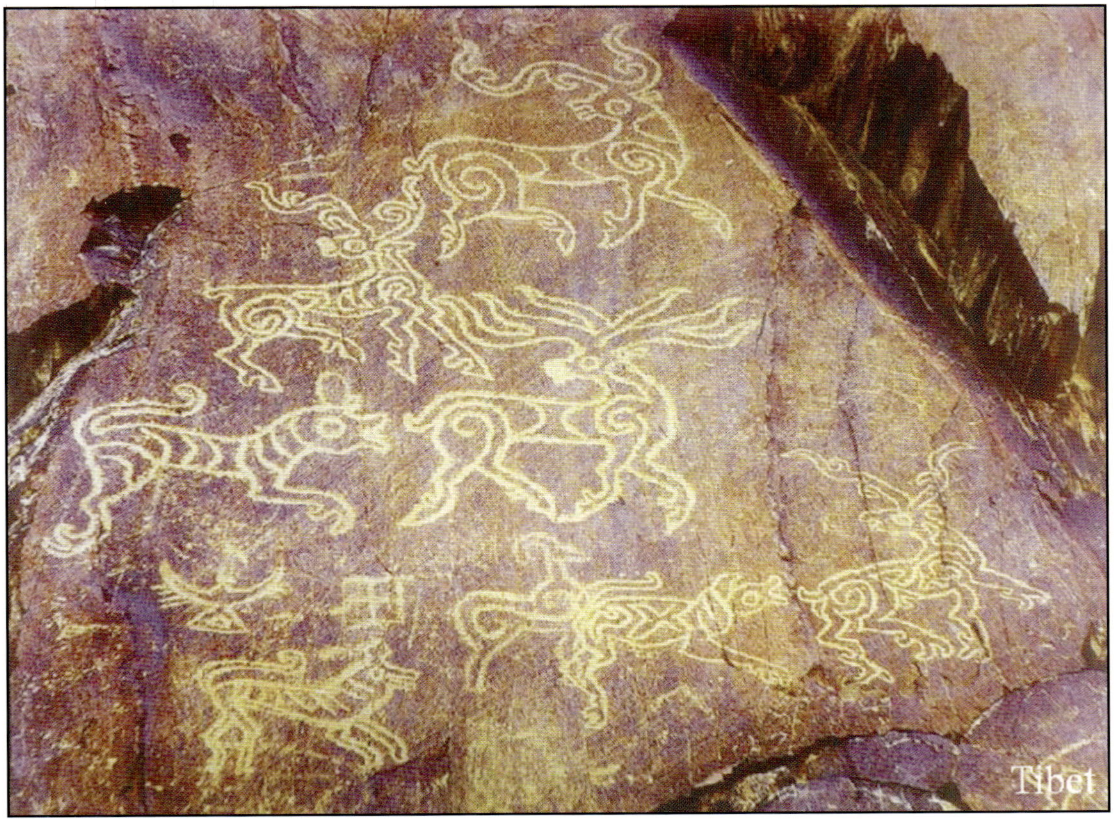

Fig. 7.3 2nd stage: 1980s-mid 1990s.

The third stage, from 1995 to 2007, was the nadir of Chinese rock art research. The shrinking of discoveries sapped researchers' enthusiasm and gradually rock art became a marginalised discipline. But this nadir helped serious researchers to take up rock art studies in the new century.

The fourth stage is from 2008 to the present. Thanks to the development of the Third National Cultural Relics Investigation of China, a number of new Rock Art sites are discovered with promotions by the government, scholars and amateurs, the depth and breadth of investigation has been upgraded (Fig. 7.5). At the same time, scientific methods have been also adopted for the recording and protection of rock art. During this period, more rock art sites were discovered in 29 provinces including Heilongjiang, Liaoning, Inner Mongolia, Hebei, Shanxi, Shaanxi, Ningxia, Gansu, Qinghai, Xinjiang, Tibet, Sichuan, Chongqing, Guizhou, Yunnan, Guangxi, Guangdong, Fujian, Jiangxi, Hunan, Hubei, Zhejiang, Jiangsu, Anhui, Henan, Shandong, Taiwan, Hong Kong and Macau. Now, rock art covers almost entire china, except 5 provinces. Most importantly, rock art has been discovered in the Zhongyuan region, which had been regarded as a place with no rock art for about 100 years. With this discovery, the notion that rock art exists only in ethnic regions, got rectify. Various new discoveries of rock art, such as Jinshajiang rock art, Xinjiang rock art, Henan cupules, human-faced rock art in Wengniuteqi of Inner Mongolia and Daxinanling's rock paintings are very significant. Chinese Scholars now extensively

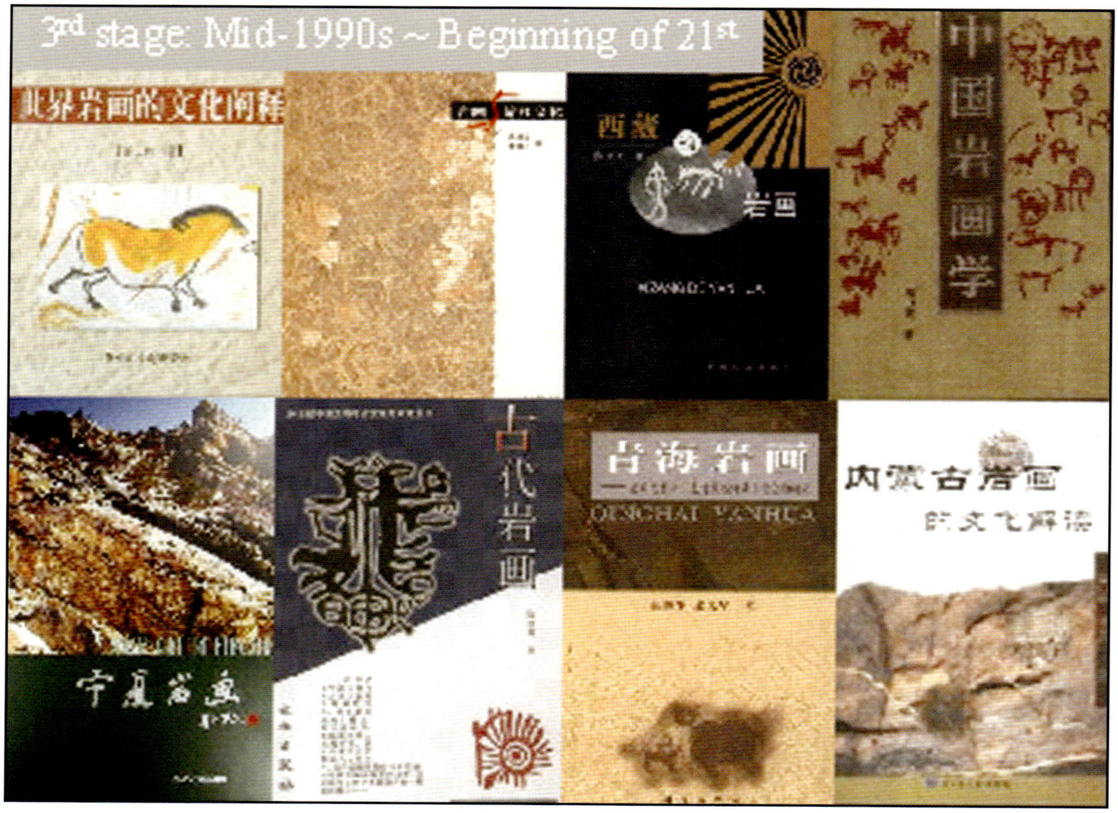

Fig. 7.4 3rd stage: Mid 1990s - Beginning of 21st Century.

exploring different research spheres and with these discoveries the research of Chinese rock art has stepped into a new prosperous stage.

THE INVESTIGATION AND PRACTICE OF CHINESE ROCK ART

The investigation practice of Chinese rock art, mainly adopted by the archaeologists in various provinces and regions, includes field work and scientific recordings. A majority of the newly-discovered rock art has been unearthed, investigated and recorded by archaeologists during survey of national cultural relics. Supported by policies and funds, these professionals employ archaeological field work as the main approach, search and gather first-hand rock art resources in divided areas and then describe these rock art resources while dating and trying to establish a staged, regionalised and classified archaeological file.

Comparative studies on regions are also conducted with a view to figure out differences of content and style and corresponding reasons for the same. Institutes represented by RARAC of the Minzu University of China (MUC) have actively collaborated with local archaeological sections to conduct comprehensive investigations and come up with scientific records of the latest-discovered rock art sites. This has opened up new prospects in universities and research institutions in the country. Between April and May 2012, RARAC created panels of up to 30 persons including undergraduates, masters and

PhD fellows to carry research on petroglyphs in the cupules in Fangcheng, Biyang and Wugang in Henan Province (Figs. 7.6 & 7.7).

Field work for Chinese rock art involves seven steps—identification, location, measurement, recording, photographing, tracing and rubbing. Its goal is to acquire standard, systematic and scientific data base on rock art to ensure the objectivity of these data with setting up of comprehensive identity files of rock art in a wide range of places. This is considered as the fundamental work of rock art research and is the most accepted method in which Chinese rock art research is completed. This data base has a inimitable and fundamental role in Chinese rock art research as it help in sorting resources systematically.

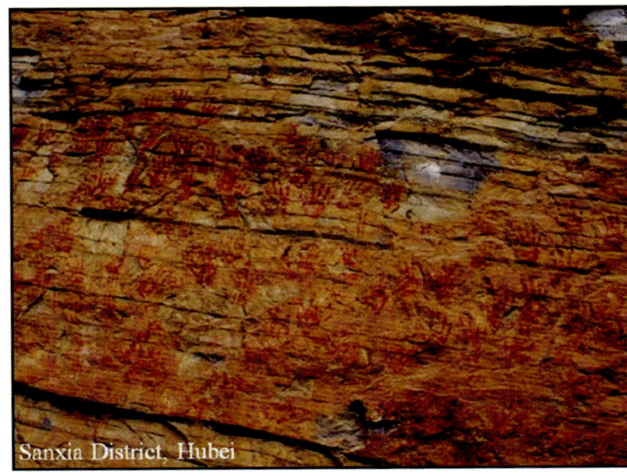

Fig. 7.5 4th stage: Beginning of 21st - till present.

For documentation and scientific recording of rock art in china many methods are adopted by the scholars that include making inventory records and digital documentation through photography and videography. The site inventory includes the rock art site's Chinese name, exclusive number, specific location, GPS coordinates (longitude, latitude and altitude), direction of the rock art, size of the images, theme and content (animals, humans, tools, patterns, symbols, plants and others), number of images, state of conservation, production methods (pecking, engraving, painting and others) and descriptions of the natural and human environment

Fig. 7.6 RARAC investigation in cup marks of Henan.

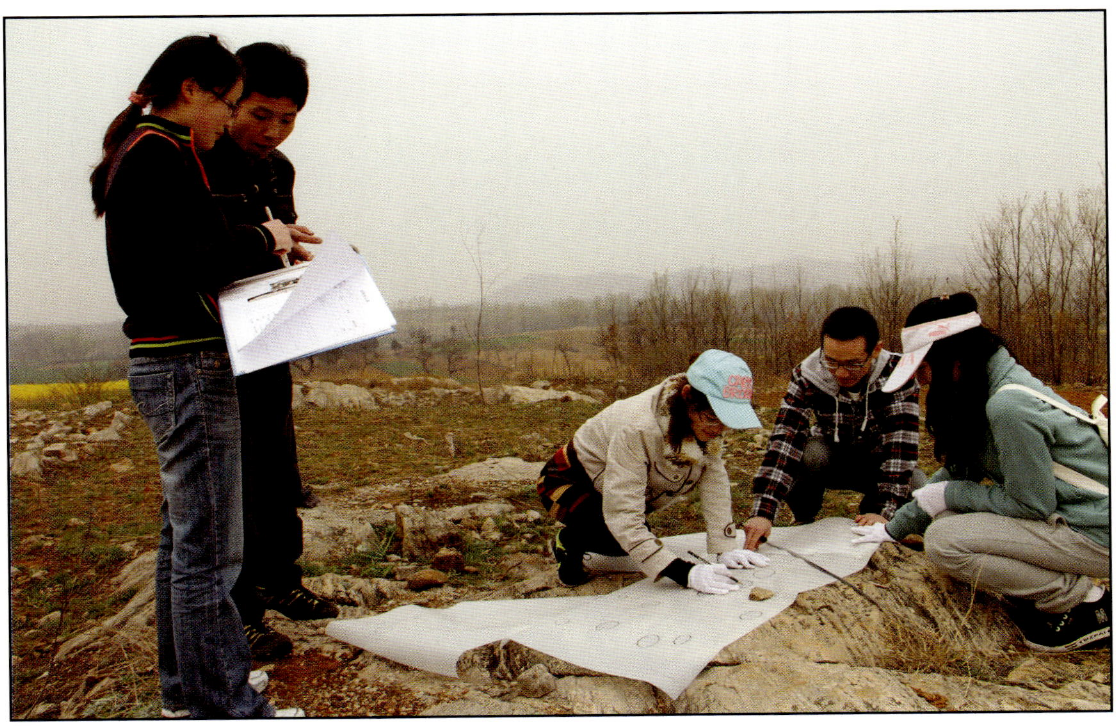

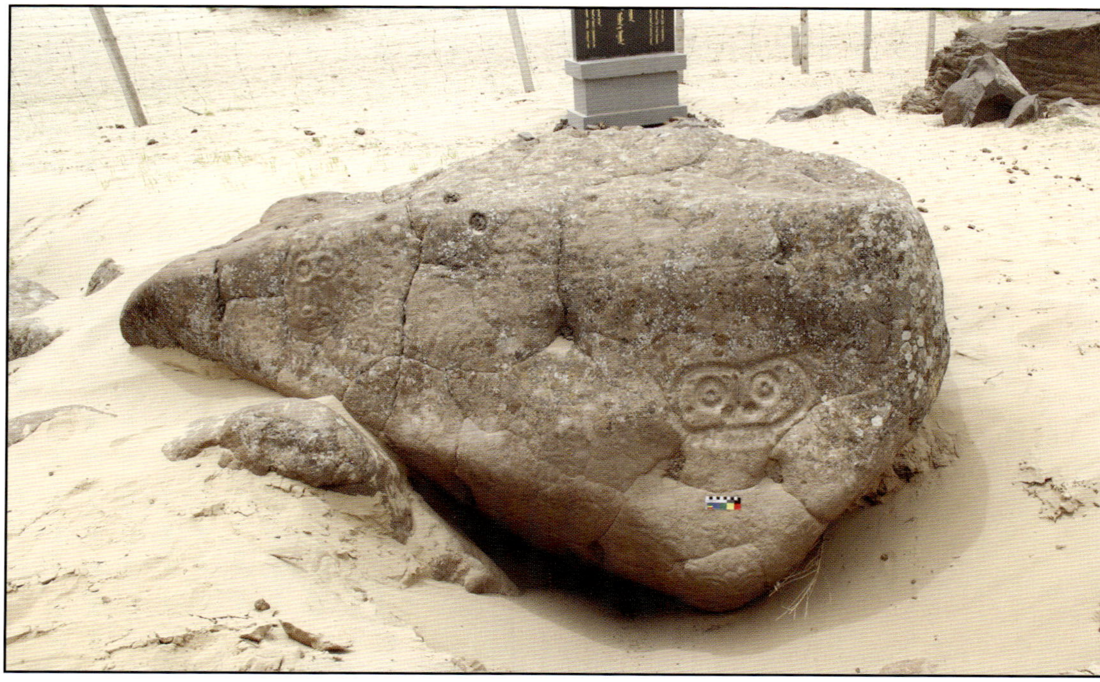

Fig. 7.7 Depiction of human face, Ongniud, inner Mongolia.

surrounding the rock art site. Video documentation includes photos (overall view, close shot, picture of the rock, panorama of image and details), tracing, grid cartography, rubbing, sketching and video recording (2D and 3D).

THEORETICAL STUDY OF CHINESE ROCK ART

Rock art sites in China depicts life scenes like hunting, sacrifices and war that are inextricably intertwined with the development of ethnic cultures of china. These have great research value to study the formation of the unity in the pluralistic society of China. Since the 21st century the theory and method of Chinese rock art research has demonstrated a trend of diversity, and inclusive multi-disciplinary research principles have broadened the horizons of the study of rock art. Scholars are no longer satisfied with the display of material or by discussions on general issues; instead, they study from comprehensive perspectives by virtue of cross-disciplines like archaeology, cultural anthropology, ethnology, folklore, history, art, religious studies, mythology, semiotics, geography, physics, chemistry, statistics and so on.

Scholars in diverse disciplines and from different cultural backgrounds choose different methods and perspectives. Among archaeological methods, there are researches on regionalisation and classification of rock art by using archaeological typology and on dating rock art by using technical methods of archaeological chronology; a study of rock art from an ethnological angle takes advantage of the results of archaeological research and knowledge about the discipline, focusing on topics, such as Aboriginal art, production and living styles, social forms and regional beliefs on the basis of field work. Some amateurs also concentrate on the discovery of rock art and research of carving methods while others try to interpret the meanings of rock through rock art images. The theoretical exploration of rock art is largely focused on 'Aboriginal thinking mode', 'pan-shamanism' and 'language of images and representational system of symbols'.

Based on theoretical research, Chen Zhaofu made a systematic introduction to the discovery and research of Chinese and global rock art in the 1990s; Gai Shanlin elevated Chinese rock art research to the height of discipline construction, which led to progress in scientific recording, description and a comprehensive study of regionalised research; Song Yaoliang, linked Chinese rock art with world rock art, did cross-national research and helped in initiating new research thoughts. In recent years, there has also been more research from diverse perspectives by Chinese scholars; literature too has benefited from this. *Origin of Art* by Emmanuel Anati has been translated into Chinese with the aim to introduce more research of world rock art to Chinese readers and scholars. RARAC has invested funds and organised professionals to edit and translate *Translation series of Rock Art*. In the new century re-discovery of rock art; topics associated with styles, themes and content, chronological dating and periodisation and interpretations are the main research interest of the scholars.

In the 20th century, it was claimed that most Chinese rock art appeared in peripheral ethnic regions or places where ancient ethnic minority groups lived. According to regional characteristics of rock art in different places, Chinese scholars came to different conclusions and proposed different ways of regional distribution of rock art. Chen Zhaofu, Tang Huishen and Song Yaoliang were in favour of dividing it into three parts as the North, Southwest and Southeast coastal areas; Li Fushun, Li Yongxian, Ban Lan, etc. advocated systems of the North and South; Gai Shanlin proposed a system of dividing it into four parts called quartering into the agriculture and forestry region of the Northeast, prairie region of the North, mountainous area of the South and the coastal area of the Southeast (Fig. 7.8). At the beginning of the 21st century, Zhang Yasha suggested the quartering of the northern prairie system, the Qinghai-Tibet Plateau system, southwestern mountainous area system and the southeastern coastal system. Plus, a large quantity of petroglyphs in the cupules and some rock art which had images and symbols were discovered in the Henan province in central China. This has changed the frontier distribution of Chinese rock art and will reconstruct Chinese rock art's mode of regional distribution.

Chinese rock art contains hunting, nomadism, integrated economy, farming and oceanic culture. When it comes to rock art in different regions, scholars have proposed their own classification systems. In 2006, Zhang Yasha did a typological study of Tibetan rock art by its images, skills of production and artistic characteristics from an iconographic perspective of the art discipline, alongside research methods of ethnology, history and religion studies. As for ethnic belongings of rock art in different places, scholars believe that it was made by indigenous people. Current researchers viewpoint is that, there were about a dozen owners of rock art including ethnic minorities like Hun, Turk, Xianbei, Donghu, Tibetan, Mongolia, Baiyue, Baipu and Qiang.

For research on chorological periodisation, scholars have attempted to study production methods, themes and content, styles and types, state of conservation, colours

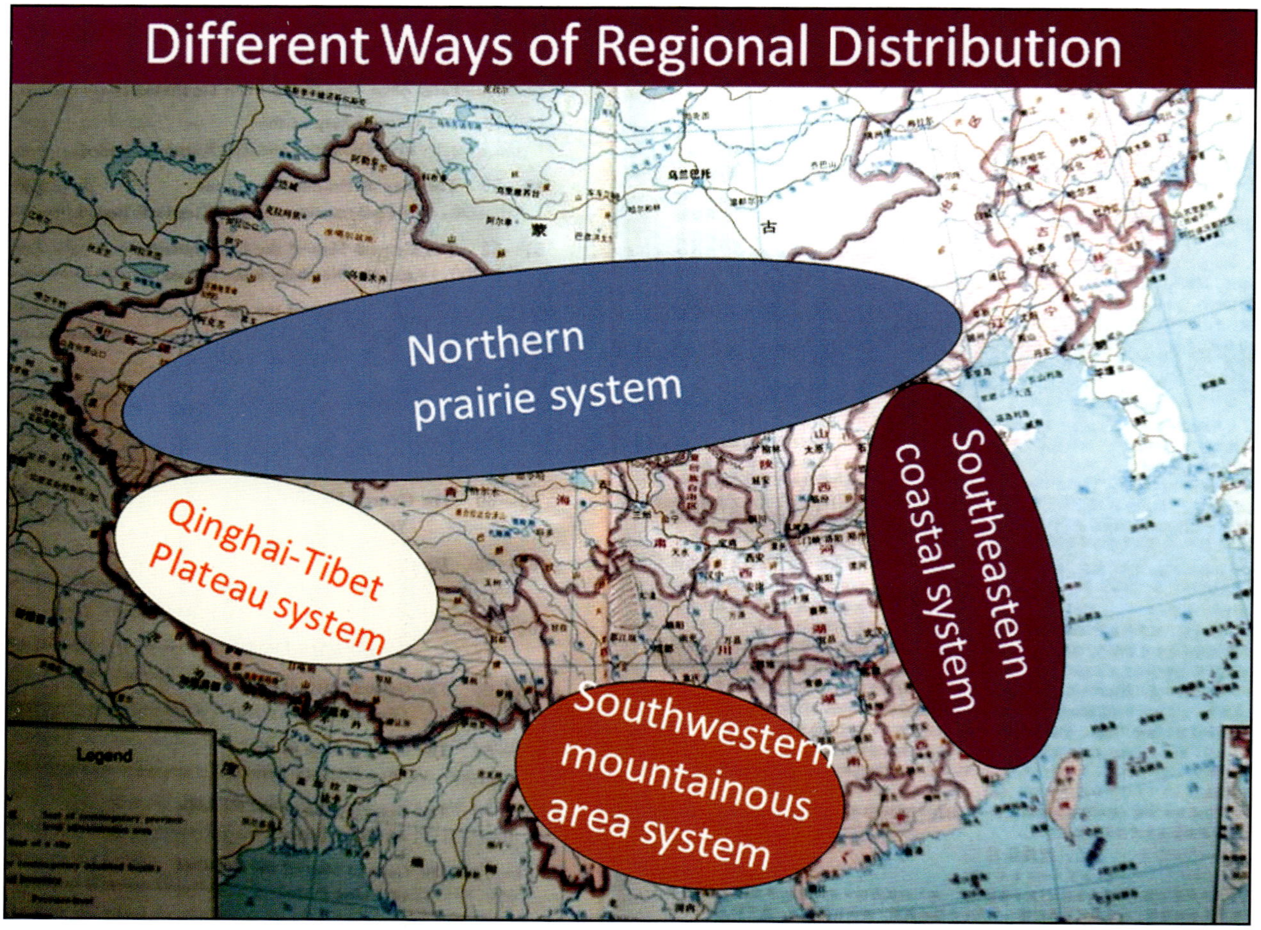

Fig. 7.8 Different ways of regional distribution.

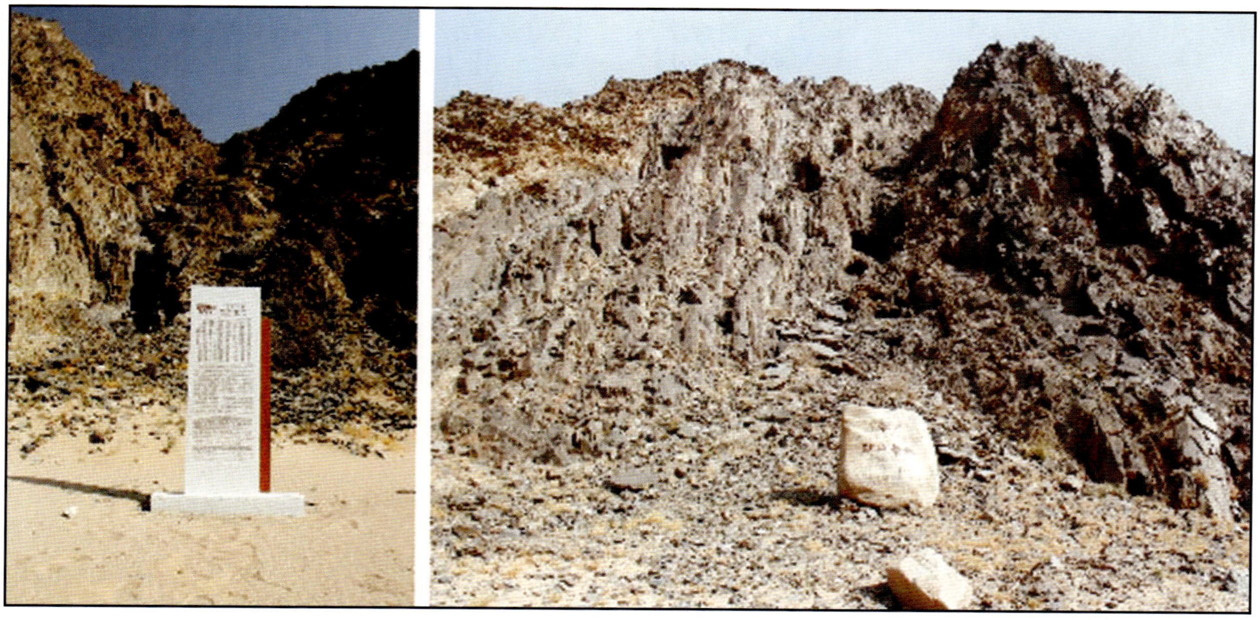

Fig. 7.9 In-situ conservation at rock art site.

and other aspects and to associate these with Palaeontology, Palaeo-anthropology, geology, typology, ethnology, folklore, archaeology of history and geography, aesthetics, religion studies and other various disciplines to make comprehensive comparisons in order to make preliminary assumptions about the date of the rock art that has been discovered in different places so far. Some scholars define the chronology of early rock art by extinct animals of zoo-archaeology. Some scholars have tried to date rock art with C14, micro-erosion dating, uranium series method, glacial striae in the 4th period while others date by Xanthoria elegans (link) Th. Fr of Lichen. However, all these methods have considerable errors when deciding the date of the rock art. That most rock art cannot be dated accurately or measured and to a large extent, it constrained deep research on the subject. Due to this bottleneck, researchers can only come up with various cultural/ethnographical interpretations of rock art and as these are based on fragmented chronological periods and scattered in various regions hence cant be scientifically proved. Chinese rock art researchers are facing a crucial issue of finding an effective solution to date rock art in China.

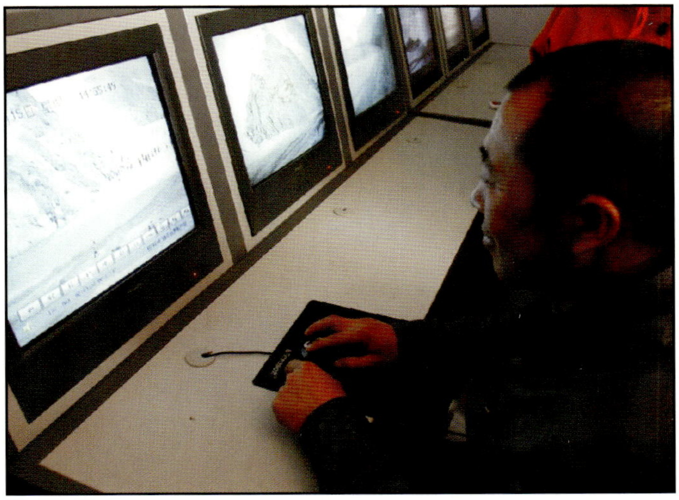

Fig. 7.10 Monitoring station in Yin Mountain, Inner Mongolia.

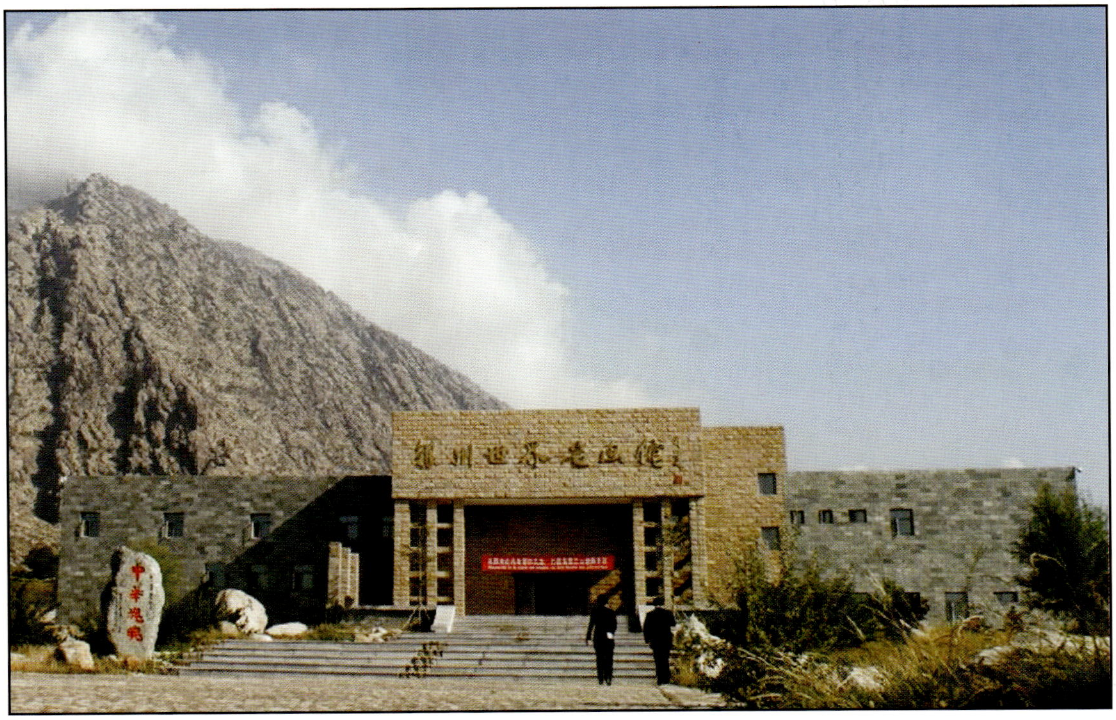

Fig. 7.11 Yinchuan World Rock Art Pavilion.

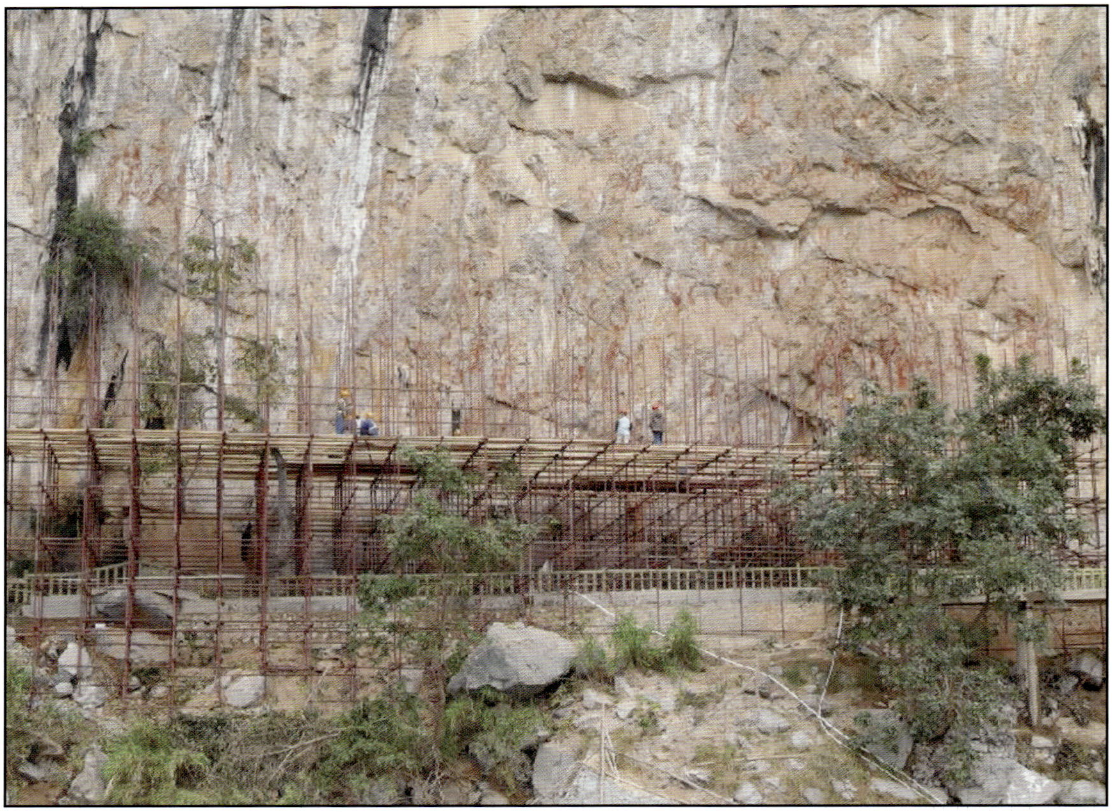

Fig. 7.12 From 2009-Huashan Rock Art Conservation Project (HRACP).

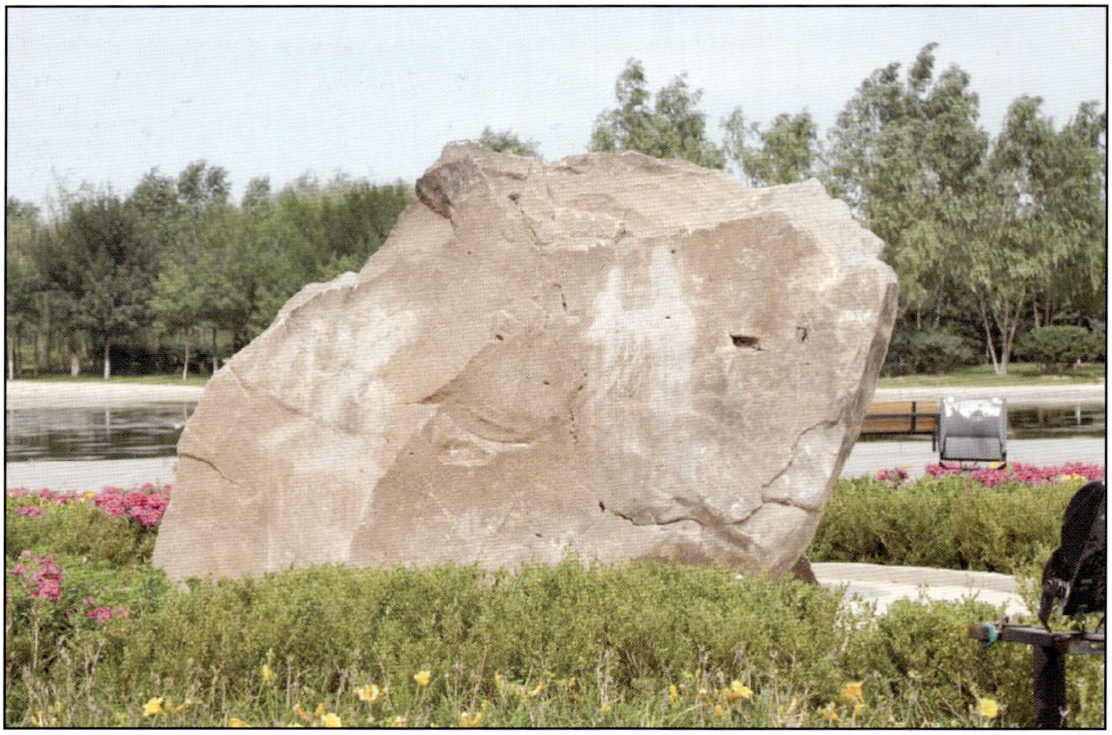

Fig. 7.13 Migrated/salvaged rock art into a park.

THE CONSERVATION AND MANAGEMENT OF ROCK ART

In China conservation and management of rock art has become especially important because of status quo of Rock art researches. Many Rock art sites are now coming into light and at the same time these are under threats of destruction by natural as well as man made factors. In general people are aware of the conservation requirement of rock art sites. The Chinese government has also started allocating funds and technical support for preservation of rock art in which juxtaposition of policies of conservation, preservation and dissemination through education are particularly emphasised.

CONSERVATION OF ROCK ART

The people and the government in china gave importance to the protection and preservation of their cultural heritage including rock art sites. In China, conservation process for the rock art includes: investigation and documentation, obtaining detailed information through a literary description and video recordings; in situ conservation methodologies to protect the rock art of which adopts approaches like tele-monitoring of sites or building a site museum if feasible to avoid ecological changes, modern construction and other man-made damages to rock art; and relocation or transplantation of rock art sites considering the nature and requirement of site specific which can not be preserved/protected in situ and have threats of urban development or construction of dam or water reservoir etc.

The Conservation work of the rock art in Jiangjunya of Lianyungang, Jiangsu province, Helanshan, Ningxia province, Yinshan, Inner Mongolia, Huayanshan and Guangxi province has got major investments and started much earlier than the other rock art sites (Fig. 7.9). In order to solidify fracture and deformation of rocks containing rock art, caused by explosions used in the coal industry in this area a pre-stressing force anchor rope is used to gave protection to the general cliff/rock portrait at Lianyungang in Jiangsu province. Bayanzhuoer region in Inner Mongolia employed remote-controlled video devices powered by solar energy to monitor rock sites in remote areas (Fig. 7.10). The Yinchuan World Rock Art Pavilion in Ningxia province was established in 2008 and opened to the public; this is the first rock art museum built in-situ in China. About 2,000 sq m of exhibiting area makes the pavilion the largest rock art museum in the world (Fig. 7.11). Since 2009, Guangxi has initiated the Huashan rock art conservation project and set out to bond and solidify the cracking rock in Huashan. In addition, due to the construction of a reservoir and power station in the Yin river basin in the Chifeng region, Inner Mongolia, the Jinsha river basin in Yunnan province, Yangtze river basin in the Guizhou and Sichuan provinces, rock art has been relocated.

THE MANAGEMENT OF ROCK ART

The issue of management of rock art and its application was proposed only a few years ago. Rock art, as a representation of the cultural and ecological environment in different areas in China, is the sum of life, customs, concepts, beliefs, skills and art consistently accumulated by different ethnic groups' in the past hundred or thousand years. Rock art provides a vivid depiction of life and cultural formats inherited by generations. This unique cultural resource created by the predecessors of different ethnic minorities, boast of rich multiple characteristics and are great cultural tourism resource and able to fulfill the need of tourists at psychological level. However, blindly catering to cultural tourism will undermine the ecological environment and the original ecological culture will be subject to deterioration. These are some of the management challenges possessed by the rock art sites. Therefore, the tourism development at rock art sites should be carried out from the perspective of holistic culture.

We need to collaborate with archaeological and museological sections to carry out systematic rock art investigation and recording. Also sort out the material systematically and publish it with the help of professional teams and methods for the purpose of creating awareness. Simultaneously, awareness about protection of rock art among the authorities and the general public should be increased by inter-disciplinary theoretical research. We also need to cooperate with tourism management authorities to develop the cultural tourism industry. These aspects call for related sections to establish specialised teams. This is the sole way to preserve China's rock art heritage and for the benefit of the present society.

The cultural tourism should be managed keeping in mind the principles of protection, development and planning. Some people are paying attention to the construction of a rock art database, (considering that rock art as a cultural heritage can be developed into a new model of professional inquiry), cultural communication, disseminating education and commercial development in the Internet era. They have contributed greatly to the establishment of virtual museums online and offered a wide array of relatively feasible solutions. Others are proposing that setting up of an 'archaeological park' is the best solution for the management of rock art sites. Currently, this model is being gradually developed in the hope that it will advance Chinese rock art's research and conservation as well as generate socioeconomic benefits through tourism (Fig. 7.12).

For example, Helanshan rock art in Ningxia, which is being promoted by the region's autonomous tourism bureau, as this rock art site is combined with the tourist circuit of the area. With the opening of the Yinchuan World Rock Art Pavilion, it has started holding an annual Helanshan Rock Art Festival, which aims at using rock art to facilitate research, conservation and development of rock art by building a public platform for communicating about culture among the government, media and the public. Huashan rock art in Guangxi province is clustered along the banks of River Zuo and has been especially developed into a rock art tourist attraction which explores a new model of cultural tourism. RARAC has formed specialised project teams and undertaken a national research project with the focus on conservation and management policy, research of rock art and the construction of a database. Since the development and management of rock art involves commercial implications, this calls for further attention and devotion from all sections of the community and the government (Fig. 7.13).

CONCLUSIONS

The study of Chinese rock art as a discipline has its own place in Chinese academic circles. This can be seen in the increasing number of institutions and scholars involved in investigation and research of rock art. This shows the development of the field in depth and breadth.

However, study of rock art faces many opportunities and challenges. In the 21st century, as we embrace the pluralism epoch, pure scientific research and interpretation of rock art will be taken on the agenda. With the continual enhancement of China's economic power and an increase in investments in culture, there have been upsurges in scientific research projects, publications, news and web pages relevant to rock art. However, the unresolved problem of dating rock art is still the main bottleneck in the research of Chinese rock art. Further, the differences between Chinese culture and its foreign counterparts results in the phenomenon of different academic cognitions. For instance, in China the English phrase 'rock art' is also synonymous with 'rock & roll'. This has affected domestic Chinese researchers' online search and resulted in a wrong notion of rock art popularise in the country

REFERENCES

Anati, Emmanuel (2010), *World Rock Art—the Primordial Language*. Oxford: Archaeopress, Gordon House.

Chen, Fan (2010), *On Physical Protection of Rock Art-A Case Study of Rock Art Protection in Cangyuan, Yunnan Province*. China Three Gorges Tribune.

Lifeng, Zhu, Yang Qinglin and Sun Xiaoyong (2012), *New Century of Rock Art in Internet Age—Guidelines of Digital Development of Chinese Rock Art*. Chinese Folk Art.

Shanlin, Gai (1995), *Rock Art Studies*. Beijing: Bibliographical Documents Publishing House.

Xihong, Shu and Xiangshi, Li (2007), *Rock Art and Nomadic Culture*. Shanghai: Ancient Books of Shanghai Publishing House.

Yaoliang, Song (1992), *Prehistoric Face Rock Paintings of China*. Shanghai: Sanliang Publishing.

Yasha, Zhang (2006), *Rock Art in Tibet*. Xining: Qinghai People's Publishing House.

Zhaofu, Chen (1991), *History of Rock Art in China*. Shanghai: Shanghai People's Publishing House.

This paper is translated by Yang Xiaoyi from Chinese to English.

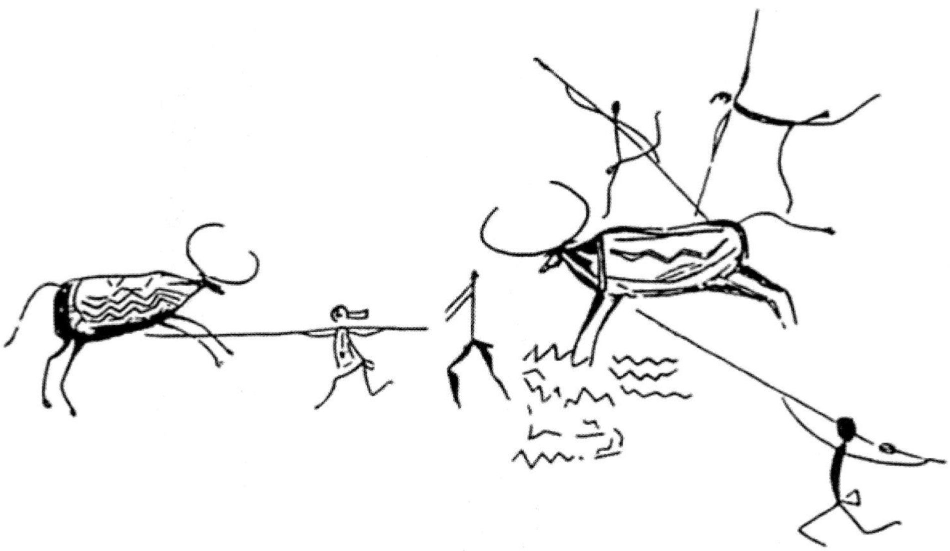

8

Distinct Dominant Traits in the Rock Art of Eastern India with Special Reference to the Rock Art of Southern Bihar and Adjoining Jharkhand

A.K. Prasad

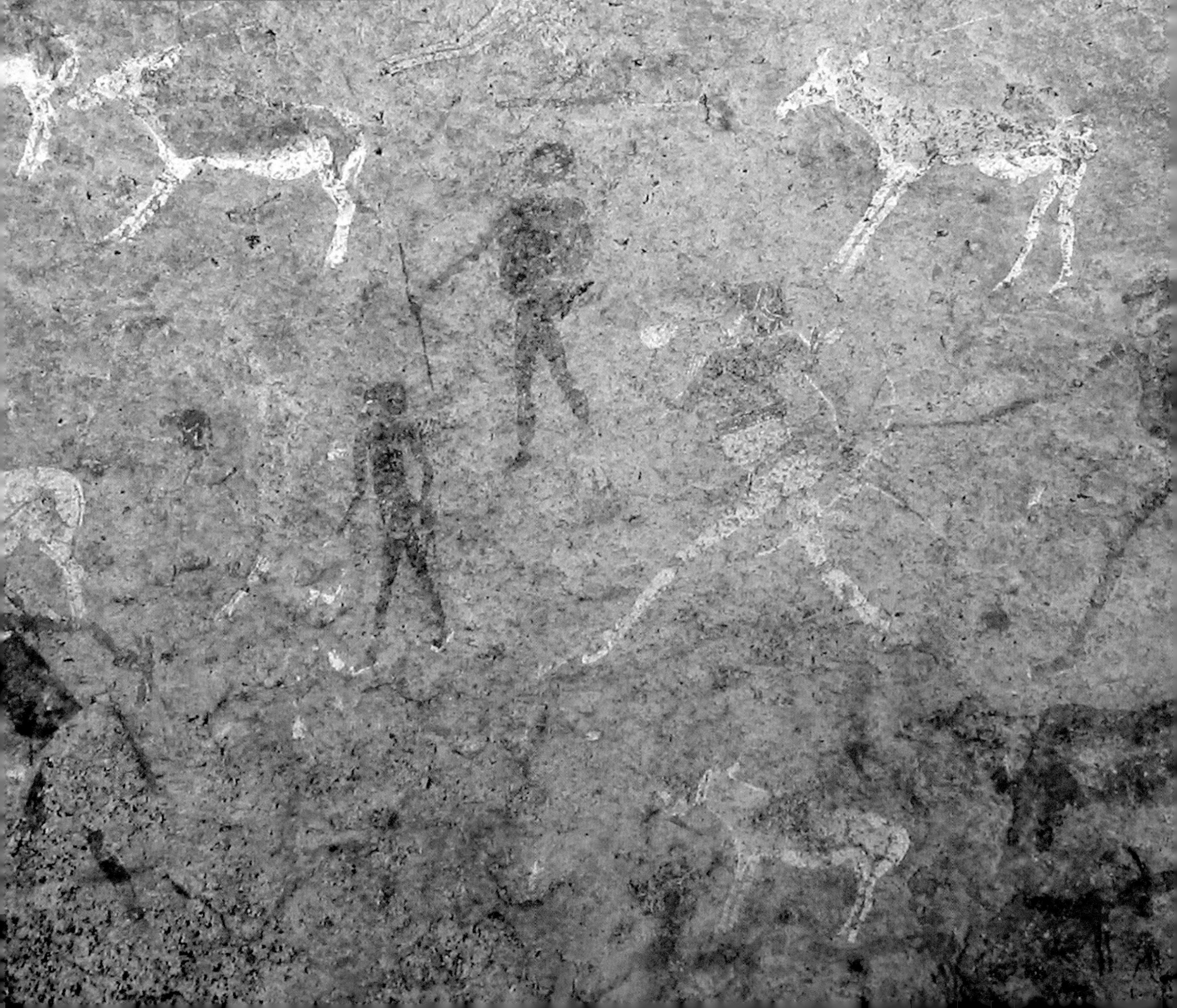

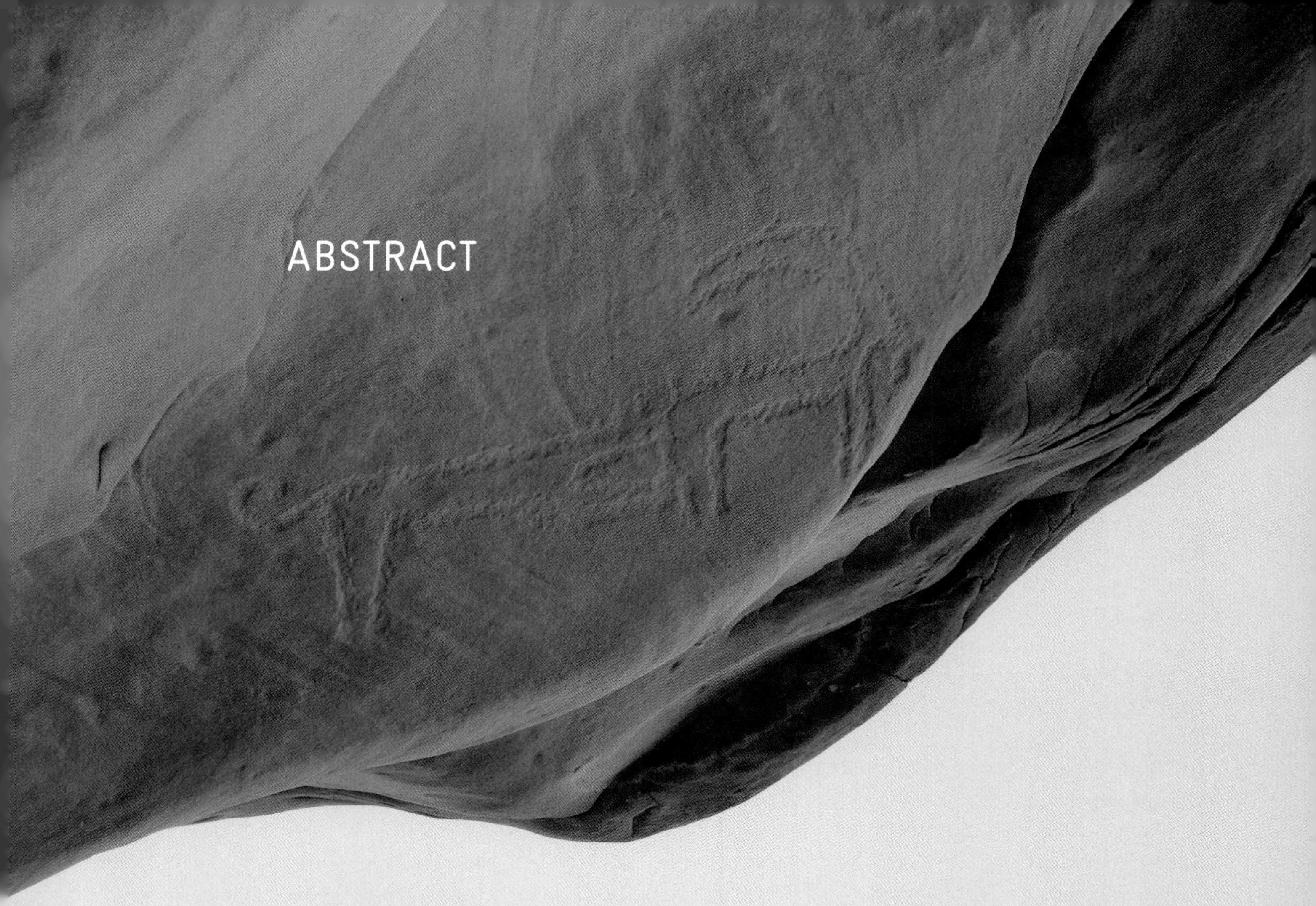

ABSTRACT

When we think of the Indian rock art, a picture of the central Indian rock art region emerges with three main characteristics—dynamism and vigour of 'S' type figures, almost equal depiction of human and animals and a presence of mixed motivational aspects. However, Dr. Prasad's original discovery of about 90 rock shelters/caves/open rock surfaces containing prehistoric rock paintings, engravings and ancient rock inscriptions in the remote, inaccessible and dangerous Vindhyan hills in Nawada, Jamui, Gaya and Nalanda districts of Bihar and the adjoining Giridih and Kodarma districts (now in Jharkhand) during the 1990s points towards the prevalence of different motivational, thematic and stylistic traits in eastern India.

INTRODUCTION

India is one of the six richest rock art regions in the world, others being South-western Europe, North Africa, South Africa, Australia and Russia. Except a few states in the north-east rock art is found in almost all the states in India. The rock art sites in eastern India are located mainly in the tribal belts of the Chotanagpur Plateau- a northern extension of the Vindhyan ranges. The Chotanagpur Plateau encompasses parts of the modern states of Bihar (southern parts), Jharkhand, Odisha (north- western portion) and West Bengal (Purulia district).

Major concentration of rock art in eastern India is found in the very remote, inaccessible and extremely dangerous forested hills in Nawada and Jamui districts in Bihar and adjoining Giridih, Kodarma and Hazaribagh districts in Jharkhand. Rock art sites with majority of Petroglyphs in Odisha are located in its western districts of Sundargarh, Sambalpur Jharsuguda, Kalahandi, Mayurbhanj and Suvarnapur (Map 8.1).

A large number of prehistoric rock paintings and petroglyphs discovered in Bihar, Jharkhand and Odisha during the last two decades point towards prevalence of some distinct thematic, motivational and stylistic traits in eastern India. In the present paper it would be an endeavour to briefly describe these special traits which distinguish the rock art of eastern India from other Indian rock art regions particularly the rock art of Central India.

In the present state of Bihar Prehistoric rock paintings were discovered for the first time by the author in the Ranigadar forest on 22nd January 1994. Subsequent explorations by him in this region during the next four years resulted in discovery of 86 painted rock shelters/caves containing prehistoric rock paintings, petroglyphs, cup marks and rare ancient inscriptions. 10 open rock surfaces comprising of important engravings, 13 Stone Age tools factory sites, four megalith sites and four Buddhist cave monasteries were also discovered besides the rock paintings and rock inscriptions (Prasad, A. K. 2003 -04). The area of discovery forms part of Nawada and Jamui districts in Bihar and Giridih and Kodarma districts in the newly carved out state of Jharkhand. Five rock shelters/caves containing rock paintings, four Buddhist cave monasteries and five Palaeolithic tools factory sites were also discovered by the author in the Rajgir-Giriak-Jethian hills in Nalanda and Gaya and Nawada districts during the field work in 2010 (Prasad, A. K. 2011). Some Rock shelters/caves containing prehistoric rock paintings have also been reported in the Kaimur hills (an extension of the Mirzapur rock art region in Uttar Pradesh) in Kaimur and Rohtas districts in Bihar (not described in the present paper as it forms part of the Central India rock art region).

In the present state of Jharkhand, before the discovery of prehistoric rock paintings in Giridih and Kodarma districts by the author, a rich rock art site was reported slightly earlier in Hazaribagh district during 1991. The reported site- Isco was brought to notice of a school teacher by his students. The information reached Bulu Imam, an environmentalist who not only announced the find to the press but also found several more painted rock shelters/caves in this region. Besides Isco other important rock art sites are Thethangi, Nautangwa and Saraiya (Neumayer, E.1994-95).

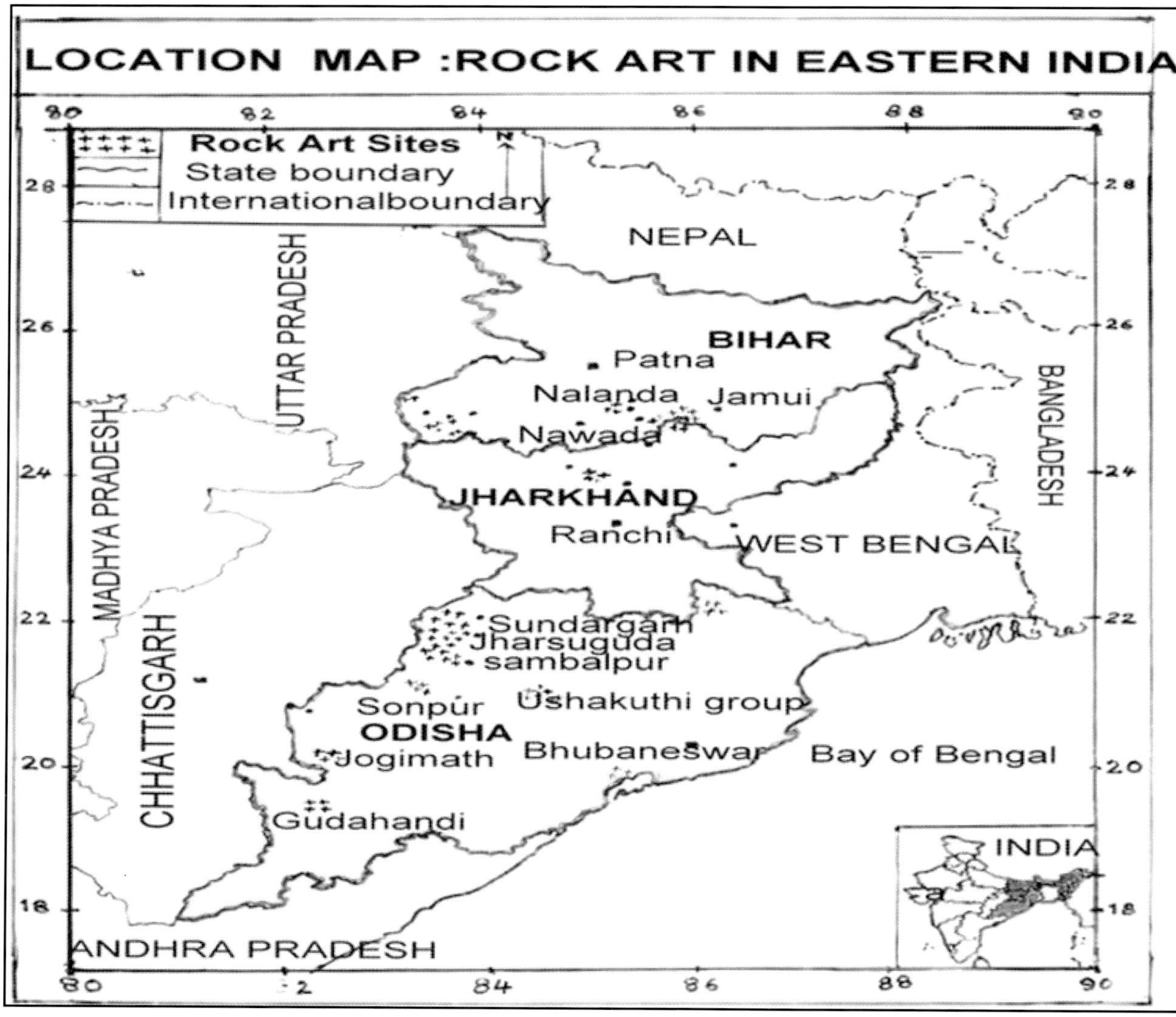

Map 8.1 Major rock art sites in eastern India (Bihar, Jharkhand and Odisha).

In Odisha evidences of rock engravings were reported much earlier in 1933 by K. P. Jayaswal from the rock shelter of Vikramkhol in the Jharsuguda district (erstwhile Sambalpur district) but it did not cause any long standing interest and only during the 1970s and 1980s further rock art was observed in Sambalpur and Sundargarh. Neumayer and Bahera also reported about five painted rock shelters during 1992-93. Subsequently Sadasiba Pradhan took up extensive explorations in this region which has resulted in reporting and documentation of 40 new rock art sites along with the earlier 15 rock art sites in Odisha. Out of the 55 rock shelters 31 contain engravings, nine engravings along with paintings and 15 rock shelters exclusively rock paintings (Pradhan, S. 2001).

In addition to the above mentioned painted rock shelters/caves there must be many more still hidden in the remote, dangerous and vast forested hills in eastern India especially in the Jharkhand region, awaiting further extensive explorations.

GEOMORPHOLOGY OF THE CHOTANAGPUR PLATEAU

Geology

Chotanagpur marks the north-eastern projection of the Indian peninsula, being one of the major components of eastern plateaus. It is composed mainly of Archaean granite and gneiss rocks with patches of Dharwar rocks (phyllite, mica-schists etc.) on the northern and southern margins, the latter being very conspicuous in the iron ore and Kolhan series covering greater part of Singhbhum district. In the structural trough of the Damodar valley occur Gondwana rocks consisting of sand stone of great thickness with some slate and clay. The Pat land on the western margin is covered with Deccan trap which is converted in to laterite and bauxite due to weathering. The Rajmahal hills in the north-eastern fringe of the plateau are also covered with lava flows which were probably linked with the initiation of the Himalayan orogeny (Singh, R. L. 2008).

Relief and Drainage

Chotangpur virtually consists of a series of plateaus standing at different level of elevation, the highest general elevation of about 1100 m being in the mid-western portion known as the Pat lands. From here the land descends in all directions in a series of steps particularly towards the east until it merges gradually with the Lower Ganga plain.

Chotanagpur is drained in different directions by numerous rivers and streams of which the South Koel, the North Koel, the Subarnarekha, the Damodar and the Barakar rivers have developed extensive drainage basins while the Ajai, the Mor, the Brahmani, the Gumani etc. drain the Rajmahal highlands in parallel channels towards the West Bengal plain. The northern fringe of plateau is drained by numerous small tributaries of the Punpun, the Phalgu, the Sakri and the Kiul rivers towards the South Bihar plain.

Climate

Chotanagpur experiences the characteristic monsoon climate having a seasonal rhythm running through all the elements of weather. With the commencement of the hot weather in March the temperature rises sharply until May, the monthly mean ranging between 29 C and 32 C. During the monsoon season (June-October) the average rainfall ranges between 100 to above 150 cm. The cold season commences in November and lasts till February.

Population

The majority of population in Chotanagpur is rural including considerable tribal population in the different parts. There are some 25 different tribes having their own respective dialects and distinctive ways. The main tribes are Munda, Oraon, Santhal, Ho, Kharia, Birhor, Paharia and Asur. Southern Bihar and adjoining Jharkhand is inhabited mainly by the Santhals. The Birhor in small number still lead the life style of hunters and gatherers shifting frequently from one location to another. Orissa also has considerable tribal population comprising 62 tribes. The Sauras and Juangs are two important tribes known for their paintings and engravings respectively (Pradhan, S. 2001).

Flora and Fauna

Although much of the original vegetal cover has been depleted by reckless felling, some pockets of valuable forest still lie intact in the inaccessible parts of Chotanagpur. Sal (Shorea robusta) is extensively found in the interior. Other trees found are Mahua, Khair, Harra, Palas, Asan, Bel, Ber, Kalond, Piar, bamboo etc.

The strength of wild animals has gone down considerably due to illegal poaching and destruction of the forest cover. Still some of them are found in good numbers especially in the foothills. These include bear, wild boar, swamp deer, blue bull, monkey, rabbit etc. and occasionally leopard, tiger and elephant. The area is also infested with various types of snakes such as python, cobra, *Karait*, viper as well as scorpions.

DISTINCT DOMINANT TRAITS IN THE ROCK ART OF EASTERN INDIA

The rock art of southern Bihar, Jharkhand and north–western Odisha forming part of eastern India share many common features with the other rock art regions of India in respect of subject matter, colour-scheme, style, motivation, superimposition and state of preservation. However, the discovery of a large number of rock paintings and engravings in this region points towards prevalence of some distinctive thematic, motivational and stylistic traits.

DISTINCT THEMATIC TRAITS

As the subject- matter of the rock art of eastern India is concerned, it has certain very special and unique features which distinguish it from the other Indian rock art regions. The important distinctive features are described below:

1. Predominance Symbols and Intricate/Geometric signs: Symbols, intricate designs and geometric signs are important components of prehistoric art all over the world. The symbols include variations/combinations of circle, square, rectangle, wheel, cross, etc. The intricate designs comprise of rhombic meanders, concentric circles, spirals and their variants. Geometric signs mainly include grids, zigzags, dots, chevrons, curves, combinations of triangles and rectangles.

One of the biases about the early art development emanating from Western Europe is that it consists largely of 'naturalistic' images of objects, notably of large animals. This is not true to the Franco-Cantabrian region of Western Europe itself where figurative representations are outnumbered more than three times by non-figurative art (Bednarik, R. G., 1991). Closure inspection of global rock art sites shows that pre-figurative rock art preceded figurative one in most cases (Sonawane, V. H. 1997).Though the symbols/ Geometric signs/intricate designs are a typical feature of the art of the early hunters and gatherers in India, they are absent from the later art of the agriculturists and cattle-keepers (Neumayer, Erwin. 1993). However, this is not so in case of eastern India where intricate/ geometric signs remained important component of rock art right from the Upper Palaeolithic/Mesolithic period down to the early medieval era (Prasad, A. K. 2006).

In India as well as abroad generally predominance of either the animal figures or the human figures or equal proportion of both is observed in the rock paintings. However,

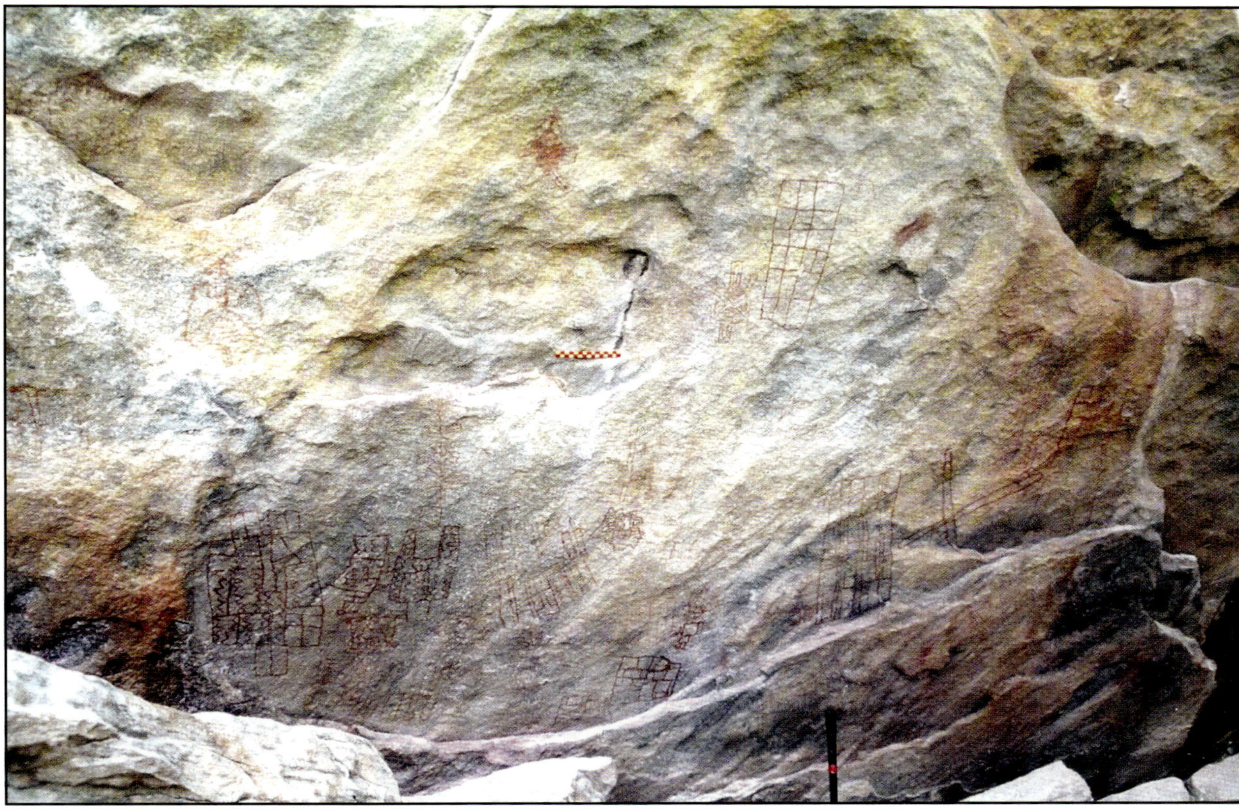

Fig. 8.1 Symbols and Intricate geometric signs from Rock Shelter XI. B.1. (Janamsthan Hills, Bihar).

in case of the eastern Indian rock art, there is obvious predominance of symbols and intricate/geometric designs. These are found in considerable numbers in each and every painted rock shelter/cave in the Nawada, Jamui, Nalanda and Gaya districts in southern Bihar (Fig. 8.1) and the adjoining districts of Giridih and Kodarma in Jharkhand (Fig. 8.2). Similar is the case in Hazaribagh and Chatra districts in

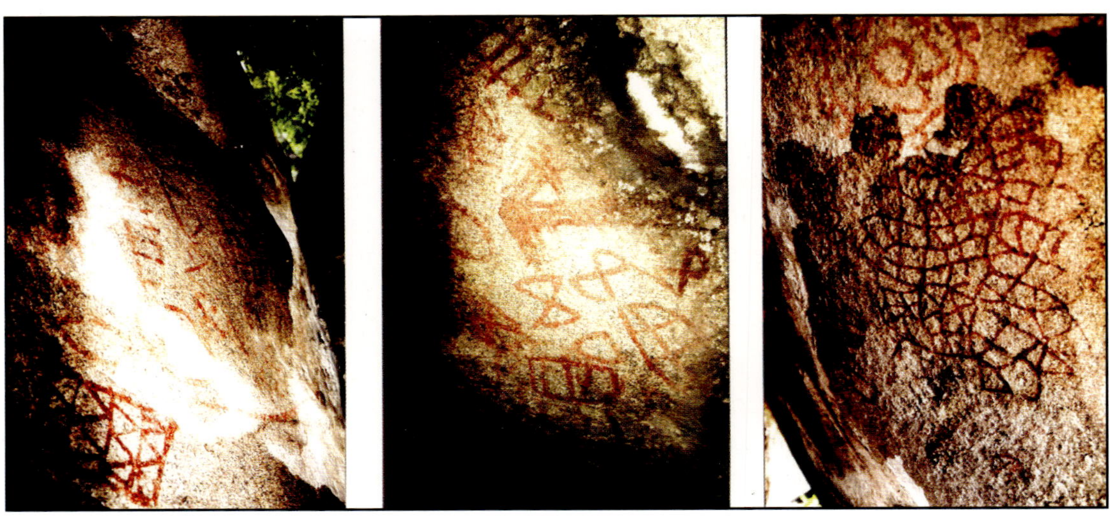

Fig. 8.2 Symbols and intricate geometric signs in Cave I.A. 8. (Bardauni, Jharkhand).

Fig. 8.3 Symbols and Intricate geometric signs from Rock Shelter. Isko, Raham and Tirthangi (Hazaribagh, Jharkhand). (Kind courtesy: Erwin Neumayer)

Jharkhand (Fig. 8.3). Here also the most eye-striking features of the paintings are the overwhelmingly geometric patterns with intricate designs of many variations (Neumayer, Erwin. 1994-95). In Odisha too the subject- matter is by and large non-figurative and non-thematic (Pradhan, S. 2001). What is seen is a host of intricate and enigmatic geometric and non-geometric patterns made of a host of spiral lines, cross-hatches, zigzag lines (Fig. 8.4).

In this aspect the rock art of eastern India differs from the cave art of Europe which is mainly zoomorphic and the rock art of Spanish- Levant, South Africa and Central India which have an almost equal percentage of human and animal figures. It also differs from the rock art of Chambal valley where animals are the most frequent subject matter (Kumar, G. 1992) and that of Mirzapur (Tiwari, R. 1990) and Kumaon Himalayas (Mathpal, Y. 1995) where human figures constitute the main body of the painted motifs.

2. Ritualistic Hunting Scenes: Another distinct feature of the eastern Indian rock art is that in the hunting scenes the archers are generally not shown engaged

in actual hunt which is so much common phenomenon in the Central Indian paintings (RS. II. C.2, XI.C.1, I.A.8. etc.). Here the hunting scenes are primarily symbolic and ritualistic in nature (Fig. 8.5).

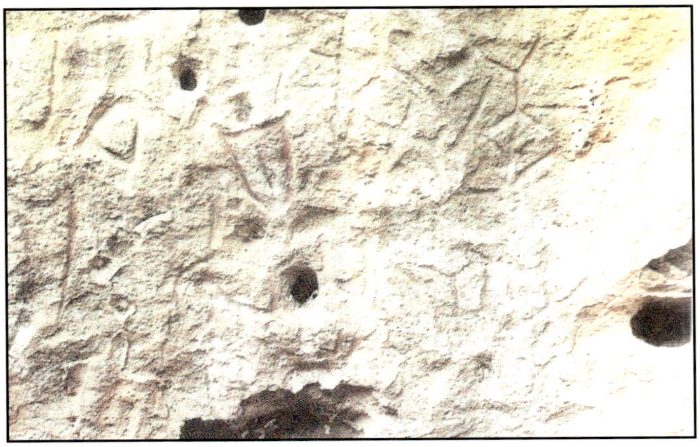

3. Frequent Depiction of Snakes: The frequent depiction of snakes in several painted rock shelters/caves in eastern India and especially the southern Bihar and adjoining Jharkhand (RS. IV. A.1, I. A. 8. X. B.1. II.D.2 etc,) is another special feature of this rock art region. Development of the 'Naga Cult' in Bihar and subsequently in whole of India may have remote links with such paintings of this rock art region. A large number of terracotta figurines found at the Chalcolithic sites of Chirand, Sonepur and some other sites in Bihar substantiate this premise.

Fig. 8.4 Engraved symbols and geometric signs from Tongo (Odisha).

4. Battle scenes between the tribal and the outsiders, so common in the Central Indian rock paintings are all together absent in the rock paintings of this region.

Fig. 8.5 Ritualistic Hunting and Dancing scenes in Rock Shelter II.C.2 (Jharanwa, Bihar).

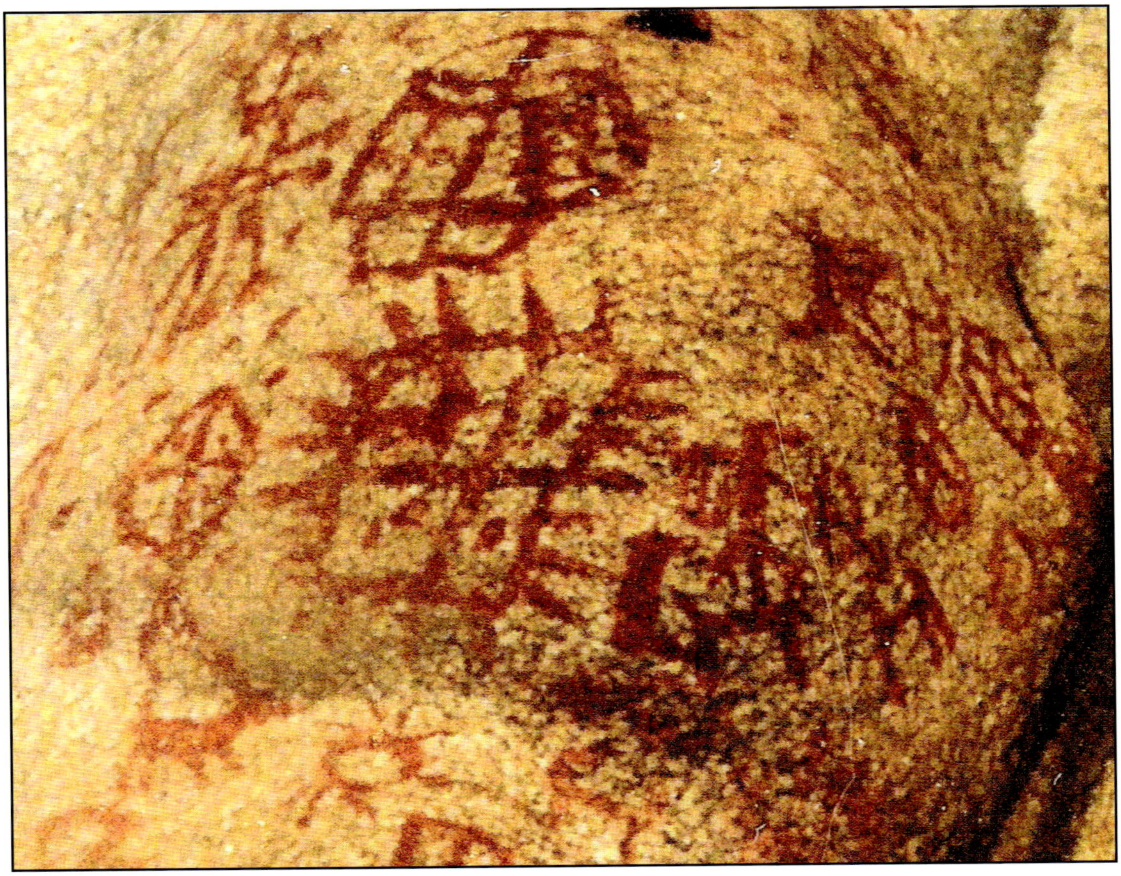

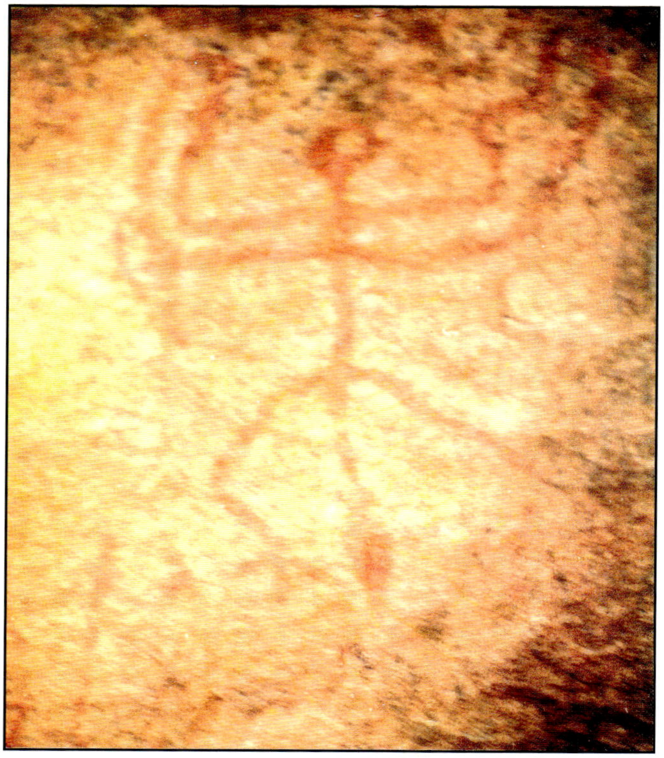

Fig. 8.6 Figure of a Shaman with enormous phallus in Rock Shelter IX.A.1 (Ghasani, Jharkhand).

5. Horse riders and humans with bow and arrows and occasionally with spear have been depicted in the rock paintings of this region but chariots or other wheeled vehicles drawn by animals, procession scenes of horse riders and elephant riders and armed warriors are absent in the rock paintings in southern Bihar and adjoining Jharkhand. Same trend is also observed in the rock art of Odisha (Pradhan, S.1995).

6. Some human figures in all other rock art sites are shown nude while others are depicted wearing some kind of cloth around their waists. But surprisingly it is all together missing in the prehistoric paintings of this region except a few figures of the goddess of fertility.

7. Phallic Human/Animal Figures are rare in Indian rock art sites but it is very common in the paintings of eastern India and especially that of southern Bihar and adjoining Jharkhand. In the rock art of these two states the Shamans/wizards are generally shown with unusually long phalluses (R.S.- I.A.8, II.A.3, IX.A.1. etc.) and occasionally even animals have been depicted with aroused phalluses (Fig. 8.6).

8. The animals are shown being hunted in herds in the rock paintings of Central India, Europe & Africa but this region's rock art contains maximum number of solitary hunted animal scenes. (R.S.- II.C.2, V.B.1, I.A.8, etc.). This feature can also be observed in the neighboring Mirzapur rock paintings.

9. In Central India intricate/geometric motifs are used for filling the body of human and animal figures where as in the rock art of eastern India they are independent patterns.

10. Kharoshti and Brahmi-Kharoshti rock inscriptions: Brahmi/Shankh inscriptions in small numbers are found in some other Indian rock art sites. However, in the rock art of southern Bihar and adjoining Jharkhand not only Brahmi and Shankh inscriptions but Kharoshti and Brahmi-Kharoshti inscriptions are also found on a very large scale (R.S.- II.A 2, III. A.2, IV.A.1, VI.A.1, X.B.1, XVI.A.11, XVII.A.5, XXV.A.2 etc.). Datable from the 1st century BCE to 8th century CE these rare rock inscriptions have important bearings on the history of India (Mukherjee, B. N.1997). As such epigraphically this rock art region is extremely important and perhaps the richest one in India as far as Kharoshti and Kharoshti- Brahmi inscriptions are concerned (Fig. 8.7).

11. Buddhist Cave Monasteries: Buddhism finds an important place in the painted rock shelters/caves in southern Bihar and adjoining Jharkhand. The Buddhist wheel of

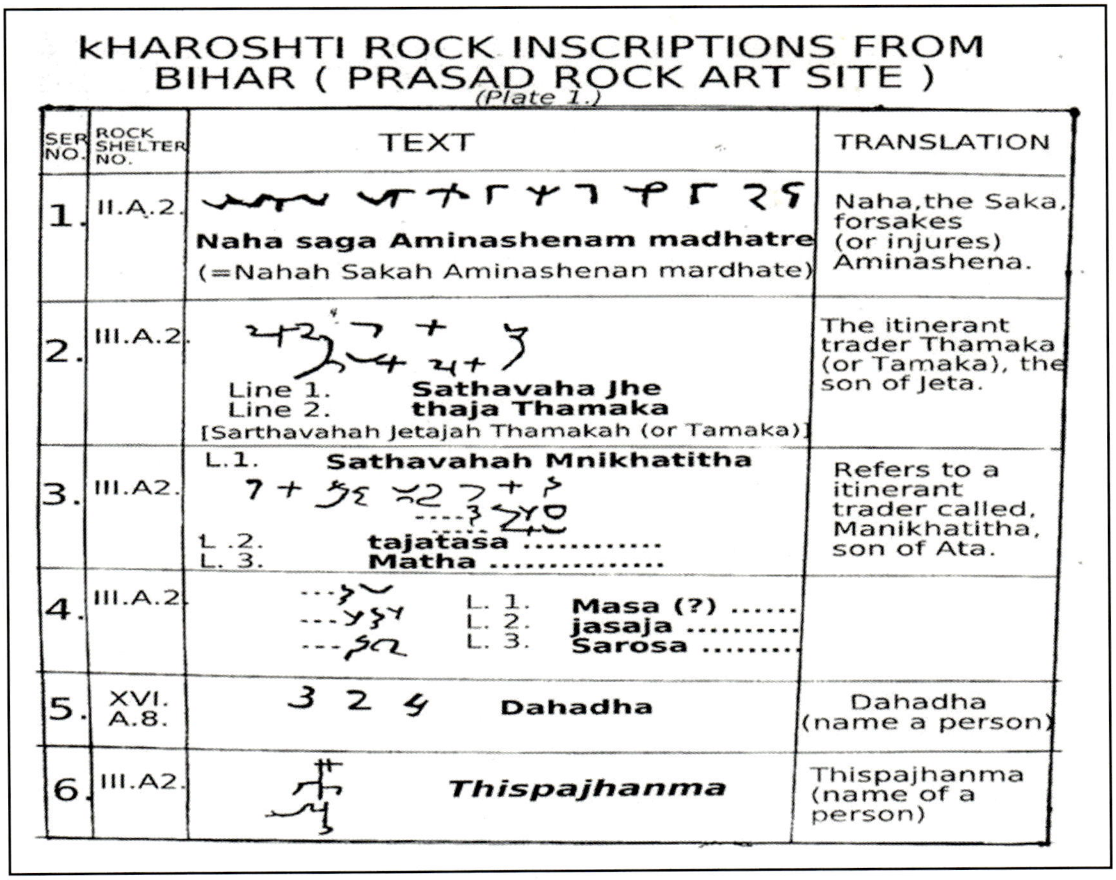

kHAROSHTI ROCK INSCRIPTIONS FROM BIHAR (PRASAD ROCK ART SITE)
(Plate 1.)

SER NO.	ROCK SHELTER NO.	TEXT	TRANSLATION
1.	II.A.2.	**Naha saga Aminashenam madhatre** (=Nahah Sakah Aminashenan mardhate)	Naha, the Saka, forsakes (or injures) Aminashena.
2.	III.A.2.	Line 1. **Sathavaha Jhe** Line 2. **thaja Thamaka** [Sarthavahah Jetajah Thamakah (or Tamaka)]	The itinerant trader Thamaka (or Tamaka), the son of Jeta.
3.	III.A2.	L.1. **Sathavahah Mnikhatitha** L.2. **tajatasa** .... L. 3. **Matha**	Refers to a itinerant trader called, Manikhatitha, son of Ata.
4.	III.A.2.	L. 1. **Masa (?)** ...... L. 2. **jasaja** .... L. 3. **Sarosa**	
5.	XVI. A.8.	**Dahadha**	Dahadha (name a person)
6.	III.A2.	***Thispajhanma***	Thispajhanma (name of a person)

Fig. 8.7 Kharoshti inscriptions from the painted rock shelters in Bihar.

Law (*Dharma chakra)* and other painted and some engraved figures connected with Buddhism are found in several painted rock shelters/ caves/open rock surfaces. Some painted caves in this region were also converted into Buddhist cave monasteries during the early historic period after minor modifications. Buddhist cave monasteries VI.A.1, VI.A.2, VI.B.1, and XII.A.1 in the Vindhyan foot hills of Kowakol and some other cave monasteries in the Giriak-Rajgir-Jethian hills discovered by the author must have played important role in the Buddhist activities for a very long span of time. The author's discovery of a Buddhist Wheel of Law (*Dharma-chakra*) engraved on the granite floor of a Buddhist cave monastery in the Ragir hills is the only one of its type discovered so far in India. The clay/terracotta tablets (Fig. 8.8) and seals containing Kharoshti- Brahmi and Brahmi inscriptions and other archaeological evidences from cave monastery VI.A.1 clearly indicate that these monasteries were continuously occupied at least from 2nd century CE to 9th/10th century CE (Prasad, A. K. 2009). These were visited by not only the local devotees but also by the pilgrims/travellers from the North- western section of the Indian sub continent.

12. **Engraved Figures of Humped Bulls:** The engraved figures of humped bulls in a triangular formation on a massive granite boulder in Rajabar forest (Fig. 8.9) in Kodarma district of Jharkhand are also a special feature of the rock art of eastern India (Prasad, A.

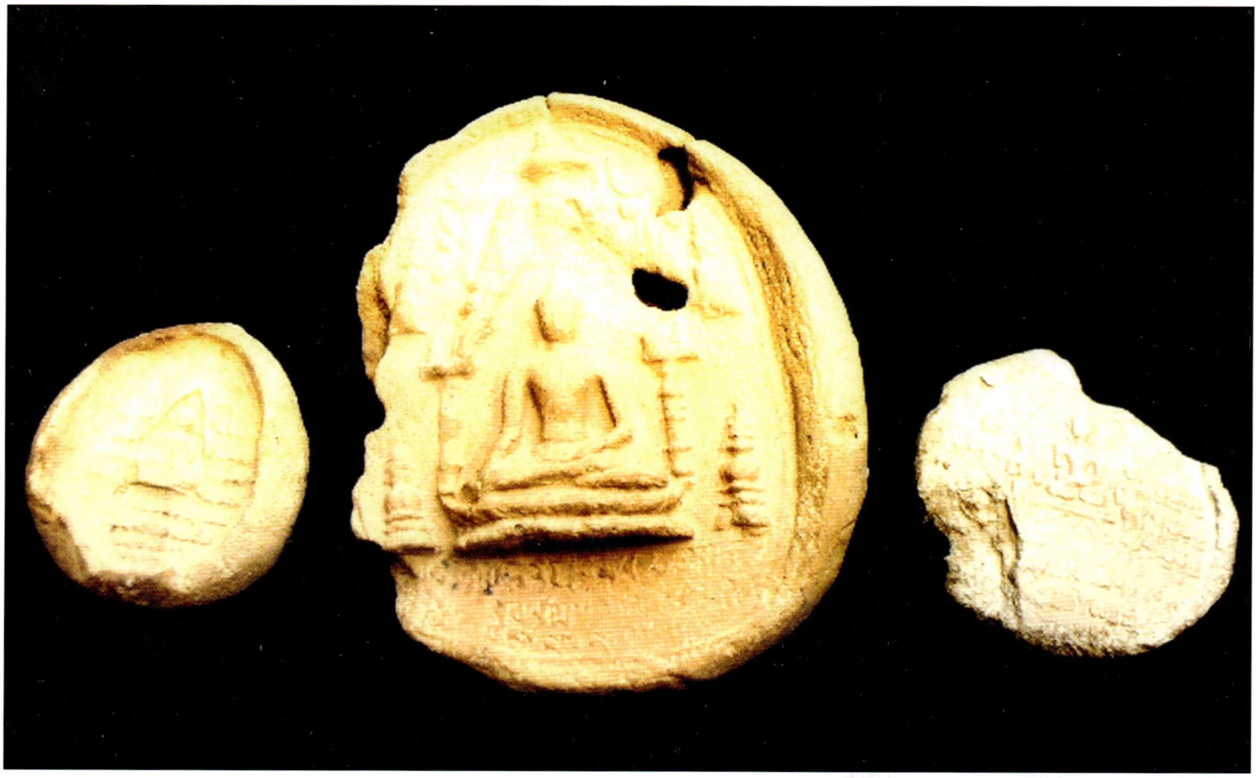

Fig. 8.8 Inscribed Clay tablets from the Buddhist cave monastery (Jogia, Bihar).

K. 2006). Surprisingly they have much resemblance with the figures of engraved humped bulls reported by Prof. Sundara in the far off rock art region of Karnataka in South India (Sundara, A. 2002).

13. Blue Colour Paintings: Use of blue colour in executing some paintings in Rock shelter XXV.A.2 in Gobindpur block of Nawada district in Bihar is another unique feature of this rock art region. This is the only rock art region in India endowed with blue colour paintings.

MOTIVATIONAL ASPECT

Motivation for prehistoric art is a controversial issue. Scholars such as Ed Lartet, M Boule, Salomon Reinach, Henri Breuil, Andre Leroi-Gourhan, Iegor Reznikoff, Michel Dauvois, Margaret Conkey, Alexander Marshack, Robert Laden, Lewis-Williams, Michel Lorblanchet etc. have come up with their own interpretations. Various suggested motives include hunting magic, religion, shamanism, totemic, sexual significance, fertility rites, communication, ceremonial symbols, calendar devices, decoration and doodling (Wakankar, V. S. and Brooks, R.R.R., 1976). However, it seems reasonable to come to conclusion that no single explanation can suffice to explain all the multitudinous forms of Palaeolthic art. Different factors probably lay behind different forms of art in different caves, different localities and so on (Ucko, P. J. and Rosenfeld, A.1967). Most probably in addition to a primary motivational factor there might be some other factors also contributing towards the creation of rock art.

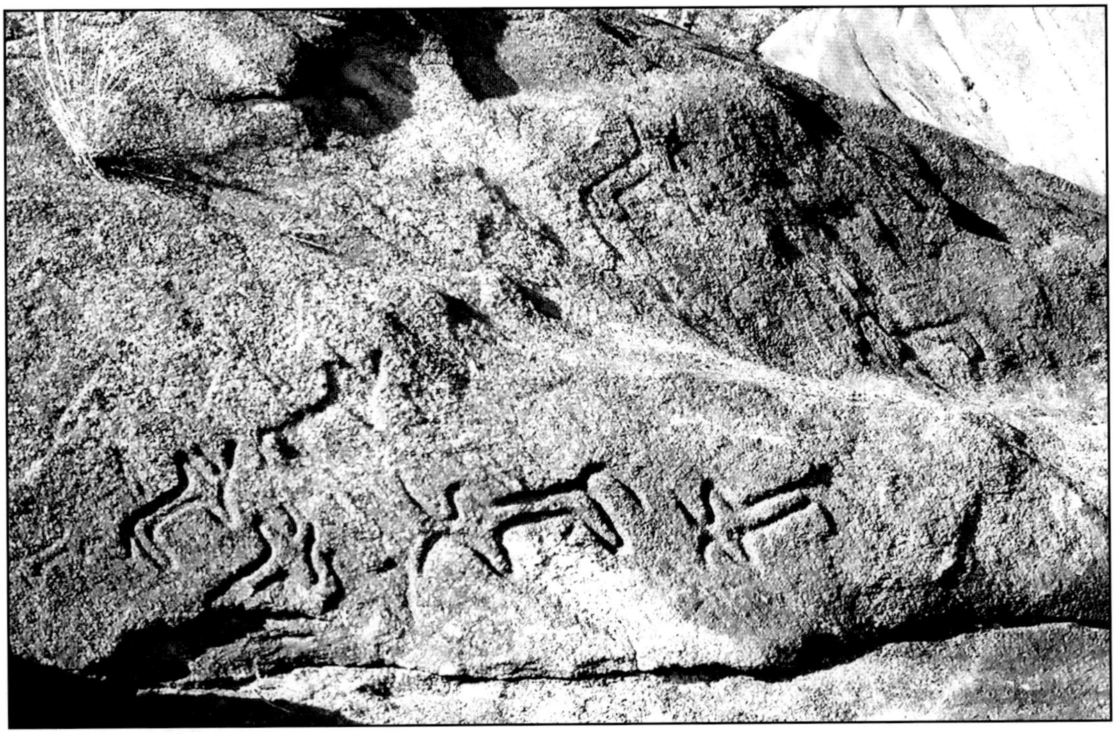

Fig. 8.9 Humped bulls engraved on a granite hillock in Rajabar forest (Rajabar, Jharkhand).

The prime motive behind making rock paintings and engravings in eastern India appears to be mainly ritualistic in which shamanism, hunting magic, religion and creative instinct have played important role. This trend is observed not only in the Upper Palaeolithic/early Mesolithic paintings but it continued throughout down to the early medieval period (Prasad, A. K. 2009). The ritualistic aspect in the rock art of eastern India is substantiated by the following factors:

1. Selection of Only One Rock Shelter Out of the Entire Cluster for Making Paintings

One of the most unique and distinctive feature of the rock art of southern Bihar and adjoining Jharkhand is that only one rock shelter out of the entire cluster of rock shelters/ caves was generally selected for making paintings. This specially selected painted rock shelter/cave was most probably considered a sacred place- a "temple" or a "community hall" for performing ritualistic and other important group activities. To a great extent this pattern is also observed in the rock art of Odisha. Although a large number of rock shelters exist in a geological formation, rock art is found in only a few of them. It is interesting to note that in Odisha the rock art sites are locally known either as *Lekhamoda* meaning rock shelter with writing or *Ushakuthi* meaning worship hall/ritual chamber (*Usha* = worship or ritual and *Kuthi* = hall or chamber) or *Ushakupa* (Usha=worship and kupa=cavity) meaning ritual cavity (Pradhan, S. 2001).

It is very interesting to observe that the tradition of using the painted rock shelters/ caves for performing rituals/other religious activities continued right from the Upper

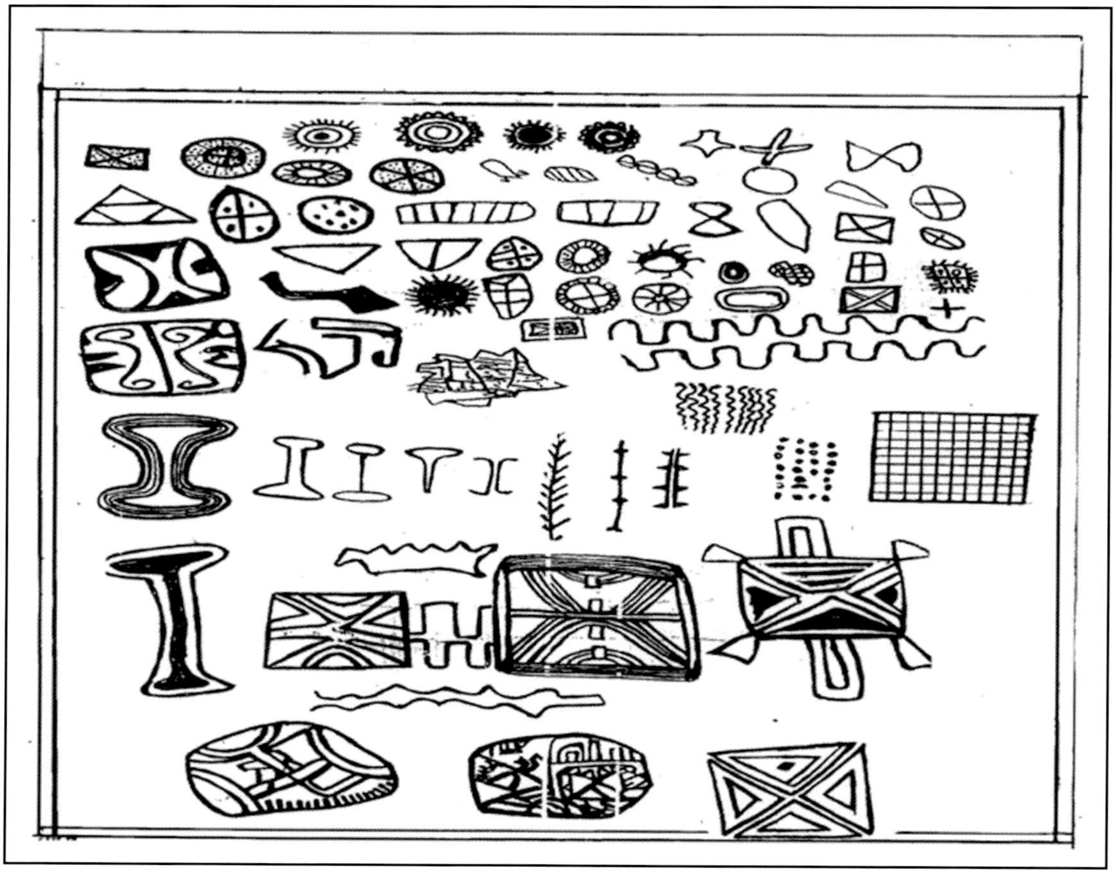

Fig. 8.10 Symbols and intricate geometric signs from the rock art of southern Bihar and adjoining Jharkhand.

Palaeolithic/Mesolithic periods down to the early medieval era. The Kharoshti and Kharoshti-Brahmi inscriptions found in various caves/shelters in southern Bihar and adjoining Jharkhand provide clear evidence that the painted rock shelters/caves continued to be used for performing local rituals during the early historical period even by the traders/travellers from the North-western section of the Indian sub-continent (Prasad, A.K. 2005-06).

2. Predominance of Symbols/Intricate/Geometric Signs

The intricate/geometric signs are considered as the most puzzling elements of Upper Palaeolithic art. For the most part, they have been explained as components of whatever hypothesis prevailed, in hunting magic or the maleness/femaleness dichotomy (Leakey, R.1996). As mentioned earlier there is obvious predominance of symbols, intricate designs/geometric signs in the rock art of eastern India (Fig. 8.10). They point towards ritualistic motive behind creation of the rock paintings. In Odisha also the repeated representation of the intricate/geometric patterns in engravings as well as in paintings gives an impression as if they are meant for transmission of some kind of a symbolic message like the Sauras (Mohapatra. 1991).

3. Depiction of Shamans in Various Forms

Shamans are found prominently depicted in the rock art of southern Bihar and adjoining Jharkhand (Caves/Rock shelters I.A.8, II.A.3, VI.A.1, IX.A.1, XI.B.1, XI.C.1, XVI.A.3 etc.). They are generally shown with heads resembling to some animal, bird or other peculiar form, spread out unusual legs and hands and generally with very big phalluses. They are surrounded by various types of symbols/geometric signs (Fig. 8.11). Some shamans are also shown on top of some unidentified animal forms. In one of the rock shelters (XI.C.1.) a Shaman is shown with five heads and five legs (Fig. 8.12). Another figure (seems female) depicted with enormous bellies probably pertains to the fertility cult.

Lewis-Williams, based on his extensive study of the art of San people of southern Africa has interpreted them as the telltale signs of shamanistic art- the images from a mind in the state of hallucination**.** He realised that the images of San art were not simple minded presentations of San life, as Western anthologists had long assumed. Instead, they were the product of shamans in a state of trance: the images were a connection with a shamanistic spirit world and were depictions of what the shaman saw during his hallucination. This is also applicable to a great extent in the context of the Santhals

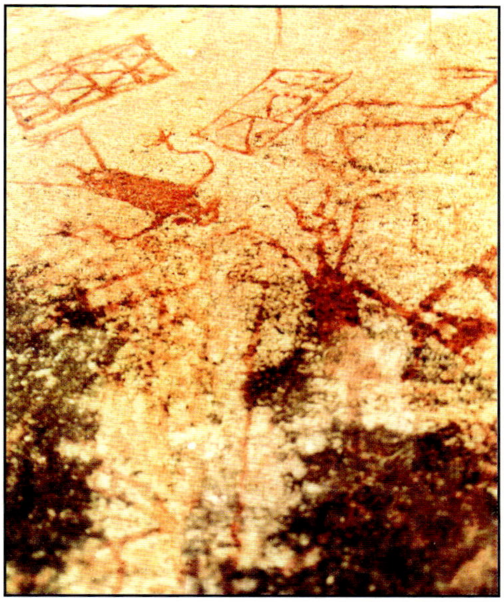

Fig. 8.11 Shamans depicted amidst symbols and geometric signs in Cave I A.8. (Bardauni, Jharkhand).

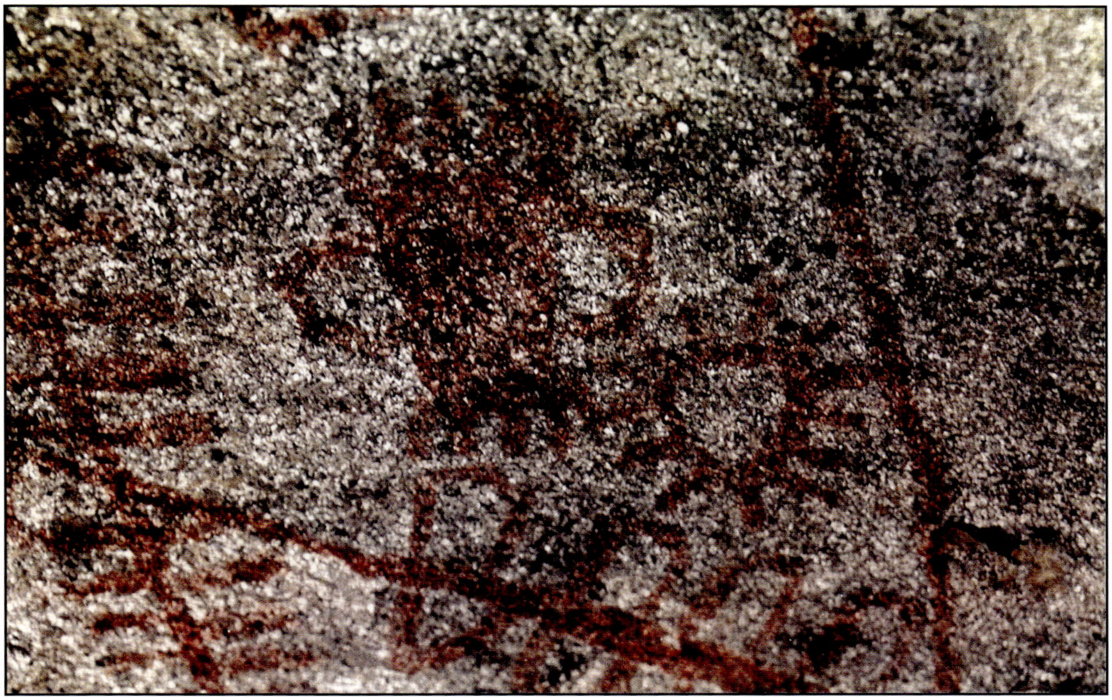

Fig. 8.12 Figure of a 5-headed and 5-legged Shaman in Rock Shelter XI.C.1. (Janamsthan hills, Bihar).

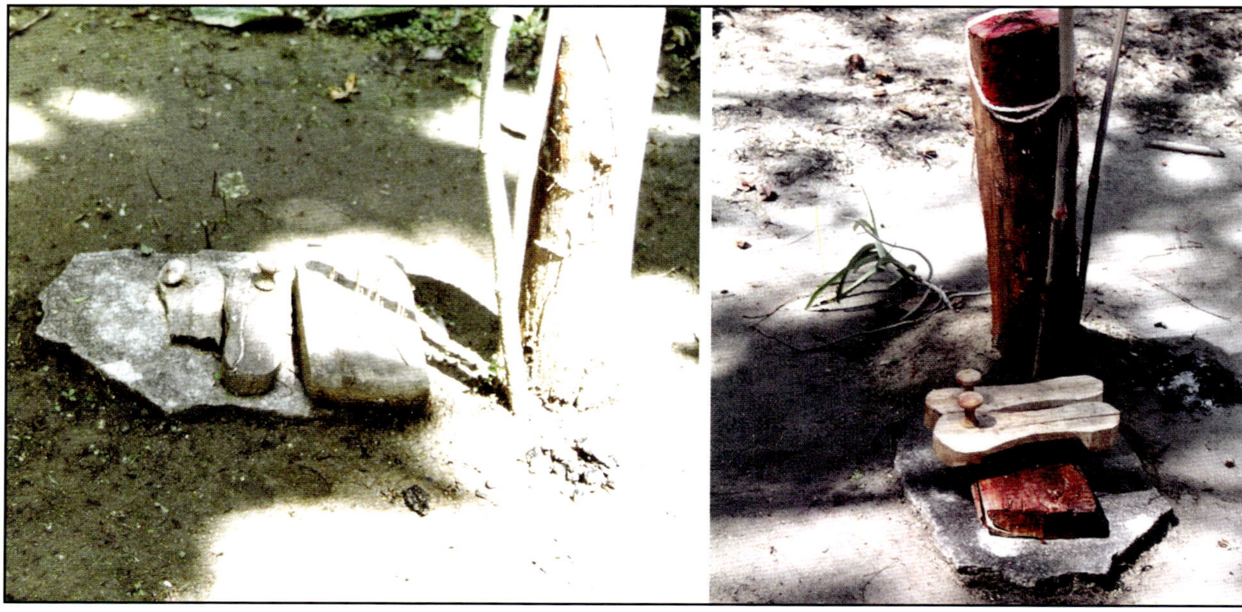

Fig. 8.13 Old and new wooden sleepers (*Kharaon*) and wooden plank containing iron nails used by the shamans (*Bhagats)* during the annual tribal ritual near Rock Shelter III.A.1 (Ranigadar, Bihar).

and other tribal communities of eastern India (Fig. 8.13). The male Shaman, locally called Bhagat and the female one known as *Bhaktini* (Fig. 8.14) still play important role in the religious, social and economic matters of the tribal communities in Bihar and Jharkhand as well as in Odisha.

4. Continuation of the Ritualistic Tradition

Plenty of epigraphic and pictorial evidences are found in the rock art region of southern Bihar and adjoining Jharkhand indicating continuation of the tradition of using painted rock shelters/caves for performing rituals even by the outsiders during the early historic period (Fig. 8.15). Various ritualistic scenes depicted in the rock paintings such as *sri-vrata* for getting favour of the goddess of wealth (Rock shelter III.A.2.), magical rites for harming opponents (Rock shelter II.A.2.), depiction of *Garuda-dhvaj* (Rock shelter III.A.2.) etc. point towards the ritualistic motive behind making rock art in eastern India (Prasad, A. K., 2005-06).

Fig. 8.14 A female shaman (*bhaktini*) performing a ritual in a Jharkhand village.

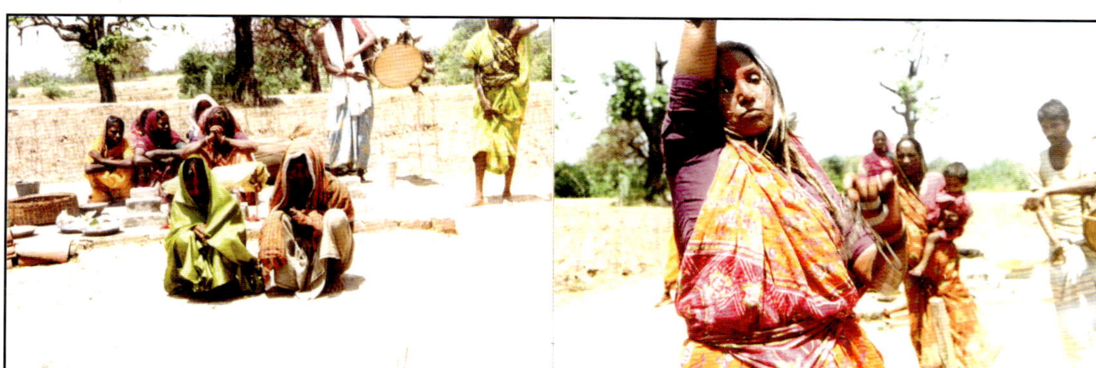

DISTINCT STYLISTIC TRAIT

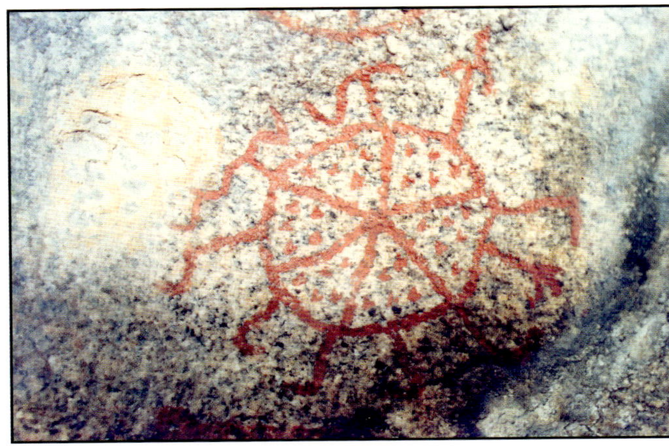

Fig. 8.15 A *Saka* trader performing a local ritual in Rock Shelter II.A.2.for harming his rival during 2nd century CE.

Though the rock art of eastern India shares with other Indian rock art regions many common features in respect of natural, geometric and schematic patterns as well as various styles such as silhouetted, decorative, partially filled and outlined, it also has a distinct stylistic feature. Here we find the figures comparatively simple and stiff instead of dynamic and vigorous as found in the Central Indian rock paintings. 'S' type figures, so common in the Central Indian rock art, are absent in the rock art of eastern India. Instead of dynamism and vigour of the 'S' type figures generally some sort of simplicity and rigidity is observed in the rock art of this region. Even the 'Stick' type figures found in some of the painted rock shelters/caves look relatively simple and static. This trend can also be observed in the rock art of Andhra Pradesh.

CONCLUSION

The rock art in eastern India has some unique and distinct features in spite of sharing some common features with other Indian rock art regions. There is obvious predominance of symbols and intricate/geometric designs. Other notable features include frequent depiction of shamans, ritualistic scenes, snakes, phallic human/animal figures and selection of generally only one rock shelte for executing paintings. All these unique features indicate towards the primary theme and motive being ritualistic in nature. Another distinctive trait is that stylistically the figures here are comparatively simple and stiff unlike the vigorous and dynamic Central Indian "S" type figures. Thus, based on the above observations it can be safely concluded that there is prevalence of some distinct thematic, motivational and stylistic traits in the rock art of eastern India. In no other rock art region in India and probably anywhere else in the world, predominance of symbols, intricate/geometric designs and ritualistic motives are so much obvious as observed in the rock art of eastern India.

REFERENCES

Bednarik, R.G. (1994), 'Art Origins', *Anthropos* 89: 169-180.

Chandramouli, N. (1994) 'Rock Art of Andhra Pradesh, South India', *Purakala* 5(1-2) 50-51.

Kumar, G. (1992), 'Rock Art of the Upper Chambal Valley', *Purakala* 3 (1-2): 17, 57.

Leakey, Richard (1996), *Origin of Humankind*. London: Phoenix, pp. 113-114.

Mahapatra, S. (1991), *Tribal Wall Paintings of Orissa*. Bhubaneswar: Orissa Lalit Kala Academy.

Mathpal, Y. (1995), *Rock Art in Kumaon Himalaya*. New Delhi: Aryan Books International, p. 61.

Mukherjee, B.N. (1997), 'Discovery of Kharoshti and Kharoshti-Brahmi Inscriptions in Bihar', *Journal of the Asiatic Society* XXXIX(3-4): 122-123.

Neumayer, E. (1993), *Lines on Stone-The Prehistoric Rock Art of India*. New Delhi: Manohar Publishers, p. 43.

Neumayer, E. (1994-95), Rock Paintings from Hazaribagh, Bihar, *Puratattva* 25: 81-83.

Pradhan, S. (2001), *Rock Art in Orissa*. New Delhi: Aryan Books International, pp. 26-27.

Pradhan, S. (1995), Rock Art in Orissa, *Purakala* 6(1- 2): 10-11.

Prasad, A.K. (2003-04), 'Important Discoveries of Prehistoric Rock Paintings, Ancient Inscriptions and Stone Age Tools in Southern Bihar and Adjoining Jharkhand', *Puratattva* 34: 69-76.

Prasad, A.K. (2011), *A Report on the Explorations in the Rajgir-Giriak-Jethian and Kowakol Hills/ Valleys: 2010* (Submitted to the ASI, New Delhi on 10th June 2011). pp. 5-51.

Prasad, A.K. 2005-06. 'Discovery of Pictorial-Cum-Epigraphic Depictions of Performing Local Rituals of the Ancient Magadha by the Traders/Travellers from Gandhar Region', *Puratattva* 36: 235-239.

Prasad, A.K. (2006), 'Rock Art in the Chhotanagpur Hills: Regional features', *Purakala* 16: 60-65.

Prasad, A.K. (2007), 'Deciphering Some Symbols/Geometric Designs in the Rock Art of Bihar and Jharkhand', in P.C. Reddy (ed.), *Exploring the Mind of Ancient Man*. New Delhi: Research India Press, pp. 357-363.

Prasad, A.K. (2009), 'Continuum in the Rock Art of Eastern India', in A.R. Sankhyan (ed.), *Asian Perspectives on Human Evolution*. New Delhi: Serials Publications, pp. 236-37.

Prasad, A.K. (2009), 'Important Discovery of Buddhist Antiquities in the Palaeolithic Caves of Magadha (South Bihar) and Adjoining Jharkhand', in S.P. Sharma and B. Labh (ed.), *The Ocean of Buddhist Wisdom*. Delhi: New Bhartiya Book Corporation, pp. 244-50.

Prasad, A.K. (2010), 'Discovery of Kharoshti and Kharoshti-Brahmi Rock Inscriptions in the Chotanagpur Hills of Southern Bihar', *Puratattva* 40: 127-134.

Singh, R.L. (2008), 'Chotanagpur Region', *India-A Regional Geography (ed.)*. Varanasi: National Geographical Society of India, pp. 650-55.

Sonawane, V. H. (1997), 'Upper Palaeolithic Art of India-A Fresh Look', *Purakala* 8(1-2): 8-9.

Sundara, A. (2002), 'Rock Art in Karnataka: Certain Geometrical Designs', *Purakala* 13(1-2): 52-53.

Tiwari, R. (1990), *Rock Paintings of Mirzapur*. Lucknow: Eureka Printers, pp. 17, 44.

Ucko, P.J. and A. Rosenfed (1967), *Palaeolithic Cave Art*. London: World University Library.

Wakankar, V.S. and R.R.R. Brooks (1976), *Stone Age Paintings of India*. Bombay: D.B. Taraporevala Sons & Co., p. 61.

9

Men and Cultures at the End of the Late Ice Age in the North of Perigord: Continuities and Ruptures

Patrick Paillet

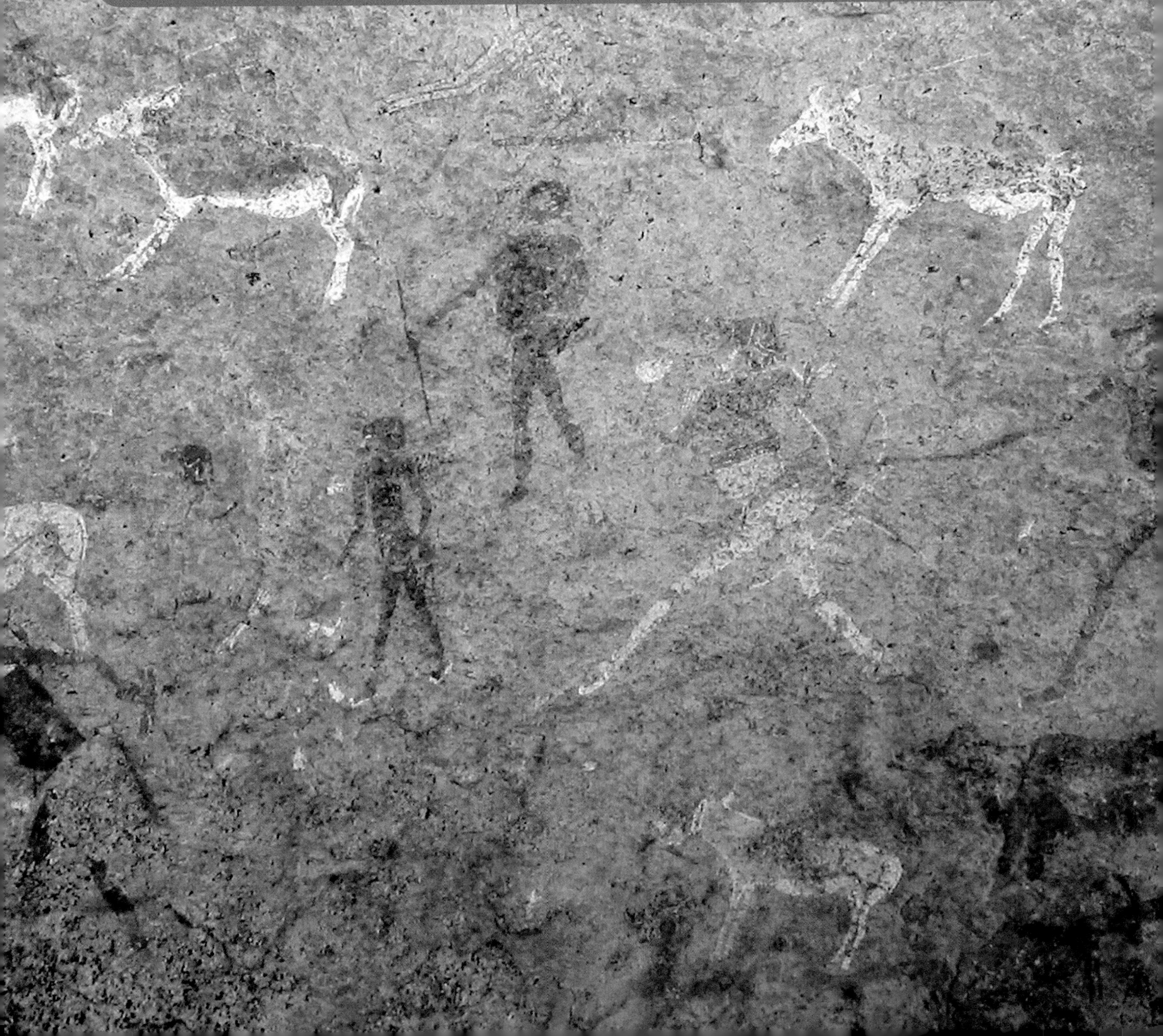

ABSTRACT

At the end of the late Ice Age, the symbolical systems moved radically in comparison with the former period particularly with the Middle Magdalenian. New geometrical or abstract representations appeared and animal and human representations became more schematised. The transformations incarnated in the artistic registers testify to the diversity of the Palaeolithic and epi-palaeolithic trajectories. They are a link with the deep climatic, environmental and cultural changes of the end of Pleistocene. The transformation and the differentiation of the environment led to a cultural gap, on increasingly partitioned territories and increasingly differentiated landscapes, inducing a part of the regionalisation of the last Magdalenian populations before the expansion of the Azilian/Laborian groups. The behaviour's symbolic systems in mutation constitute an important source of knowledge on these groups and of these societies in transition.

INTRODUCTION

In Western Europe at the end of the Magdalenian period, around 12,000 non-cal BP symbolic representations changed radically from classical realism to the emergence of geometric and abstract images. These new graphic proceedings accompanied or, more probably, were one of the consequences of the climatic, environmental and cultural changes that marked the end of the Pleistocene and the transformation of the landscape from an Ice Age environment to a temperate environment. Transformation and differentiation of human communities led to a cultural fragmentation of territories as they got more and more partitioned. At the same time, the environment got more and more differentiated, inducing some regionalisation of the last Magdalenian people. Their technical and subsistence behaviours transformed the same way that their systems of symbolic representations did. To document these changes and their impact on the spiritual life of our ancestors, we are conducting a research in a complex territory in the north of the Dordogne or Perigord, in the southwest of France.

This programme started in 2007 by the study of a portable art collection from a small cave called Rochereil (Grand-Brassac, Dordogne). It has now taken the administrative form of a Collective Research Programme, bringing together more than 15 researchers from several institutions. Ten sites, both occupation sites and decorated caves, are being studied.

THE CAVE OF ROCHEREIL IN ITS TERRITORY

The studied territory is in the northeast part of Dordogne, close to the highest part of the Aquitanian plateau. It is centred by the Dronne valley. The cave of Rochereil, that we consider the centre of our approach, is located about 10 km to the south and downstream of Brantôme (Dordogne). The cave opens in a Coniacian limestone cliff to the southeast, overlooking the right bank of River Dronne. On the opposite bank, the site of Pont d'Ambon is another important archeological deposit considered in our programme (Fig. 9.1).

The Rochereil site lies in a small cavity 3.50m in length, 3m in width and 5.50m in height; it is prolonged with an outdoor terrace square of 3.50m a side. The site was discovered and explored in 1906 and 1907 by Raoul de Ricard. In 1912 and 1921, Maurice Féaux and the Marquis Gérard de Fayolle undertook the first excavation, digging a tunnel under the main archeological layers in the Magdalenian deposits. Before the collapse of their dangerous tunnel, a rich bone and lithic collection was found. This is currently kept in the Museum of Art and Archaeology of Perigord (Périgueux, France). Between 1937 and 1939 and between 1940 and 1947, Dr. Paul-Emile Jude and Jean Cruveiller led a more systematic excavation of the site. The results were published in 1938 and 1960 (Jude and Cruveiller 1938; Jude 1960). Most of the material now belongs to the French state and is kept in the former archaeology Museum of Brantôme. The cave itself was registered as a historical monument on 1 April 1952.

Jude and Cruveiller dug in the large deposits of upper and final Magdalenian. They also discovered a very complete Azilian layer on top of the Magdalenian. Therefore,

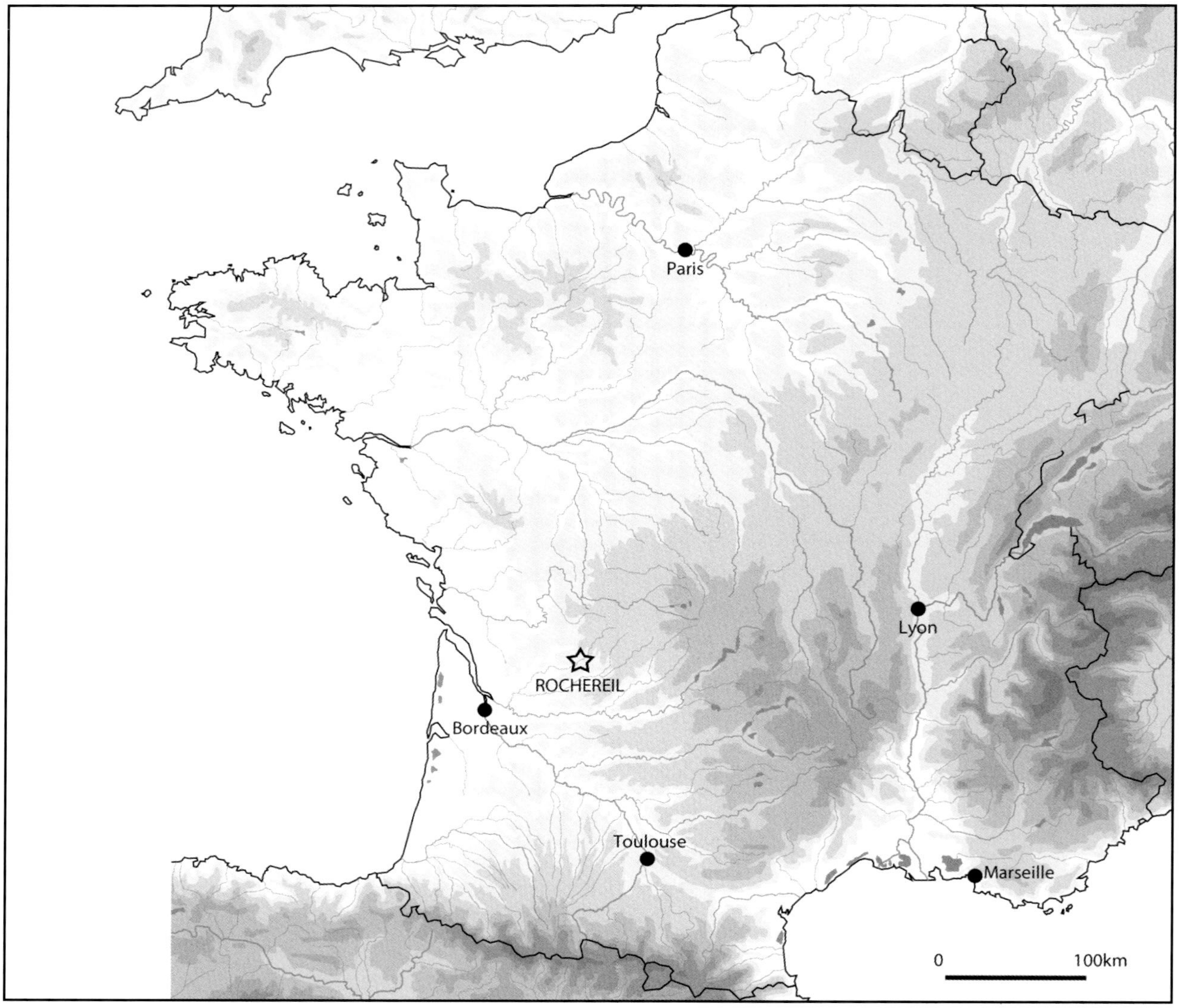

Fig. 9.1 Localisation map Rochereil. Drawing P. Paillet.

Rochereil is a crucial site as it shows the cultural changes that occurred at the end of the last glaciation. The stratigraphy as published by Jude reveals at least four layers of different colours and structures. After a first sterile layer, we find the upper/final Magdalenian layer (II), which is 0.40 m thick. It is composed of several lenses of black ash and is sub-divided on the terrace in its upper part by three ribbons of yellow limestone (flows of solifluction?). On the basis of the heterogeneity of some lithic and faunic material, this layer has been arbitrarily shared by Jude in two levels (IIa or lower level, about two-third of the layer) and IIb (top level).

Layer III (Azilian) is 1.80 m thick. It is directly superimposed on layer II, without a sterile intermediate layer. It consists of very compact clay-limestone sediment, with ochre in its middle (IIIb) and lower parts (IIIc). In its upper part (IIIa), the layer ends in a 20 cm thick black ash level. The high density of archaeological material and the apparent heterogeneity of the layer led Jude to divide it in three levels (Fig. 9.2).

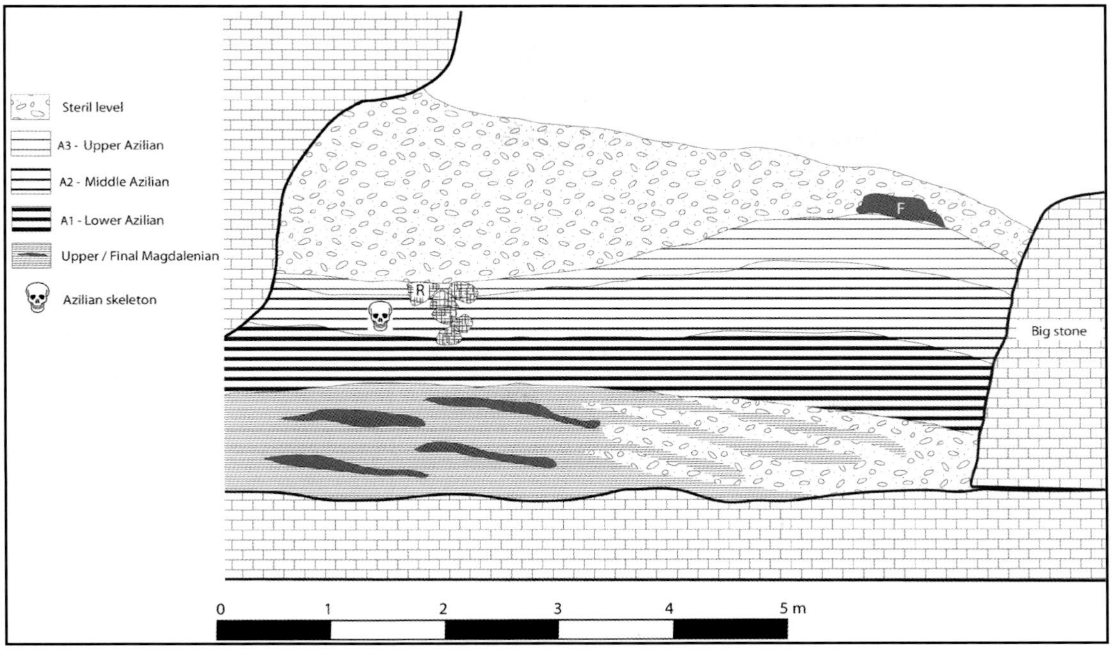

Fig. 9.2 Stratigraphy of Rochereil. Drawing P. Paillet after Jude, 1960.

Magdalenian occupations of layer II are associated with cold fauna, dominated by reindeer, horse, elk, polar fox, wolverine and lemming. The lithic industry is very rich (nearly 2,000 tools), as is the bone industry. Both characterise typical upper Magdalenian. More than 250 decorated objects (portable art) also enrich the extraordinary Magdalenian series of Rochereil. In the upper part of the occupations, an evolution towards the final Magdalenian is attested by the presence of Laugerie-Basse and Teyjat points.

A skull and a mandible of a child with pathological lesions were discovered in 1939 in the Magdalenian layer. Thus, a recent dating on a cranial fragment (11 255±50 BP, OxA-16932) corresponds to the Pleistocene/Holocene transition (Mafart 2007, 2009).

Azilian occupations of layer III are associated with a more temperate fauna with aurochs, boar, deer, beaver and rabbit. The lithic industry is well characterised by the presence of typical Azilian points. The bone industry is poor (only four harpoons and some punches and spears). Portable art is limited to a few painted pebbles and an engraved pebble (Roussot and Delsol 1970). Recently, an engraved bone has enriched the collection.

A remarkably conserved human skeleton was discovered in 1937 at the average level of the Azilian layer (Ferembach 1974). In 1939, at the same level, burned teeth and human bones were identified as those of two Azilian teenagers (Vallois 1971).

PORTABLE ART OF THE JUDE COLLECTION

The portable art from the upper and final Magdalenian levels in Rochereil, collected during the excavations by Féaux and Fayolle and by Dr. Jude, is a major collection. It is as much a reference as the contemporary sites of La Madeleine (Tursac, Dordogne) or Laugerie-Basse (Les Eyzies-de-Tayac, Dordogne). The Paul-Emile Jude collection of

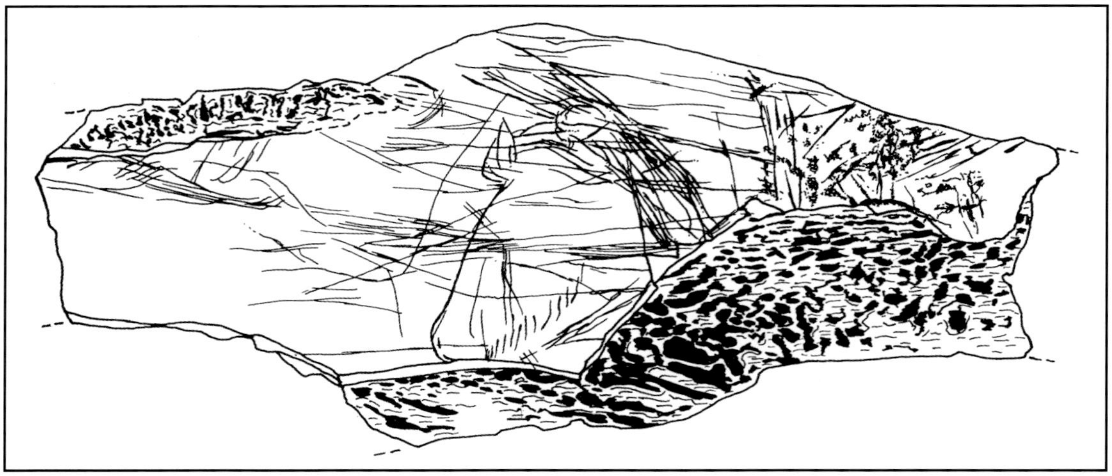

Fig. 9.3 Engraved scapula. Tracing P. Paillet.

Brantôme includes a large number of masterpieces that are the foundation of our work in terms of evolution of symbols in the region. We present them in this paper, with a comparison of several graphic forms existing in the rest of our corpus.

The Jude series includes 255 decorated objects, of which 177 (approximately 70 per cent) are unpublished. The archeo-stratigraphic origin of the portable art is not known for sure. It comes from layer II (upper and final Magdalenian). More than 40 per cent (108) of the objects have no readable or accurate indications. We simply know that a majority of them (90) were discovered in 1939 (final year of the excavation) in the sector n° 3 of the cave (the left and deeper part). The series gathers two types of organic material: bone (108) and reindeer antlers (76).

Considering bones, it appears that flat supports are the most frequent (more than 42 per cent): about 40 reindeer and bovine scapulas, as well as six fragments of mandibles of large herbivores (Fig. 9.3). Ribs were also used and transformed but to a lesser extent (17). We also found long bone fragments (13) and metapodes (7). The series also includes some engraved bird bones.

Among the antlers, sticks were mainly decorated (100 pieces). They can be intermediate tools (chisels—41), fragments of sticks (28) or spear points (22). We also note the presence of five indeterminate bevels and four points. Twenty-two objects concentrate on rough antlers. There are also 17 harpoons. The antlers of large and medium-large modules appear to have been preferentially used as support for the engravings (about 50 per cent of the objects).

Only one single lithic support has been engraved, while art engraved on lithic material is common or abundant in contemporary series that are equally important, such as those of La Madeleine, from Laugerie-Basse, of Limeuil (Dordogne). Therefore, we need to consider the selection made by Jude during the excavation, as in the modest Féaux-Fayolle collection we have found several pieces on hematite and ferruginous sand stone (Tosello 2003).

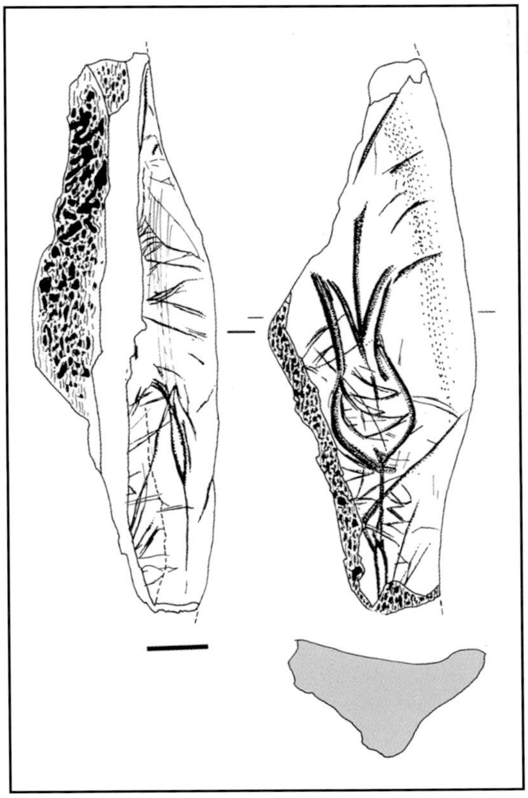

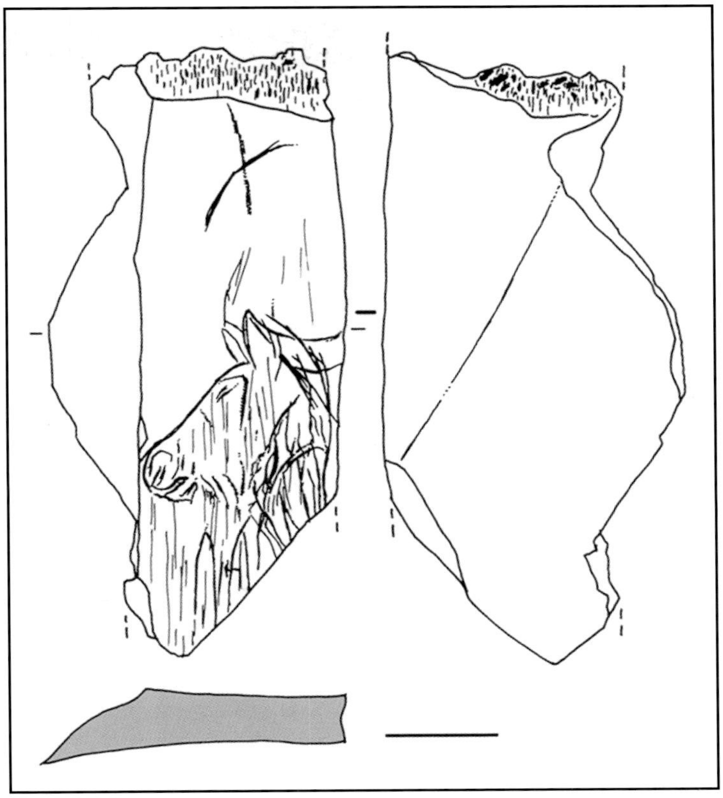

Left: **Fig. 9.4** Root-looking sign on bone. Tracing P. Paillet.

Right: **Fig. 9.5** Horse head on scapula. Tracing P. Paillet.

AN OSCILLATION BETWEEN REALISTIC AND SCHEMATIC REPRESENTATIONS

A first analysis of the 255 engraved objects shows that 197 pieces (more than 77 per cent) are decorated exclusively with signs or geometric patterns. Only 25 objects carry figurative representations and 33 combine geometric and figurative designs.

In the geometric category, there is a large majority of simple signs, such as linear or angular symbols and ramiform signs. We have also identified many leaf-like signs, composed of a main oval or lanceolate-shaped part, with its inner part filled with lines evoking veins. The body is divided in the middle by a linear path such as the petiole of a leaf. The corpus is also enriched with these exceptional forms of leaves and others that are similar to 'roots' or 'bulbs' (Fig. 9.4). These last two categories of signs, which are very elaborate typologically, are exceptional in Magdalenian art. They appear to derive graphically from figurative representations (animals or human, seen in a front view and/or vegetable designs). Signs and geometric patterns are often linked to reindeer antlers (127 including 99 on sticks) but also exist on bones (66).

On the contrary, figurative representations isolated or in association with abstract or geometric patterns, occur more frequently on bones (40) than on antlers (17). The main figurative theme, present on 16 objects, is the horse (Fig. 9.5). This is followed by indeterminate or composite animals (13 objects) (Fig. 9.6). Figures of women are not

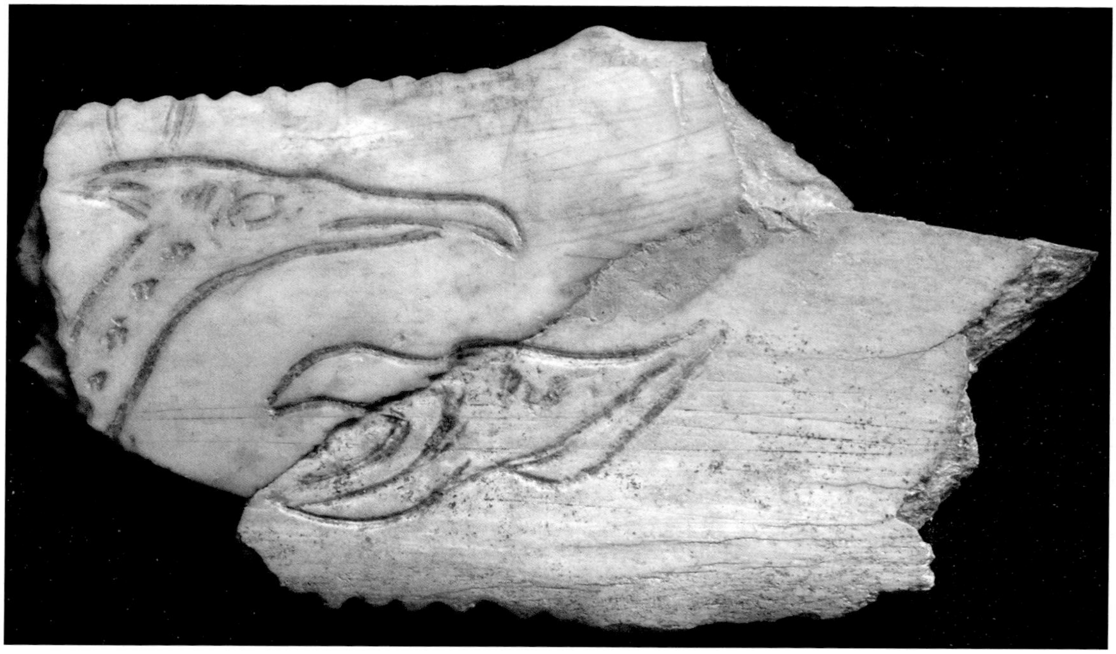

Fig. 9.6 Fantastic animals on bone. Picture P. Paillet.

rare (8), seen in front view or in profile (Fig. 9.7). We also find ibex in a front view (5), birds (4), deer (probable reindeers) (5) and aurochs (3). Bison, wolf, bear and fish complete this bestiary, which is extremely diverse in its composition.

The style of these animal representations oscillates between realistic and schematic. At the end of the Magdalenian period, the stylistic components of the representations evolved towards a stylisation in form and details. For example, horses with 'heavy jaws', known as horses 'barygnathes' were a common pattern. They are present in the graphic composition of the Rochereil collection as well as in the portable art series of the southern sites of Perigord such as La Madeleine. Another interesting expression is the goat or ibex in a front view. They are present in this collection like composite or fantastic representations. All these images co-exist with figures of a very conventional realism, inherited from graphics and stylistically of the middle Magdalenian models.

This oscillation between convention and stylisation is linked with the emergence and the development of original geometric patterns including highly structured sketches, bearing figurative inspirations. The presence of several foliated representations and ramiform signs invites us to think that plants were also a source of inspiration for the artists of Rochereil.

The art of Rochereil, rich and complex, offers a broad catalogue of themes, technical characters and contrasting styles that confer an original universe to the upper and final Magdalenian of the northern Perigord. However, it shares many things with other contemporary sites in the region, between the valleys of the Dronne to the south and the Tardoire in the north. The Rochereil series can thus be compared with the small collection of La Peyzie (Lisle, Dordogne) (Anonymous 1934; Cestac 2004; Paillet 2012), of the

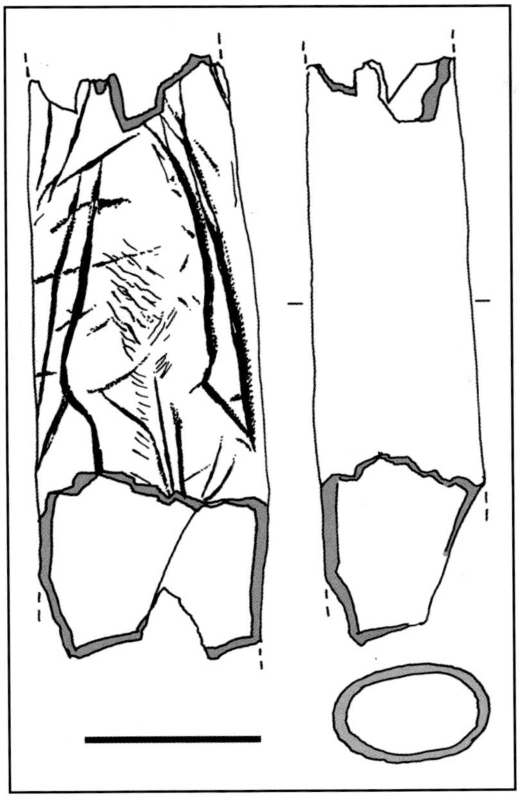

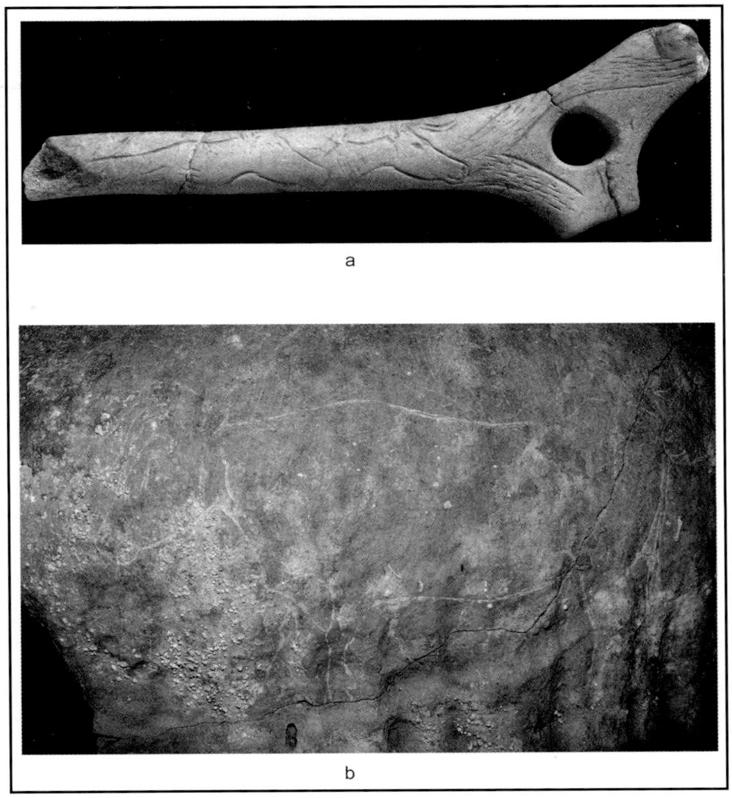

Left: **Fig. 9.7** Schematic feminine figure, seen in front view on bone. Tracing P. Paillet.

Right: **Fig. 9.8** Aurochs engraved: a- Rochereil; b- cave of La Mairie. Pictures P. Paillet.

cave of Les Oiseaux in the Rebiéres valley (Brantôme) (Pittard and Boissier 1928–1929) and of the cave of La Mairie and the rock shelter Mège (Teyjat, Dordogne) (Capitan et al. 1906, 1908). Stylistic and thematic communities can also be found in the parietal art of the same region, realised during the same time in Fronsac (Vieux-Mareuil, Dordogne) (Carcauzon 1984; Delluc and Delluc 1996; Paillet 1999), in Front-Bargeix (Champeaux and La Chapelle-Pommier, Dordogne) (Barrière 1989; Barrière and colleagues1990; Carcauzon 1985) and La Mairie (Barrière 1968, 1972; Capitan et al. 1913). These thematic and formal analogies are now discussed in more detail.

SHARED CONVENTIONS

As discussed earlier, the corpus of the portable art of Rochereil offers about 60 figurative representations, dominated by horses and indeterminate animals. Thus, deer and bovines (aurochs and bison) are not uncommon. They find an interesting echo in the cave of Les Oiseaux where an engraved bison on a long bone fragment was discovered (Paillet 1993) and in the decorated caves of Fronsac and La Mairie. The stylistic treatment of the aurochs in Rochereil is very close to the style of figures engraved on one of the stalagmite *cascades* of a panel in La Mairie (Fig. 9.8). The care taken in the treatment of anatomical details, including the barb or body segments (eye, ear, nostril, horns, etc.), is particularly remarkable on quite a few of these animal figures. The rock shelter Mège offers a stylistic

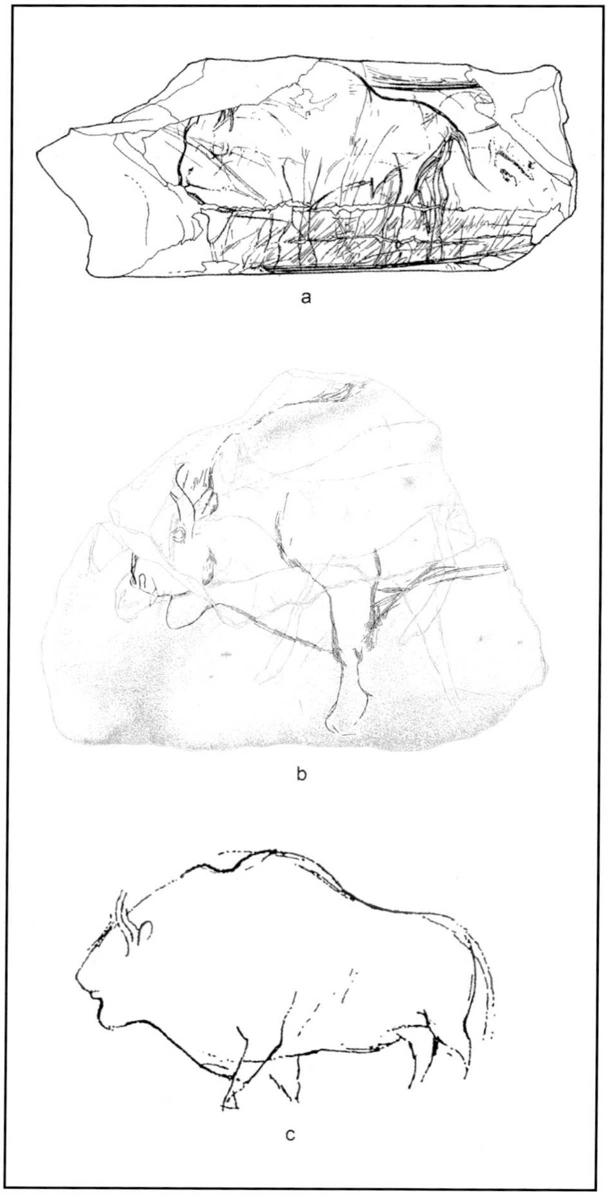

Fig. 9.9 Bisons engraved: a- Les Oiseaux; b-Rochereil; c- la Mairie. Pictures P. Paillet.

approach which is similar to what is known in the Magdalenian culture (Capitan et al. 1906).

Specific graphic and stylistic similarities can be underlined in the rendering of certain anatomical details. For instance, we can identify the beard in the 'bag' of bison from Les Oiseaux (Paillet 1993), Rochereil and Fronsac (Fig. 9.9). Other details such as the projection of the horns of aurochs are found to be identical in Rochereil and La Mairie. The alignment of some bovines, reindeer and horses also finds an echo in a particular rendering of perspective or movement, by duplication or multiplication of the lines of the animal (Rochereil, La Mairie). Finally, other analogies can be highlighted, such as figuration and utilisation of ground lines (Les Oiseaux, La Mairie).

Another graphic and stylistic group brings together what we may call 'conventions', typical of the upper and final Magdalenian. For example, in Rochereil we find a typical treatment of horses, bearing large jaws and particularly big heads. Known as 'barygnathes', these horse representations are common at the end of the late Ice Age, in the main sites of Perigord, such as La Madeleine. In Rochereil, these horses occupy the sides of several intermediate tools and spear points. They are executed by deep engravings. In La Peyzie, we know two finely engraved horses, laid on the handle of a double-bored stick. In La Mairie, two stylised horses are firmly engraved on a reindeer antler and three other horses are finely incised on the radius of an eagle. Despite small variations in their graphics, these horses are similarly stylised in La Madeleine, Laugerie-Basse, the cave Richard (Dordogne), Limeuil, Soucy (Dordogne), and the Morin rock shelter (Gironde) (Fig. 9.10).

Although very rare in Perigord, Pyrenees and on the Cantabrian coast, mountain goats and deer in back or front view are found at Rochereil, La Mairie and Mège. This shared mode of expression occurs sometimes in a schematic form (Rochereil) and sometimes in a more realistic way (La Mairie, Mège) (Fig. 9.11). In Rochereil, we studied 10 harpoons whose bases are decorated with this type of designs (Julien 1982). Another schematic ibex is engraved on a polished bone. In La Mairie, a stick bears two heads of

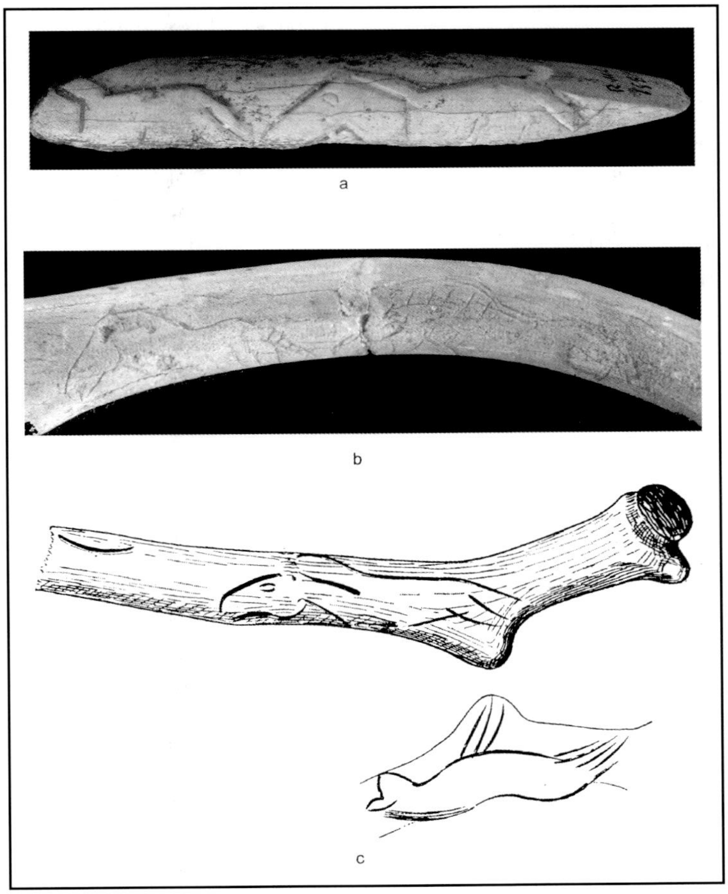

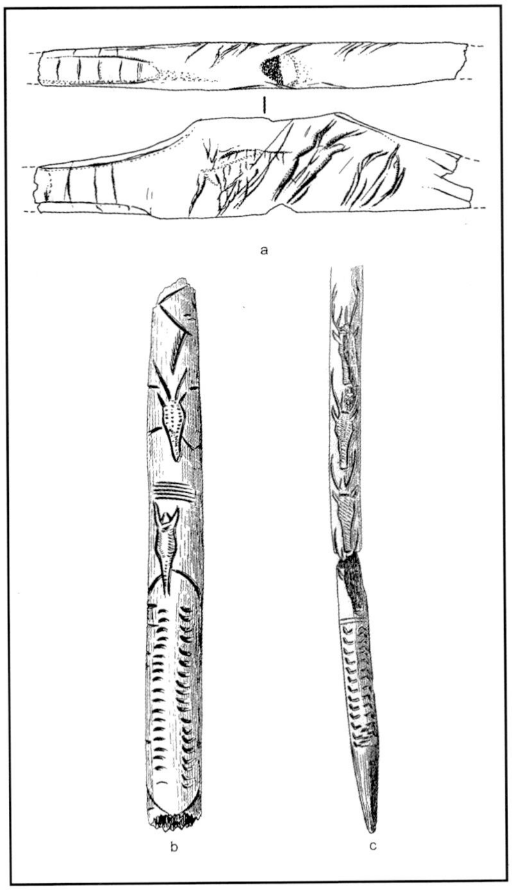

Left: **Fig. 9.10** Big head horses: a-Rochereil; b- La Peyzie; c-La Mairie. Pictures P. Paillet and Tracing H. Breuil.

Right: **Fig. 9.11** Animal seen in front view: a-Rochereil; b-Mege; c-La Mairie. Tracings P. Paillet and H. Breuil.

animals with a filling of short incisions forming the fur. In Mège, four deer heads are engraved on a spear point. To a certain extent, we can link these designs with the 'roots' figures, whose figurative origins must be underlined. Breuil (1905) considered some of them as a 'degeneration' of animal figures in front views. The various stages of the process of transformation from one form to the other are unknown, but comparisons with more realistic representations suggest these interpretative trails.

Another typical convention found at the end of Magdalenian, specifically in Perigord, is the stylised or schematic feminine figure. The image may be in profile or in front view, sometimes accompanied by *vulvae* representations. In our corpus, they are present in Rochereil, La Peyzie, La Mairie and in the caves of Fronsac and Font-Bargeix (Delluc and Delluc 1991, 1994) (Fig. 9.12).

In Rochereil we found several women corresponding to this schematic pattern. They are all engraved on bone (Paillet 2011). One object is a bird-bone bearing a figure very similar to one known in the Rond-du-Barry collection (Haute-Loire) (Fig. 9.12a). The head and neck are confused, very elongated and projected on the left side. The belly is broad and the navel is prominent. The body ends in short legs. This very schematic

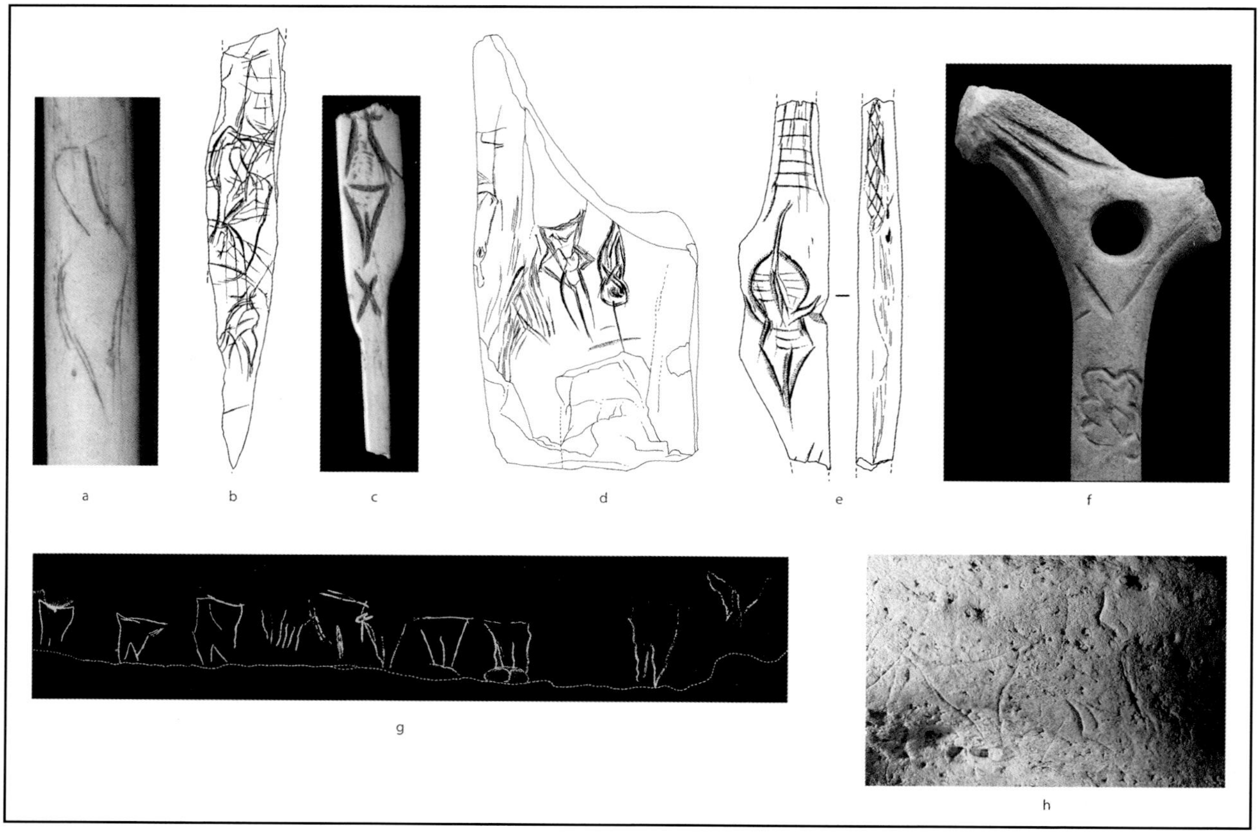

Fig. 9.12 Schematic feminine figures: a-e- Rochereil; f- La Peyzie; g- cave of Font Bargeix; h- cave of Fronsac. Tracing and Pictures P. Paillet.

representation is atypical in its form (on a three quarter view). A second object is a fragment of bone gathering at least two female schematic profiles (Fig. 9.12b). They are the same headless forms of the Lalinde-Gönnersdorf type. The third object is a small blade of bone (Fig. 9.12c). A female representation is seen in front view on the main face. It is narrow, with a breast covered by small incisions (hairs?). A great pubic triangle is also engraved, with an indication of the *vulvae*. This shape recalls schematic views of gravettian or Magdalenian women's images.

On another object, another female representation in front view can be seen (Fig. 9.12d). Despite its cursive nature, the female figure is fairly complete, with an elongated head. The body is completed by two arms outstretched on the sides. The body is also marked by prominent hips and a very round belly. The navel and the pubic triangle are shown. The two thighs are clearly separated by a large incision. By its style, its originality and its freedom of expression, this human representation is totally atypical in Palaeolithic iconography. All proportions kept, it could be linked to the naked women carved on the rock walls of La Magdeleine-des-Albis (Tarn). The anatomical realism is even more striking with the displayed gestures, evoking a fashion model. The figure is almost complete. The bust is a little more confusing than the bottom of the body. The head appears to be lowered, projected forward. Both arms are raised and folded behind

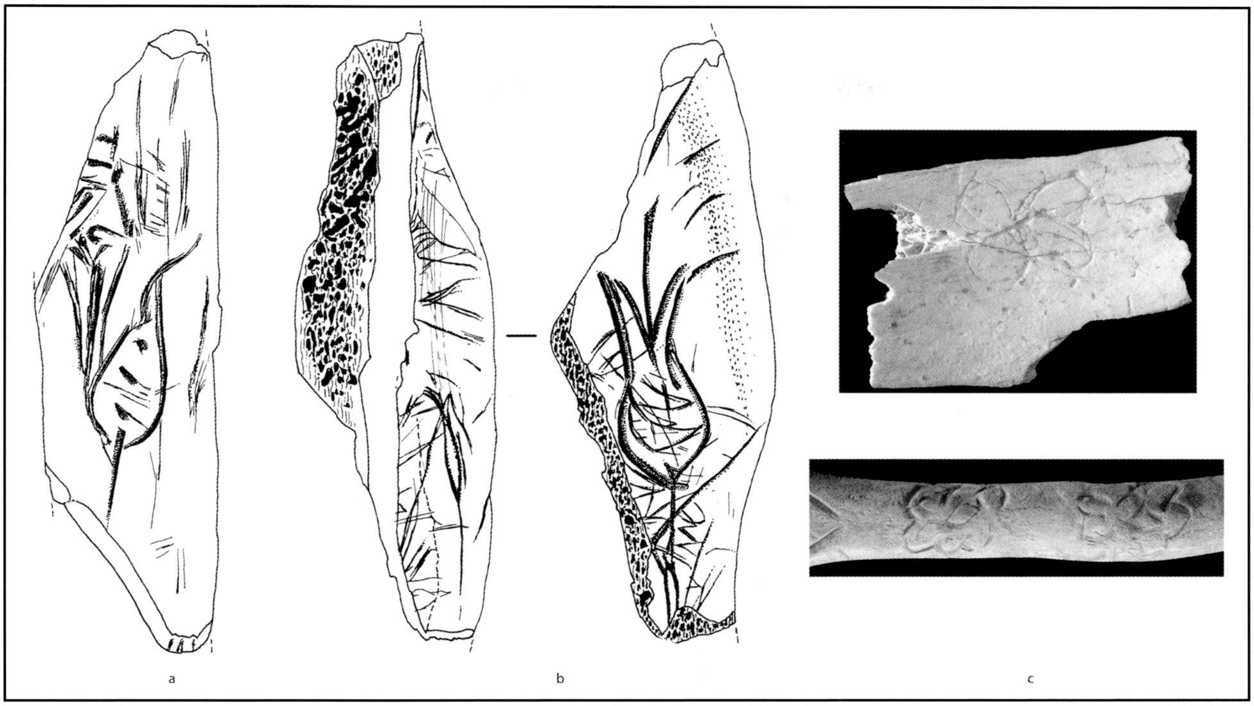

Fig. 9.13 Phytomorphes representations. Tracing and Pictures P. Paillet.

the head. But they could also be seen as being held on the hips. Such a position and movement are exceptional in Palaeolithic art. Every detail on this image is executed with perfect control linked with a big graphic economy (Paillet 2011).

The last object bearing a feminine figure is a small bone blade, decorated on both sides (Fig. 9.12e). On one side is a schematic ibex. On the opposite face, we see a strange figure, whose inspiration is probably figurative. The general form evokes a female body viewed from the front. The lower part of the body seems to outline the schematic contours of a belly, marked by three horizontal curved lines with protruding hips and legs. It could also be a more segmental representation of the body, reduced to a pubic triangle and *vulvae*. The figure is nested in an oval pattern, split in two parts by double vertical curved lines. Both parts are bound by two double curved lines, as two arms between the body and the head. The extreme stylisation of this image leads us to a prudent interpretation. An antler of La Mairie studied by Breuil also shows a possible representation of a segmental woman in front view (Capitan et al. 1908).

Two pubic triangles with a median incision are highly engraved on both sides and around the hole of one of the two is a bored stick of La Peyzie (Fig. 9.12f). These vulvar representations echo those seen on the walls of Font-Bargeix (Fig. 9.12g) and Fronsac (Fig. 9.12h). In this last cave, nearly 20 schematic female profiles (type Gönnersdorf-Lalinde) are engraved, sometimes even executed in deep engraving on the walls of two galleries. The main panel is centred by a line of four aligned figures, surrounded by a dozen other schematic female representations of variable dimensions and shapes.

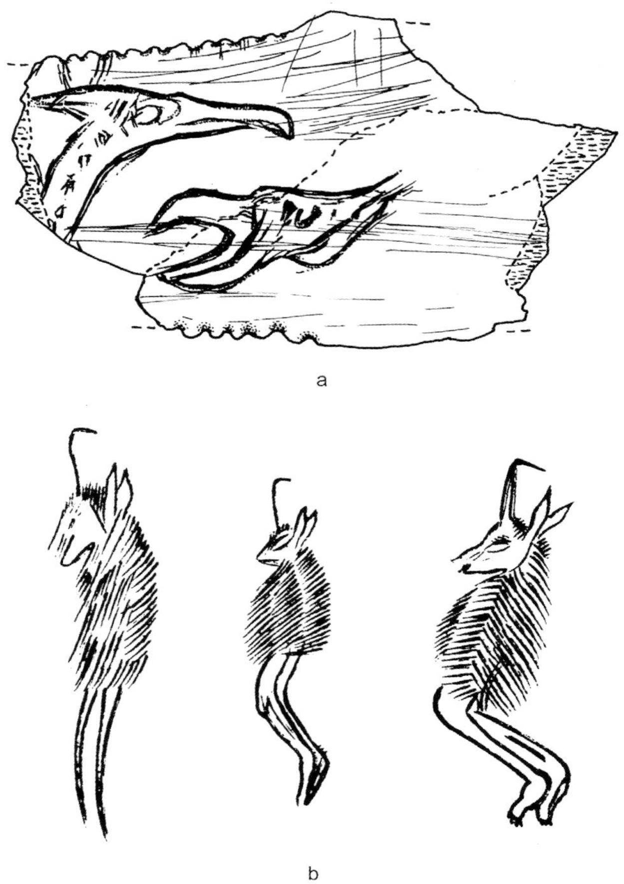

Fig. 9.14 Fantastic figures: a- Rochereil; b- Mege. Tracings P. Paillet and H. Breuil.

PHYTOMORPHES AND FANTASTIC PATTERNS

The plant signs, also reported in the contemporary series of rock shelter Morin (Deffarge et al. 1975) are numerous in Rochereil and in La Peyzie, on a bored stick. This category includes leaf-like designs (about 20 representations on antlers and bones) (Fig. 9.13a) and 'roots' patterns (Fig. 9.13b). Some others images also evoke flowers with four or six petals (Fig. 9.13c). All of them can complete the inventory of 'phytomorphes' described by Breuil (1906).

To complete this review of the symbolic catalogue of the Magdalenian sites of northern Perigord, we must mention the case of the rare composite or fantastic representations. In Rochereil, they are present on a bone blade fragment and in Mège, on a double-bored stick, realised on a deer antler (Capitan et al. 1909) (Fig. 9.14). This object presents two horses, three swans, a cow and three composites that are nicknamed 'little devils'. They are developed from a chamois head, an undetermined animal body and human legs. The aesthetic and symbolic character of this iconographic device is similar to the engravings on the Rochereil bone blade, with its two fantastic and original bird figures.

CONCLUSIONS

The upper and final Magdalenian of northern Perigord, between Dronne and Tardoire, has offered several sites of occupation and several decorated caves. They show an interesting development of shared modes of expression. They accompany the Palaeo-environmental and climatic change, as well as the demographic evolution of the end of the late Ice Age. These links, identified by the symbolic, thematic and formal analogies that we have just described, appear to be maintained within networks of circulation and exchanges well implanted and established at a certain distance from the well-known sites of the valleys of the Dordogne and Vézère.

To measure the territorial dimension of these occupations from the end of the late Ice Age, to assess their mobility and the nature of potential contacts with the south of Perigord as well as the Charente on the northwest, by the natural axis of the Dordogne and Charente, we follow technical and subsistence behaviours and their systems of symbolic representations. In a territory where the combination of portable and parietal art is exceptional, this study of the symbolic organisation of the Magdalenian can be considered a particularly valuable documentary source. As a part of this research we will also take into account analogies with middle and long distance sites, to know in particular whether there are continuities and/or ruptures in technical and thematic representation systems, especially in the world of the upper and final Magdalenian. By correlating the circulation of objects, such as portable art, with the intellectual universe expressed on cave walls, we gain a dynamic vision of prehistoric societies, creating a human and cultural geography of the Magdalenian-Azilian transition, inside this incredible framework of the northern Perigord.

REFERENCES

Anonyme, Peyzie (la) (1934), *Congrès préhistorique de France*. Périgueux, pp. 73-75.

Barrière, C. (1968). *Les Gravures de la grotte de la Mairie à Teyjat*. Toulouse, T.X.: Travaux de l'Institut d'Art préhistorique.

—— (1972), *Grotte de la Mairie à Teyjat, une nouvelle petite gravure*. Toulouse, T: Travaux de l'Institut d'Art préhistorique, pp. 204–205.

—— (1989), La Font-Bargeix, Champeaux-et-la-Chapelle-Pommier, Dordogne: Outillage, matériaux, faune. *Travaux de l'Institut d'Art Préhistorique*, t.31, Toulouse le Mirail, pp. 39-143.

Barrière, C. et al. (1990), La grotte ornée de la Font-Bargeix (Champeaux-et-la-Chapelle-Pommier, Dordogne). *Travaux de l'Institut d'Art Préhistorique*, t.32, Toulouse le Mirail, pp. 9-47.

Breuil, H. (1905), La dégénérescence des figures d'animaux en motifs ornementaux à l'époque du renne. *Compte-rendus de l'Académie des Inscriptions et Belles Lettres,* 1905, pp. 105-120.

—— (1906), Exemples de figures dégénérées et stylisées à l'époque du renne. *Compte-rendus du XIIIe Congrès d'Anthropologie et d'Archéologie préhistoriques*, Monaco, 1906, pp. 394-403.

Capitan, L. et al. (1906), L'abri Mège, une station magdalénienne à Teyjat (Dordogne). *Revue de l'Ecole d'Anthropologie de Paris*, 16ème année, t.6, Paris, pp. 196-212.

—— (1908), La grotte de La Mairie à Teyjat (Dordogne). Fouilles d'un gisement magdalénien. *Revue de l'Ecole d'Anthropologie de Paris*, 18ème année, t.V, pp. 153-73 et pp. 198-218.

—— (1909), Observations sur un bâton de commandement orné de figures animales et de personnages semi-humains. *Revue de l'Ecole d'Anthropologie de Paris*, 19ème année, t.2, Paris, pp. 62-77.

—— (1913), Les gravures sur cascade stalagmitique de la grotte de la Mairie à Teyjat. *Congrès international d'Anthropologie et d'Archéologie préhistoriques*. Compte-rendu de la XIVe session, Tome I, Genève, 18 p.

Carcauzon, C. (1984), Une nouvelle découverte en Dordogne: la grotte préhistorique de Fronsac. *Revue archéologique Sites*, n°22, pp. 7-15.

—— (1985), La grotte de Font-Bargeix. *Revue archéologique Sites*, n°30, pp. 3-20.

Cestac, A.M. (2004), Autour des fouilles de la vallée de la Dronne dans la première moitié du XXe siècle. La Peyzie, Rochereil, La Chèvre. *Bulletin de la SHAP*, t. CXXXI, pp. 157–73.

Deffarge, R. et al. (1975), Art mobilier du Magdalénien supérieur de l'abri Morin à Pessac-sur-Dordogne (Gironde). *Gallia-Préhistoire*, Tome 18, n°1, pp. 1-64.

Delluc, B. (1996), La grotte ornée de Fronsac (Vieux-Mareuil, Dordogne): inventaire des úuvres. In Mohen J.P. *La vie préhistorique*, Dijon, éditions Faton, pp. 416-421.

Ferembach, D. (1974), Le squelette humain azilien de Rochereil (Dordogne). *Bulletins et Mémoires de la Société d'Anthropologie de Paris*, t.2, série XIII, pp. 271-291.

Jude, P.E. (1960), *La Grotte de Rochereil. Station magdalénienne et azilienne.* Archives de l'I.P.H., Mémoire n°30, Paris.

Jude, P.E. and J. Cruveiller (1938), La grotte et l'homme de Rochereil. *Bulletin de la SHAP*, t.LXV, pp. 190-197.

Julien, M. (1982), *Les harpons magdaléniens.* XVII° supplément à Gallia-Préhistoire, CNRS, Paris, 306 p.

Mafart, B. (2009), Une reconstitution surprenante d'un fossile humain: la mandibule magdalénienne du crãne d'enfant Rochereil III. *Paleovol*, 8, pp. 403-412.

Mafart, B., G. Guipert, C. Alliez-Philip and J.J. Brau (2007), Virtual Reconstitution and New Palaeopathological Study of the Magdalenian Child's Skull of Rochereil, *Paleovol* 6: 569-579.

Paillet, P. (1993), Un objet inédit provenant de la "grotte des Oiseaux" dans le vallon des Rebiéres (Commune de Brantôme, Dordogne). *Antiquités Nationales*, 25, pp. 7-15.

—— (1999), *Le bison dans les arts magdaléniens en Périgord.* XXX° supplément à Gallia-Préhistoire, CNRS, Paris, 480 p.

—— (2011), Les figurations féminines de la grotte de Rochereil. *Catalogue de l'exposition "Mille et une femmes de la fin des temps glaciaires"*, Réunion des Musées Nationaux – Grand Palais, Musée national de Préhistoire, Les Eyzies, pp. 118-119.

—— (2012), Deux bãtons percés inédits de la Peyzie. PALEO (sous presse).

Pittard, E. and G. Boissier (1928–1929), Une nouvelle station magdalénienne: la grotte des Oiseaux. Vallon des Rebiéres (Dordogne). *Archives suisses d'Anthropologie générale*, tome V, n°2, Genève, 1930, pp. 216-221.

Ricard, (de) R. (1906), Instrument de silex magdalénien de Rocheroeil (Dordogne). *Bulletin de la SPF*, t.3, pp. 256-257.

Tosello, G. (2003), *Pierres gravées du Périgord magdalénien.* XXXVIe supplément à Gallia-Préhistoire, CNRS, Paris, 584 p.

10

Megalithic Monuments and the Context of Rock Art in North-East India

Dwipen Bezbaruah

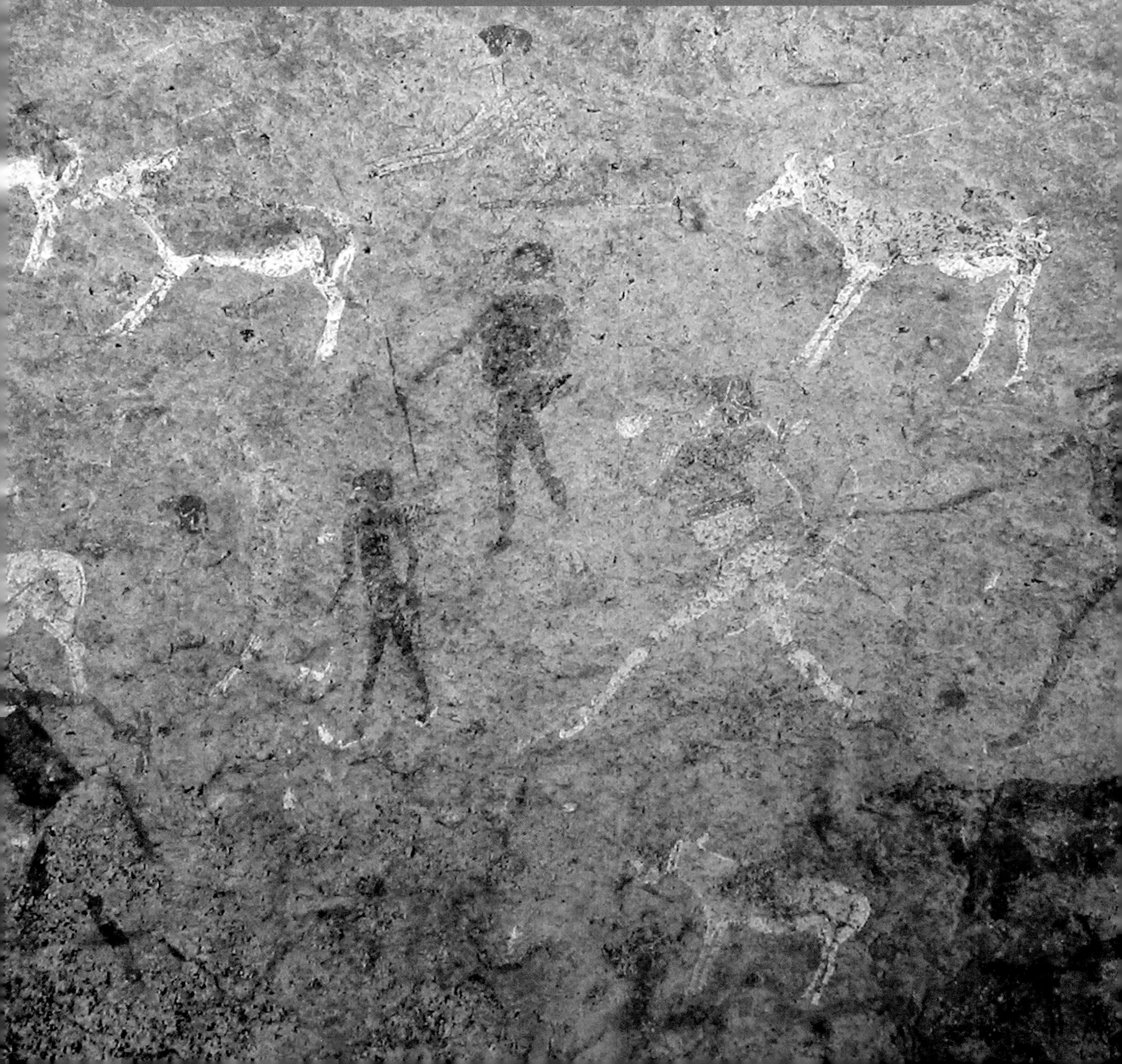

ABSTRACT

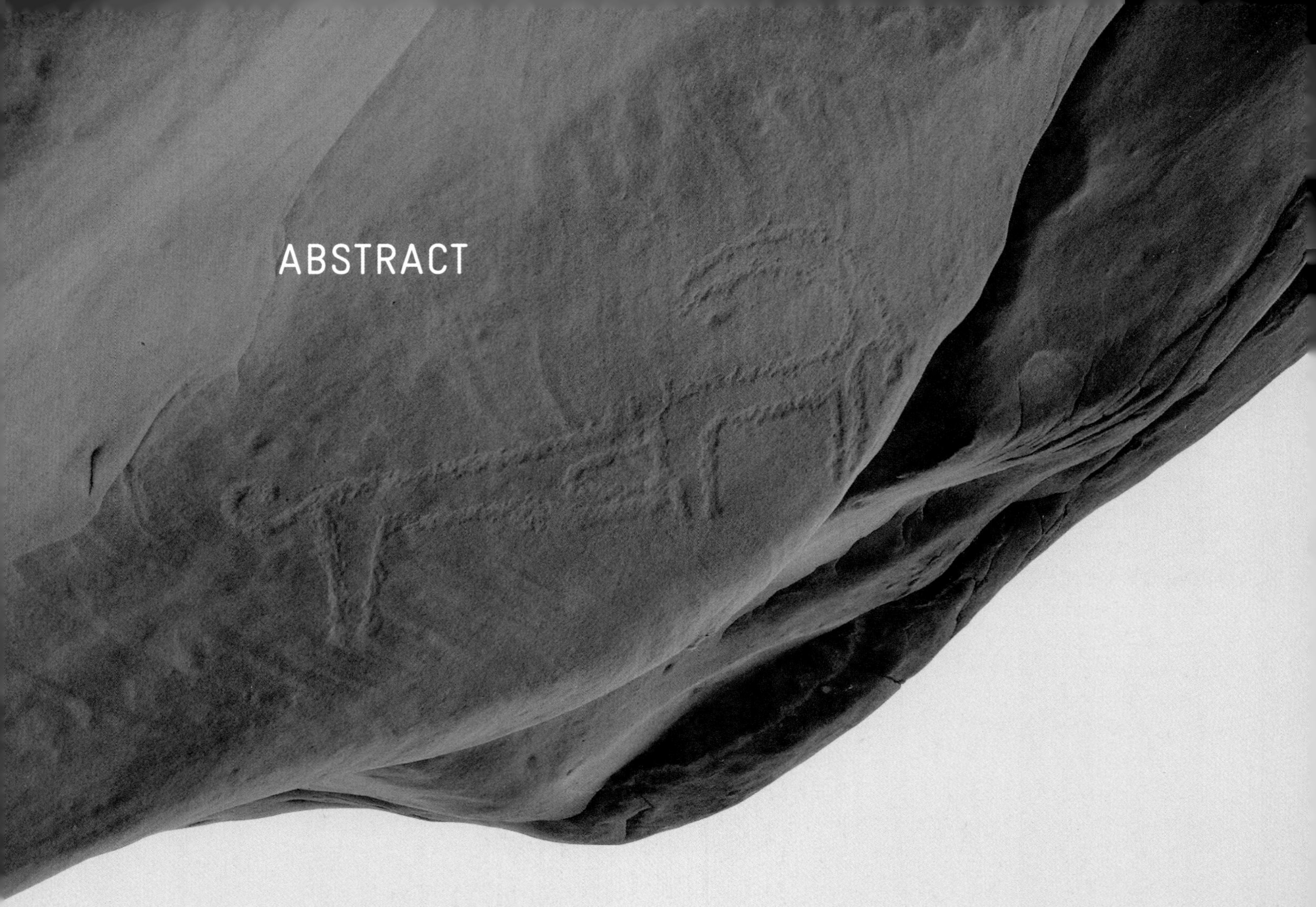

In North East India we have evidence of rock art only in the form of rock engravings from Manipur, possibly belonging to the earliest phases of history. Similarly, from Assam also we have reporting of rock impressions belonging to historical phases. However, there is the occurrence of high concentration of megalithic remains in this region particularly in the hilly terrain of Khasi-Jayantia hills of Meghalaya, North Cachar hills and Karbi Anglong in Assam and in Manipur and Nagaland. There is also reporting of engravings and other impressions on some megalithic remains. Evidence till date indicates that the rock art of North East India is not very old and consists of engravings. The non-occurrence of rock paintings is also a matter of scholarly probe. Dr. Bezbaruah's paper discusses these aspects in detail on the basis of secondary evidence and primary data collected by him.

From the perspective of the geo-environment, North-East India consists of two distinct zones—Himalayan and non-Himalayan—with the Brahmaputra valley forming the intermediary catchments of demarcation. The non-Himalayan region consists mainly of the hilly terrain of Nagaland, Manipur, Mizoram, Tripura and Meghalaya and the broad plains of Barak and Imphal valleys; this merges into the southern hill ranges. The Himalayan region consists of Arunachal Pradesh and its southern periphery which merges into the north bank of river Brahmaputra and the foothills of Bhutan in Assam. The concept of Zomia developed by Scott (2010) for the great Southeast Asian massif wherein he includes the non-Himalayan highland of North-East India may be cited as an instance of relevance. He considers the Zomia as a geo-cultural unit inhabited by diverse ethnic communities which have had commonalities of life through the ages.

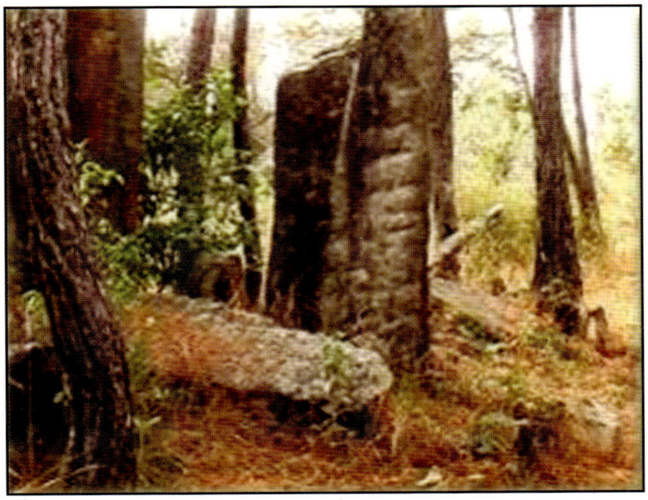

Fig. 10.1 Grooved stone, Umnoi, South Khasi Hills.

It should, however, be noted that there are micro variations within the geo-environmental sphere of the non-Himalayan region. Considered from the viewpoint of prehistoric archaeology, the non-Himalayan region has so far proven to be significant with a majority of the Stone Age sites in the North-East found here; some sites with a distinct context have also been reported from this region. Another archaeological significance of this region is the presence of numerous megalithic remains. The megalithic remains are mainly recorded in the hilly terrains of Nagaland, Manipur, North Cachar and Karbi Anglong in Assam and in eastern Meghalaya (Figs. 10.1-10.4). Commenting on the megalithic remains of Manipur, P. Binodini Devi (2005) says that these monuments are concentrated in the high hills of Chandel, Senapati and Tamenglong and in Ukhrul districts. In North Cachar hills, megaliths have been reported from Nenglo, Bolasam, Kobak, Derebora and Kartong (Mills

Fig. 10.2 Fallen grooved stone, Umnoi, South Khasi Hills.

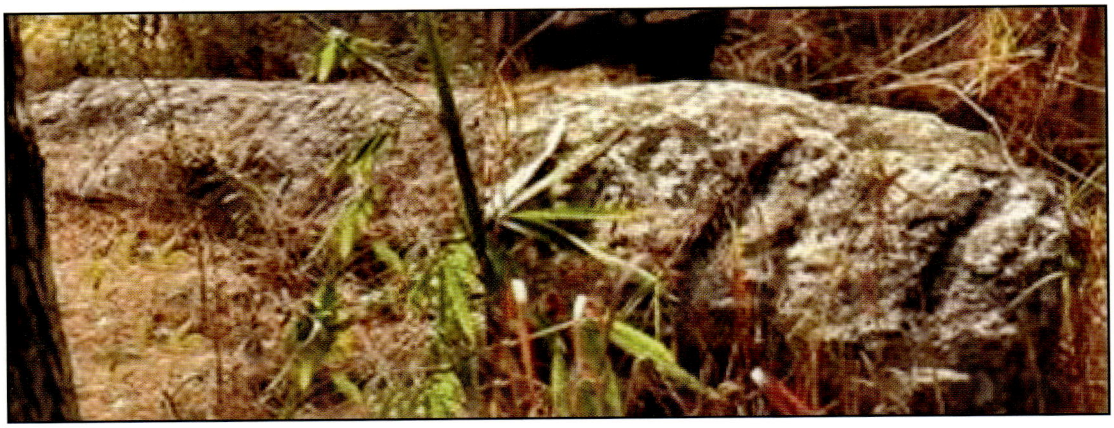

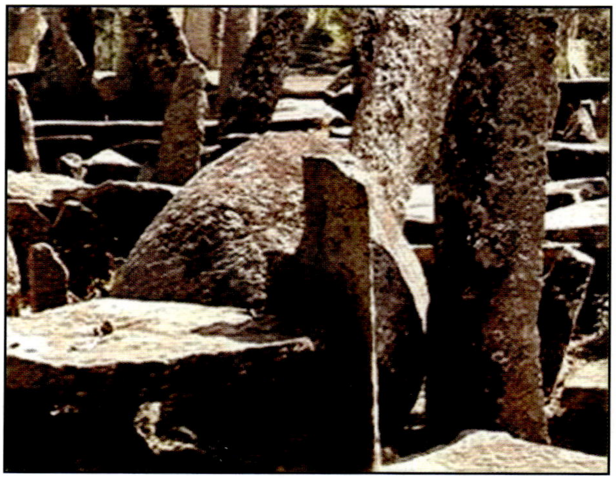

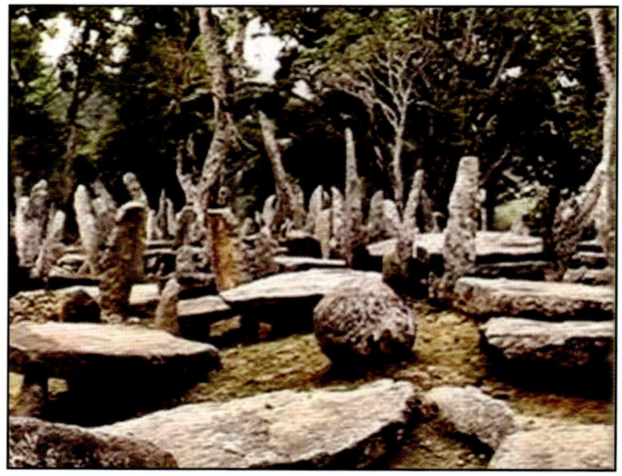

Left: **Fig. 10.3** Megalithic remains, Nartiang, Meghalaya.

Right: **Fig. 10.4** Megalithic remains, Nartiang, Meghalaya.

and Hutton 1929). Megalithic remains have also been recorded in Kamarpha, Rongali, Nongjrong, Mukhrow, Umcherra, Bowlagog, Habang, Umteli, Opthernala, Jorshala, Locrew and Mauslai in Karbi Anglong (Bezbaruah 2005). In Meghalaya, megaliths are concentrated in Cherapunji, Maoflong, Lailong, Kote, Laitkhor, Jowai and Nartiang (Godwin Austen 1872).

It is thus clear that on the spatial plane there is a continuous tract of a megalithic belt extending from Nagaland through Manipur bordering North Cachar and Karbi Anglong in Assam up to western Meghalaya (Figs. 10.5-10.10). Haimendorf (1945) has extended this belt in the east up to mainland Southeast Asia and in the west to the East Indian territory inhabited by Mundari speaking populations. Ethnologically, this region is the abode of diverse communities at various levels of subsistence with cultivation as the core practice. Various ethnic communities such as different Naga groups like Aos, Angamis, Rengma, Mao and Maram; Karbis from Assam; and Khasis from Meghalaya who inhabit this region are socio-culturally attached to the megalithic tradition. Among these communities the Khasis are linguistically close to Southeast Asian Austric speakers with conspicuous matrilineal socio-cultural characteristics.

Left: **Fig. 10.5** Rectangular serial grooves, Surya Pahar, Goalpara, Assam.

Right: **Fig. 10.6** Series of dots, Surya Pahar, Goalpara, Assam.

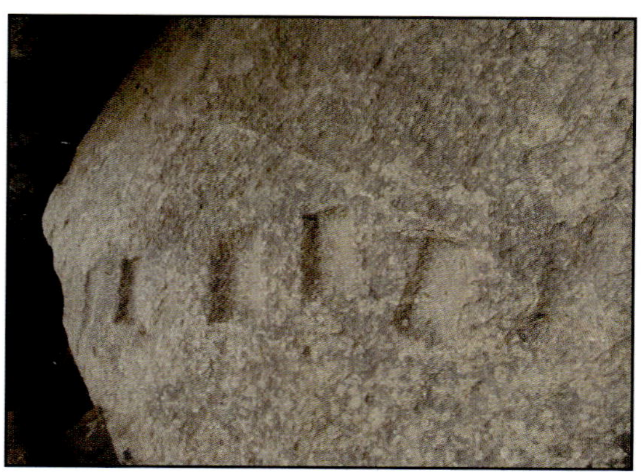

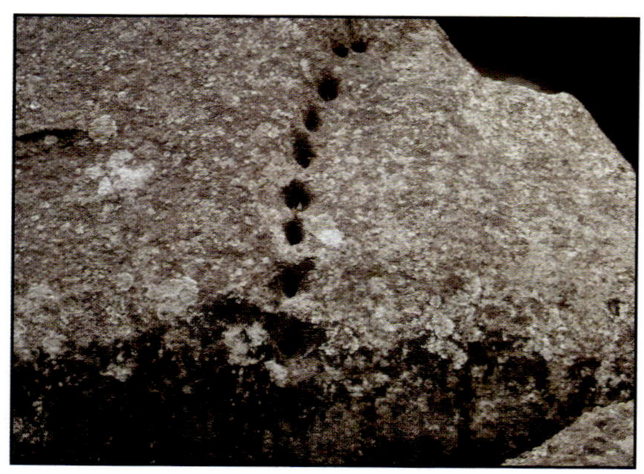

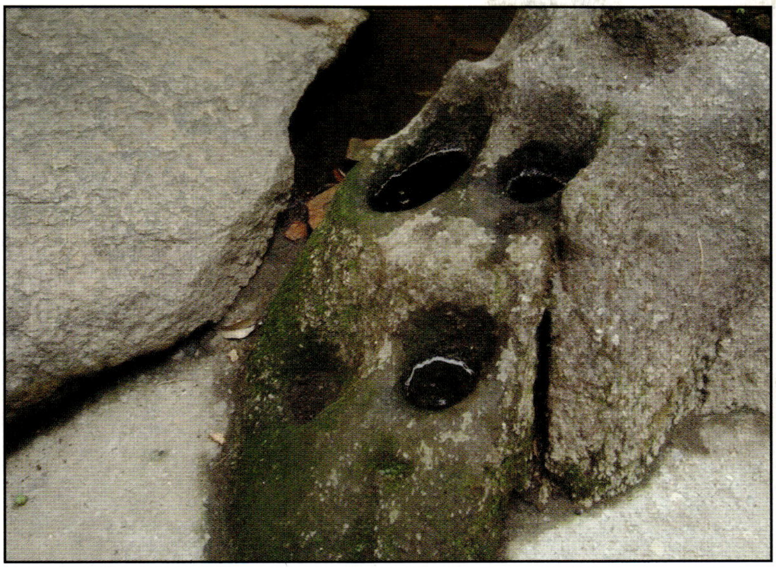 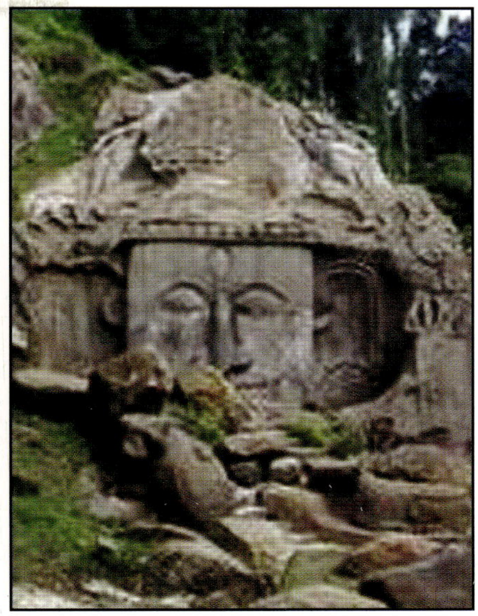

Left: **Fig. 10.7** Cup marks, Surya Pahar, Goalpara, Assam.

Right: **Fig. 10.8** Rock cut human face,Unakoti,Tripura.

There is insufficient evidence of the prehistoric period in North-East India. Whatever little evidence is available comes from the hilly terrains of Garo and Khasi hills in Meghalaya, the Khowai valley in Tripura, Ukhrul caves in Manipur and Parsi Parlo in Arunachal Pradesh. No evidence of prehistoric habitation has been recorded in the highly disturbed valleys of Brahmaputra and Barak rivers in Assam. According to some scholars, the history of human activities in North-East India is not very old. Besides the adjacent territories of South East Asia also do not have enough evidence of earliest prehistoric rock art. In North-East India, till date we have evidence of rock art in the form of rock engravings from Manipur possibly belonging to the earliest phases of history (Figs. 10.7 & 10.8). Similarly from Assam, rock engravings and impressions besides megalithic monuments belonging to the historical period have been reported (Fig. 10.8). There is an occurrence of high concentration of megalithic remains in this region particularly in the hilly terrain of Khasi-Jayantia hills in Meghalaya, North Cachar hills and in Karbi Anglong in Assam, Manipur and Nagaland (Figs. 10.9-10.15). Engravings or petroglyphs and other impressions on some megalithic remains have also been reported. The evidence till date indicates that rock art in North-East India is not very old and consists only of engravings (Figs. 10.16-10.21).

From Mally's reports it has been noticed that petroglyphs dominate pictographs in Malaysia. Pamela Guntman (2007) also points to rock carvings and engravings belonging to the later part of history in Myanmar. The proximity of Southeast Asian territories as far as rock works are concerned can be gauged by these examples.

As mentioned earlier, the megalithic tradition in North-East India on the macro level has a non-Himalayan geo-cultural trait. Geo-environmental parameters like lithological compositions also play a determining role in the occurrence of megalithic remains. This is the reason why prolific megalithic remains are noticed in western Karbi Anglong and

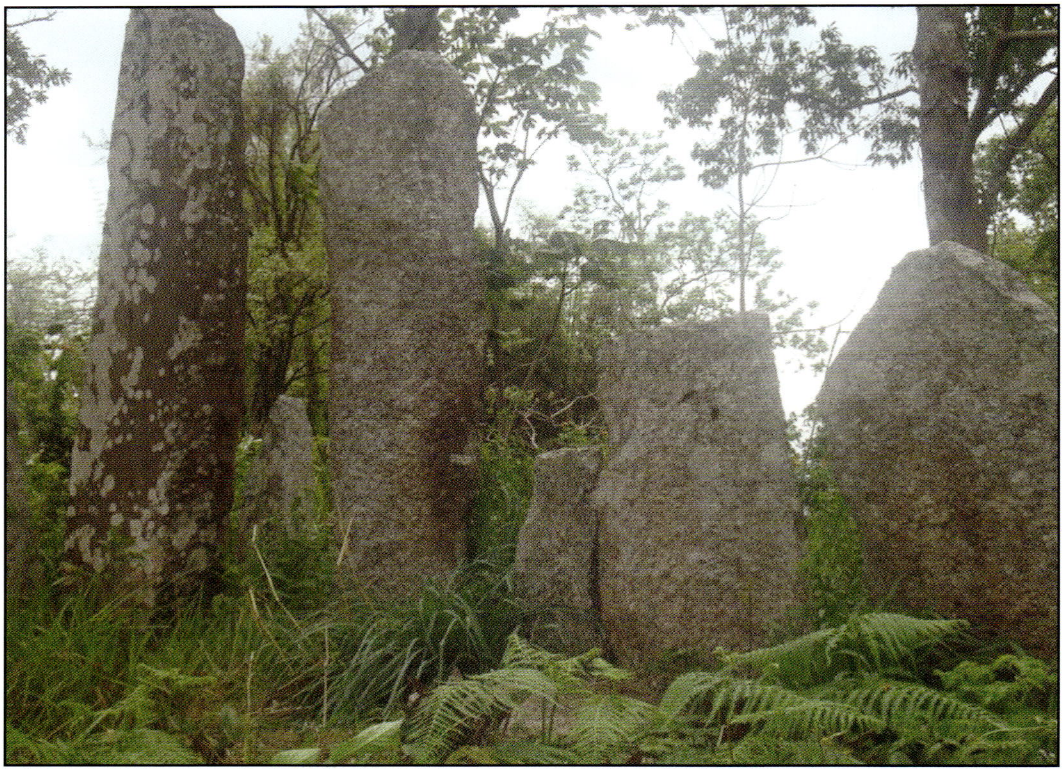

Fig. 10.9 Stone alingment, Umat, Karbi Anglong, Assam.

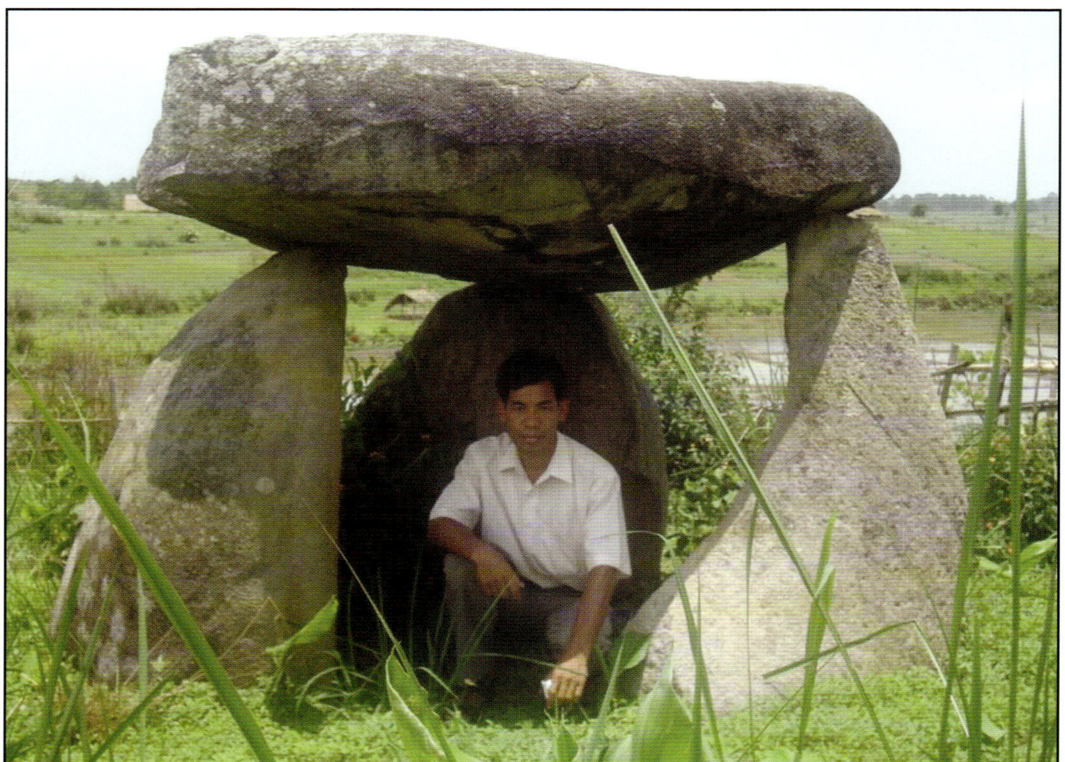

Fig. 10.10 Table stone: Nongjrong,Karbi Anglong, Assam.

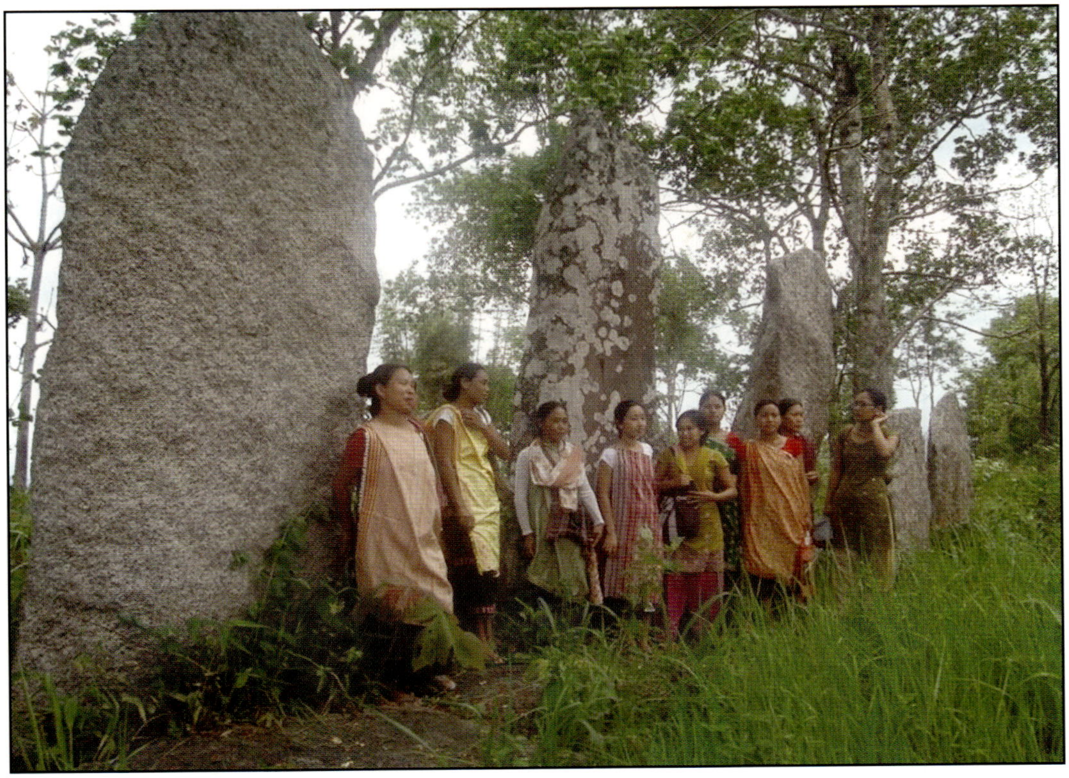

Fig. 10.11 Stone alingment, Umat, Karbi Anglong.

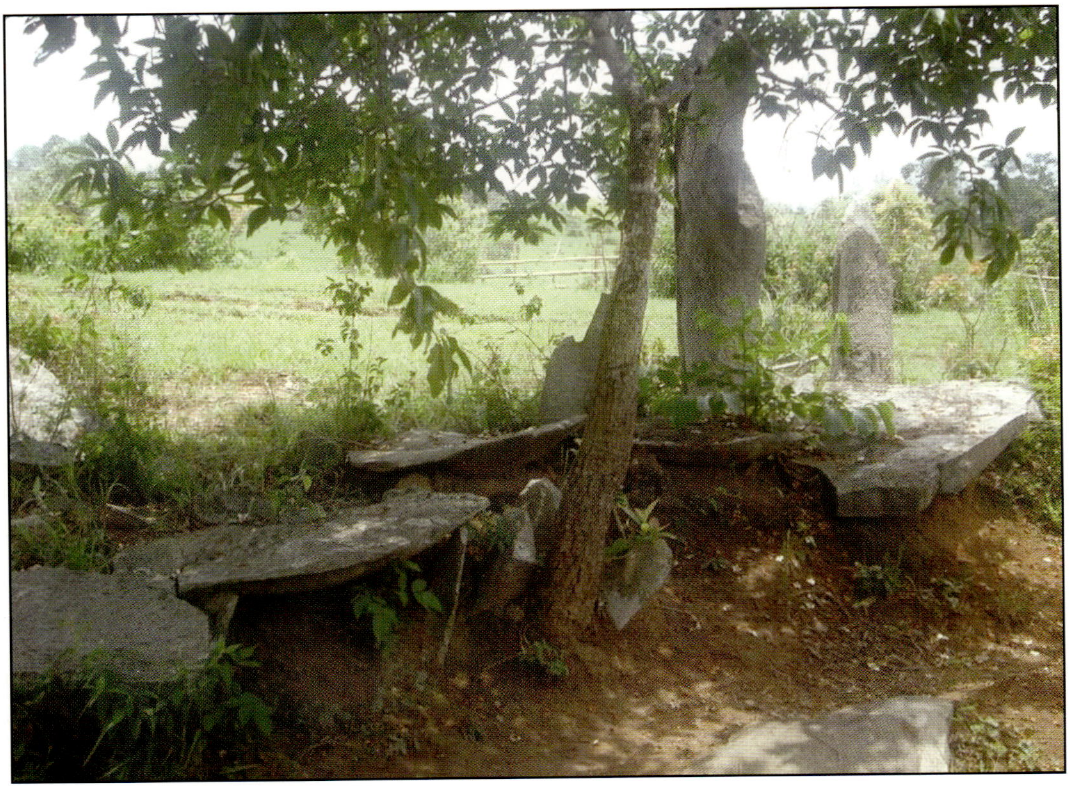

Fig. 10.12 Megaliths, Nongjrong, Karbi Anglong.

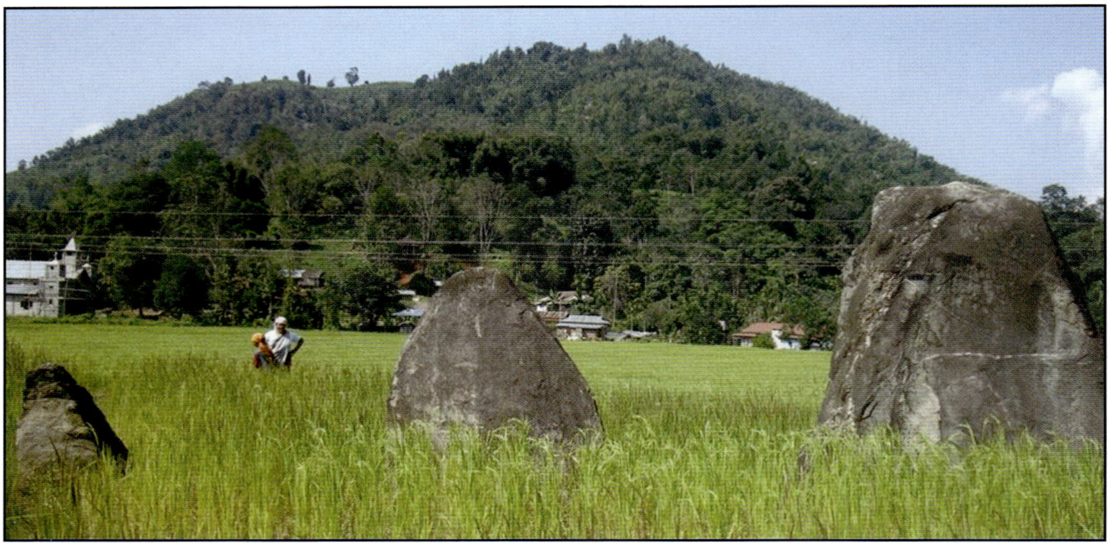

Fig. 10.13 Monoliths in agricultural field, East Khasi Hills.

Fig. 10.14 Megaliths, Nongjrong, Karbi Anglong.

not in its administrative counterpart, the east Karbi Anglong, although both are tied politically and ethnically as the same unit but they are distinct as far as lithological characteristics are concerned (Bezbaruah 2005). GIS mapping of the megalithic remains in western Karbi Anglong using SRTM (Shuttle Radar Tomography Model) for elevation has indicated that this is a high altitudinal phenomenon with a majority

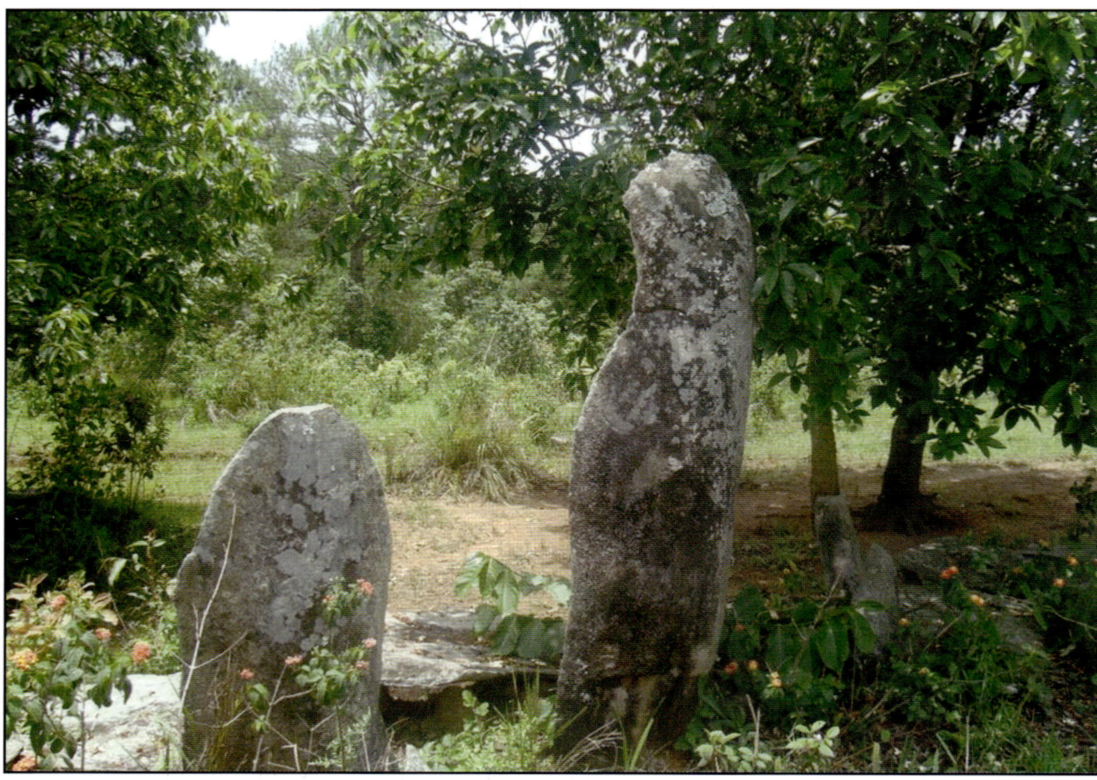

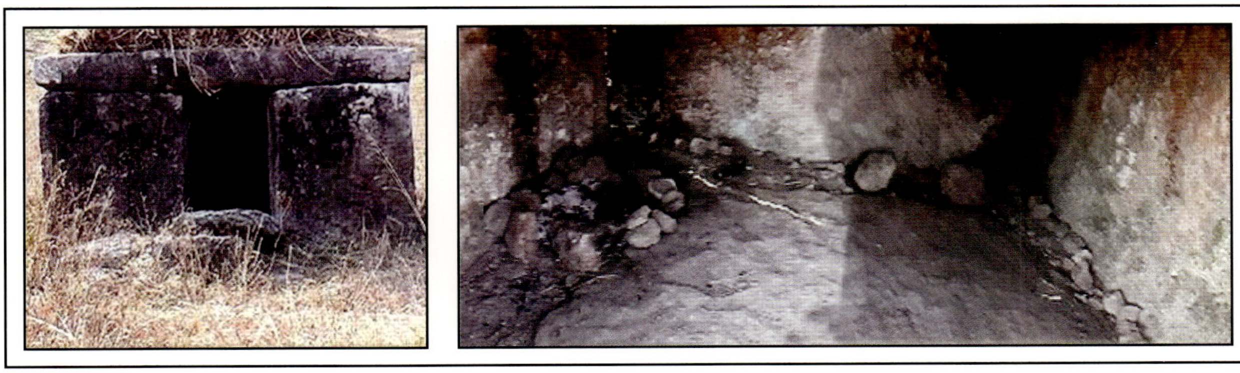

Fig. 10.15 Mawsmai stone chamber, South Khasi Hills.

of the sites lying at altitudes ranging from 700 m MSL (above mean sea level) to 1,200 m MSL (Bezbaruah 2009).

P. Binodini Devi's (2005) investigation in Manipur and S.N. Rao's (1993) study in Khasi hills have also indicated that megalithic remains in Manipur and Meghalaya respectively are located at high altitudes. The site micro environment in western Karbi Anglong reveals it to be associated with water sources (tributaries and streams) in this sub-tropical region and primary rock types like gneiss, quartzite and phyllites belonging to the Shillong group. The situation in the Naga inhabited hills in Manipur and Nagaland is different to a certain extent as it lies in a geological belt with secondary rocks. The impact of the litho-environment in determining the shape and size of the megaliths in this region is a fact to be considered critically. Careful observation and comparison of the monoliths from the Naga hill and from Manipur with the ones from the primary rock-occurring areas of Khasi hills and its continuation in Karbi and North Cachar hills of Assam reveal some interesting facts. There are more monoliths with a roughly circular and thick base and body in Naga hills as these generally happen to be naturally occurring pieces of secondary rocks unsuitable for detaching. A majority of the monoliths from Karbi Anglong as well as Khasi hills have a roughly triangular thin base and elongated body being detached from the parent primary rock. The erection of historical monoliths in Dimapur (now in Nagaland) with engraved designs was easier due to the local availability of secondary rocks. Like the other monoliths these too are

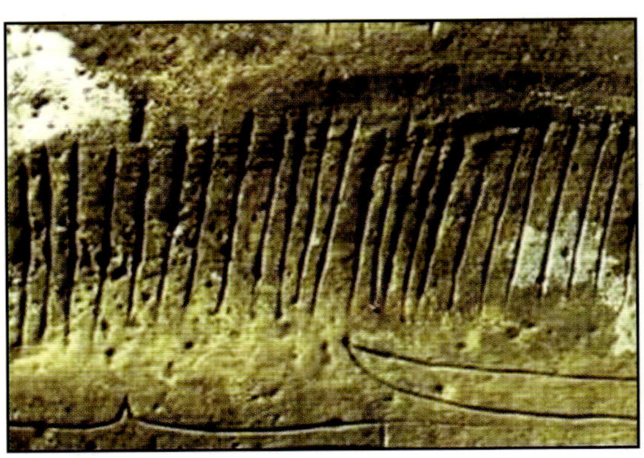

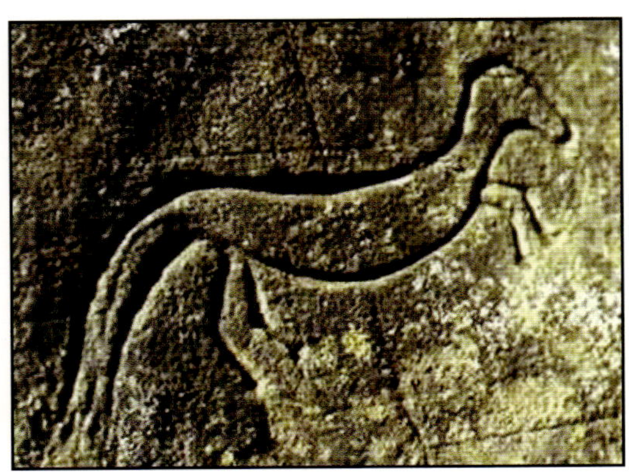

Left: **Fig. 10.16** Series of lines Khoupum, Tamelong districts, Manipur (Photo: IGNCA).

Right: **Fig. 10.17** Engraving of horse, Khoupum, Tamelong districts, Manipur (Photo: IGNCA).

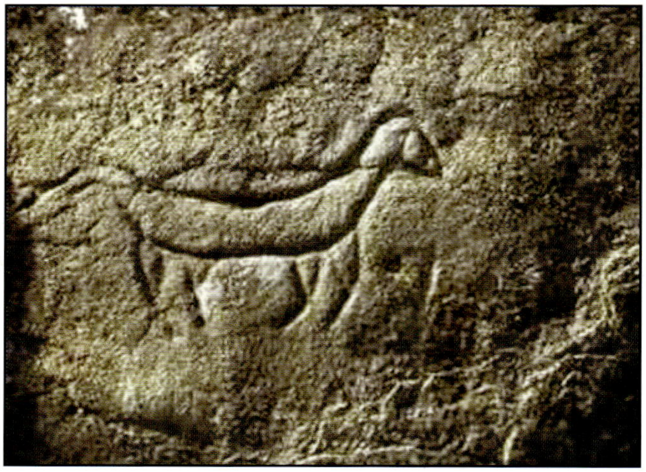

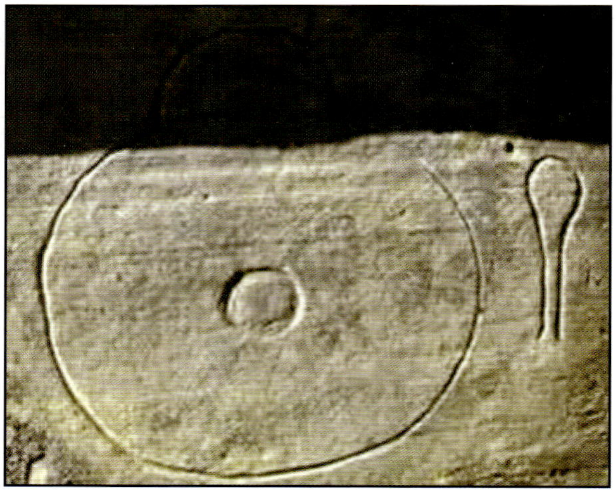

Left: **Fig. 10.18** Engraving of horse, Khoupum, Tamelong districts, Manipur (Photo: IGNCA).

Right: **Fig. 10.19** Unidentified object, Khoupum, Tamelong districts, Manipur (Photo: IGNCA).

made of comparatively soft secondary rocks and have a thick cylindrical base with deliberate engravings.

Whether the megalithic tradition is a prehistoric legacy or a reinvention among the mentioned ethnic communities of North-East India has baffled scholars for long. Pending a focused investigation, available data seems to endorse the hypothesis of continuation.

The fact of structural similarities between the ancient dilapidated and recently erected ones together with the spatial continuity of the tradition mentioned earlier is a relevant fact to support this thinking. What Perry (1918) terms dissoliths (structures in Indonesia) are structurally similar to the single pieces of standing stones with flat table stones in front reported frequently in Khasi as well as Karbi hills. Structural variations of the megalithic types along with such elaborate ceremony as bone deposition recorded by Roy (1963) prevalent among the Khasis indicate the primitiveness of the tradition. It is worth mentioning in this regard that the Khasis, Nagas as well as the Karbis have distinct ethno-lingual terms for megalithic

Left: **Fig. 10.20** Engraving of horse, Khoupum, Tamelong districts, Manipur (Photo: IGNCA).

Right: **Fig. 10.21** Unidentified object, Khoupum, Tamelong districts, Manipur (Photo: IGNCA).

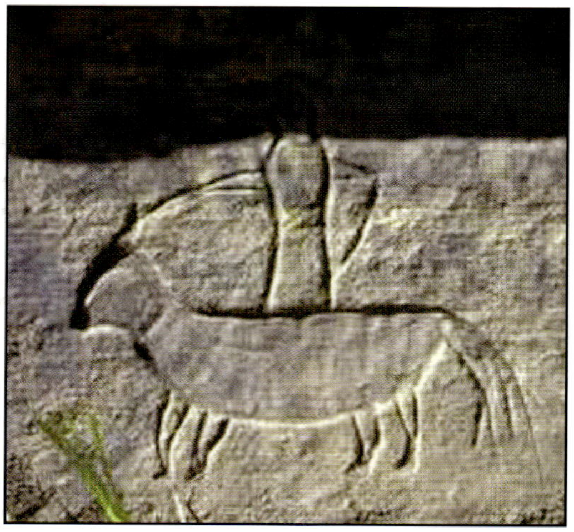

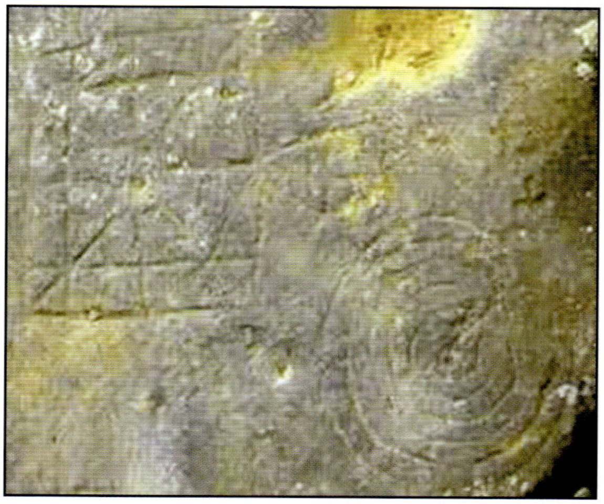

types. For instance Rao (1993) records nine different types of memorial stones and three types of funerary stones among the Khasis all of which have distinct local terms of cultural significance.

Similarly the Angami Nagas as recorded by Hutton (1926) have four types of commemorative stones each having a culturally ascribed term. Rao (2010) has put forward further logic on the structural and cognitive role of megaliths in societies in North-East India. He borrows the concept of MVS (Monstrous Visual Syndrome), a phenomenon explained in the context of state societies of North East Africa, performed by monoliths and brings into discussion similar types prevalent among the Khasis and the ones erected during the reign of Kachari at Dimapur, now in Nagaland. The seeds of state according to him were sown in these societies and were well reflected by the erection of monoliths.

Today we are nearer to the conclusion that this tradition was carried out by migrating groups of people from the south-eastern territory during the juncture of transition to the Christian era and settled possibly in two centres of diffusion—one bordering the present Myanmar in the Manipur-Nagaland highland and the other in Khasi hills. Karbi Anglong and North Cachar hills are the touching peripheries of the centres. Since its initiation in the highland, the tradition has undergone spatio-temporal expansion in this region, the remnants of which are retained by certain communites in an altogether different context. Investigations on rock art have to be carried out in the backdrop of this discussion for systematic documentation and meaningful dissemination of knowledge in the days to come.

REFERENCES

Bezbaruah, D. (2004), 'Megalithic Ruins in Karbi Anglong District of Assam: A Study in the Context of Karbi Culture', Unpublished Ph.D. thesis, Gauhati University.

—— (2005), 'Megalithic Remains of Karbi Anglong, Assam: An Appraisal', *Bulletin Department of Anthropology, Dibrugarh University*, p. 61.

—— (2008), 'Fresh Look into the Megalithic Remains of Karbi Anglong', Paper presented at a seminar on Pre and Proto History of North East India.

Devi, Binodini P. (2005), 'Distribution of Megalithic Traditions and Ethnography in Manipur', *Abstract Volume, National Seminar on Megalithic Tradition in Ethnography and Archaeology in India*, p. 7

Furer Haimendorf, C.Von (1945), 'The Problem of Megalithic Culture in Middle India', *Man in India*, XXV(2): 73-90.

Godwin Austen, H.H. (1872), 'On the Stone Monuments of the Khasi Hills Tribes and Some of the Peculiar Rites and Custom of the People', *Journal of Anthropological Institute* I: 122-43.

Guntmen, Pamela (2007), 'Rock Art and Artisan in the Lemro Valley, Arakan, Myanmar', *Antiquity* 81: 655-74.

Mills, J.P. and J.H. Hutton (1929), 'Ancient Monoliths of North Cachar', *Jr. Asiatic Society Bengal*, XXV: 285-300.

Perry, W.J. (1918), *The Megalithic Culture of Indonesia*. Manchester, p.33.

Rao, S.N. (1993), 'Megalithic Practices among the Khasi and Nagas', in J.P. Singh and G. Sengupta (eds.), *Archaeology of Northeastern India*. New Delhi: Vikas Publishing House, pp. 106-25.

—— (2010), 'Rise of Civilisation in North East Africa and Megalithic Tradition in North East India', Second DN Majumdar (jr.) Memorial Lecture, Guwahati.

Roy, D. (1963), 'The Megalithic Culture of the Khasis', *Anthropos* 58: 520-56.

Scott, C. James (2009), *The Art of Not Being Governed, an Anarchist History of Upland Southeast Asia*. New Delhi: Orient Blackswan Private Ltd.

11

Pagoda-Shaped Depictions in Tibetan Rock Art

Zhang Yasha

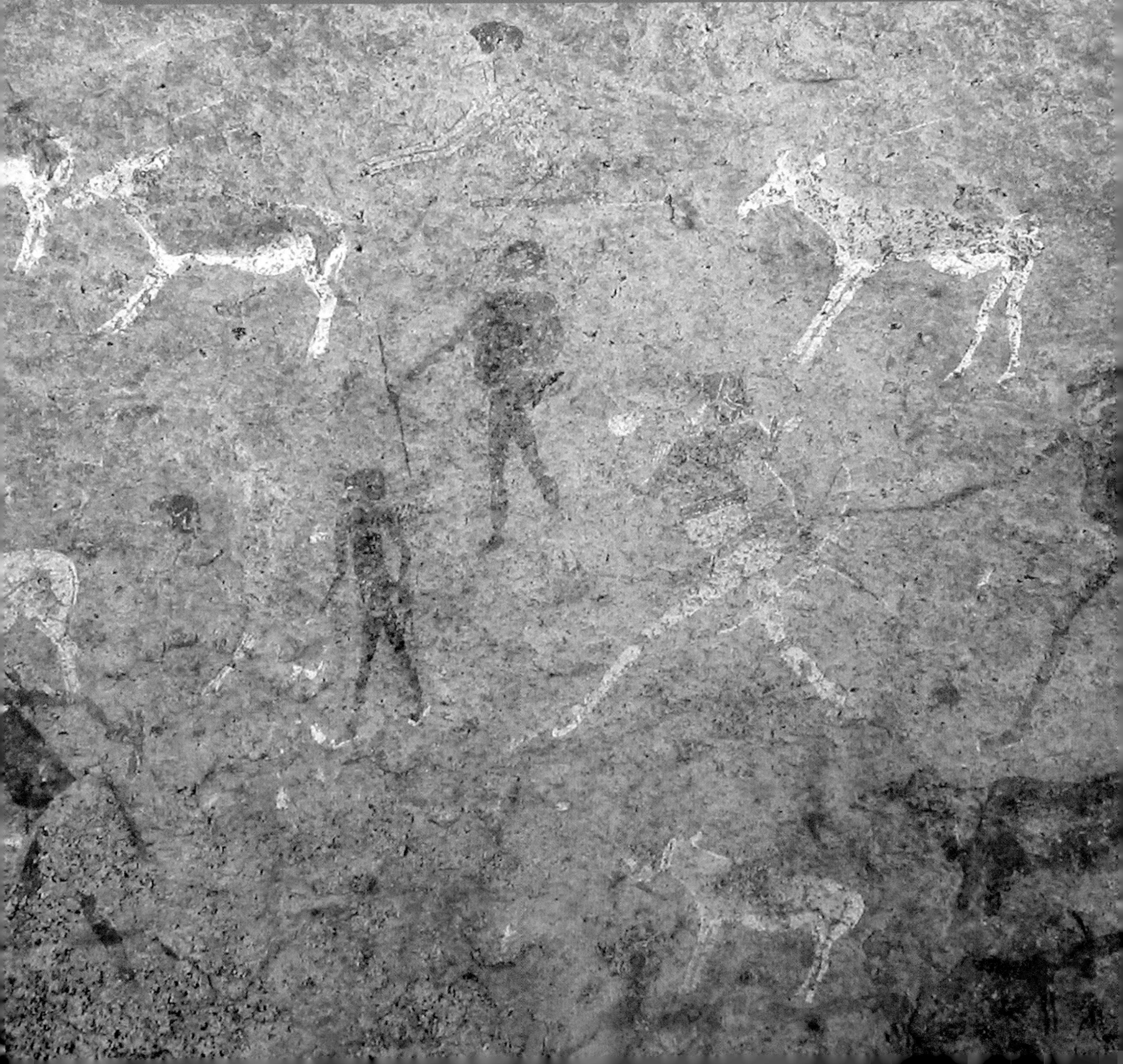

ABSTRACT

Tibetan rock art is mainly distributed in the northern plateau, featuring images involving hunting for wild yaks, worship of Khyung and original altars of Bon religion. Rock art, Megalithic relics, Megalithic monuments, bronze animal statuettes and abundant Microlithic tools collectively comprise the cultural heritage of northern Tibet in the Chalcolithic period. Those who executed the rock art belonged to the Qiang ethnic tribe, who migrated westwards during 2500–1000 BP *and made a living by taming horses and hunting for wild yaks. They blazed a salt-traded road in the northern Tibetan grassland, thus becoming a powerful ethnic group at that time. Their stories, as demonstrated in rock art, relate to the epic of Gesar, female country, Zhang-Zhung's kingdom (an ancient country established by them in the westernmost Qiang Tang), the yak's tribe, and story of horses and other legends of the ancient plateau.*

INTRODUCTION

In 2004, the author and her colleagues went to the Helanshan ranges in Ningxia to conduct a survey of rock art of the area as member of the Rock-Art Research Center, Ethnology and Sociology College of the Central University for Ethnic Minorities. In the central and northern sections of the Helanshan ranges, the group noticed many 'pagoda-shaped' depictions of the Xixia period (1038–1227). These depictions are mainly of two types. Examples of the first type are rather simple and irregular, but they are more numerous than the second type. The second type has been identified as Buddhist pagodas of Tibetan Buddhism in its early period. The first types are mainly found in the central and northern sections of the gullies of the Helanshan mountains (the central section of the Helanshan mountain range is near the city of Yinchuan, and its northern section is near Mt. Shizuishan). A large number of pagoda-shaped depictions are found in the Jiucaigou Gully in the northern section (Fig. 11.1) (Li Xiangshi and Zhu Cunshi 1998). Pagodas of the second type are similar to the 'Kadamkyi Chorten' pagodas often mentioned by Mr. Su Bai in his works. Up to the present, depictions of the second type are found only in the Laobagou Gully of Shizuishan area in the northern section of the Helanshan range (Su Bai 1996) (Fig. 11.2). These two types of Xixia pagoda shapes are different from each other in their outward appearance.

According to Su Bai's investigation and study, Kadamkyi Chorten pagodas were prevalent in Tibet and in the Hexi Corridor during the 12th–14th centuries. They appeared in monasteries in Tibet proper and in some cave temples (the stone carving of the Mati Monastery at Zhangye and the frescoes in the Yulin Grottoes at Anxi) in the Hexi Corridor simultaneously, and they are a typical form of Tibetan Buddhist pagodas of the second propagation period of Tibetan Buddhism by the end of the Yuan dynasty. According to our study over the past years, the earliest Kadamkyi Chorten images that appeared in Tibet must be those that are seen in the rock art at Rutok, Ngari (Fig. 11.3). They were made before the 11th or 10th centuries or even the 9th century, but they appeared in frescoes in monasteries in U-Tsang (dbus-gtsang) no later than the 11th century**.** This kind of pagoda with its unique form might not necessarily have come from India. They appeared in Gandhara in Central Asia as early as the 2nd century. Therefore, it is quite natural to estimate that this kind of Buddhist pagodas came to the western part of the Qinghai-Tibet Plateau by way of some Buddhist countries in Central Asia, and then spread to Gansu and Qinghai by way of the hinterland of Tibet. During the period of Xixia, they had already arrived at the Hexi Corridor.

We have also been very concerned with the extension of this shape of pagodas eastward and northward. By theoretical inference, the spreading of Kadamkyi Chorten pagodas must not have stopped after they reached Dunhuang, Anxi or Ganzhou; they might have reached the territory of Xixia or even the Mongolian territory. The discovery of rock art of Kadamkyi Chorten justifies our inference. According to our theory, it is not difficult to give a reasonable explanation for this discovery. However, the discovery of Kadamkyi Chorten depictionss in Helanshan, Ningxia, was not limited to the study of rock art (it also falls in the category of Buddhist rock carvings). It is necessary to mention

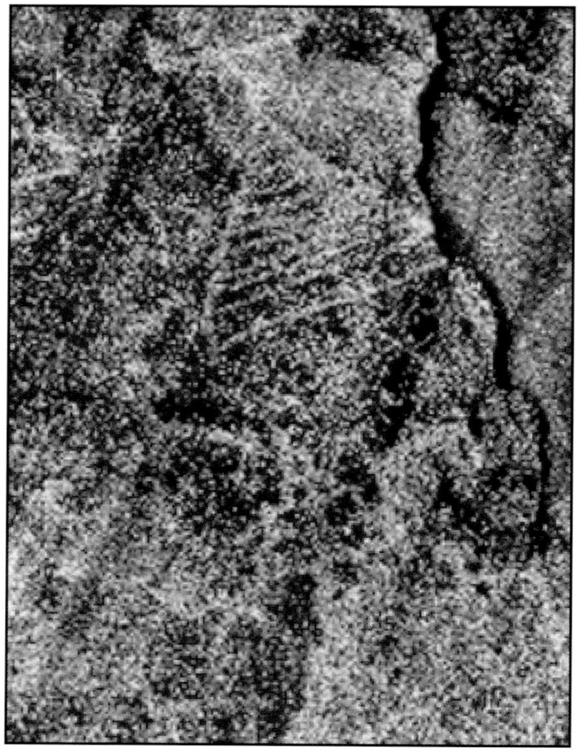

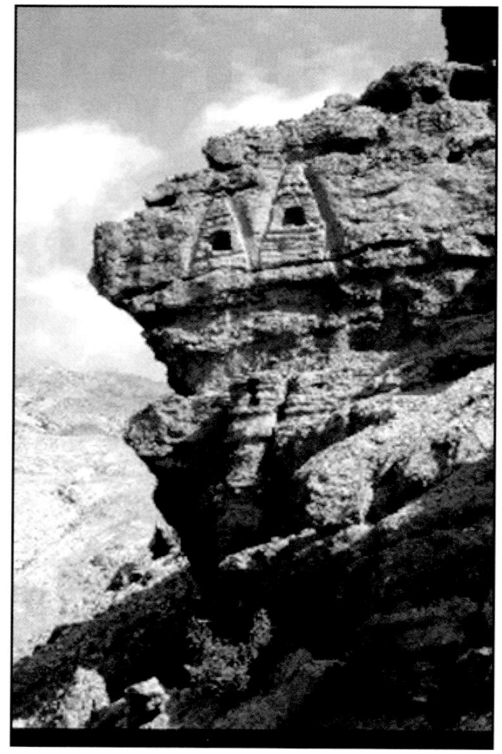

Left: **Fig. 11.1** Pagoda-shaped stone carving in the Jiucaigou Gully in the Helanshan mountain range, Ningxia.

Right: **Fig. 11.2** Pagoda-shaped stone carving in the Laobagou Gully in the Helanshan mountain range, Ningxia.

here that they had a close relationship with the first type of pagoda-shaped petroglyphs found in the Helanshan.

Since the Dangxiang people (*Mi-nyag* in Tibetan) founded the Xixia kingdom with Yinchuan city as its capital, and Tibetan Buddhism flourished and prospered during the middle and later periods of the Xixia kingdom, it was quite natural that the Tibetan pagoda-shaped depiction of the early period be found within the boundary of Xixia. But we were happily surprised by the discovery of the first type of rock art in the Helanshan ranges in Ningxia (Fig. 11.4). These kinds of depictions did not seem to be related to Tibetan Buddhism but appeared in the central part of the populated areas of the Xixia people, and as such contain more cultural connotations.

These pagoda-shaped depictions seem to be nearer to the Bon religion. The appearance of these remains in Xixia reflects at least two facts: (i) the similarity of the depiction of the Dangxiang people and those in the Qinghai-Tibet Plateau, and (ii) The pagoda-shaped altar that appeared in the Bonist sacrificial ceremony had already emerged in the Buddhist culture.

In addition, because of the accuracy of the dates in the Xixia period, the discovery of the Xixia pagoda-shaped rock petroglyphs is helpful in ascertaining the dates of Tibetan rock art.

The similarities between the petroglyphs of the Xixia Dangxiang people and the petroglyphs discovered in the Qinghai-Tibetan Plateau prove that these depictions are

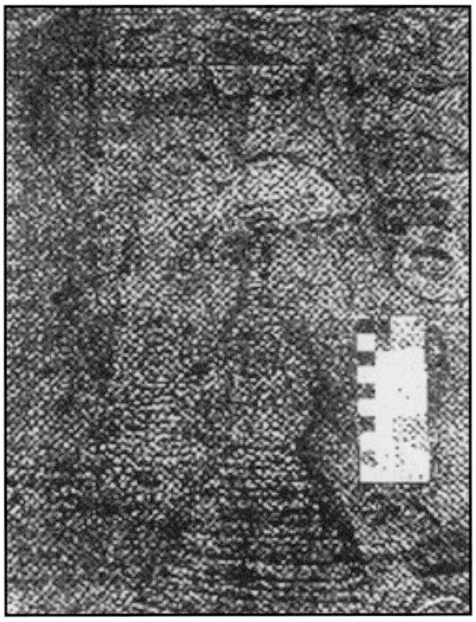

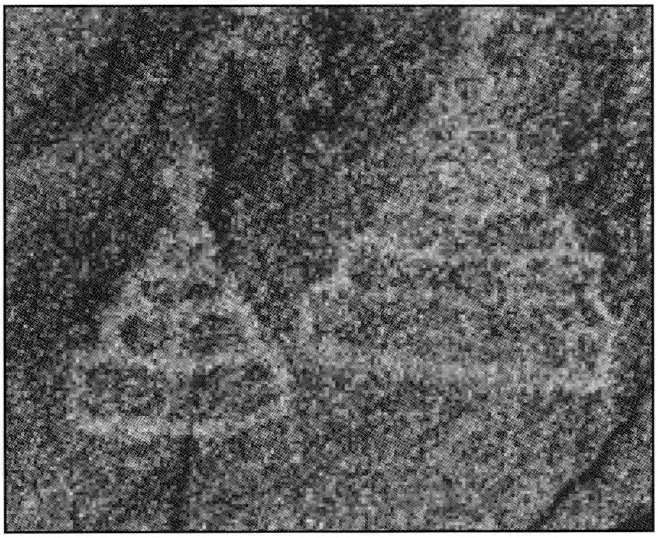

Left: **Fig. 11.3** Buddhist pagoda, Ladrodrang rock painting site, Ngari, Tibet.

Right: **Fig. 11.4** Pagoda-shaped depictions in the Jiucaigou Gully, Helanshan Mountain, Ningxia.

made by Qiang people who inhabited the northern part of the Qinghai-Tibet Plateau. The producers of Tibetan rock art were ethnic Qiang people who lived in Changtang in northern Tibet about 3,000–1,000 years ago. The two most important ethnic groups of the Qiang people were the western Women kingdom and the northern Shangshung kingdom. It seems that the Sumpa people and the Dangxiang people to their northeast were not involved in the production of petroglyphs (although the rock art around Qinghai Lake was obviously related to the Tuyuhun people). However, judging from the fact that the pagoda-shaped depiction of the Qinghai-Tibet Plateau exist in Xixia petroglyphs in the Helanshan range (in addition, there are some very typical Qinghai-Tibet Plateau patterns of yaks), the Dangxiang people were also the producers of the Qinghai-Tibet Plateau rock art. The Sumpa people were probably one of the peoples who depicted yaks.

PAGODA-SHAPED DEPICTIONS IN TIBET ART

The origin of both these types of pagoda-shaped rock carvings discovered at Helanshan, Ningxia, may be found in the rock art of Tibet. In other words, they originated in the Qinghai-Tibet Plateau. Obviously, they were the work of the Dangxiang people, who in ancient times lived in the eastern part of the Qinghai-Tibet Plateau but moved eastward continuously. There are many designs of pagoda-shaped depiction in Tibet. About the date of these pagoda-shaped depictions, scholars tend to attribute them to the Tibetan Buddhist culture. Thus, the dates of all the sites where pagoda-shaped depiction appeared were defined as the Tubo dynasty period or even later. However, as to the pagoda-shaped petroglyphs in Tibet, there are the following problems that should be discussed: (i) Are there pagoda-shaped rock paintings in Tibet, without exception, Buddhist stupas?, and (ii) Did the Tibetan aboriginal religion have a pagoda-shaped sacrificial altar or construction? The key to the problems obviously lies in whether the Tibetan pagoda-shaped rock paintings belonged to the Buddhist culture of the Tubo period or to a pre-Buddhist period, that is, the Bon cultural period.

Judging the rock art of the plateau as a whole, it seems unreasonable to say that a majority of the rock art belong to the pre-Buddhist cultural period while the pagoda-shaped patterns belong to the Buddhist cultural period. It is true that the six-word Lamaistic charm *Om-mani-padme-hum* was carved on the side of some pagoda-shaped pictures. But there are two possible reasons for this: firstly, the six-word Lamaistic charms were added at a later time, that is to say, the date of the petroglyphs cannot be ascertained by the existence of the six-word *dharani.* Secondly, a few pagoda-shaped depictions surely might be works of the Buddhist cultural period, but a majority of the depictions are still the work of the Bon cultural period. Our reasons for this include:

1. A majority of the pagoda-shaped depiction in Tibetan rock art are different in shape from Buddhist stupas. Up to the present, a great number of pagoda-shaped patterns in Tibet are quite different from Buddhist stupas prevalent in India or Central Asia, including others in the western regions of China.
2. The Bon religion in Tibet used a pagoda-shaped stone altar, whose fundamental characteristics are stone terraced pagoda-shaped constructions.

Tibetan rock art were made 3,000–1,000 years ago. This was in the Chalcolithic age (in archaeological terms), or the Small kingdom period and the Tubo dynasty period in Tibetan history. Tibetan rock art has a historical developmental period of more than 2,000 years. Compared with ancient symbols of Yungdrung, trees, the sun and the moon, the pagoda-shaped depiction are a product of a rather late period. However, we should say that a majority of the pagoda-shaped petroglyphs were made in the Bon culture period, but pictures of this kind were under Buddhist influence in the later period. The patterns of the pagoda-shaped altar of Bon religion must have emerged in the first millennium of the Christian era.

About 2,000–1,300 years ago, the Bon symbol system was almost fully developed. A prominent feature of this period was the adding of the pagoda-shaped sacrificial symbol into the Bon symbol system. About 1,200 years ago (the Tubo period) and after that, Buddhist cultural impact was clearly shown in the rock art of Bon religion, and the Bon sacrificial altar also has a great resemblance to the Buddhist pagodas. That is to say, during a period of 1,000 years, the pagoda-shaped depiction in Tibet experienced periods of birth, formation, evolution and finally perfection. What are worthy of attention are the Qinghai rock depictions. During this period, they gradually separated from the main part of the Qinghai-Tibet rock art, and began moving on the road to decline. The main part of the plateau rock art is concentrated in the western and northern part of Tibet (from Rutok in Ngari and extending eastward to the Namtso Lake/*gnam-mtsho* in the north of Tibet), that is, the Changtang (*byang-thang*) region.

EVOLUTION OF PAGODA-SHAPED DEPICTIONS IN TIBET

In the ancient remains, we found the pagoda-shaped small bronzes of personal adornments [called *toja (thog-lcags)* in Tibetan, which means 'stone dropped from the

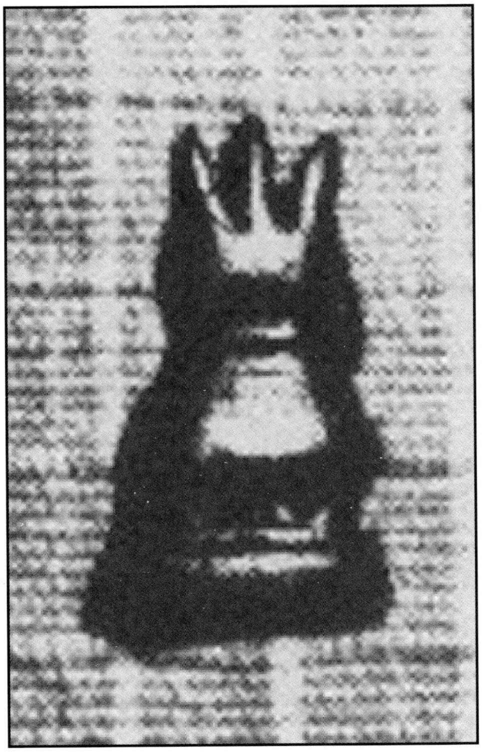

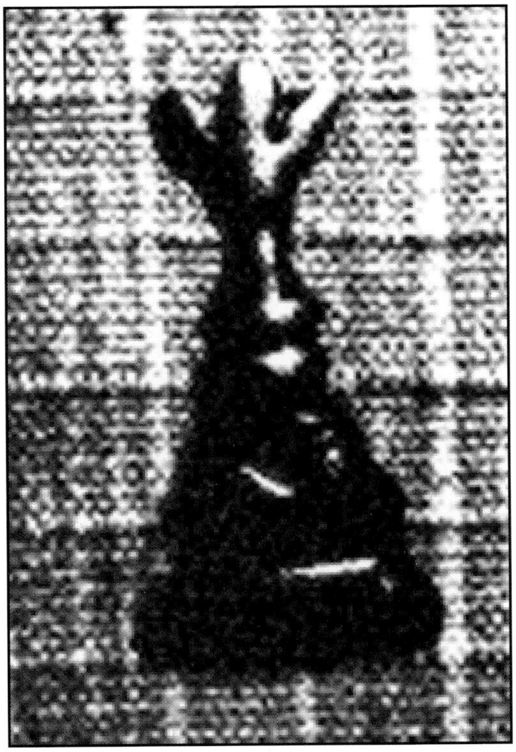

Fig. 11.5 (*left*) and **Fig. 11.6** (*right*) are pagoda-shaped articles, called "togia (thog-lcags)" in Tibetan, meaning "stone dropped from sky". They were small bronze decorations of religious connotation in ancient times.

sky'] near the altars of the Bon religion. The ancient northern part of the plateau had its own tradition of a sacrificial altar. Sacrificial altars of this kind consisted of two parts: the main body and the top of the altar (Figs. 11.5 & 11.6). Its main body is like a cone and the top is like a trident and the connotation of the same remained mysterious/ unknown. It is interesting that we have found similar pagoda-shaped altars in the western Ladrodrang rock-painting site in Rutok (Figs. 11.7 & 11.8).

The original form of the Bon altar might be related to the stone sacrificial pillar (Fig. 11.9), which was prevalent in the west and north of Tibet. As early as the beginning of the 20th century, some foreign investigation teams and Tibetologists found a lot of man-made, single-stone pillars and altars made of stone. During 1989–1992, the Tibetan Cultural Relics Survey team discovered a number of remains and named them 'Megalithic remains' or 'Megalithic buildings'. American Tibetologist, Vincent Bellezza has been conducting a survey of ancient Shangshung cultural remains in the north of Tibet since 1995. His reports done in 1999 and 2000 provide a great number of pictures and photos of stone altars and stone buildings of the early period. All this pictorial data clearly proves that the Bon culture in the Changtang grassland was well developed. It goes without saying that there were a rather large number of early Bon stone altars or stone buildings in the north of the plateau; they and the rock engravings in the north of Tibet belonged to the same period.

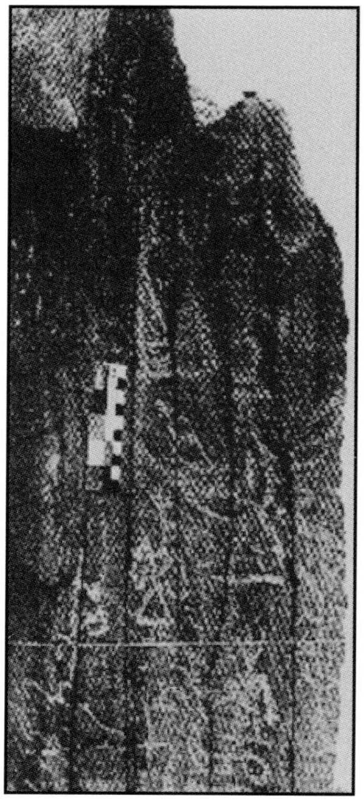

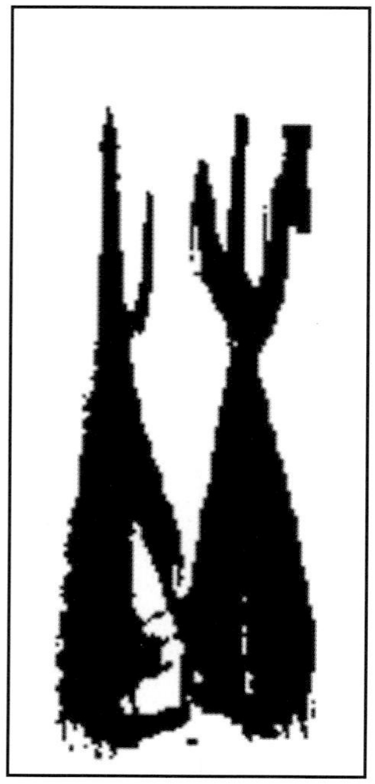

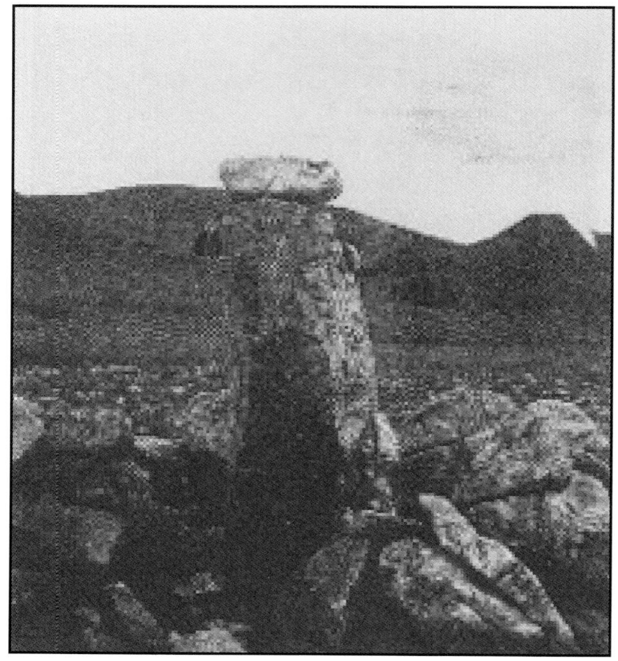

Left: **Fig. 11.7** The symbols of eagle, pagoda, tree and Yungdrung on ladrodrang rock art in Rutok County.

Centre: **Fig. 11.8** Line drawing of pagoda-shaped patterns.

Right: **Fig. 11.9** An ancient sacrificial pillar made of a single stone in the Northern Tibet.

The Bon altar of the early period is more like a sacrificial pillar. Fig. 11.7 is a set of religious symbols found at the Ladrodrang rock art site at Rutok. The picture consists of a number of representative symbols—the sun, moon, Yungdrung, trees, pagoda patterns, eagle, bird-man and bird-witch. Among this set of symbols, most peculiar are two pagoda-shaped patterns, which are quite similar to the early Bon sacrificial pagodas shown as 'togo' (stone dropped from the sky). The main bodies of these two pagoda-like images are like cones, and their tops are like tridents.

That the early stage sacrificial pagoda (or sacrificial pillar) of Bon religion emerged in the west of Tibet instead of the north of Tibet is a very interesting problem worthy of study. It shows that the origin of the pagoda-shaped patterns might be related to a Central Asian culture or Kashmir culture. The two pagoda-shaped objects depicted with a set of other symbols are unique to Bon religion, which means a new item (pagoda-shaped pattern) has been added to the symbols. In the Ladrodrang rock painting site at Repang Lake in Rutok county, there are not only patterns of early period Bon sacrificial pillars, but what is more important is that more than ten other pagoda-shaped items display the influence of Bon sacrificial pagodas. Judging from this, it is without doubt that the Ladrodrang site is one of the most important rock art sites in the west of Tibet.

The sacrificial altar looks like a sacrificial pillar (Fig. 11.9), but later it developed towards the form of an altar. The sacrificial pillar transforming into an altar should have been the first stage of the evolution of the Bon pagoda. The key change was that the pagoda was no longer made from a single stone, but was made with many stones.

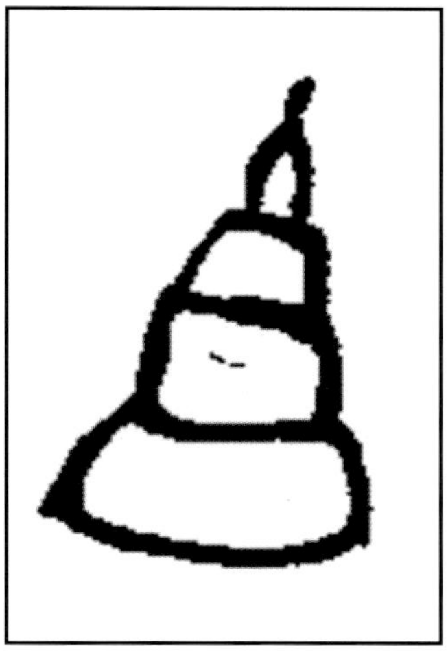
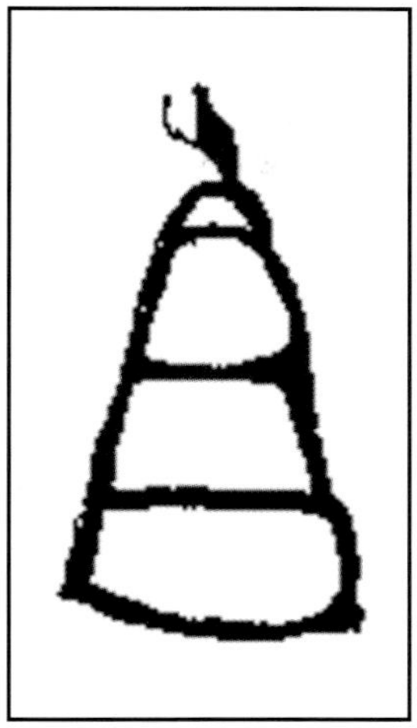
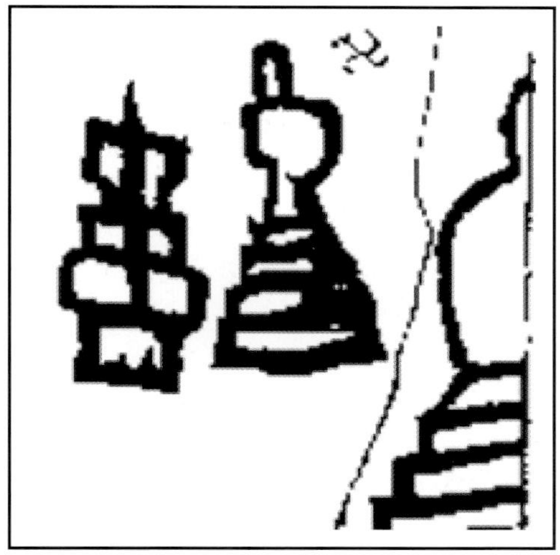

Left & Centre: **Figs. 11.10 & 11.11** Pagoda at Ladrodrung, Rutok County, Western Tibet.

Right: **Fig. 11.12** Pagoda at Ladrodrung Rutok County. Western Tibet.

Figs. 11.10 & 11.11 are altars made of several layers of stones. It seems that there was no strict regulation about the number of stones needed to complete an altar. For instance, the altar in Fig. 11.10 was made of four large pieces of stones, while that in Fig. 11.11 was made of three pieces. The pagoda in Fig. 11.12 has a big belly, which is wider than the top and the bottom. This is unique. The top of the altar is no longer a trident, but a thing with a pointed head.

When the main body of the altar evolved into a five-terraced form, the Bon altar came to its final form. John Vincent Bellezza said the 'five-terraces' of the stone altar of Bonism might be a representative of the five elements (water, fire, metal, wood and earth) that made up the cosmology of Bonism. This kind of a relatively regular form appeared at the Drakpuk rock art site. Like the Ladrodrang rock art site, Drakpuk is also located in the region of Repang Lake. The pagoda-shaped construction on the Drakpuk rock art site has distinct Bonist characteristics—the altar was made of five pieces of big stones, every piece of stone smaller than the one below it, and a pair of yak horns were placed on the top of the altar (Fig. 11.13). There are seven pagoda-shaped patterns in Fig. 11.14, the biggest one of which consisted of five stone layers and a pair of yak horns on its top. The other six pagoda-shaped altars are composed of only four layers. These seem to demonstrate that at that time, there was no strict regulation on the number of layers in a pagoda. Above the rock depictions of altars are pictures of two animals. The centre one is of a deer and the right one is of probably a sheep. Fig. 11.13 has a terraced ladder with a top having a pair of yak horns; probably on the right is an unfinished picture of a pagoda. It must have been in the third stage of the evolution of pagoda altars in west Tibet that the pagoda was fixed at five terraces and yak horns were offered at its top. This is a clear Bonist cultural characteristics. The custom of offering yak horns on altars or important piles which exist in Tibetan-inhabited areas up to the present is, without doubt, related to Bonism. Thus, at least by this period, the pagoda-shaped depictions in rock art may belong to the pre-Buddhist period.

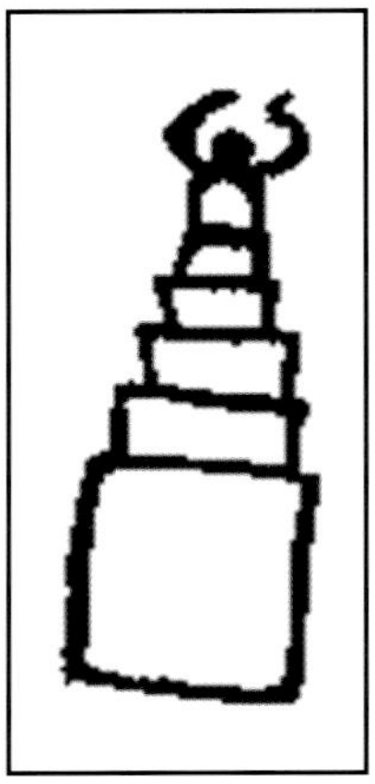

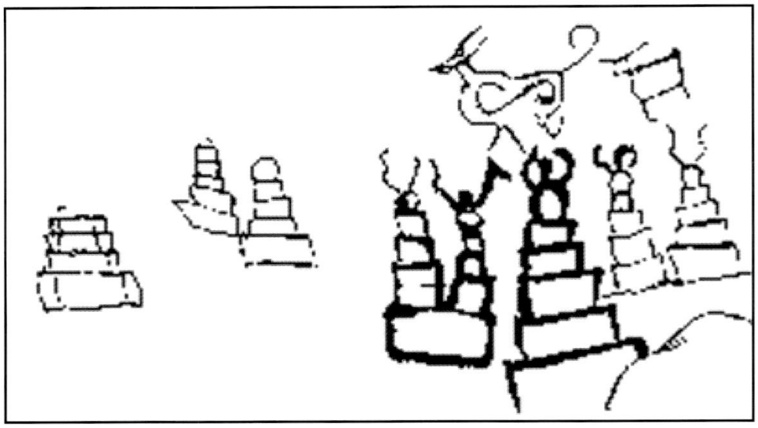

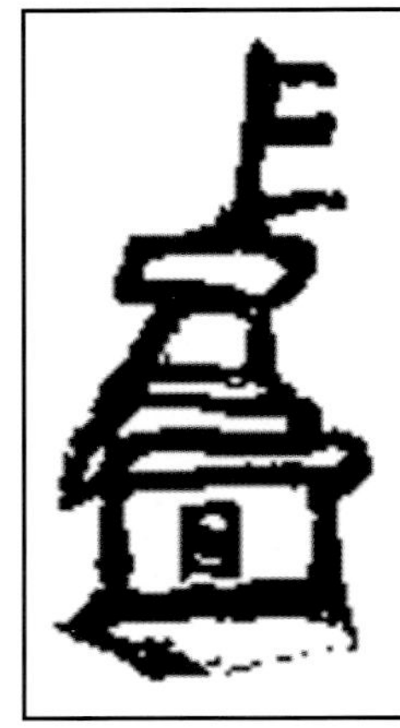

Left: **Fig. 11.13** Pagoda at Dradong, Rutok, Western Tibet.

Centre: **Fig. 11.14** Pagoda-shaped rock depictions at Dradong, Rutok, Western Tibet.

Right: **Fig. 11.15** Rock art depictions at Dradong, Western Tibet.

IMPACT OF EARLY-PERIOD BUDDHIST PAGODAS ON THE BON PAGODA ALTARS

From what period did the Buddhist pagoda begin to have a notable impact on Bon sacrificial altars? Judging from the process of the development of pagoda-shaped depictions in the west regions probably started from the 4th stage of the development of the Bon pagoda. The most important change that occurred in the 4th stage is a 'round altar' which appeared on the five-terraced altar. Its appearance should be regarded as a result of Buddhist impact (Fig. 11.16). Its appearance seemed an insignificant change, but in reality it was a very important one because there was no round altar of this kind in the early period. Here, the question arises at what time did the Bon altar get influenced from Buddhist pagoda? Did it begin during the Tubo dynasty?

According to the chapter an 'Women Kingdom' in the *History of the Northern Dynasties*, at least in the period of the southern and northern dynasties (5th and 6th centuries), the western 'Women Kingdom' had already felt the impact of Buddhism. What is worthy of notice is that in the same period, the Tubo to the east of the Women Kingdom also began to have contact with the Buddhist culture. According to Tibetan documents, during the reign of Tubo Tsenpo Lhatotori Nyantsan (about the 5th century, at the same time as the Women Kingdom was recorded in the *History of the Northern Dynasties*), a Buddhist monk went to Tubo to do missionary work, but the Tubo Tsenpo, it seems, did not accept his doctrine. The monk left a few Buddhist sacred books behind when he left.

Although King Lhatotori Nyantsan did not accept Buddhism, he worshipped the scriptures as sacred and he got the Buddha's protection for this. Tsenpo Lhatotori Nyantsan recovered his youthful vigour at the age of 80 and lived till the age of 120. It is because of this that Tibetan historians say that in this period of time 'Tibet began to have orthodox Buddhism'. The chapter on Women Kingdom in the *History of the Northern Dynasties* says that the Women Kingdom 'worshipped Asura and Spirits of Trees'. It adds that in the Women kingdom in the west of Tibet, except for the worship of tree spirits and the

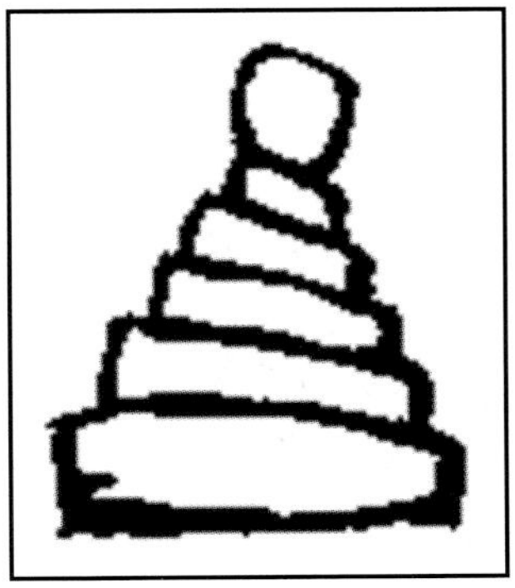

Fig. 11.16

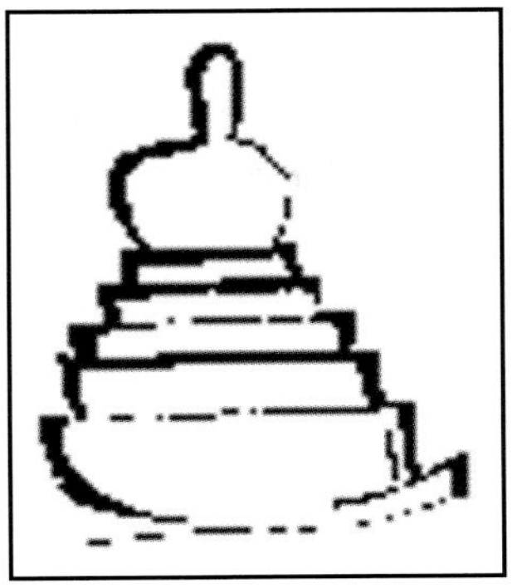

Fig. 11.17

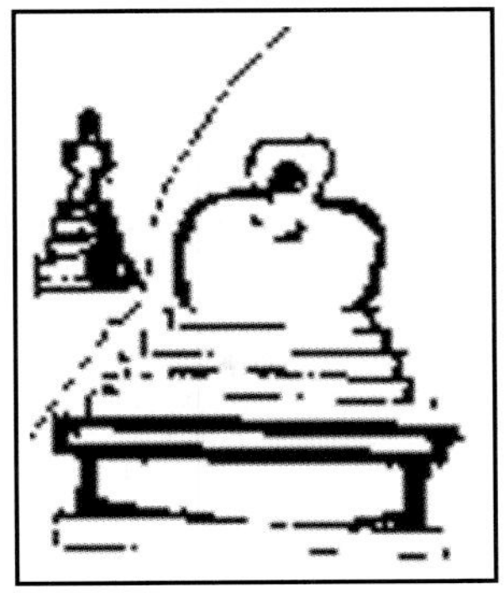

Fig. 11.18

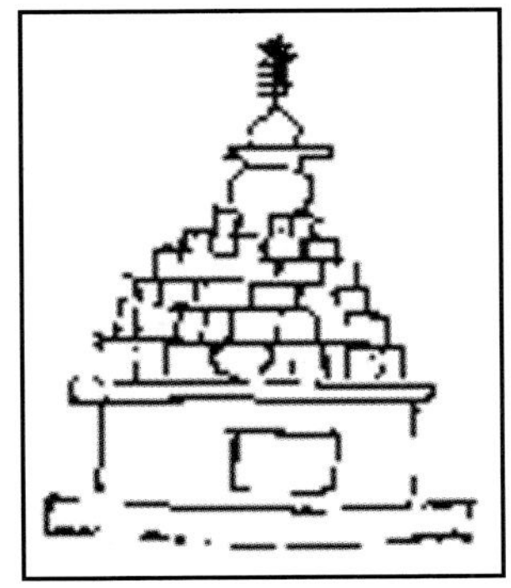

Fig. 11.19

Figs. 11.16-11.19 Pagoda-shaped depictions at Ladrodrang rock site, in Rutok county, Western Tibet.

custom of bird divination, their main religious practice was the worship of Asura. Geographically, the Women Kingdom bordered Kashmir and the Indus Valley in the west, and the kingdom of Khotan in the north. Buddhism was prevalent in these two places. It was in Kashmir that the Buddhist Fourth Gathering was held, and the Buddhist culture was prosperous in this area. In neighbouring areas, such as the Spiti Valley and Swat area, Buddhist statues made in 2-3 century BCE have been found. The rock paintings in the Spiti area and in Rutok were of the same type. In ancient times, the kingdom of Khotan was the first area in China which received Buddhism, which was introduced in Khotan around the 1st century. The introduction of Buddhism in Khotan was closely related to Kashimira (present-day Kashmir).

Owing to the fact that the kingdoms west and north of the western kingdom of Women were Buddhist, it was quite possible that Buddhism spread to the kingdom of Women by way of these areas. Chinese historical documents clearly indicate that the western kingdom of Women had close contacts with northern Hindus. From this it is clear that the Women Kingdom in the western part of Tibet might have received the Buddhist culture before the period of Tubo Kingdom (Tang dynasty) because it was under the influence of Buddhism from North India and Kashmir. However, there is no record of when this influence began. The *History of the Northern Dynasties* and the *History of the Sui Dynasty* have similar records; the form of the pagoda had been fixed at least in the southern and northern dynasties (420–589). In our opinion, the Bonist altar first appeared in the west of Tibet, but then it was under the influence of Buddhism. It was because the neighbours bordering west Tibet, such as North India, Kashmir, Khotan and Nepal were all Buddhist countries. Hence, west Tibet became the key place for the Bonist pagoda (altar) culture to emerge, develop and evolve.

The five-terraced pagoda with a round top first appeared at Karin Banre (also called Banre) in the Repang district of Rutok county (Fig. 11.16). At first sight, there is no major difference from the Drakpuk rock altar, but the round top itself is a great change. However, other things might appear on the round top of the pagoda. For instance, on a Ladrodrang rock art, a pillar appeared on the round top; on another Ladrodrang altar, there is a flat platform on the round top on which are images of the sun and the moon. The appearance of the round top is the 4th stage of the development of pagoda-like patterns, and it is an important stage to show that Bonist altars began to feel the influence of the Buddhist pagoda. A square base placed under the five-terraced pagoda completed the 5th stage of the development of the Bonist pagoda. This stage made the Bonist pagodas look much like Buddhist ones (Figs. 11.17-11.19).

There are a few Buddhist pagoda patterns at the Ladrodrang rock painting site: on a rock surface, there are three pagodas side by side. The six-syllable *dharani* in Tibetan is painted on the base of each pagoda. The body of each pagoda is in three sections, at the centre of the second section are Sanskrit letters; at the top are sun-and-moon patterns, which are in the prototype of Bonism. Obviously, Buddhist pagodas have also absorbed some traditional Bonist patterns.

DEVELOPMENT ORDER AND CHARACTERISTICS OF PAGODA-SHAPED PICTURES IN NORTH TIBET

The earliest Bonist pillar form pagoda pictures have not been found in rock paintings in north Tibet, because this kind of pagoda only began in the 3rd stage in west Tibet. Judging from the material that we have, Bonist sacrificial altar rock paintings came into being in the Rutok district in west Tibet, and then they developed towards relatively regular Bonist models. When it came into the 3rd stage, that is, when the Bonist pagoda was basically formed, it gradually spread to north Tibet. In other words, pagoda-shaped rock paintings first appear in chiseled rock art; after they came into maturity, they spread to north Tibet.

The pagoda-shaped rock art of north Tibet is mainly concentrated in the caves on the shore of Namtso Lake (*gnam-mtsho*), especially on the Greater Tashi (*bkra-shis*) Island and Lesser Tashi (*bkra-shis*) Island (the latter was also called Dong Lake) on the eastern shore of Namtso Lake. The rock paintings in the caves of these two islands are numerous and unique, and their forms are varied. Surely it can be said

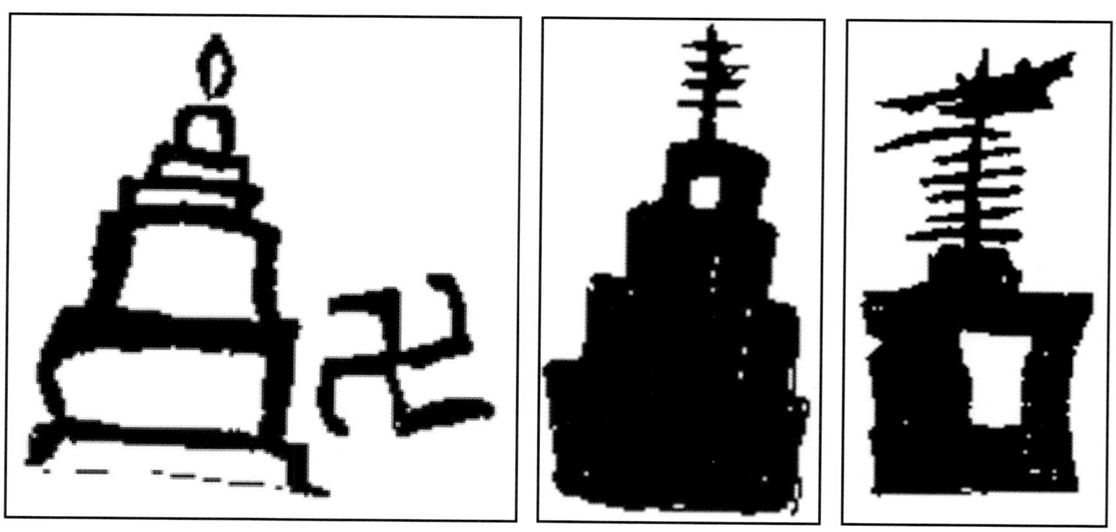

Left: **Fig. 11.20** Pagoda and Yungdrung depiction in a cave of Drashi Island in Namtso Lake of Northern Tibet.

Centre & Right: **Figs. 11.21 & 11.22** Pagoda-shaped depiction in the cave of Drashi Island in Namtso Lake of Northern Tibet.

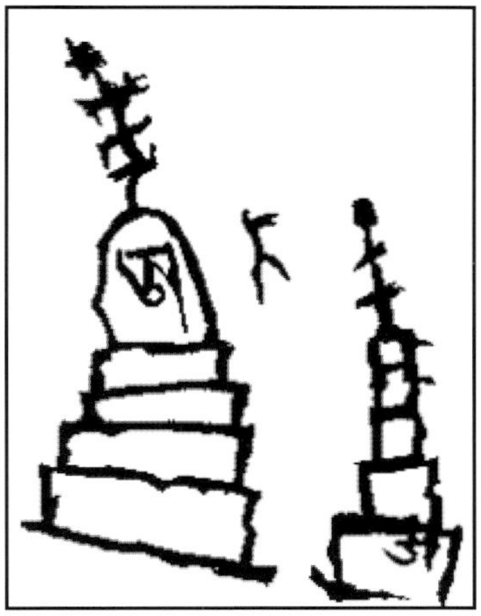

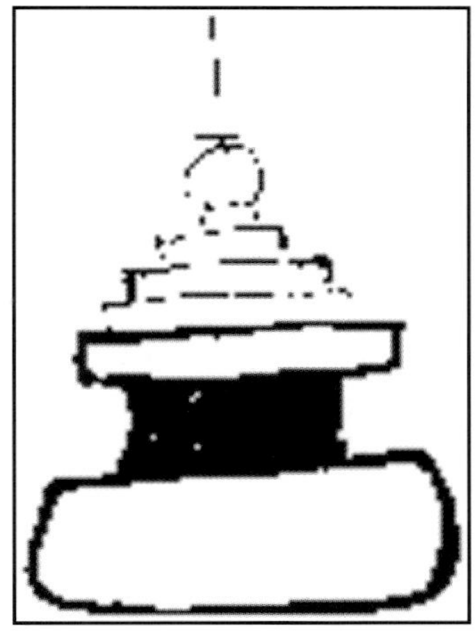

Left: **Fig. 11.23** Pagoda and Yungdrung depictions in the cave of Drashi Island in Namtso Lake of Northern Tibet.

Centre & Right: **Figs. 11.24 & 11.25** Pagoda shape depictions in Eastern Island (also called lesser Drashi Island) in Namtso Lake of Northern Tibet.

that the pagoda-shape of west Tibet represents the early and middle stages of the Bonist sacrificial rock art, while the pagoda-shaped pictures in the caves on the shore of Namtso Lake represent the later stage of the Bonist pagoda culture. The 3rd stage of Bonist rock pictures was a period in which the Bonist pagoda-shaped altar attained maturity. An example (Fig. 11.20) may be found in rock art in the caves of Tashi Lake. The form of this pagoda was identical to that of the 3rd stage in west Tibet. The forms of Yungdrung indicate clearly that this type of pagoda had a special relationship with the Bonist sacrificial altar.

Although the rock art of the pagoda-shaped altars of north Tibet was introduced from west Tibet, they began to follow a path of their own in development. They formed their own unique systems; the distinctions between them gradually became clear. On the altars in west Tibet, Drakpuk rock art sites are yak horns, while this kind of sacrifice has never been found in north Tibet. The sacrifices on the altars in north Tibet are trees (or something like plants) (Figs. 11.21 & 11.22). This kind of altar and trees are also found at the Donshampo rock art site, but these seem to be the pictures of the later stage, because there are Tibetan letters on the pagoda (Fig. 11.23). The pagoda-shaped depictions of the 4th stage of north Tibet were different from those of west Tibet. They all had a round top, but the round top of north Tibet pictures always had an aerial-like straight line (Fig. 11.24). The same is true of the pagoda-shaped depiction of the 5th stage of north Tibet (Fig. 11.25). However, this kind of pagoda is similar to later Buddhist pagodas.

The Bonist pagoda of the later stage in north Tibet presents a free style, with various characteristics; the sacrificial culture is prominent with strong mystical elements. Fig. 11.26 is a cave art of a Bonist sacrificial pagoda on the Lesser Tashi Island. On the base of the pagoda are two Yungdrungs, and three more around the body of the pagoda. The most conspicuous is the human form standing on the altar, but we do not know whether it is a witch or a sacrifice. Fig. 11.27 is similar to Fig. 11.26; on its top is probably a human form or a strange symbol. The base and body of the pagoda are also quite

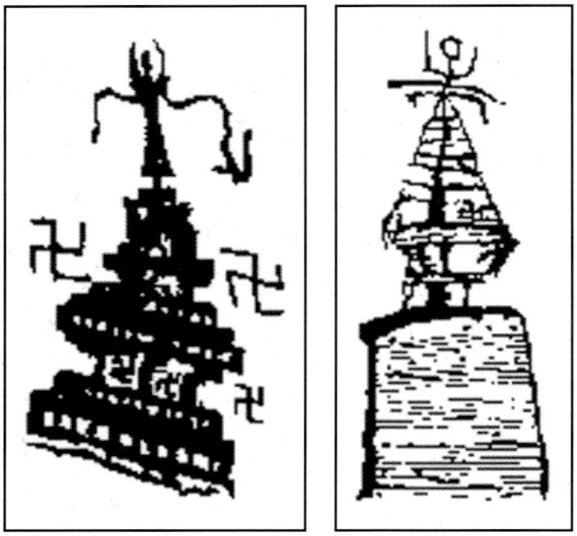

Figs. 11.26 & 11.27 Rock paintings on lesser Drashi Island, in the eastern shore of Namtso Lake, Northern Tibet.

strange; it looks like a terrace with many signs representing various spirits. The pagoda-shaped depictions in the caves on Tashi Lake on the eastern shore of Namtso Lake in north Tibet not only have various shapes and mystic symbols, but also have Yungdrung symbols, characteristic of the Bon culture. Bird (eagle) worship also has a spectacular representation in northern Tibetan rock art.

In the Ladrodrang rock art in Ngari, north Tibet, an eagle and early-stage pagoda sacrificial rituals co-existed; but, generally speaking, rock art of western Tibet seldom put pagoda altars together with eagle-worship. This indicates that eagle (or bird) worship was an important cultural character of the ancient civilisation of Shangshung (this has been confirmed by rock art of Tibet). But the picture of the eagle (or bird) seems more related to witchcraft (to pretend to be a bird-man or adorn the witch with bird mask or bird-feathers) of witches (Bon followers), while the pagoda altar itself was the object of worship by Bon followers.

An example of combining pagoda-worship and bird-worship appeared in the cave at Namtso Lake in north Tibet (Fig. 11.26). This bird-shaped pagoda is more of a sacrificial altar than a pagoda, and it represents more directly the idea and custom of Bonist bird worship. On the right of Fig. 11.26 are two bird-shaped sacrificial altars, on whose top, it seems, are some vegetables. In front of these bird-shaped pagodas is an animal with a tree-branch (?) on its head. This seems to signify that the animal was a deity, or it means the animal was a sacrifice. The Greater and Lesser Islands in Namtso Lake are Bon rock art sites, with a big collection of pagoda-shaped pictures, which means that this area is a major Bonist cultural centre in north Tibet. John Vincent Bellezza conducted a field trip here to collect a number of folk legends, and proved that Namtso Lake was the northern Tibetan Bonist cultural centre for a long time. The pagoda-shaped depictions on the Greater and Lesser Tashi (*bkra-shis*) Islands have proved his viewpoint from the angle of cultural relics.

(This paper has been translated by Chen Guansheng)

REFERENCES

Bai, Su (1996), *Tibetan Buddhism and Temple Archaeology*. Beijing: Cultural Relics Publishing House.

Bellezza, John Vincent (2002), *Antiquities of Upper Tibet: An Inventory of Pre-Buddhist Archaeological Sites on the High Plateau* (Findings of the Upper Tibet Circumnavigation Expedition, 2000). Delhi: Adroit Publishers.

Tucci, G. (1987), *Tibetan Archaeology* (Chinese translation by Xiang Hongjia). Lhasa: Tibetan People's Publishing House.

Yongxian, Li (1998), *Primitive Arts in Tibet*. Chengdu: Sichuan People's Publishing House.

12

Spatial Distribution of Petroglyphs of Ladakh

Tashi Ldawa Thsangspa

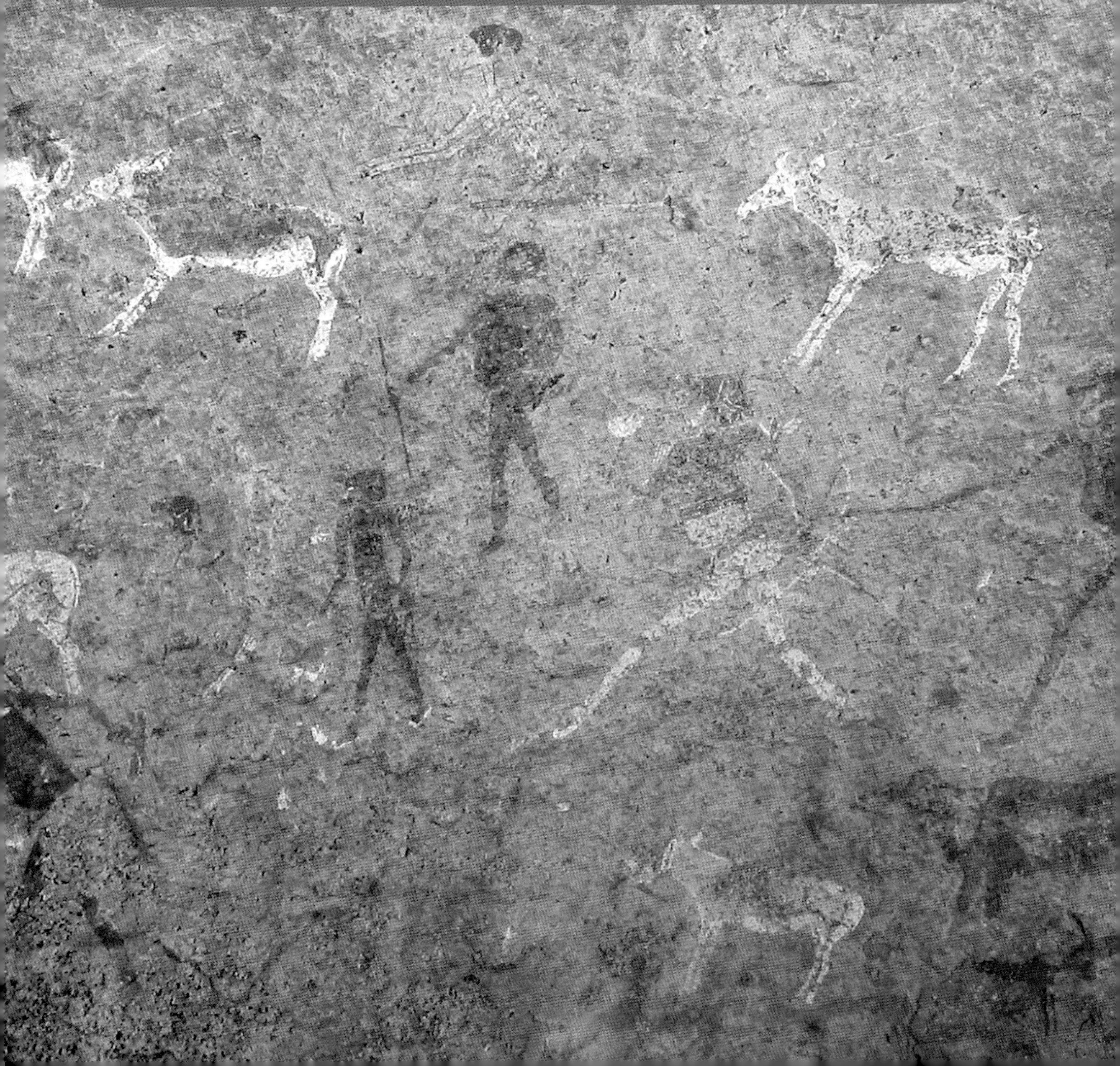

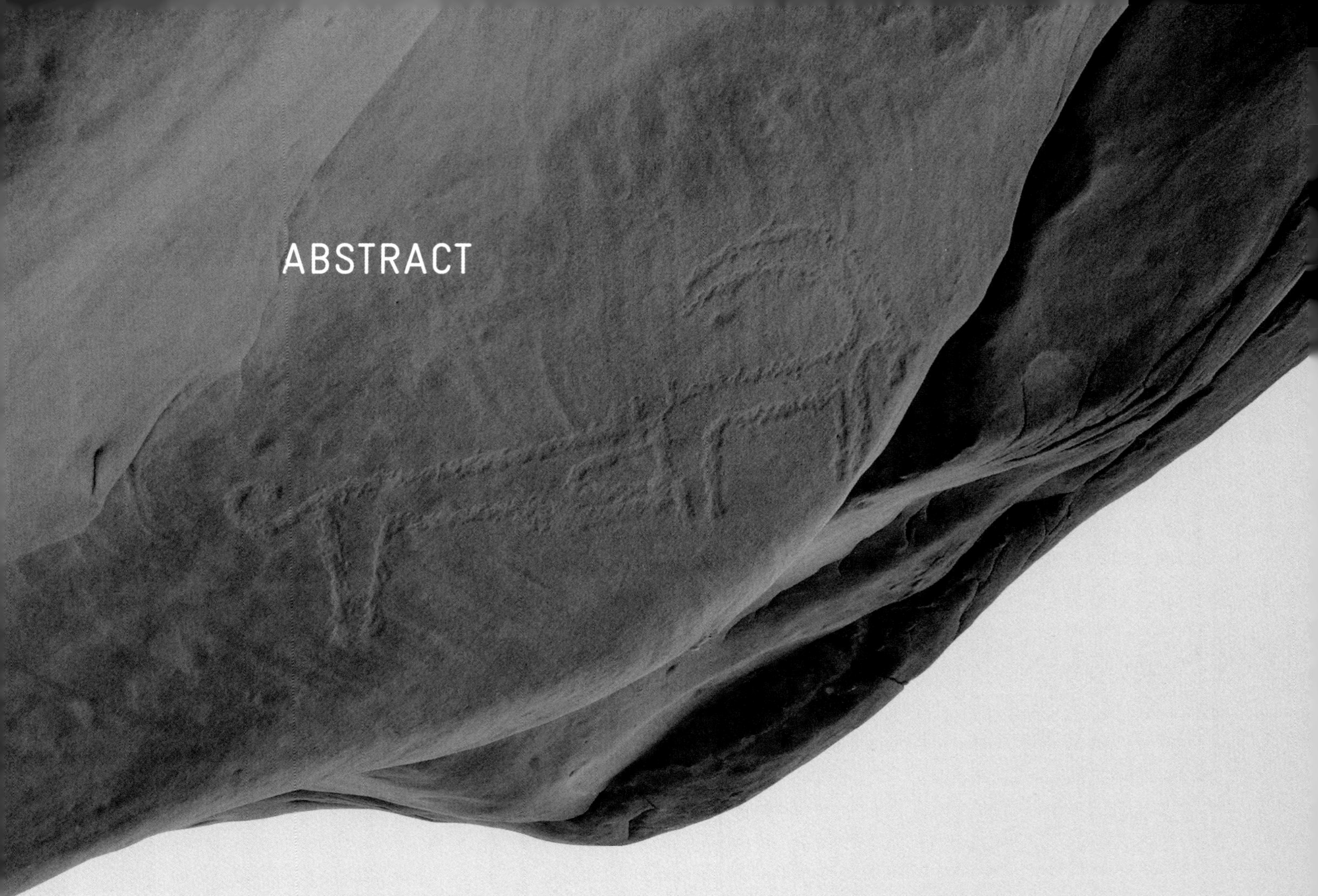

ABSTRACT

Reports of subjugation of Ladakh by Tibetans in the 7th or 8th centuries show that Ladakh had a settled population during that period. Recent reports of petroglyphs confirm that the region was visited by nomadic pastoralists, tribes and others even before the Christian era. Of the thousands of petroglyphs that we have discovered in the last 15 years, many have been studied simultaneously by scholars. The discoveries make us believe that this art can be categorised into two: one, made by local inhabitants probably residing in a particular oasis village and the other by foreigners like herders, traders, travellers, pilgrims and invaders. The former type made by locals is found in and around villages or in high pasture lands (doks). Moreover, their style and subject is so widely prevalent that some of these representations appear formulaic throughout the region. This paper reports on only those art forms that we consider exotic, incongruous and primarily belonging to the pre-Buddhist period. Broadly, we have generalised that the exotic petroglyphs are confined to the routes which existed during prehistoric times. There is no doubt that some of these art works show homogenous character with neighbouring states, but still there are many which show no resemblance to any cited literature and hence need further research.

INTRODUCTION

Ladakh constitutes the northernmost region of the state of Jammu and Kashmir and forms a part of the Himalayas, approximately between 32 and 36 degrees north and 75 to 80 degrees east. This high-altitude cold desert is situated between the Karakoram and Greater Himalaya ranges. Ladakh forms a barrier between Central Asia and Peninsular India. However, there are many interconnecting routes through some formidable passes. These passes join various river valley systems within Ladakh. To the north lie some of the key passes—the Karakoram Pass through which a vital feeder route connects the southern arm of the Silk Route at Yarkand. It is also referred to as the 'Gates of India' (Hopkirk 1980). Leh, the capital and major town in Ladakh since ages, subsequently connects Kashmir, Tibet, Himachal and mainland India. As such, Ladakh was termed 'the crossroad of high Asia' (Rizvi 1983). In this light, inevitably, Ladakh has also become a crossroad of cultures of various nations and states.

The earliest settlers in Ladakh were considered to be mixed Indo-Aryan populations, often referred to as Dards and Mons (Francke 1907), who penetrated the area from the west. Ladakh and Zanskar were populated by Dards until the 7th and 8th centuries CE (Bruneau, personal communication). The history of the Dards and their migration to Iran and the Indian subcontinent from the north and north-west dates back to around 2nd millennium BCE (Harmatta 1999). Petech (1977) believes that the process of Tibetan settlements did not begin until the 10th century, from the east. However, Denwood (1995) argues that the process of Tibetan settlements in Ladakh could have started in the 7th century or earlier. Thus, the inhabitants of Purig near Kargil, which is geographically farther from Tibet (as compared to Leh), retained the features nearest to those of the earlier stratum.

Whatever little pieces of Ladakh's early history have been put together do not give us a clear picture so that we can recreate the distant past. In such circumstances, we have an enormous number of petroglyphs which may supplement scarce archaeological and historical sources. However, until recently work on petroglyphs was hardly carried out in a serious manner. Although the author has been documenting and researching for more than 15 years, he has yet to learn how to interpret; do a chronological analysis and above all do ethnographical studies. He has attempted the spatial distribution of rock art, particularly in relation to ancient routes through the valleys of Ladakh in this paper. Being neither a historian nor an archaeologist, the main focus is on the protection of rock art. For more than 15 years he has seen many rock art disappeared to so-called modern development. The author hopes that some of them will be preserved through this publication.

LADAKH: CROSSROADS OF HIGH ASIA

Ladakh, the land of the passes, inadvertently also means the 'land of mountains'. The passes through these mighty rugged and difficult mountain ranges connect different valleys, through which oasis villages have prospered. These villages established vital linkages, while the routes changed their functions with time: for survival, prosperity,

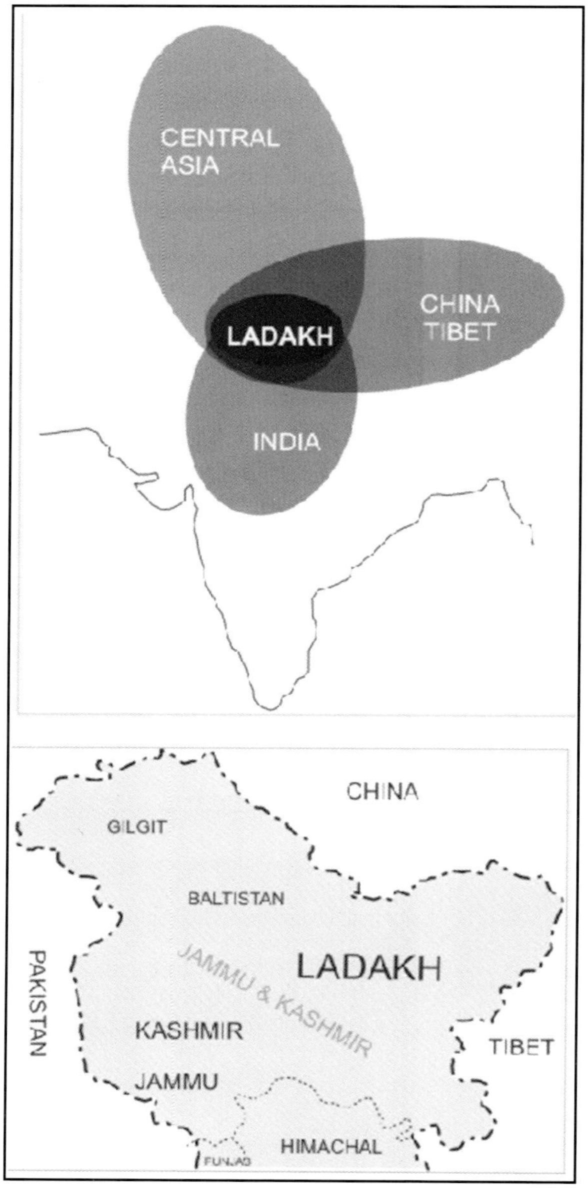

Map 12.1 General map of Ladakh.

pilgrimages, adventure, trade and even for escaping and invading. Art, ideas and thoughts were also commodities that passed through along with men and material.

The ancient network of the Silk Route has a history of about 2,000 years; it connected Rome to Chang'an, the capital of China (Rizvi 1983). Silk may have been one of the primary commodities, but enormous varieties of other commodities were also traded. The route gave birth to many trading posts, which prospered in their own right. Rizvi writes: 'With the passage of time, though political conditions varied, and with them the fortunes of the traders, trade itself must never have come to a standstill. ...when some routes were rendered impassable by war and general lawlessness, the traffic in goods and commodities continues. ... And so it went on, century after century, until well on into the twentieth. Gradually, a network of routes developed, linking every major town and production area with all the others.... For much of history, it was the nodal point of a whole complex of trade routes...'

The content of the trade is out of the scope of this paper but it essentially consisted of either local products or long-distance consignments of small-bulk and high value goods. On the other hand, trade was inevitable for people striving in a harsh environment. For example, the Changpa nomads (eastern Ladakh) were rich in livestock (so also their by-products) while the geography did not allow any agricultural practices. So residents of lower Ladakh (Sham) bartered their agricultural product with Changpas. Leh, the centre of Ladakh, soon established its worth for both traders and travellers. The traders recovered and replenished their supplies to go further or to go back with their trade-offs.

Rizvi (1983) writes, 'In spite of its seeming isolation, Ladakh was, as a result of the trade carried on over the Karakoram Pass, very much part of a wider world.' However, with the present documentation of rock art and with further scope for research, one may assert that Ladakh was a part of a wider world since the prehistoric period.

The routes that criss-crossed Ladakh were:

a. From north, via Nubra Valley, one of the important routes touched eastern Turkestan/Xinjiang (that is, Yarkand, Kashgar etc.). It crossed the Karakoram range

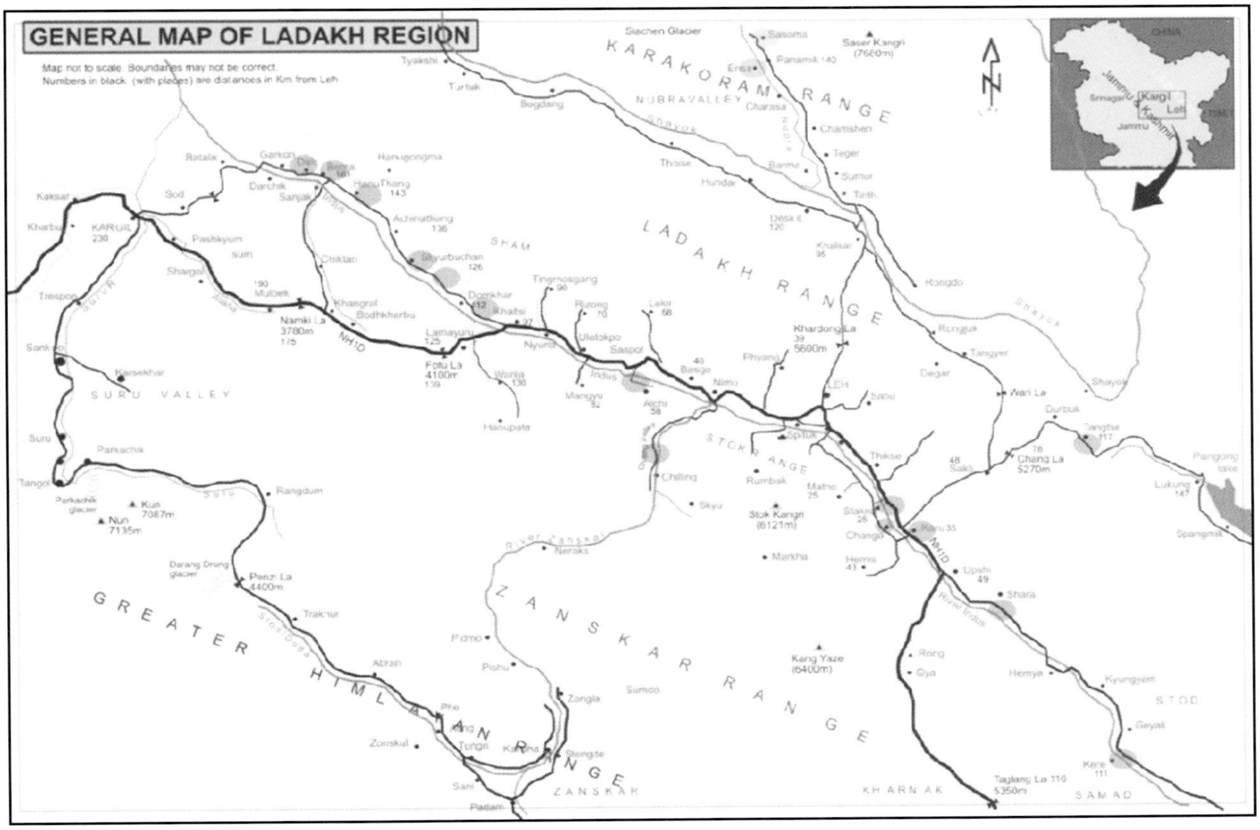

Map 12.2 General map of Ladakh showing spatial distribution of rock art style. Note: Most of the sites reported in the paper are marked by a shaded circular mark. Numbers with name of places are distances in kilometres from Leh.

through Saser La (pass) and the Karakoram Pass, ultimately touching the southern arm of the Silk Route through Central Asia.

b. To the east, a couple of routes ultimately touched Lhasa in Tibet.
c. To the west, the routes either along the Shayok or the Indus River (with its tributary Suru from Kargil) touched Skardu (Baltistan). Another route touched Kashmir via Zoji La.
d. To the south, the route cut through Zanskar Valley with routes on either sides touching Himachal or Punjab.

The mountain ranges and the valley system of Ladakh run in the south-east and north-west directions, or for convenience, we can say in the east-west direction. Geographically, the eastern part of Ladakh is at a higher altitude and in continuation with the Tibetan Plateau showing nomadic pastoral activities, while as you go west the altitude falls and settled agriculture systems are more prevalent. Political boundaries apart, the geographic landscape is in continuum with Baltistan to the west. However, the little oasis villages were separated from each other and many remained cut-off from each other for the long winter months. This isolation, particularly between valleys across high mountain ranges, must have brought differences in their cultures. Thus, in different regions of Ladakh, we can still find some spatial differences in cultures, dialects, habitations and even in some social practices.

The present paper deals only with the stylistic distribution of rock art in Ladakh and therefore only those figures are presented that are uncommon and peculiar in their distribution in the sites or valleys of Ladakh. To start with, a question may be raised: why are art forms not uniformly distributed, or in other words why did some valleys have some peculiar type of art, which was not present in others? Beyond valleys, there is some rock art which is site-specific or boulder-specific. Although the author agreed that he may not been able to provide any reasoning for this, he would still like to present some general observations on the spatial distribution of petroglyphs in Ladakh. No scaling has been done and some of the figures are extracted from their wider contexts. All the figures are drawn by superimposition on digital photographs.

Stylistically, the rock art of Ladakh depicts both realistic as well as unrealistic forms. The entire collection consists of various representations of animals, humans and various other motifs and forms.

The wild figures include dong or yak (usually with a hairy body and a bushy tail), wild sheep (horns curved back or sideways), ibex (horns curved back and upwards), stags (antlers), tigers/leopards (or felines with their jaws open), elephants, birds, lizards and snakes. Domesticated animals include horses (raised mane), camels (double humped), and dogs (tailed curled on the body). Social events like hunting, fighting, dancing and strange group activities are also depicted. Despite these, a good number of engravings also represent signs and symbols. They include geometric decorations, zigzags, meanders, concentric circles and combinations thereof.

Another important and major class of representation consists of engravings of unrealistic forms. Such figures consist of anthropomorphic forms, disproportional human forms or human forms with certain parts exaggerated, animal-human conflations and strange signs and symbols associated with some scenes. As such, these figures convey more than mere figures of human or human-like forms. Anthropomorphic figures, whenever discovered, are usually found in particular sites and often in association with vast numbers of other similar depictions. Of late, mask-like figures have been found in plenty, particularly in Nubra Valley.

UPPER INDUS VALLEY

River Indus flows through Ladakh, entering from Tibet in the east and flowing out through Batalik in the west, almost flowing about 400 km or so in the region. Since there is significant difference in altitude from the east to the west, habitation patterns also differ significantly. Therefore, for our convenience we have divided the Indus Valley into Upper and Lower. We have a couple of significant sites on the bank of the Indus in the Upper Indus Valley. One such site is at Kere (and a nearby site), about 110 km from Leh. It is a tiny site on the right bank on an outcrop of a rock from the river. There are hundreds of figures, many of them showing scenes of hunting. Many of the individual or group figures consist of animals. The animal figures on this stretch significantly represent

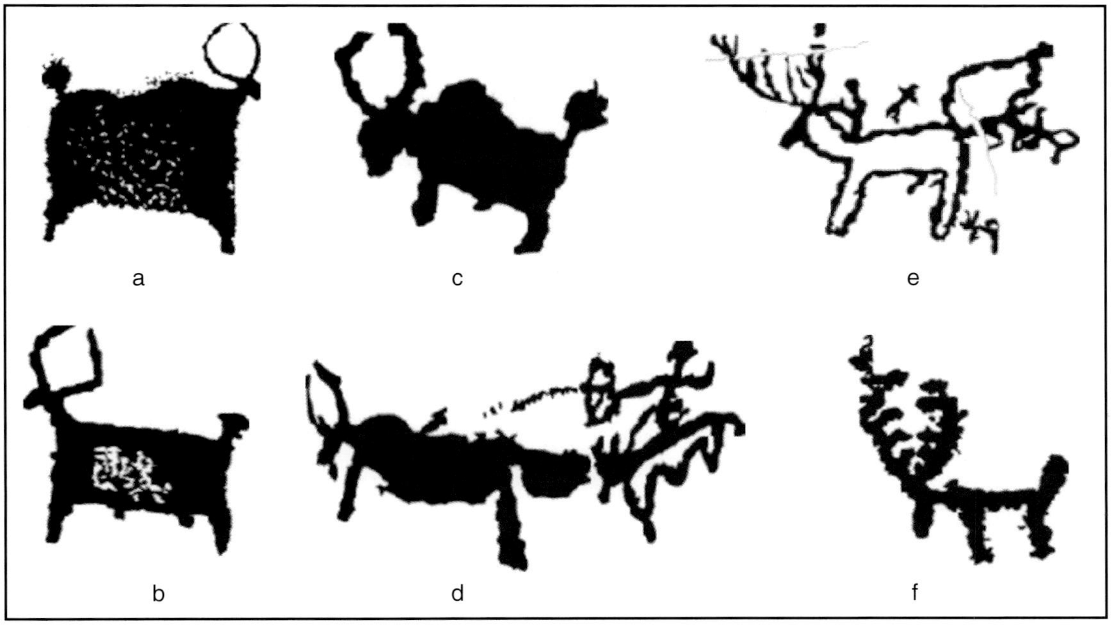

yaks and animals with antlers, probably a species of deer. Although, to the east of Ladakh in the entire Changthang area yak is a predominant domesticated species. However, no species of any deer (or any species with antlers) are found in Changthang (Figs. 12.1 & 12.2).

Another site about 60 km from Leh is near Shara village (Figs. 12.3 & 12.4). Again, on the right side of the river, there are two huge boulders with similar figures. These figures, particularly because of their size, cannot be compared to any other figures. These are

Fig. 12.1 Yaks (above) and deer representations from Kere site.

Fig. 12.2 An entire panel of the boulder near Kere.
Note: Yaks, wild sheep/goats and hunting scenes and S-shaped geometric symbolic signs are also peculiar to this site.

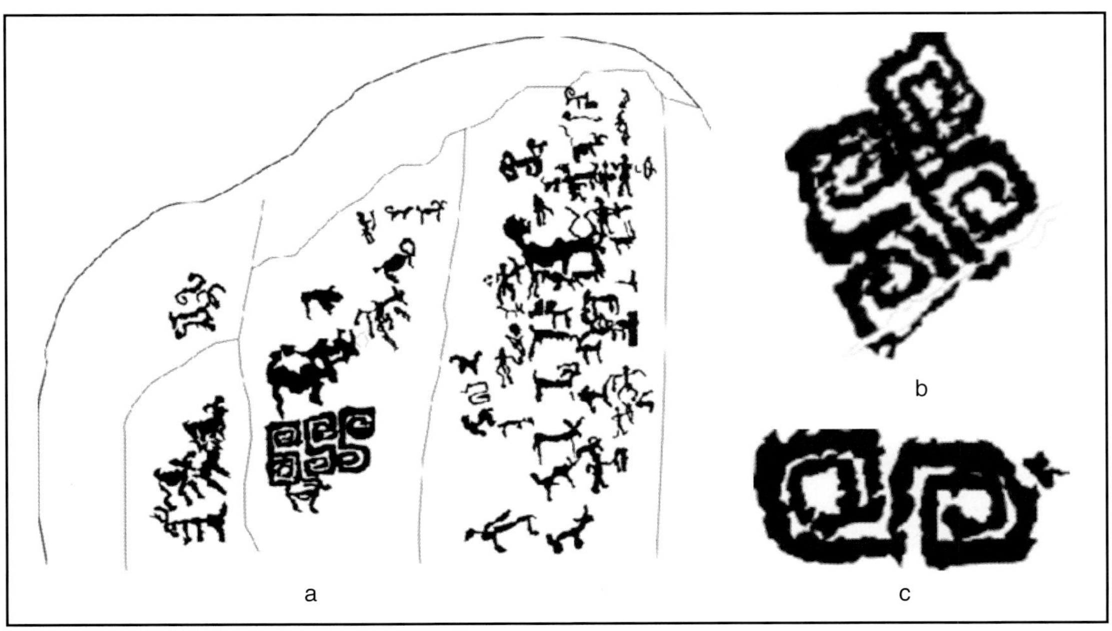

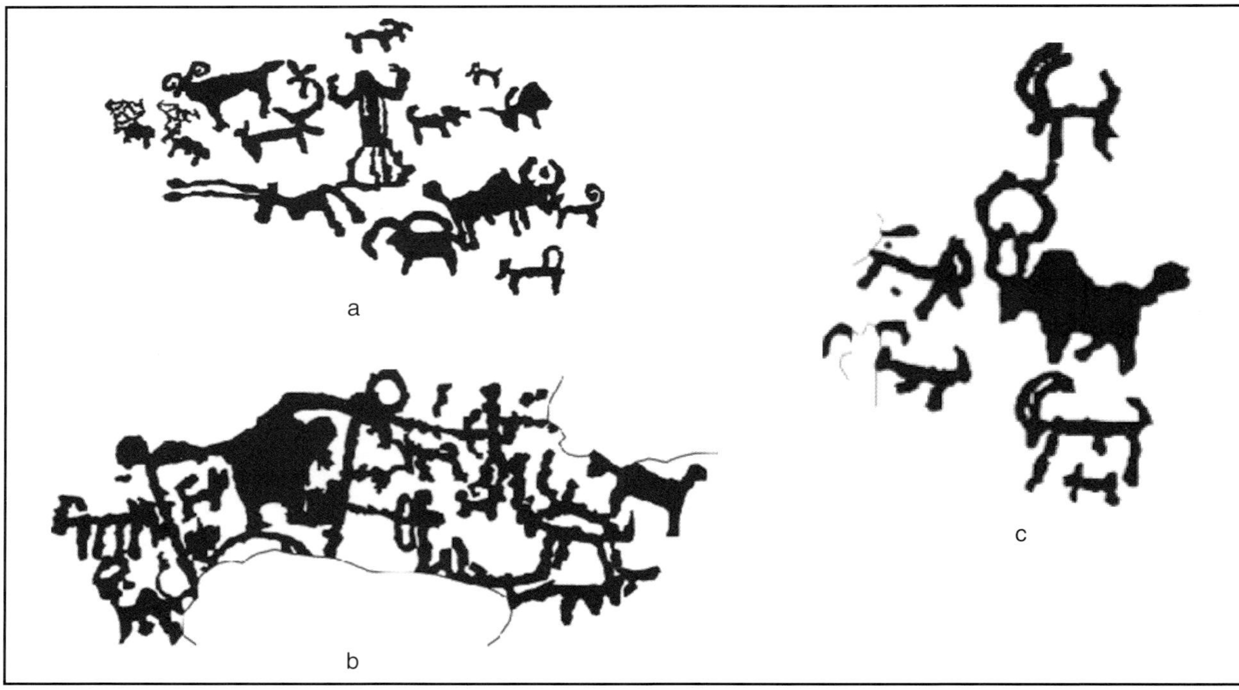

Fig. 12.3 Figures from Shara site.
Note: The site has yak, deer, wild sheep/goat and some anthropomorphs. Figure (a) has now been lost.

large figures more than 1 m in height, with some kind of geometric symmetry. Around 100 m away, there is another site with more than a dozen boulders representing various types of figures. Another unusual one is the 13 hand-prints on one of the vertical boulders. Hand-print is a common subject, even in Ladakh but this one is stylistically distinct with long fingers. It is associated with yaks and stick-like human figures. This site has lost quite a few of the engraved rocks for upcoming high-tension electric towers. Similar activities and road widening is likely to take more of a toll.

Fig. 12.4 Unknown signs and symbols at Shara site
Note: Figure (c) is little more than a metre in height.

Another site, 'Theme Park' at Kharu (Figs. 12.5 & 12.6), on the right side of Indus is an enclosure of about a dozen engraved boulders erected by the army. Yak and hand-prints are among the prominent figures found here. Hunting scenes and deer are also represented

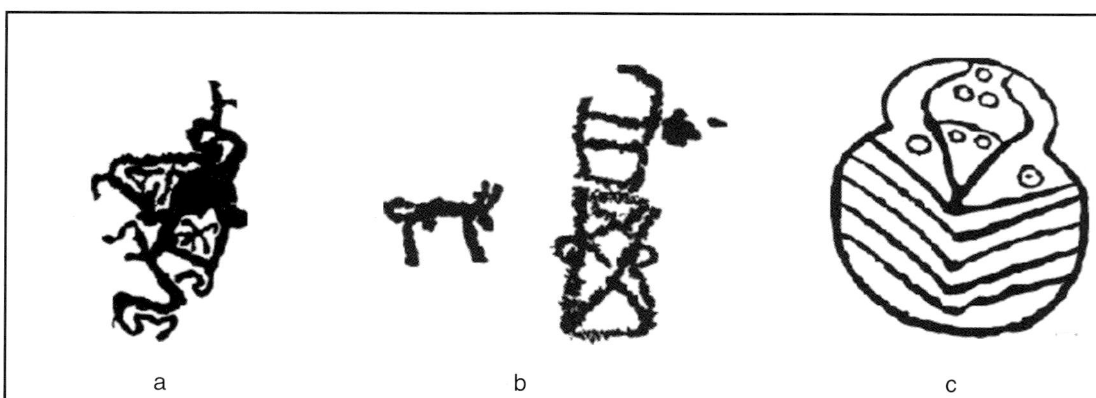

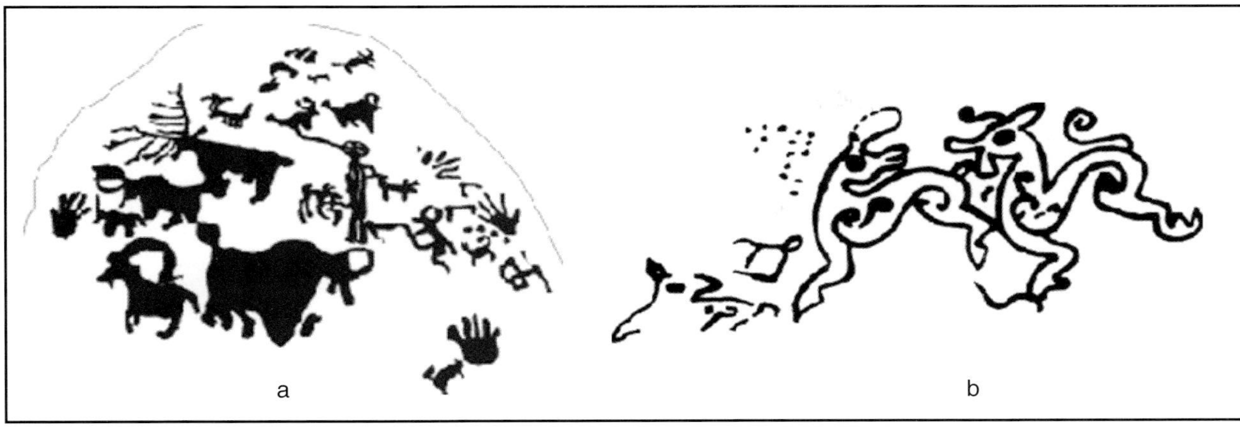

Fig. 12.5 Kharu site has more than a dozen engraved rocks. Note: Yak, deer, hand-prints and anthropomorphic figures are prominent. The second is a typical subject of predator chasing a prey.

among the many figures. However, one of the beautiful figures outside the park is of a predator chasing a prey, reminding one of 'animal style' figures. Nearby, there is another deer figure of animal style.

The deer figures representing 'animal-style' like figures show their presence in plenty at Domkhar (Lower Indus). However, outside Domkhar, these are rare. From Stakna bridge to this site at Kharu, we found three such figures, one of which is now destroyed for road pavement.

Another site on the left bank of the Indus, near Changa village, has numerous boulders representing yak, ibex, deer and hunting scenes (Fig. 12.7). There are a couple figures that are represented by dots, a rare style of carving.

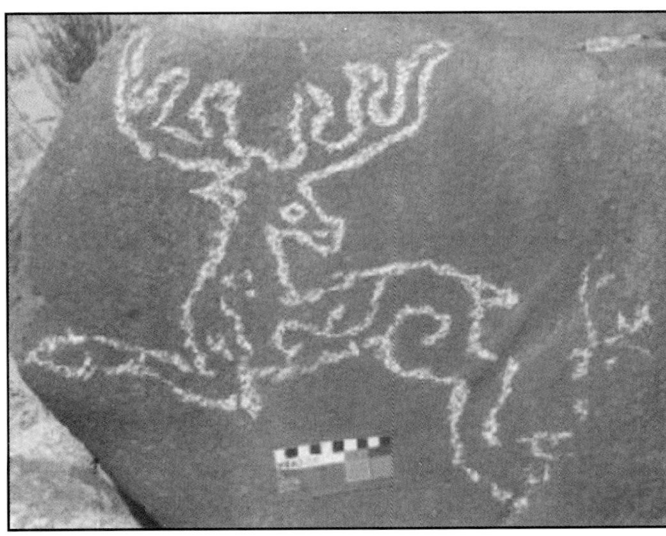

Fig. 12.6 A representation of an elegant deer near Kharu park.

LOWER INDUS VALLEY

There are numerous figures along the Lower Indus; they are almost spread all along the Indus river for about 150 km. It is also true that most of the ancient routes pass along this river. Although there are scores of sites on the entire stretch, each with as many as dozens of rocks, some of the individual rocks consist of hundreds of engraved figures. Despite many common and uniform types of figures found almost all over Ladakh, this stretch also contains some peculiar specialities. Further, within these peculiarities, some sites show area- or boulder- specific figures that are not seen elsewhere.

Except for a few, most of the sites mentioned here stretch from Khaltse to Dah, along the Indus river. Khaltse village was a major junction for different routes—one of the routes crosses the river into a side valley, leading to Srinagar via Kargil or to Zanskar

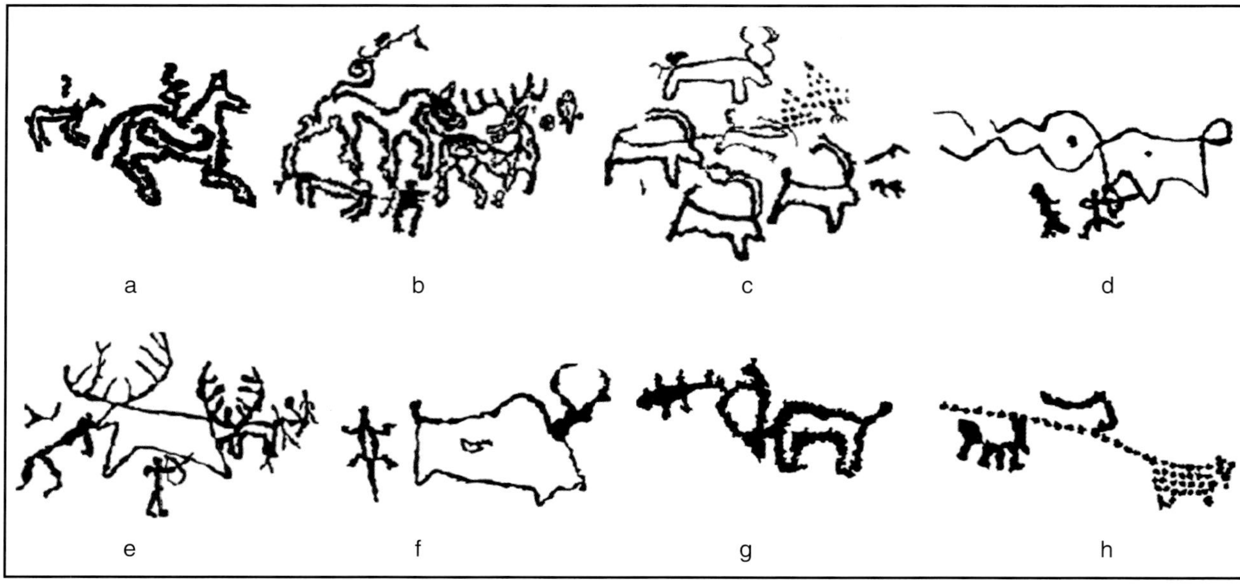

Fig. 12.7 Changa site.
Note: Figure (a) shows 'S' type of curls in the body. b. shows a predator chasing a deer. (c), (d) and (e) show yaks, wild goats, deer and hunting scenes. (f) and (g) show yaks; each of them also has a rare figure of lizard-like animals. (h) shows an animal represented with dots.

via Wanla. Today modern roads also follow this ancient route. It was here that Francke reported a Kharoshti inscription about 100 years ago; it is not found any more.

One of the peculiar sites before Khaltse is Alchi Thang. Unfortunately, most of the boulders with rock art depictions have been broken for construction needs. One boulder, about a kilometre from this site down the Indus on the left bank, has one of the most strikingly peculiar figures in Ladakh (Fig. 12.8).

Two lion figures near Khaltse bridge are of a peculiar style. However, both of them have been cut and removed by a private collector and have been put in a restaurant in Khaltse. A few kilometres further, there are a few more rocks with strange anthropomorphic figures, including some ritualistic figures (Figs. 12.9 & 12.10).

Fig. 12.8 A site on the left bank of Indus near Alchi.
Note: The boulder is partially buried in the sand.

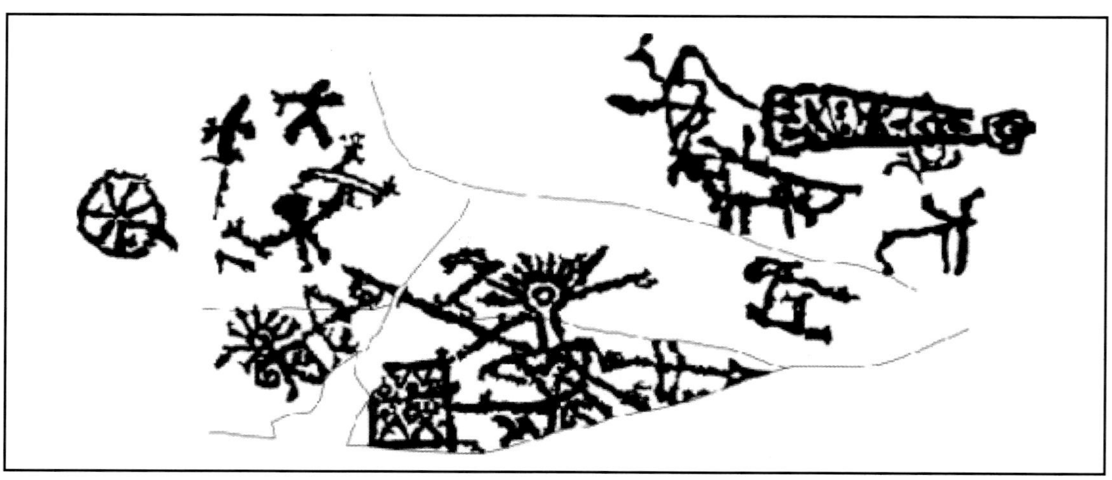

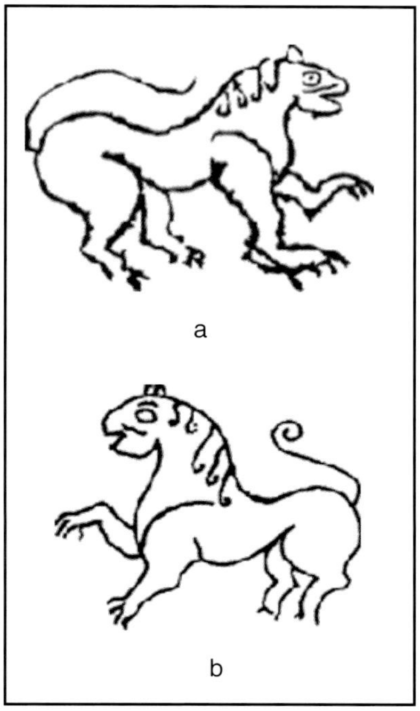

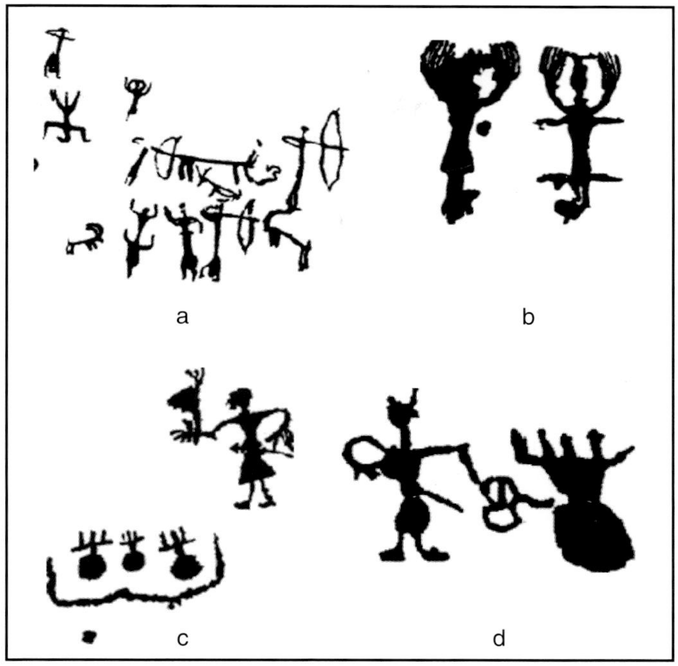

Left: **Fig. 12.9** Figures from near Khaltse bridge.
Note: These two lion figures are the only ones of their type in subject and style found in Ladakh.

Right: **Fig. 12.10** A rare representation of anthropomorphic figures, a few kilometres away from Khaltse bridge.
Note: Anthropomorphic figures from Khaltse along the Indus are greater in number and in variety.

In Domkhar village, about 112 km from Leh, a distinguished site in Ladakh contains one of the finest collections of rock art, both in artistry and antiquity and hence the author calls it the 'Domkhar sanctuary' (Figs. 12.11 & 12.12). The foremost subject of the site has 'animal-style' figures in their extreme beauty and perfection. These figures generally consist of elegant curves and spiral hooks. Many are shown standing on tip toe. At least in Ladakh, there is no comparison to this site. The obvious question is, with a few rare exceptions, why is such a style confined to one single site? One of the reasons may be the close proximity of the two banks of the Indus, a vital link for river-crossing, a probable waiting place.

Between Skyurbuchan and Achinathang, at another desolated site on the right bank of the Indus is found one of the most intriguing figures. One of them seems to be a ritualistic figure consisting of several human beings with raised hands (Fig. 12.13a). The figures depicted are incomplete, as the boulder is partially buried under the debris of road construction. Nearby, there are several more figures (12.13b and 12.13c) showing a rare representation of animal-human conflation. At Skyurbuchan, there is another site with scores of figures, but much of it has been vandalised with names and figures (Fig. 12.13d). One of the scenes shows a hunting figure associated with several other figures. One of the human figures has dots around the body; another has a rounded body; and a few more have raised hands.

One of the most concentrated engraved boulders is found a little after Hanu Thang, at an isolated site on the right bank of Indus. There are several engraved rocks and

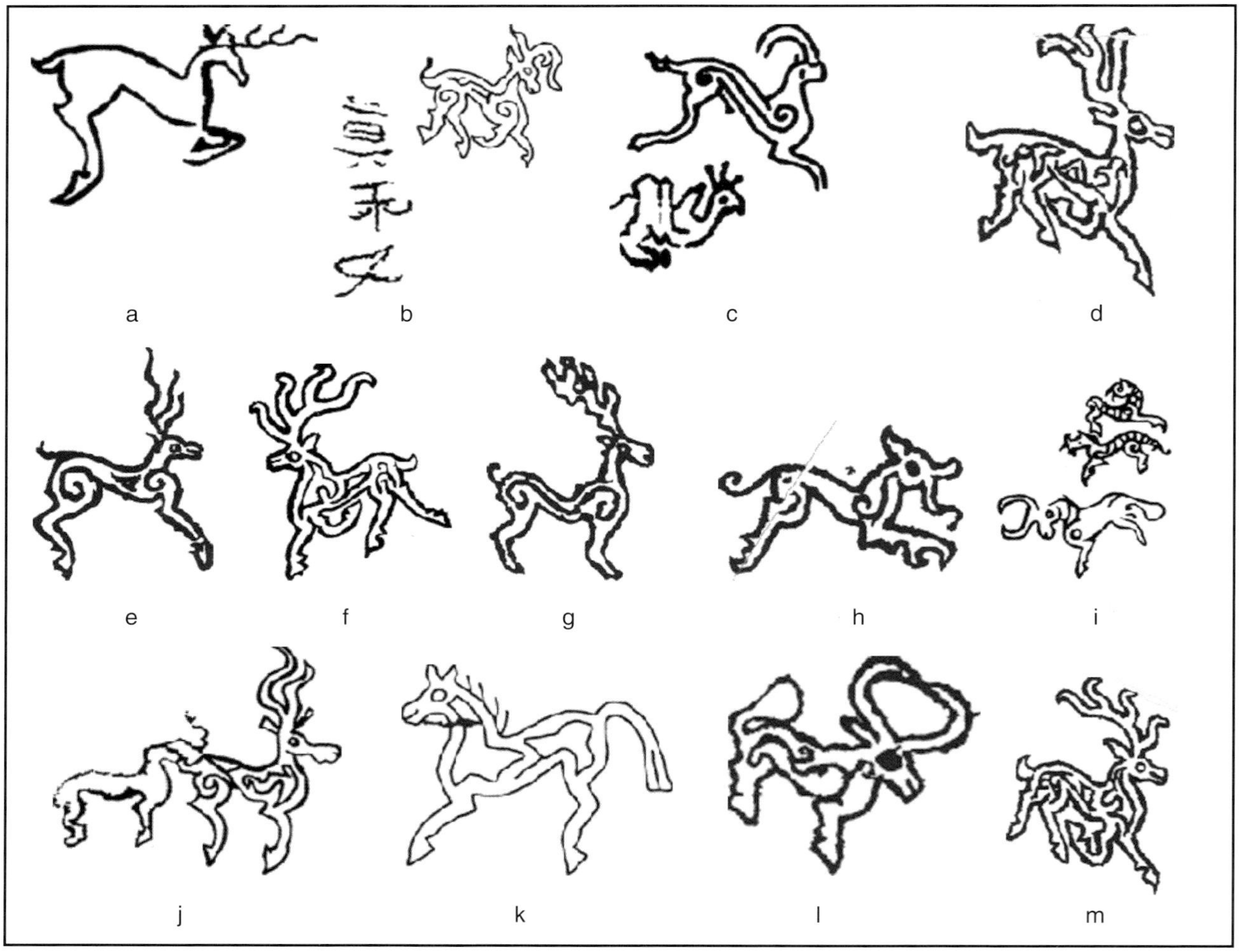

Fig. 12.11 'Animal style' at Domkhar Sanctuary.
Note: The figures represent deer, ibex, yak, horse and feline. The Chinese inscription on one of the figures (b) seems to be a later addition.

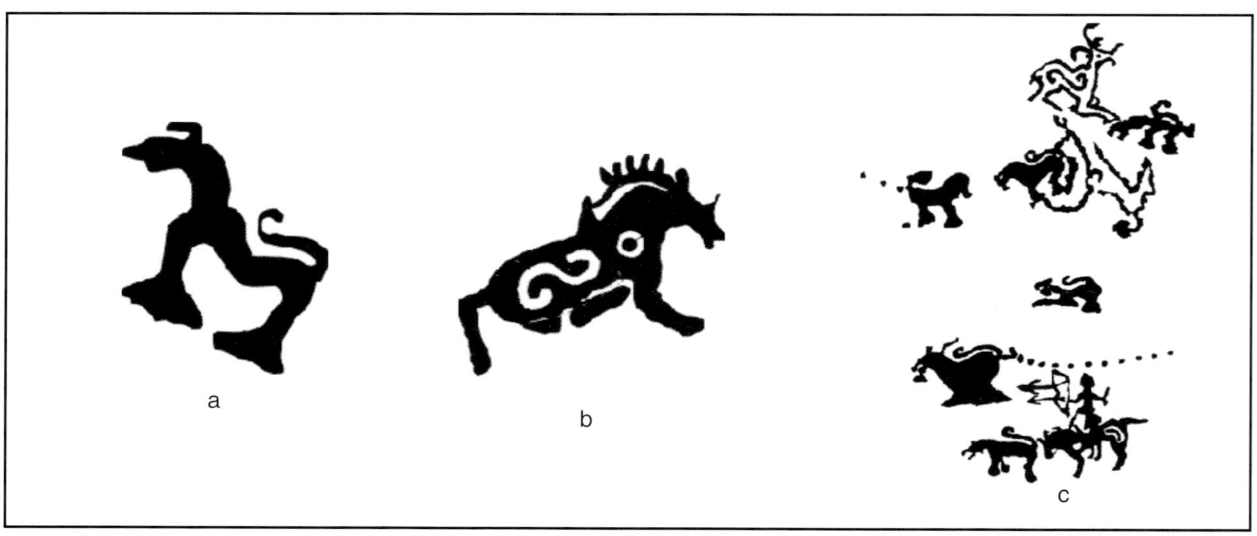

Fig. 12.12 Some of the other stylistically distinct figures from Domkhar Sanctuary, including decoration of the body by blank spaces.

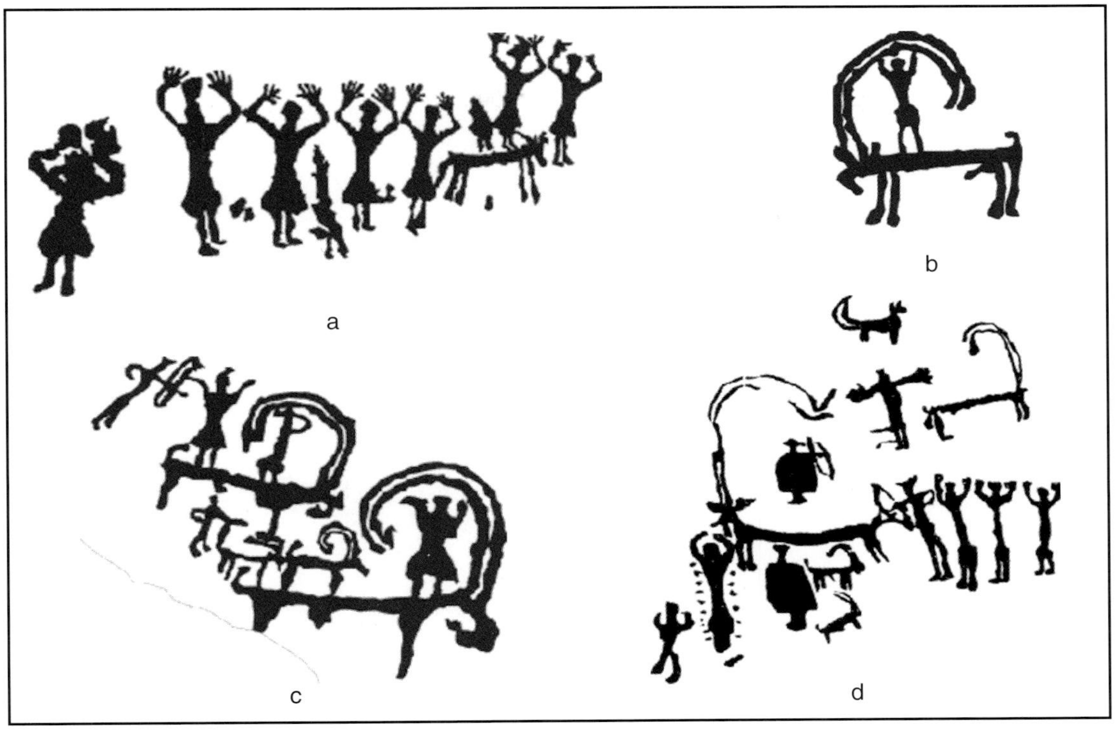

Fig. 12.13 (a-c) Depiction from a site between Skyurbuchan and Achinathang: A rare human representation, including animal-human conflation figures. (d) figures from Skyurbuchan.

boulders. One of them is a 'Big Boulder', which is more than two storeys high, with the base touching the riverbank (Figs. 12.14 & 12.15). It has a 30 foot wide slant surface with hundreds of figures engraved on it. Nearby, on another boulder is a flat rock with an outline of a human figure. A little above these there are a few more boulders, one of them showing a giant-like figure with stretched hands and some foot and hand-prints.

The Big Boulder contains hundreds of figures, with a couple of Kharoshti inscriptions in a corner (Figs. 12.16 & 12.17). Many of the figures represent hunting scenes, while an equal number also show social scenes with strange human forms along with anthropomorphic figures. Some of the animal forms are stylistically very different.

At Bema and Dha, there are a few more interesting sites with peculiar anthropomorphic figures not seen elsewhere in Ladakh (Fig. 12.18 a-c).

CHILLING VALLEY

Chilling Valley forms along the last stretch of the Zanskar River before it confluences with the Indus River near Leh. Much of the later part of this river, which cuts through the Zanskar range, forms a deep gorge, which is impassable along the bank. There are about six sites along the last stretch of the river, spanning about 25 km. There are several routes passing through the valley before it narrows down leading to smaller villages on the northern face of the Zanskar range. Despite many common figures, it is quite

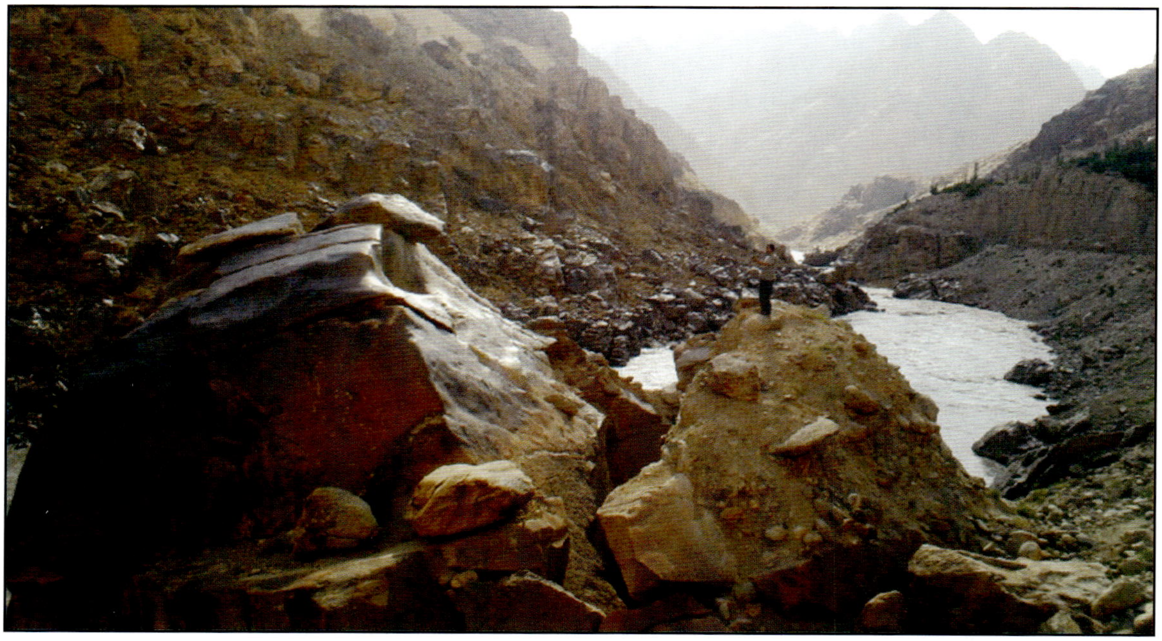

Fig. 12.14 The Big Boulder along the right bank of the Indus River.
Note: The flattish inclined shining face has engravings on the entire surface.

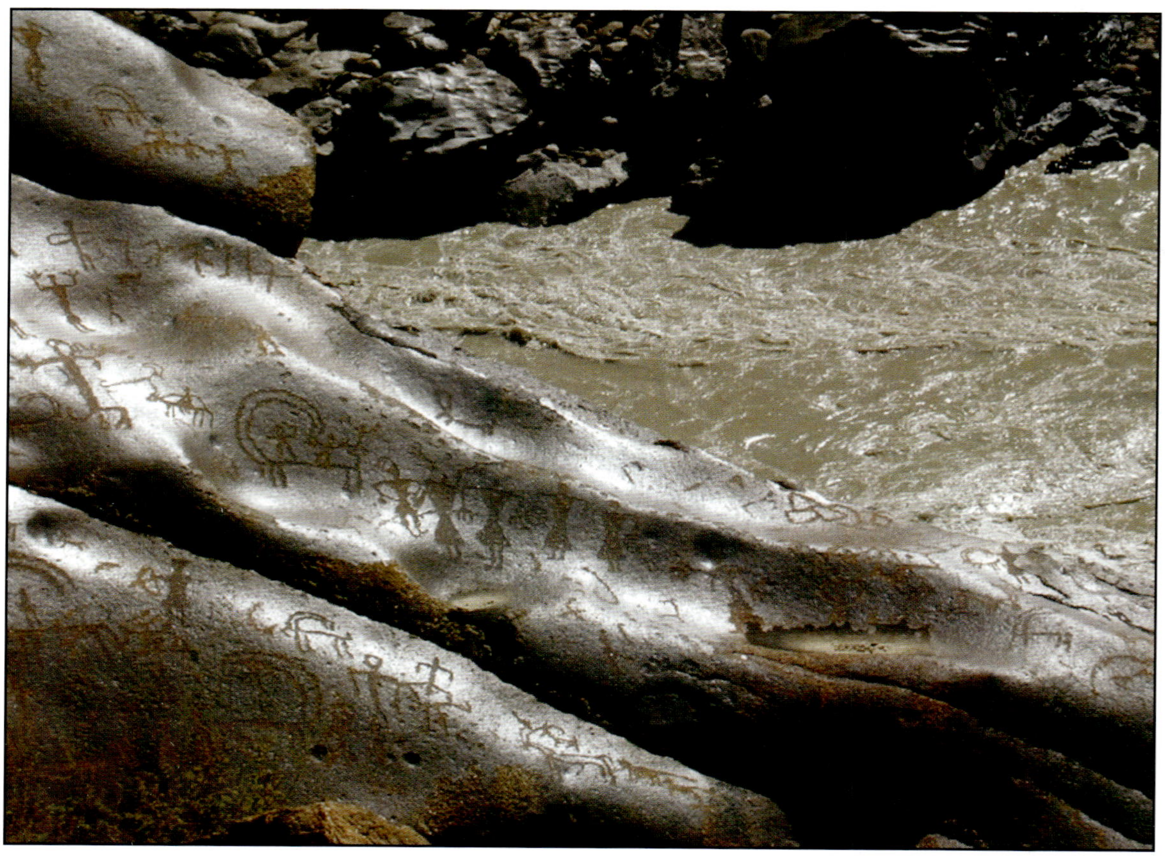

Fig. 12.15 A small part of the Big Boulder.
Note: Kharosti inscription on the left upper corner is also seen.

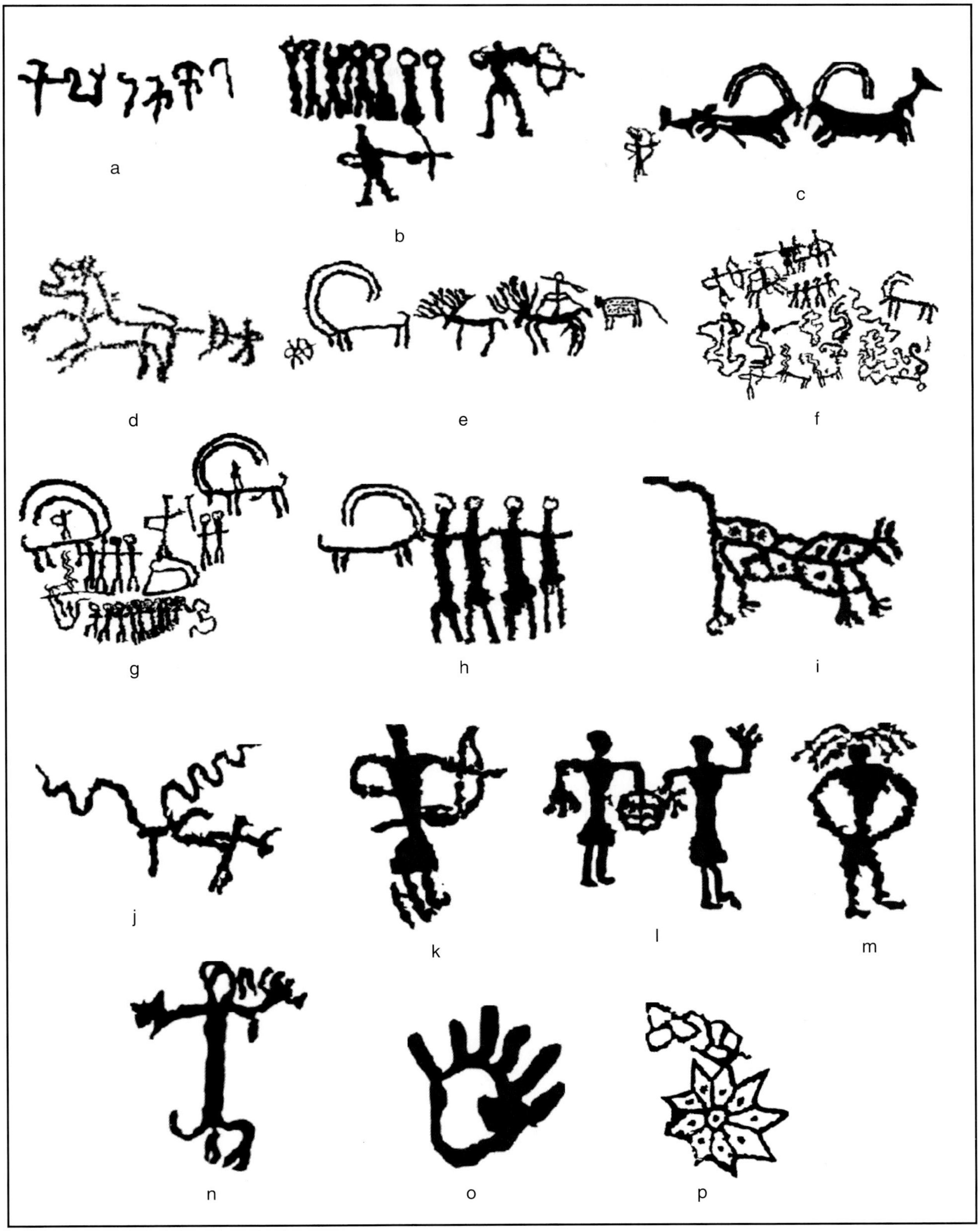

Fig. 12.16 Figures from Big Boulder.
Note: There is an amazing assemblage of variety and number on a single boulder.

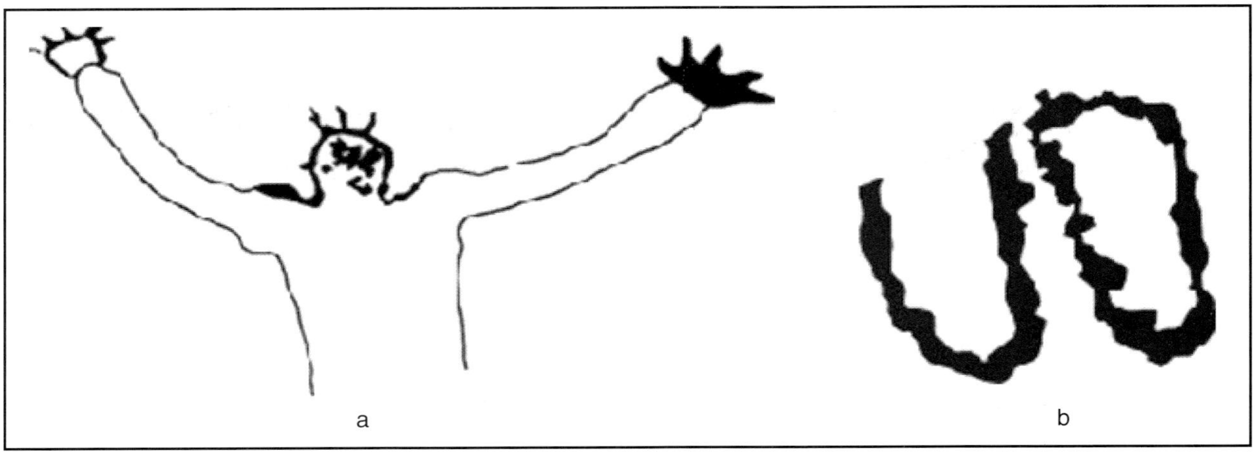

Fig. 12.17 A giant figure and a footprint near the Big Boulder.

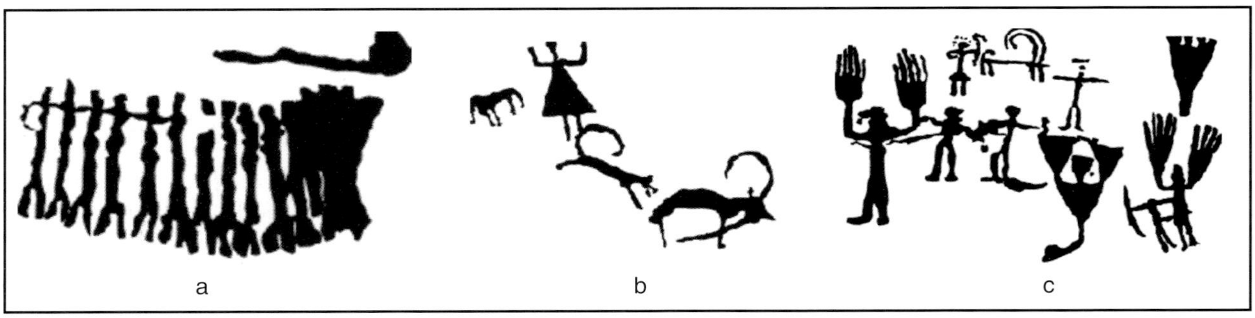

Fig. 12.18 Figures from Bema (a-b) and (c) figure from Dha.

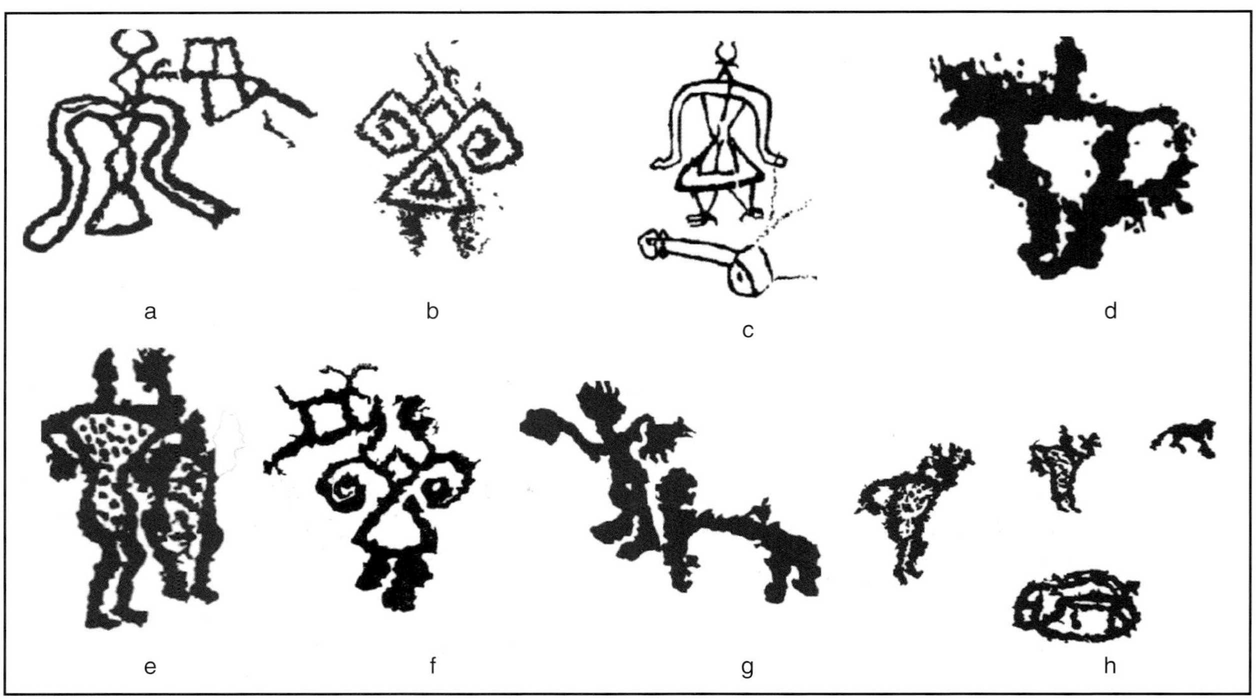

Fig. 12.19 (a-h) Anthropomorphic forms from Chilling Valley are comparatively unique.

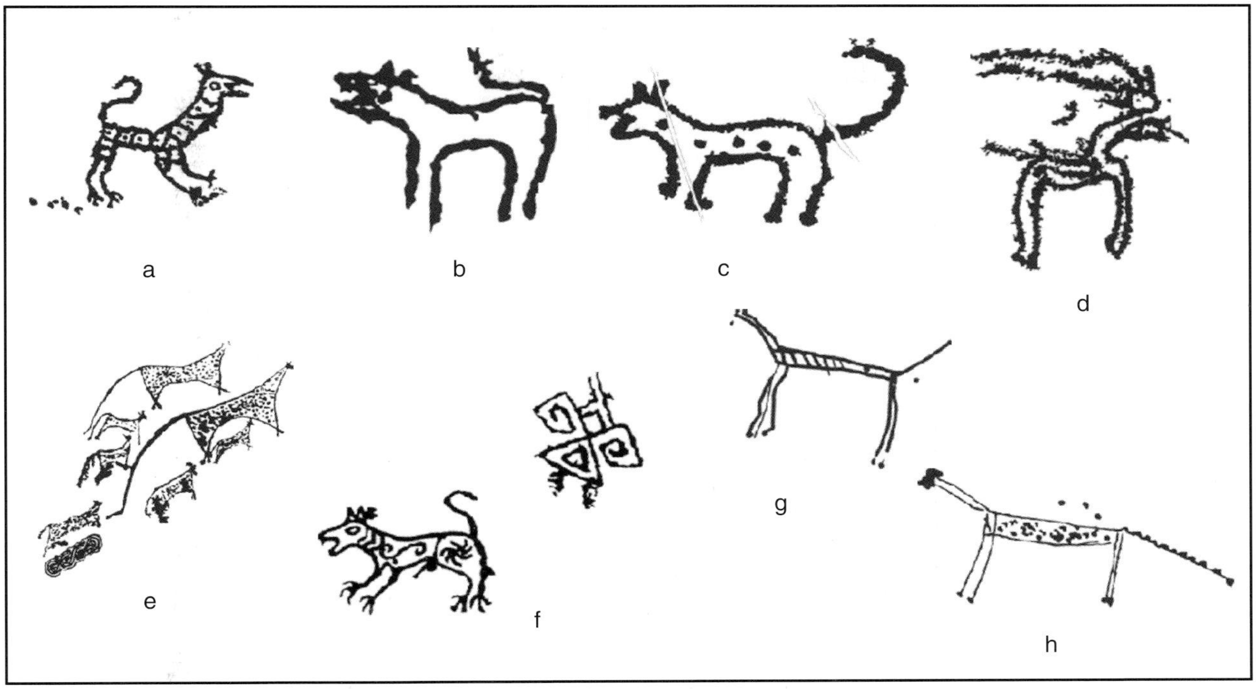

Fig. 12.20 (a-h) Animal figures of Chilling Valley also show some different style of engravings.

interesting to see that a significant number of the rock art figures of this valley do not show any similarities with any other sites in Ladakh (Figs. 12.19-12.21).

TANGTSE

Tangtse is one of the largest settled villages in the Changthang region. Historically, it falls on one of the routes towards Tibet via Rudok and Gartok. Understandably, it shows one of the finest collections of rock art with signs and symbols and with a good number of inscriptions. The site is also one of the most studied ones. There are three main boulders, about a size of large room, in the middle of the village. These boulders consist of hundreds of carvings with many types of signs and symbols. There are also inscriptions in various scripts (Figs. 12.22-12.25).

Around the village, there are several more boulders with equally interesting carvings. One of the finest is of a predator chasing a prey, which is very similar to the figure found in Renmudong, Tibet of Iron Age (WuJunkui 1987).

Fig. 12.21 (a-d) Bird or bird-like figures from Chilling Valley is also rare in Ladakh.

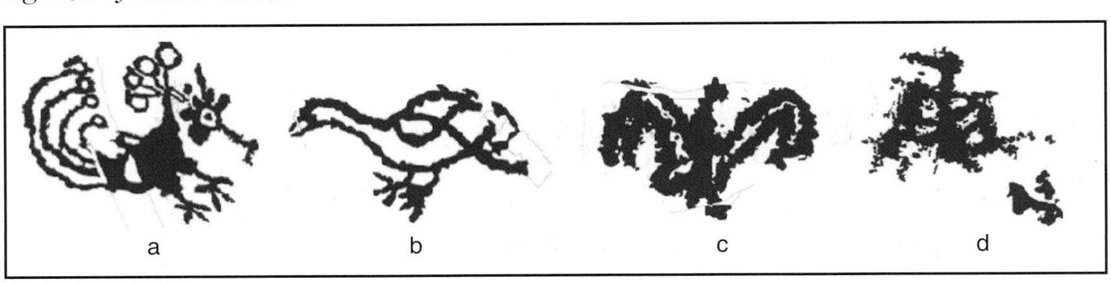

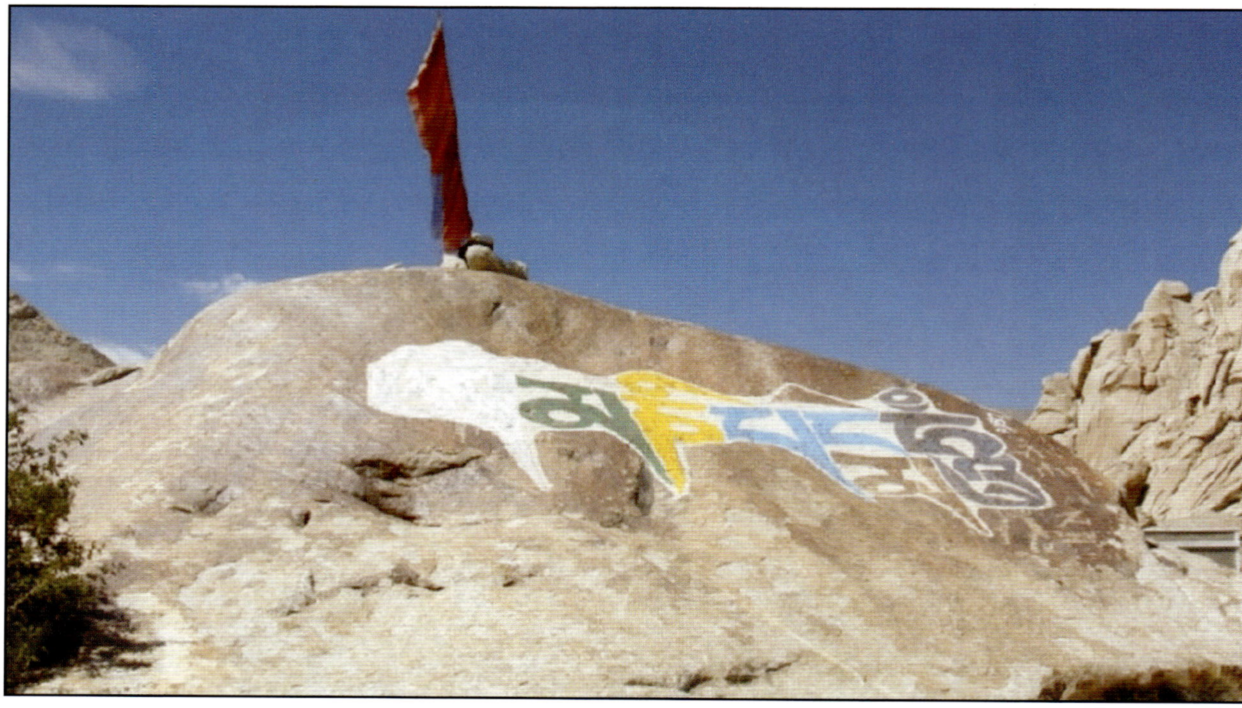

Fig. 12.22 One of the boulders with signs and symbols. Note: This is superimposed with engraved and painted Buddhist mantras.

NUBRA VALLEY

Nubra Valley has one of its routes via Karakoram Pass connecting to the famous Silk Route. It was near Sasoma village, on the left bank of Nubra River, where the route had its base for a long and arduous journey to Yarkand. Near Sasoma there are several sites and one of the primary elements of the engravings are, understandably, horses and camels, the beasts of burden on this trail. The stylistic representation of horses with raised manes and with male organs is very typical of this site (Fig. 12.27).

Another site of interest is Ensa around the Murgi tokpo (stream), on the right bank of Nobra River. The site is a conglomerate of thousands of blackened boulders, with hundreds of them having carvings. The entire site is cut by the Murgi tokpo. In fact, during heavy discharge from the stream the water flows all around the site. There is no doubt that this single site has the largest collection of petroglyphs in Ladakh. The mask-like figures, which we considered rare after finding a few at Sasoma site many years earlier (Thsangspa 2007), were found in plenty at Ensa (Figs. 12.28-12.31).

The enormous number and peculiar stylistic representation at Ensa are puzzling, particularly from the point that the site is away from ancient routes and it also did not have any large pasture land for pastoralists (Fig. 12.32). Even the present villages on the right side of Nobra River are squeezed between the river and the mountain with very limited land.

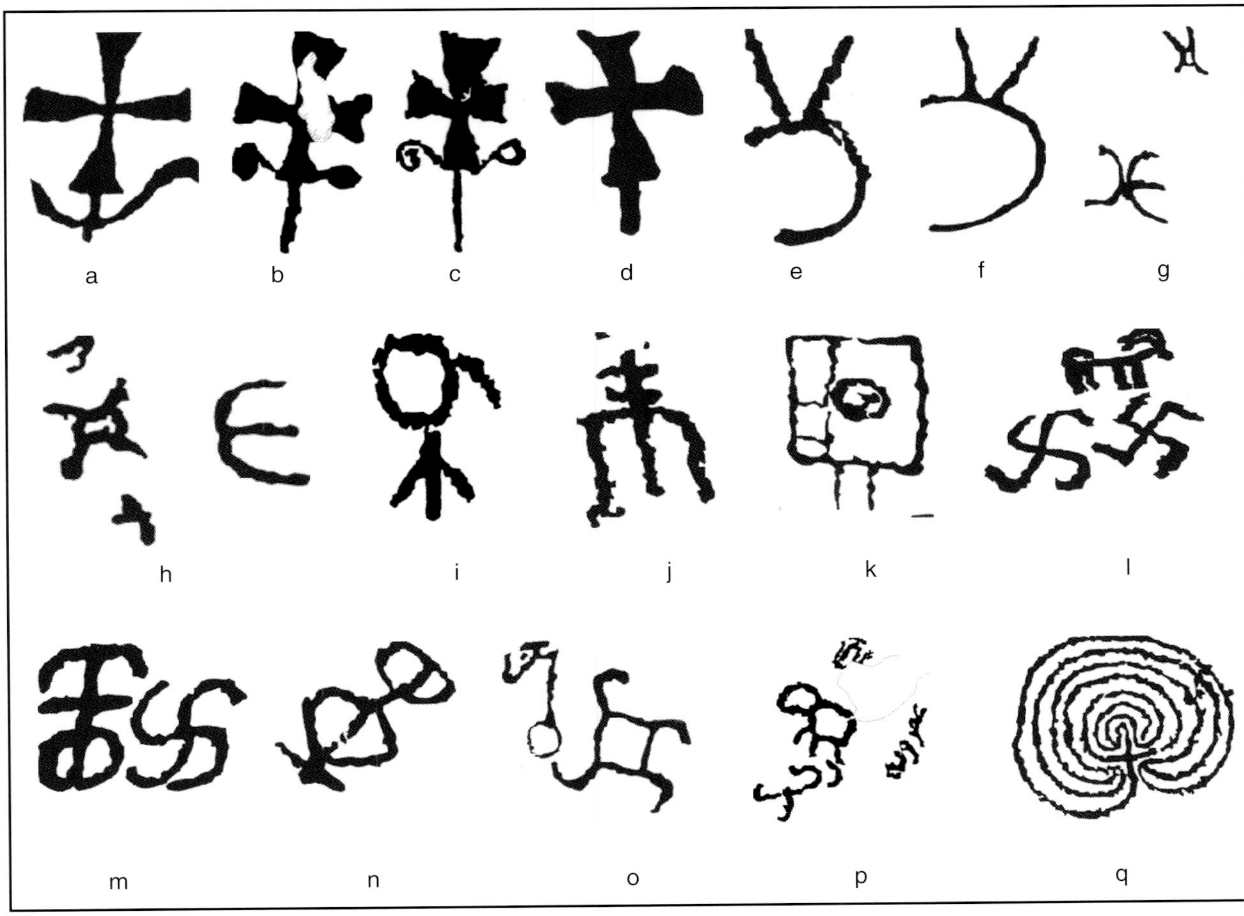

Fig. 12.23 Signs and symbols on the main three boulders in the middle of the Tangtse village.
Note: The first four figures represent a Christian cross.

SPATIAL SIGNIFICANCE

Rock art (petroglyphs) in Ladakh is spread throughout its length and breadth. However, we can broadly make a general remark on the differences in its spatial distribution, with some exceptions. There are two types of rock art: one by the river valleys area along the ancient routes. The other type is found in pasture land where, the author believes, the ancient routes did not touch. There is a significant difference between these two categories. The rock art depictions along the river valleys or the routes are stylistically peculiar and are very

Fig. 12.24 A scene of a predator chasing prey with stylistically drawn figures is one of the finest representations at Tangtse site.

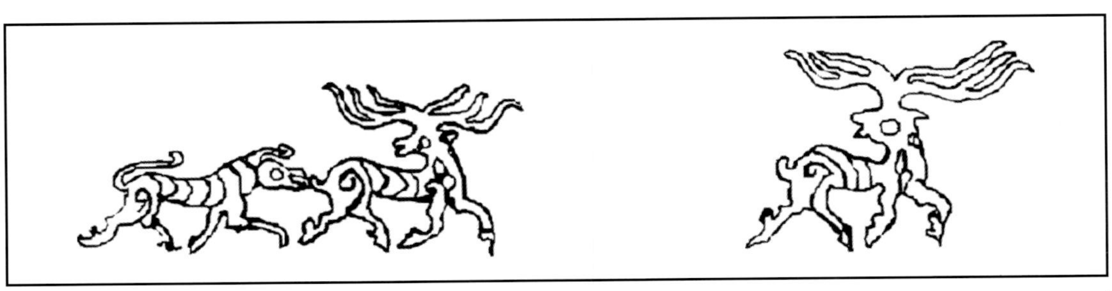

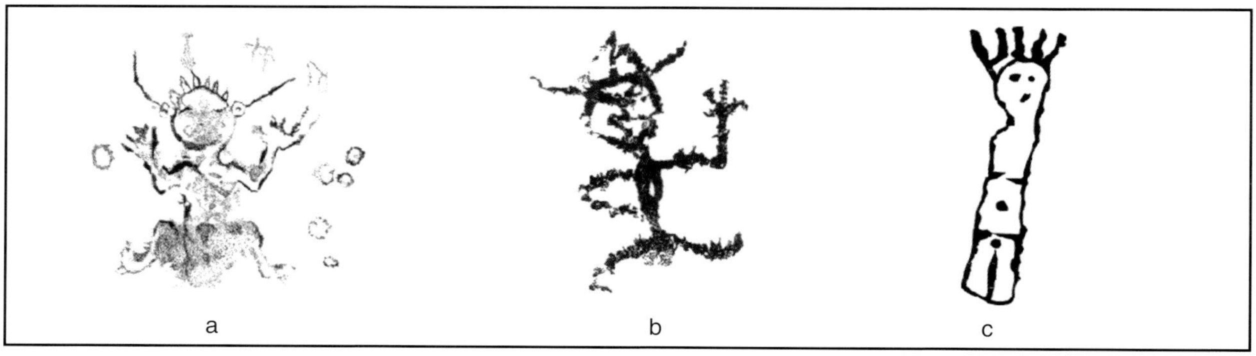

Fig. 12.25 Anthropomorphic figures seen near Tangtse village are rare in style.

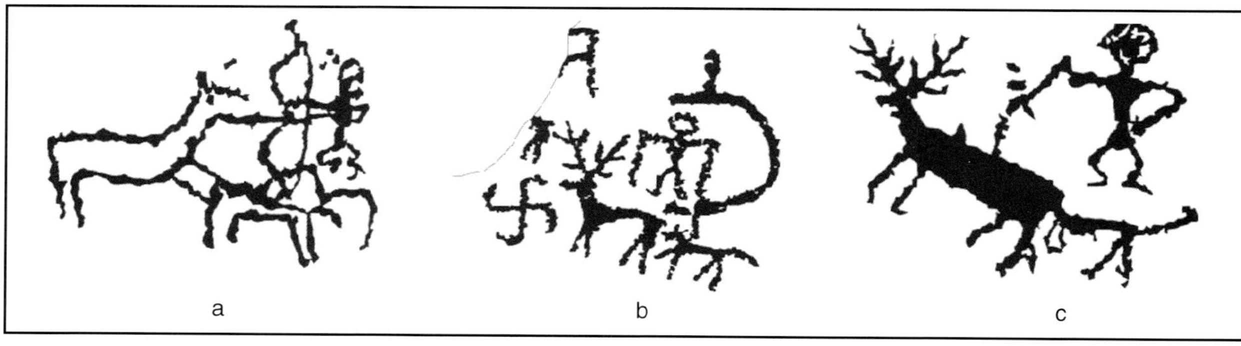

Fig. 12.26 (a-c) Hunting scenes from the main boulders.

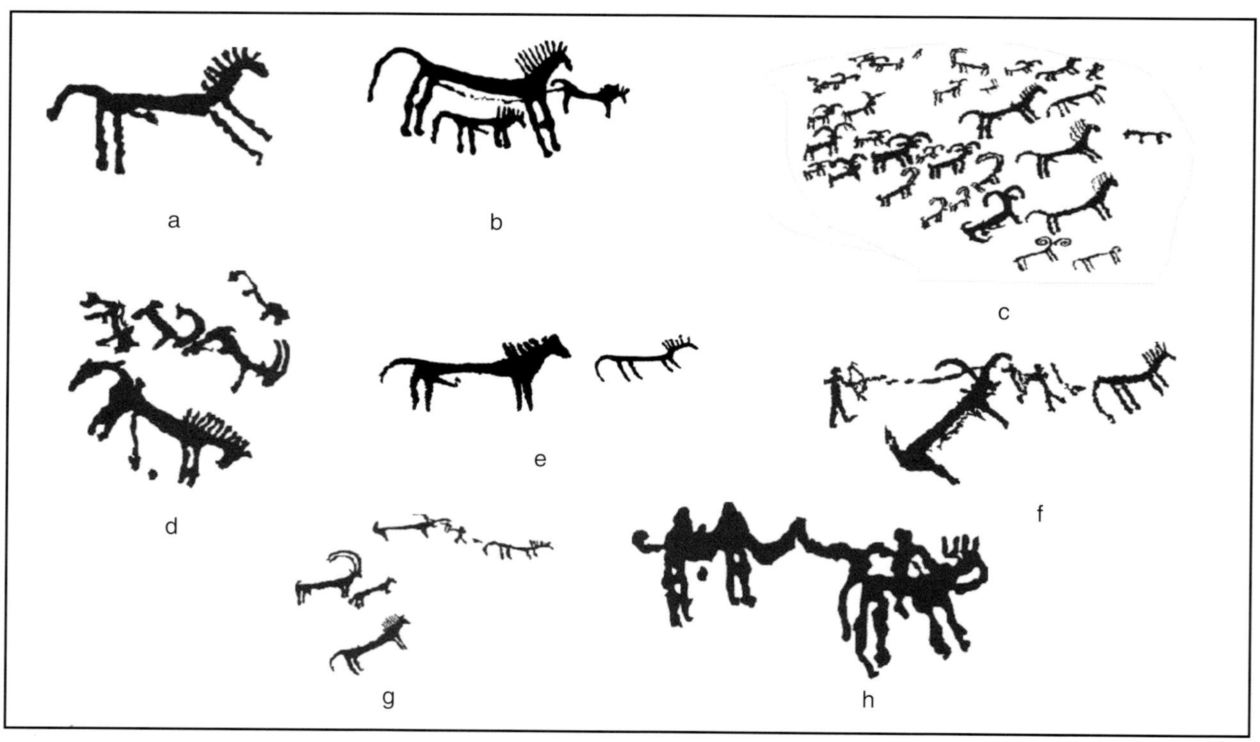

Fig. 12.27 Figure of horses along with hunting scenes are common at the Sasoma site.
Note: Such a stylistically distinct representation of horses is not found elsewhere in Ladakh.

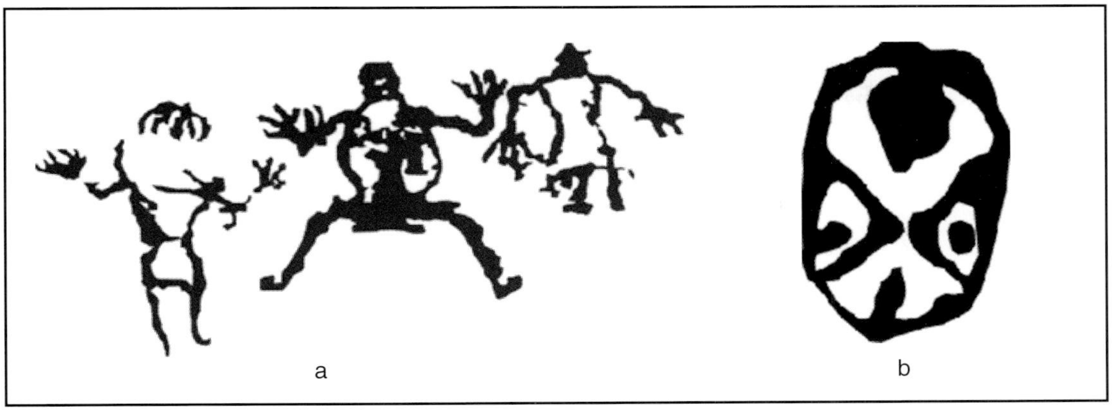

Fig. 12.28 (a) A rare representation of giant-like human forms; (b) represents one of the six mask-like figures near Sasoma.

rarely repeated in any other place. The other type on vast pasture land subjectively and stylistically depicts some uniformity. This is represented by wild goat, ibex, yak or hunting scenes. We are yet to analyse if such differences in rock art could make any difference to the ethnic identity of the carvers. Due to the large number of petroglyphs, the present paper analyses only the former type of rock art, i.e., along the routes.

Barnes (2007) writes, 'Rock art is also selective—it does not represent life in its entirety, but emphasises particular aspects of it.' Therefore, the rock art of Ladakh certainly shows some uncertain functional roles that it played, but on the other hand at many places it shows some peculiar aspects, not represented or repeated elsewhere, thereby giving a puzzling spatial significance.

The significance of the landscape is associated with various places like rivers, plateaus, passes and peaks. Many of them are associated with certain gods or spirits, representing Buddhist cultural practices of Ladakh. Encountering important locales in the course of social

Fig. 12.29 Ensa site (the little blackened oval island-like on the slope) is seen from the other side of the Nobra River.

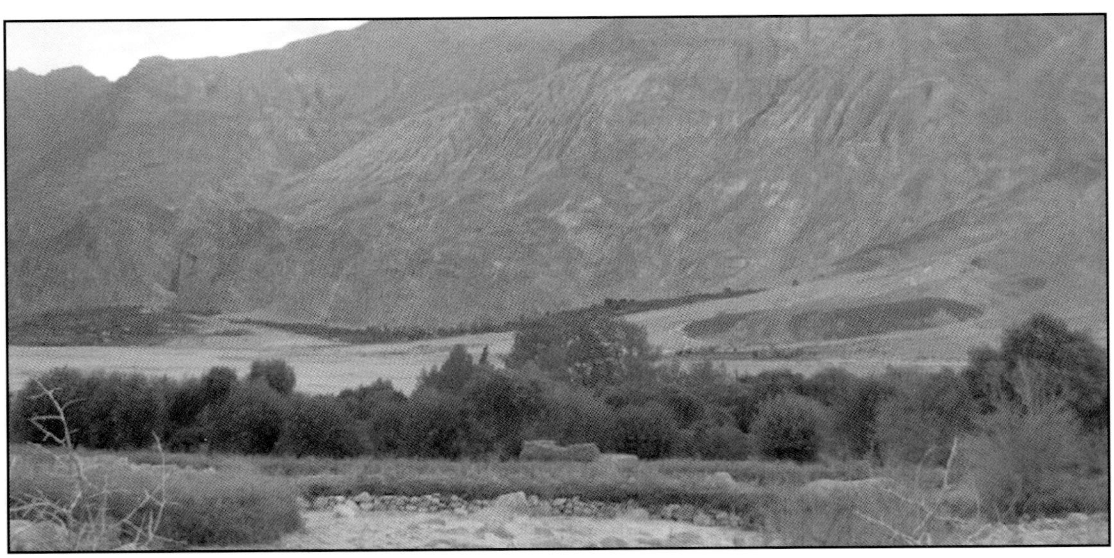

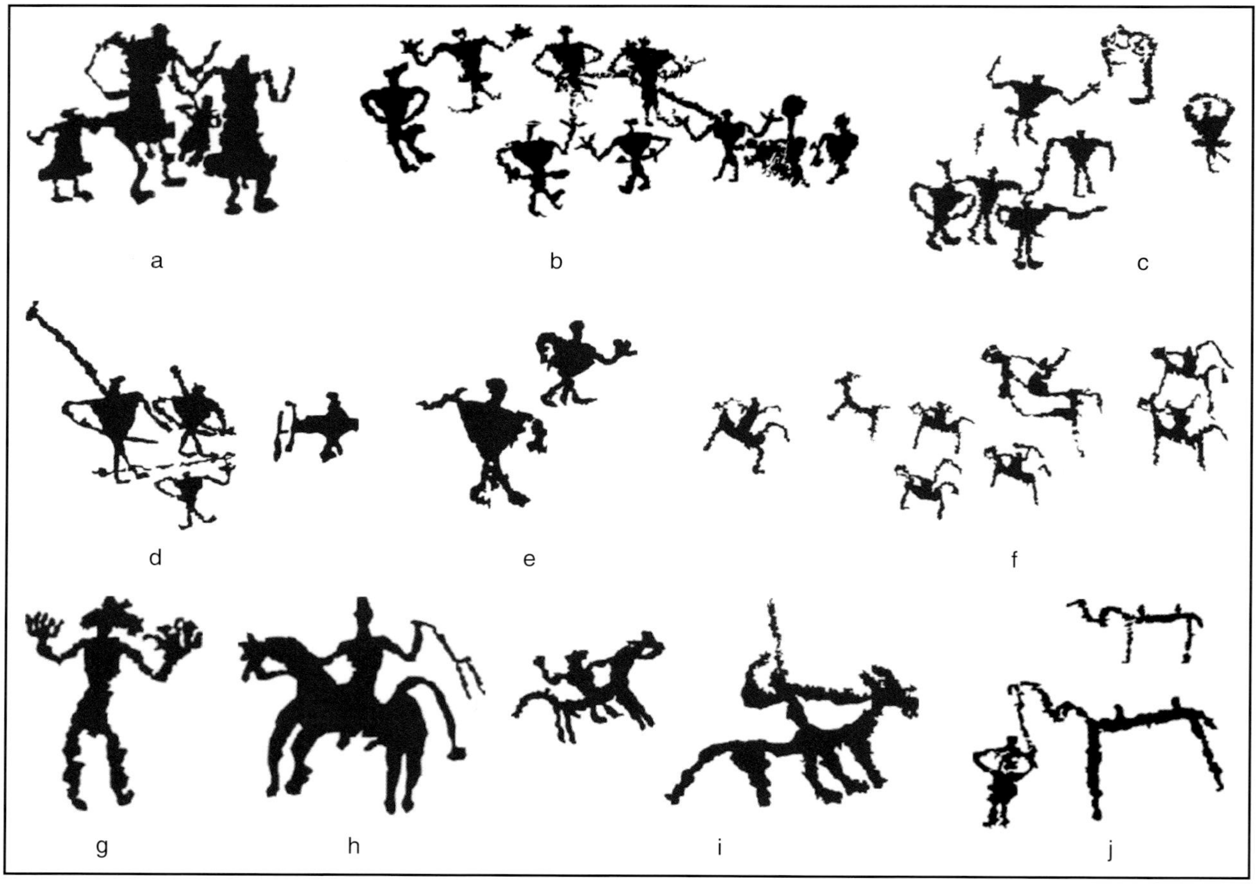

Fig. 12.30 The human forms found at Ensa site are in fact a stylistic representation that seems confined to this particular site.

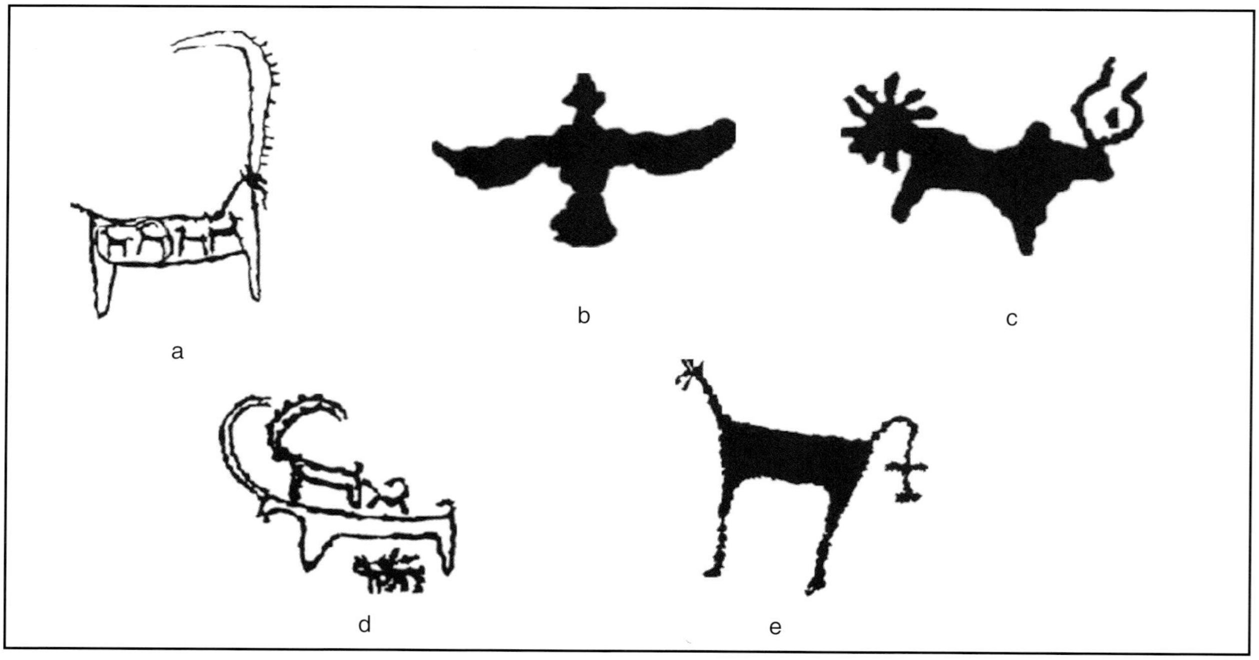

Fig. 12.31 Some of the animal figures at Ensa are stylistically peculiar.

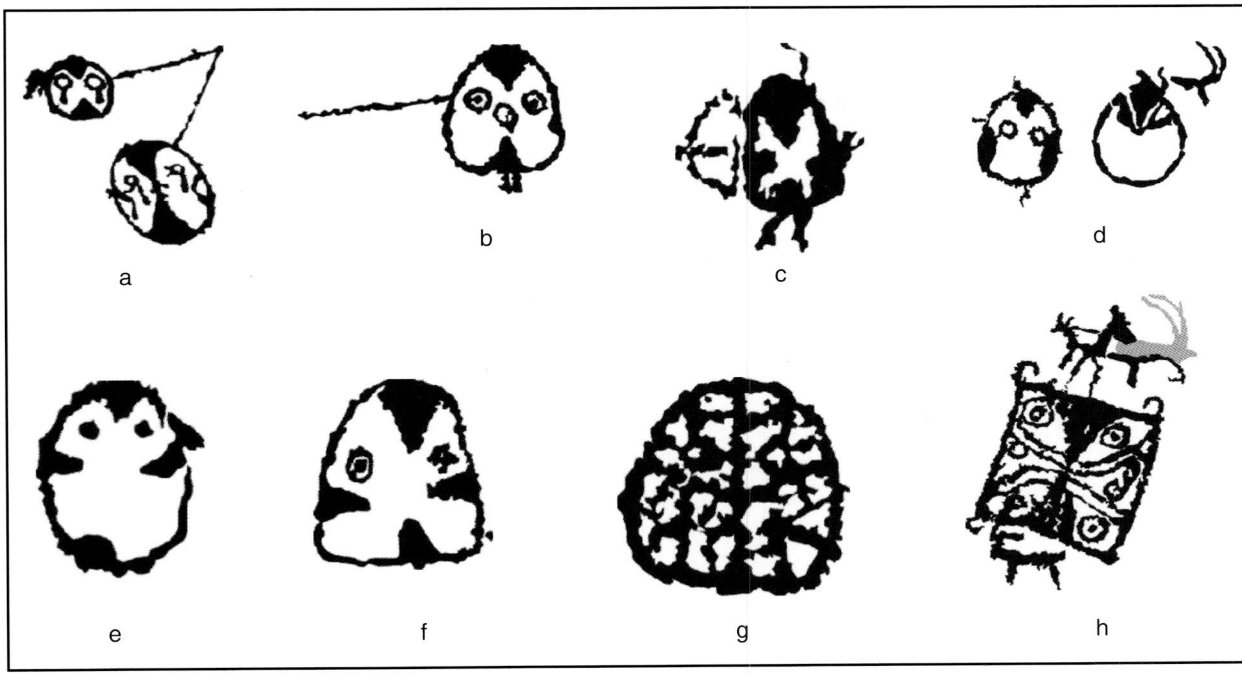

Fig. 12.32 Some of the mask-like figures from Ensa site. Note: The first few figures give a clue that the mask-like figures are associated with hunting.

routines act as a mnemonic device for social history (Basso 1996). Establishing the landscape context of the rock art helps in determining the kind of audiences it was intended for and thus the kind of social relationships it may have negotiated (Bradley 2000). Uniformity in the subject and style of rock art is quite prevalent, from Ladakh to European caves, that is, hand-prints, hunting scenes, etc. In Kenya, nearly every region has at least one type of rock art; there is no concentration of rock art sites in one area from which it was deduced that people were sparsely distributed (Odak 1992). Representation of particular species specific to a particular region is also common in rock art, so are hunting scenes. The present paper discusses only the rock art of Ladakh that is uncommon in its subject, style and distribution, particularly along with the ancient routes. It was puzzling to note as to why some sites were prolific in a particular style and pattern of rock art. For example, 'Domkhar Sanctuary' has a collection of rock art that is almost exclusive to that particular site. On the other hand, the entire Lower Indus Valley has plenty of anthropomorphic figures, incomparable to other anthropomorphic figures elsewhere in Ladakh, which is very rare. We are yet to ascertain if such differences are due to a distinct regional identity, probably determined by isolated smaller ecological units in this Himalayan part.

Animal style figures were seen in plenty in Domkhar Sanctuary. Although quite a few were found in various other sites in Ladakh like Tangtse, Kharu, Stakna, Changa and Zanskar, but their presence in these areas was restricted to one or a couple of figures in isolation. Animal style figures show some peculiar patterns: standing on tips of hoofs, body decorated with volutes, often with S-shaped designs and a few showing a predator chasing a prey. Animal style with elegant curves and spiral hooks is also reported from the northern areas of Pakistan (Jettmar and Thawalt 1987) often dated from 4th to 6th century BCE. Other animal style figures (including a predator chasing a prey) of deer, ibexes, felines and bovines is reported from Renmudong, Tibet, belonging to Iron Age (WuJunkui 1987). Such figures with spiral hooks in the body or on the tip of the hoofs are also reported from Minusinsk area belonging to 5th-4th century BCE (Jettmar and Thawalt 1987) and Mugur-Sargol, Siberia of Iron Age (Jettmar and Thawalt 1987).

The large number of mask-like figures found particularly in Nubra Valley is a puzzling phenomenon, although mask like figures have been reported from Ladakh (one from Char in Zanskar (Francfort et al. 1992), another from rGya (Vohra 1990) and even from the northern areas of Pakistan (two from Chilas on the Indus) (Jettmar and Thewalt 1987). However, the masks from Nubra Valley surpass all others, particularly in terms of their affinity with the Okunuv culture. These 'mascoids' are considered a characteristic motif of the Okunuv culture in south Siberia, which began in the 3rd millennium BCE (Jettmar and Thewalt 1987). At Sasoma we found around six mask-like figures on a rock surface, half buried in the ground. Ensa (in Nubra) is another site which is astonishing. It has plenty of masks like figures, both in terms of numbers and variety. However, as shown in Fig. 12.32 a, b, and c, the first few figures give us a clue that the mask-like figures are associated with hunting or human forms. At the same site, human forms (Fig. 12.30) show a stylistic peculiarity although human forms with a triangular upper body are also reported from far east Russia (Brentjes 1999).

It was understandable that some of the sites had a particular style and subject. For example, inscriptions, signs and symbols on the boulders at Tangtse were probably because of its location, being a major village on the Leh-Lhasa (via Gartok/Rutok) route. Likewise, representations of horses and camels at Sasoma are also understandable. The site was a base for the Leh-Yarkand route.

Searight (2004) divided Morocco into zones and found 'certain types of engravings were concentrated in certain areas and that little mixing took place'. She concludes that 'the rock art sites were associated with "useful places", high altitude pasturages and passes in the mountains, passages between mountain chains, ridges providing vantage-places from which to observe the surrounding plains, or water sources... it was proposed that the engravings could define territories, proclaim ownership, indicate the presence of water (not always immediately visible), commemorate heroes or battles'. We could also propose that some sites have some particular significance. Chilling Valley and the Lower Indus Valley with many anthropomorphic figures demonstrate some kind of magico-religious beliefs that might have prompted hunter-gatherer populations to engrave for survival in the harsh environment. Rock art was used to decorate sacred places or in waiting areas before a dangerous passage or to mark landmarks or cairns (Francfort 1992). Commenting on rock art from Lower Indus, Vohra (1990) presumes that the location might have formed an 'ethnic sanctuary'. These boulders, engraved with symbols and imbued with magical powers, provided an appropriate atmosphere for a socio-religious gathering.

These spatial differences raise a doubt: did these valleys develop their own traditions of engravings as something autochthonous or whether they were influenced, imitated or

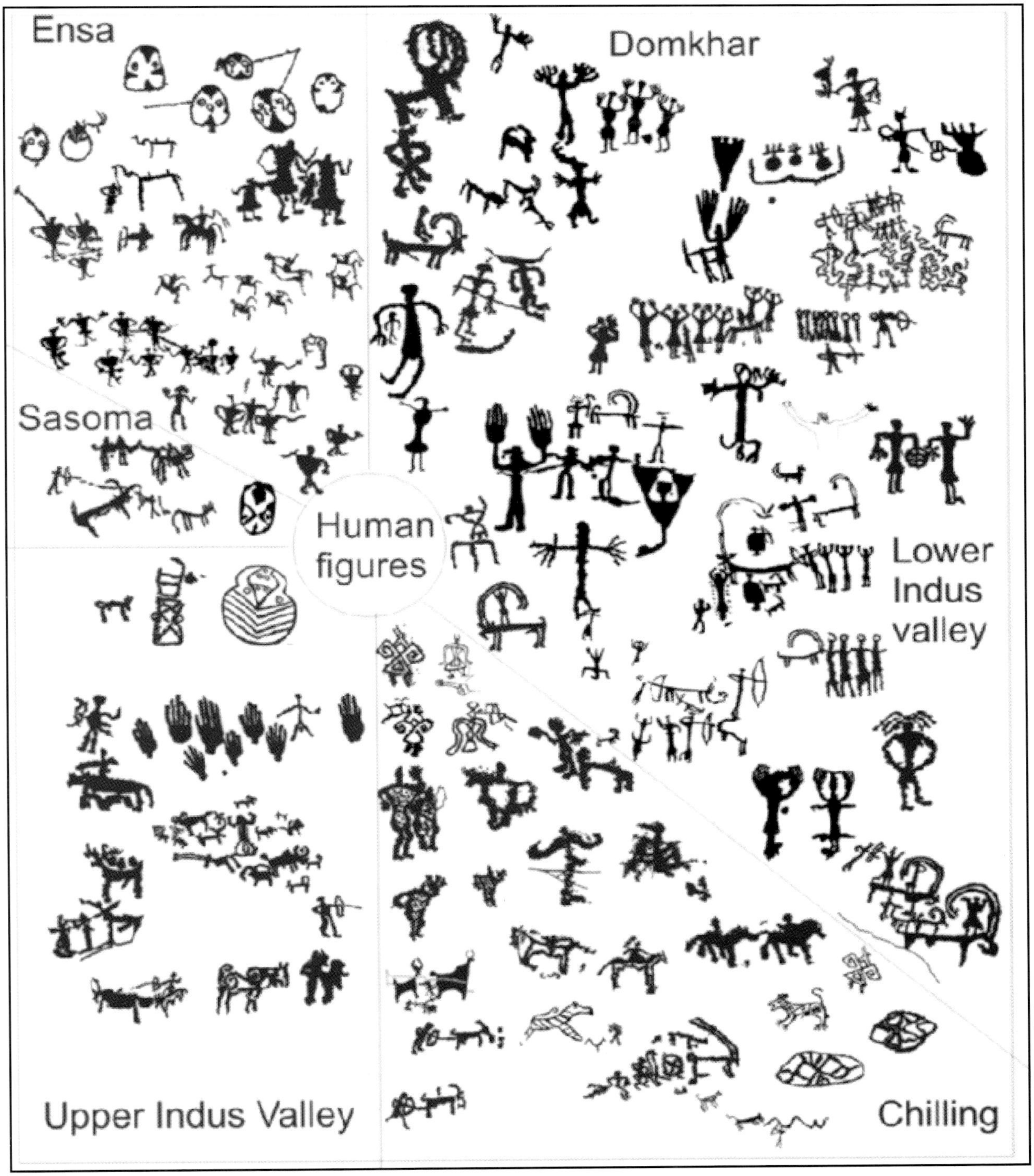

Fig. 12.33 A general classified representation of human (or anthropomorphs) and other human associated figures from different regions/sites.
Note: The distribution pattern in terms of style and subject can be broadly outlined. Ensa and Sasoma falls in Nubra Valley, Domkhar is actually a part of Lower Indus Valley and Chilling Valley is included in the Upper Indus Valley.

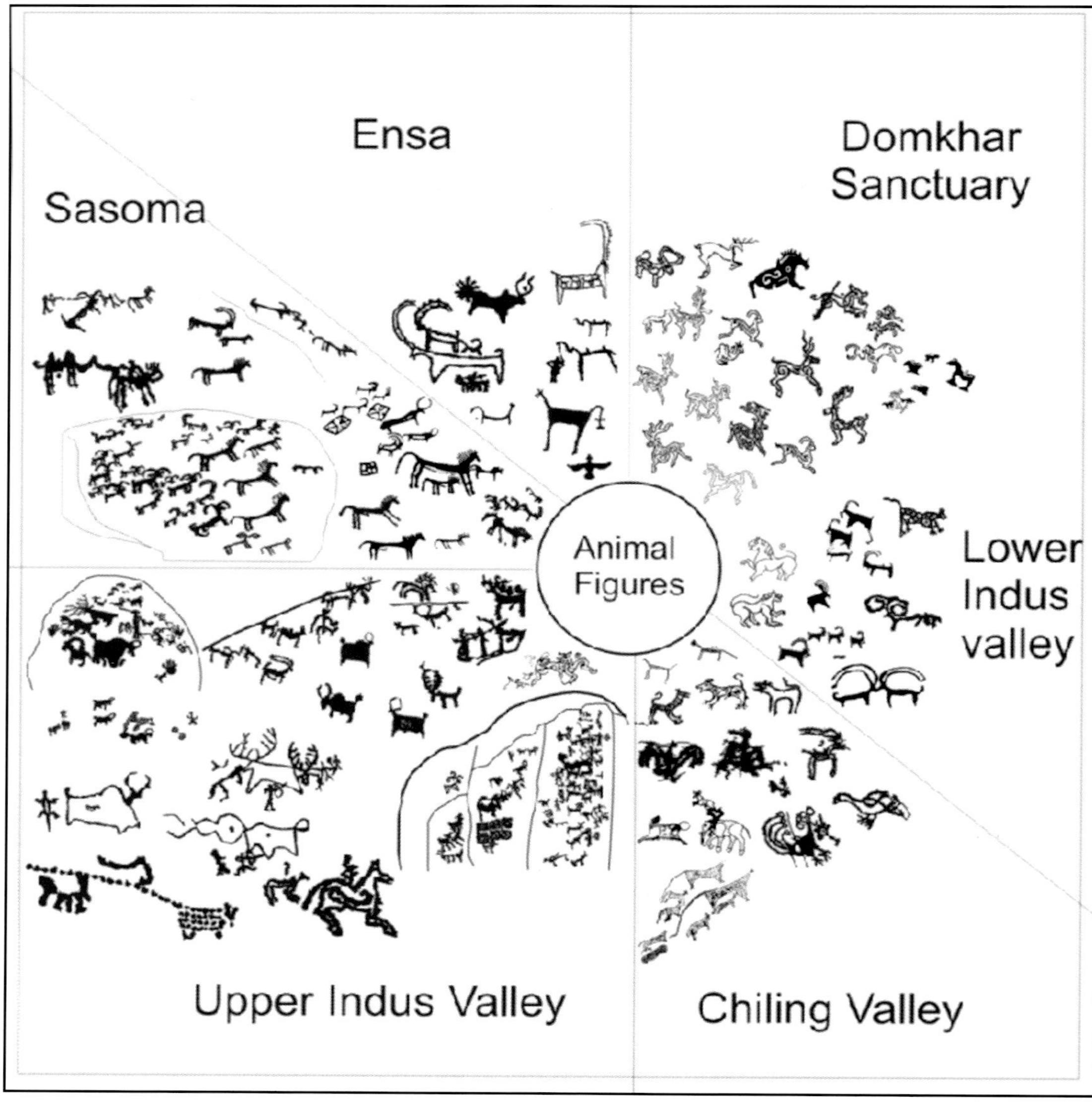

Fig. 12.34 A general classified representation of animal or animal-like figures from different regions/sites. Note: The distribution pattern in terms of style and subject can be broadly outlined.

modified from another tradition. We also doubt if many of the rock art elements reflect the environmental and ecological conditions that they were made in.

CONCLUSION

Whatever the purpose and reason, the author believes that there are significant differences in the spatial distribution of the rock art of Ladakh in the valleys or along the ancient routes. Moreover, there are some site-specific engravings, which may or may not fall on ancient routes. Such sites emphasise the importance of the particular space. Therefore, the rock art of Ladakh should be studied beyond a comparative analysis, which many authors have done with reference to elements from Central Asia. The deliberate distortion of figures, exaggeration of body parts, animal-human conflation, etc. transcend realism. Such figures must have a core essence of their being engraved on a particular rock or site. On the other hand, this art is no longer an integral part of our lives today. Most of the people of the present generation are oblivious of its presence; some even fail to recognise a boulder that they have been passing by since the last 50 years.

More importantly, the present paper has tried to highlight the variety and number of petroglyphs found in Ladakh and to bring to the notice of the world that this rock art is disappearing. It is being broken down, vandalised and weathered, and therefore the author invites experts to help in protecting it.

REFERENCES

Basso, Keith H. (1996), *Wisdom Sits in Places: Landscape & Language among the Western Apache.* Albuquerque: University of New Mexico Press.

Bradley, Richard (2000), *An Archaeology of Natural Places.* London: Routledge.

Brentjes, Burchard (1999), 'Rock Art in Russian Far East and in Siberia', Asia, TRACCE (online Rock Art Bulletin) No. 11.

Francke, A.H. (1907), *A History of Western Tibet.* London: S.W. Partridge.

Francfort, Henri-Paul, Daniel Klodzinski and Georges Mascle (1992), 'Archaic Petroglyphs of Ladakh and Zanskar', in Michel Lorblanchet (ed.), *Rock Art in the Old World, IGNCA Rock Art Series-I.* New Delhi: IGNCA and Aryan Books International.

Harmatta, J. (1999), 'The Emergence of Indo-Iranians: The Indo Iranian Languages', in A.H. Dani and V.M. Masson (eds.), *History of Civilisations of Central Asia,* Volume 1. Delhi: Motilal Banarsidass Publishers Pvt. Ltd.

Hopkirk, Peter (1980), *Foreign Devils on the Silk Road: The Search for the Lost Treasures of Central Asia.* Oxford: Oxford University Press.

Jettmar, K. and V. Thewalt (1987), 'Between Gandhara and the Silk Roads: Rock Carvings along the Karakoram Highway', Discoveries by German-Pakistani Expeditions 1979–1984. Mainz am Rhein: Verlag Philipp Von Zebern.

Odak, Osaga (1992), 'Kenya Rock Art Studies and the Need for a Discipline', in Michel Lorblanchet (ed.), *Rock Art in the Old World, IGNCA Rock Art Series-I.* New Delhi: IGNCA and Aryan Books International.

Petech (1977), *The Kingdom of Ladakh c. 950–1842 A.D.* Roma: IsMEO.

Rizvi, Janet (1983), *Ladakh. Crossroads of High Asia.* Delhi: Oxford University Press (revised and expanded edition 1996).

Thsangspa, T.L. (2007), 'A Short Note on Some Petroglyphs of the Nubra Valley', in John Bray and N.T. Shakspo (eds.), *Recent Research on Ladakh.* Leh: J&K Academy of Art, Culture and Languages, International Association of Ladakh Studies.

Vohra, R. (1990), 'Antiquities of the Southern Arteries of the Silk Route: Ethnic Movements and New Discoveries'. Paper Presented at a Conference on the Anthropology of the Himalayas and Tibet.

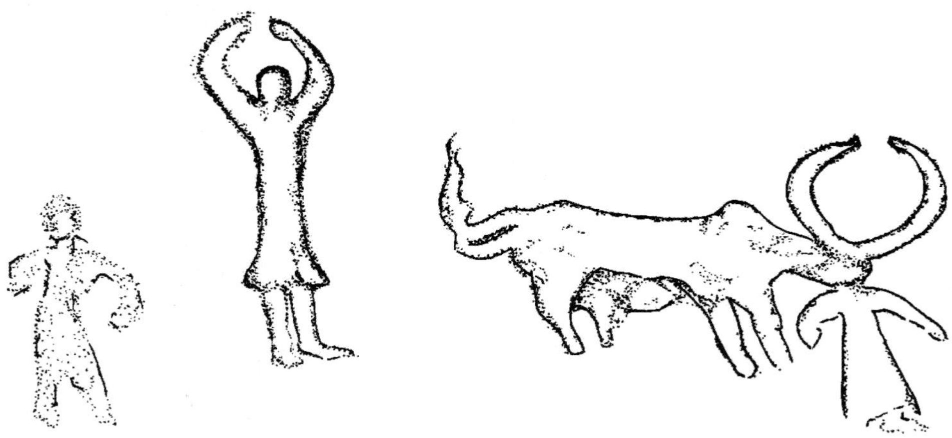

13

Rock Art and Its Cultural Context—Recent Evidences in Tamil Nadu, India

K. Rajan

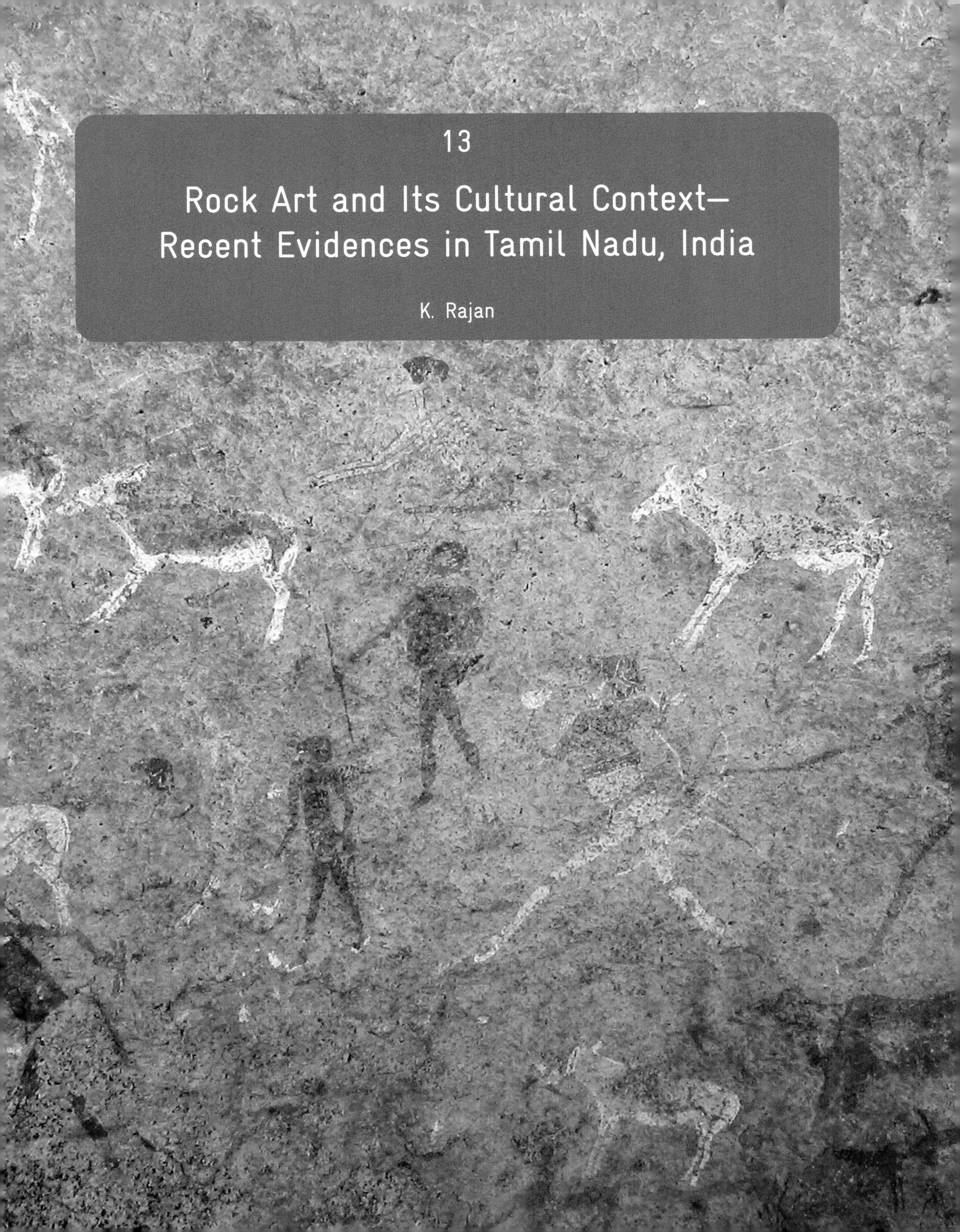

ABSTRACT

Recent discoveries made in the southern tip of peninsular India provide a new insight into the cultural context in which these art forms were developed. Rock art was found in different cultural contexts stretching from Microlithic times down to early historic times. The discovery of more than 100 rock art sites executed on rock shelters and Iron Age Megalithic monuments, particularly on dolmens, suggests their cultural preferences. The distributional pattern suggests that this rock art was generally associated with two types of inhabitants. The rock art found in dense forests as one can notice in Anjanad Valley and a lower Palani hill of the Western Ghats, is suggestive of the hunter-gatherer community living on forest products. The other rock art sites located at the foothills and outcrops of the plains are suggestive of the agro-pastoral community living in semi-arid zones. The excavations conducted at Paiyampalli, Mallapadi, Mayiladumparai and Thandikudi provide good scope to situate them within a specific chronological and cultural frame. A majority of the rock art sites are located in isolated places away from habitation mounds suggesting their ritual status. However, despite the presence of a large number of rock art sites in different ecological zones, the study of rock art in Tamil Nadu has not received sufficient academic attention, though the limited documentation carried out on these art forms provides a restricted understanding of their cultural wealth. Dr. Rajan's paper attempts to present a status report on the geographical distribution, socio-cultural contexts, themes, context and chronological evolution of this rock art.

INTRODUCTION

Rock art is an expression of subsistence patterns, belief systems, thought processes, philosophy of life and surrounding eco-systems. In a nutshell, it is the representation of the rich life-ways of prehistoric communities. Rock art was produced at different levels, which depended upon the level of the progress made in the daily lives of the people executing this rock art. Moving from a sedentary to a settled life (or one may say the transformation from hunter-gatherers to agro-pastoral life) was bound to have an impact on the life system. The changes in perceptions led to a change in representation. As a result, when researchers come across rock art they try to understand the total concept of the lives of past communities based on the location of a rock shelter, the colours of the pigments used, spatial distribution of the representations or expressions within a complex and the overlaps thus going beyond its aesthetic value. Rock art, therefore, is not just about expressing 'things', but it represents ideas, sublime thoughts and values. Rock art serves as an important source material for understanding the 'mental world' of past societies through their dynamic expressions. This non-verbal language, communicated through an everlasting medium, provides insights into the world of a bygone era. The study of rock art in Tamil Nadu, particularly in recent years, has attracted the attention of a number of academicians, artists and amateurs from different fields. Curiosity about this ancient form of art has resulted in the discovery of more than 75 sites in Tamil Nadu with paintings (petrographs) and engravings (petroglyphs) executed on the surface of rock shelters and Iron Age (megalithic) graves, particularly dolmens. Unlike in the northern part of India, where rock art is dated back to the later Palaeolithic times, according to available evidence, South Indian rock art seems to have first appeared in Mesolithic times, but continued through Neolithic, Iron Age, and early Historic times (Map 13.1).

HISTORY OF RESEARCH

Since the first discovery of rock paintings in 1880-1881 by Archibald Carlleyle in the Kaimur range of Bihar region, several rock art sites have been brought to light in different parts of India. Though several sites have been identified, these identifications have been sporadic in nature as the one discovered by Fawcett in 1901 at Edakkal in Wayanad region of Kerala. Unlike other rock art sites in the contemporary world, Fawcett's discovery is unique, as Edakkal is the only site that represents rock engravings on a massive scale; it also remained the only site discovered for over a century till the discovery of Perumukkal in Tamil Nadu. Irrespective of its uniqueness, scholars miserably fail to locate rock art in Kerala and Tamil Nadu during the pre-independence era. The study of rock art as a discipline emerged only in the post-independence era. The discovery of a cluster of painted shelters at Bhimbetka in 1957 by V.S. Wakankar had a tremendous impact on the study of rock art in India. The discovery of rock paintings at Mallapadi in Dharmapuri district by K.V. Raman in 1978 during an excavation programme opened a new vista in the study of rock art in Tamil Nadu. Pon. Arasu, a then prehistoric archaeologist from the Tamil Nadu State Archaeology Department, took initiatives under the direction of R. Nagasamy and documented nearly ten sites in a short span of time, particularly in the area in and around Tirukkoyilur in the south Arcot region. However, the discovery of Kilvalai paintings near Villupuram with certain graffiti marks identical to the Harappan/ Indus script by Bagur Kuppusamy in 1984 generated great interest among archaeologists and linguists. The symbols provided a new dimension to the study. Archaeological officers posted in different districts made considerable efforts to locate rock paintings. For instance, R. Poongundran, then Registering Officer of Nilgiri district, discovered several sites in Nilgiri hills. Likewise, R. Krishnamurthi, the Archaeological Officer of Dharmapuri district, discovered paintings on the inner surface of the orthostats of the dolmens at Maharajakadai and Mallachandram. This discovery provided a new direction to our understanding of this rock art. Until the discovery of dolmen paintings, rock shelter paintings were hypothetically associated with, the archaeological sites of Microlithic, Neolithic or Iron Age. The paintings executed on the inner surfaces of orthostats, generally against the porthole of the dolmen, put to rest debates about its possible chronology. The dolmen paintings also suggested that the white pigment might be associated with the Iron Age culture. V. Vedachalam, while documenting the Tamil-Brahmi inscriptions engraved on the rock shelters associated with Jain beds, brought to light a few sites in Madurai region. His findings suggested that earlier rock shelters occupied by prehistoric and proto-historic communities were re-occupied by Jain monks. R. Paundurai (1986) of Tamil University consolidated the available data on rock art and published a monograph. Pulavar Duraisamy, a school teacher in Kaveripakkam, discovered several rock art sites in Dharmapuri district between 1986 and 1988. Pulavar Duraisamy was involved in mango plantations and also in marketing mangoes. As a result, he discovered several sites in a mango-growing area. But due to his limited knowledge, he largely ignored the associated cultural material. To pursue this issue, the author in association with Pulavar Duraisamy and T. Subramaniam, the then Archaeological Officer of Dharmapuri district, carried out archaeological surveys in the region and placed certain sites within a definite chronological framework. For 15 years, between 1990 and 2005, there was a lull in rock art research. Only a few sites were added to the list. However, the Tamil Nadu State Archaeology Department initiated a programme to re-survey and document all the available rock art sites in Tamil Nadu and the consolidated report was published as a monograph (Sridhar 2005). However, recently between 2005 and 2007 a few researchers like K.T. Gandhirajan, R.N. Kumanan, M. Saranya, K. Kumar (2005a, 2005b) and Valliyammal (2005) have brought to light several sites. K.T. Gandhirajan as part of a project funded by the Central Institute of Classical Tamil, concentrated in and around Kollegal taluka of Nilgiri district and brought to light one of the largest rock art sites at Karikkiyur near Kollegal in the Niligiri hills. K. Kumar carried out surveys in the Vellore region between 2005 and 2007 and reported several sites. R.N. Kumaran and M. Saranya as a part of their PhD programme noticed rock art sites for the first time in the Palani hills of Kodaikanal region in 2007. Irrespective of these 'discoveries' and rock art studies, Tamil Nadu lacks a systematic approach including ethical/faithful documentation and micro-level analyses. This is due to the lack of data on the cultural context of the sites. Further, there have been only limited excavations at the sites yielding rock art. The excavations at Paiyampalli, Mallapadi and

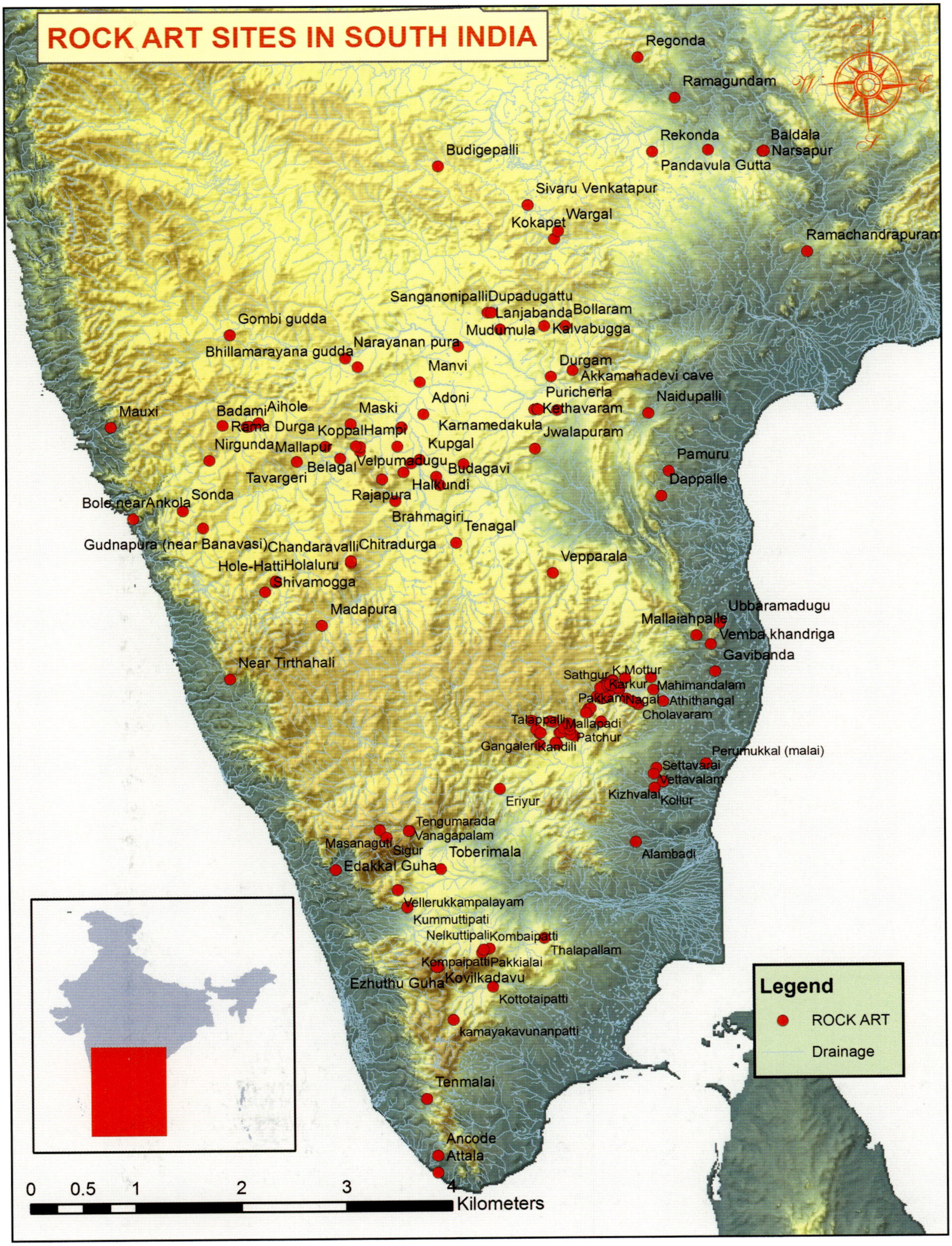

Map 13.1 Rock art sites in South India.

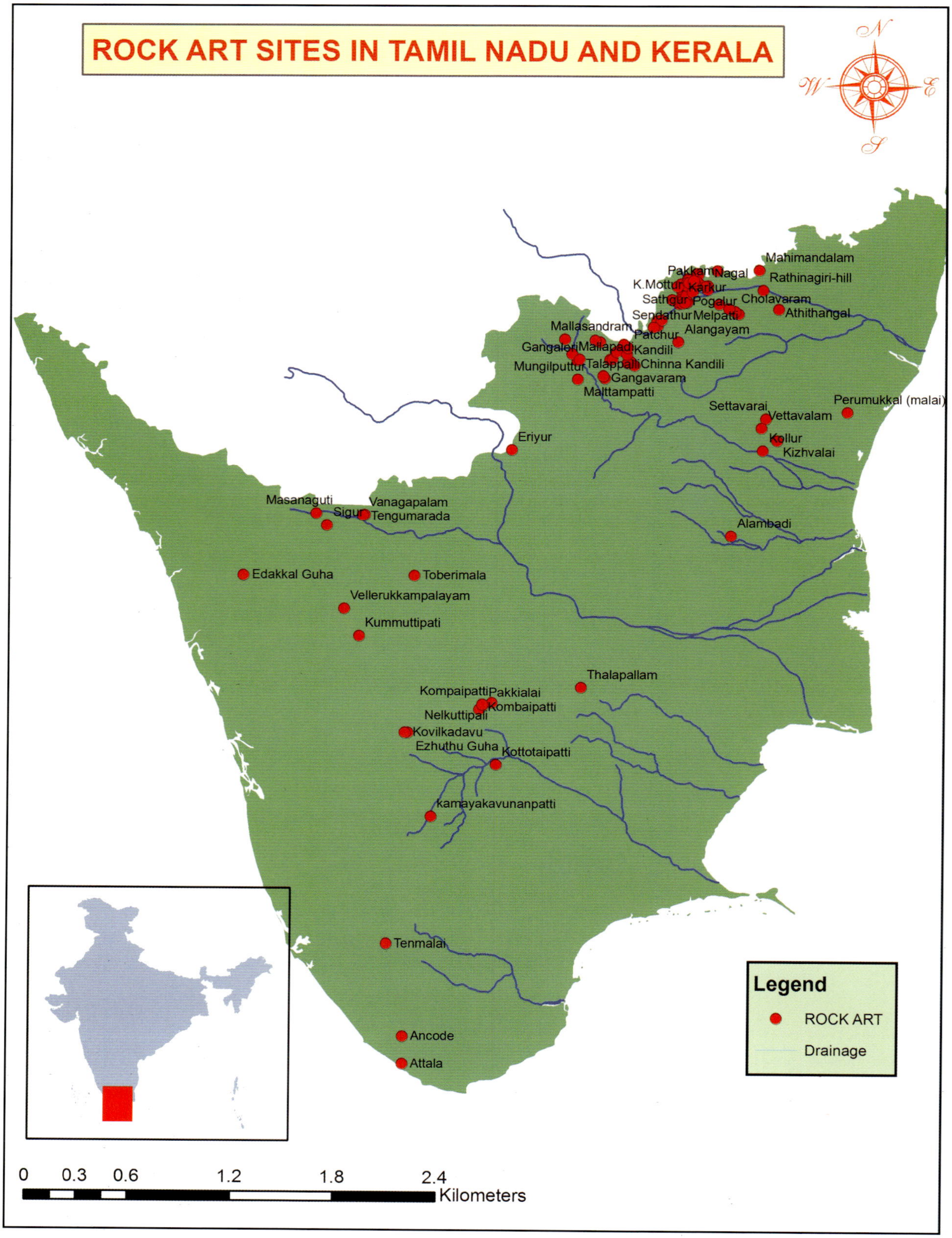

Map 13.2 Rock art sites in Tamil Nadu.

Mayiladumparai have helped in finding out an association between rock art and its cultural contexts. The contextual position of each representation within a complex and inter- and intra-regional associations of these expressions have not been properly studied and understood. A majority of the studies stand as mere documentations of the rock art rather than placing it in a concrete and understandable spectrum.

CHRONOLOGY AND DISTRIBUTION

Till date, nearly 120 sites are known to have yielded paintings executed in rock shelters and 'megalithic' tombs in Tamil Nadu (Table 13.1). Only a few of these sites have engravings. Rock art is witnessed throughout the region with a higher concentration in the northern part of Tamil Nadu (Map 13.2). This scenario is probably due to limited explorations carried out in the southern region. In the recent past, several Palaeolithic sites have been discovered beyond the traditional Palaeolithic centres of Kortalaiyar Valley, in Chingleput, Vellore, Dharmapuri and Ariyalur districts. The discovery of a number of Palaeolithic and Mesolithic tools in the lower Kaveri Valley in sites like those at Kilkolattur (Figs. 13.1-13.4), Kattur and Peraiyur is an eye-opener. Likewise, several Mesolithic sites have been discovered throughout Tamil Nadu (Figs. 13.5 & 13.6). The new discoveries of Palaeolithic sites suggest that prehistoric people intensively inhabited Tamil Nadu but limited explorations restricted to specific geographical zones have hindered our understanding about the spread and nature of these sites. However, their transformation from one cultural phase to another differs considerably if one considers the nature of data recovered all over Tamil Nadu. Rock art sites are found mainly in association with Mesolithic, Neolithic and Iron Age cultures and to some extent with the early Historic culture. In the Mesolithic and Neolithic contexts, they occur on open rock shelters located within the vicinity of the settlements or within their wandering spaces. In the context of Iron Age, they are found both on rock shelters as well as on orthostats of graves, particularly dolmens. The late Iron Age phase in Tamil Nadu understandably overlaps with the early Historic phase. Some of the paintings, though associated with the later Iron Age phase, do reflect historical elements. The period around the 6th *c.* BCE could be treated as the overlapping phase. Some rock paintings are noticed in the caves associated with Jain beds engraved with early Historic Tamil-Brahmi inscriptions. Whether these paintings are contemporary or prior to Jain occupations are yet to be assessed. In all probability, Tamil Nadu has a long rock art tradition starting from the Mesolithic and extending up to the historical phase. A majority of the rock shelters were in continuous occupation for a long period, which resulted in overlapping of evidence, and in a few cases the defacement of earlier rock art. An analysis of superimpositions, spatial and stylistic elements of the rock art and associated archaeological material in a stratified context have helped to date the paintings to some extent. The excavations conducted in an open rock shelter associated with rock paintings at Mayiladumparai could be cited as a fine example of this (Rajan 2004: 74-89). However, this method could not be applied as a universal rule to all the shelters as the content, themes, philosophy and the pigments used for the paintings vary through time. Artefacts like Mesolithic tools, Neolithic celts

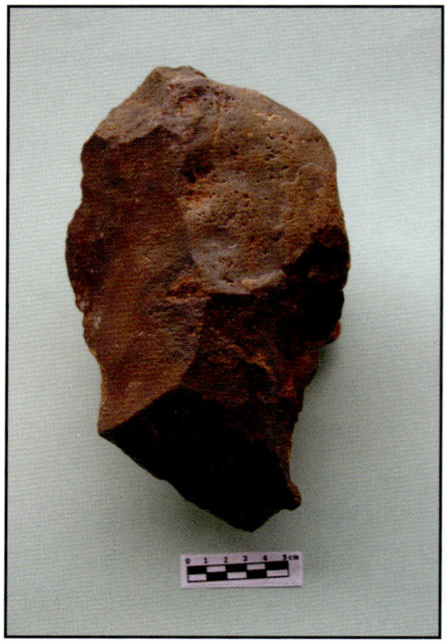

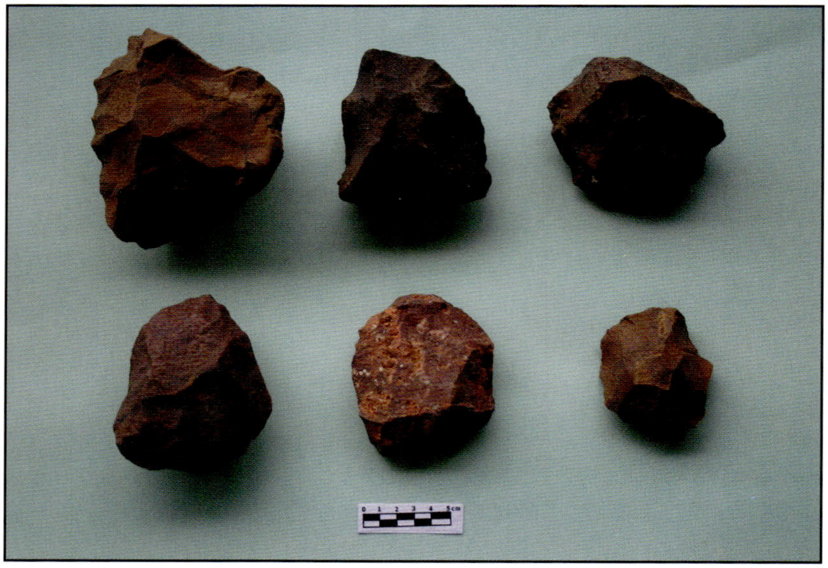

Left: **Fig. 13.1** Kilkolattur: Palaeolithic tools.

Right: **Fig. 13.2** Kilkolattur: Middle Palaeolithic tools.

and Iron Age habitation material were recovered from a majority of the rock shelters and also from the vicinity overlooking the shelters. Mayiladumparai (Fig. 13.7), Munandipatti, Ulkombai, Kilvalai (Fig. 13.8), Perumukkal, Mallapadi and Paiyampalli (Fig. 13.9) can be cited as fine examples in this category of sites.

With regard to engravings, Tamil Nadu has very limited evidence but Perumukkal engravings are the best examples of this category (Fig. 13.10). There are sporadic engravings in rock shelters at Mayiladumparai, Tirumalpadi, Chinna Kandili, Chennarayanpalli, Mahimandalam, Athithangal and Rathinagiri. Excavations carried out in a shelter with engravings at Mayiladumparai suggest that these engravings belong to the Neolithic phase. The Perumukkal engravings are identical in all respects to those found in the Edakkal caves in Kerala. But the former's cultural association is yet to be ascertained though claims have been made for its prehistoric origin. Besides the usual engravings on the walls of the shelter, cup marks are noticed on the capstones of the Iron Age (megalithic) cist burials at Karubayanahalli and Vedarthattakkal in Krishnagiri district. Cup marks were also seen for the first time on the boulders of a stone circle entombing a cist burial at Velliripatti near Melur in Madurai district and at Surai, Chandrapuram and Odugattur in the Vellore region. Recently, Mulli Mani of the Archaeological Survey of India excavated a rock shelter at Malayadipatti near Pudukottai and he associated these marks with Palaeolithic times though such tools could not be observed in the region. Other than Malayadipatti, none of the Palaeolithic sites have so far yielded any remnants of rock art in Tamil Nadu.

In Tamil Nadu, traces of rock art were found in the districts of Dharmapuri, Krishnagiri, Vellore, Tiruvannamalai, Coimbatore and Madurai with much concentration in the former three districts. Any new addition to the list in future may change the present concentration of rock art in northern Tamil Nadu. The northern part, particularly Dharmapuri and Vellore

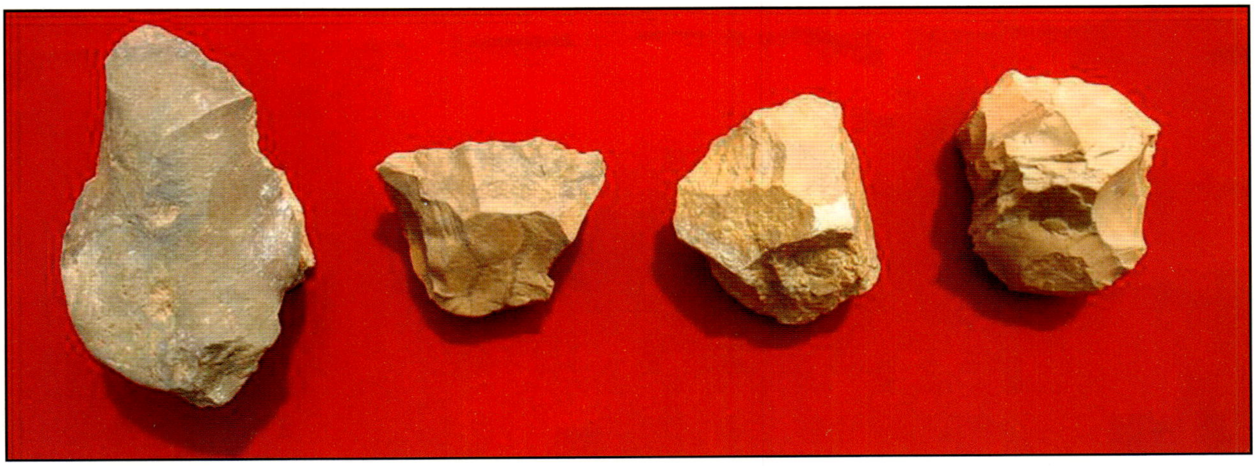

Fig. 13.3 Kilkolattur: Middle Palaeolithic tools.

districts, have paintings of Mesolithic and Neolithic phases. The findings at Mayiladumparai, Paiyampalli and Mallapadi are the best examples in this category. These sites are located in the landscape, which is an extension of the Mysore Plateau. Palaeolithic tools were recovered from Varatanapalli and Kappalavadi in Krishnagiri district. The earliest paintings associated with the Mesolithic phase could be seen at Mayiladumparai in Krishnagiri district. The tradition continued in the Neolithic phase and much of the evidence surfaced in the Iron Age as seen at Kilvalai in Tiruvannamalai district. The late phase of Iron Age culture in Tamil Nadu overlaps with the early Historic phase. The cultural transformation from one cultural phase to another is not uniform across this region. Uneven ecological settings in the area might have led to an uneven development in the cultural process. The southern part of Tamil Nadu, particularly the area south of river Vaigai, did not witness the Neolithic phase. Though, quite a number of Neolithic celts have been recovered from surface explorations, we hardly have conclusive to say conclusively about the Neolithic phase. Recent excavations conducted at Mangudi (Shetty 2003) and Teriruveli reveal that this region transformed directly from Mesolithic to Iron Age. This is contradictory to the scenario in the northern parts of Tamil Nadu. Very few explorations and a negligible number of excavations have been conducted in this region. So future explorations and issue-based excavations may change this scenario. As the present evidence goes, the rock paintings found at sites like Sirumalai, Mayiladumparai, Ulkombai and Munandipatti could be associated with the Mesolithic phase.

In the case of Iron Age, the picture is somewhat clearer. The area under study witnessed inhabitants belonging to different social/occupational groups. The earliest groups were mainly involved in hunting and cattle-rearing, while the later groups were engaged in agriculture. The former groups generally settled down on hillocks, whereas the latter groups occupied riverine tracts, which were suitable for agriculture. Though both the groups followed the practice of raising Iron Age (megalithic) tombs for the dead, there seem to be architectural and cultural variations in their funerary rites. The groups that occupied the hillocks or foothills generally built dolmens and dolmenoid

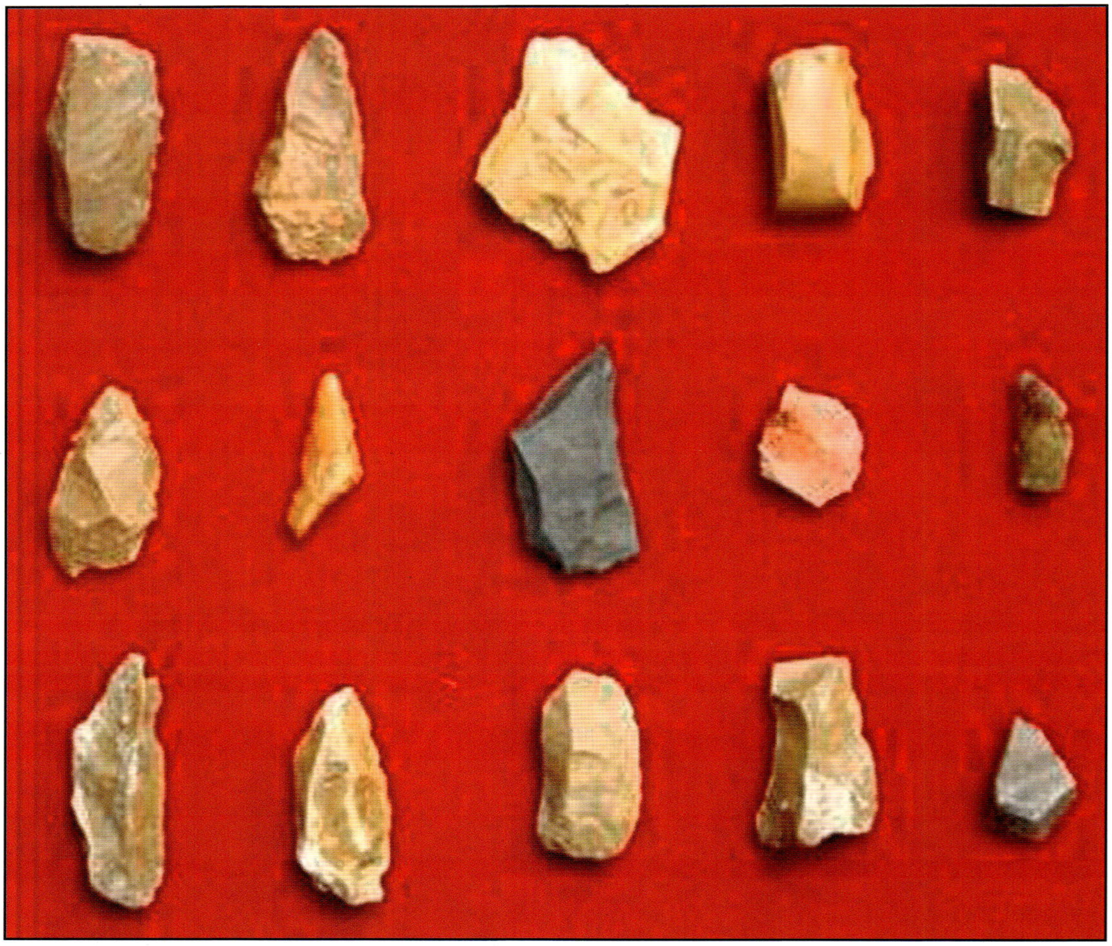

Fig. 13.4 Kilkolattur: Middle Palaeolithic tools.

cists. Their main water sources were small tanks and perennial ponds. The inhabitants settled on the plains adopted urn burials and stone circles entombing cist or urn burials (Rajan 1992a: 35-47). The size, type and location of the burials and the associated habitations indicate that in Tamil Nadu rock art was adopted by the people who were actively involved in cattle raising or who had a rudimentary form of an agro-pastoral economy rather than those associated with agriculture. Most of the paintings were noticed on rock shelters and dolmens. The rock shelters were generally located in the middle part of the hillocks and in the vicinity of habitation mounds and Iron Age graves, thereby exposing their close relationship. Most of the habitation mounds normally lie on the flat surface of a hillock, whereas the rock shelters were located a little away from the habitation mounds. Non-availability of any cultural material in these shelters clearly suggests that they did not witness long-term human occupation, and instead they were used occasionally on specific times. It probably suggests their ritualistic role. Some of the shelters are still used for worship by local communities. For instance, at Mallachandram in Dharmapuri district and at Kilseppuli in Tiruvannamalai district, even today during festival time, particularly in the Tamil calendar month of Karthikai

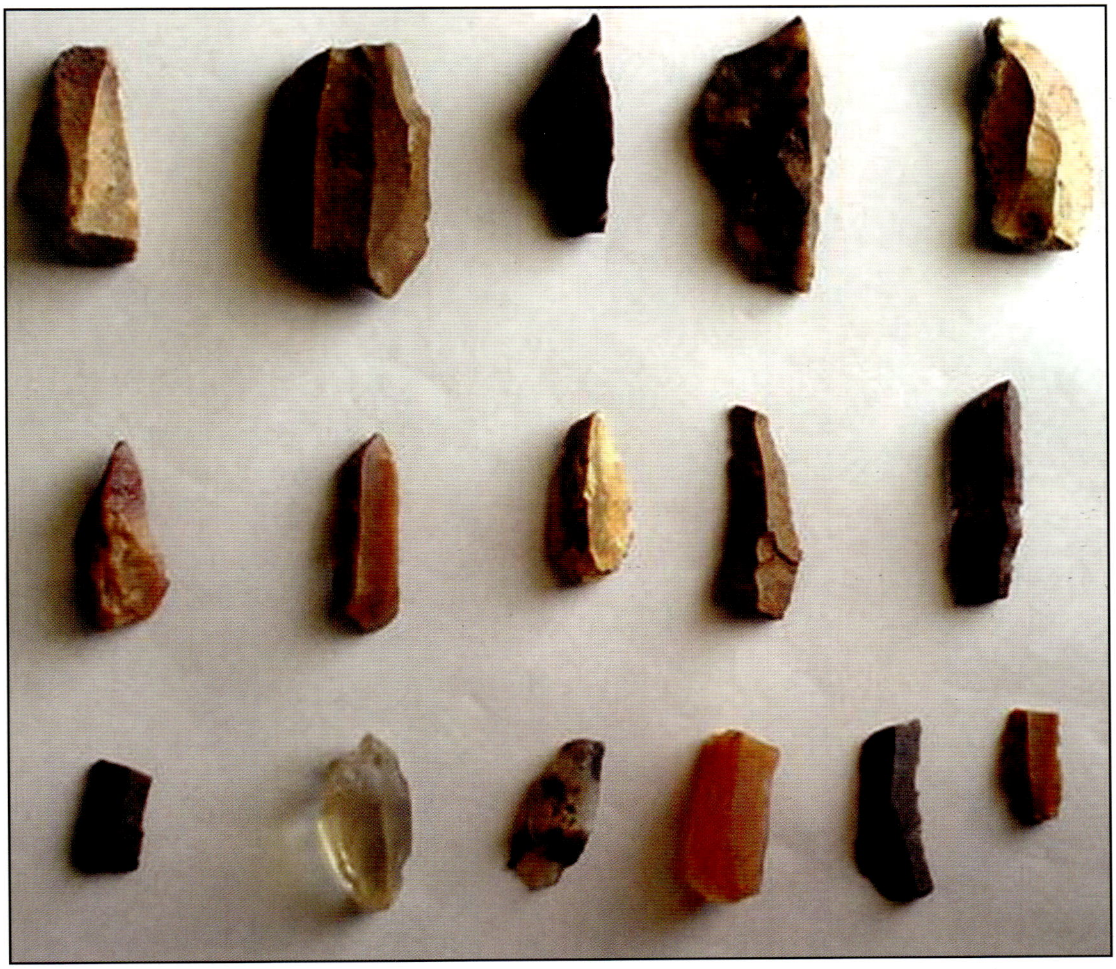

Fig. 13.5 Tirutangal: Microlithic tools.

(November-December), inhabitants from the village first light a lamp in the dolmen/rock shelter and then begin celebrations at home. The living tradition explicitly indicates the continuity and the importance of the rock shelters. It seems that in ancient times, too, Neolithic or Iron Age people visited these shelters on specific occasions to perform such rituals. The ethno-archaeological observations show the spiritual importance attached to the shelters. The close observation of various rock art sites suggests such an association. Chronologically, earlier rock art sites were found in the north-eastern part of Tamil Nadu, in Krishnagiri taluka of Dharmapuri district. It seems that the idea slowly penetrated into Tiruvannamalai district through the Chengam Pass. The tradition of painting Iron Age tombs was discarded and this practice was carried out only on the rock shelters. For instance, in Dharmapuri district, nearly 90 per cent of the rock art sites were found in association with dolmens. Out of 18 dolmen sites, nearly 14 sites were reported with paintings (Fig. 13.11) (Rajan 1991: 37-52). Hence, it is clear that this art was well received and absorbed in the historical period also.

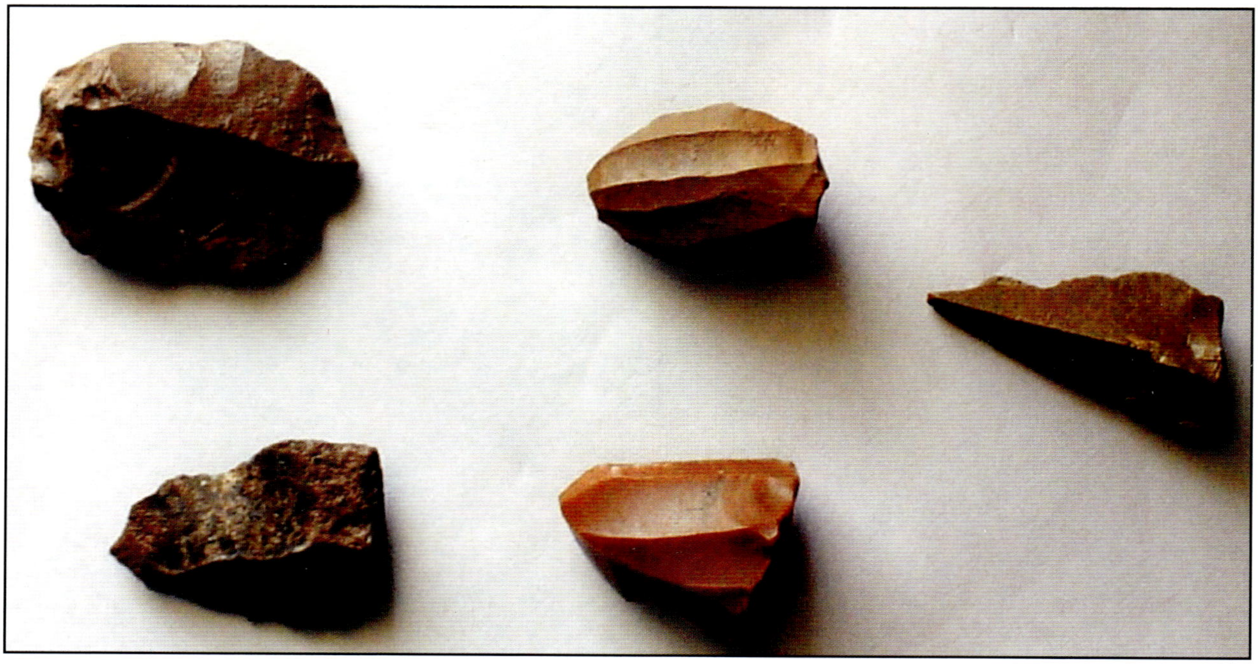

Fig. 13.6 Tirutangal: Microlithic tools.

PIGMENTS

Rock paintings were made invariably by using both white and red pigments as observed at Kilvalai, Chettavarai, Alambadi, Oramanagunta, Mayiladumparai and Oppatavadi. At Mayiladumparai and Oramanagunta, paintings in red pigment superimposed by white pigment are seen, thereby suggesting an earlier date for the red pigment. This indicates that the paintings were drawn on the shelters at a date earlier than the one for the graves. It is probable that the paintings with red pigment belonged to the Neolithic period. However, this needs to be probed further and authenticated with concrete evidence. The non-availability of paintings in red pigment in Iron Age tombs and their superimposition by white pigment suggests their earlier date. The type, position and techniques indicate that they were executed in different locations in the same shelter.

MOTIFS AND THEIR CONTEXT

There is negligible difference between the motifs found on the dolmens and those found on the rock shelters. The former have numerous human figurines involved in fighting, whereas the latter have scenes depicting social gatherings. The figures are done either in flat wash or in outline. While executing the paintings on the interior surface of the dolmens, the painters preferred the western orthostat first and then the northern, southern, and finally, the eastern orthostats. Generally, the paintings are seen on the western orthostats against port-holes. Paintings in the rock shelter are generally found on the ceiling, but a little inside from the edge. Interestingly, at Mayiladumparai the rock shelter was devoid of any natural light and the paintings were found in the darker part of the shelter.

THEMES

Cattle Raids

Paintings at several sites including Mayiladumparai, Oppattavadi, Oramanagunta and Konavakkarai depict scenes of warriors heading for cattle raids. In these cases, the warriors are generally seen mounted on the cattle and holding weapons such as swords, javelins, lance like objects and shields. In a few cases, the victorious hero is shown with a head-dress or a square box and mounted on cattle. The square box may also indicate the memorial stone raised for the slain hero involved in cattle retrieval. These themes recall later day hero-stones found in the study area. At Konavakkarai, the hero is shown as being large, whereas the rest are comparatively small in size (Paundurai 1986: 34-36). This scheme of depiction is well illustrated in later day hero-stones too.

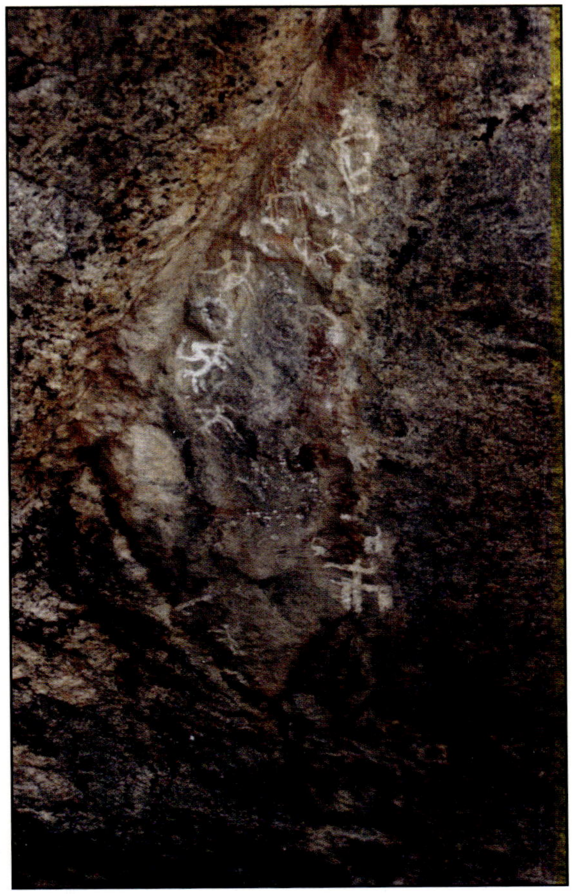

Fig. 13.7 Mayiladumparai: Rock paintings.

Hunting Scenes

Hunting scenes are shown in different patterns. Here, the archer holds a bow and arrow above his head in a position of charging the arrow upwards. In one scene, four hunters encircle a deer standing in the centre. The horns of the deer are depicted with branches, which suggest attention to detail on the part of the painter. In another scene, a hunter kills an animal by piercing it with a lance-like object. It should be recalled here that memorial stones were also raised for heroes who were killed while hunting or fighting wild animals (Rajan 1992b). There are a number of such memorial stones called *pantrikuttipattankal*, *pulikuttipattankal* and *yanaikutti pattankal*, indicating stones erected for men who were killed by a boar, a tiger and an elephant respectively (Nagasamy 1975: 45-49).

Other Scenes

Besides fighting scenes, tilling of land, dancing in a row, riding a horse and cattle rearing (Fig. 13.12) are some of the other scenes portrayed in rock art. In one instance, the fighting scene involving a horse rider (?) is depicted. The contenders fight with a shield in one hand and a rein of the horse in the other. Sometimes, they hold long lance-like objects. While depicting dancing scenes, the painters preferred to draw human figures in a row. In one case, a house is drawn in front of a row of four human figures depicted in a dancing posture. In one painting, a plant is depicted emerging out of a square box recalling the 'tree and rail tree' symbol of punch-marked coins (or Buddhist tradition?).

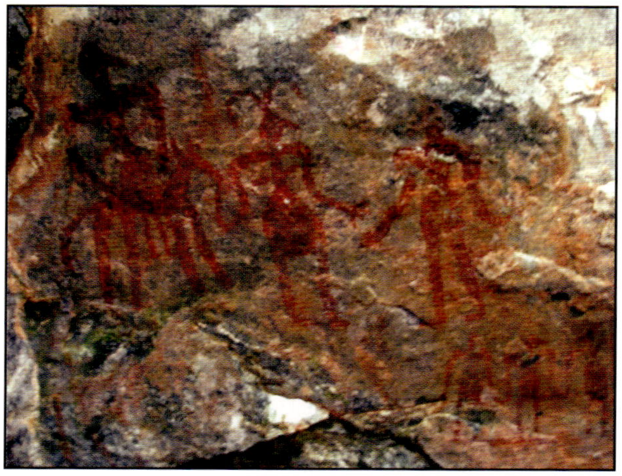

Fig. 13.8 Kilvalai: Rock paintings.

Interestingly, the paintings observed at Kuruvinayanapalli had symbols with 12 square boxes formed out of five vertical and four horizontal strokes. Out of the five vertical strokes, the inner three strokes end with arrow marks. Four human figures are also depicted, two each on either side of the symbol. In addition, two human figures and one animal are also seen. The boxed symbol with an arrow mark in the centre is similar to the symbols depicted in the fertility stone, locally called *sanniyasikal* of later times. The animal depicted on one side of this motif may be a symbolic representation of an animal, which was made to cross the feature represented in the motif, probably in order to increase fertility. Some other symbols like stars, human genitals, flower motifs and circles with a dot were also found.

Symbols

Another important aspect of the study is the graffiti found in association with various themes. At Kilvalai, five symbols were found (Samy 1984: 71-72) and such graffiti was also found at Vettavalam, Tirumalai, Kurralapadai and Podikaimalai. The Panaikkarans, a contemporary 'tribal' population, worship the

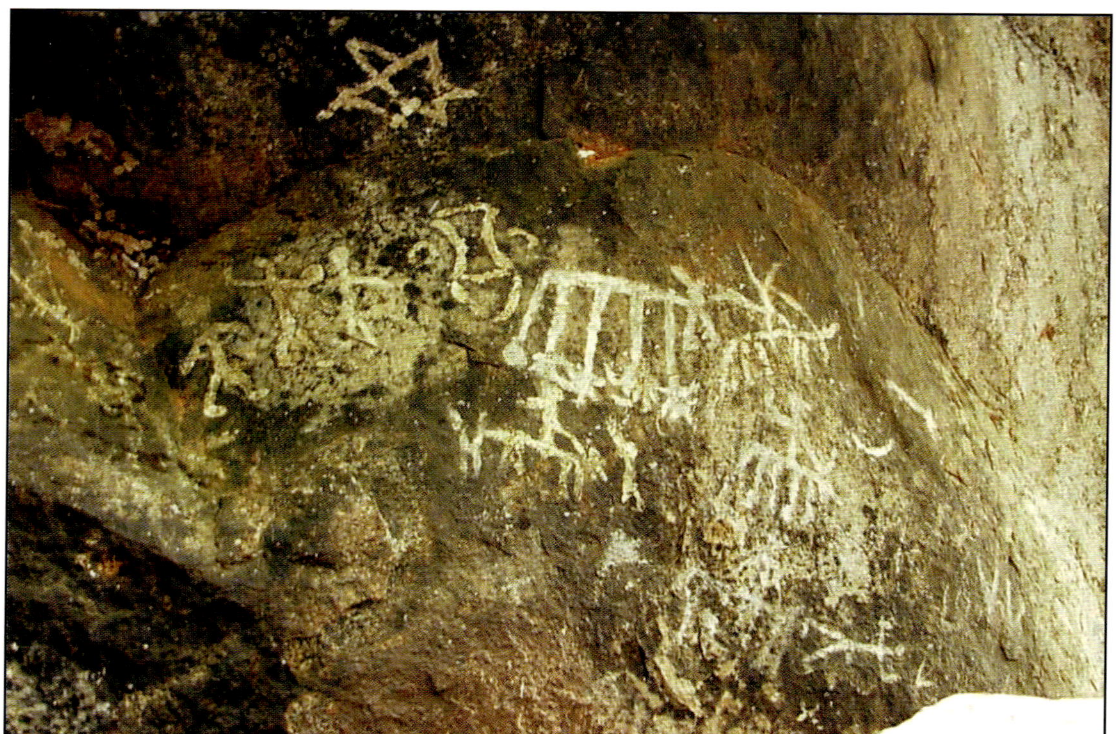

Fig. 13.9 Paiyampalli: Rock paintings.

symbols found at Podikaimalai. Recently, engravings were found on the rock shelters at Perumukkal and Tirumalpadi. These engravings are identical to the paintings found elsewhere. It is possible that in the course of time, instead of painting, people began engraving to make their art last forever.

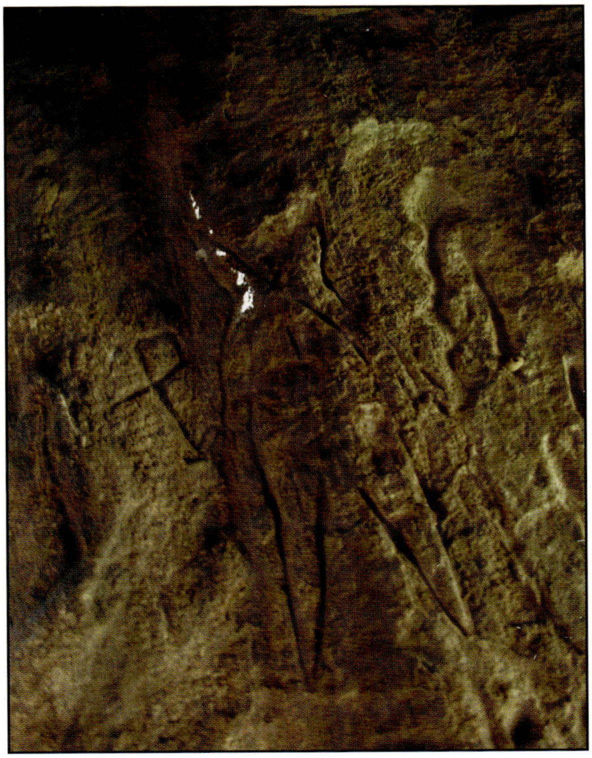

CONCLUSIONS

Situating rock paintings in proper socio-cultural contexts, studying their evolution or transformation within a specific chronological frame, systematic documentation and proper protection are still wanting as far as the rock art of Tamil Nadu is concerned. The varied nature of the paintings and their association with contemporary cultural material can provide enormous data for understanding past societies in the right perspective. The unprotected nature of the rock shelters and of Iron Age dolmens has exposed them to a great deal of vandalism. As long as the rock art sites are not discovered, they remain in a good state of preservation. Discovery of the sites and their subsequent publication invites human pressure on the sites in the name of documentation, filming, curiosity and ritual initiations. This kind of destruction will lead to the loss of these precious and

Fig. 13.10 Perumukkal: Rock engravings.

Fig. 13.11 Mallachandram rock paintings.

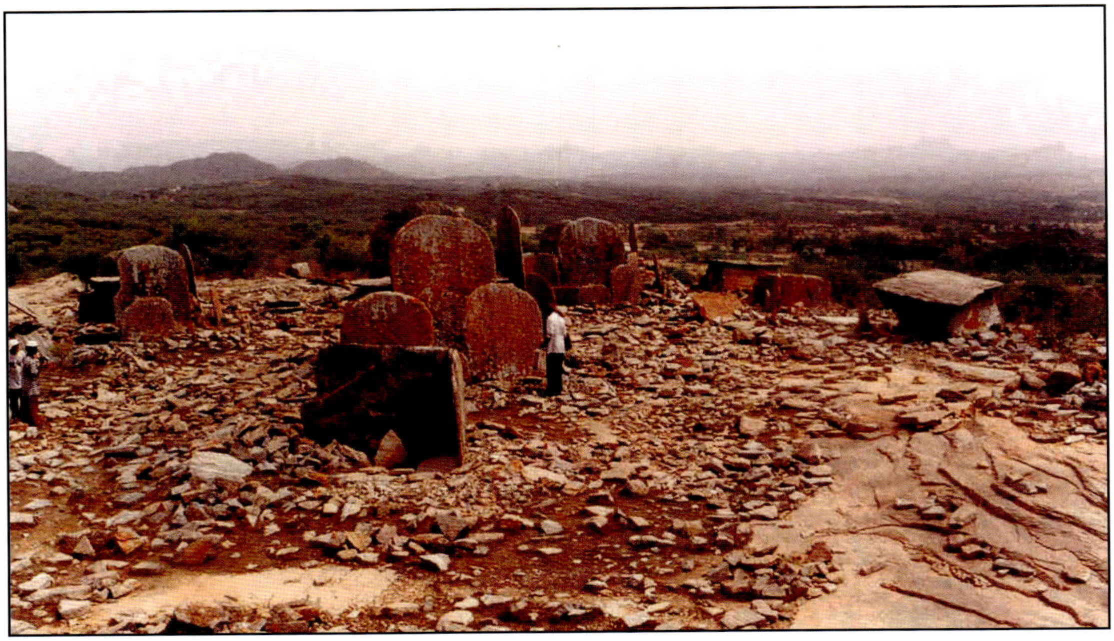

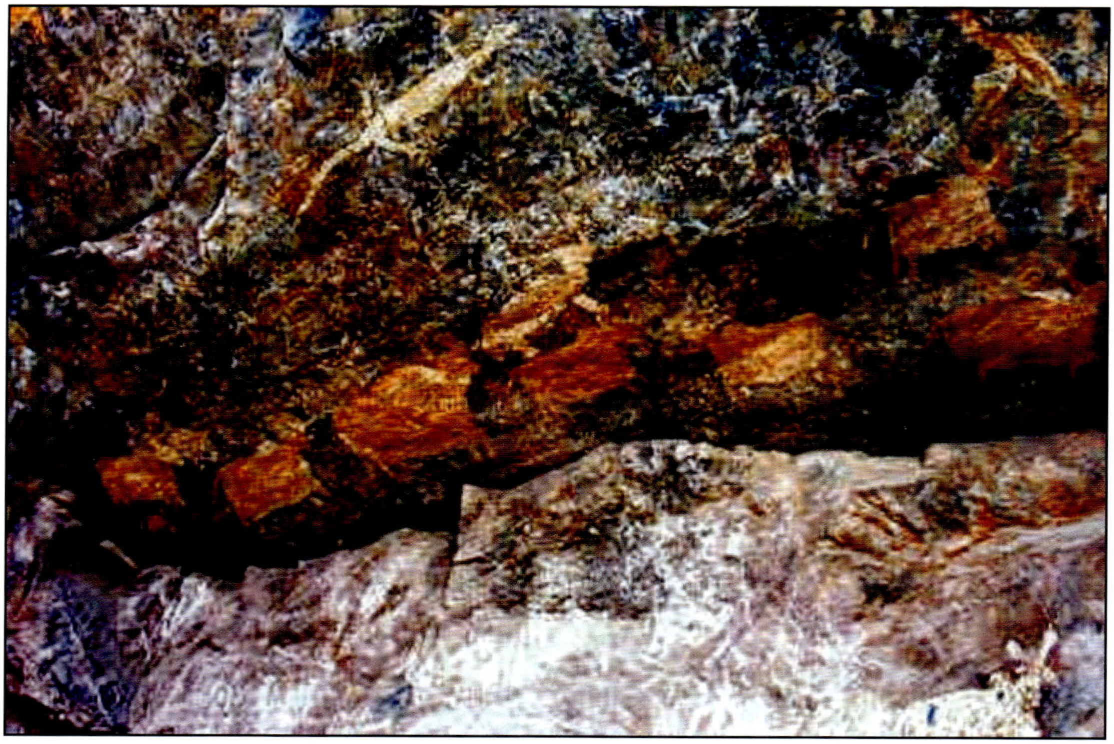

Fig. 13.12 Mavadaippu rock paintings.

tangible cultural properties in the near future. Urgent steps are needed from the government to protect these valuable archaeological remains.

Table 13.1 Rock Art Sites in Tamil Nadu.

S. No.	Site	Taluk	District	Culture	Colour of Pigment	Description
1.	Alambadi	Tirukkoliyur	Villupuram	Iron Age	Red White	Animal figurine mainly deer, bull and boar
2.	Alangayam	Vaniyambadi	Vellore	Early Historic	White	Horse-rider, human figures, bird, star, trident and religious symbols.
3.	Alanguppam (three rock shelters)	Gudiyattam	Vellore	Early Historic	White	Human figure, symbols, geometric design, etc.
4.	Anaigundu (near Sempalli)	Gudiyattam	Vellore	Iron Age	White	Human and animal figures, geometric designs and religious symbols.
5.	Anaipatti	Dindukal	Madurai	Early Historic	Red	Horse-rider, cart, deer, Human figures
6.	Andimalai	Krishnagiri	Krishnagiri	Iron Age	White	Human figures

S. No.	Site	Taluk	District	Culture	Colour of Pigment	Description
7.	Appukkal	Vellore	Vellore	Iron Age	White	Human and animal figures
8.	Athithangal	Arcot	Vellore	Historical	Engravings	Geometrical designs and symbols.
9.	Attakuddai	Krishnagiri	Krishnagiri	Iron Age	White	Birds, human figures with weapons
10.	Chandra-puram	Tirupattur	Vellore	Iron Age/ Neolithic	Red ochre and White	Human and animal figures, geometrical desings, dancing female figures, floral designs, hand and footprints, cup marks.
11.	Chennarayan-palli	Gudiyattam	Vellore	Iron Age	White & Petroglyphs	Hunting scene, horse-riders, human and animal figures, geometrical designs, totemic symbols and petroglyphs.
12.	Chinnapalam-pakkam	Vellore	Vellore	Iron Age	White	Human and animal figures, geometric symbols
13.	Chinna-Damal-Cheruvu	Gudiyattam	Vellore	Early Historic	White	Trident and religious symbols
14.	Chinna Kandili	Tirupattur	Vellore	Iron Age	White and Petroglyphs	Horse-rider, human figures, petroglyph and peacock figure.
15.	Chokkarishi-kuppam (Molugu-gundu)	Gudiyattam	Vellore	Historical	White	Symbols and geometric design
16.	Cholavaram (two rock shelters)	Vellore	Vellore	Iron Age	White	Patha (foot) symbols, floral designs, animal figures, geometric and religious symbols, hand print and enigmatic signs.
17.	Eachampattu	Vaniyambadi	Vellore	Early historic	White	Trident, symbols and designs.
18.	Elayanagaram	Vaniyambadi	Vellore	Historical	White	Star, trident and religious symbols.

S. No.	Site	Taluk	District	Culture	Colour of Pigment	Description
19.	Erthangal (four rock shelters)	Gudiyattam	Vellore	Iron Age	White	Human figures, floral, men on animal back, geometrical designs, symbols and graffiti marks.
20.	Gittapalli	Gudiyattam	Vellore	Historical	White	Star symbols and geometrical designs
21.	Iduhatti	Kothagiri	Nilgiri	Iron Age	White	Animal and human figures, geometric designs
22.	K. Mottur	Gudiyattam	Vellore	Historical	White	Trident and symbols.
23.	Kamalapuram	Gudiyattam	Vellore	Iron Age	White	Human figures, abstract figure, symbols and geometrical designs.
24.	Kamaya-Kavundan-patti	Uttama palayam	Madurai	Iron Age	White	Human figures and cattle
25.	Kandli	Tiruppattur	Vellore	Iron Age	White	Human and Animal figures, horse-rider, bird and human figures, engraving of a peacock
26.	Karikkiyur	Kotagiri	Nilgiri	Early Historic	Red and White	A procession of bison, monkeys clambering up a tree branch, a herd of deer grazing, human beings welcoming one another with outstretched arms, a battle scene with men aiming at each other with bows and arrows, men on horseback engaged in battle, a shoulder-clasping dance after a successful boar-hunt, a man with a mask, the depiction of sun and its rays, a spiral, a tiger fighting another animal, and a man and his dog sleeping.
27.	Karkur (two rock	Gudiyattam	Vellore	Iron Age	White	Human and animal figures, dancing girl,

S. No.	Site	Taluk	District	Culture	Colour of Pigment	Description
	shelters)					bird figures, geometric designs and symbols. Dancing scene, human and animal figures, geometric symbols
28.	Karungala-kudi	Melur	Madurai	Early Historic	Red	Horse and bull
29.	Kidaripatti	Melur	Madurai	Iron Age	Red	Human and animal figures
30.	Kilvalai	Tirukkoyilur	Villupuram	Iron Age	Red and White	Dancing scene and graffiti
31.	Kollur	Tirukkoyilur	Villupuram	Iron Age	Red and White	Human and animal figures
32.	Kombapatti	Kodaikanal	Dindugal	Iron Age	White	Wild animals
33.	Konavakkarai	Coonur	Nilagiri	Iron Age	White	Hunting scenes and cattle raiders
34.	Kothakuppam (four rock shelters)	Gudiyattam	Vellore	Historical	White	Symbols, trident and geometrical design
35.	Kothamari-kuppam (four rock shelters)	Gudiyattam	Vellore	Iron Age	White	Human figures, man on animal back, lady with child and symbols.
36.	Kottamitta	Gudiyattam	Vellore	Early Historic	White	Trident and symbols
37.	Kottarama-dugu	Gudiyattam	Vellore	Historical	White	Trident and religious symbols
38.	Kudumipatti	Gudiyattam	Vellore	Iron Age	White	Symbols and designs.
39.	Kuliratti	Virudhu-nagar?	Virudhu-nagar	Iron Age	Red and White	Animal and human figurines, geometric symbols
40.	Kumbavarai	Kothagiri	Nilgiri	Iron Age	White	Human and animal figures
41.	Kumuttipati	Coimbatore	Coimbatore	Iron Age	White	Human and animal figures
42.	Kuruvi-nayanapalli	Krishnagiri	Krishnagiri	Iron Age	White	Human figures, geometric symbols
43.	Lakshmi Ammal Puram	Gudiyattam	Vellore	Iron Age	White	Symbols and geometrical designs.
44.	Lingundram (three rock shelters)	Gudiyattam	Vellore	Early Historic	White	Fish figure, geometrical designs and animal figures.

S. No.	Site	Taluk	District	Culture	Colour of Pigment	Description
45.	Maharaja Kadai	Krishnagiri	Krishnagiri	Iron Age	White	Human and animal figures
46.	Mahimand-alam hill	Katpadi	Vellore	Historical	Petroglyphs and White painting	*Patha* symbol, cup marks and symbols in white pigment.
47.	Malaipatti	Usilampatti	Madurai	Iron Age	White	Human and animal figures, geometric designs
48.	Malayampattu (three rock sheleters)	Vaniyambadi	Vellore	Iron Age & Historical	White	Human figure, geometrical design, tridents and symbols.
49.	Mallachand-ram	Hosur	Krishnagiri	Iron Age	White	Human and animal figures, archer, plant house
50.	Mallapadi	Krishnagiri	Krishnagiri	Iron Age	White	Horse-riders and human figures with weapons
51.	Mavadaippu	Pollachi	Coimbatore	Iron Age	White	Tiger, a deer with straight horns, anthropomorphic figures marching inside a circle, an elephant seizing a man with its trunk while another man is chasing it
52.	Mayiladum-parai	Krishnagiri	Krishnagiri	Microlithic Neolithic Iron Age	Red and White	Human and animal figures, human with weapons
53.	Meenur	Gudiyattam	Vellore	Early Historic	White	Human figure and geometrical symbols.
54.	Melakuppam	Vaniyambadi	Vellore	Early Historic	White	Religious symbols and graffiti marks.
55.	Melpatti	Gudiyattam	Vellore	Iron Age	White	Human figure, stars, graffiti marks, trident, designs and symbols like Tamil Brahmi script.
56.	Modikuppam	Gudiyattam	Vellore	Iron Age	White	Human and animal figures, geometric designs, horse-rider.
57.	Moongilpudur	Krishnagiri	Krishnagiri	Iron Age	White	Human and animal figures

S. No.	Site	Taluk	District	Culture	Colour of Pigment	Description
58.	Morasapalli	Gudiyattam	Vellore	Historical	White	Geometrical designs.
59.	Mudippinay-anapalli	Hosur	Krishnagiri	Iron Age	White	Human and animal figures, man holding bow and arrow, geometric symbols
60.	Munandi-ppatti	Andipatti	Teni	Iron Age	Red and White	Human and animal figures
61.	Mungappattu	Gudiyattam	Vellore	Iron Age	White	Human figure and symbols
62.	Muttupatti	Tirumang-alam	Madurai	Iron Age	White	Human and animal figures
63.	Muttuppatti	Madurai	Madurai	Early Historic	White	Animal figures
64.	Nagal (two rock shelters)	Gudiyattam	Vellore	Iron Age	White	Human figures, trident, religious symbols and geometrical designs.
65.	Nalanganallur (Boligundu)	Gudiyattam	Vellore	Iron Age	White	Human figure, insects and geometrical patterns.
66.	Nalanganallur (Gummimalai)	Gudiyattam	Vellore	Iron Age	White	Geometrical design, graffiti marks and symbols.
67.	Namalaigundu (Chokkarishi-kuppam)	Gudiyattam	Vellore	Iron Age	White	Human figures, animal, animal riders, birds and geometrical design.
68.	Nayanur	Tirukkoyilur	Villupuram	Iron Age	Red	Animal figures
69.	Neganurpatti	Gingee	Villupuram	Iron Age	White	Human and animal figures
70.	Netterimalai	Katpadi	Vellore	Neolithic/ Iron Age	Red and White	Two human figures and geometric symbols
71.	Oppathavadi	Krishnagiri	Dharmapuri	Neolithic (?)	Red and White	Archer, bird, elephant, human and animal figures and geometric symbols
72.	Oramanagunta	Krishnagiri	Krishnagiri	Iron Age	White	Human and animal figures, man seated on a cattle, bird
73.	Othikuppam	Krishnagiri	Kishnagiri	Iron Age	White	Men in row
74.	Pachur	Tirupattur	Vellore	Iron Age	Black and White pigment	Human figures, boat symbol, floral designs, birds and religious symbols.
75.	Padiyandal	Tirukkoyilur	Villupuram	Iron Age	Red and White	Human and animal figures

S. No.	Site	Taluk	District	Culture	Colour of Pigment	Description
76.	Paikkal	Kothagiri	Nilgiri	Early Historic	White	Human and animal figures
77.	Paiyampalli	Tiruppattur	Vellore	Iron Age Early Historic	Red and White	Human and animal figures, fighting scenes, elephant, horse
78.	Paiyampalli (Sothaimalai)	Tirupattur	Vellore	Iron Age/ Neolithic	Red ochre and White	Human and animal figures, fighting scene, enigmatic symbols, animal riders, mythical figures
79.	Pakkam	Gudiyattam	Vellore	Iron Age	White	Human figures, trident and religious symbols.
80.	Panan parambu	Chenkottai ?	Tirunelveli	Early Historic	Black	Bull in circle, dancing figures, elephant
81.	Paravaikkal	Gudiyatham	Vellore	Iron Age	White	Human and animal figures, geometric symbols
82.	Paravakkal (six rock shelters)	Gudiyattam	Vellore	Iron Age	White	Human figures, marching scenes, animal figures and geometrical designs.
83.	Perumukkal	Tindivanam	Villupuram	Iron Age	—	Engravings of human and animal figures, cup marks
84.	Pogalur (eight rock shelters)	Gudiyattam	Vellore	Iron Age	White	Birds, human and animal figures, geometrical designs, tridents, totemic symbols, reptiles, etc.
85.	Poonkulam (two rock shelters)	Gudiyatham	Vellore	Iron Age	White	Human and animal figures, geometric symbols
86.	Rajakuppam	Gudiyattam	Vellore	Historical	White	Symbols and designs
87.	Rathinagiri hill	Wallajapet	Vellore	Iron Age	White	Human and animal figures, geometric designs and rock engravings.
88.	Ratnagiri	Vellore	Vellore	Iron Age	White	Human and animal figures
89.	Salakkora	Kothagiri	Nilgiri	Iron Age	White	Human and animal figures
90.	Samarishi-kuppam (Pandava-rparai) (two rock shelters)	Gudiyattam	Vellore	Early Historic	White	Human figure and symbols.

S. No.	Site	Taluk	District	Culture	Colour of Pigment	Description
91.	Sanniyasi-guddai (Meenur)	Gudiyattam	Vellore	Historical	White	Trident and symbols.
92.	Sempalli	Gudiyatham	Vellore	Iron Age	White	Birds, human and animal figures, geometric symbols
93.	Sempalli (Anuppala-gundu) (three rock shelters)	Gudiyattam	Vellore	Iron Age	White	Birds, human and animal figures, geometrical designs, trident, enigmatic signs, etc.
94.	Sempalli hill	Gudiyattam	Vellore	Iron Age	White	Human and animal figures, geometric designs.
95.	Sendathur	Gudiyattam	Vellore	Historical	White	Trident and religious symbols.
96.	Settavarai	Gingee	Villupuram	Iron Age	Red and White	Human and animal figures, hunting scene and cattle raid
97.	Seykundram	Gudiyatham	Vellore	Iron Age	White	Human and animal figures, geometric symbols
98.	Sikur	Otacamund	Nilgiri	Iron Age	Red and White	Human and animal figures
99.	Sirumalai	Dindukal	Dindukal	Iron Age	Red and White	Human figures, hunting and fighting scenes
100.	Sivanatha-puram	Vellore	Vellore	Iron Age, Early Historic	Red and White	Human figure and symbols.
101.	Sundasingam	Kothagiri	Nilgiri	Early Historic	White	Human and animal figures
102.	Sundeku-ppam	Krishnagiri	Krishnagiri	Iron Age	Red and White	Human and animal figures
103.	Tattakuzhi-kadu	Kodaikanal	Dindugal	Iron Age	Red and White	Animal and human figures, geometric symbols, hunting scene and dancing scene
104.	Thalapalli	Krishnagiri	Krishnagiri	Iron Age	White	Star, Human and animal figures, bow and arrow, fighting scene
105.	Thattaparai	Gudiyatham	Vellore	Historical	White	Religious symbols and designs
106.	Thengu Marahada	Kunnoor	Nilgiri	Iron Age	White	Human and animal figures

S. No.	Site	Taluk	District	Culture	Colour of Pigment	Description
107.	Tirumalai	Sivagangai	Sivagangai	Iron Age	Red	Human and animal figures, fighting and dancing scenes
108.	Tirumalpadi	Wandiwash	Tiruvanna-malai	Iron Age (?)	—	Engravings of human and animal figures
109.	Tiruvadavur	Madurai	Madurai	Early Historic	Red	Circle
110.	Tondur	Gingee	Villupuram	Early Historic	White	Human and animal figures
111.	Udayarnattam	Villupuram	Villupuram	Iron Age	Red and White	Human and animal figures
112.	Ulkkombai	Andippatti	Teni	Mesolithic	White	Human and lnimal figures
113.	Upparapalli hill	Gudiyattam	Vellore	Iron Age	White	Human figures, symbols and designs.
114.	Vairangalmalai	Gudiyattam	Vellore	Early Historic	White	Human figures and symbols
115.	Veersettipalli (Durga-mmalai)	Gudiyattam	Vellore	Iron Age	White	Human figure, bird and symbols
116.	Vellerikombai	Kotagiri	Nilgiri	Iron Age	White	Stylised human and animal figures
117.	Vellerukkan-palayam	Coimbatore	Coimbatore	Early Historic	White	Human and animal figures
118.	Vettavalam	Tiruvanna-malai	Tiruvanna-malai	Iron Age	Red	Human and animal figures
119.	Vikkaramang-alam	Usilampatti	Madurai	Early Historic	White	Human figures
120.	Yerpettu	Kothagiri	Nilgiri	Iron Age	—	Engravings of human beings and tree

REFERENCES

Baldwin Brown, G. (1928), *The Art of Cave Dweller*. New Delhi: Cosmo Publications.

Brooks, R.R.R. (1975), 'Reconstruction of Stone Age Paintings', *Archaeology* 28(2): 92-97.

Chandramouli, N. (1987), 'An Analytical Study of Rock Paintings at Kethavaram, Kurnool District', *Proceedings of the Andhra Pradesh History Congress, XIth Session, Nagaram,* Guntur.

—— (2002), *Rock Art of South India (With Special Reference to Andhra Pradesh)*. Delhi: Bharatiya Kala Prakashan.

Dayalan, D. (2003), 'Rock Art in Tamil Nadu and Its Archaeological Perspective', in *Kalpavrksa, Essays on Art, Architecture and Archaeology*. Delhi: Bharatiya Kala Prakashan, pp. 134-57.

Dikshit, S.K. (1956), 'Rock Shelters in Vindhya Pradesh', *Indian Archaeology—A Review*, pp. 56-69.

Duraisamy, P. and R. Mathivanan (2002), *Dharmapuri parai oviyangalil sinduveli eluttukkal* (Tamil). Chennai: Sekar Pathippagam, pp. 85-87.

Fawcett, F. (1901), 'Notes on the Rock Carvings in the Edakkal Cave, Wynad', *Indian Antiquary* XXX: 309-21.

Gandhi, M. and P. Venkatesan (1995), 'Rock Paintings Discovered', *The Hindu*, 28 July.

Gordon, D.H. and R. Allchin (1935), 'Rock Paintings and Engravings in Raichur, Hyderabad', *Man* 55: 97-99.

Kasinathan, Natana (1985), 'Prehistoric Paintings in Tamil Nadu, UNESCO', *Courier*, p. 2.

Kumar, K. (1991), 'Paiyampalliyil Perunkarkala Kugai Oviyangal', *Dinamani*, 24 March.

—— (2000), 'Athithangal Kalvettu', *Avanam* 11: 11.

—— (2002), 'Rathinagiri Parai Oviyangal', *Avanam* 13: 187-88.

—— (2005a), 'Karkur Parai Oviyangal', *Avanam* 16: 124-25.

—— (2005b), 'Netterimalai Tholliyal Chinnangal', *Avanam* 16: 128-31.

—— (2006a), 'Modikuppam, Puthiya Karkala Marrum Irumbukala Urirukkai', *Avanam* 17: 151-53.

—— (2006b), 'Melpatti Parai Kuriyidugal', *Avanam* 16: 217-18.

—— (2007), 'Pogalur Parai Oviyangal', *Avanam* 18: 137-38.

—— (2010), 'Paiyampalli–Sothaimalai marrum Pachur Oviyangal', *Avanam* 21: 147-51.

Mathivanan, R. (1995), *Indus Script Among Dravidian Speakers*. Madras: International Society for the Investigation of Ancient Civilisations, p. 95.

Mathpal, Y. (1984), *Prehistoric Rock Paintings of Central India*. New Delhi: Abhinav Publications.

—— (1990), 'Rock Paintings of Bhimbetka and Karnataka, Theme, Style and Technique', in A. Sundara (ed.), *Archaeology in Karnataka*. Dharward: Karnatak University, pp. 269-76.

Mathpal, Yashodhar (2007), 'Mythical Creatures in Indian Rock Art', in S.P. Shukla, R.S. Bish, M.P. Joshi and Prashant Srivastava (eds.), *History and Heritage*, In Honour of Prof. Kiran Kumar Thaplyal, Vol. 1. Delhi: Agam Kala Prakashan, pp. 441-18.

Nagasamy, R. (1975), *Dharmapuri Kalvettukkal* (Dharmapuri Hero stones). Chennai: Department of Archaeology, Government of Tamil Nadu.

Natarajan, Avvai and Natana Kasinathan (1993), *Art Panorama of Tamils*. Chennai: Department of Archaeology, pp. 29-34.

Neumayer, E. (1983), *Prehistoric Indian Rock Paintings*. New Delhi: Oxford University Press.

—— (1992a), 'Rock Pictures in Orissa', *Puratattva* 22: 13-24.

—— (1992b), 'Rock Art in India', in Michel Lorblanchet (ed.), *Rock Art in the Old World*. New Delhi: Indira Gandhi National Centre for the Arts, pp. 215-47.

—— (1993), *Lines on Stone: The Prehistoric Rock Art of India*. New Delhi: Manohar Publishers and Distributors.

Pandey, S.K. (1993), *Indian Rock Art*. New Delhi: Aryan Books International.

Paundurai, R. (1986), *Tamilagap Parai Oviyangal* (Tamil). Madras: Sekar Publications.

Pradhan, Sadasiba (2001), *Rock Art in Orissa*. New Delhi: Aryan Books International.

Powell, T.G.E. (1966), *Prehistoric Art*. London: Thames and Hudson.

Rajan, K. (1991a), *Archaeological Gazetteer of Tamil Nadu*. Thanjavur: Manoo Pathippakam.

—— (1991b), 'Archaeology of Dharmapuri District, Tamil Nadu', *Man and Environment* XVI(1): 37-52.

—— (1991c), 'Rock Painting in Dharmapuri District, Tamil Nadu', *Purakala* 2(2): 51-70.

—— (1994), *Archaeology of Tamil Nadu (Kongu Country)*. Delhi: Book India Publishing Co.

—— (2008), 'Rock Art in South India—A Status Report', *Purakala* 18: 5-22.

Ramabrahmam, V. (1995), 'Evidence of Megalithic Art in Chittoor District, Andhra Pradesh History Congress', *Proceedings of the Nineteenth Session*, Anantapur, pp. 22-23.

Ramamurthy, D. (1988), 'The Rock Paintings of Central India: An Approach through Myth', *Man and Environment* XII: 75-107.

Raman, K.V. (1976–1977), 'Excavation at Appukkallu, District North Arcot', *Indian Archaeology—A Review*, pp. 47-48.

—— (1977–1978), 'Excavation at Mallapadi District Dharmapuri', *Indian Archaeology—A Review*, p. 50.

—— (1981), 'Ancient cave paintings in Tamil Nadu', *Man and Environment* V: 16-24.

—— (1983), 'The Prehistoric Beginnings in Tamil Civilization', *Quarterly Research Journal of the Tamil University* I (4): 24-27.

—— (1983–1984), 'Exploration in District North Arcot', *Indian Archaeology—A Review*, pp. 77-78.

Rao, L.S. (2003), 'Indian Prehistoric Rock Art: A Few Observations', in A.K. Sharma et al. (eds.), *Pura Prakasa*, Dr. N.A. Desai Commemoration Vol. I. Delhi: Bharatiya Kala Prakashan.

Rivett Carnac, J.H. (1879), 'Prehistoric Remains in Central India', *Journal of the Royal Asiatic Society of Bengal* 48: 4-11.

Samy, P.L. (1984), *Tamilnattil Sinduveli Eluttoviyam*, (Harappan Scripts in Tamil Nadu), Madras.

Sankalia, H.D. (1978), *Prehistoric Art in India*. Delhi: Vikas Publishing House Pvt. Ltd.

Sharma, A.V.N. (1964), 'Rock Paintings from Kambakkam, South India', *Quarterly Journal of Mythic Society* LV(2): 43-46.

Sharma, R.K. and Rehaman Ali (1980), *Archaeology of Bhopal Region*. Delhi: Agam Kala Prakashan.

Shetty, Ashok Vardhan K. (2003), *Excavations at Mangudi*. Chennai: Department of Archaeology, Government of Tamil Nadu.

Sridhar, T.S. (ed.) (2005), *Rock Art of Tamil Nadu*. Chennai: Department of Archaeology, Government of Tamil Nadu.

Sundara, A. (1968), 'Rock Shelter, Hire Benakal Hills, Raichur', *Indian Archaeology—A Review, 1967-68*, p. 67.

Thamaraikkannan (1989), 'Chandrapuram parai Oviyangal (Tamil)', *Dinamalar*, 9 May.

Trivedi, H.V. (1959), 'Rock Shelters in District Mandasor', *Indian Archaeology—A Review*, p. 72.

Valliyanmmal, M. (2005), 'Panan parambu parai oviyam', *Avanam* 16: 132-33.

Wakankar, V.S. (1991), 'Rock Art of South India', in C. Margabhandu, K.S. Ramachandran, A.P. Sagar and D.K. Sinha (eds.), *Indian Archaeological Heritage, K.V. Soundara Rajan Festchrift*, Vol. I. Delhi: Agam Kala Prakashan, pp. 63-90.

Wakankar, V.S. and Robert R.R. Brooks (1976), *Stone Age Painting in India*. Mumbai: D.B. Taraporevala Sons & Co.

14

Rock Art of Kaimur and Its Authors: New Evidence

B.R. Mani and Shanker Sharma

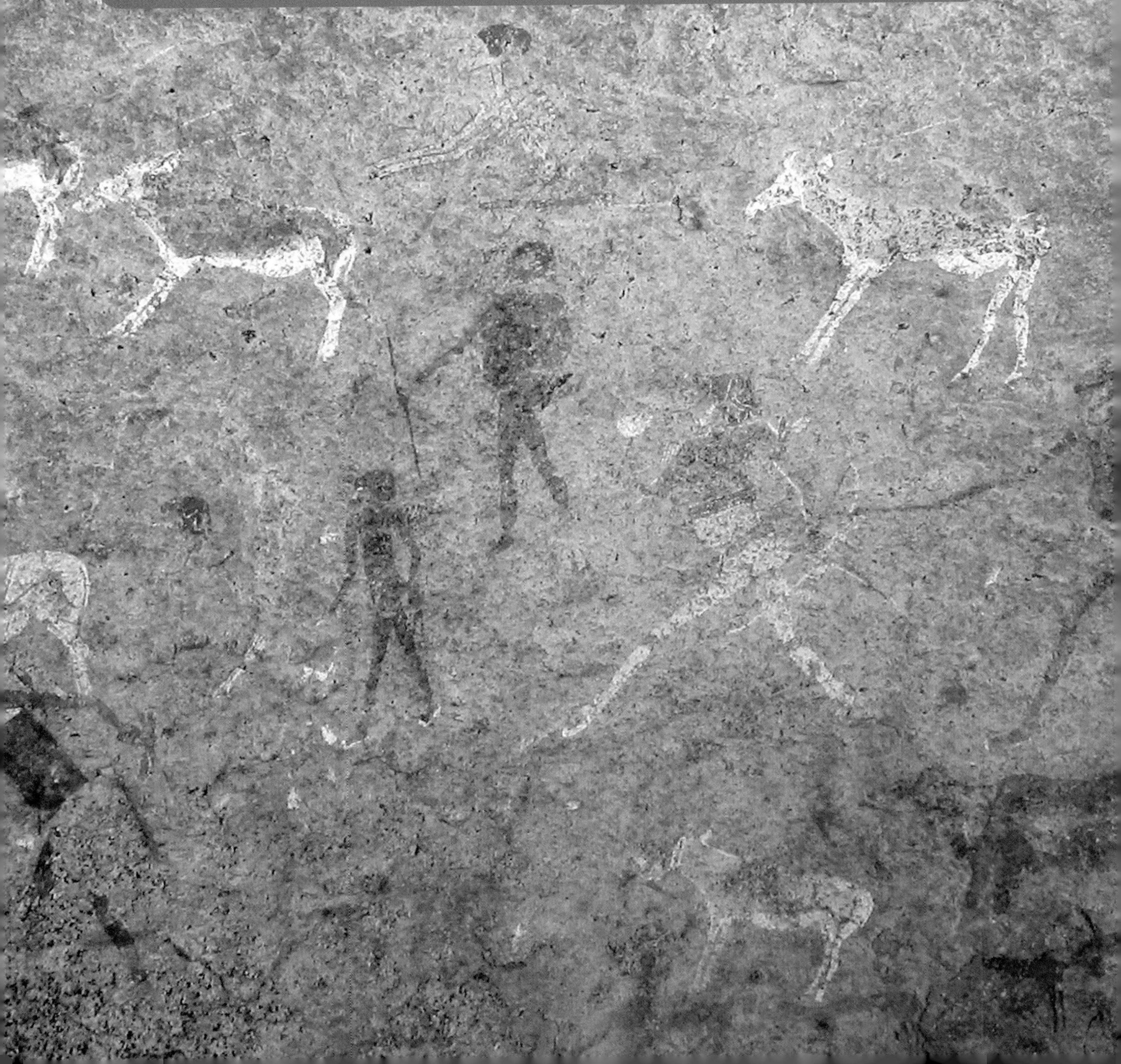

ABSTRACT

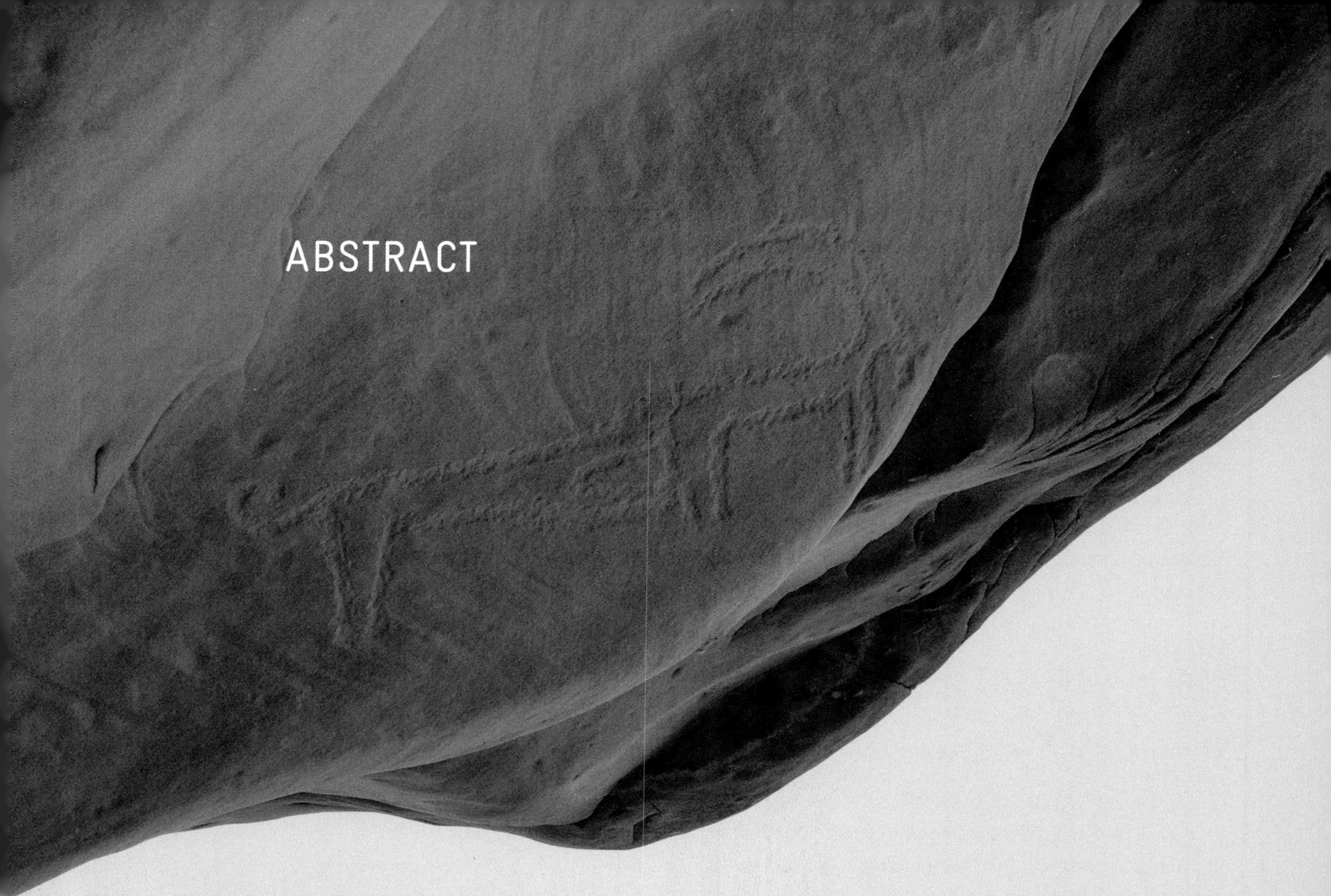

In spite of a diversified ancient culture and civilisation, Kaimur's geographical terrain, which has rich material of the culture of the past, could not be studied for a long time in terms of rock art. However, the region has been investigated from time to time by many researchers and a large number of rock art sites have been identified as belonging to the Epi-palaeolithic, Mesolithic, Neolithic and Chalcolithic periods followed by the Historical period in Mirzapur, Chandauli, Kaimur and Rohtas within the region and also in its outer orbit in Allahabad district. The subjects of the paintings include hunting-gathering scenes, domestication of animals, fighting animals, war scenes, scenes of festivity, astronomical, geometrical, floral and religious symbols, Buddha in a preaching posture and painted records of early Brahmi script from the Historical period. Among the engravings, deer, chess pattern and games have been noticed. Some of the paintings have been noticed in superimpositions. X-ray paintings belonging to Mesolithic and Chalcolithic periods have also been reported. Recent exploration conducted by the authors in the region, on the border of Uttar Pradesh and Bihar, show all these aspects of rock art.

INTRODUCTION

In recent archaeological investigations conducted by the authors in Kaimur hills on the border of Uttar Pradesh and Bihar, a number of rock shelters, rock paintings, and other archaeological remains were found. A fresh interpretation in light of previous findings and also new findings of rock art and archaeological sites helps in solving some issues related to the authorship of the paintings depicted on the rocks in the region. This study traces the indication of some ancient line of communication in the area on the basis of supported material evidence from early times to the Historical period. The route travelled by Buddha for the first time after his enlightenment at Uruvela (Bodh Gaya) to the place of his First Sermon at *Ishipattana* (Sarnath) is an issue of debate among scholars and these recent discoveries add some new information to that.

The Kaimur hills are the cradle of ancient culture, which emerged with the activities of primitive men (Chaudhary 1966: 49). It is remarkable that in the region between the valleys of Chandraprabha (Mirzapur) and Karmnasa (Chandauli) were found Middle Stone Age tools and microliths and also Megalithic burials at the noteworthy sites of Dagmagapur, Drummondganj, Dudhi, Hathwani, Hema-kachar, Kon, Muralia, Paraspani, and Raja-ki-Chauki in Mirzapur district and Hathinia-Pahar and Kaurihar in Varanasi district (*IAR* 1962-63: 32). Two-third of the rock art sites are located in the sandstone belts of the Vindhyas (Mathpal 1995: 8) while the most important region concerning rock art is the Vindhyan range. Geologically, these mountains consist of sedimentary quartzite and basaltic trap rock. All the paintings here are found in the quartzite region (Neumayer 2001: 15). The rock art of the Vindhyas can be divided into the art of the hunter-gatherers and that of the pastoralists and agriculturists. Of these, the latter is recent (Neumayer 2001: 216).

The noteworthy findings of recent explorations are rock art in the form of pictographs and petroglyphs, inscriptions, ancient settlements, pond and sculptures, etc. Among the paintings that were discovered, prehistoric rock paintings belonging from the Mesolithic to Neolithic periods followed by the Chalcolithic and Historical periods were noticed in many rock shelters on various hills. A large number of prehistoric rock paintings executed in various places clearly indicate a dense population in this region since the Mesolithic period. The region was further occupied by Neolithic and Chalcolithic communities, who lived a somewhat settled life as agro-pastoralists. They expressed their artistic acumen in the rock shelters in the form of pictographs and petroglyphs. Some remains of wattle-and-daub and undressed stone houses are located on the foothills near the shelters. Paintings belonging to the Historical period depict various aspects representing war scenes, hunting scenes, games and amusement, but the significant one is the painting of the Buddha in a preaching pose flanked by stupas. There are three minor rock edicts of Asoka—Sasaram, Ahraura, and the recently discovered Basahan—all within the Kaimur range. Hence, on the basis of archaeological findings, ancient literary references, and other favourable physical factors, some light can be thrown on: (i) the ancient line of communication in the region; (ii) Buddha's travelling route through this region; and (iii) the authors of rock art in the Kaimur region.

GEOMORPHOLOGY AND ECOLOGY

The Kaimur Plateau is situated between lat. 24° 24' N and 24° 52' N. It has a width of about 32 km and an average height ranging from 420 to 510 m. It is an evenly undulating plateau merging gradually at many places with the Ganga alluvium (Sharma et al. 1980:1). Geologically, Kaimur hills, which have a forest cover on the eastern fringe of the Vindhyan range, consist of sedimentary rocks. The presence of stones like sandstone, quartzite, chert, chalcedony, agate, carnelian, jasper, quartz, and other fine-grained rock in the nearby region offered man a rich supply of raw materials at various stages of his existence. Haematite ore is another supplementary material available in the area (Sharma et al. 1980:1). Towards the north of the area is alluvial soil. The alluvial deposit is of tertiary and quaternary age, and mostly consists of sand, silt, and clay with occasional gravel beds (Singh 2004:2).

The Kaimur Plateau is the mother of several rivers and water streams flowing towards the Ganga plains. The Karmnasa River flows about 10 km north-west from these settlements. The river has a course of about 125 km in the north-east direction, which finally merges in the Ganga near village Chausa in Bihar (Choudhary 1966: 11). This is a tributary of the Ganga which rises near Sarodas in Kaimur hills in Bihar and flows in Mirzapur via Robertsganj and enters district Chandauli on the southern border of tehsil Chakia. The Karmnasa descends from the plateau at Chhanpathar by a fall of 300 feet of which the lower portion (100 feet high) is perpendicular. The river runs almost dry after February but boats ply on it during the rainy season (Choudhary 1966: 11). The main tributaries of Karmnasa river are Chandraprabha, Guruwat, Dharmavati, and Bajarigoria, which emerge from the Kaimur range (Tripathy 2009: 8–11). Gurwat River consists of water channels named Labgora and Khargora. Khargora meets Gurwat near Chainpur and at the same point river Gurwat meets Karmnasa. The origin of river Durgawati is 5 km away towards the east of the origin point of Karmnasa and to the north of Son River is another tributary of river Karmnasa. There are some natural depressions in the back side of the rock shelters in Osarighat hills as well as in the north-west of Gharwa Pahari, which store natural water during the rainy season and are dry at the end of the spring season. It also provides water for farming in the plains particularly for *rabi* crops like wheat and barley. A big lake behind the Osarighat and Bharkon Baba ki Pahari stores a large volume of water and releases this through a palaeo-channel in the south-east area of the plains.

FLORA, FAUNA AND THE INHABITANTS

Sediments of different ages have been converted into fertile fields and must have been covered before the beginning of agriculture by grasses and shrubs. In addition to grasses and shrubs, the flora on the plateau includes bamboo *(bambusa)*, *tendu* (*Diospyros Melonoxylona*), *khair* (*Acacia Cateclm*), and *mahua* (*Madhuka Indica*); there is long grass, chiefly spear grass kush (*Poa Cymosuroides*), the *khaskhas* (*Andropogon Muricatus*) and *Diospyros, Terminallia, Boswellia, Sterculia Fatida* trees. Wild fauna like tiger (*Panthera Tigris*), leopard (*Panthera Pardus*), bear (*Malurses urinus*), monkey (*Cerco-*

Pithecidae), *nilgai* (*Baslaphus trago camelus*), *chital* (*Axi-saxis*), deer (*Cervidae*), and jackal (*Canis Awreusinn*) are noteworthy (Choudhary 1966: 24-30).

The climate in the region is characterised by a long and hot summer, a fairly pleasant monsoon, and a cold season; normal rainfall in this area is 50 mm, while heavy rainfall of 256 mm is recorded during the monsoon season (Choudhary 1966: 24-30).

The Kharwar people live in the area of Adhaura, a tribal community which considers itself as a *kshatriya* clan and traces its origin to Khairagarh in Madhya Pradesh (Tripathy 2009: 6). The Kaimur Plateau and the forest regions were inaccessible and contained a large number of the aboriginals and the semi-tribes (as they still do), and the people of this area had a great belief in witchcraft (Chaudhary 1966: 698). The forested area of the Kaimur Plateau is mainly inhabited by tribes and semi-tribes like Agariya, Gond, Kharwar, Chera, Oraons, Bhuiyans, and Karias and they live mostly in mud houses. In Mirzapur district, tribes like Bongas, Bhutiyas, and the above-mentioned tribes use paintings on the outer walls of their houses.

PREVIOUS FINDINGS OF PREHISTORIC EVIDENCE

There are four rock shelters with paintings found near Banda village in Rohtasgarh, which are locally known as Mithaiyaman, Mangarua, Chamainman, and Lunnerbigahiyaman. They are all located near water sources. All paintings are done in red oxide. The scenes include hunting, gathering, and depiction of some birds. Similar paintings were traced at Phulvariaghat, Gitaghat, Kadimkund, Singaykund, Badkikapari, Bundhikhoh, and Jamaniamand (Cockburn 1883: 56-64, 94).

The Ganga Valley comprises a 0.5-m thick highly consolidated gravel formation with small-sized calcium carbonate and sand. This gravel, according to a study in Belan and Son Valley, contains upper Palaeolithic tools dated to about 24000–18000 BCE on the basis of carbon dating (Pal 2009). For the chronology of the Mesolithic culture in north-central India, three dates deserve special attention and these are from Baghor. The Baghor formation has yielded fresh upper Palaeolithic artefacts and the earliest date of 100,000 BP is assignable to the lower Palaeolithic period here. The Mesolithic cultural chronology of north-central India has three dates from Baghor-II in the Son Valley. A date reading 6380±220 BCE (Possehl and Rissam 1992: 461) was obtained from Lekhahia rock shelter-I; in Mirzapur district two AMS C-14 dates of about 6420 BCE (Lukacs 1996: 103-11) were obtained. These dates will help in understanding the emergence of the Mesolithic culture in the area in the first half of Holocene, if not at the close of Pleistocene (Pal 2009).

Table 14.1 Stratigraphy of the Prehistoric Culture in Belan and Son Valley.

Chronology	Time
Lower Paleolithic	100000 BP
Middle Palaeolithic	58000–45000 BP
Upper Palaeolithic	39000–20000 BP
Epi - Palaeolithic.	20000–16000 BP
Mesolithic	10,000–8,000, BP
Neolithic	6000–3000 BP

The antiquity of the Neolithic and Chalcolithic culture of the Vindhyas in the Ganga plain has been determined on the basis of C-14 dates from excavated Neolithic sites like Koldihwa, Mahagara, Kunjhum, Lahuradeva, and Tokwa (Mirzapur) (Pal 2009).

Excavations at Lekhahia on the Kaimur, at Chopanimando in Belan Valley, as well as the exploration of a large number of sites in the Ganga Valley and the Vindhyan area have shown the absence of geometric tools in the early horizon of the excavated sites and in the surface collection of most of the explored sites. A majority of the explored sites in the Vindhyas and the Ganga Valley belong to early Mesolithic or the non-geometric Microlithic phase (Sharma et al. 1980:15).

THE MIGRATION ROUTE

The two main rivers that drain the northern plateau of the Vindhyas are Karmanasa and Tons (with Belan and its tributaries). Black chert is the principle raw material at the sites in the Karmanasa system: Baira-doomuhawa (lat. 25° 2" N. long. 83° 11" E.) in Varanasi district is the most important settlement of the Epi-palaeolithic and the Mesolithic periods found so far. The material from Garhwa (lat. 25° 23' 30" N. long. 82° 57' E.) in the Ganga Valley in Varanasi district, situated at a distance of 48 km from Baira-doomuhawa on the Chandraprabha (a tributary of the Karmanasa), has yielded Epi-palaeolithic tools of the same material. Evidently, the raw material was brought to the Ganga Valley from Karmanasa River (Sharma and Pal 1980:8).

The Neolithic site of Senuwar is located on the right bank of river Kurda, about 7 km south of Sasaram in Rohtas district, Bihar. The Senuwar site lies in an area close to the alluvial plain in the vicinity of the foothills of Kaimur (Varma 2004: 478). Radiocarbon dates available for the lower levels of the neo-Chalcolithic phase of Senuwar are 1770±120 BCE. Keeping in view the dates, the beginning of Senuwar I-B may be fixed around 1800 BCE and the beginning of I-A may be placed around the beginning of the 3rd millennium BCE (Varma 2004: 487). Senuwar can be linked with the Belan Valley Neolithic complex ceramic traditions and other cultural components. All the ware found at Senuwar is associated with the twin sites of Koldihwa and Mahagara showing remarkable similarity in fabric, surface treatment, and to some extent in typology. In addition, other cultural assemblages also show similarities between Senuwar I-A and the Mahagara-Koldihwa complex (Singh 2004: 23). A site named Masahi belonging to the upper Palaeolithic period lies in the plains of the northern cliff of Kaimur hills (Singh 2004: 11).

While dating the Belan Valley Neolithic complex is another complicated issue particularly Koldihawa Neolithic as G.R. Sharma claimed their high antiquities with precisely three dates —5440±240 BCE, 4530±185 BCE, and 6570±210 BCE. J.N. Pal believes that these dates do not belong to the Neolithic strata of the site; he believes that the Neolithic of this area could be of about 3rd-2nd millennium BCE rather than earlier, which is also in accordance with the dating of the Neolithic culture of the Ganga plains.

The middle Palaeolithic industries might have been in existence in Karmanasa Valley in the Naugarh area of Chandauli district. Numerous rock shelters in Mirzapur district, particularly one rock shelter in Mura hills near village Lahriyadih, those located in the hill range lying north of the Son and those in the Sandag forest (around villages Baralia and Kuraila about 25 km south-east of Robertsganj) from there, provide evidence of upper Palaeolithic tools (Roy 1963:10). The excavations at Morahana Pahar, Baghaikhor, and Lekhahia (all in Mirzapur district) have revealed a sequence from the non-geometric pre-pottery stage to the geometric type associated with the pottery stage (Verma et al. 1974: 73-75).

In Varanasi district, two sites of Bankat-Bhikari-Rampur and Garhawa, belonging to the Mesolithic period, have been reported. The rock paintings in Mirzapur district are dominated by hunting scenes related to the story of ancient man (Roy 1963: 10). In the region between the valleys of Chandraprabha (in Mirzapur) and Karmanasa (in Chandauli), which are notably rich in Middle Stone Age tools, were found microlithic tools and Megalithic burials on the banks of both the rivers and at the foot of the isolated hillock. Microliths consisting of simple and parallel-sided blades, blunted back blades, lunette, and burins were found at several sites, noteworthy amongst which are Bhainsaur, Dagmapur, Durumundganj, Dudhi, Hathwani, Hemakahar, Kone, Murariya, Parspani, and Raja-ki-chauki in district Mirzapur and Hathania Pahar and Kaurihar in district Varanasi. Rock shelters with painting in red ochre depicting scenes of hunting, dancing, and other rituals were found at Baga Pahari, Baghai Khor, Bedia, Kharipathari, Lekhania, Marchahia, and Thar Pahara in district Mirzapur. In some cases, evidence of superimposition of paintings was also observed (*IAR*, 1962-63: 32). In the painted rock shelters of the Lekhahia group in district Mirzapur and Khusiyar Ghat ki Pahari in district Rewa (Madhya Pradesh), four stages of evolution of the paintings are determined: outline, filings with oblique lines, solid filings, and the use of white colour (*IAR*, 1963-64: 49). Similar paintings in Kaimur hills on the border of Uttar Pradesh and Bihar were also noticed by the authors.

EXPLORATIONS AND FINDINGS

A large number of archaeological sites in the study area belonging from the prehistoric to the early Historical period were noticed. These are located in the Kaimur Plateau under Rohtas and Kaimur districts in Bihar and Chandauli and Mirzapur districts in UP. The Senuwar settlement revealed the assemblage of antiquities belonging to the neo-Chalcolithic period (2nd millennium BCE) determined on the basis of C-14 dates (Chakrabarti 2001: 276). Some microlithic tools and their associated antiquities have been found at Garhawat in Krishnapur village in Kaimur. A number of sites have been found belonging to the Chalcolithic and NBPW periods in Rohtas and Kaimur districts in Bihar. The evidence of Ashokan inscriptions (Sahsaram, Basahan, and Ahraura) and stupa mounds are situated in the area. The paintings depicting Buddha on rock ascribed to the Gupta period (4th-6th *c.* CE) are noteworthy evidence in Kaimur of the Historical period.

Table 14.2 Archaeological sites including rock art sites in Kaimur and its surrounding.

District	Name of the sites
Rohtas	Singai Kund, Badaki, Kapari, Bundhi Khoh, Jamania Mand, Chandan Shahid, Chhamahiya hill*, Tarachandi, Luner Bigahiya Maan, Gita Ghat, Kadim Kund, Fulwariya, Amilo Hill*, Bannu Khoh*, Gandke Khoh Hill*, Kachhuar Maan*, Meethai ya Maan, Mangarua Maan, Chanain Maan, Inarbighahiya Maan*, Kohabarwa Maan*, Mushaharwa Maan*/Kachhuwar Maan, Banar Sabha Hill, Majhor Maan*, Gupta Dham.
Kaimur	Kokhardan*, Rauta, Sarodog, Madra, Prewa, Badki Goriya*, Pravara hill*, Mokari Khoh hill*, Patesar, Dewane Mokwa, Jhapia hill/Lekhania, Garhawat, Nindaur, Dihguleriya*, Nandena, Shyamagarh*, Ramgarh, Badargarh, Rajandih, Basahan.
Chandauli	Ghurahupur, Yogini ki Mand, Osari ghat, Gahadas Shahpur, Bangarh, Banarsiya Minor.
Mirzapur	Baba Pahari, Baghaikhor, Bediya, Kharipathari, Lekhania, Marchhahiya, Thar Pahara, Lehariyadih, Sahabiya, Munibaba, Panchmukhi, Kanda Kot, Chand Manawa, Kohbar, Ghor Mangar, Maldariya, Mahadariya, Chunar
Allahabad	Ramgarhawa, Chhatarpalia, Chandatari, Lakhaar, Chandawa

Note: ** Sites explored by Sachin Kr. Tiwary (Paper presented jointly with Shanker Sharma in IAS, ISPQS, IHCS 2011 conference at Thrisur, Trivandrum, Kerala).*

PREHISTORIC SITES

Artefacts belonging to middle Palaeolithic industries are found in Karmanasa Valley, Naugarh area of Chandauli district, and Sandag forest (around villages Baralia and Kuraila about 25 km south-east of Robertsganj) where evidence of upper Palaeolithic tools is found. Morahana Pahar, Baghaikhor, and Lekhahia (Mirzapur district) revealed a sequence from a non-geometric pre-pottery stage to geometric types associated with the pottery stage. Baira Doomuhawa, Varanasi, and Garhwa on Chandraprabha River yielded settlements of the Epi-palaeolithic and Mesolithic periods. Bankat-Bhikari-Rampur and Garhawa in Varanasi revealed antiquities belonging to the Mesolithic period. In the region between the valleys of Chandraprabha, Varanasi, and Karmanasa River (Chandauli), microlithic tools consisting of parallel sided blades, blunted back blades, lunette, and burins were found. Senuwar revealed tools of Neolithic and Chalcolithic affinities.

Table 14.3 Some Reported Prehistoric Sites in the Ganga Valley.

District	Culture			
	Epi-pala-eolithic	**Mesolithic (Non-Geometric)**	**Mesolithic (Geometric)**	**Neolithic/ Chalcolithic**
Pratapgarh	Mandah, Salhipur, Suleman Prabatpur	Aip ka purwa, Akoa (Akhaua), Akhohia, Amuwahi, Andewari, Ankaripur, Asudi, Atarsand, Bani, Baladih, Balipur, Baron, Banpurwa, Bansi ka Purwa, Basauli, Chamrupur, Dalapur, Elahi ka dih, Garahi, Haidarpur, Jahanpur, Kaharia, Lakhipur, Madha-i-sarai, Nagapur, Pachauri, Rajpur, Sadhaipur, Taradih, Usrapur, Warikalan	Bachhuha, Balapur, Dharampur, Hainsipariya, Jetapur, Kanjkhas, Mahadaha, Misirpur II, Pura Nagaiya, Raigarh, Sarai Nahar Rai, Sobhipur, Utras	Koldihwa, Mahagada, Kunjhum, Lahuradewa, Tokwa (Ganga Plain) Lekhahiya (Kaimur), Chopanimando (Belan Valley)
Allahabad	Ahiri	Bhikhampur, Kurha, Maharudih, Jamunipur	Bichhiaw	——
Sultanpur	——	Hathauratal, Garayen, Rahgaipur, Sultanpur	——	——
Jaunpur	——	Dhanikpurwa, Kaithora, Pure Gange Mani	——	——
Varanasi	Garhwa	Bankat Bhikhari Rampur	Lohina, Nagguli, Pura Gambhirshah	——

RECENT DISCOVERIES

Prehistoric rock paintings have Mesolithic and Chalcolithic cultural traits. Most of the Mesolithic paintings are expressions of the relationship between human beings and animal life. The depiction of paintings shows a hunting and gathering lifestyle (Fig. 14.1). Some noteworthy paintings belonging to the Chalcolithic period depict cows (Fig. 14.2). A painting depicted over a ceiling in the Osarighat hills makes a mysterious circle and bridge (Fig. 14.3) that is painted in white, buff colour, and red ochre. The depiction of fighting bulls (Fig. 14.4) shows the idea of a contest among animals for supremacy. This idea was already known to prehistoric society and hence its expression in rock art. Mesolithic people have given more expression to the challenges that they faced in life through rock art. The execution of paintings by Mesolithic painters is sometimes found in very inconvenient places like high rock walls or ceilings, which could only have been done by using elaborate ladders and scaffoldings. A figure of a dog in petroglyphs (Fig. 14.5) at the Bhitari Gharwa Hill is a rare example of its kind in the region and can be ascribed to the Historical period; it is contemporary of the paintings of Buddha. Historical paintings in rock shelters on Bhitri Gharwa Pahari in Ghurhoopur village depicting the Buddha in a preaching posture flaked by stupas (Fig. 14.6) and five Buddhas in a series (Fig. 14.7) painted in a tradition similar to that of the Sarnath School of Sculptural Art of the Gupta period have also been discovered recently.

Important archaeological evidence has also been discovered, which reflects the existence of Buddhism in the region in later times also. In spite of Buddhism, there are several paintings of animals and other aspects of human activities in various shelters on Osari Ghat Hill, which have been executed over Chalcolithic paintings.

ASHOKAN MINOR ROCK EDICT

The nine-line Ashokan Minor Rock Edict (Fig. 14.8) was discovered recently at a hilltop in the Kaimur range at Bharkon Baba Pahari within the jurisdiction of Basahan village in district Kaimur, Bihar. The important feature of this inscription is its location, as it is engraved on an outer surface and has neat alphabet in Asokan Brahmi script. Near it, a number of paintings are depicted on the ceilings of some shelters including a human chain formed by girls and some palm impressions. There are a number of such types of shelters where paintings are observed in different localities. Some of the paintings are depicted in superimposition (Mesolithic by Chalcolithic and Historical periods). Some war scenes depicted in the shelters belong to the Historical period.

On the foothill towards the north of the Ashokan inscription, a stupa mound and a pond (Fig. 14.9) on the east of the stupa were discovered by these authors. A large number of potsherds are scattered on the surface of the mound. The mud mortar paved stone block masonry is perhaps the main circumambulatory of the stupa observed in the northern cutting section. Among the pottery are red wares, mostly fragments of bowls and vases, which can be ascribed to the 3rd century BCE.

ANCIENT SETTLEMENT SITES

A huge mound in village Nindaur is situated about 8 km north-west of the Minor Rock Edict; this has a multi-cultural deposit. The brick structure may be ascribed to the Kushan period including the evidence of Buddhist, Hindu sculptures and terracotta from the early Historical period. A headless statue in *dhyana* (meditation) posture is another important finding in Kaimur sandstone. The mound of Banersia Minor is situated about 3.5 km north of the Minor Rock Edict, where some artefacts of the Chalcolithic and early Historical period have been observed.

DISCUSSION

I. Ancient Line of Communication in the Region

The ancient line of communication is well established in the Indian subcontinent on both the external and internal trade links (Lahiri 1999: 230). The early Historic trade route in

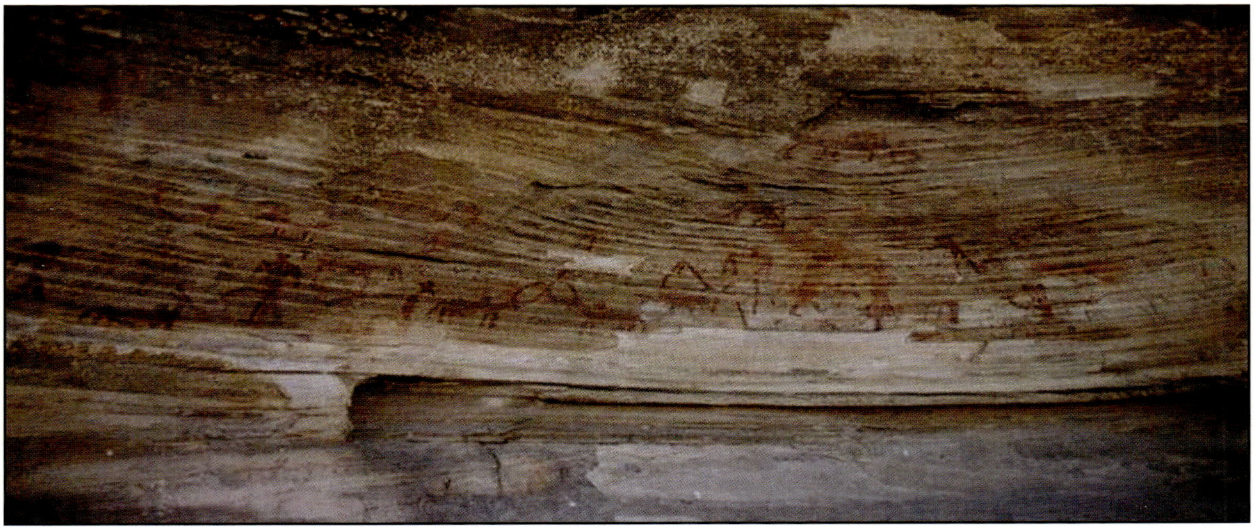

Fig. 14.1 Hunting scene, Osari Ghat Hill.

the region falls under the northern trans-regional route known as *Uttarapatha*. It is mentioned in literature that this ran across the Indus and Gangetic plains to the port of Tamralipti on the eastern coast; however, it had two major sectors—northern and southern. Varanasi is in the southern sector. Evidence of movement along the *Uttarapatha* is ound in *Vinaya*-III. It states that from Rajgriha, one road led to Varanasi and further west to the cities of Prayag, Mathura, and Taxila through Gaya along which Buddha journeyed to Rishipattana (Sarnath) (*Vinaya*-III: 2 and Pandey 1963: 197-98) The Grand Trunk Road is probably the same ancient route, and it runs through Dhanbad, Barahi, Gaya, Sasaram, and Varanasi (Grierson 1893: 16-198). According to the Ariyeopariyesana-sutta, of *Majhjhima Nikaya*, 'there was already in the time of the Buddha a high road *(Adhanmagga)* that connected Uruvela with Gaya proper and extended westward as far as Benaras and its vicinity'. Information gleaned from the *Vinaya Mahavagga* (*Mahavagga:* 4) suggests that this high road, used for caravan traffic, stretched downwards as far as the distant land of Ukkala (modern Odisha) (Barua 1934: 162). Pali literature further provides us with images of routes of communication

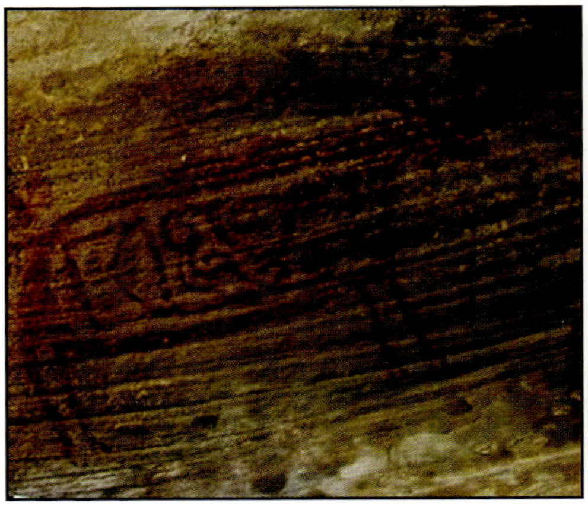

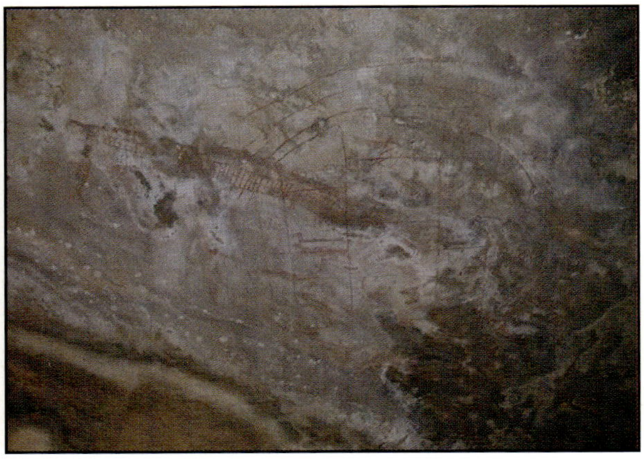

Left: **Fig. 14.2** Depiction of cow, Osari Ghat Hill.

Right: **Fig. 14.3** Mysterious circle and bridge, Osari Ghat Hill.

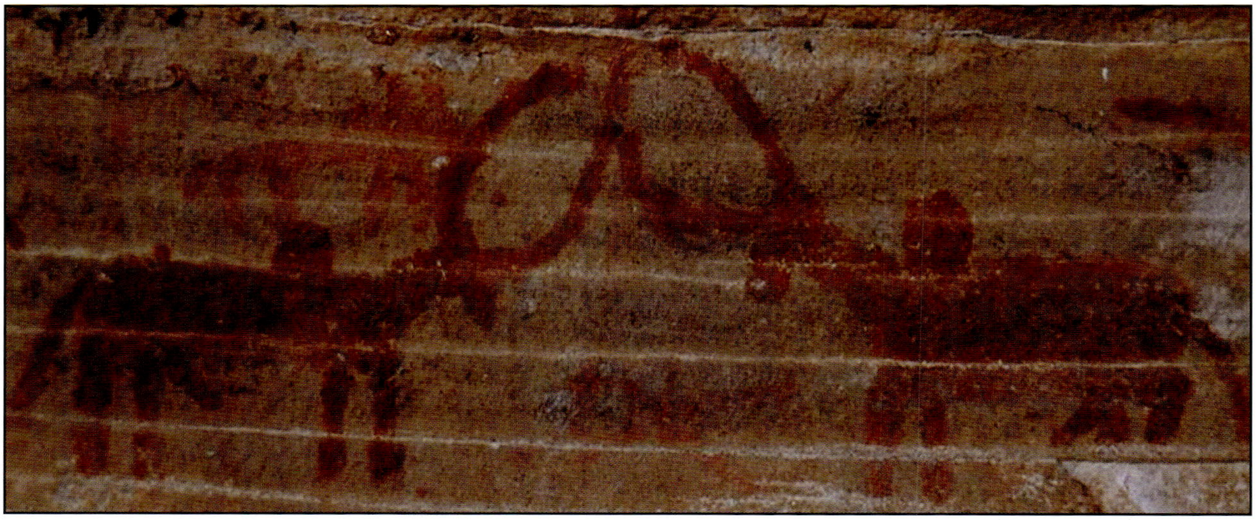

Fig. 14.4 Depiction of fighting bulls, Osari Ghat Hill.

that the Buddha and his wondering *bhikkhus* must have followed. A road runs from Tamralipti to Varanasi via Ranchi and Palamu. Romila Thapar states that the existence of a tomb near Sahsaram gives us an idea that there was a route from Patna up to the Son Valley across the plateau to Jabalpur, and then down the Narmada Valley to Bharoch. Sahsaram was then an important town on the northern edge of the plateau. Rupnath is located on Kaimur hills near Salimabad in Madhya Pradesh (now in Chhattisgarh) while Ahraura is in Varanasi near Chakiya. There was a route that led to MP and Rohtas district at the same time. Ahraura was probably on the route from Magadha to the west coast, as were

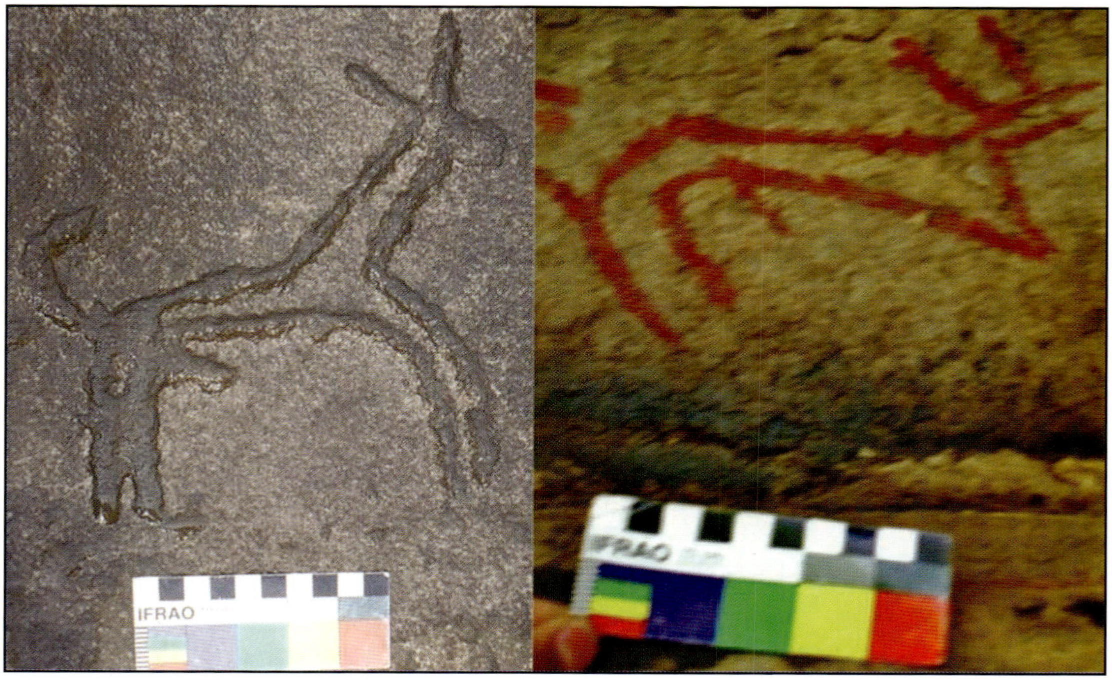

Fig. 14.5 Dog in petroglyphs & pictograph, Ghurhoopur (Courtesy: Sachin Kr. Tiwary).

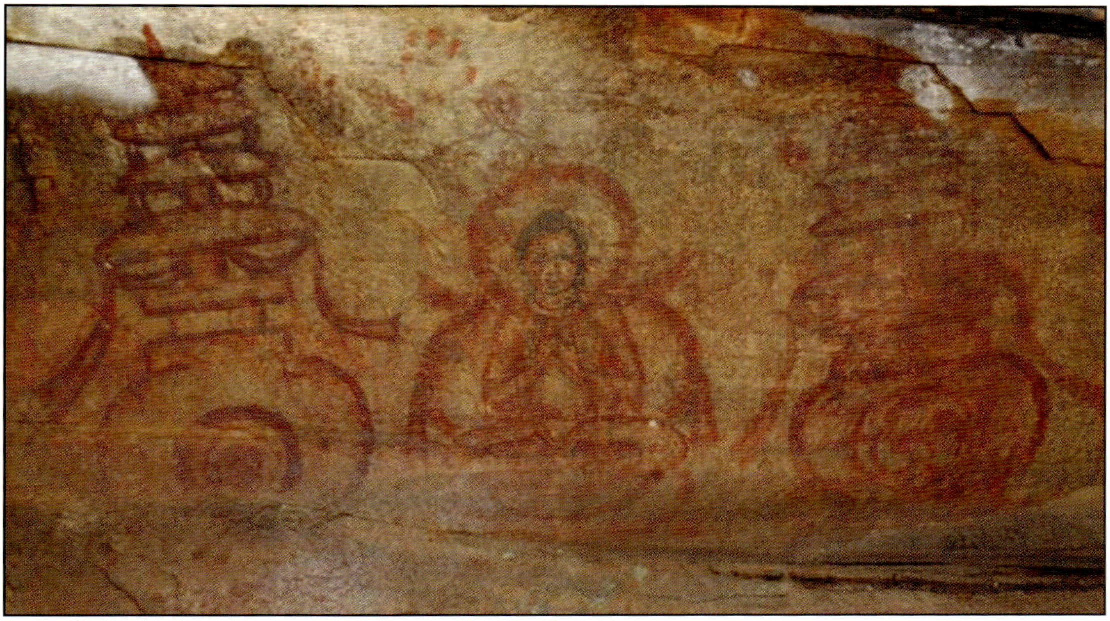

Sahsaram and Rupnath. It was due to the fear of *atvikas* that *sarthavaha* that *caravan* leaders travelled in large groups. During Buddha's time two merchants, Tapassu and Bhallaka, travelled from Odisha to central India (Davidz 1998: 209). The Gaya-Benaras road seems to have struck the Benaras-Rajgir Road at Sonbhadra on the old Son and passed through Konch across Morhar at Pali to avoid the two branches of rivers, which

Fig. 14.6 Buddha in preaching posture flanked by stupas, Ghurhoopur.

Fig. 14.7 Buddha in a series, Ghurahoopur.

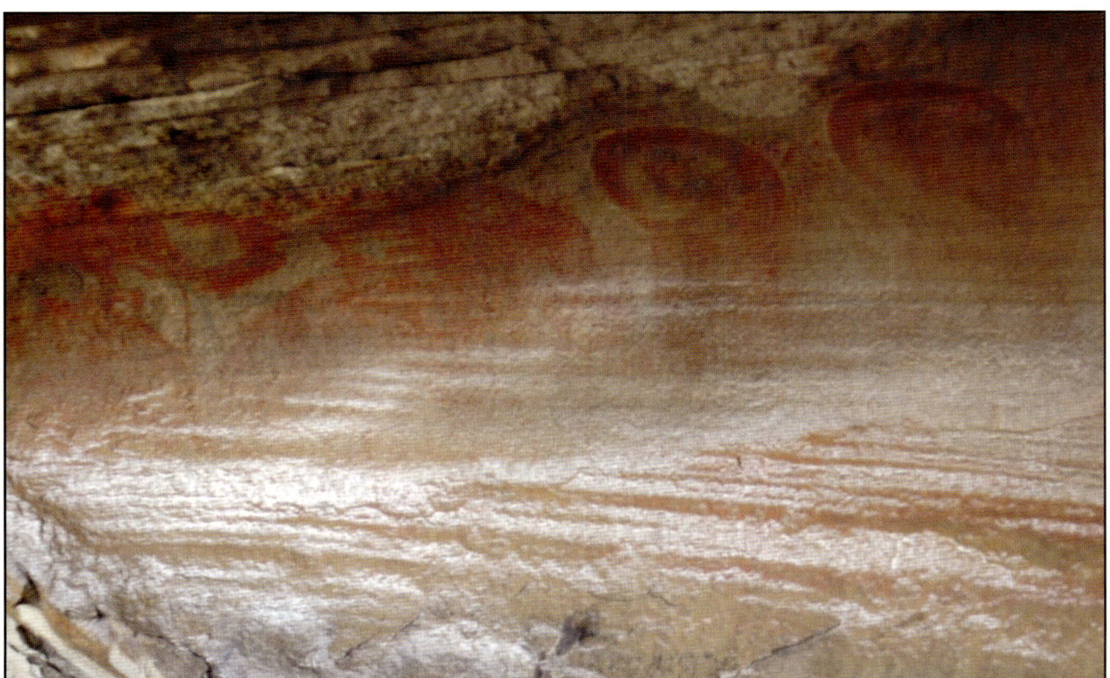

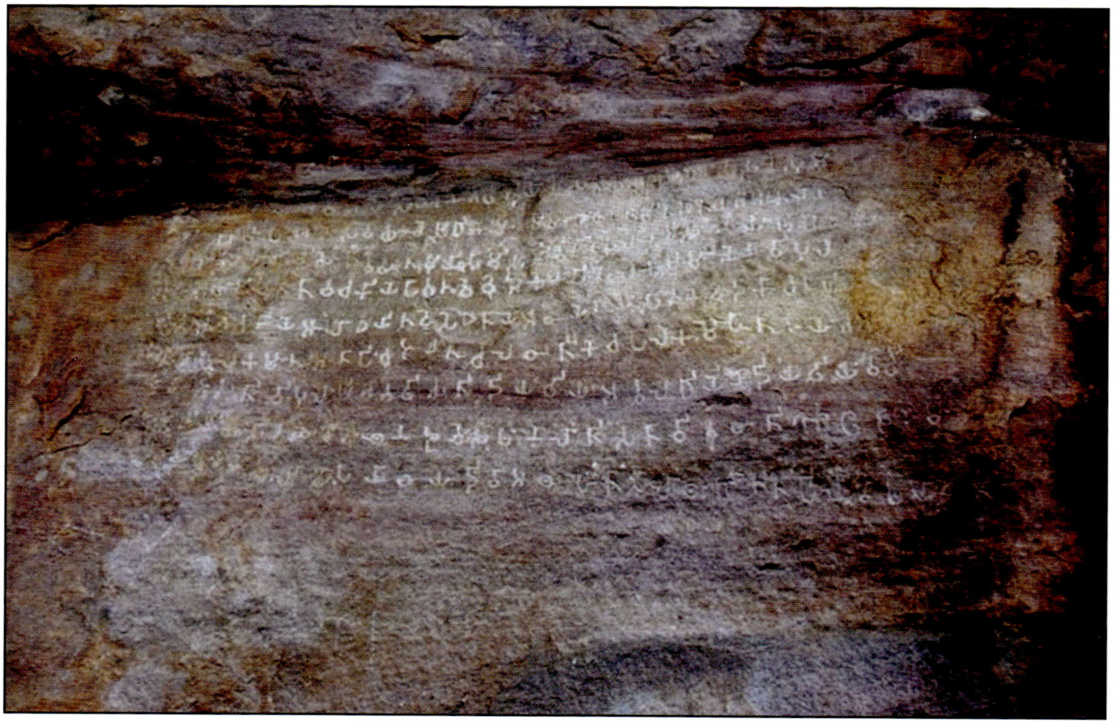

Fig. 14.8 Ashoka Minor Rock Edict, Basahan.

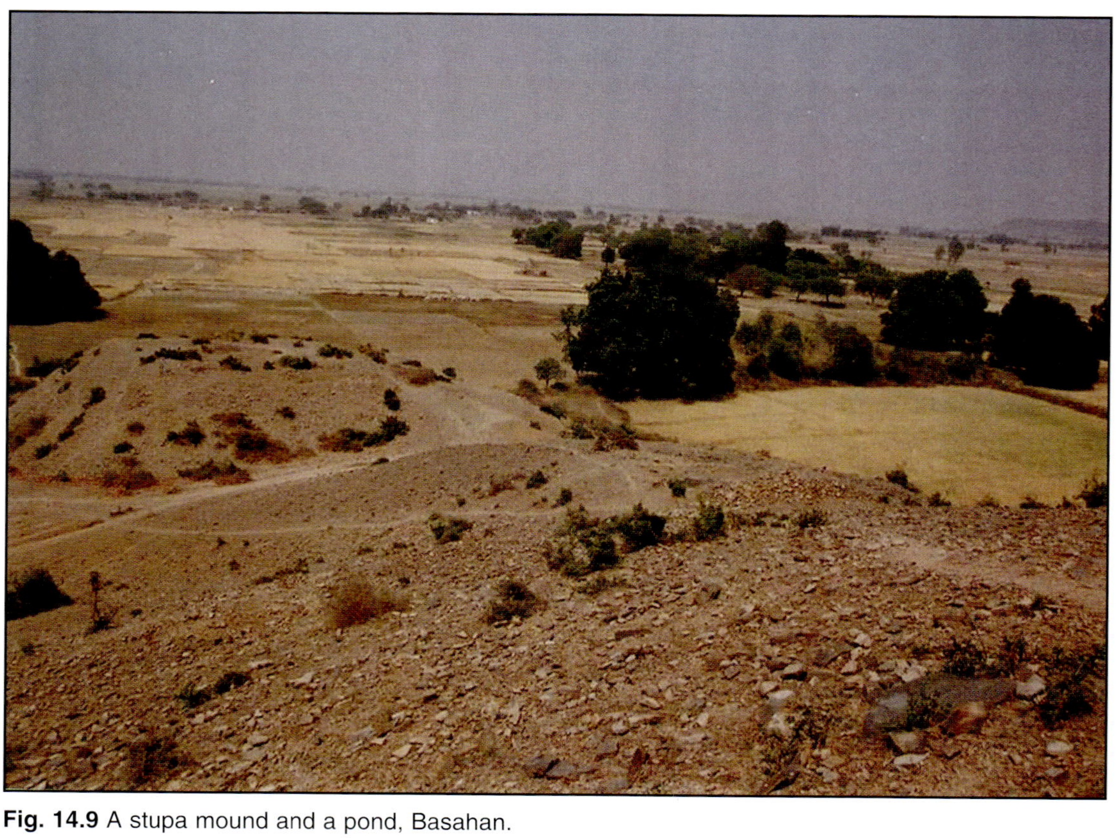

Fig. 14.9 A stupa mound and a pond, Basahan.

it could meet if it had to cross either above or below. The Benaras-Rajgir road seems to have crossed the old Son at Sonbhadra, Morhar at Ghejan, and Falgu and the Patna-Gaya road at Jaru (Barua 1934: 113-14). Between Mirzapur and Gaya, Son River which, is navigable, might have been used for communication (Hunter 1876: 23).

II. Evidence of the Existence of Buddhism and the Buddha Passing through This Route for the First Sermon at Ishipatana (Sarnath) after His Enlightenment

The location of the Minor Rock Edict of Emperor Ashoka at Sasaram and Basahan (Ramesh Ravishankar 2011: 1-4) in Kaimur and Ahraura in Mirzapur suggests that this route was popularly associated with Buddhist followers attracting the attention of Ashoka for inscribing rock edicts when he actively propagated *dhamma* post his association with Buddhist *samgha* (Thapliyal 2009:9).

After investigating all the material—authentic literary sources; archaeological remains; geo-echo factors; support system in the route for facilitating human movement; existence of contemporary tribal and semi-tribal communities and the continued use of land by man without any hiatus which allowed human movements and alternate supportive routes parallel to it—we have been able to identify the shortest possible route between the two destinations and the most probable one undertaken by Buddha while moving to the place of his First Sermon.

III. The Authors of Rock Art in Kaimur Region

The large number of prehistoric rock paintings and shelters clearly indicate dense population in this region since the Mesolithic period. People settled in this region due to a number of favourable factors like the existence of a large numbers of water bodies near the natural shelters and other ecological factors and also because raw material for making stone tools was available in the Karmanasa system.

The depiction of fighting bulls is perhaps one of the expressions of the artists who showed the idea of contest among animals for supremacy. This idea was already known to Mesolithic society. The Mesolithic people tried to explain their activities in life. A petroglyph depicting deer is also ascribed to this period. The artists gave an expression to their challenges of life through rock paintings.

The region was also occupied by Chalcolithic communities and they led a well-settled life here as agro-pastoralists; they have depicted their wide experiences in rock shelters in the form of pictographs. Some X-ray paintings (might be of a cow) also support this idea. Chalcolithic paintings were sometimes executed in superimposition overlapping earlier paintings.

Perhaps, they were living in either wattle-and-daub houses or houses constructed of undressed stone as can be seen near village Ghurhupur along the Osari Ghat Hill. The site is spread over 2 km in which potsherds and some burnt clay pieces have also been noticed. In some cases, the debris of stone structures was also carried out for constructing modern houses.

Further, the excavation of the Senuwar site on the course of river Durgawati (about 40 km south-east of these settlements) has unveiled Neolithic (*c.* 2200–1950 BCE) and

Chalcolithic (*c*.1950–1300 BCE) evidences, the material culture from the twin site Koldihwa-Mahagara. This typologically shows more affinity with Senuwar. So, it could be considered that the Senuwarian- Neolithic communities had the first settlement in this region and; that they either migrated from the Gangetic plains from the Koldihwa-Mahagara cultural complex and settled in this Kaimur region. Similarly, cultural migration via Son Valley from the Baghor formation to this region may also be considered and a conclusion may be drawn that the influence of the cultures in this region during the Mesolithic period could have travelled through the lower Son Valley and flourished in the plains of the northern lower foothills of the Vindhyas at the sites of Mahagara-Koldihawa complex. In this cultural mobility, the prehistoric community could have settled in this region along the Kaimur ranges.

As far as the paintings of the Historical period are concerned, they are of general and court art in nature. The general nature of the paintings can be seen in aspects like expressions of life and the activities of the common people including depiction of games and amusement by society as a number of settlements are located in its orbit and in the surrounding areas that belong to the early historic and later periods. However, stylistic paintings of war scenes may be an expression of a community associated with ruling societies as the size of these paintings is large. A petroglyph perhaps depicting a dog could only be possible to execute with hard metal tools like iron, which can be ascribed to the historical period.

The paintings depicting Buddha in series and preaching poses flanked by stupas along with painted inscriptions in Brahmi belonging to the Gupta period found near Ghurhoopur village might be done by some Buddhists followers or by the royal order that can be placed under the category of court art in the rock art, as the same has been represented in Fresco and Tempera rock paintings in Ajanta rock-cut caves under the Gupta-Vakataka period. The shelter having large space may be used for meditation purpose and thus led to the depiction of such paintings in large sizes. It is also possible that for the Buddhist followers those who used to go through this route in Kaimur for *Sambodhiyatra* (route of the enlightenment) and *Dharmachakrapravartanayatra* (route of the turning the wheel of law) from Bodh Gaya < Sarnath < Bodh Gaya perhaps painted and engraved their desired subject. This kind of paintings can also be placed under the nature of court art. On the basis of this hypothetical fact, it can be assume that the credit of the execution of these paintings in the shelters of the Kaimur can be given to the above communities and to the settlers who were either living permanently or temporarily camped in and around the region.

A comprehensive study of both the paintings and material reported through explorations indicates that the authors of the rock art in Kaimur were settled in its vicinity itself and impressed their art on rock in the region. This is supported by the fact that in this region the excavated sites such as Senuwar bear the evidence of Neolithic and Chalcolithic cultures. Remains of cultures from the middle of the 2nd millennium BCE are extensively found with early historical material at a number of sites in the region including Nindaur. Association of the rock art with Buddhist monastic establishments is also quite prominent. All this taken together suggests that the authors of the rock art were local inhabitants who settled in the region from at least Mesolithic times. During the early historical period, the travelling monks must have also contributed to this art during the period of their *Varshavasa* (staying during rainy season).

ACKNOWLEDGEMENTS

We express our deep gratitude to late Sushil Tripathy, a press reporter who lost his life in due coverage of archaeological evidence including rock paintings and shelters available in the vicinity of Ghurhupur village in Kaimur in the year 2008. It was his effort to bring into limelight of the historical paintings on rock of Buddhism influx. We are extremely thankful to *Shri Sachin Kumar Tiwari* for providing the list of some recently discovered rock art sites in Kaimur in respect of Bihar and Shri K.K. Jha and Rajiv Kumar of Archaeological Survey of India for providing photographs.

REFERENCES

Barua, B.M. (1934), *(Revised) Gaya and Buddha-Gaya, Vol. II, Book-I.* Calcutta: Cotton Press, pp. 62, 113-14.

Chakrabarti, D.K. (2001), *Archaeological Geography of the Ganga Plain: The Lower and the Middle Ganga.* New Delhi: Orient Blackswan, p. 276.

Choudhary, P.C. Roy (1966), *District Gazeteer Shahabad*, p. 11.

Cockburn, J. (1883), 'On the Recent Existence of Rhinoceros Indicus in the North Western Provinces', *Journal of the Asiatic Society of Bengal* 52(2): 56-64, 94.

David, R. (1998), *Buddhist Birth Stories: Jataka Tales.* New Delhi: Sristhi Publisher and Distributers, p. 208.

Grierson, G.A. (1893), *Note on the District of Gaya and Buddha-Gaya*, Bengal Secretariat Press, pp. 16-198.

Hunter, W.W. (1876), *A Statistical Account of Bengal-II, IV*, Delhi, p. 23.

I.A.R. (1962–63), Exploration in District Allahabad, Banda, Mirzapur and Varanasi, p. 32.

I.A.R. (1963–64), Exploration in District Allahabad, Mirzapur and Rewa (M.P.), p. 49.

Lahiri, N. (1999) (Reprint), *The Archaeology of Indian Trade Routes up to 200 B.C.* New Delhi: Oxford India Paperback, pp. 230, 232.

Mathpal, Yashodhar (1995), *Rock Art in Kumaon Himalyas.* New Delhi: IGNCA, p. 8.

Neumayer, Ervin (2001), 'Rock Art in India', in Michel Lorbelanchet (ed.), *Rock Art in the Old World.* New Delhi: IGNCA.

Pandey, M.S. (1963), *Historical Geography and Topography of Bihar.* Delhi: Motilal Banarsidass, pp. 197-98.

Ramesh, K.V. and T.S. Ravishankar (2011), *Epigraphia Indica*, XLIII, New Delhi: ASI, pp. 1-4.

Roy, T.N. (1963), *The Ganges Civilisation*, New Delhi, p. 10.

Sharma, G.R., V.D. Misra, and J.N. Pal (1980), *History and Archaeology*, I (1-2), Department of A.I.H. Culture & Archaeology, Allahabad University, Allahabad, p. 15.

Sharma, S. and S.K. Tiwari (2010), Paper Presented on 'Ancient Route in Kaimur Range: In Light of New Evidences', Lucknow, Joint Annual Conference of IAS, ISPQS and HIS, 28-30 December.

Singh, B.P. (2004), *Early Farming Communities of Kaimur.* Jaipur: Publication Scheme.

Thaper, R. (2012), *Ashoka and the Decline of the Maurya*, Oxford University Press, pp. 235-36.

Thaplyal, K.K. (2000-01), 'Observations of Buddha and Rishabhanath as Avatar of Vishnu', in S.M. Mishra (ed.), *Puravritta, Vol. I.* Lucknow: Lucknow University.

——. (2009), *Jnana-Pravaha Monograph–I, A New Asokan Inscription from Ratanpurava*. Varanasi: *Jnana-Pravaha,* Centre for Cultural Studies and Research, p. 9.

Tripathy, Hawaldar (2009), *Dakshin Bihar Ki Nadiyan: Dhar aur Kachhar*, II. Patna: Bihar Hindi Granth Academy, p. 8.

Varma, R.K., V.N. Misra and M.S. Mate (1974), *Indian Pre-history*. Pune, pp. 73-75.

Verma, B.S. (2004), *Pre Historic Archaeology of Bihar*. Patna: Directorate of Archaeology and Museum, Bihar, p. 478.

Watters, Thomas (1996) (Reprint), *On Yuan Chwang's Travels in India, Vol. II*. Delhi: Munshiram Manoharlal, p. 48.

15

Petroglyphs in Seeta Valley, Sindh

Zulfiqar Ali Kalhoro

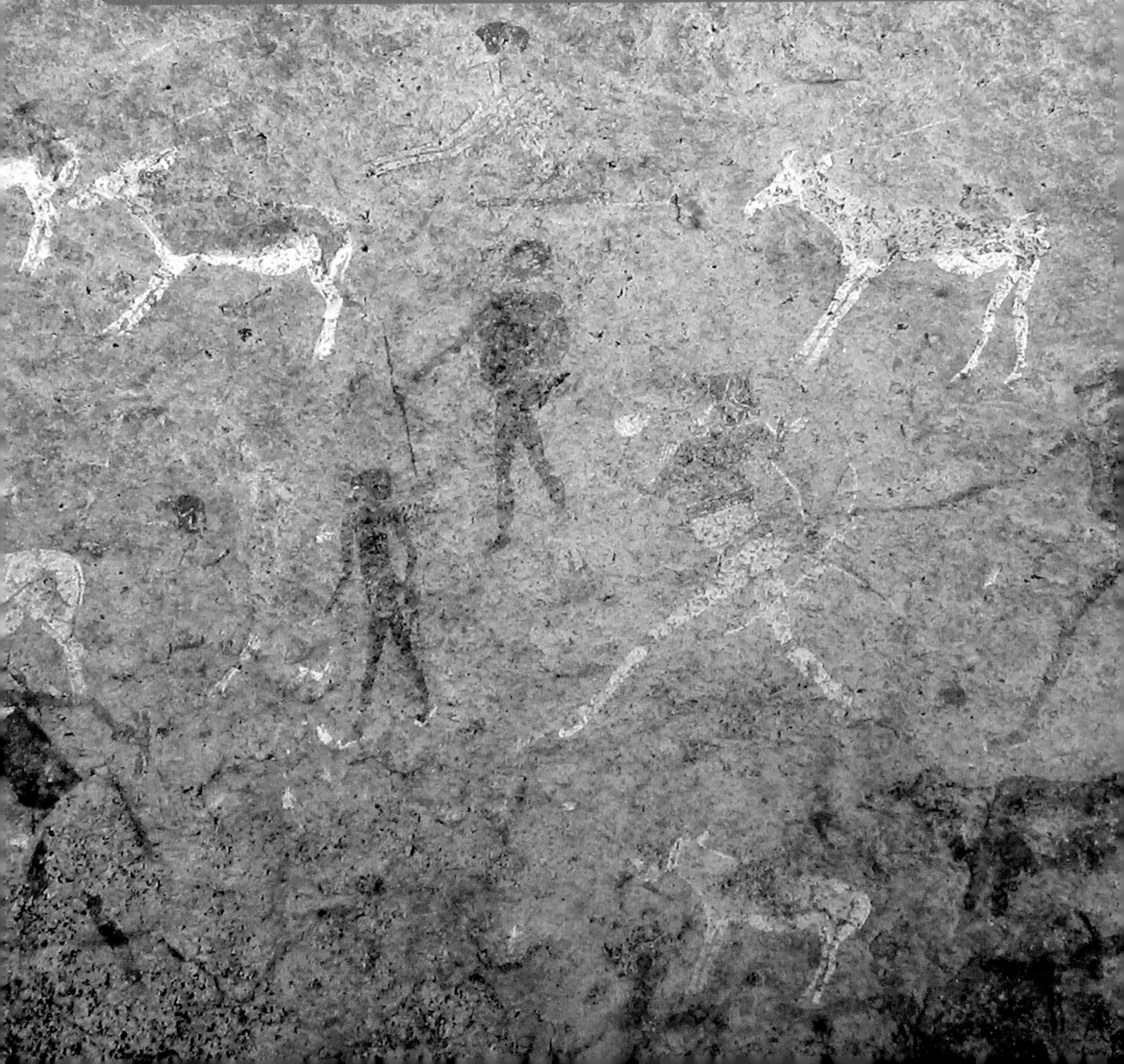

ABSTRACT

The discovery of rock art in the Khirthar mountain range is the turning point in the archaeology of Sindh. Dr. Kalhoro's paper deals with the rock carvings in Seeta Valley, which lies 80 km west of Larkana city and 70 km from Mohenjo-Daro. It discusses and interprets the rock carvings of Seeta Valley, which is noted for Indus period petroglyphs where one finds the most interesting petroglyphs of a horned deity with dancers. The dancing scenes are a recurrent theme in the petroglyphs of Seeta Valley.

INTRODUCTION

Rock engravings in Sindh do not exist in isolation. There are archaeological remains, graveyards and gabarbands lying close to them but, surprisingly, petroglyphs or rock engravings in Sindh are not known to the scholars working on Sindh. The Khirthar and Lakhi ranges abound in petroglyphs. Majumdar (1934) was the first archaeologist to record petroglyphs in the Lakhi range at Dalh, which he briefly mentioned. He believed that they were scratches and drawings of the modern period. He also explored lower *nai* (hill stream) Gaj but did not mention any of the rock art sites lying close to the settlement sites of Rohel Ji Kund, Chhute Ji Kund, Nagzani Ji Kund and Jaro Kalat.

Ansari (2011) first noticed the petroglyphs in Seeta Valley in 1990 and wrote a series of articles in local newspapers. Rashid also visited one rock art site in Seeta Valley in 1996 and wrote an article in a leading English daily. Later in 2002, Abro systematically documented a few rock art sites in Seeta Valley and he traversed the lower valley of Mazarani, Keharji, Chhanhar, Nari, Kukrani and Naing. The author went into 15 valleys in search of petroglyphs and documented the rock carvings and paintings. This includes the valleys of Angai, Nari, Mamani, Heghan, Gaj, Makhi, Khurbi, Sallari, Radh, Sughro, Chhanhar, Keharji, Mazarani, Gerelo and Seeta. The author explored the entire Khirthar range and traversed every *nai* (hill stream) of the Khirthar to document petroglyphs and pictograms, ancient and medieval period graveyards, ancient dams (gabarbands), terraces and megaliths.

There are many archaeological remains in these valleys. However, one finds more archaeological remains in Gaj Valley, some of which were documented by Majumudar (1934). One such site is Rohel Ji Kund, which is an Amrian site with Nal influence (Krishna Deva). Majumdar was killed by an absconder at this site while he was busy documenting the site. Krishna Deva (1949) completed and published his survey of the Gaj Valley and plains lying east and northeast of Gaj. They mentioned in their report two sites of Rajo Dero (Amrian) and Pai Jo Kotirio, which exist in the plains lying east and northeast of Nain Gaj. Pai Jo Kotirio was also documented by Majumdar. According to him, the site belonged to the Amrian period. He made three trenches at the site and found a large number of plain and some painted and incised potsherds, terracotta bangles, cakes, toy-cart frames, shell bangles, perforated potsherds, a couple of flints and a terracotta bull-figurine (Krishna Deva 1949:14).

Majumdar also mentioned other sites that lie in the main valley of Gaj. They include the sites of Rohel Ji Kund, Chutti Ji Kund, Nagzani Ji Kund and Jaro Kalat. Near all these sites are situated rock carvings. At Rohel Ji Kund, a few small boulders depicting a bull, Bactrian camel and other images were found.

West of the Jeandi Shah, which is an Indus period site, are six rock art sites in the Shakloi Dhoro (Kalhoro 2010).

Apart from *nai* Gaj, one also finds archaeological remains in the Nari Valley which have not been mentioned by archaeologists. Majumdar (1934) only documented and discussed the Wahi Pandhi site which is on the right bank of Nain Nari. He could not go deep inside the valley. The Wahi Pandi site is located where the Nari debouches from Khirthar hills into the plains.

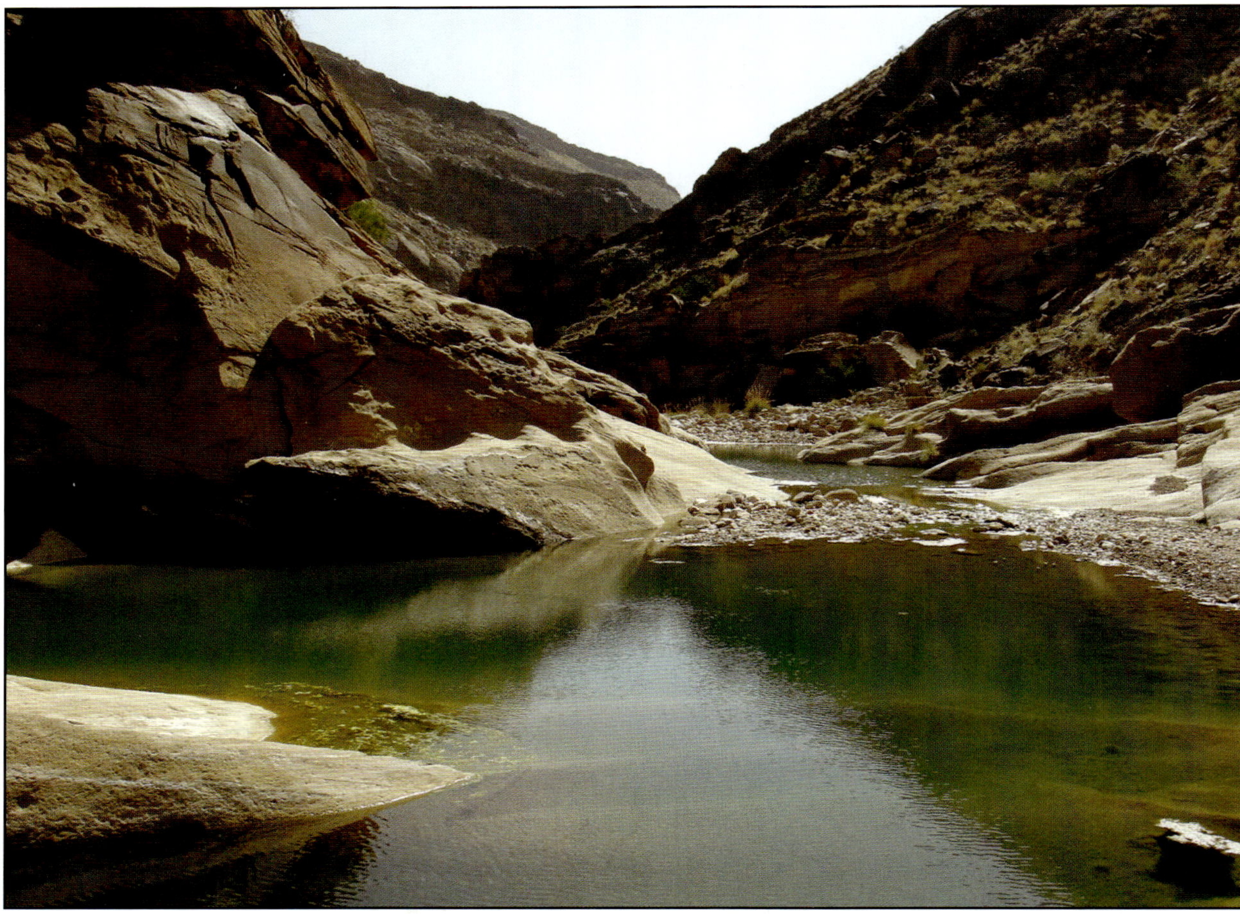

Fig. 15.1 View of Seeta Valley.

On the top of the Khotho hill in Nari, there are remains of structures. There are, in fact, remains of four rooms. A few plain red potsherds are lying on the ground. At walking distance from the Khotho remains are rock engravings at Sarwan, Chuchar, Jhudri and Kalri.

There are also found archaeological remains in Sallari Nain, which lies south of Seeta Valley. These sites are locally called Sallarkot and Khazani wari Buthi. The former is a site of Amrian period while the latter of the historic period, probably of the Kushan period (Kalhoro 2011).

Likewise, the Seeta Valley is also home to archaeological remains of ancient gabarbands (ancient dams), which indicate its antiquity. These gabarbands lie in close proximity to the rock art sites.

PETROGLYPHS IN SEETA

Ansari (1996) first discovered petroglyphs in Seeta Nai. He only mentioned the petroglyphs of Seeta Dath and Chitan Wari Bhar. Later, Rashid (1996) also mentioned the petroglyphs of Chitan Wari Bhar. Abro (2006) documented more rock art sites in Seeta Valley and discussed five rock art sites. The author discovered seven more rock art sites in Seeta Valley, so now there are 13 rock art sites in Seeta Valley: six located in the main Seeta Nai (valley) and seven in subsidiary valleys (*dhoras*) of Seeta. Before we discuss the rock art sites in Seeta, the term Seeta should be discussed.

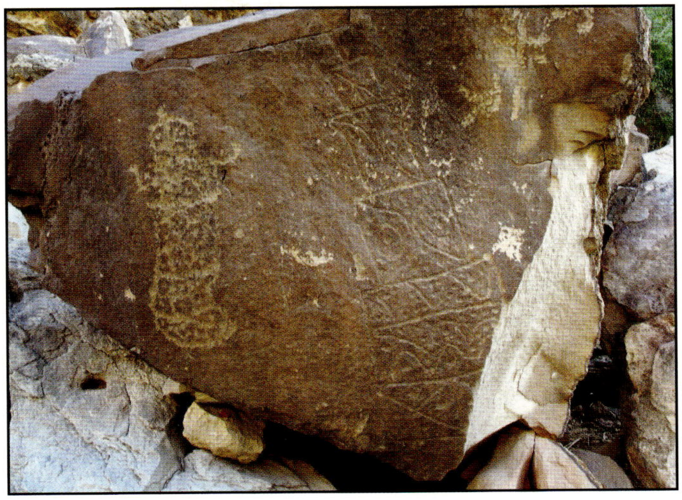

Fig. 15.2 Stupa images at Seeta Dath.

There are several local interpretations regarding the term Seeta. Some local people believe that Seeta is named after the famous character Sita who was Rama's wife from the epic *Ramayana*. Others have a different explanation for the term Seeta and believe that the word is derived from *seet,* meaning cold or pleasant region. This valley is famous for pleasant weather in hot summer months and many people spend the hot summers in Seeta Valley. The most famous and highest peaks of the northern Khirthar range are also close to this valley, which includes the Dog's Tomb rising 6,800 feet and Darharo rising 6,000 feet MSL. Seeta Valley had been the ancient route for traders and pilgrims. People still frequent this route to go to Baluchistan. Along this ancient route are found many rock art sites and gabarbands (ancient dams and wall terraces).

METHODOLOGY

To explore the nature of the rock art phenomena, the author focused on Seeta Valley where there are several rock art sites. The author first photographed all the rock art sites and later tracings were prepared. According to the author, the petroglyphs in Seeta Valley represent the interaction of inhabitants surrounding these sites as well as the visitors. The author tried to show the same and attempted to prepare a tentative chronology. Finally, while concluding, he gave descriptions and interpretations of the images. The author also briefly discussed the themes and motifs found in the rock art of Seeta Valley. There are 13 rock art sites in Seeta and its subsidiary valleys. However, the author only described six major rock art sites.

1. Seeta Dath

This rock art site is located at the mouth of the valley. It situated near two hamlets of Gancha and Chandia tribes who serve as porters for the visitors to the Dog's Tomb or Darharao. Dath is a word derived from Sindhi language, which means a jaw. At this site, the valley becomes narrow and takes a sharp turn. This site has sandstone and limestone rock formations. There are also loose boulders with petroglyphs. There are some large boulders, too, where people visiting from the lower valley take rest. The lower valley is called Tuni, which runs in the plains of Kachho while the upper valley which begins from Dath is called Seeta Valley (Fig. 15.1). People usually rest at this site and make

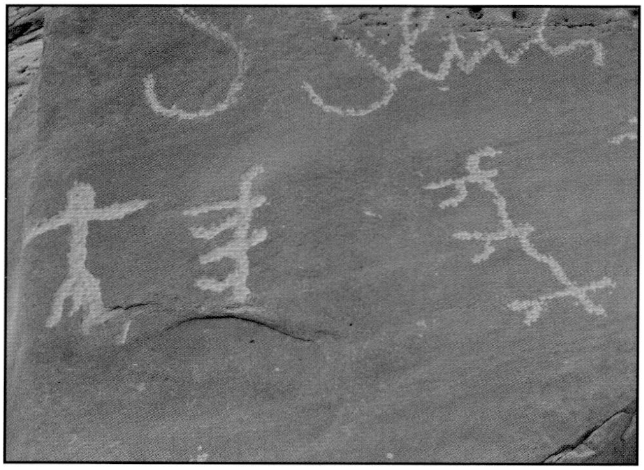

engravings. One can also find modern graffiti along with old and ancient petroglyphs. The modern engravings include the names of individuals and petroglyphs of animals. There are six boulders depicting images of animals, humans and buildings. As one approaches the Dath of the valley, one comes across a huge boulder with tower-like stupa images (Fig. 15.2).

The second boulder depicts ibex and camel images, which are from the medieval period and were drawn by travellers. Close to these animal images are some geometric designs. The third boulder depicts interesting petroglyphs of dancers. There are two rows of dancers who are shown dancing possibly before a deity or a tribal chief (Fig. 15.3). In each row, there are three dancers hand in hand. This is possibly a ceremonial scene. A hierarchy is visible among the figures with the deity being taller than the others. The deity or tribal chief is shown with genitals and extended arms. The figure is larger than those of the dancers. The dancing scenes are the special feature of the rock art of Seeta Valley. They can be found in two other rock art sites, which the author will discuss later. There is another interesting engraving of a snake near the petroglyphs of the dancers. On the fourth boulder, there are only three engravings. There is an interesting petrogylph on this boulder. A snake is shown attacking or approaching a man. The man is stunned by the sudden appearance/attack of the snake and the snake's mouth is fully open for its prey (Fig. 15.4). These snakes are locally called *bala* (literally meaning a large snake or dragon), which bite both humans and animals. There have been several incidents of snakes biting people in the recent past which are still fresh in the memories of the local population. Seeta Valley is notorious for poisonous snakes. Interestingly, people have made engravings of these harmful snakes. However, one does not find petroglyphs of snakes in other valleys of

Fig. 15.3 Dancing figures at Seeta Dath.

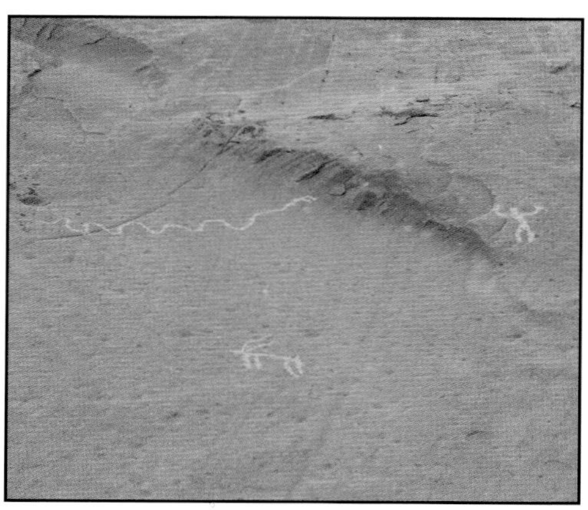

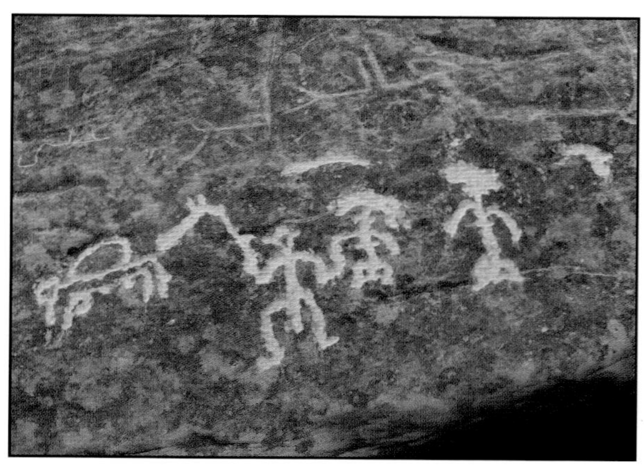

Left: **Fig. 15.4** Snake and man motif at Seeta Dath.

Right: **Fig. 15.5** Engravings of a man with two women at Seeta Dath.

Khirthar, Bado and Lakhi ranges or even in the Maher hill in Karachi district, although one finds many petroglyphs and pictographs there.

The fifth boulder depicts a man with two women. The man is shown holding the bridle of a camel in one hand and a woman's hand in the other. Both women have headgears with two dots on either side of their chests representing breasts (Fig. 15.5). (Modern engravings, mostly names of individuals can also be noticed here.)

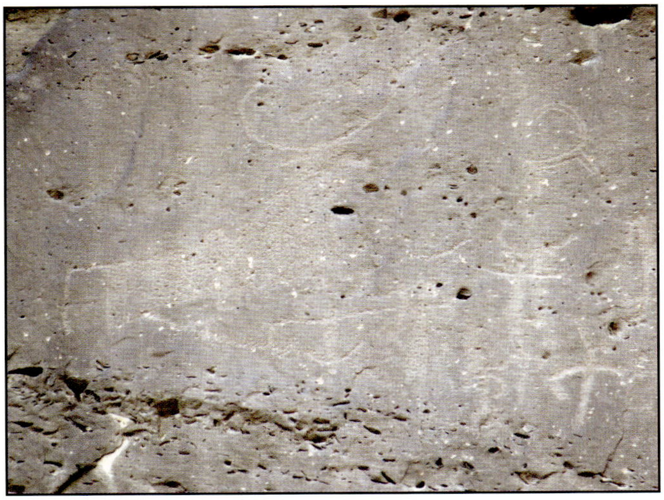

Fig. 15.6 Human figures with raised hands before the bull at Chitan Wari Bhar.

The sixth boulder only bears camel and ibex images. Some of these are ancient while the other images are from the medieval period. Ancient petroglyphs of animals are drawn with heavy patina while the medieval ones are drawn are with light patina.

2. Chitan Wari Bhar (Engraved Cliff)

This site is located at walking distance from the Seeta Dath rock art site. It is just 500 m from Seeta Dath. There is a cliff which is fully covered with petroglyphs mainly from Mesolithic and Neolithic periods. The cliff faces the west. Petroglyphs are present on the cliff at a height of 30 feet from the riverbed. There is a large horizontal panel containing images of animals, cattle and humans. On the left or the northern side of the cliff, there are images of wild bulls with human figures which are shown with raised hands as if worshipping or invoking some deity. There are at least five such petroglyphs of males with raised arms (Fig. 15.6). This scene possibly represents a religious ceremony, apparently invoking the deity for some boon. It is also likely that they are calling upon the help of the deity for domestication of the bovid, which is drawn close to the figures of males with raised arms. The depiction of the bull is unrealistic with a large rectangular body and a short head and almost

Left: **Fig. 15.7** Arrows pointed to the anthropomorph figure of woman giving birth to a child.

Right: **Fig. 15.8** Arrows pointing to the bull images on the panel at Chitan Wari Bhar.

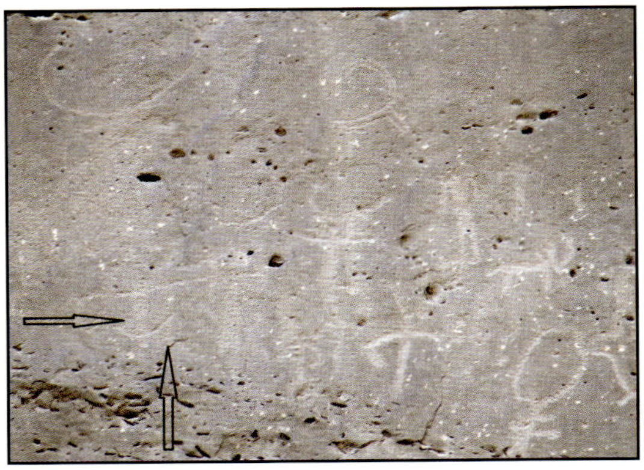

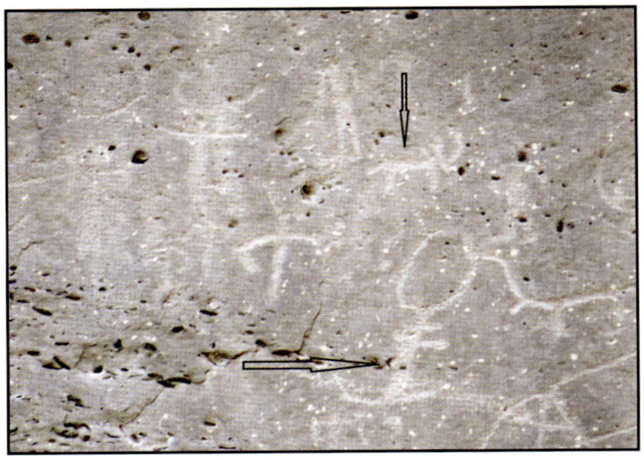

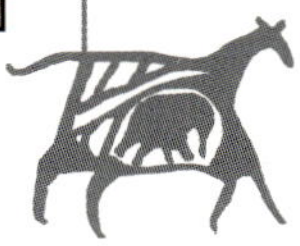

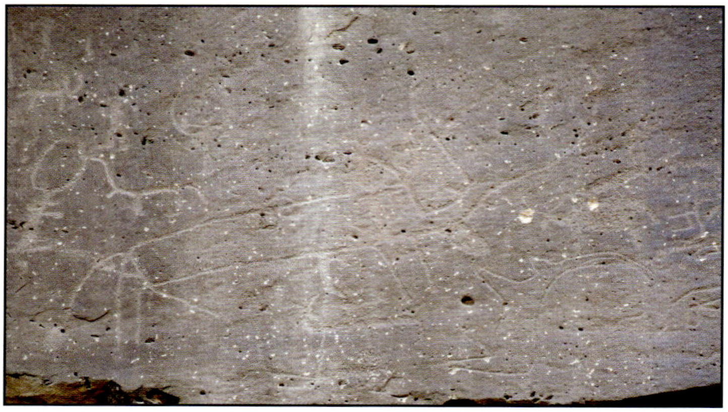 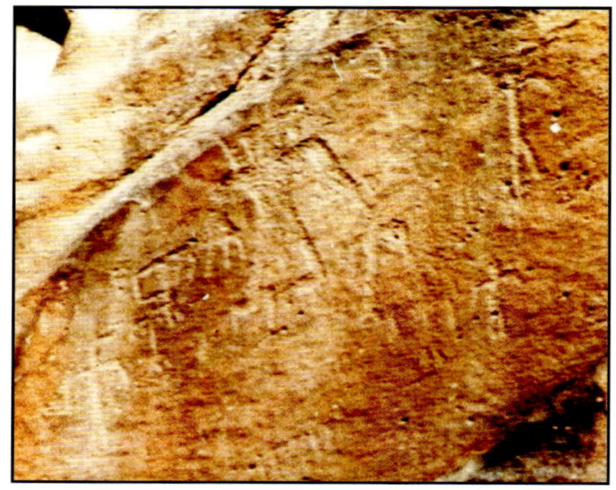

Left: **Fig. 15.9** Bull and ibex images on southern panel at Chitan Wari Bhar.

Right: **Fig. 15.10** Masked figure, possibly the head of a hunting band or guardian deity of Seeta Valley.

non-existent legs, which appear to be attached with the body of the bull. The horns, on the other hand, are large and in a crescent shape. Below the image of the bull and on the left side of the human figures with raised hands is the image of a woman who is shown giving birth to a child (Fig. 15.7). This is a very interesting petroglyph of a birth scene.

There are several other bull images that are drawn small as compared to the single large one. One bull image is drawn in a vertical position as if it is falling down. Close to this image is the line drawing of another bull. There are several other human figures between these bull images like an archer, a male figure which is shown in movement, etc. All the male figures are shown very tall. All the bulls in this panel appear as though they were not domesticated at the time when the artist drew these images (Fig. 15.8). Likewise, the southern side of the panel also depicts images of other animals, cattle and humans. The large bull image almost covers the whole of the southern side of the panel. The bull is shown with a large body and prominent large genitals. Before the petrogylph of the bull are images of ibex, a male figure and a bull. The ibex are drawn with large prominent sexual organs (Fig. 15.9).

South to this large panel, there are three other panels. The first panel depicts two images of ibex and a human. The second panel depicts images of an ibex and a snake. The third panel depicts the most interesting petrogylph of a masked deity or tribal chief or head of a hunting band (Fig. 15.10). Or, it is likely that this was the guardian deity of the valley, as it was very dangerous and difficult for travellers to cross Seeta Dath and Chitan Wari Bhar without encountering dragons and snakes. This deity who is drawn at a height of 30 feet from the ground level is visible from a distance. It is likely that it protected the devotees from the poisonous snakes and harmful dragons of Seeta Valley. It is very difficult to interpret the actual meaning of this image.

3. Kari Laki

At a distance of a few hundred kilometers from Chitan Wari Bhar is located the rock art site of Kari Laki. The word Kari Laki means black pass. It was the abode of ancient artists who drew figures on a height of 30 feet from the ground level. This is a sandstone ridge with black and brown patinas. There are four panels on Kari Laki. Three panels face north while the fourth faces west.

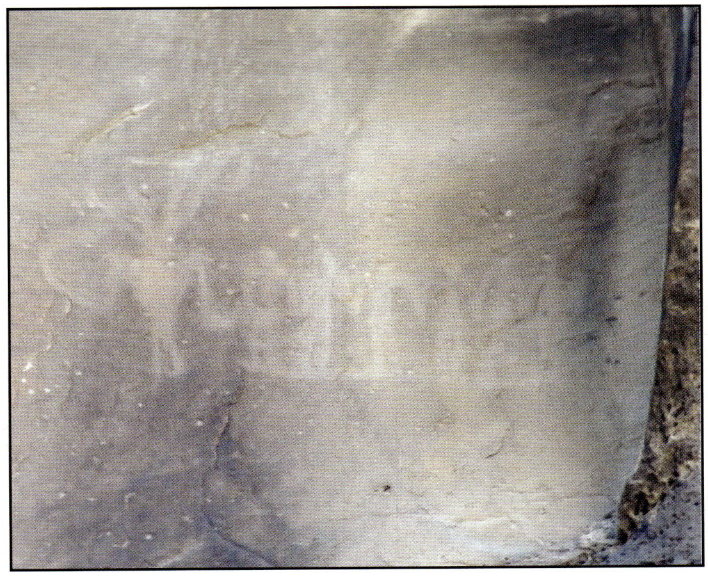

Fig. 15.11 Masked figure with dancers at Kari Laki.

The first panel that faces north has the most amazing petroglyph, which represents a dancing scene. Six dancers are shown hand in hand before a masked figure. The masked figure appears to be the deity of the dancers (Figs. 15.11 & 15.11a). One finds a ritual scene with seven females on Indus seals too (Dale 1991: 141). But, in the petroglyphs of Kari Laki, the artist only drew six dancers before the masked figure. It is likely that this is the same legend that one finds on Indus seals. The petrogylph of the masked figure is interesting. The body of the figure is triangular shaped and even the mask that the figure is wearing is triangular with two lines possibly representing horns rising from the left and right of the mask. One also finds masks in the petroglyphs of Seeta but masked figures are very rare in the rock art of Sindh. There are only three specimens in the rock art of Seeta Valley where one finds masked figures. The figure which is drawn at Chitan wari Bhar is also shown wearing a mask. However, the mask of the figure that is drawn at Kari Laki is more complex and interesting. Another interesting feature of the masked figure is an object that it is holding in its right hand, possibly a magical wand. All the dancers are shown standing on the base. One can figure out from the buns of the dancers that they are females.

The second panel which faces north depicts another interesting petroglyph. It shows a wild bull, which is shown hitting a female. It is

Fig. 15.11a Drawing of a masked figure with dancers at Kari Laki (drawing by Badar Abro).

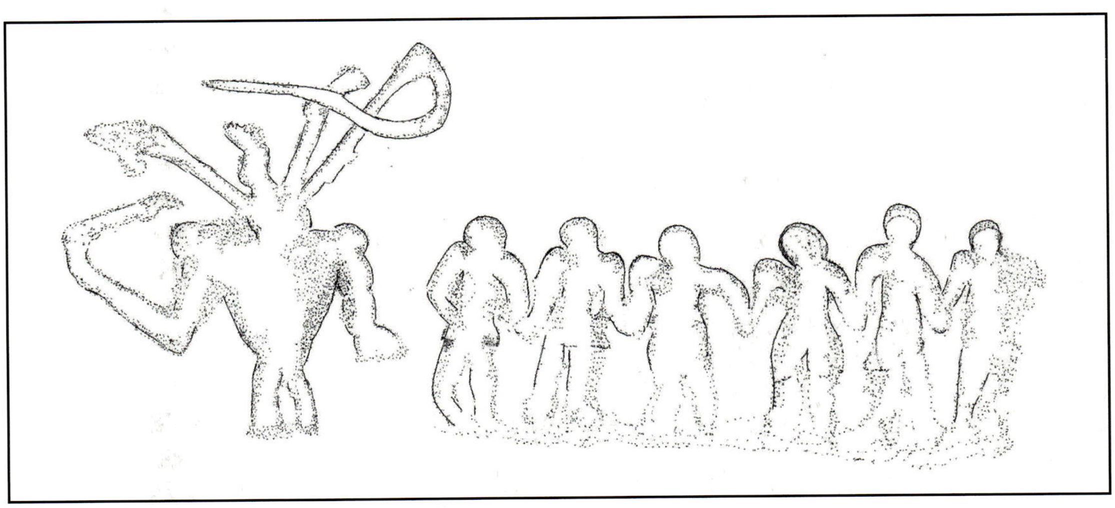

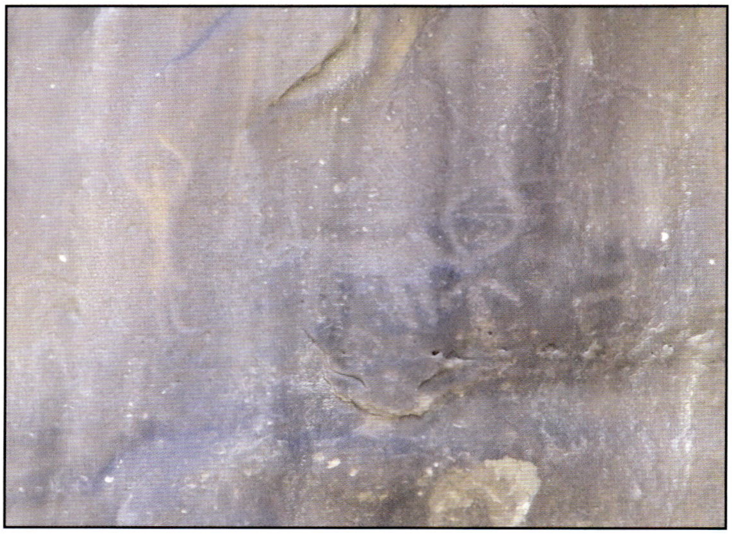

Fig. 15.12 Wild bull hitting the women at Kari Laki.

interesting to note that the bull is also shown hitting and dragging a female. A man behind the wild bull is depicted crying with his hands raised indicating that he is stunned by a sudden attack of the bull on the female (Figs. 15.12 & 15.12a). This shows that the bull was not domesticated at that time. Above the depiction of the bull and the female, there is a petroglyph of a mask which appears to be of an earlier time than the wild bull and the female. There are several other petroglyphs but all these are very faint and it is difficult to identity them.

Close to these engravings are two other panels, both of which face north and depict images of ibexs. The ibex are shown with joined legs. They are also shown with small heads, large horns and prominent genitals. All these petroglyphs are peckings.

Apart from the four panels facing north, there is one large panel facing west. This panel only depicts zoomorphs. Ibex are in a majority. All of them are shown with large horns and prominent sexual organs. There is also a depiction of a wild bull in the same panel (Fig. 15.13). The horns of the bull are shown forward as if it was going to hit something. There is also a petroglyph of a camel. Two jackals are also shown in a separate panel close to the large one.

Besides the petroglyphs on the Kari Laki cliff, there are several other engravings on the large flat rock surface on the left side of the Seeta riverbank. One finds only images of camel-riders and travellers. The travellers are shown on camels. Interestingly, the artists have

Fig. 15.12a Drawing of wild bull hitting the woman while the man behind is stunned by the sudden attack.

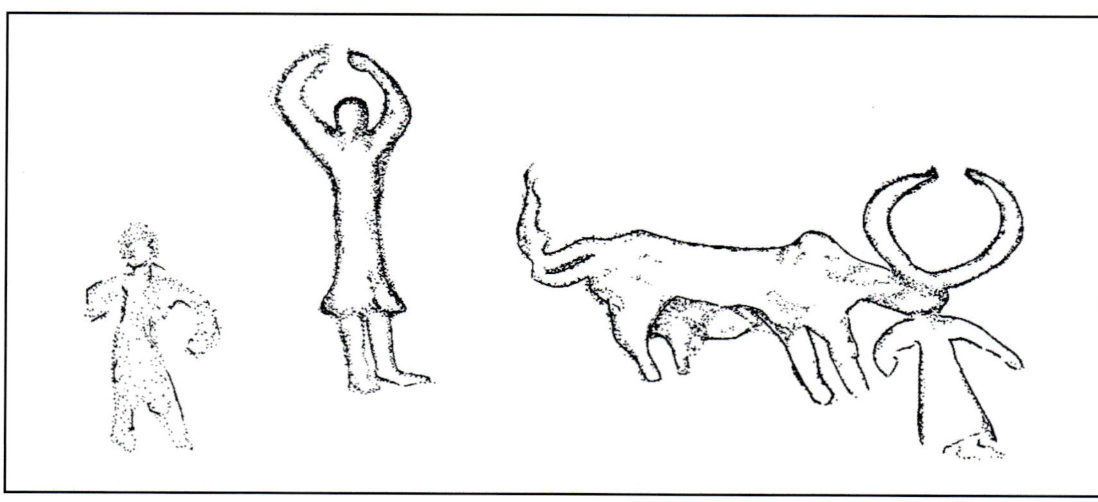

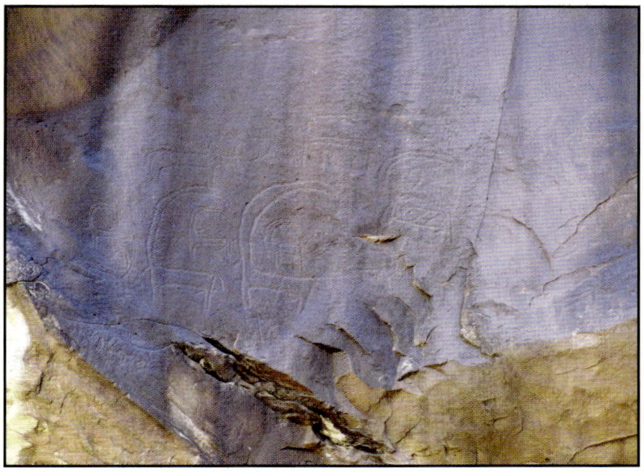

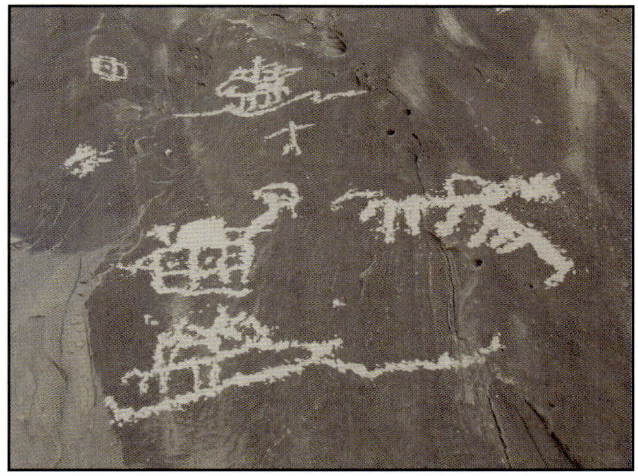

Left: **Fig. 15.13** Panel showing the ibex and a wild bull at Kari Laki.

Right: **Fig. 15.14** Camels are shown travelling on the routes or paths.

also drawn a path or road on which these camels are shown travelling (Fig. 15.14). The horizontal lines underneath the camels represent the path. It is likely that these may be royal caravans. The figures seated on the camels appear to be royals, as one finds some headgear representing crowns. Apart from these royal caravans, there is a depiction of a male with outstretched arms. It appears to be either a demon or a shaman (Fig. 15.15). Ibex images also appear on the same rock surface.

There is an interesting petroglyph of a female who is shown being kidnapped by a camel-rider. The man is shown holding the arm of the woman very tightly and the woman appears to be struggling to set herself free. Below this engraving is a petroglyph of a camel, which is depicted with persons holding its bridle. The first person appears to be a male while the second is a female. They are trying to pacify the camel that appears to be wild.

4. Shaho Kumb

This rock art site lies 500 m from Kari Laki. There are only two petroglyphs on the cliff facing south. The cliff is located on the left

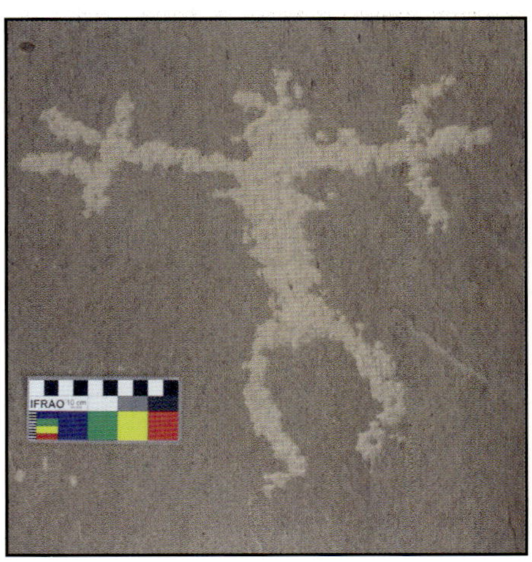

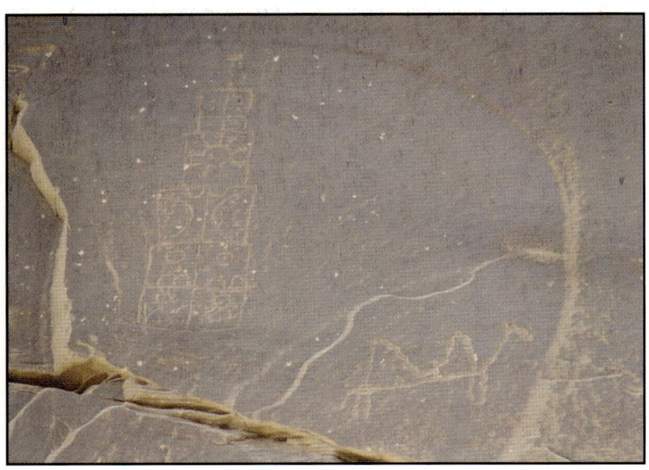

Left: **Fig. 15.15** The petroglyph of a shaman or demon at Kari laki.

Right: **Fig. 15.16** Petroglyphs of stupa and Bactrian camel at Shaho Kumb.

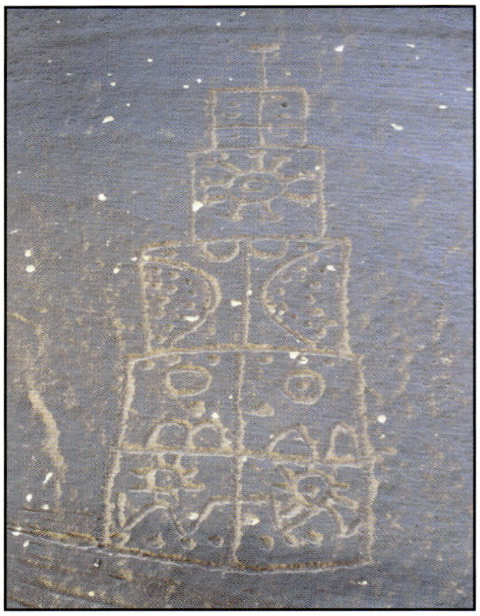 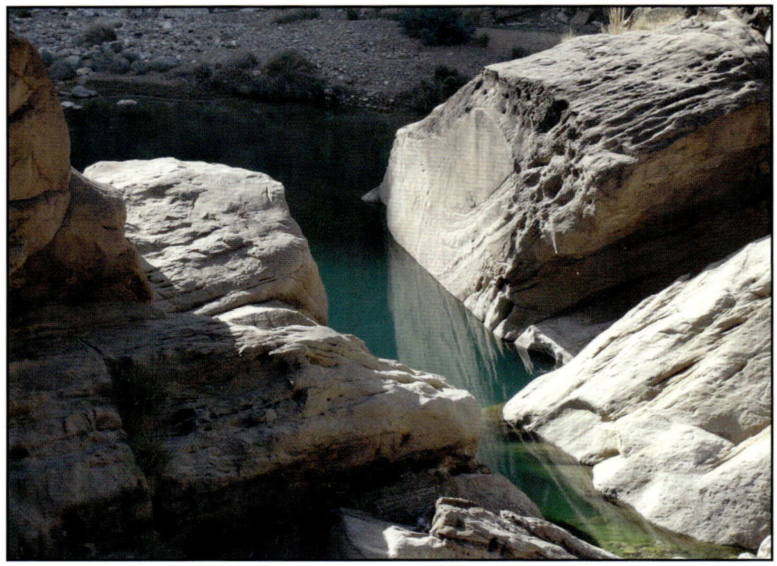

Left: **Fig. 15.17** Stupa image at Shaho Kumb.

Right: **Fig. 15.18** View of Hayar Kumb.

bank of the river. There is only one panel depicting a Bactrian camel and stupa (Fig. 15.16). This is the only petroglyph of a Bactrian camel found in Seeta Valley. However, images of humped camels are numerous in other rock art sites in the Khirthar range. The representations of Bactrian camel are only found in the rock art sites of Mazarani, Khurbi and Gaj valleys.

The stupa image is also very interesting. It is drawn as a multi-storeyed building with six terraces (Fig. 15.17). It is likely that the decoration on the stupa represents decorative and moulded bricks that were used in the stupa built in different part of Sindh (Cousins 1998). The lower storey depicts sun motifs and likewise the last or the seventh storey also depicts a large sun motif. The stupa images found in Seeta Valley have their own distinctive style. This distinctive feature is the decorations found on every storey of the structure. Stupa images found in other valleys lack detailed decorations as seen on the stupas in Seeta Valley. Two stupa images at Seeta Dath also fall in this category of decorated stupas.

5. Hayar Kumb

This rock art site is located 400 m from Shaho Kumb. There are a few petroglyphs on the flat rock surface which lies on the left bank of Seeta Nai. Here, a large amount of water accumulates at the Hayar, which is locally called kumb. It is a very deep kumb and is located in the middle of the riverbed, making it impossible for anyone to cross. Rather, people cross Hayar Laki (pass) to reach the other side of the river (Fig. 15.18). As one ascends the Laki, there is large flat rock surface where there are petroglyphs. At Hayar Kumb, there are eight petroglyphs. The more interesting depiction is that of man who is shown combating a leopard (Fig. 15.19). He is shown holding a sword in one hand and a shield in the other. The leopard appears to be ready for attack. Even the man is ready

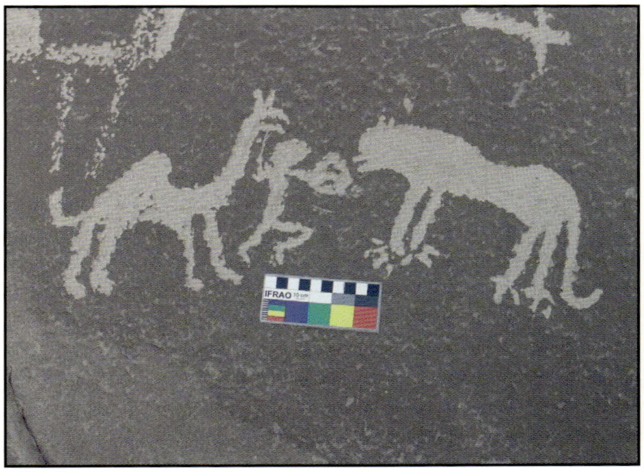

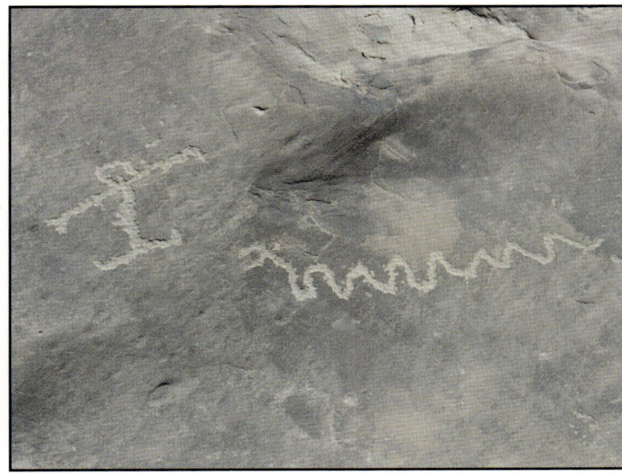

Left: **Fig. 15.19** The petroglyphs of a man and predator combat at Hayar Kumb.

Right: **Fig. 15.20** Snake and man motif at Hayar Kumb.

to face the predator with of one his knees placed down in the position of a fight. This petroglyph is made by the scratching technique. Close to these petroglyphs are engravings of snakes; there is a group of three snakes engraved on the rock. Frequent images of snakes at almost every rock art site show that Seeta had a number of snakes in the valley.

A little further to the east of these petroglyphs of snakes is the depiction of a man who appears to be surprised by the sudden appearance of a snake (Fig. 15.20). The snake is shown as if about to attack the man who appears to be saving his life from the fast approaching snake. There are two such depictions of a snake attacking a man in Seeta Valley—one at the rock art site in Seeta Dath and the other at Hayar kumb.

6. Beelo Kumb

As one goes up, the valley becomes narrow. However, at Beelo kumb it becomes wide again (Fig. 15.21). There are a few rock shelters at Beelo kumb, which serve as a refuge for travellers and shepherds from the scorching sun in the hot summer. There are two rock shelters which are covered with petroglyphs here. One of the rock shelters faces east while the other faces west. The eastern rock shelter depicts interesting petroglyphs. One finds animal images and fighting scenes, not to mention dancing scenes here. Buddhist stupa images are also found on the rock shelter. Before the stupa image, there is a group of dancers (Fig. 15.22). These dancers are shown dancing possibly before a deity or a tribal chief. The deity is shown wearing an interesting mask. The masked figure is standing before the two groups of dancers. There are three dancers with their hands linked together and all the dancers appear to be in movement (Fig. 15.23). On the right of the masked deity are two dancers—one female and one male. But they are shown facing the rider and archer and not the masked deity (Fig. 15.23a). This may represent the community ritual dance possibly performed for a hunt or for other purposes. Before this dancing scene are carvings of a trident (*trisul*) or possibly a trident-shaped symbol and stupa. This dancing scene is linked with the religious symbols of a stupa and *trishul*. However,

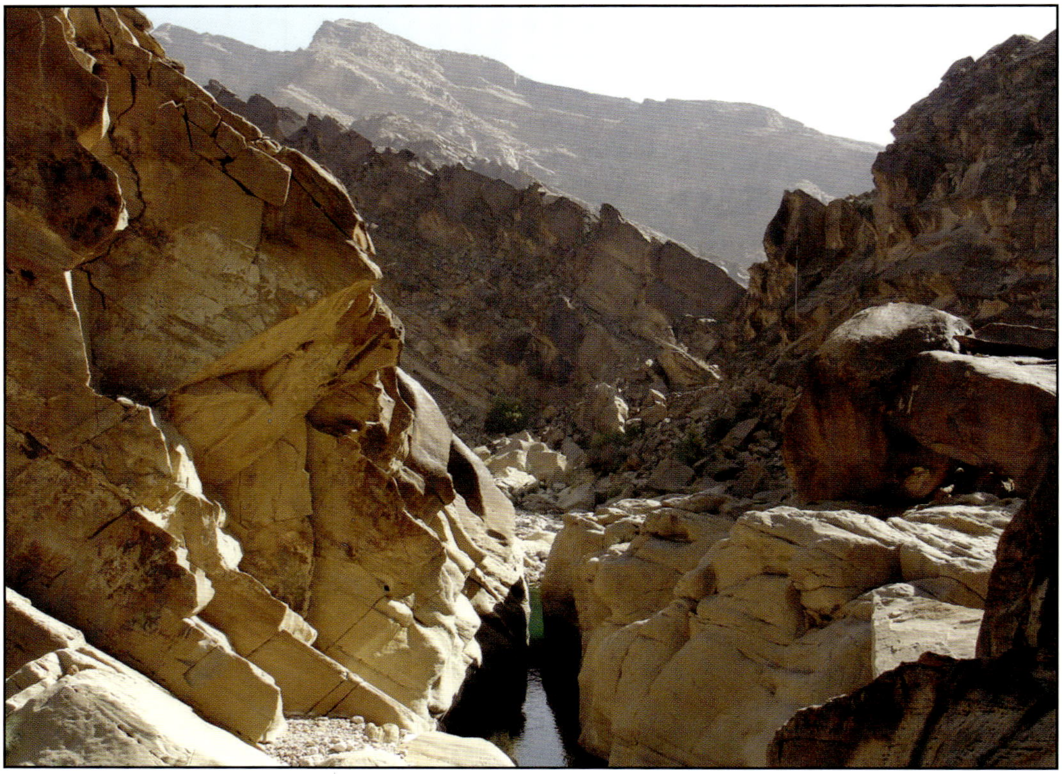

Fig. 15.21 General view of rock shelter at Beelo kumb.

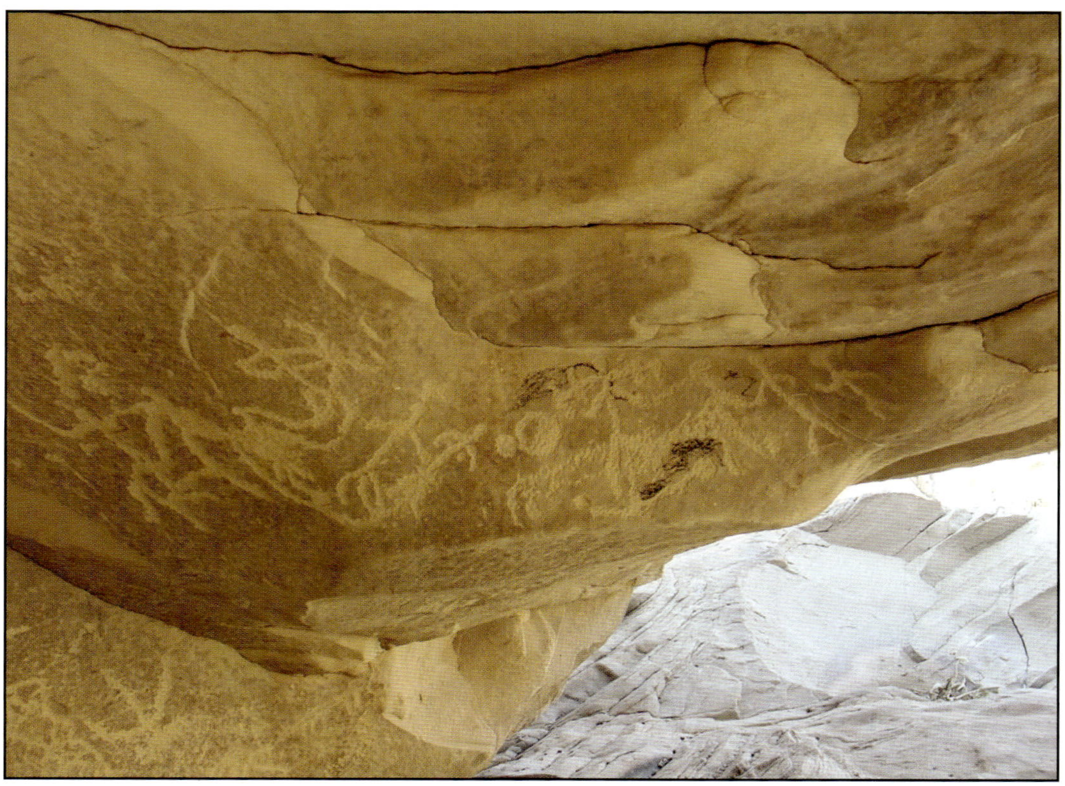

Fig. 15.22 The petroglyphs of masked figure and dancers in the rock shelter at Beelo kumb.

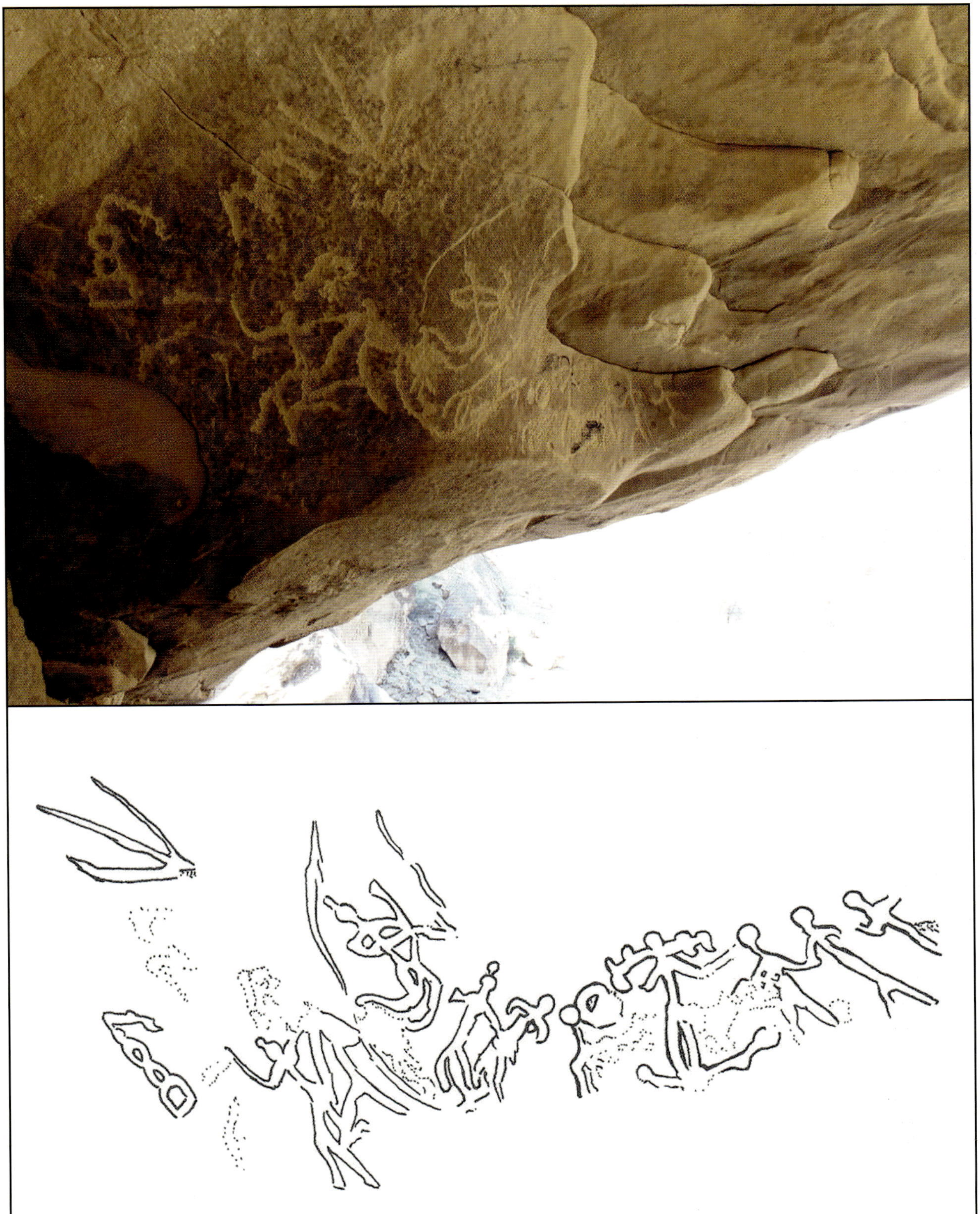

Fig. 15.23 Masked figure with dancers. A stupa and trident can also be seen in the photo.

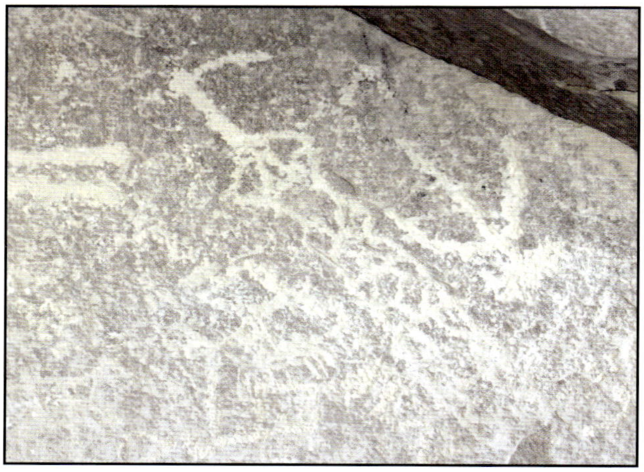

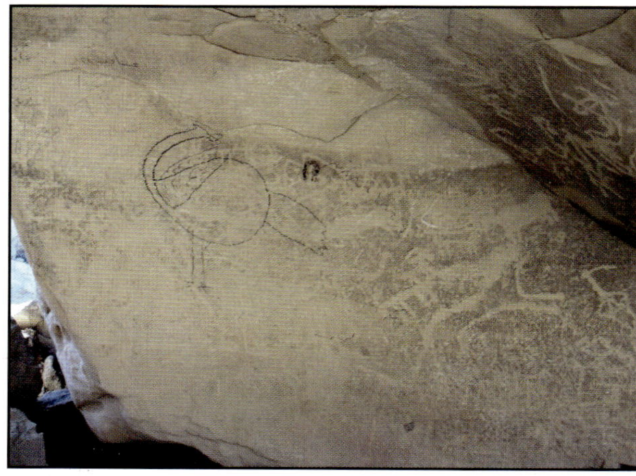

Left: **Fig. 15.24** A Stupa and trident sign in the rock shelter at Beelo kumb.

Right: **Fig. 15.25** Superimposition and juxtaposition of the petroglyphs. However, two cows can be seen in the panel.

it is more probable that these dancers are Buddhists performing a ritual dance. The petroglyph of a warrior with a sword suggests that the entry of a new faith in the valley and those dancers might have sought divine help in the form of a ritual dance to protect their faith. One can argue that before the Arab conquest of Sindh, Buddhists and Hindus were the two main religious groups not to mention the Zoroastrians. It is more probable that the warrior might be an Arab Muslim who conquered the Budhia, the land of the Buddhists, and the Hindus were also subjugated by the followers of a new faith. As is apparent from the panel, the two religious symbols associated with Buddhism and Hinduism are shown behind the warrior indicating probably that he has conquered the land of the powerful religious groups who ruled in pre-Islamic Sindh.

The most interesting feature of the dancing scene is the mask. We need to carefully study the artefacts, especially the masks of pre-Islamic Sindh, to reach any conclusion. But, unfortunately, we do not have any masks of pre-Islamic Sindh to compare the one depicted in the rock art of Beelo Kumb with. Although, we have masks—some also from the Indus period—but they differ from those of Seeta Valley. All the masked figures depicted in the rock art sites of Chitan wari Bhar, Kari Laki and Beelo kumb are different in form from those discovered from Mohenjo-Daro and Harappa. The masks found in Mohenjo-Daro and Harappa are all round or oval-shaped while those of Seeta Valley are rectangular, square and triangular. However, there are two petroglyphs of round masks at Kari Laki and Beelo kumb. The stupa near the masked figure is a three-storey building with a streamer. It is a very image of a small stupa. Close to this stupa is another stupa, which is tower like. It is quite tall with five terraces or storeys and is surmounted with an *anda*. The dome of the stupa is surmounted with a finial (Fig. 15.24). On the right side of the stupa image is a petroglyph of the trident-shaped sign. On the left side of the stupa image are several images of animals and cattle.

There is superimposition and juxtaposition of images on the panel, thus making it difficult to identify the images (Fig. 15.25). There are only two images clearly identifiable, which are of cows and can be clearly identified. These drawing are made by the abrading technique. Apart from the images of cows, there is an image of an ibex that is being

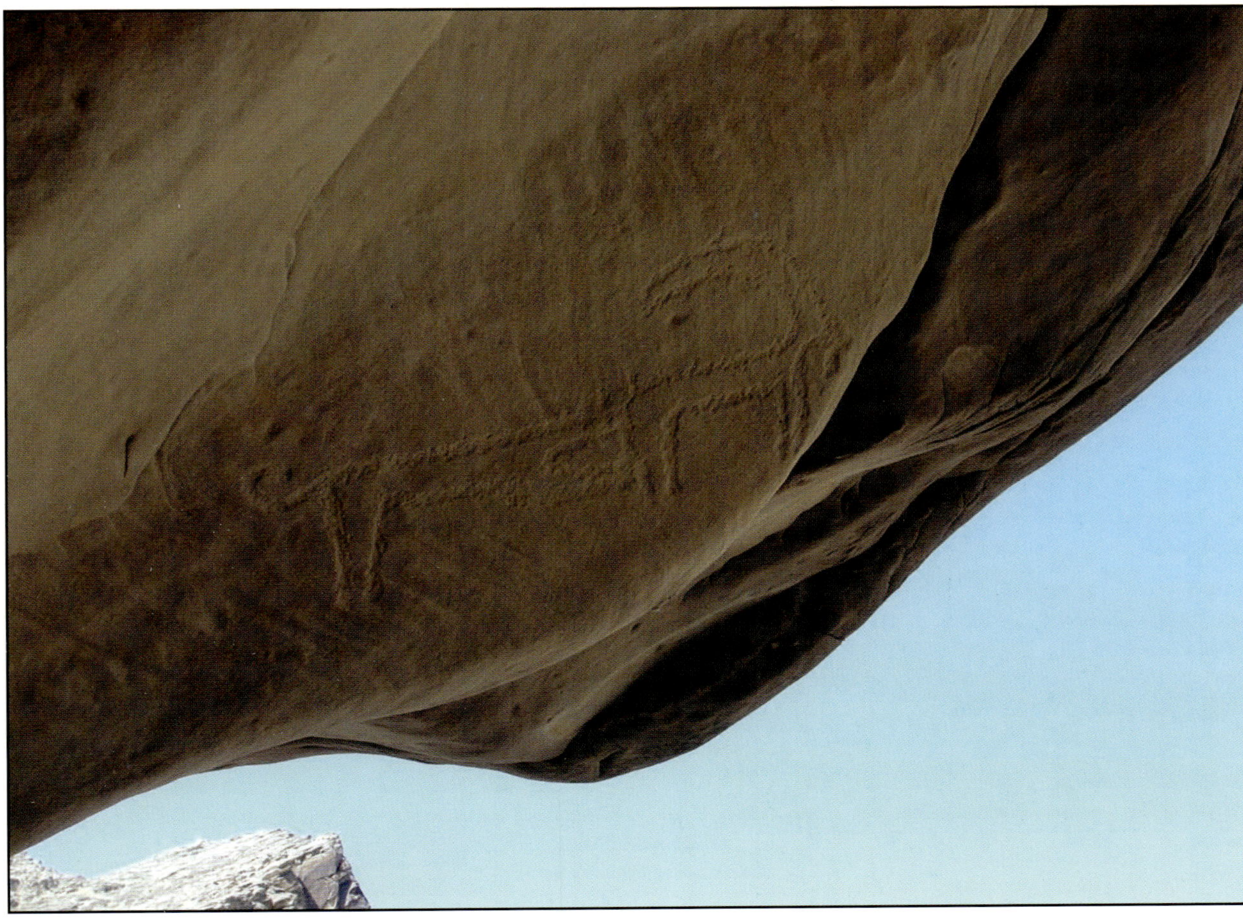

Fig. 15.26 Petroglyph of a predator attacking ibex at Beelo kumb.

attacked from behind by a predator. The predator is shown overcoming the ibex from its hind side. The hind side of the ibex is shown in the mouth of a predator, possibly a leopard (Fig. 15.26).

The outer walls of the rock shelter are full of names from the modern period. Travellers and literate shepherds have left their imprints in the form of their names. On the north of the main rock shelter is another small rock shelter, which depicts three anthropomorphs (Fig. 15.27). These are really interesting figures. One of the figures is shown with outstretched arms with the hands moved down. Another figure is shown in a similar style but with its hands almost touching the feet. The third figure is also shown in the same style with its hands down. All these figures are possibly of magicians who are shown performing some magic. All the three figures are shown in a row. The author believes that they are probably shown performing some act of magic.

He would like to mention two signs here; one is on the exterior wall of the main rock shelter and the other is in the interiors of a small rock shelter at Beelo kumb. The first sign appears to be a mask, which is round in shape with an ear on the left (Fig. 15.28). This mask is different in shape from the one drawn on Kari Laki, which is oval and the earliest representation of masks in the Seeta Valley (Fig. 15.29).

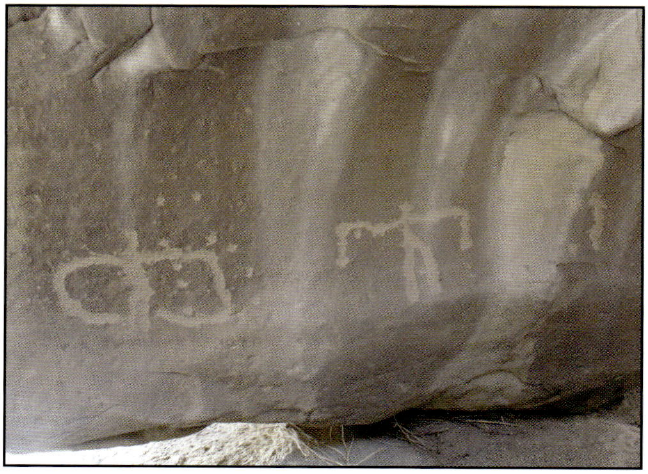 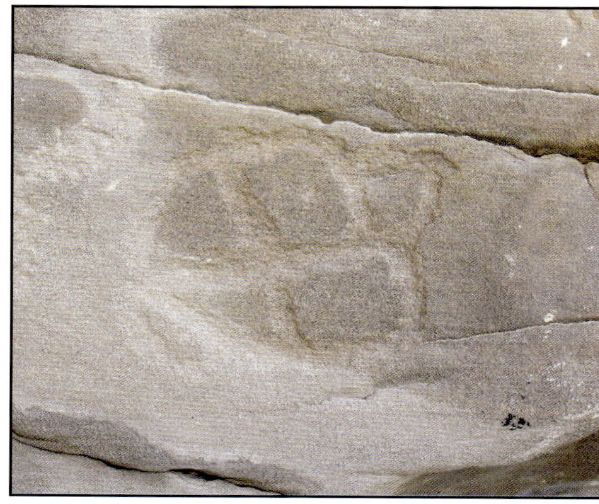

Left: **Fig. 15.27** Anthropomorphic figures in rock shelter at Beelo kumb.

Right: **Fig. 15.28** Petroglyphs of mask or geometric sign at Beelo kumb.

The other sign is very complex and difficult to interpret (Fig. 15.30). It looks as if an anthropomorph is shown with a wheel. Therefore, the author calls it an anthropomorph with wheel. It is a complex sign to interpret.

Finally, the author would like to discuss the few animal images and anthropomorphs on the cliff which faces north. There are three ibex images and a leopard; all the figures are shown with legs joined (Fig. 15.31). Below these petroglyphs is the image of a man who is shown being bitten by a snake. The snake has jumped to bite the hand of the anthropomorph. This is the most ancient petroglyph if one compares it with two other similar snake-and-man motifs in Seeta Valley.

There is a legend of Beelo and Hayar associated with these two rock art sites. Beelo and Hayar, after whom both kumbs are named, were two women who jumped in the kumbs to save their honour (*izzat*) after their men suffered defeat at the hands of Amir Zunun Beg of Qandhar. Amir Zunun Beg frequently invaded the western part of Sindh during the reign of the last Samma ruler Firoz Shah (*c.* 1508–1520 CE). There are no petroglyphs to support the legend of Beelo and Hayar. The author believes that the legend is from the pre-Islamic period, which was later Islamised by the present inhabitants in Seeta Valley. These two female characters symbolise their weakness and may refer to their subjugation by the people of a new faith with reference to Arab Muslims. These followers of the new faith were Arab Muslims who conquered the land of the Buddhists and Hindus. It is likely that these two female characters are linked with these two religious groups who proved very weak in resisting Arab invaders. A similar story also echoes in the Nali/Nari Valley, which lies about 150 km south of Seeta Nai where two women, Sado and Mazo, jumped into the kumb when their men lost the battle. This kumb is named after these women. This battle was fought between two Baloch tribes, the Rinds and Lasharis. But again, this is a pre-Islamic story which was Islamised by the people living in Nali and other neighbouring valleys of Khirthar. The terms Sado and Mazo refer to the arrival of a new faith in the valley, thus replacing the old faith which was followed by the Buddhists. Therefore, the new faith belongs to the Arab Muslims who conquered the land and converted some people too. The Buddhists, Hindus and Zoroastrians were among the loser group who lost their land and even religion to the Arab Muslims.

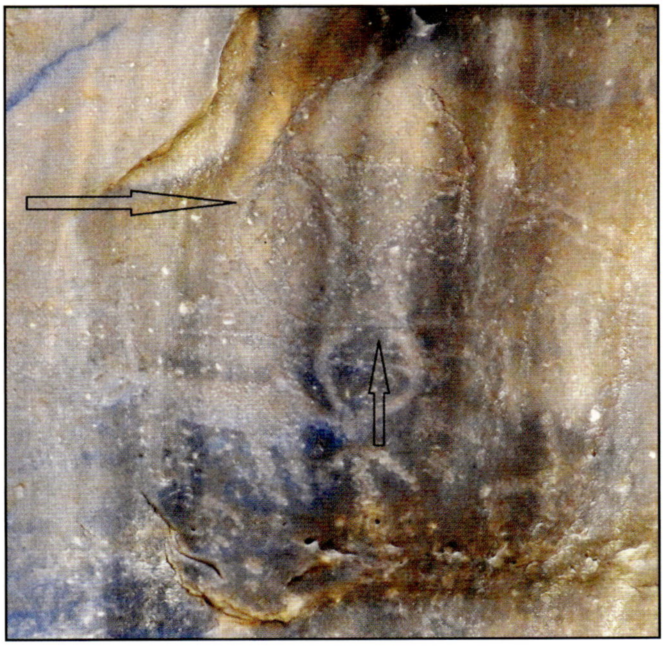

Fig. 15.29 Arrows pointed towards the representation of mask at Kari Laki.

TENTATIVE CHRONOLOGY

The rock art of Seeta Valley is difficult to date with precision. Scientific dating has not been carried out. However, the use of different tools and techniques, the variable amounts of weathering and the changes in style and iconography indicate that the images were produced over an extended period of time.

Therefore, the author propose three main periods—Mesolithic-Neolithic (10000 BCE–4000 BCE), Chalcolithic-Bronze Age and Iron Age (4000 BCE–600 BCE), and the Historic Period (500 BCE to the modern period). The Historic Period is further sub-divided into eight phases corresponding to dynastic rules of foreigners and local rulers. Therefore, the following phases correspond accordingly—Phase 1, Achaemenian, Mauryan and Bactrian Greek dynasties (519 BCE–70 BCE) Phase 2, Scytho-Parthians and Kushan dynasties (70 BCE–175 CE), Phase 3, Sassanian and Buddhist Rais dynasties (283 CE–641 CE), Phase 4, Brahman and Arab dynasties (Umayyad, Abbasid Governors and Habaris (671–1011), Phase 5, Soomra and Samma dynasties (1040 CE –1524 CE), Phase 6, Arghuns, Tarkhan and Mughal dynasties (1524–1737 CE), Phase 7, Kalhora and Talpur dynasties (1680–1843 CE), Phase 8, British period (1843–1947 CE), and Phase 9, the contemporary period.

The representations of particular animals (now domesticated) and humans (with masks and particular dresses), purported objects (bow, arrow, etc.), buildings (stupas, etc.) and practices (dancing scenes,

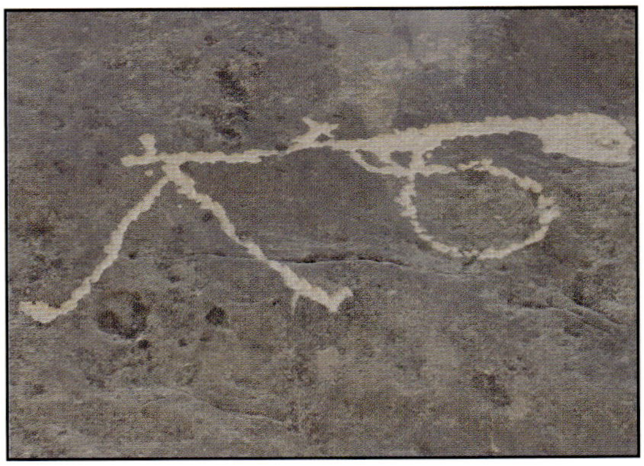

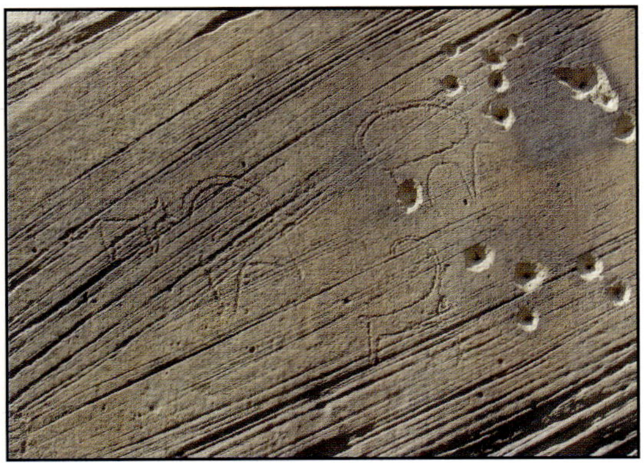

Left: **Fig. 15.30** Anthropomorph with wheel.

Right: **Fig. 15.31** Panel showing ibex and predator.

etc.) provide data to help date the petroglyphs of Seeta. On the basis of style and iconography, many petroglyphs at Chitan wari Bhar and Kari Laki can be placed in the two periods—Mesolithic-Neolithic and Chalcolithic, Bronze Age and Iron Age. All the wild cattle can be placed in the Mesolithic period where we know that the domestication of cattle occurred in the Neolithic period and we have evidence from Mehrgarh in Baluchistan for this (Meadow 1991).

Representations of masked figures at Chitan Wari Bhar and Kari Laki were drawn in the Bronze Age. Even the legend of Kari Laki is of Bronze Age. The depiction of snakes and man was possibly done during the Bronze and Iron ages. The one at Beelo kumb was drawn during the Bronze Age while those of Seeta Dath and Hayar kumb were made in the Iron Age. The representation of Bactrian camel appears to have been done during the dynastic rule of the Achaemenians or the Syctho-Parthians. The dancing scene at the Beelo kumb was done during Phase 3 of the dynastic rule of Sassanian, Buddhist. Even the stupa images were drawn during this phase. The dancing scene at the Seeta Dath was done in Phase 5 during the Arghun, Tarkhan and Mughal dynasties. Representations of ibex, camels and horses appear to have been drawn in Phases 4 and 5 during the Soomra, Samma and Arghun, Tarkhan and Mughal dynasties. Several of them were also made in Phase 6 during the Kalhora and Talpur dynasties. Some fighting scenes appear to have been drawn during the dynastic rules of Kalhoras and Talpurs. All the names of individuals and some of the drawings of camels and ibex were made in Phase 8 or in contemporary times. This means that the tradition of rock art still continues in Seeta Valley.

CONCLUSION

The petroglyphs of Seeta Valley can be placed in three periods and further sub-divided into eight phases. Only the petroglyphs found in the main Seeta Valley were studied and those found in the subsidiary valleys were not part of this study. The remains of several gabarbands in the valleys provide valuable information about those who drew the petroglyphs on the cliffs and boulders in the valleys. Archaeological remains and artefacts found from those sites in the Khirthar piedmont also provide valuable information about the designs and motifs with some similarities with those depicted on the cliffs, boulders and rock shelters of Seeta Valley.

Representations of wild cattle are numerous in the rock art sites of Chitan Wari Bhar, Kari Laki and Beelo kumb, which suggest that cattle were not domesticated at that time. The domestication of cattle occurred in the 7th millennium BCE in the Mehrgarh. Later, when the cattle were domesticated, one finds several depictions of cattle on the pottery from Mehrgarh, early Indus and mature Indus period sites. Representations of masked figures are also very interesting. The legends associated with them are probably of the Indus period. One of the dancing scenes with seven dancers resembles those found on Indus seals.

The theme of dance is frequently found in various rock art sites of Seeta Valley. The snake and man motif is also peculiar to this valley, which is found in the rock art sites of Seeta Dath, Hayar kumb and Beelo kumb.

REFERENCES

Abro, Badar (2007), 'Petroglyphs in Khirthar', in Karim Khawaja (ed.), *Mountains of Sindh*. Karachi: Peoples Doctors' Forum.

Ansari, Ishtiaq (2011), *Gorakh: The Beautiful Resort of Sindh* (trans. Noor Ahmed Janjhi). Hyderabad: Kavita Publications.

Cousins, Henry (1998), *The Antiquities of Sindh*. Karachi: Sindh Culture and Tourism Department.

Dales, George F. (1991), 'The Phenomena of Indus Civilisations', in Michael Jansen, Maire Mulloy and Gunter Urban (eds.), *Forgotten Cities on Indus: Early Civilisation in Pakistan from 8th to the 2nd Millennium BC*. Mainz: PHVZ.

Deva, Krishna and McCown (1949), Further Explorations in Sindh: 1938. *Ancient India*. 5: 4-3.

Lambrick, H.T. (1986), *Sindh: A General Introduction*, (3rd edition). Jamshoro: Sindhi Adabi Board.

Kalhoro, Zulfiqar Ali (2009), 'Rock Carvings and Inscriptions of Sado Mazo in Johi, Dadu (Sindh, Pakistan)', *Journal of Asian Civilisations* 32(2): 94-125.

—— (2011), 'Rock Carvings of Shakloi Dhoro (Nai Gaj, Sindh)', in *Proceedings of the International Workshop on Gandharan Cultural Heritage*, 1-3 December 2010, Islamabad: Taxila Institute of Asian Civilsations, pp. 305-29.

—— (2011). 'Initial Report of the Archaeological Survey of the Sallari Valley, Khirthar, Sindh', *Journal of Pakistan Historical Society* LIX (3): 79-96.

Majumdar, N.G. (1934), *Exploration in Sindh: Memoirs of Archaeological Survey of India*. Kolkata, No. 48.

Meadow, Richard H. (1991), 'The Domestication and Exploitation of Plants and Animals in the Greater Indus Valley, 7th-2nd Millennium BC', in Michael Jansen, Maire Mulloy and Gunter Urban (eds.), *Forgotten Cities on Indus: Early Civilization in Pakistan from 8th to the 2nd Millennium BC*. Mainz: PHVZ.

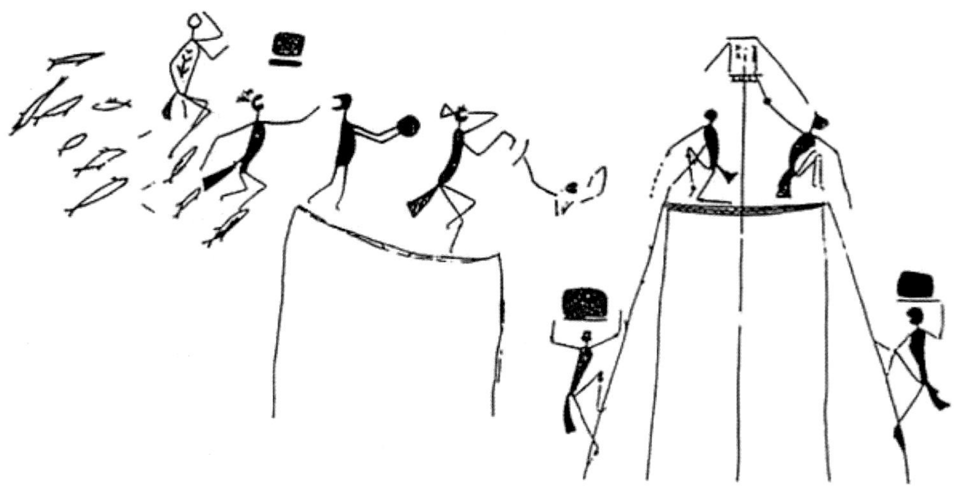

16

Decorated Rock Shelters of Gawilgad Hills, District Betul, Madhya Pradesh

Nandini Bhattacharya-Sahu and Prabash Sahu

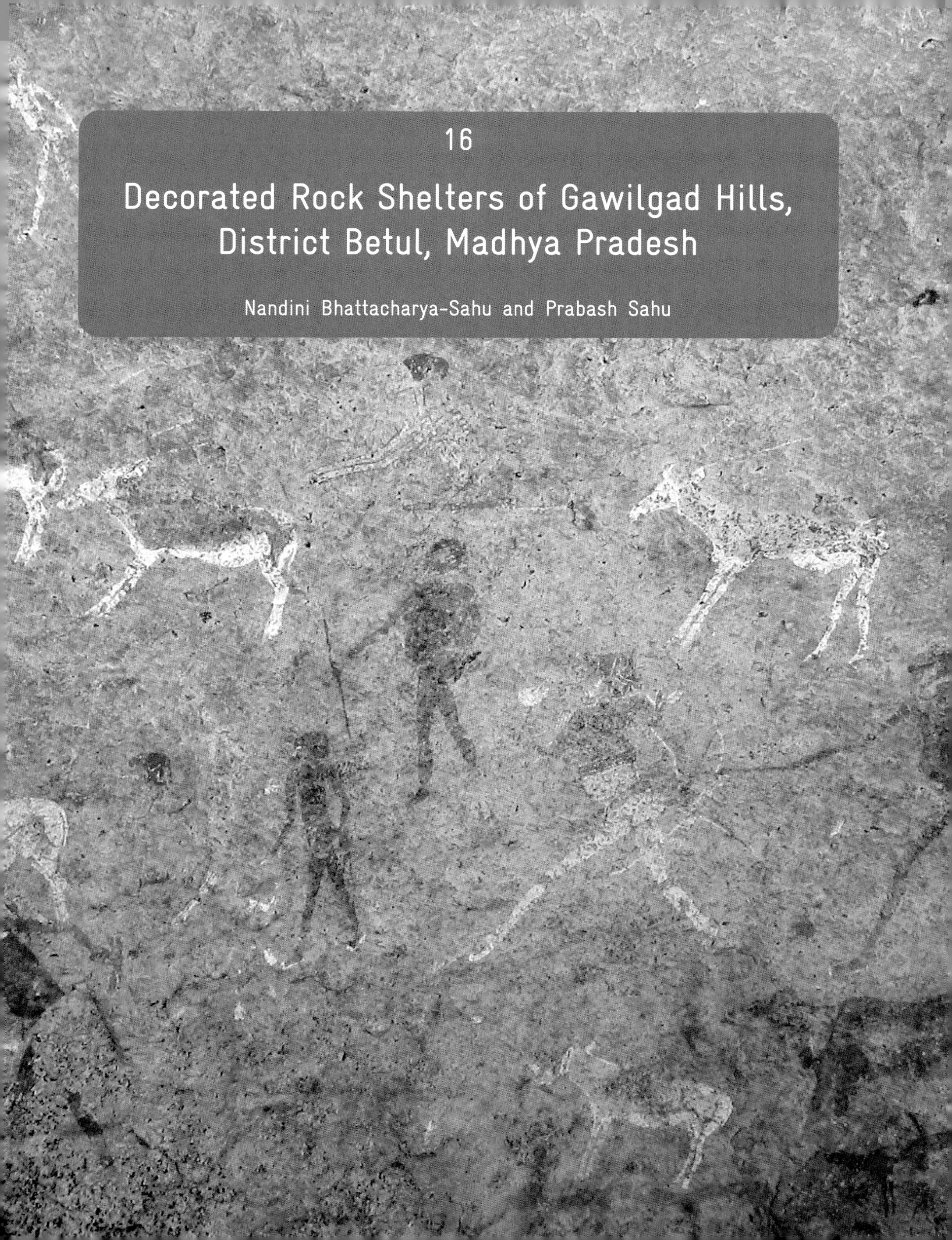

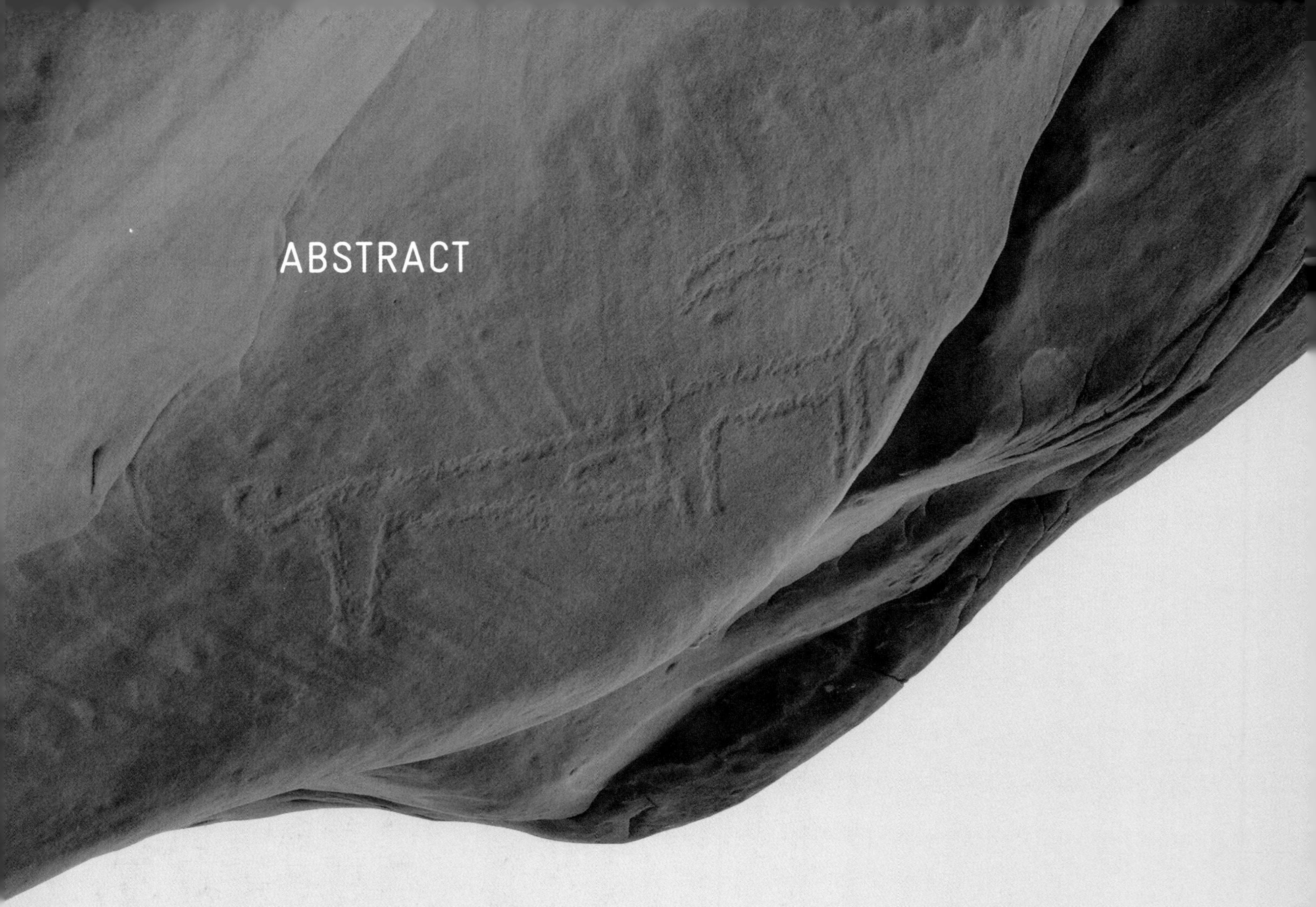

ABSTRACT

The Prehistory and Excavation Branch-I of the Archaeological Survey of India, Nagpur, recently carried out explorations in the Atner tehsil of Betul district, Madhya Pradesh and reported 18 decorated rock shelters in the ortho-quartzite formations of the Gavilgarh Hills, a member in the Satpura range. These shelters contain pictographs and petroglyphs on their walls and ceilings. Seven groups of rock shelters, in different localities over the sprawling hills and cliffs, have been identified. All the shelters contain a rich variety of pictographs, sometimes superimposed on the engravings, mostly in burnt sienna in red hue and seldom in white. Though the paintings mostly depict natural motifs, especially the faunal world like boar, nilgai (Boselaphus tragocamelus, an antelope found in the Indian subcontinent), deer, sambar (a type of deer), spotted deer, bull, monkey, rabbit, monitor lizard, tortoise, fish, vultures and stick-shaped human figurines are also present. The paintings also depict some geometrical designs like festoons and honeycombs.

With the discovery of painted rock shelters by Archibald Carlleyle, First Assistant in the Archaeological Office from Sohagi Ghat in the Mirzapur district of Uttar Pradesh (then United Provinces), and petroglyphs from Almora, Uttarakhand, in the first half of the 19th century, a new era of archaeological research began in India. Soon, eminent European and Indian researchers like Vincent A. Smith, John Cockburn, Percy Brown and Manoranjan Ghosh reported many new rock art sites all over the subcontinent, especially in India (Chakravarty and Bednarik 1997). The year 1957 marked the discovery of the Bhimbetka group of rock shelters—the most commended attribute in the diorama of Indian rock art studies, by V.S. Wakankar (1975) and his team in the Raisen district of Madhya Pradesh. Since then, these shelters, now nearly 800 in number, have been steadily discovered and studied by an array of scholars. These bear paintings from the upper Palaeolithic to the Medieval times and engravings from the lower Palaeolithic to the Mesolithic periods. The assiduous efforts of researchers and scholars, both of Indian and foreign origin, like M. Ghosh (1932), S. Tiwari (1975), K.K. Chakravarty (1984), A. Sundara (1984), Yashodhar Mathpal (1984), S.K. Pandey (1993), Rakesh Tiwari (1990), Giriraj Kumar (1996), Erwin Neumayer (1983), R.G. Bednarik (1993) and Michel Lorblanchet (1993), to name a few, have brought to light more than 5,000 rock art sites in the entire subcontinent.

Steadily, over the last 50 years and more, the discipline of rock art studies has gained good momentum with more number of rock art sites being studied and interpretations being derived from varied perspectives. The domain of rock art sites in India has grown manifold over these years. Notwithstanding the diverse geological structuring of a vast landmass, rock art in various forms has been reported stretching across from Kerala in the south to Ladakh and Zanskar Valley in the north and from Gujarat in the west to Odisha in the east and Assam, Manipur in the north-east. However, their assembly mainly in the Vindhyas and Kaimurs of Madhya Pradesh and Uttar Pradesh in the central region, bespeaks the affinity of the artists with sandstone. These shelters were formed when horizontally laid sandy sediments, under due pressure and atmospheric conditions, metamorphosed into tough ortho-quartzite (Neumayer 1983: 6). These rock shelves were, in due course, exposed and disturbed by various agencies like tectonic upheavals and weathered by weathering agents to form themselves into huge rock structures, cliffs, rock shelters and caves. The prehistoric artist found a readymade canvas to execute his artistic thoughts in various forms on the walls and ceilings of these shelters, most commonly using iron oxide or geru nodules. The later chemical reaction between the pigment and the quartzite walls of the shelters ascertained the near permanent visibility of his art. Thus, the pictures remained visible even after the pigments eroded.

This paper aims to discuss a relatively unknown patch bearing beautifully decorated rock shelters in the Gawilga hills of the Satpura Range in Central India. At the outset, it is also submitted that an attempt to determine the chronology of rock art in the study area has been made purely based on stylistic comparisons with other rock art sites in Central India.

The research is primarily based on the works of Neumayer, Wakankar and Giriraj Kumar. The claims have their bases in the lithic assemblages found either from the floors of the rock shelters or from their vicinity.

The Satpura, a hill range that rises in the eastern part of Gujarat near the Arabian Sea coast, runs through the states of Maharashtra and Madhya Pradesh to the east till Chhattisgarh, dividing the valleys of the Narmada and Tapi rivers. The range parallels the Vindhya range to the north, and these two east-west ranges divide the Indian subcontinent into the Indo-Gangetic plain in northern India and the Deccan Plateau in the south. According to one belief, the name Satpura connotes *Sat Putra*, in Sanskrit, signifying the seven sons of the Vindhya range, or according to another, Satpura, meaning seven folds, perhaps, signifying the numerous parallel ridges of the range. The Gawilgad hills, a part of the Satpuras, so named from the fortress situated on one of the southern spurs, begin near the confluence of the Purna and Tapi in Madhya Pradesh and pass through the Melghat tehsil in Amravati district in Maharashtra to Betul district in Madhya Pradesh. The hills are composed of the Deccan trap except that in the south-easterly section a line of fault exposes the sedimentary beds from beneath the Deccan trap. Sandstone outcrops are thus found in good abundance in the Gawilgad hills. The oldest geological formations comprising unclassified metamorphic are exposed on the southern margins of Gondwana sandstones, forming the southern scarp of Gawilgad hills. Found in the overlying trap are veins of cryptocrystalline materials like chalcedony and agate suitable for prehistoric dwellers for their needs. The explored area is a well-preserved compact block of forest with immense floral and faunal wealth. The area borders the Melghat Tiger Reserve in Melghat tehsil in Amravati district. The important floral varieties are *teak* (*Tectona grandis*), *tiwas* (*Ougenia dalbergioides*), *shisham* (*Dalbergia latifolia*), *bija* (*Pterocarpus marsupium*), *saj* (*terminalia tomentosa*), *dhawda* (*Anogeissus latifolia*), *tendu* (*Diospyros melanoxylon*), *beheda* (*Terminalia belerica*), *amba* (*Mangifera indica*), *bor* (*Zizyphus jujube*), *palas* (*Butea frondosa*), *babul* (*Acacia Arabica*), *khair* (*Acacia catechu*) and bamboo (*Dendrocalamus strictus*). The important garden trees are lemon, orange, sweet lime and banana. The area is equally rich in fauna, both wild and domesticated ones. Important among these are black monkeys (*Semnopithecus entellus*), red monkeys (*Macacus rhesus*), wild cows (the calves let loose, and they take refuge in the forest and become wild), tigers (*Felis tigris*), leopards (*Felis pardus*), panthers (*Felis panther*), jungle cats (*Felis chaus*), hyenas (*Hyaena striata*), wild dogs, Indian sloth bears (*Ursus vel melurus ursinus*), Indian bisons or *gaur* (*Bos vel gaveus gaurus*), *sambhar* (*Rusa aristotelis*), *chital* (*Axis maculates*), barking deer (*Cervulus muntjac*), blue bulls (*Portax pictus vel boselephas tragocamelus*) and the four-horned antelopes or *chausingha*. Interesting species of birds are also found in good numbers in the area; some of the rare ones are orange fly catcher (*Ochromela nigrorufa*), tickell's blue-red breast (*Cyornis Tickellia*) and Malabar whistling thrush (*Myiophonus Horsfieldii*).

In the months of January-February 2012, the Prehistory Branch of the Archaeological Survey of India, Nagpur, under the aegis of this season's Central Advisory Board for Archaeology (CABA), approved the project of 'Explorations in the Tapti Purna Valley', meant to cover the archaeologically rich valley in the states of Maharashtra and Madhya Pradesh reached Amravati district in Maharashtra, while covering the two rivers from their confluence backwards. Taking a cue from the article by Vijay Ingole et al., the team decided to visit the four reported painted rock shelters. They were joined in their explorations by a team from the Archaeological Survey of India's Excavation Branch-I, Nagpur, comprising two members. The shelters and the hills are accessible from village Dharul, as it is situated on the state's border. A board in the village marks the border with its two sides showing the two states of Maharashtra and Madhya Pradesh. In Maharashtra, the village is in the revenue jurisdiction of tehsil Morshi, district Amravati and in Madhya Pradesh it is in the Atner tehsil, district Betul. The hills housing the rock shelters, in terms of revenue jurisdiction, fall under Atner tehsil, district Betul, Madhya Pradesh.

The average height of the hills where the shelters are situated is 600–800 m. Approach to the shelters is an arduous path, which needs mountaineering skills and equipment. However, the commendable effort on the part of the team having no such skills is praiseworthy. The shelters are strewn over a large portion of Gawilgad hills, from Bairam ghat, tehsil and district Amravati to Salbardi, a place of religious importance, divided between the districts of Betul and Amravati in Madhya Pradesh and Maharashtra. The team began its explorations by revisiting the earlier reported shelters and came across 14 more. The preliminary phase of the work was conducted in an area of about 20 sq. km. As this article is being written, further work is continuing in the region, with the certitude of finding many more rock shelters.

These shelters present vivid artistic representations, mostly in the form of paintings and sometimes in the form of petroglyphs. Though the authors, as part of the team, visited 18 rock shelters with decorations, they claim credit, on behalf of their Director General, for the discovery of 10 new ones. Of the 18, eight had already been reported earlier by two different agencies (also refer to K.A. Pawar et al. 2012). Inside the shelters, mostly the walls and occasionally the ceilings bear paintings, starting from the prehistoric to the modern times. The petroglyphs have been executed on the walls of the shelters. Artefacts, assignable to the upper Palaeolithic and Mesolithic industry, were found from the surface inside some shelters as well as from their immediate vicinity and from the approach paths of some others. This paper discusses all the 18 rock shelters and the other findings as studied during our brief tours.

The shelters carry petroglyphs in the form of engravings, bruisings, peckings and pictographs in the form of stick figures, outlines and solid and X-ray figures. For the convenience of study and recording, the fairly large area of the exploration was demarcated and classified into distinct zones. Though the base was essentially village Dharul, ascends to these zones were from different directions. These zones were labeled according to local terms and as per the norms prevalent in the Archaeological Survey of India, abbreviated for ease. The shelters were then numbered using abbreviated zone names followed by the numbers assigned to the shelters. The shelters in a given zone were numbered in a clockwise pattern, for example, the first shelter in the Gaimukh group was numbered GMK 1. The groups which have been identified till now are—Mungsa Dev Group (MSD), Kosumb Gufa Group (KMG), Kukadsa Dev Group (KSD), Ambadevi Group (ABD), Telkan Group (TKN) and Gaimukh Group (GMK). The shelters vary in size from 26 m x 8 m x 9.5 m (largest) to 8.5 m x 2 m x 4.25 m (smallest). The shelters generally face south, south-east and south-west (Fig. 16.1).

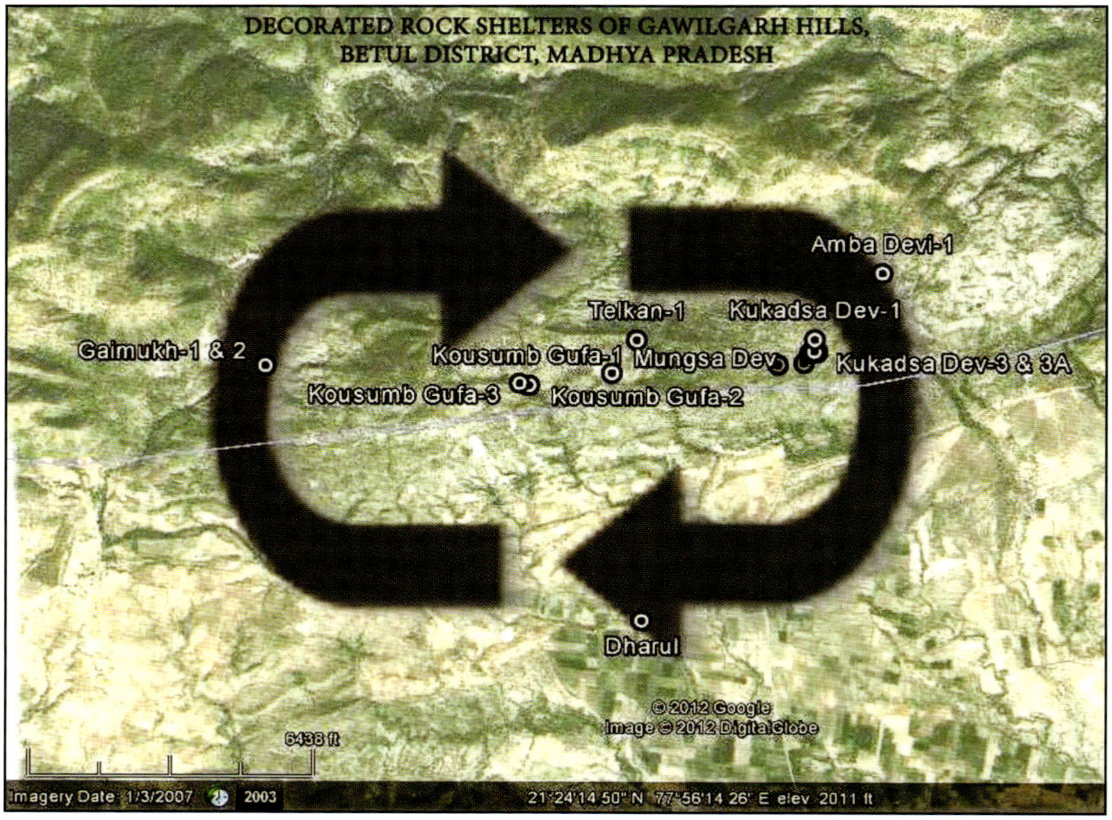

Fig. 16.1 Decorated rock shelters of Gawilgarh hills (Source: www.google.com/earth).

Petroglyphs including engravings, pecking and bruising were noticed in a few of the shelters, as distributed in three of the groups' shelters of MSD, KSD and ABD. A rarity in terms of Indian rock art studies noticed in these shelters is the depiction of a larger variety of subjects other than the commonly seen cupules in most instances. The petroglyphs comprised cupules and engravings, deeply engraved into the rock surface, most commonly depicting groups of *gaur* (*Bos vel gaveus gaurus)*, in various moods and activities like grazing, running, climbing a slope and indulging in playful pranks; other herbivores like *chausingha* and deer also find prominent place in the subject repertoire. All these have been very astutely and sharply depicted by the artist on the hard rock surface. The various stages of their movement are clearly discernible by the diverse positions of their tails and limbs. Petroglyphs in the form of pecking show common herbivores like herds of deer, *barasingha* and *chausingha* in various positions and the bruising comprise simple faunal and geometric motifs.

The paintings, found largely on the walls and sometimes on the ceilings, appear to have been made out of iron oxide nodules or geru. Mostly executed in red, burnt sienna and occasionally in white, which have been taken into cognisance by the authors while discussing the time-frame of the respective art, they depict a good range of faunal and geometric motifs. The absence of floral representation, as observed in the reported paintings, though situated within a dense forest, is intriguing. Depictions of stylised tortoise, deer, dog, bull, wild boar, vulture/bat, rabbit, ox, monitor lizard, donkey, *chital, nilgai* and *sambar* are common in the shelters. Geometric designs, which also comprise natural elements like the honeycomb, are depicted in almost all the groups. Paintings in red are the earliest, stylistically assignable to the Mesolithic period, which have been superimposed at some places by paintings in burnt sienna, stylistically assignable to the Chalcolithic period. Paintings identified as Mesolithic, mostly in weak red, are in turn found to superimpose engravings in some instances, thereby postdating the petroglyphs.

The team, in its initial stages of work, collected upper Palaeolithic tools like blades, bladelets, borer-cum-scraper and fluted cores made on material like chert, agate and quartz, and Mesolithic tools from the surface of the rock shelters as well as their immediate vicinity.

A description of the rock shelters discovered by the team (numbers 1–10) as well as those already reported and revisited by the team (11–18) is given in Table 16.1.

Table 16.1 Description of the Shelters.

Sr. No.	Shelters	Geo-coordinates*	Nature of remains
1.	Gaimukh 1	Lat. 21° 24' 11.40" N; Long.77° 54' 28.20" E	Traces of painted animals
2.	Gaimukh 2	Lat. 21° 24' 11.40"N; Long. 77° 54' 28.20"E	Paintings of boar, *nilgai*, honeycomb, etc.
3.	Telkan 1	Lat. 21° 24' 17.22" N; Long. 77° 54' 31.74" E	Paintings of honeycomb, stylised tortoise, donkey and lithic tools
4.	Kukadsadev 1	Lat. 21° 24' 14.46" N; Long. 77° 56' 38.53" E	Traces of painted bull
5.	Kukadsadev 4	Lat. 21° 24' 14.10" N. Long. 77° 56' 37.62" E	Paintings of wild boar and palm impression
6.	Kukadsadev 4A	Lat. 21° 24' 14.64" N; Long. 77° 56' 35.82" E	Painted geometric design
7.	Kukadsadev 7	Lat. 21° 24' 11.46" N; Long. 77° 56' 23.16"E	Engravings showing bovine groups and paintings
8.	Ambadevi 1	Lat. 21° 24' 33.84" N; Long. 77° 56' 58.08" E	Engravings and paintings of bull,Deer and honeycomb
9.	Kosumb Gufa 2	Lat. 21° 24' 7.68" N; Long. 77° 55' 30.36" E	Paintings of stylised tortoises and geometric designs
10.	Kosumb Gufa 3	Lat. 21° 24' 9.72" N; Long. 77° 55' 25.38" E	Paintings of tortoise, rabbit, monkey, etc.
11.	Mungsadev 1	Lat. 21° 24' 9.78" N; Long. 77° 55' 51.42" E	Paintings of bovine groups, cupules and lithic tools

Sr. No.	Shelters	Geo-coordinates*	Nature of remains
12.	Kosumb Gufa 1	Lat. 21° 24' 7.78" N; Long. 77° 55' 37.74" E	Paintings of boar, tortoise, bull, elephant and stylised human
13.	Kukadsadev 2	Lat. 21° 24' 15.90" N; Long. 77° 56' 38.88" E	Painting of grazing bovines
14.	Kukadsadev 3	Lat. 21° 24' 14.34" N; Long. 77° 56' 38.40" E	Paintings of boar, fish and elephant
15.	Kukadsadev 3A	Lat. 21° 24' 14.76" N; Long. 77° 56' 37.32" E	Paintings of boar, deer, tortoise, palm impression and lithic tools
16.	Kukadsadev 5	Lat. 21° 24' 15.90" N; Long. 77° 56' 36.12" E	Paintings of honeycomb, doe, mythical animal with elongated body and lithic tools
17.	Kukadsadev 6	Lat. 21° 24' 11.82" N; Long. 77° 56' 36.24" E	Engravings of bull, deer; paintings of mother and child, monitor lizard, donkey, stick human figures, cupules and lithic tools
18.	Telkan 2	Lat. 21° 24' 6.34" N; Long. 77° 56' 12.41" E	Paintings of rabbit, dog, vulture/bat, monitor lizard and geometric designs

Note: * Readings taken with the help of Garmin GPSMAP 76CSx

GAIMUKH GROUP (GMK)

GMK 1: (21°24'11.40" N; 77° 54' 28.20" E): This is a shallow rock shelter, facing north-west. The shelter is not in a very good state of preservation. Traces of paintings are visible; among them a stick figure (Fig. 16.2) is discernible, though we cannot make out whether it is an animal or a human.

GMK 2: (21° 24' 11.40" N; 77° 54' 28.20" E): This shelter is in a far better state of preservation than GMK I. It has a rich repertoire of paintings, assignable on stylistic grounds majorly to the Mesolithic and a few to the Chalcolithic periods. Boar, a characteristic member of the Mesolithic design repertoire, is shown filled up with a chevron design and a long snout. An elephant drawn on the ceiling is shown with a cross dividing the interior and an incurved trunk, facing left. The rapid motion is shown with the help of a hind limb that is raised a bit. Superimposed on the Mesolithic boar are Chalcolithic geometric designs. Also depicted in this shelter are a herbivore with a long neck, probably a *nilgai*, honeycomb and an antelope shown with an x-ray depiction of its internal organs in the form of a spiral.

KOUSUMB GUFA GROUP (KMG)

KMG 1: (21° 24' 7.78" N; 77° 55' 37.74" E): In a fairly good state of preservation, this shelter offers a vivid picture of the Mesolithic canvas. A life-size antelope is depicted over the entire ceiling of the cave. Mesolithic artists, true to their style of emphasising

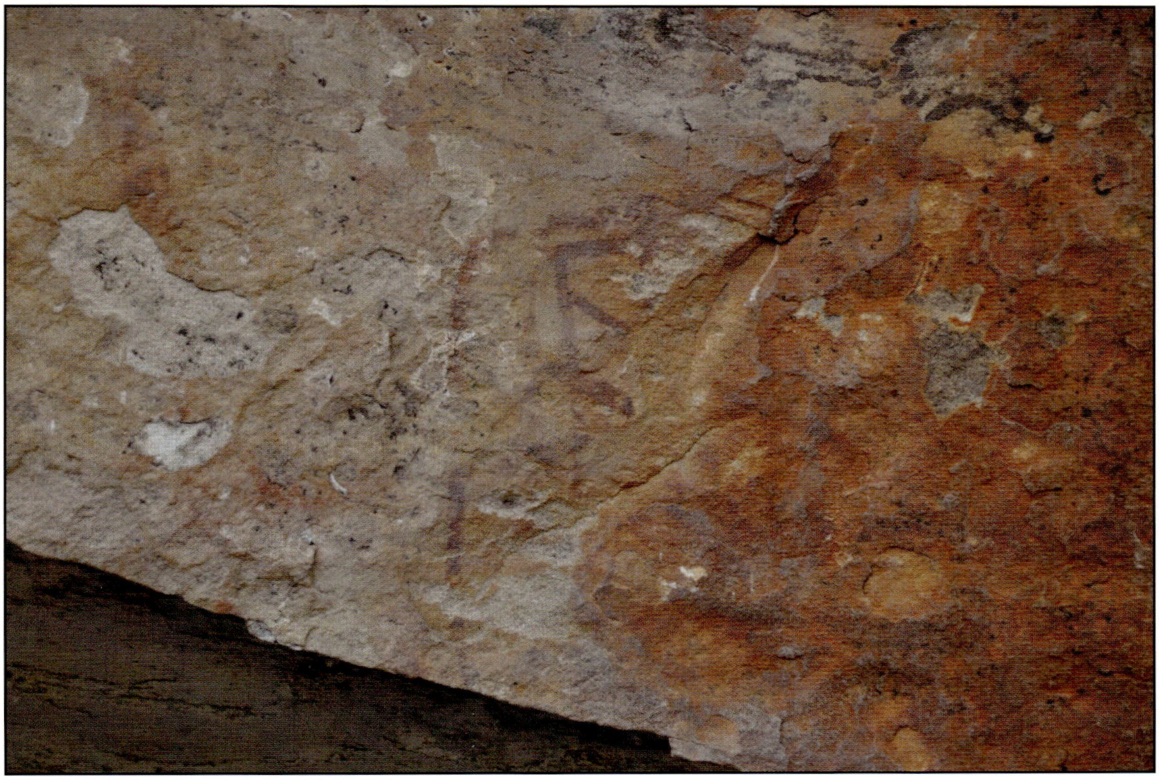

Fig. 16.2 Stick figure, Gaimukh 1.

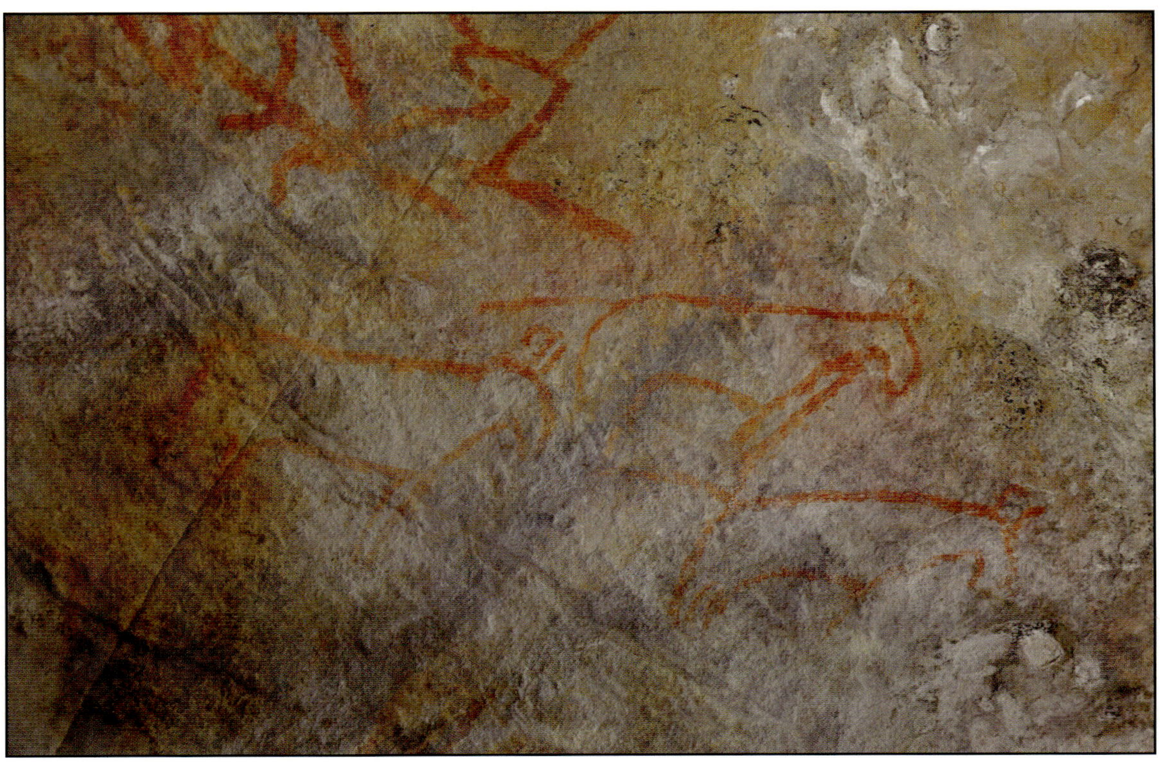

Fig. 16.3 Big cat with horns (?), Kousumb Gufa 1.

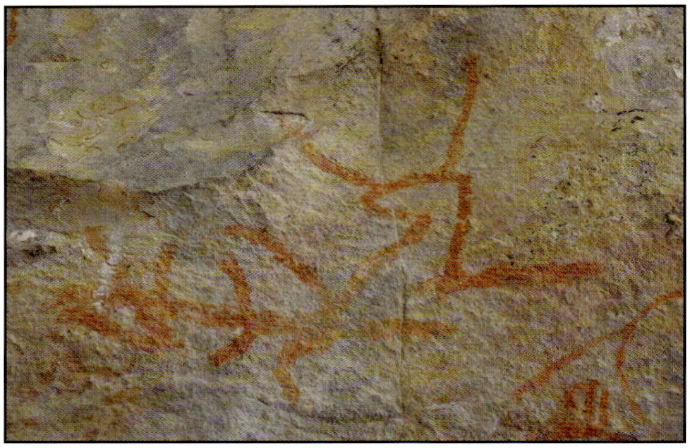

Fig. 16.4 Herbivore shot by an arrow/spear, Kousumb Gufa 1.

the horn, have shown figures resembling big cats with horns (?) (Fig. 16.3). A herbivore is shown shot by a typical Mesolithic arrow/spear in one of the panels (Fig. 16.4). Fishing nets hint at their subsistence pattern. The Chalcolithic element is mainly represented by one humped bull; an ithyphallic cult figure with upraised hair is shown with splayed fingers and a boar venerating or facing a tortoise.

KMG 2: (21°24' 7.68" N; 77°55' 30.36" E): As KMG I and most other shelters in the area, this shelter too appears to have been in use in the Mesolithic as well as Chalcolithic periods. However, due to profuse leaching action, the earlier paintings are not very clear. In later times, an array of animal hides is depicted on the wall (Fig. 16.5).

KMG 3: (21° 24' 9.72" N; 77° 55' 25.38" E): This shelter appears to have either been used less or decorated less, as excavations can only speak about the period of occupation. Except a herbivore, probably of the Mesolithic period, showing a spiral representing the internal organs with a little raised tail, no other depiction is worth discussing.

KUKADSA DEV GROUP (KSD)

KSD 1 (21° 24' 14.46" N; 77° 56' 38.53" E): The shelter is in a bad state of preservation, wherein traces of paintings could be noticed, but nothing was discernible.

Fig. 16.5 Animal hides, Kousumb Gufa 2.

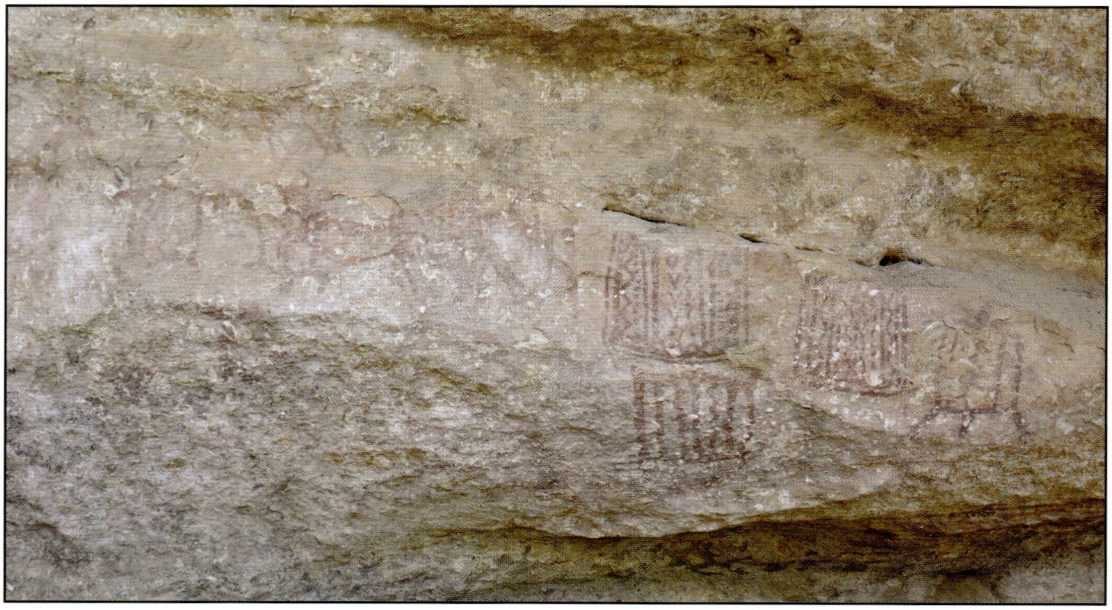

KSD 2 (21° 24' 15.90" N; 77° 56' 38.88" E): In a better state of preservation than KSD I, the only coherent panel in this shelter represents a group of humans, drawn in stick style, one amongst them showing a rotund body. One person is seen active in a somewhat bending posture. The paintings are Mesolithic.

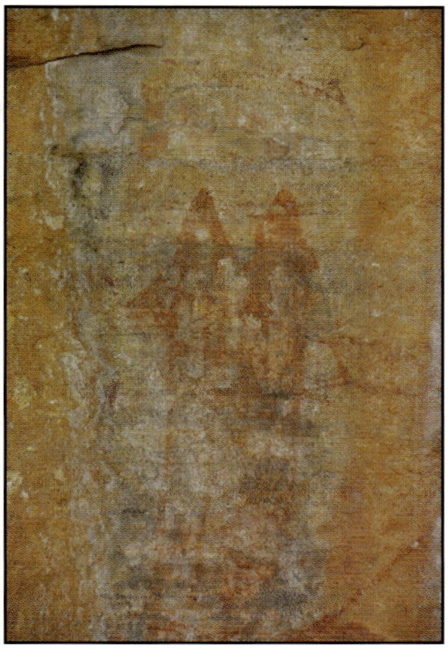

Fig. 16.6 A pair of fish, Kukadsa Dev 3.

KSD 3 (21° 24' 14.34" N; 77° 56' 38.40" E): The shelter holds a few intelligible examples of Chalcolithic superimposition over Mesolithic art; a bovid with a checkered body is drawn over a simple geometric box design. Among the few other design elements are a pair of fish, stylistically of the Mesolithic period (Fig. 16.6). An impression of a right palm on one of the walls of the shelter appears to be Mesolithic. An antelope, represented by a linear stick style, is shown following a stick-figured human being, the antlers of an antelope very prominently shown. Microliths made on crypto-crystalline material like chert, chalcedony and quartz like bladelets, fluted cores and points were found in the near vicinity of the shelter.

KSD 3A (21° 24' 14.76" N; 77° 56' 37.32" E): The mushroom-shaped shallow shelter has at least two prominent panels of pictographs, facing east and west. The panel facing west appears to have been used both by the Mesolithic and Chalcolithic people alike. A lot of superimposition is evident on the rock canvas; at least two phases are well discernible on close examination. Honeycombs have been depicted by artists of both the periods, however differing in style of execution. The panels facing west show an antelope with its internal organs depicted as a spiral facing a tortoise with a very stylised shell. These two are drawn over pictures from

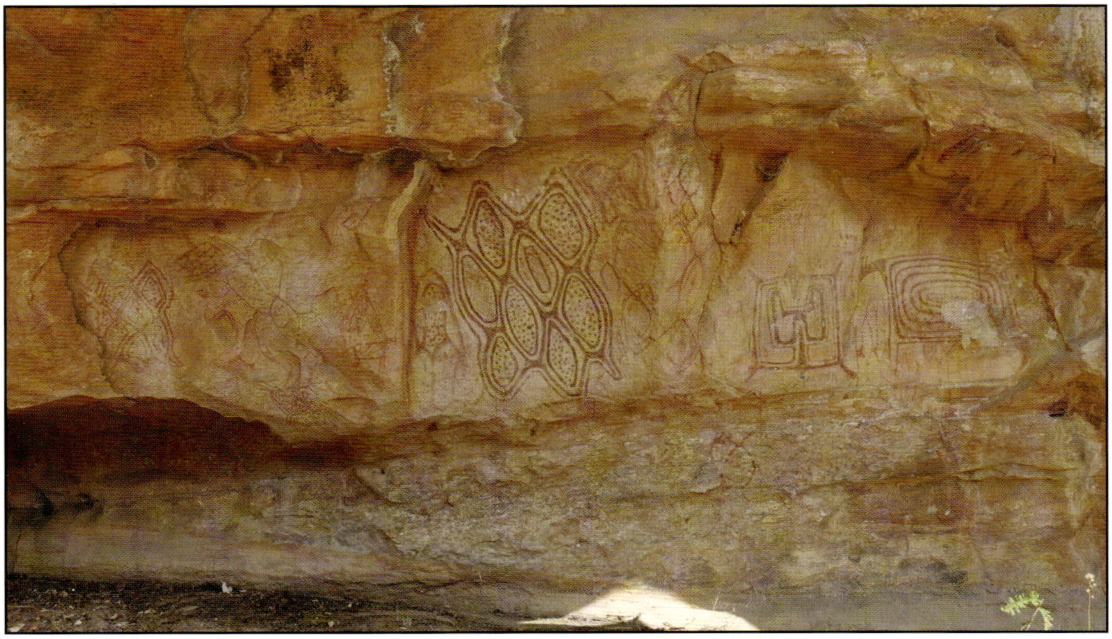

Fig. 16.7 Mesolithic figures superimposed by later figures of antelope and deer, Kukadsa Dev 3A.

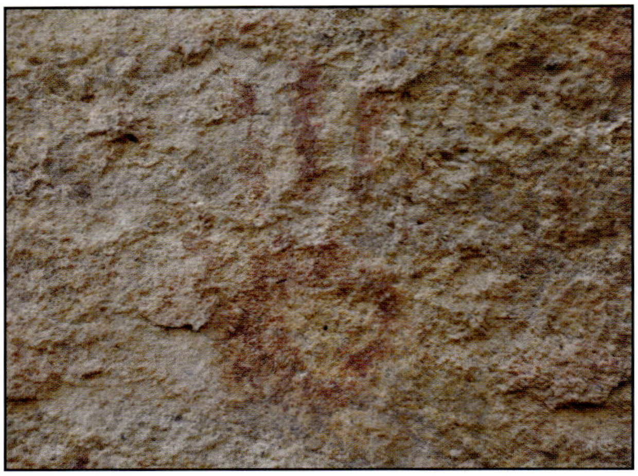

Fig. 16.8 Right palm, Kukadsa Dev 4.

the earlier period, which can be very clearly seen. An ithyphallic stick figure is seen belonging to the Mesolithic period between the antelope and the tortoise. Also seen are more elements like a pair of fish and other unintelligible elements beneath the antelope and tortoise (Fig. 16.7). Besides, there is a running antelope, the internal organs represented by a spiral, belonging to the Mesolithic period. The lower panels show an elongated-bodied animal, which appears to be a *dhol* (wild dog). The panels facing east have incomprehensible pictographs, much destroyed due to weathering and water actions. A right palm's print appears on one of the walls, apparently of Mesolithic affiliation (plate 13; 0261).

KSD 4 (21°24' 14.10" N; 77°56' 37.62" E): This shelter and the one above this are not in a very good condition and the paintings are scanty and worn out. A right palm impression is seen on one of the walls (Fig. 16.8) and traces of faint paintings can also be seen.

KSD 4A (21° 24' 14.64" N; 77° 56' 35.82" E): The paintings in this shelter are obscure and almost worn out. Not much could be studied; neither could a tentative periodisation be done. However, the traces of paintings noticed show common motifs painted in red ochre.

Fig. 16.9 Geometric motif, Kukadsa Dev 5.

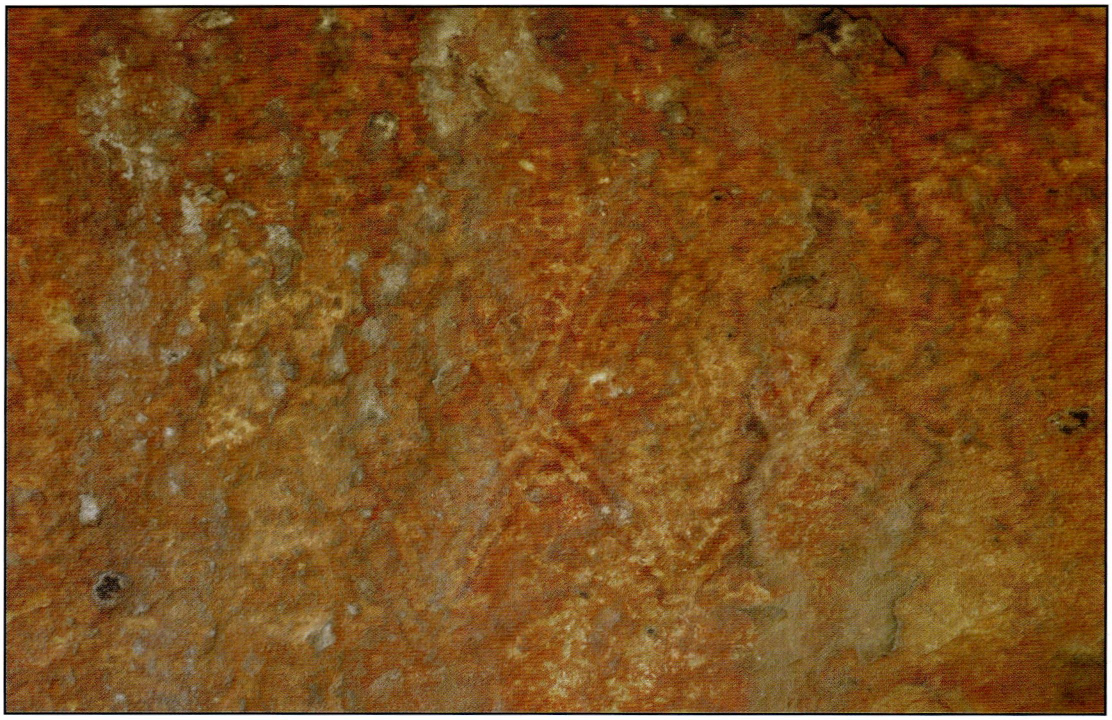

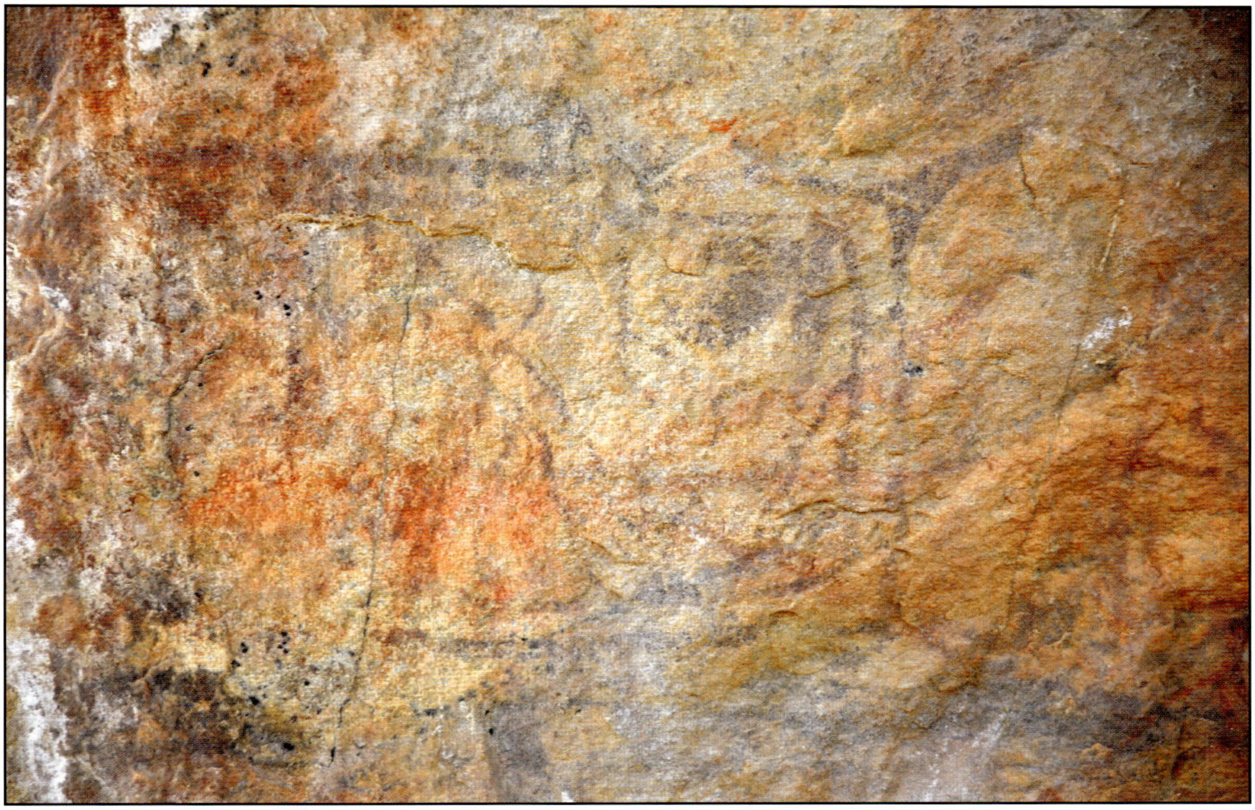

Fig. 16.10 Ithyphallic stag with raised tail, Kukadsa Dev 5.

KSD 5 (21° 24' 15.90" N; 77° 56' 36.12" E): This shelter, shaped like a mushroom and nicknamed the 'mushroom shelter' by the team, is a rich album of paintings, pertaining to the Mesolithic and Chalcolithic periods. The Mesolithic design elements comprise abstract geometric designs (Fig. 16.9) and animal motifs. The Chalcolithic elements are more vibrant in this shelter than those noticed elsewhere in the group. A peacock with splayed plumes and an antelope, probably depicted as being pregnant, carrying another animal figure within, an ithyphallic stag with a raised tail superimposed on Mesolithic paintings (Fig. 16.10) and a stag with a raised tail are worth noting.

KSD 6 (21° 24' 11.82" N; 77° 56' 36.24" E): This shelter is a gallery that was used for millennia by artists from the upper Palaeolithic to the Chalcolithic times. The walls of the shelter show beautiful examples of rock art in the form of engravings being superimposed by Mesolithic paintings, which in turn are superimposed by Chalcolithic paintings (Fig. 16.11). The engravings in the shelter essentially depict herbivores, chiefly herds of Indian bison or *gaur* and antelope with sharp antlers. The herd of *gaur*s is shown performing various activities (Fig. 16.12) like standing, walking, grazing and playfully pouncing over each other. The artist has very meticulously engraved the high convex ridge between the horns, the prominent ridge on the back and a medium length tail reaching the hocks. Antelopes are the other herbivores depicted through engravings in the shelter. Like the *gaur*s, the antelopes have also been depicted with much deftness,

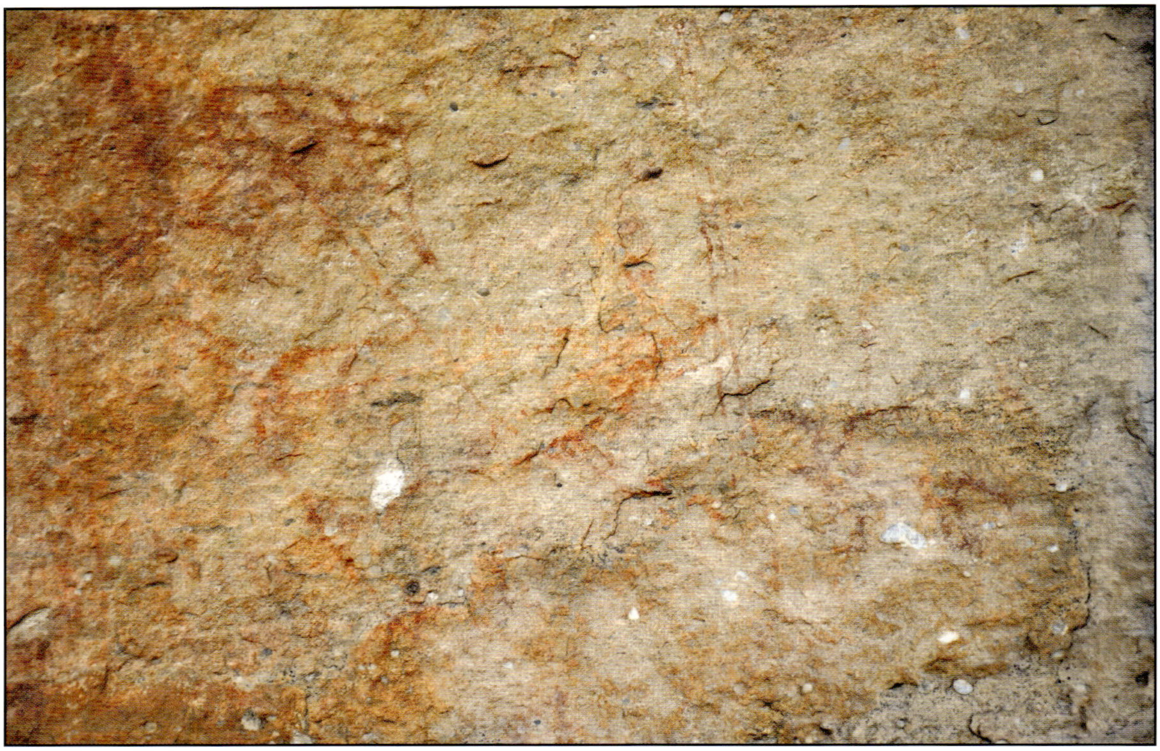

Fig. 16.11 Superimposition of paintings over engravings, Kukadsa Dev 6.

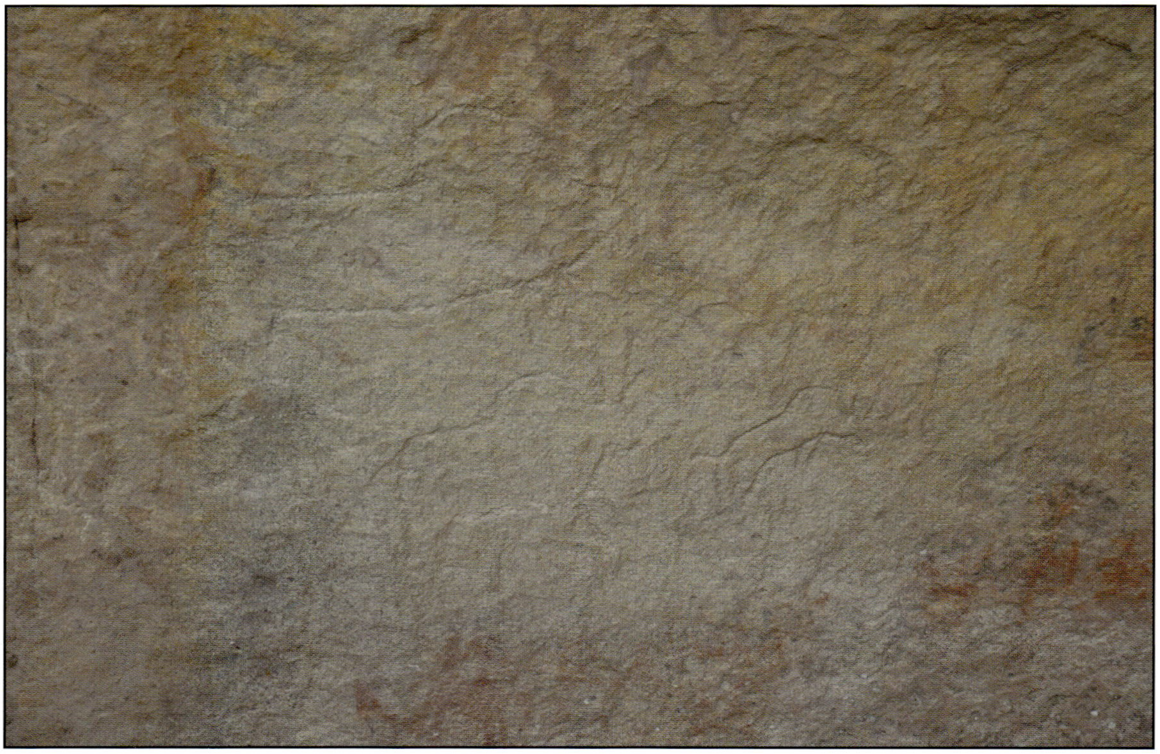

Fig. 16.12 Herd of *gaurs*, Kukadsa Dev 6.

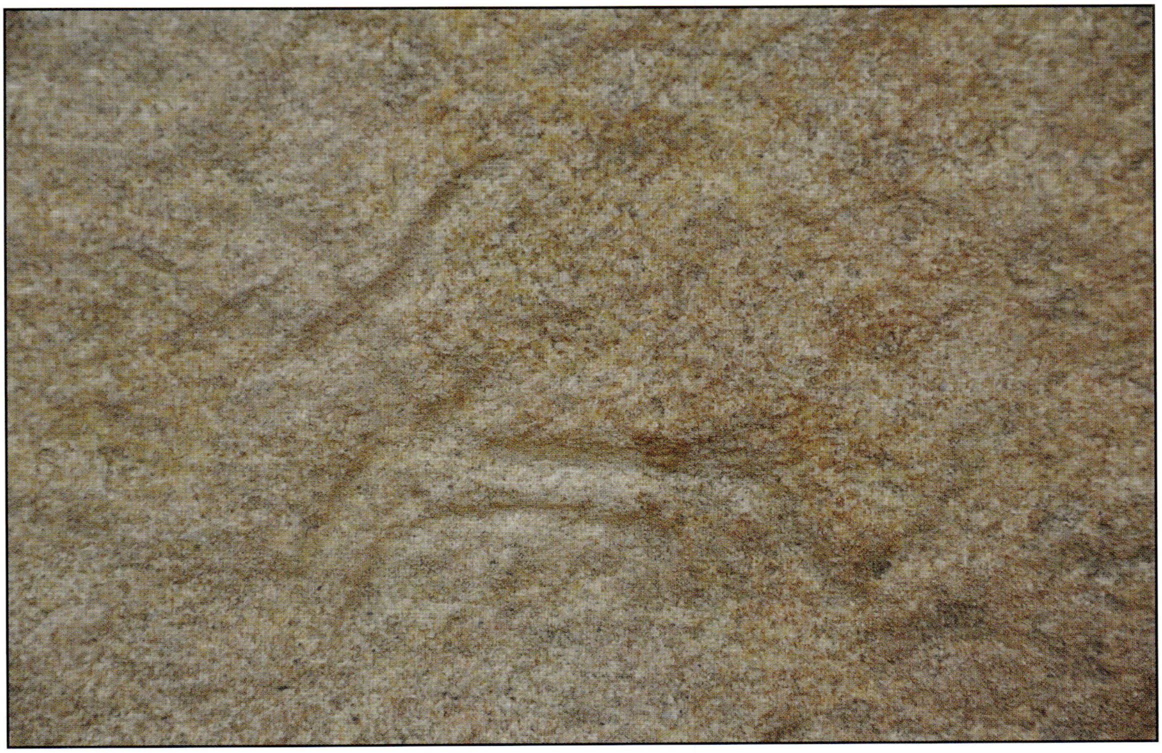

Fig. 16.13 Engraved antelopes, Kukadsa Dev 6.

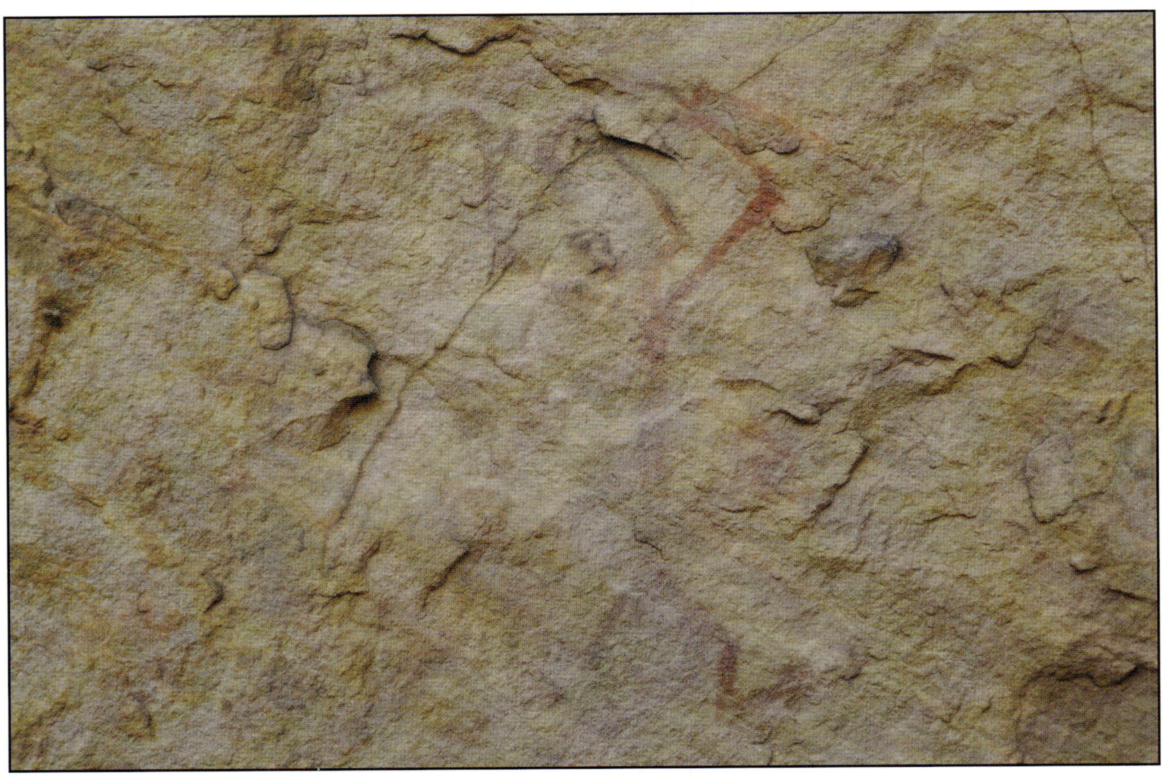

Fig. 16.14 Hunter with spear, Kukadsa Dev 6.

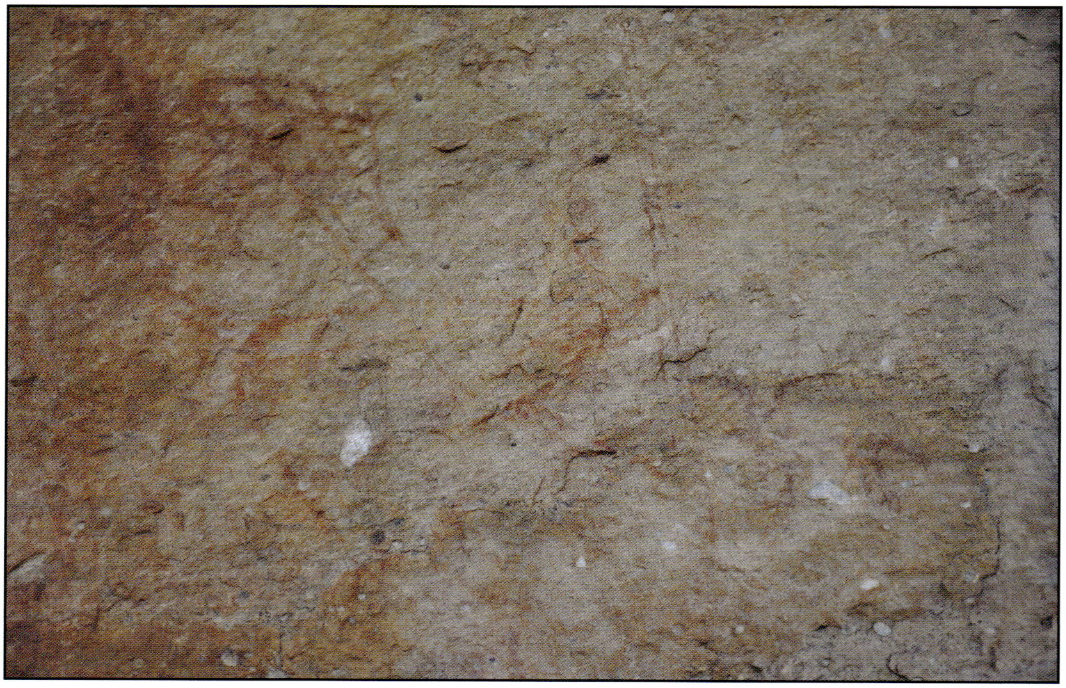

Fig. 16.15 Superimposition of paintings, Kukadsa Dev 6.

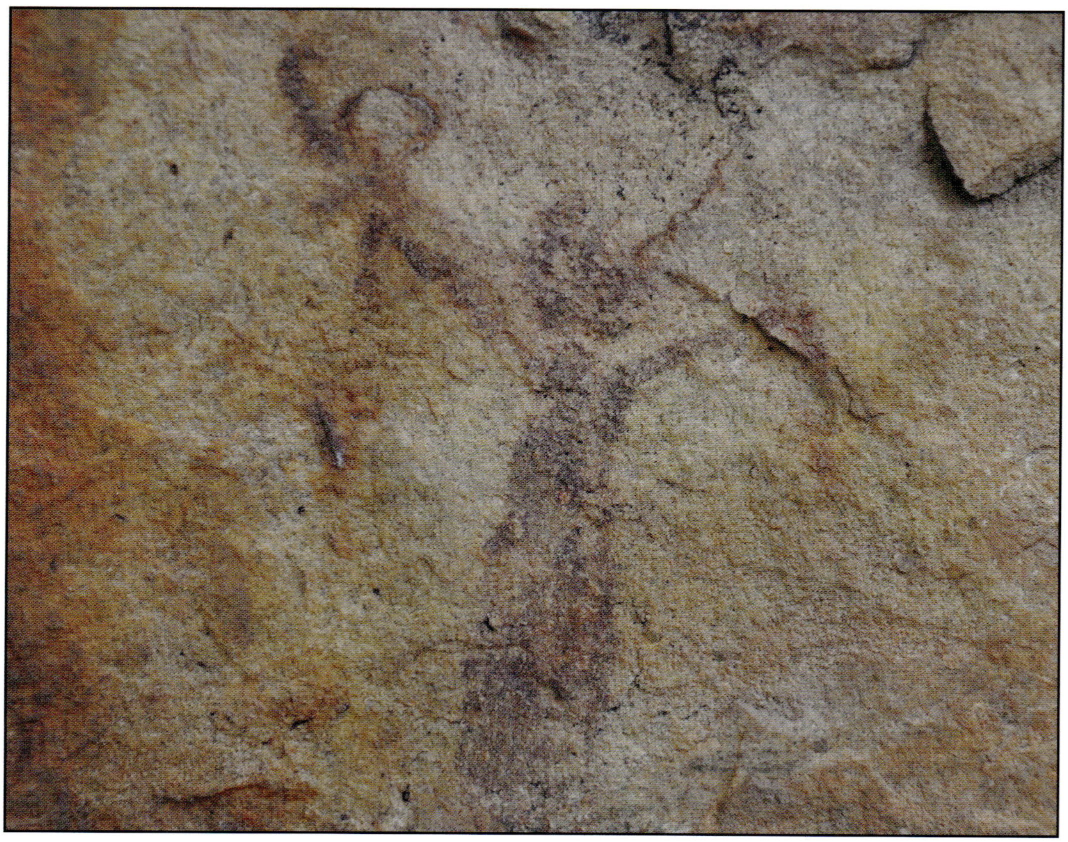

Fig. 16.16 Victor and vanquished, Kukadsa Dev 6.

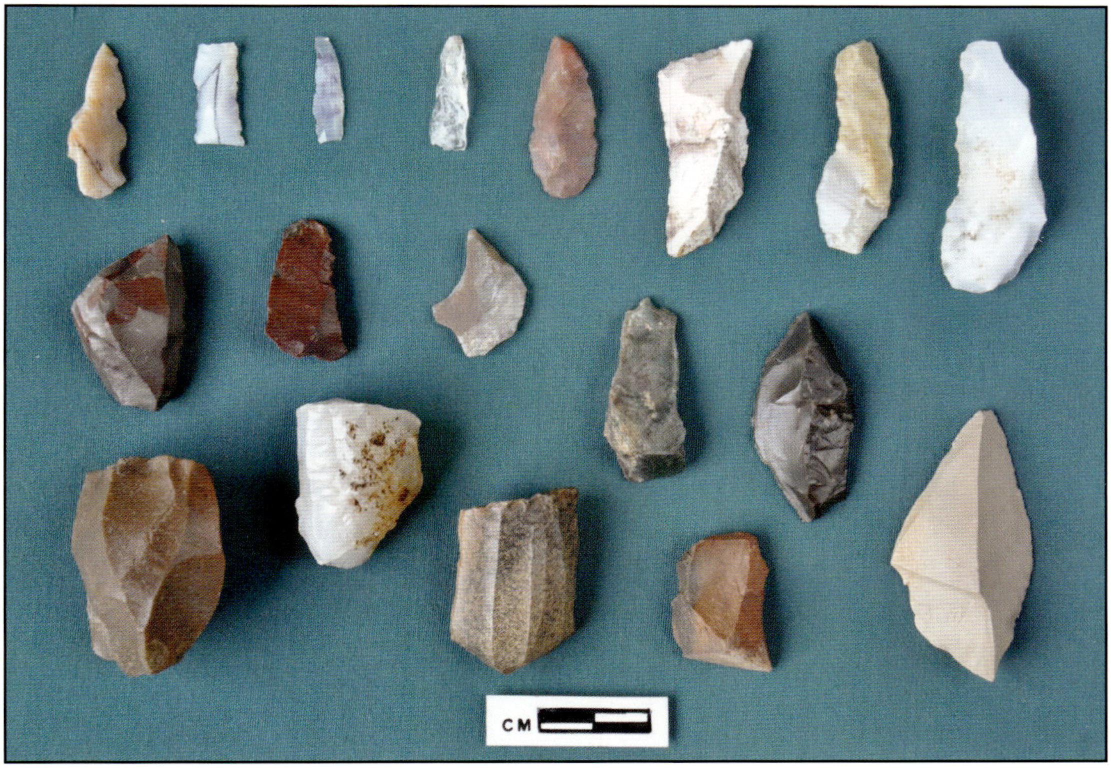

Fig. 16.17 Upper Palaeolithic tools, Kukadsa Dev 3 and 6.

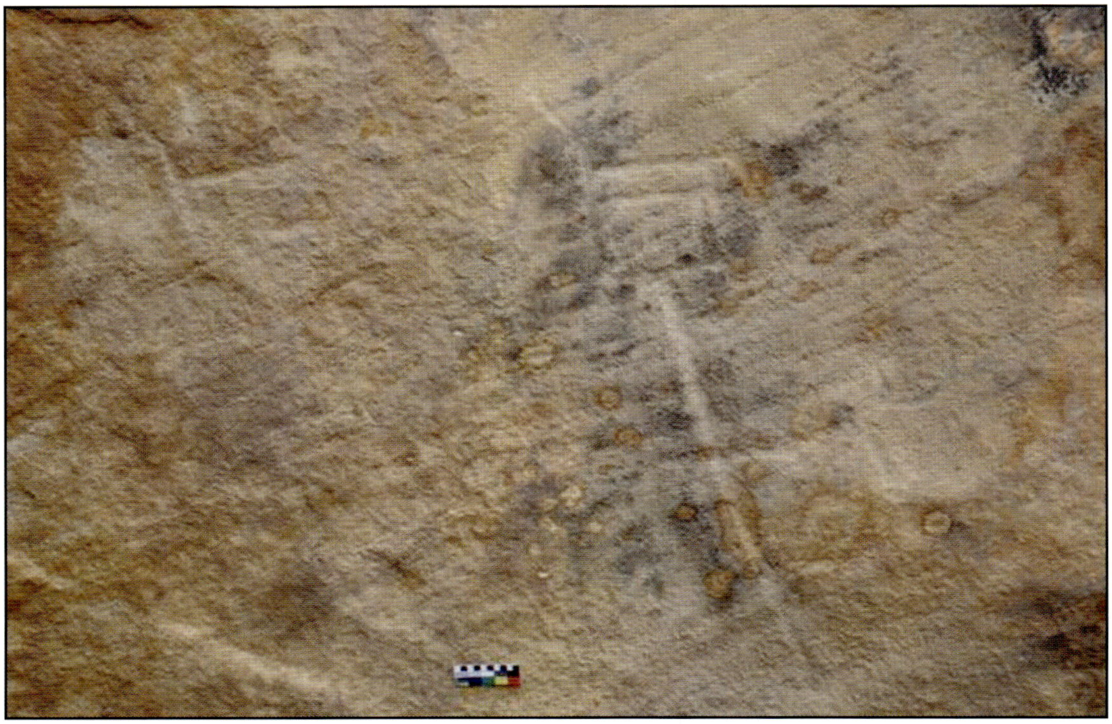

Fig. 16.18 A herd of deer, Kukadsa Dev 7.

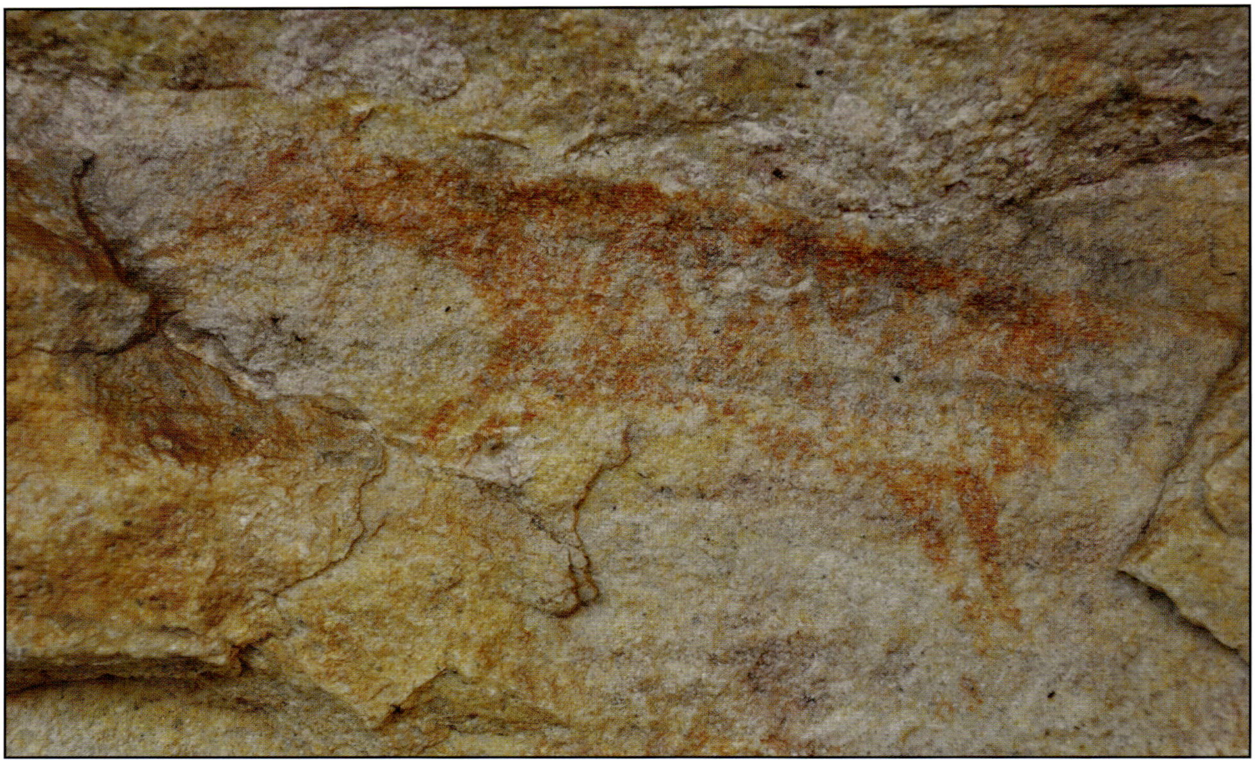

Fig. 16.19 A wild dog, Kukadsa Dev 7.

even carving the slightly wavy pair of antlers on the hard surface (Fig. 16.13). The robust and huge *gaur*, which sometimes reaches a height of about 7 feet from the ground, is shown in all its might by the engraver on the shelter wall. Mesolithic artists occupied the shelter after the generation of engravers and took to the canvas for representing the images in their mind. A stick human figure on the wall probably shows a hunt chase, where only the hunter is seen running with a spear-like object held up high over the head to his left (Fig. 16.14). Some more incognisable stick figures could also be marked out. The stick figures, depicting a human group, were drawn over the engraved upper Palaeolithic *gaur* herd by later Mesolithic man (27; DSC no. 0588). Mesolithic art was again superimposed by later artists in the Chalcolithic period (Fig. 16.15). The later artists drew many interesting panels and figures like a human figure wearing a gown, perhaps a female, both hands upraised and holding aloft another smaller human figure representing a pair of the victor and the vanquished (Fig. 16.16). There are also a few lesser depicted animals like a donkey and a camel besides regular depictions like antelopes with splayed antlers, to mention a few. Upper Palaeolithic tools were found from the surface inside the shelter as well in its immediate neighbourhood. Made on material such as chert, chalcedony and jasper, the tool kit was represented by awl/borer, knife point, simple blade and point (Fig. 16.17).

KSD 7 (21°24' 11.46" N; 77°56' 23.16" E): This double-storeyed shelter again shows continuity from upper Palaeolithic to the Chalcolithic periods. A feature worth noting is the use of the upper storey perhaps as a watchtower, as no rock art was seen on its

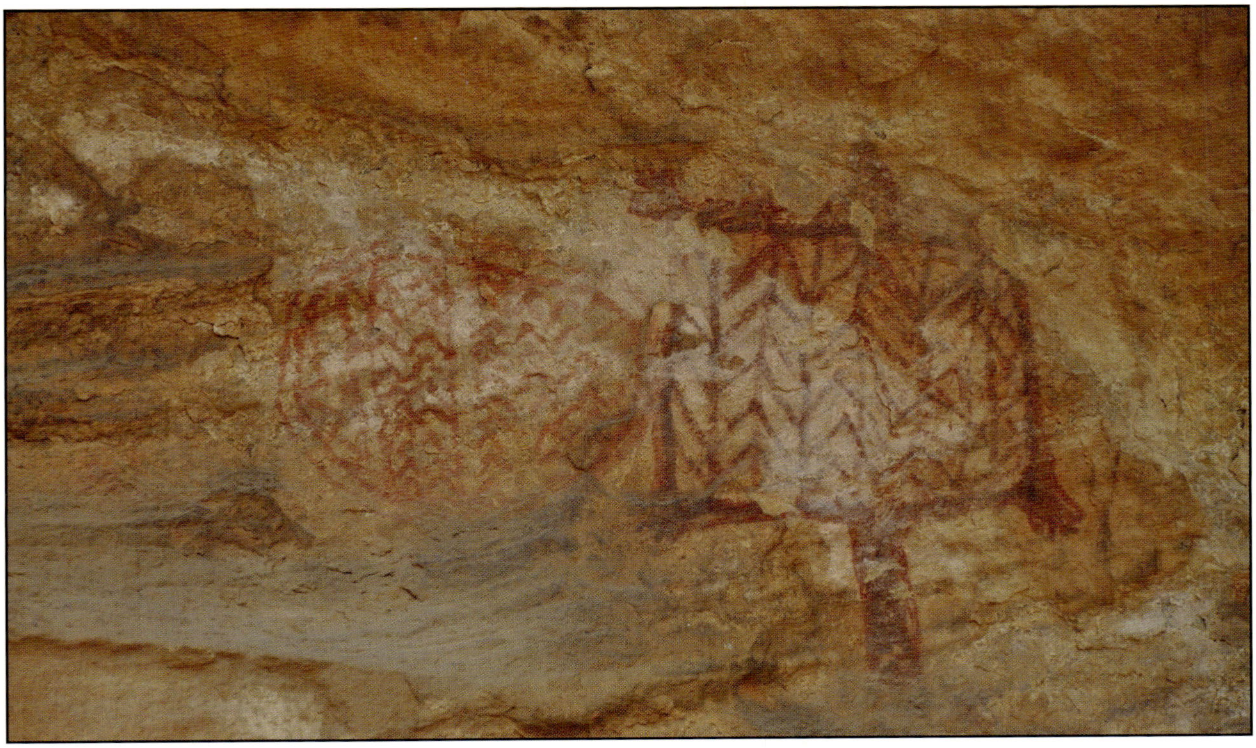

Fig. 16.20 A stylised lizard, Telkan 1.

walls. A herd of deer made by pecking and engraving, signifies the earliest bunch of inhabitants, the upper Palaeolithic people on the walls of the lower shelter (Fig. 16.18). They were succeeded by Mesolithic people, whose presence is marked by design elements like a series of dotted diamonds, a bovid with its front portion eroded by leaching and salt encrustation, the body filled with horizontal lines, prominent ears and some stick figures. The Chalcolithic paintings of this shelter are represented by the painting of a *dhol* (wild dog) (Fig. 16.19), drawn on the salt-encrusted wall just beneath the Mesolithic bovid figure. However, unlike KSD 6, which shows superimpositions between the arts of the different periods, this shelter did not yield any such example.

TELKAN GROUP (TKN)

TKN 1 (21° 24' 17.22" N; 77° 54' 31.74" E): The south-east facing shelter seems to have been preferred more by people in the Mesolithic period as compared to the Chalcolithic period. The nearly obliterated Mesolithic paintings show a chase scene where a stick human figure is shown running with his left hand held high, as if driving away some creature. Another panel shows a deer or antelope, with a raised tail, chasing a human; all the creatures are shown in stick forms. Among other motifs of this period are chains of designed diamonds. Later art is represented by geometric motifs and a stylised lizard (Fig. 16.20). The inhabitants of the Gawilgad hills appear to have been impressed by the tortoise and reptiles like lizards in their vicinity. The walls of the shelters bear frequent representations of these in Mesolithic as well as Chalcolithic times. The area around the

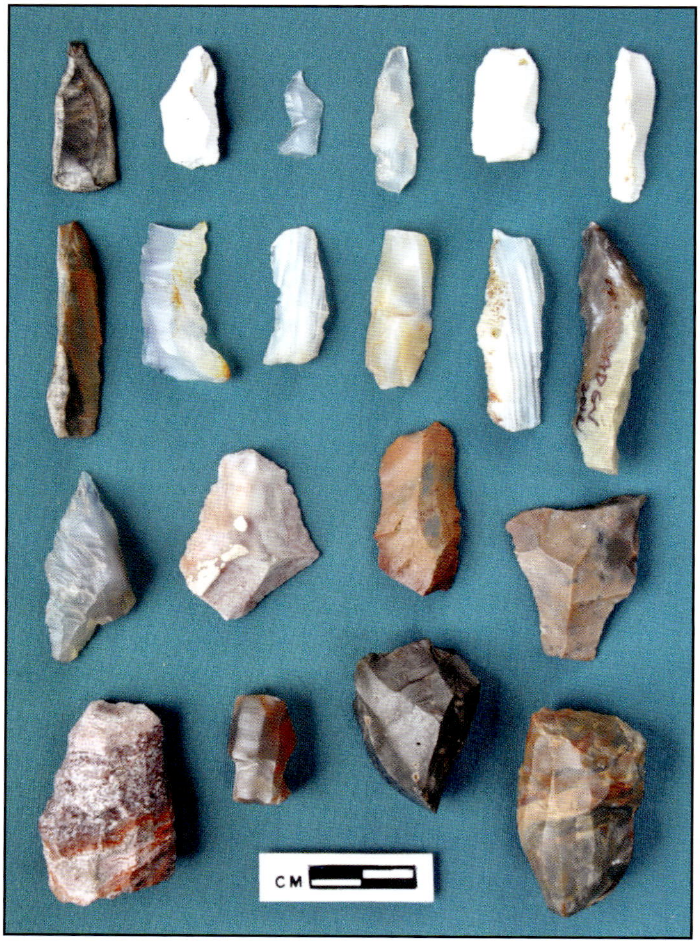

Fig. 16.21 Upper Palaeolithic and Mesolithic tools, Telkan.

shelter and also within it yielded upper Palaeolithic and Mesolithic artefacts all made on crypto-crystalline materials. The upper Palaeolithic repertoire was represented by notched scraper, points and blunted backed blade and the Mesolithic by bladelets and fluted core (Fig. 16.21).

TKN 2 (21° 24' 6.34" N; 77° 56' 12.41" E): In a better state of preservation than the TKN 1 shelter, this shelter houses many rare pictographs like depiction of a prey bird, rabbit and monitor lizard and misses out on some regular ones like deer and antelopes. The shelter has Mesolithic as well as Chalcolithic paintings on its walls. The Mesolithic repertoire is represented by beautiful geometric motifs arranged in a floral design (Fig. 16.22), rabbit and a bird of prey, discernible by the span of its wings. A long-necked animal is shown with a rectangular body, which may be a stylised representation of a grazing donkey (Fig. 16.23), a donkey, a monitor lizard (Fig. 16.24) and so on. The Chalcolithic assemblage comprises elements like a fox, two long-necked animals drawn in a composite style having a single rectangular body with two heads, a rabbit, monitor lizard and other geometric motifs.

MUNGSADEV (MSD) (21° 24' 9.78" N; 77° 55' 51.42" E)

This was a single shelter and was found to be the one with plenty of recent encroachments. The pictographs were defaced and tampered with. A small shrine of some local deity is housed there and as a result it is prone to unwanted intrusions. The shelter was witness to some fine works of art by the upper Palaeolithic, Mesolithic and Chalcolithic people. A broken slab of stone at the entrance of the shelter shows cupules, one of which is deep. The floor of the shelter also shows an arrangement of cupules, two of these being deeper than the others (Fig. 16.25). One of the walls shows a deeply incised rectangle, resembling the engraved deer of KSD 6 (Fig. 16.26). Bruisings depicting linear square-bodied animals are seen on the upper panel of one of the walls, together with evanescent Mesolithic paintings. The Mesolithic artist made a beautiful deviation from his regular practice of depicting animals in isolation. Seen here is a long-necked crane or ostrich, besides a pair of fish, perhaps communicating the bird's intention of eating the pair

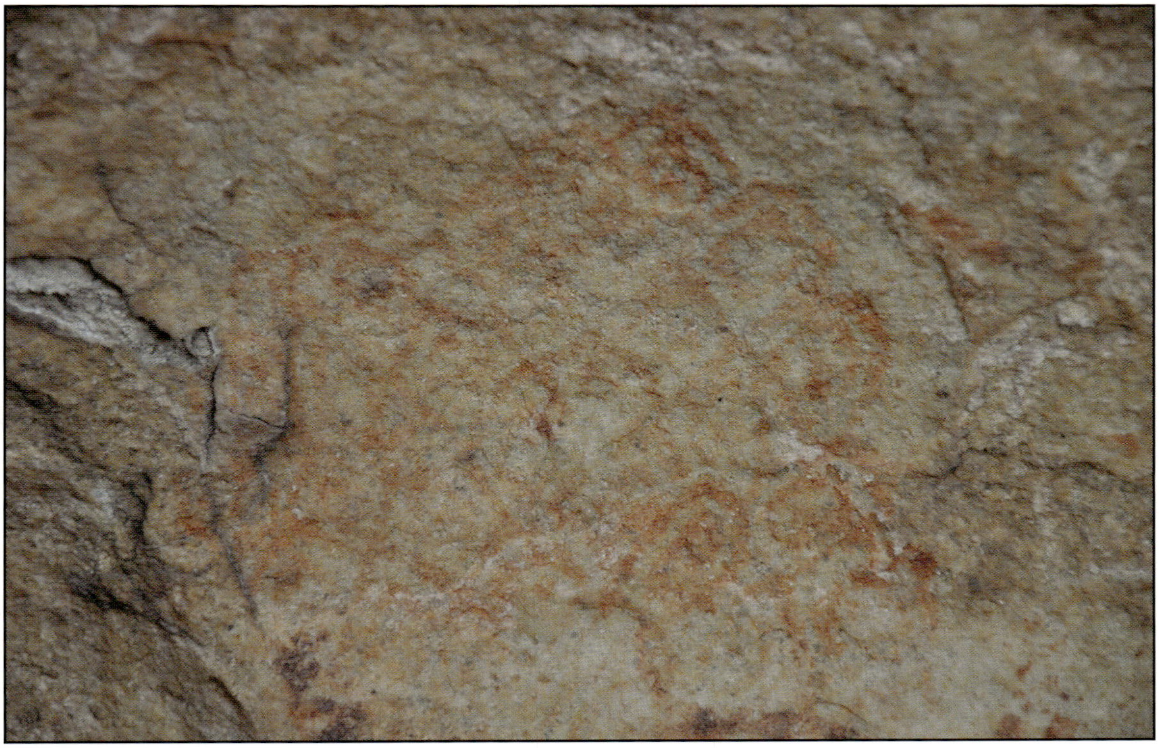

Fig. 16.22 Geometric motif, Telkan 2.

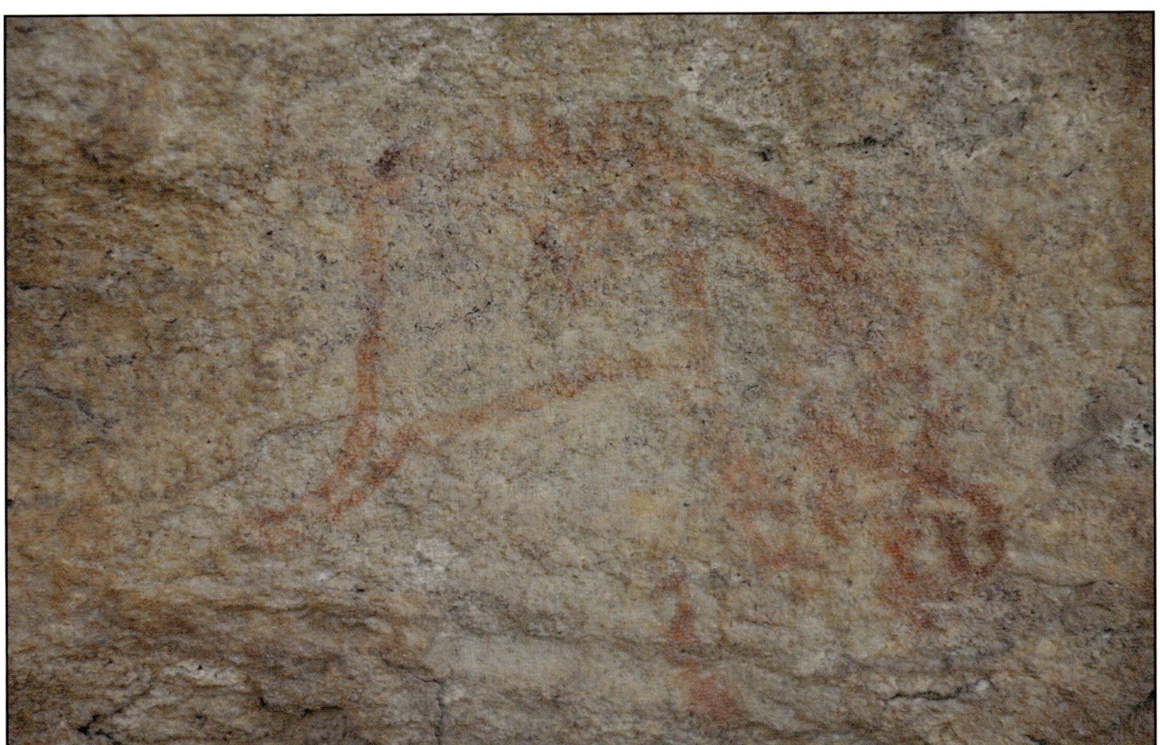

Fig. 16.23 A grazing donkey, Telkan 2.

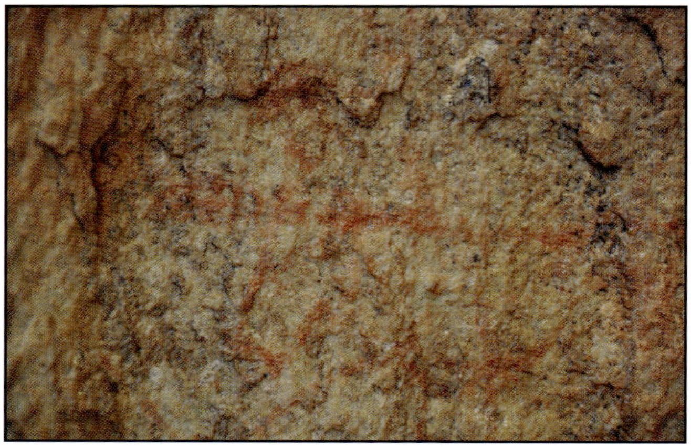

Fig. 16.24 A monitor lizard, Telkan 2.

(Fig. 16.27). Superimposition of Mesolithic paintings on upper Palaeolithic cupules is evinced again in one of the walls where the Mesolithic antelope has been tampered with and provided with a white outline in later times. An array of stick figures in white also adorns the walls of this shelter, which have not been noticed so far in the other shelters. Apart from a few more geometric designs, many of which have been given a white outline in later times, the paintings have faded away. The Chalcolithic people also added pictures to the album of this shelter in the form of ox with completely filled in bodies and a herd of deer, which has been ruthlessly vandalised by people visiting the shelter. Lizards, connected diamonds and beehives are the other patterns of the Chalcolithic period noticed here. Apart from the lithic periods, the shelter has recent paintings done in red and white on the walls. These paintings appear to have been executed after the shrine was instituted and pilgrims began visiting the shelter. The most common motif of these, which is still very much in vogue, is referred to as *Godhani.* The residents of the nearby villages are mainly from the Gond tribe and decorate the walls of their huts with similar designs, especially during festivals. The shelter as well as its immediate neighbourhood yielded upper Palaeolithic and Mesolithic artefacts made on chert, jasper, chalcedony and quartz. Tools like awl/borer, point, backed blades, simple blades, an engraver with a notch for better grip represented the upper Palaeolithic tool assemblage and bladelets, fluted core and points in bladelets, represented the Mesolithic assemblage. Also recovered were fluted cores, of both the periods (Fig. 16.28).

AMBADEVI GROUP (ABD)

The group gets its name from the now famous shrine of Ambadevi, housed in a huge shelter which might have contained rock art. However, since being enshrined, the walls of the shelter have been coloured and the floors tiled. Any traces of rock art in any form are no longer available. It was worth noting that the shelter, the biggest of all those reported here, contained a perennial spring inside. The team visited an adjacent shelter and named it after the most famous feature in that area, the shrine of Ambadevi.

ABD 1 (21° 24' 33.84"N; 77° 56' 58.08"E): The shelter appears to have been in regular use from the upper Palaeolithic period as a beautiful decoration made by engravings occupies space on one of the walls. The motif, a combination of cupules enclosed by wavy lines, sometimes spiraling like a double helix (Fig. 16.29), appears to be of upper Palaeolithic times. This is deducted from a comparative analysis with engravings and superimpositions in other shelters. The place was much in use during Chalcolithic times as beautiful art of this period adorns the shelter walls. Stick figures in

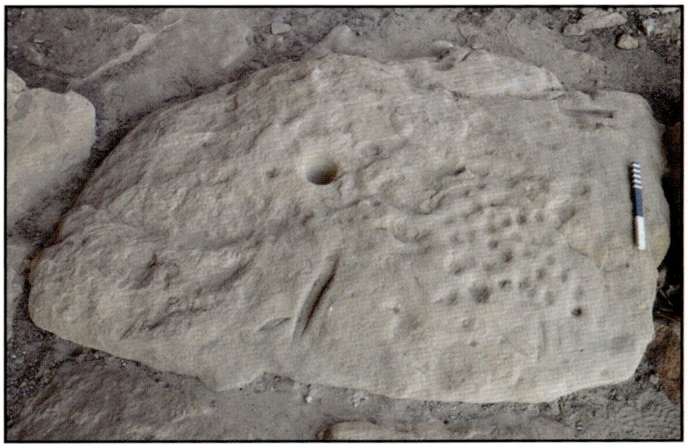

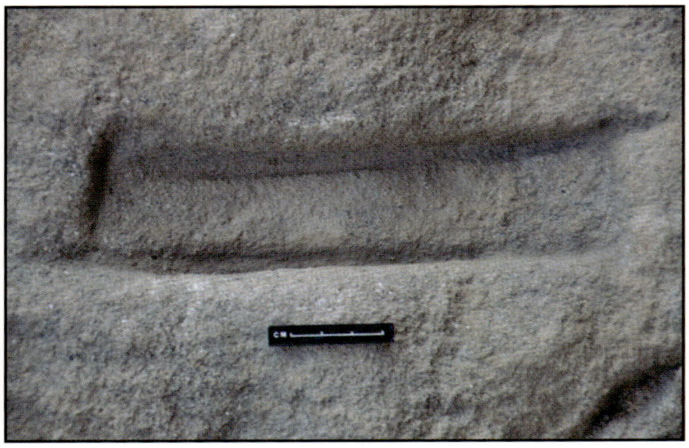

Left: **Fig. 16.25** Cupules, Mungsadev.

Right: **Fig. 16.26** Engraved rectangle, body of a deer (?), Mungsadev.

various postures, monitor lizards, geometric motifs and beehives are good representations of Mesolithic art. Of special significance is a figure, identified by the team as that of a scorpion, belonging to the Mesolithic period (Fig. 16.30). Later art assignable to the Chalcolithic period is found superimposed over earlier art, like in one instance a humped bull made by bruisings is superimposed on stick dancing figures (Fig. 16.31). The *barasingha,* seemingly depicted in the Chalcolithic period, was noticed only in this shelter in the studied area. One of the walls of a hut appears to have been decorated with festoons, which continue on the shelter wall (Fig. 16.32). A humped bull with prominent horns and a hump, an elephant with an upraised trunk (Fig. 16.33) are especially worth mentioning in the Chalcolithic

Fig. 16.27 A pair of fish and a crane/ostrich (?), Mungsadev.

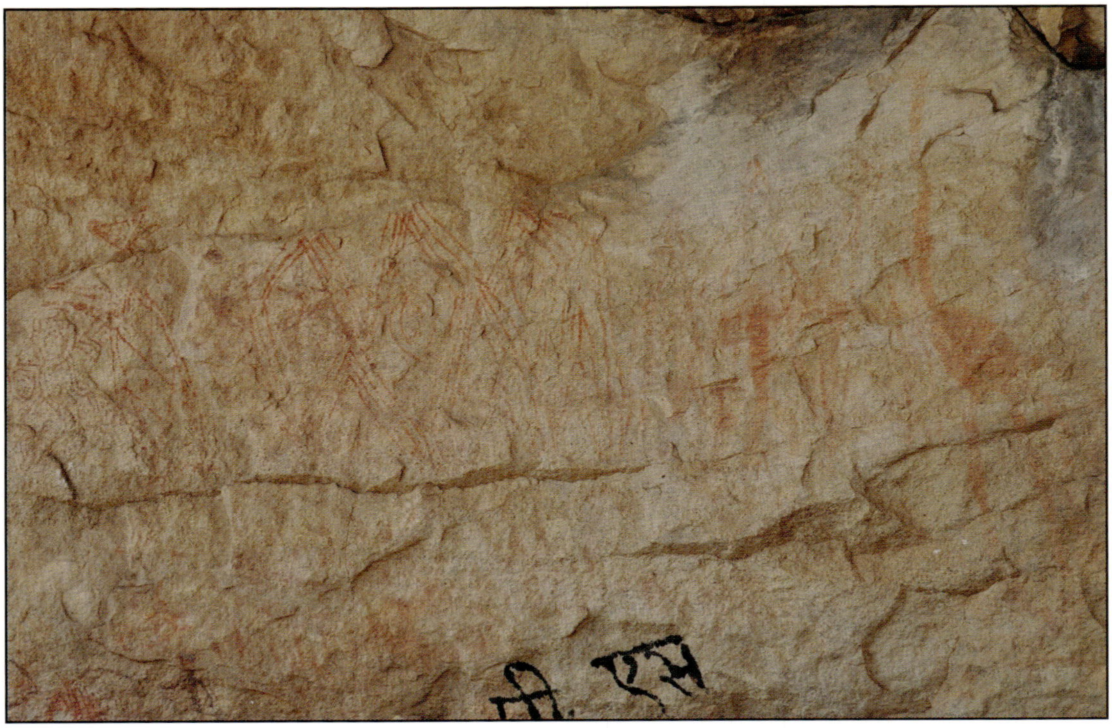

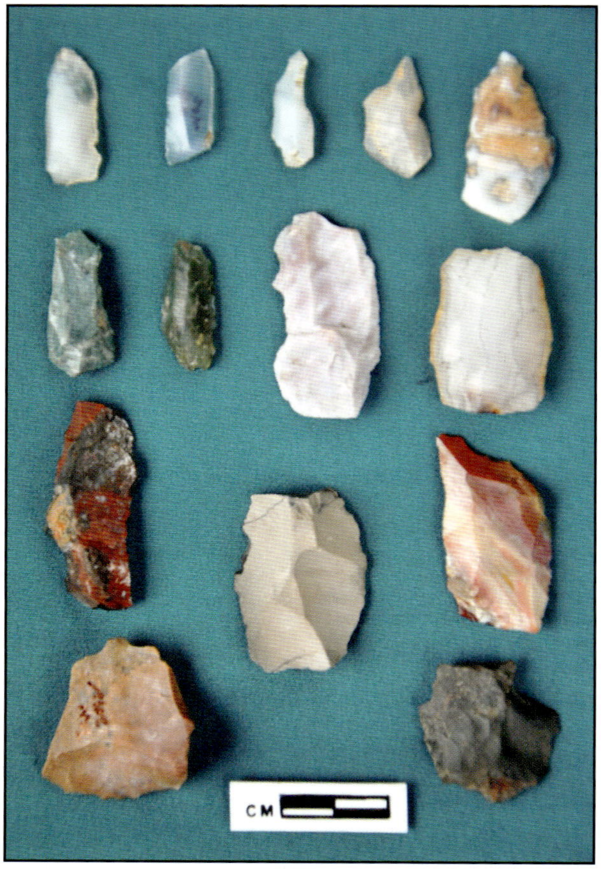

Fig. 16.28 Upper Palaeolithic tools, Mungsadev.

repository. Another humped bull with very prominent horns and a hump is painted at the entrance wall of the shelter.

To surmise, it can be said that human beings in prehistoric times resided in these rock shelters in Gawilgad hills, overlooking the Tapi Valley for a fairly long period in continuation. Of all the aspects of rock art studies worldwide, the most challenging one, as also admitted to by scholars, has been that of dating them. However, it is reiterated that an attempt to assign dates to the rock art discussed here is primarily based on three perspectives—comparative analyses with various rock art sites in Central India; evidence of superimposition of the depictions in the reported shelters; and the lithic assemblage found from and in the vicinity of the rock shelters. Much fieldwork, and if need be, excavations in the floors of the shelters, are required to come up with dates with certitude. An intriguing thought which crosses the authors' minds is the complete absence of representations from the plant kingdom though those from human and animal kingdoms are fairly large. This appears to be a paradox, as the shelters are in the middle of a dense forest with lush vegetation growth. This remains an enigma, as most of the rock shelter sites with reported pictographs, all over India, though situated usually in forests, are partisan in their content of faunal art as

Fig. 16.29 A double helix, Ambadevi.

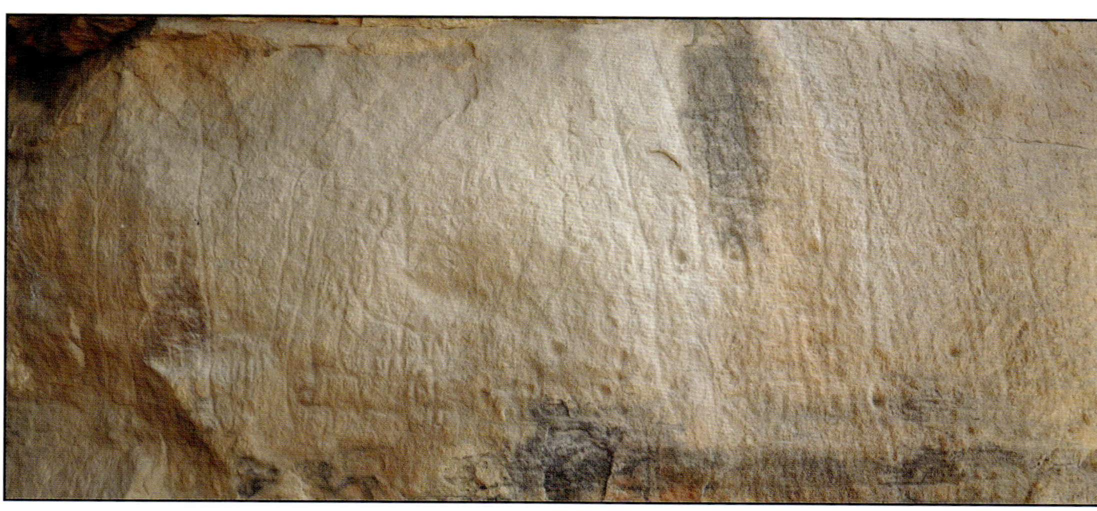

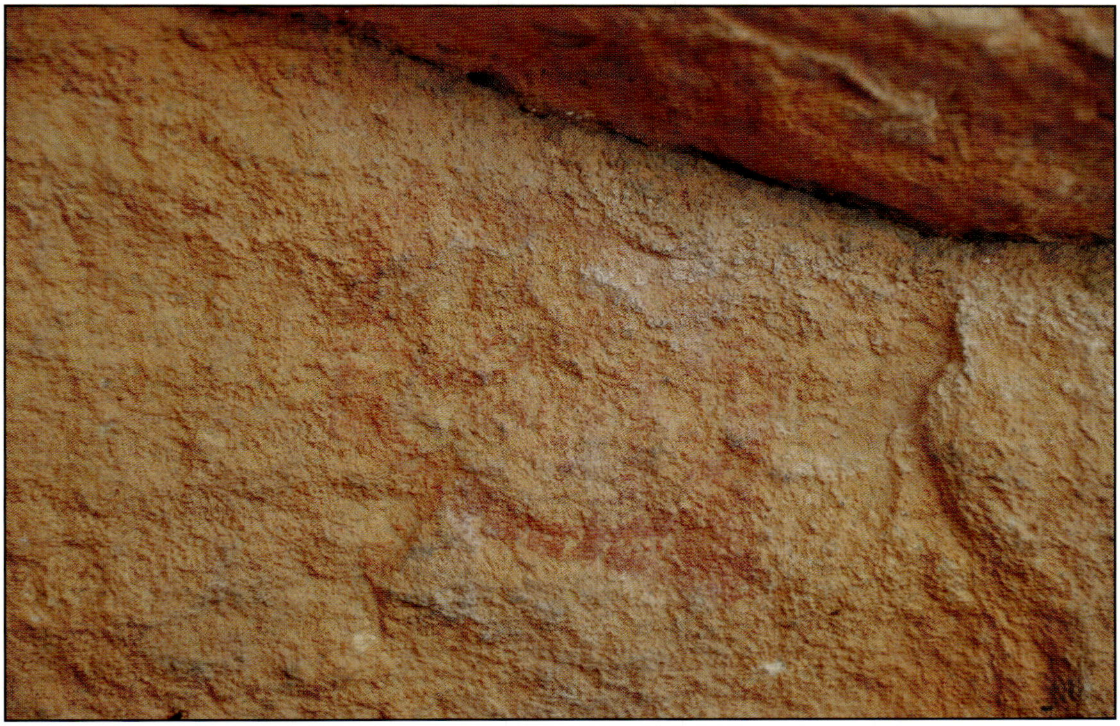

Fig. 16.30 A scorpion, Ambadevi.

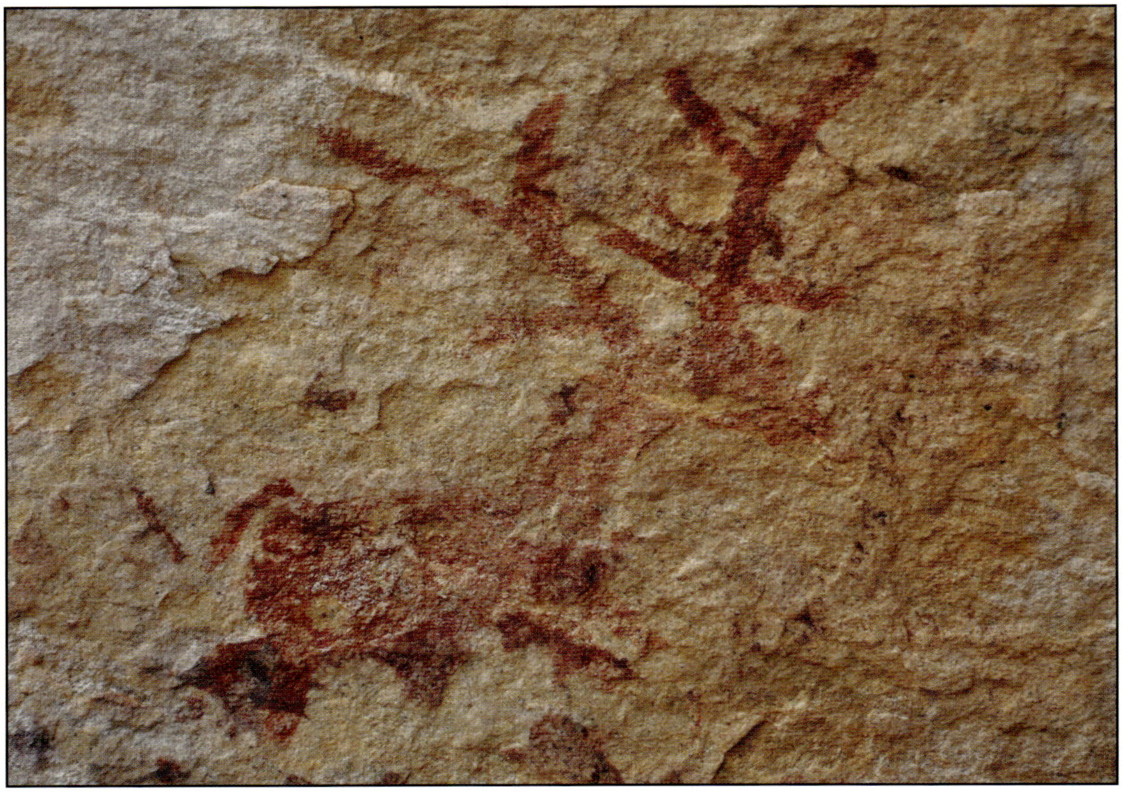

Fig. 16.31 *Barasingha*, Ambadevi.

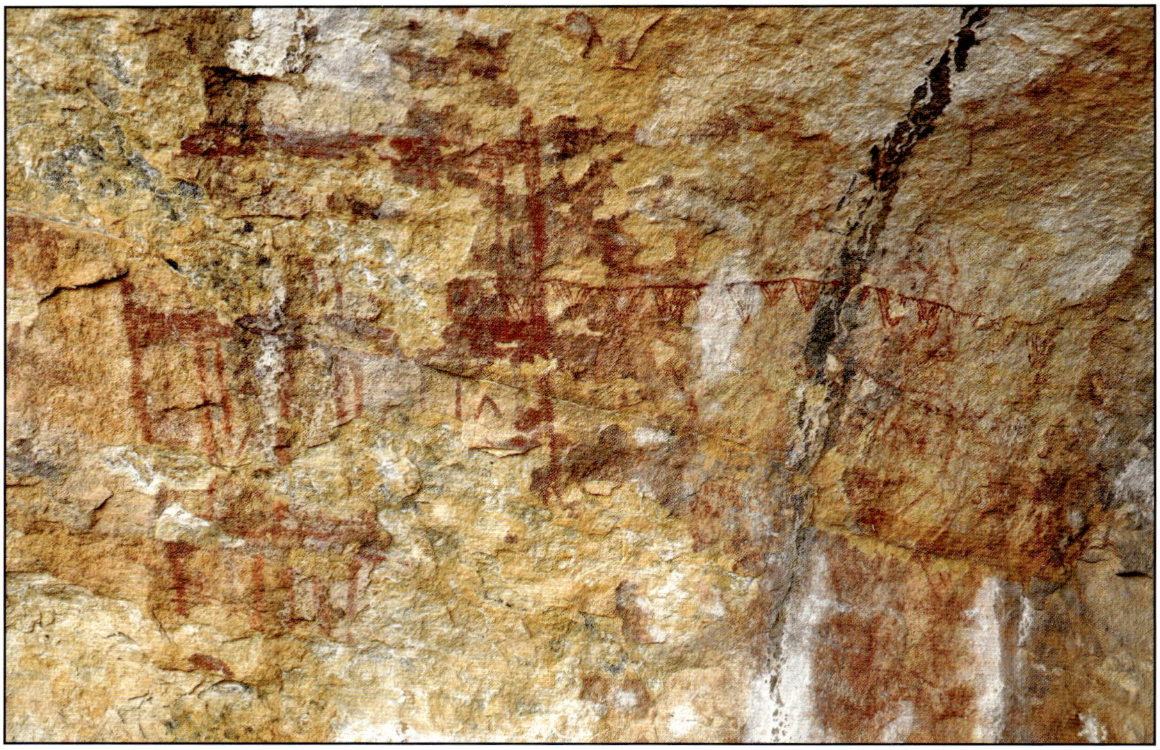

Fig. 16.32 A hut with festoons, Ambadevi.

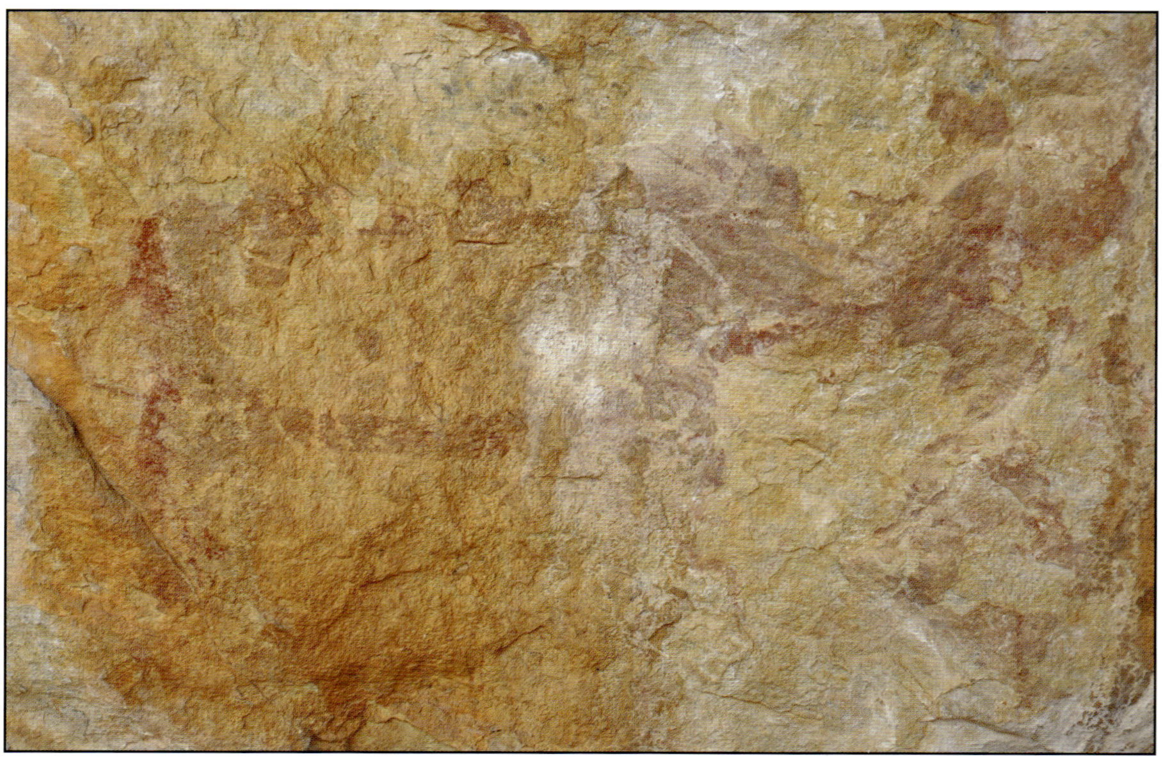

Fig. 16.33 An elephant with an upraised trunk, Ambadevi.

compared to the floral art of the place. The subsistence economy of hunting and gathering by prehistoric people is attested to by the paintings of hunting, fishing nets and beehives on different shelters. The collection of honey is one of the primary occupations of the present-day tribes of Gonds and Korkus inhabiting the area. This and many more such traits remain to be explored, deciphered and interpreted in the area of study. Arresting human vandalism, coupled with the vagaries of nature, are an integral part of protecting these shelters, as many of these have either been converted or are on the verge of being converted to shrines inviting hordes of ignorant visitors, damaging and defacing the invaluable relics.

ACKNOWLEDGEMENTS

The first author is grateful to the Director General, Archaeological Survey of India, for giving permission to work in the Tapti-Purna valley. Special thanks are due to Dr. B.R. Mani, Additional Director General of the Archaeological Survey of India, for his guidance and constant encouragement. The team comprising Shri Gajanan Katade, Dr. K.M. Girhe, P.L. Janbandhu, Dr. V. Gedam, Ms. Ekta Dharkar, R.G. Deshpande, M.S. Kadhao of the Prehistory Branch and Shri Manohar Kambe of the Excavation Branch I, Nagpur, deserves special thanks for the arduous task of discovering and documenting the rock shelters. Without their efforts and enthusiasm, the present work could not have been done. Shri N.K. Nimje, Senior Photographer, Prehistory Branch, was of much help in preparing the plates of tools; thanks are also due to him. The most important receivers of our acknowledgement and heartfelt thanks are the villagers of Dharul, especially S/s Ashok Kumre, Raju Kumre, Shyamrao Dhurve, Balu Dhurve, Gunwant Iwne and Shankar Dhurve who guided us through the difficult terrains and made our work a unique experience.

REFERENCES

Bednarik, R.G. (1993), 'Palaeolithic Art in India', *Man and Environment* XVIII(2): 33-40.

Chakravarty, K.K. (ed.) (1984), *Rock Art of India*. New Delhi: Arnold Heinmann.

Chakravarty, K. and Robert Bednarik (1997), *Indian Rock Art and Its Global Context*. Delhi: Motilal Banarsidass.

Ghosh, M. (1932), *Rock Paintings and Other Antiquities of Prehistoric and Later Times*. New Delhi: Memoirs of Archaeological Survey of India 24.

Ingole, V.T. et al. (2007), 'Discovery of Painted Rock Shelters from Satpura-Tapti Valley', *Purakala* 17: 153-58.

Kumar, G. (1996), 'Dara ki Chattan: A Palaeolithic Cupule Site in India', *Rock Art Research* 13(1): 38-46.

Lorblanchet, M. (ed.) (1993), *Rock Art in the Old World*. New Delhi: Indira Gandhi National Centre for the Arts.

Mathpal, Y. (1984), *Prehistoric Rock Paintings of Bhimbetka, Central India*. New Delhi: Abhinav Publication.

Neumayer, E. (1983), *Prehistoric Indian Rock Paintings*. New Delhi: Oxford University Press.

Pandey, S.K. (1993), *Indian Rock Art*. New Delhi: Aryan Books International.

Pawar, K.A. et al. (2011), 'Painted Rock Shelters at Dharul, in the Uppper Tapi Basin, Madhya Pradesh', *Man and Environment* XXXVI(2): 45-50.

Sundara, A. (1984), 'Some Selected Rock Paintings from North Karnataka', in K.K. Chakravarty (ed.), *Rock Art of India*. New Delhi: Arnold Heinmann, pp. 137-48.

Tiwari, S. (1975), 'Jaora: The Shelter of the Largest Rock Painting in India', *Prachya Pratibha* 3 (2): 93-96.

Tiwary, R. (1990), *Paintings of Mirzapur*. Lucknow: UP State Archaeological Museum.

Wakankar, V.S. (1975), 'Bhimbetka: The Prehistoric Paradise', *Prachya Pratibha* 3 (2): 7-29.

17

Prehistoric Rock Art in the Vindhyas in Uttar Pradesh and Adjoining Areas, North-Central India

J.N. Pal

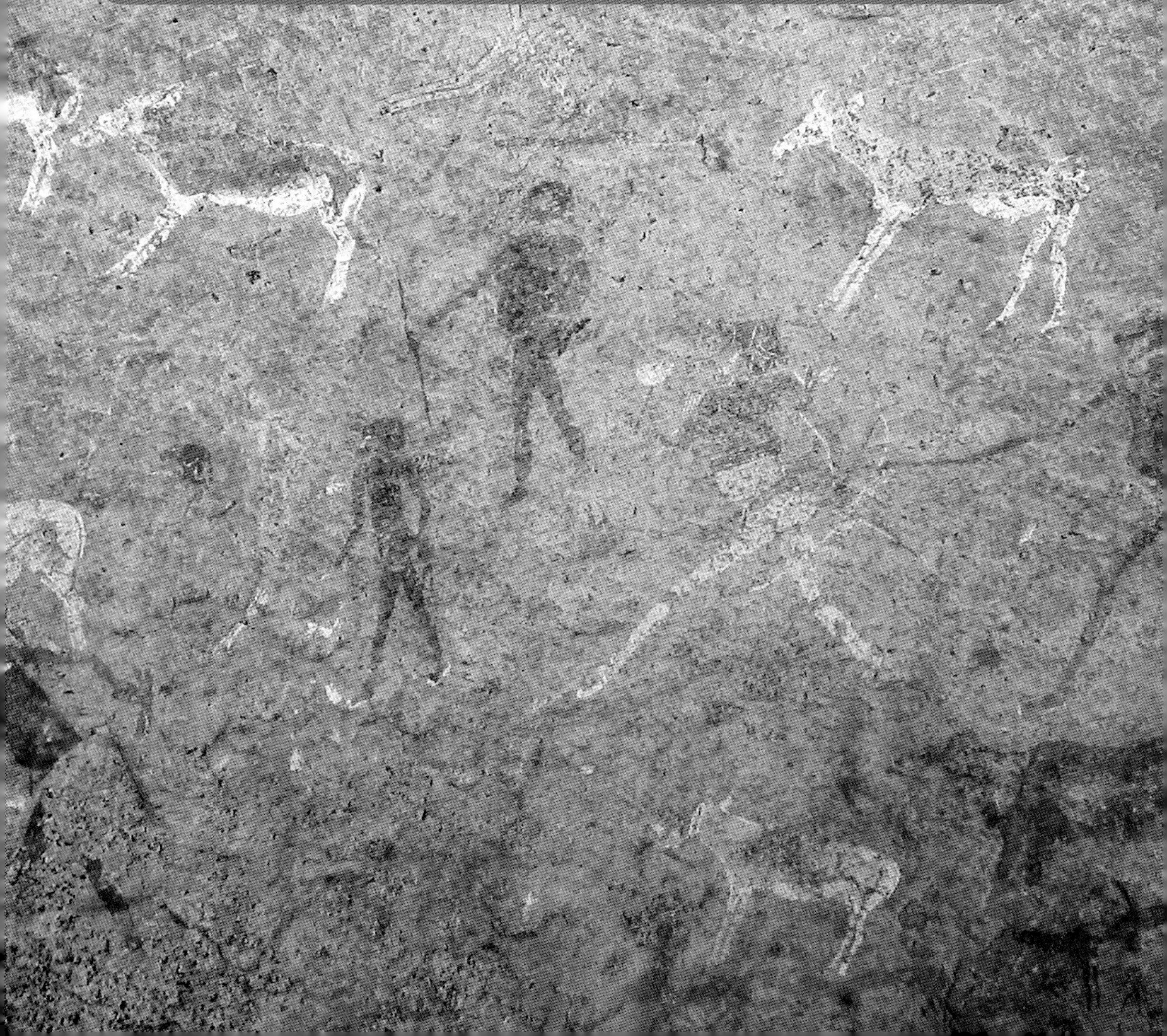

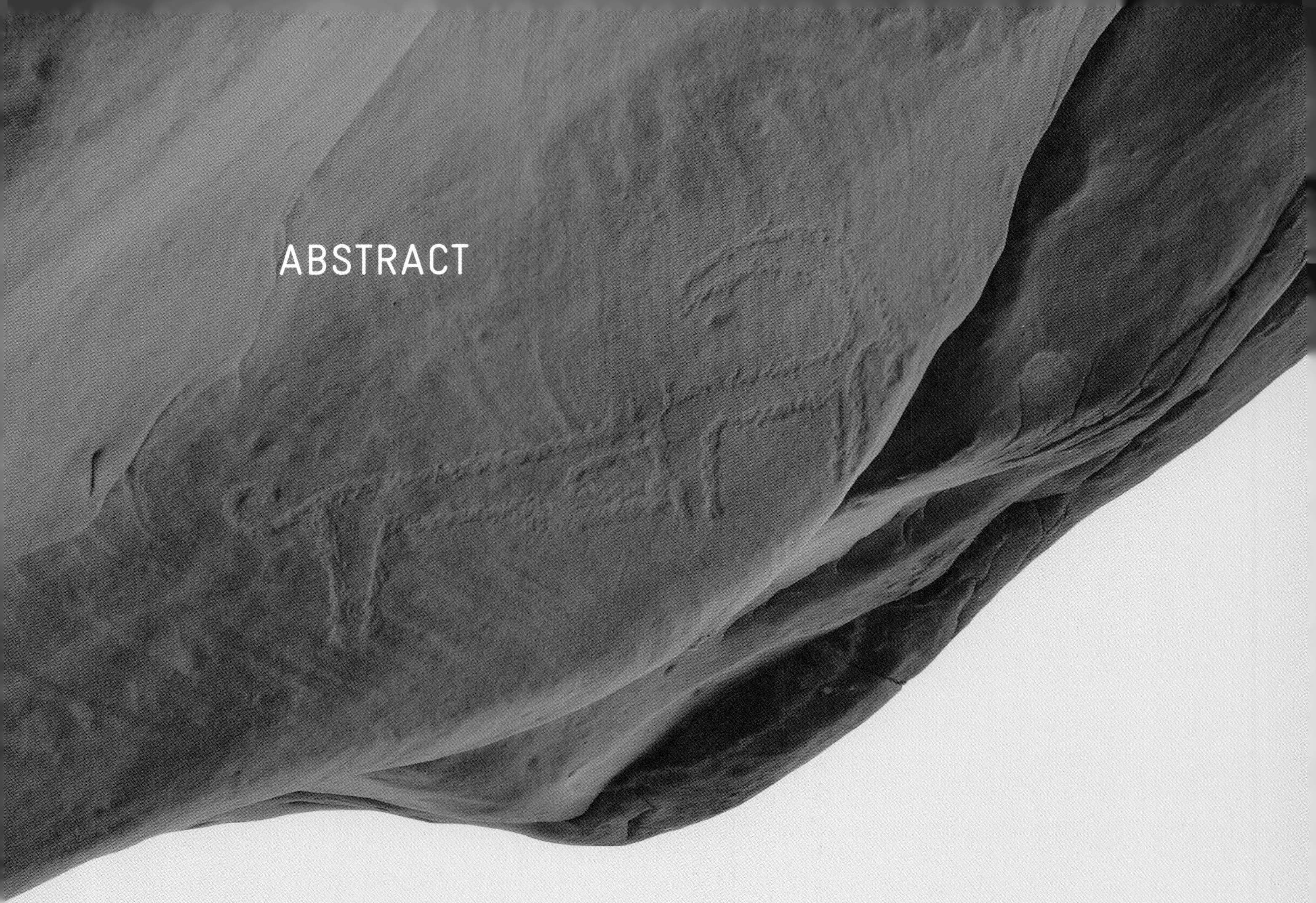

ABSTRACT

The Department of Ancient History, Culture and Archaeology, University of Allahabad, has conducted intensive archaeological investigations in the middle Gangetic plain and the adjoining Vindhyan Plateau lying to the south of the Gangetic plain for the last five decades, which has resulted in bringing to light ample data to reconstruct the life of prehistoric man right from the emergence of man in the region. The archaeo-geological studies have revealed significant results regarding the palaeoclimate of the region. Excavations of primary context prehistoric sites, especially Mesolithic rock shelters and open-air settlements, have yielded ample evidence to reconstruct the life ways and subsistence pattern of Stone Age man. Evidence of art activities has also been discovered right from the lower Palaeolithic period in the Vindhyas. The present paper tries to give a synthesis of such activities.

The north-central Vindhyas where intensive archaeological researches have been conducted include the districts of Chandauli, Allahabad, Mirzapur and Karwi in Uttar Pradesh and Rewa, Satna and Sidhi in Madhya Pradesh. The area is hilly and is characterised by stepped formations gradually rising from the north-east to the south-west. Its diverse and rugged topography is made of granite gneiss, sandstone and serrated ridges of quartz reefs. Presently, the climate of the area is characterised by a hot summer (March to June), rainy season (July to September) and cold winter (December to February). The region, lying to the south of the Ganga and Yamuna rivers, has archaeologically been one of the most investigated areas in India.

The geological, palaeontological and archaeological studies carried out in the region during the last five decades have revealed valuable evidence to reconstruct the Stone Age culture. Significant contributions in this field were made from 1980 and 1982 by a multidisciplinary research team from the Department of Ancient History, Culture and Archaeology, University of Allahabad and the Department of Anthropology, California University, Berkeley, USA, the Department of Earth Sciences, Macquire University, Australia and Birbal Sahni Institute of Palaeobotany, Lucknow. In the western part of the northern Vindhyas, known as Baghelkhand, archaeological investigations were also carried out by Banaras Hindu University, Varanasi, and Deccan College, Pune. The area of rivers Belan, Adwa, Tons, Son, Chambal, Paisuni and their tributaries being perennial sources of water provide a natural habitat for a variety of animals and plants in the river valleys. With reference to prehistoric archaeology, Belan and Son river valleys are the most important. The explored area in these valleys measures 19,000 sq. km and the geological and archaeological deposits are preserved in the river sections right from the middle Pleistocene to the early Holocene periods. Evidence of Palaeolithic, Mesolithic, Neolithic and Chalcolithic cultures along with transitional and transformational phases is very significant for understanding the developmental process of the cultures. The longest quaternary geological and cultural sequence has been worked out in the valleys of Belan and Son.

Belan along with its tributaries has a 61-km wide valley. Bounded by the Kaimurs in the south and the plateau in the north, an area of about 5,400 sq. km has been extensively explored and quaternary formations examined. The cliff section of the Belan with an average height of 18 m rests on the eroded and laterite plated Vindhyan rock and is divisible into 10 units (Misra 1977; Pal 1997; Sharma 1973).

The Son Valley was explored in an area of 13,601 sq. km in its middle reaches in Sidhi district in Madhya Pradesh and Mirzapur and Sonbhadra districts in Uttar Pradesh, where it flows to the south of Kaimur. The quaternary deposits of the middle Son Valley, as recorded from the nearly 30-m thick river section, is represented by four alluvial and three widespread loess formations (Clark and Williams 1990; Williams and Royce 1983). These formations have been named after the type sites: (i) Sihawal formation further sub-divisible into (a) Sihawal formation gravels and (b) Sihawal formation silt, (ii) Khuteli formation, (iii) Patpara formation, (iv) Baghor formation with two units (a) coarse member and (b) fine member, and (v) Khetaunhi formation (Williams et al. 2006). It is interesting to note that Khuteli formation, sandwitched between Sihawal and Patpara formations, has been identified in recent studies (Williams et al. n.d.).

The palaeo-environment during the Acheulian culture is inferred on the basis of basal formations in river valleys (Pal 1997). The basal gravels of Belan and Son (Unit 1 of Belan and gravel of Sihawal formation of Son) represent high energy fluviatile bedload deposits in a semi-arid climate with intermittent, erratic rainfall and sparse to absent plant cover (Williams and Royce 1983). The silt resting on it (Unit 2 of Belan and clay of Sihawal formation of Son) represents a relatively dry climate, which was deposited by low energy streams unable to carry coarser material.

Cemented gravel II with cross-finger deposits and intervening silts and sands of Belan and Patpara formation of Son, belonging to the middle Palaeolithic period, indicate highly effective discharge of rivers at least seasonally, moist conditions followed by a return of drier conditions.

During the period of upper Palaeolithic and Epi-Palaeolithic, upper gravels of Belan (III and IV) and coarse and fine members of Baghor formation of Son were the result of an intermediate flow regime within a low sinuosing bedload inter-tropical and phase change from bedload to suspended load regime at some stage in the terminal Pleistocene to early Holocene period. On the basis of OSL and C-14 dates, different Stone Age cultures have been dated (Pal et al. 2005) (Table 17.1).

Table 17.1 Different Stone Age cultures.

S. No.	Formation in the Son Valley	Geological Units in the Belan Valley	Culture	Period
1.	Sihawal Formation	Belan Units (a), (b)	Lower Palaeolithic	$\geq$ 100 K
2.	Khunteli Formation	Belan Unit (c)	Middle Paleolithic	75 ka
3.	Patpara Formation	Belan Unit (d)	Middle Palaeolithic	58-45 ka
4.	Baghor Formation (Coarse member)	Belan Unit (e)	Upper Palaeolithic	39-20 ka
5.	Baghor Formation (Fine member)	Belan Unit (f)	Epi-Palaeolithic	20-16 ka
6.	Khetaunhi Formation	Belan Unit (f)	Microlithic	10-8 ka
7.	Khetaunhi Formation	Belan Unit (g)	Neolithic	6 – 3 ka

A large number of sites ranging in age from lower Palaeolithic to early Historic have been located and a number of them have been put to excavation (Map 17.1). The excavated sites of Palaeolithic and Mesolithic cultures are:

Lower Palaeolithic: Sihawal II (Kenoyer and Pal 1983) and Nakjhar Khurd (Misra et al. 1983) in the Sidhi district in Madhya Pradesh in the Son Valley; Manigara (Misra et al. 1983) in Mirzapur district in Uttar Pradesh in Adwa Valley and Maihar (Pal and Pandey 1992-93) in Satna district in Madhya Pradesh in Lilji Valley.

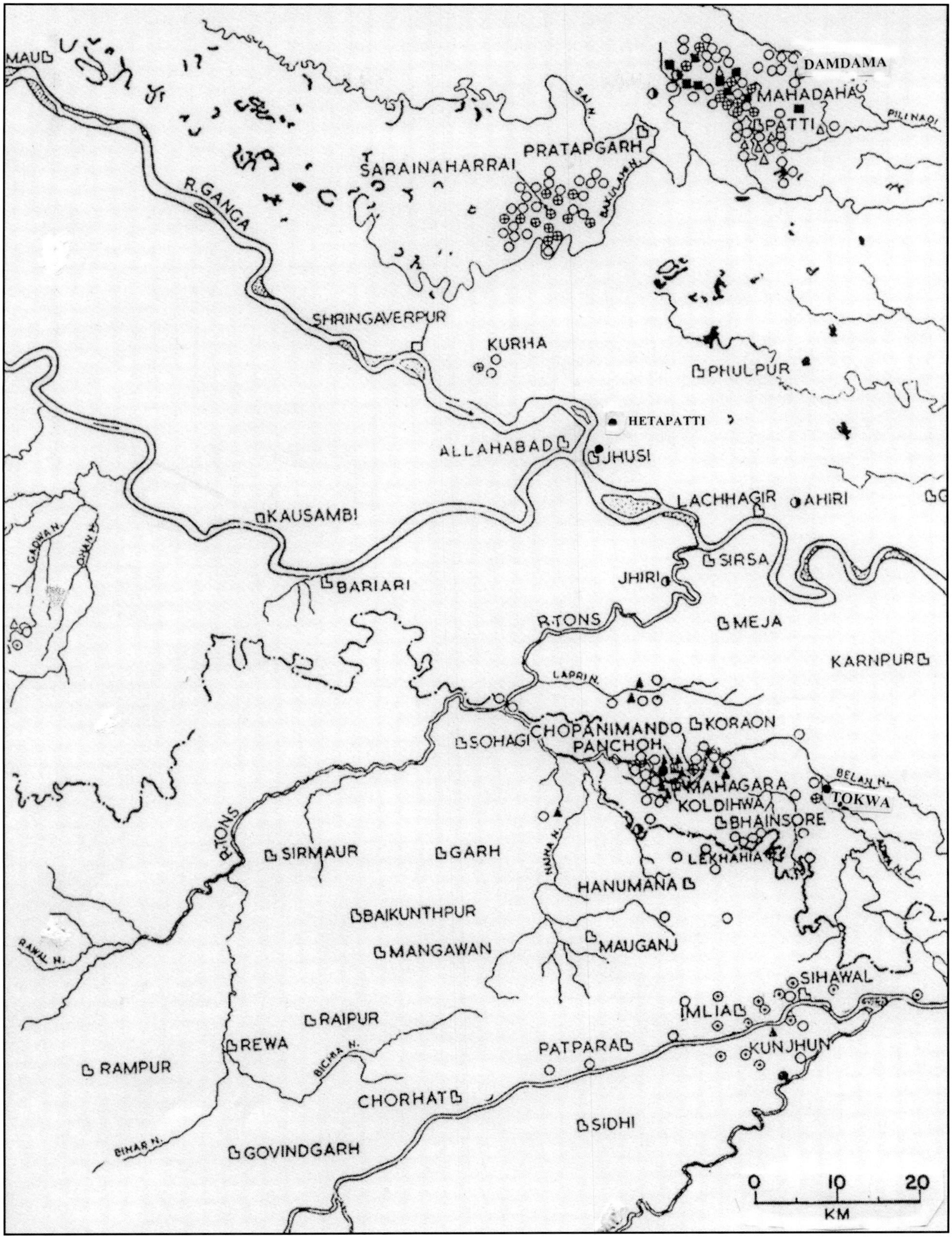

Map 17.1 Distribution of sites.

Middle Palaeolithic: Patpara in Sidhi district in Madhya Pradesh in Son Valley (Blumenschine et al. 1983); Baidha (Pal and Gupta 2002-03) in Mirzapur district in Uttar Pradesh and Maihar II and III (Pal and Pandey 1992–93) in Satna district in Madhya Pradesh in Lilji Valley.

Upper Palaeolithic: Baghor I (Kenoyer et al. 1993), Baghor III (Clark and Drieman 1983) and Rampur (p.c.) in Sidhi district in Madhya Pradesh in Son Valley; Maihar IV (Pal and Pandey 1992-93) in Satna district in Madhya Pradesh in Lilji Valley.

Mesolithic: Morahana Pahar (Varma 1964, 1965, 1977: 244-47, 1986), Baghai Khor (Kennedy 1990; Varma 1964: 342-43, 1965, 1986) and Lekhahia (Misra 1977: 53-57, Sharma 1965) and Lahariadih (Pant 1982) in Mirzapur district, Bhadahwan Pahar (Misra 1977: 179-80) in Chandauli district, Chopani Mando (Sharma and Misra 1980) in Allahabad district in Uttar Pradesh and Baghor II (Sussman et al. 1983), Ghagharia Rock shelter I (Brandt et al. 1983), Kunjhun II, Medhauli (*IAR* 1982-83: 57-58) and Banki (Misra et al. 1992-93) in Madhya Pradesh.

Though biological remains have not been found during excavations of primary context sites of Palaeolithic culture, some of these have yielded interesting evidence of art activities. Symmetrically manufactured, standardised and beautiful artefacts made with skill right from the Acheulian period were utilitarian and also art objects. However, evidence of art activities in the form of non-utilitarian art objects has been discovered right from the lower Palaeolithic period in the Vindhyas. The Palaeolithic sites yielding art objects are: Maihar I (lower Palaeolithic), Lohanda Nala in the Belan Valley (upper Palaeolithic) and Baghor I in Son Valley (upper Palaeolithic).

Maihar I: The primary context of the Acheulian site of Maihar is located in an almost flat land between Maihar temple hillock and Lilji River in Maihar sub-division in Satna district in Madhya Pradesh. An area of 36 x 24 was gridded in 1 x 1 m squares for horizontal excavation and 226 squares in 1987, 100 squares in 1988 and 67 squares in 1992 were exposed. A test trench of 1 x 2 m area was also excavated up to a depth of 1.73 m. The whole deposit is divisible into 3 main layers:

Layers (1) and (2) having a thickness of 57 to 76 cm are post-Acheulian deposits. Layer (3), divisible in two units— (3) and (3A), is the real Acheulian deposit. Layer (3) is a yellowish silt deposit of 25 to 30 cm containing besides fresh Acheulian artefacts weathered shale fragments, pallets coated with laterite and laterite nodules. Layer (3A) with a thickness of 20 to 40 cm is a mottled clay deposit containing in situ artefacts and shale fragments. This layer rested on the bedrock and there are bigger sandstone and quartzite blocks on the bedrock. It is interesting to note that these stone blocks are also unabraded.

Most of the artefacts recovered from the Index trench are made on quartzite while in other squares, besides quartzite, sandstone has also been used for manufacturing the artefacts. The artefact-manufacturing areas were identified where bigger stone blocks were used as anvils. Hammer stones along with cores, flakes, chips and tools in different stages of manufacture were lying around these anvil stones. The tools include cleavers, scrapers, retouched flakes, retouched chunks, retouched cores, spheroids, handaxes, knives, choppers and borers.

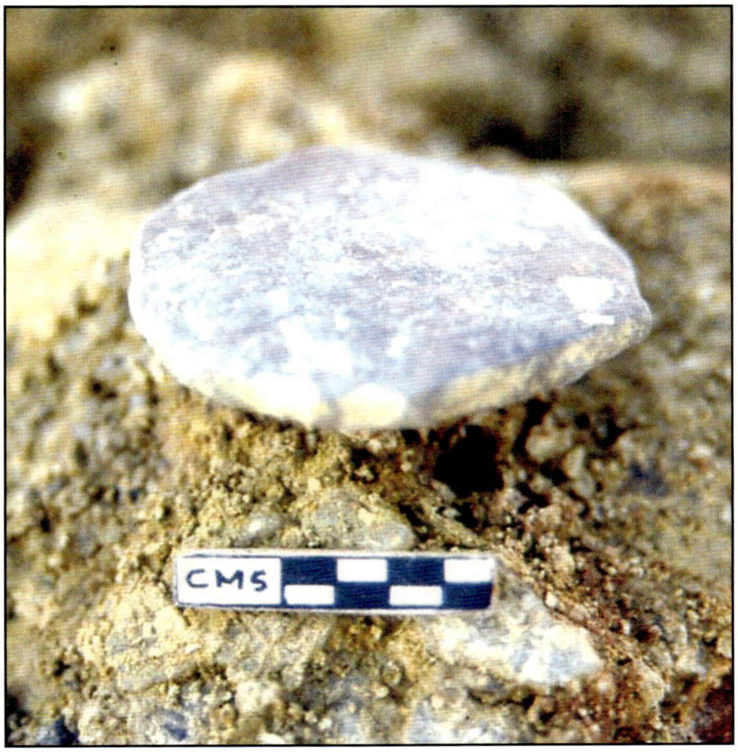

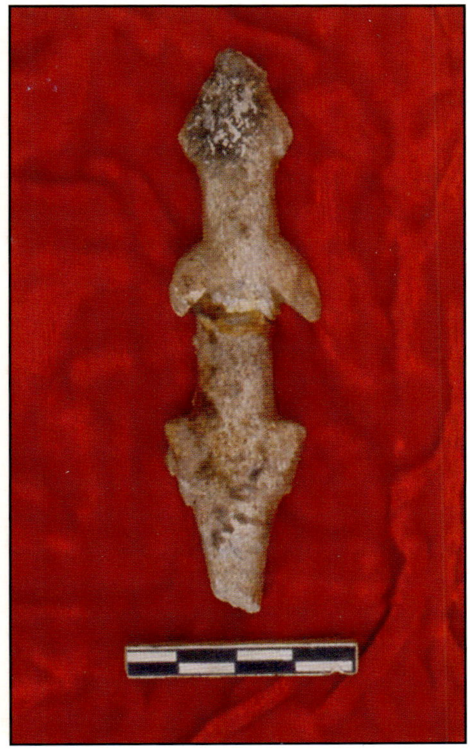

Left: **Fig. 17.1** Flaked disc with symmetrical alternate flaking on periphery.

Right: **Fig. 17.2** Bone art object, Lohanda Nala, Belan Valley.

Among the most interesting discoveries of the Acheulian culture is a symmetrically shaped disc from the Index trench with alternate flaking on its periphery (Fig. 17.1). This non-utilitarian stone object is a rare evidence of art activity in the Acheulian period. The disc may be a game object for children. In this connection, it may be mentioned that the site has yielded miniature cleavers that were also game objects for children rather than being functional cleavers.

Lohanda Nala in Belan Valley: The third cemented gravel of the Belan Valley (Unit 6) is the geological horizon of upper Palaeolithic culture. From the eroded surface of this formation in Lohanda Nala, a tributary of Belan, a bone object (Fig. 17.2) was found in association with unabraded upper Palaeolithic artefacts (*IAR* 1970-71, Misra 1977). Though doubts have been expressed about its being a human figurine or mother goddess (Gupta 1979-80), it is generally accepted on the basis of different features that it is definitely a female figurine (Sankalia 1974: 184). This bone figurine may be that of the mother goddess and like his distant cousin in Europe, the upper Palaeolithic man of Belan Valley was expressing himself through the medium of art (Misra 1977).

Baghor I: The upper Palaeolithic site of Baghor I is situated at a distance of about 1 km south of the Kaimur and 5 km north of Son on the bank of a small nala emanating from Kaimur at a distance of about 4 km north-east of Medhauli village in the Gopad-Banas sub-division of Sidhi district in Madhya Pradesh. The site was excavated in 1980 (Kenoyer et al. 1983) and 1982 (Pal 1980-81).

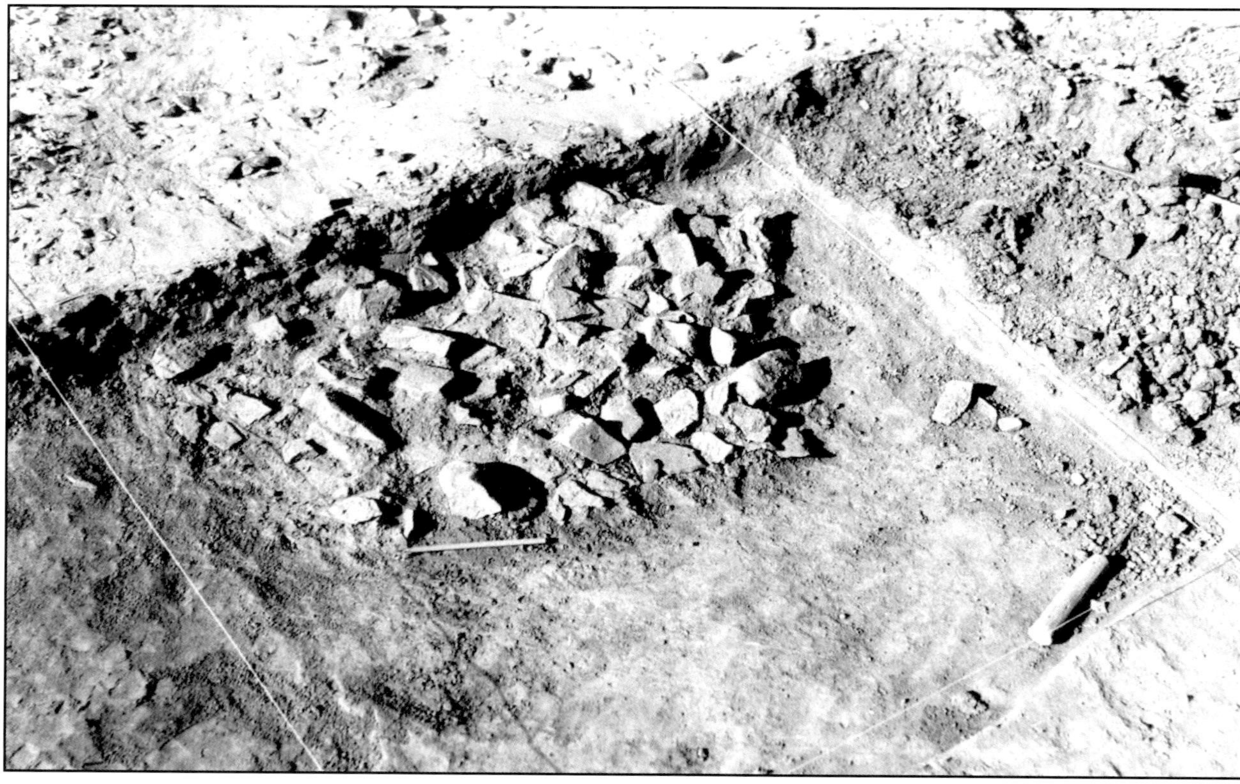

Fig. 17.3 Triangular ferruginous stone with concentric triangles, Baghor I.

The site was extended in an area of 660 sq. m and it was excavated in an area of 284 squares. Stratigraphically, the total deposit is divisible into three layers. Layer (1) with an average thickness of 35 cm is a sandy clay loam of orange colour. Layer (2) with an average thickness of 20 cm is greyish brown clay. Layer (3) composed of dark grey clay loam varies from 7 to 10 cm in thickness. This layer is the artefact-bearing horizon, the overlying layers being devoid of any in situ artefacts.

The excavated occupation surface shows some interesting features. In the heavily concentrated artefact area, a large number of nodules, cores, flakes, blades and debitage were accumulated along with finished and semi-finished tools. Mostly on the periphery, hammer stones and anvils were found along with chert and chalcedony nodules, cores, flakes and blades. One interesting thing is that the nodules are heat-treated before manufacturing was started. A number of artefacts are marked with heat-spalled surfaces. Besides unmodified waste (flakes, blades, core rejuvenating flakes, core trimming flakes, chunks and cores) and modified waste (modified/edge damaged blades, flakes, chunks, choppers, bored stone, lower grinding stone and hammer stone), a number of tools were found from the artefact-bearing horizon. The finished tools include straight-backed blades, convex-backed blades, double-backed blades, partly backed blades, half-backed and half-denticulated blades, straight-backed and truncated blades, convex-backed and truncated blades, partly backed and truncated blades, truncated blades, backed and denticulated blades, denticulated blades, denticulated blades with distal truncation/double

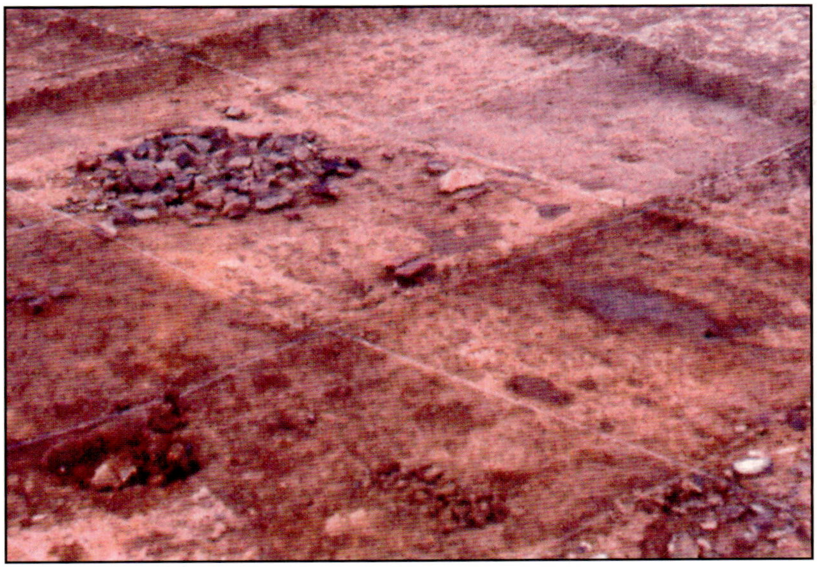

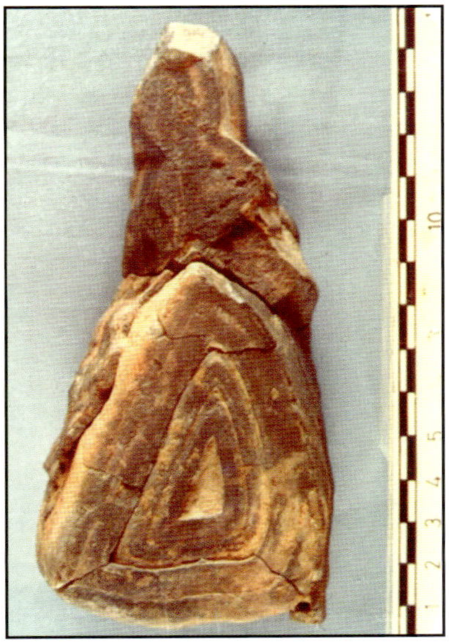

Left: **Fig. 17.4** Circular platform of the shrine, Baghor I.

Right: **Fig. 17.5** Triangular ferruginous stone with concentric triangles, Baghor I.

truncation, blades with ouchtata retouch, blades with normal retouch, blades with inverse retouch, scalene triangles, trapeze, parallelogram, drill, percoir, retouched flakes, side scrapers, end scraper, convex side scraper, round and double side scraper and transverse scraper-cum-bec. The excavation revealed interesting evidence of conjoining the blades/flakes with respective cores. There are many finished tools, which are so similar that they demonstratively show that these were removed from the same core by a similar technique using equal force of percussion.

One of the most important finds of the 1982 excavation was the discovery of a probable shrine of mother goddess at the end of the excavation. In squares I-9 and I-10 (2 x 1 m), as in other squares, tool-manufacturing waste with some shaped tools and sandstone rubbles were exposed. After lifting the exposed artefacts during the removal of the underlying debitage, numerous pieces of sandstone rubble interspersed with numerous chert artefacts were encountered (Fig. 17.3).

After lifting the chert artefacts, we discovered that sandstone rubble formed roughly a circular platform about 85 cm in diameter. In the centre of this platform was a fragment of a natural, ferruginous laminated stone, the colour of which ranges from light yellowish red to dark reddish brown. Additional fragments of the same stone were found lying next to the first fragment and two pieces were found on the periphery of the platform while one fragment was 90 cm to the south of the centre of the platform (Fig. 17.4). So far, ten fragments have been found and they all join together to form a triangular-shaped natural stone—15 cm high, 6.5 cm wide and about 6.5 cm thick (Fig. 17.5).

As seven fragments of the central part of this stone were found at the centre of the platform, it could be said that the complete stone, as it is attractive due to laminated coloured concentric triangles, was placed originally in this central position and was worshiped as mother goddess. Being weak in physical structure due to lamination, the stone cracked, broke apart and scattered on the platform.

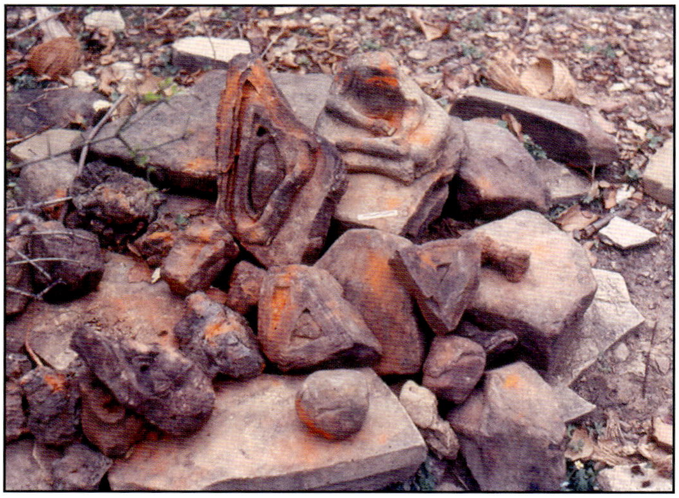

Fig. 17.6 Shrine of mother goddess at Kerai near Baghor I.

It is interesting to note that the present tribal inhabitants of the area, especially the Kols and Baigas, worship this type of colourful natural stones with concentric laminations as the mother goddess. The central position of the stone on the platform, its striking similarity to the stones worshipped at Kerai-ki-devi (Fig. 17.6) and in the shrine below a Neem tree in Medhauli village and other such shrines in the area, and the immediate and spontaneous recognition of its significance by the local inhabitants all indicate that there is very strong probability that this structure and the triangular stone represent a shrine of the mother goddess.

In the absence of radiocarbon dates and other datable material, the chronology of the upper Palaeolithic culture at the site is not fixed. But geologists are of the view that Baghor I is within the upper part of the coarse member of Baghor formation, which may tentatively be dated to about 18000 BCE on the basis of a C-14 date reading 20,135±220 BP, obtained from the main yellow-brown loess formation containing shells (Williams and Clarke 1995).

Evidence of stone discs manufactured by alternate flaking, standardised and beautiful miniature cleavers from the excavation of Maihar, mother goddess made of bone from Belan and natural triangular stone discovered from a circular platform (shrine) at Baghor I is some evidence to show that the Palaeolithic hominid and upper Palaeolithic man had aesthetic sense like that of man of later times.

The Mesolithic term for the culture lying between Palaeolithic and Neolithic was given by A.C.L. Carlleyle, who discovered microliths for the first time from Kaimur in Mirzapur district. One of the rock shelters discovered by Carlleyle was Morahana Pahar. Some of the shelters were excavated by him (Carlleyle 1883). On the walls and ceilings of the rock shelters, Carlleyle noticed paintings, which appeared to him 'to illustrate in a very stiff and archaic manner scenes in the life of the ancient stone chippers; others represent animals or hunts of animals by men armed with bows and arrows, spears and hatchets' (Smith 1906: 187). Carlleyle's contemporary, J. Cockburn (1883, 1899), studied the rock paintings and fossil fauna found in this region. The site of Morahana Pahar was excavated afresh by R.K. Varma of Allahabad Universiy. The excavations of rock shelters and open-air settlements of the Mesolithic period by University of Allahabad yielded four stages of development of the Mesolithic culture: (i) Non-geometric microlithic aceramic, (ii) Geometric microlithic aceramic, (iii) Geometric microlithic with pottery, and (iv) Diminutive microlithic with pottery (Misra 1977; Varma 1964). Some of the excavated rock shelters and open-air occupational sites in the area like Chopani Mando and Ghagharia have produced engraved designs on bone and stone objects. Rock paintings have been one of the important sources for reconstructing the life of Stone Age man. In India, according to prehistoric art historians like V.S. Wakankar, the beginning of rock paintings has been ascribed to the upper Palaeolithic period. It is undoubtedly accepted that rock painting activity was at its peak during the Mesolithic period (Varma 2002). There are a number of natural rock shelters in the Vindhyan area, both plain and painted, which have attracted pre-historians right from the later half of the 19th century. In our study area, these have been located in Banda, Karwi, Allahabad, Mirzapur, Sonbhadra in Uttar Pradesh and Sidhi, Sahdol and Rewa districts in Madhya Pradesh. Of the painted rock shelters, mention may be made of Sarhat, Malawa, Kuriyakunj, Amawa, Uldan, Bargarh, Markundi, Majhawan, Kauakhoh and Chitrakut in Karwi; Ramgarhwa, Chhatarpalia, Chandatari, Lakhahar and the Chandawa group of rock shelters in Allahabad; Sahabia, Bediya, Ladbedia, Baga, Baghaikhor, Marchahwa, Khari Pathari, Munnibaba, Lekhahia (Bhainsore area), Panchmukhi, Kandakot, Chanmanwa and Lakhania (Rajpur area); Lakhania, Kohbar, Ghora Mangar, Maldaria, Mahadaria (Ahraura area); and Tharpahara (Chunar Area) in Mirzapur district and Gahala-Shahpur on the bank of Karmanasa in Varanasi district. Among the important sites in Madhya Pradesh, mention may be made of Ghaghria. The painted rock shelters bear paintings on the walls and ceilings in red ochre, white and black pigments. The red ochre colour ranges from deep red to dull red. The paintings have been done either in outline or flat wash. It seems that the paintings were executed by spreading the liquid or semi-liquid pigment by a brush or a pad. The painted motifs include hunting scenes, group dance, animals, particularly stag and bovids and palm impressions. The rock shelters and rock paintings in north-eastern Vindhyas could not be documented in detail as was done for those around Bhimbetka (Varma 1984). Rakesh Tewari explored several important painted rock shelters in Mirzapur district (Tewari 1990). R.K. Varma completed a detailed and systematic documentation of rock art of north-eastern Vindhyas recently and is publishing an illustrated monograph on it.

R.K. Varma, who studied the rock paintings of undivided Mirzapur district in 1963-64 in detail, has divided the paintings in five groups on the basis of the technique of presentation, state of preservation and superimposition (Varma 1965: 75-76, 1984). The first and earliest group has been termed as imitative, naturalistic in which the animals represented are in life-size and in natural postures. No human figures or hunting scene have been observed in this group. The colour is burnt red and the paintings are covered with a thin coating of patina. The paintings of this group are generally superimposed by those of the later period.

The second group of paintings is termed as stylistic or suggestive and they are found in large numbers in the area. No attention was paid to the proportion. Variety of subjects, animals, single or in small groups, hunting scenes, trap scenes, animals with riders and human figures form the subject matter of this group.

The paintings in the third group are symbolic in which pictures are reduced to an angle, a circle, a dot, a spiral line or a loop. The fourth group contains animals or human figures executed in white colour.

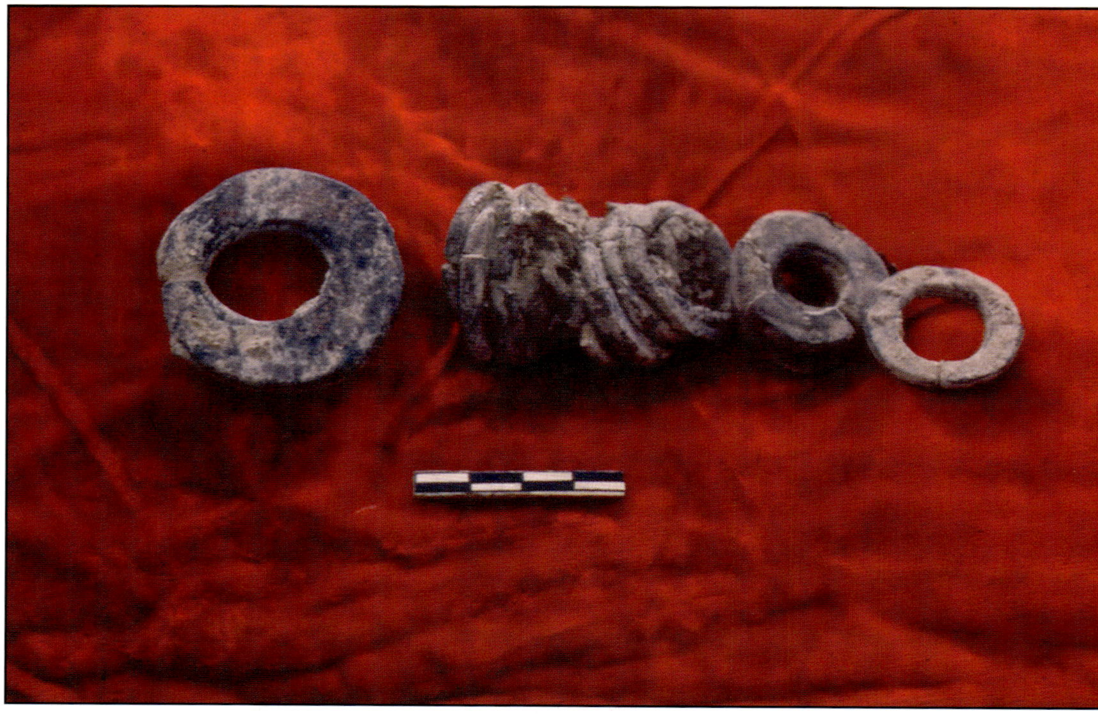

Fig. 17.7 Ornaments made of antler, Mahadaha.

The last group of paintings depict caparisoned animals, yoked bulls, war scenes and processions, etc. The subject matter, technique and appearance clearly suggest that these belong to the post-Mesolithic period farming cultures and continued up to the historical period. Sometimes, black pigment was used in these paintings.

The first four groups of rock paintings in the rock shelters in the Vindhyas are a valuable source of knowledge for constructing the subsistence pattern of the Mesolithic hunting-gathering society, as is reflected by various ways of hunting, trapping and gathering, etc. (Varma 1996). Rock art, especially the paintings, throw welcome light on the hunting methods during the Mesolithic period. Ferocious big games like rhinoceros, bison and boars were hunted in groups by spears and harpoons. Scenes of small games like deer are shown being hunted by bows and arrows (Varma 2002, 2012).

A majority of the Mesolithic sites in the Ganga plain were apparently temporary settlements yielding only unmodified waste and finished tools, but a few are marked by thick occupational deposits with rich cultural material and biological remains which indicate semi-sedentary settlements. A few of these sites, namely Sarai Nahar Rai, Mahadaha and Damdama, all in Pratapgarh district, have been excavated and the data obtained in combination with geo-morphological research, have enabled the reconstruction of human adaptations in the early Holocene period in the Ganga plain. Evidence of artistic activity has also been obtained from these excavated sites of the Ganga plain (Gupta 2002; Pal 2002).

Numerous nodules of haematite and ochre with rubbed surfaces have been found from the excavations of Mesolithic sites in the Ganga plain. As ochre was used for executing

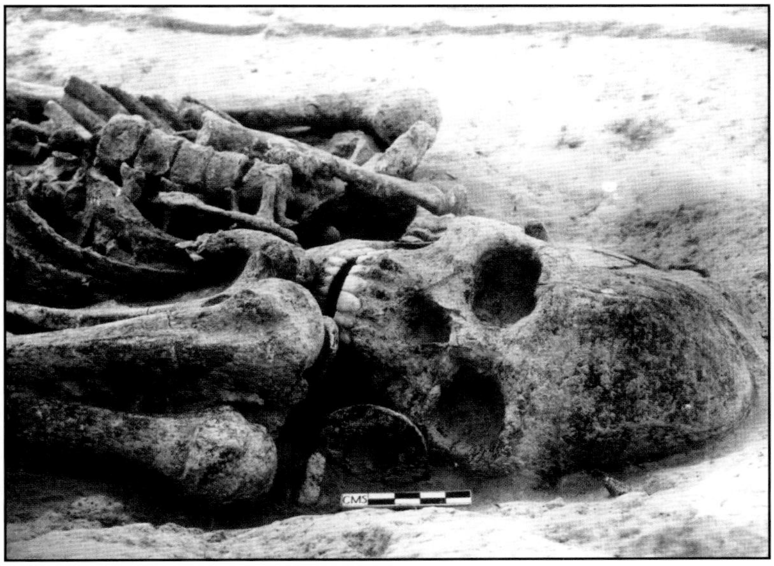

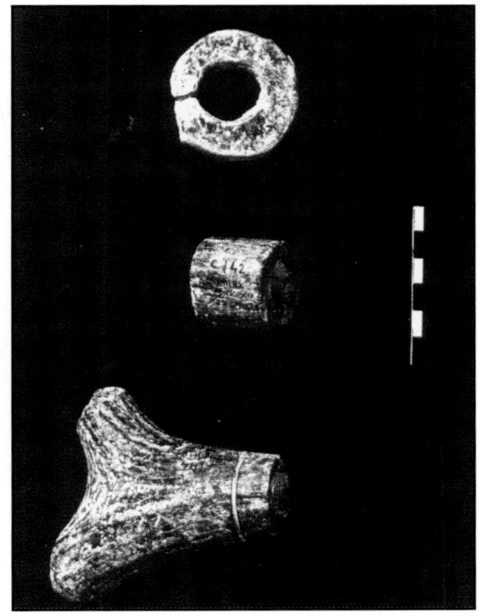

Left: **Fig. 17.8** Male skeleton wearing earring, Mahadaha.

Right: **Fig. 17.9** Ornaments in different stages of manufacture, Mahadaha.

rock paintings in the hilly region, it may be presumed that the Mesolithic inhabitants of the Ganga plain also made paintings, possibly on animal skins. It is also possible that ochre was used to paint the face and other parts of the body as tribal people do even today on some special occasions. Seven circular marks on a bone object found at Damdama deserve special attention (Gupta 2002). In one of the human burials, seven haematite nodules were placed as offering. The Mesolithic people of the Ganga Valley were also fond of wearing ornaments like earrings, necklaces and pendants made of bone, antler or ivory (Fig. 17.7). However, wearing of ornaments was not a common practice, as only a few graves have yielded ornaments (Fig. 17.8). It may be assumed that these belong to people who enjoyed a special position in society. Evidence of different stages of manufacture of ornaments at Mahadaha is significant (Fig. 17.9).

CONCLUSION

Beautifully made mini-cleavers and other artefacts made with skill, as obtained from Maihar in the Vindhyas, were utilitarian; but they were also art objects. The discovery of a symmetrically shaped disc from Maihar is also one of the early art objects of the Acheulian people. The mother goddess bone figurine from Belan and a natural triangular stone discovered from a circular platform at Baghor-I are also indicators of the aesthetic sense and religious beliefs of upper Palaeolithic man. A developmental sequence in the lithic technology obtained from excavated rock shelters and open-air settlements can be treated as definite evidence of their cultural advancement, which is also seen in their rock paintings. The painted rock shelters in the Vindhyas showing different activities of their life and objects made on bone and stone having engraved designs also provide evidence of art activities. The Mesolithic people of the Gangetic plain expressed their aesthetic sense on portable objects in the form of stone and bone art objects, as is evident from bone ornaments and heavily rubbed/used ochre nodules.

REFERENCES

Blumenschine, R.J., S.A. Brandt and J.D. Clark (1983), 'Excavation at Analysis of Middle Palaeolithic Artefacts from Patpara, Madhya Pradesh', in G.R. Sharma and J.D. Clark (eds.), *Palaeoenvironments and Prehistory in the Middle Son Valley*. Allahabad: Abinash Prakashan, pp. 39-100.

Brandt, S.A., J.D. Clark, J.A. Gutin and B.B. Misra (1983), 'Rockshelters with Paintings on the Top of the Kaimur at Ghagharia and an Account of the Excavation and Analysis of the Mesolithic Occupation at the Ghagharia I Shelter', in G.R. Sharma and J.D. Clark (eds.), *Palaeoenvironments and Prehistory in the Middle Son Valley*. Allahabad: Abinash Prakashan, pp. 205-39.

Carlleyle, A.C.L. (1983), 'Notes on Lately Discovered Sepulchral Mounds, Cairns, Caves, Cave-Paintings and Stone Implements', *Proceedings of the Asiatic Society of Bengal* (February), p. 49.

Clark, J.D. and R. Drieman (1983), 'An Occurrence with Small Blade Technology in the Upper Member of the Baghor Formation at the Baghor III Locality', in G.R. Sharma and J.D. Clark (eds.), *Palaeoenvironments and Prehistory in the Middle Son Valley*. Allahabad: Abinash Prakashan, pp. 197-204.

Clark, J.D. and M.A.J. Williams (1990), 'Prehistoric Ecology, Resource Strategies and Culture Changes in the Son Valley, Northern Madhya Pradesh, Central India', *Man and Environment*, XV (1): 120-33.

Cockburn, J. (1883), 'On the Recent Existence of Rhinoceros Indicus in the North-West Provinces, and Description of an Archaic Rock Painting from Mirzapur, Representing the Hunting of an Animal', *Journal of the Royal Asiatic Society of Bengal* 52: 56-64.

—— (1883), 'A Short Account of the Petrographs in the Caves and Rock Shelters of the Kaimur Range in Mirzapore District', *Proceedings of the Asiatic Society of Bengal* 52: 125-26.

—— (1899), 'Cave Drawings in the Kaimur Range, North-West Provinces', *Journal of the Asiatic Society of Bengal* 18: 89-97.

Gupta, M.C. (2002), 'Mesolithic Bone Objects of the Middle Gangetic Plain', in V.D. Misra and J.N. Pal (eds.), *Mesolithic India*. Allahabad: Department of Ancient History, Culture & Archaeology, University of Allahabad, pp. 306-12.

Gupta, S.P. (1979-80), 'The Alleged Upper Palaeolithic Bone Mother Goddess from Belan', *Puratattva* 11: 116.

Kenoyer, J.M., J.D. Clark, J.N. Pal and G.R. Sharma (1982), 'An Upper Paleolithic Shrine in India', *Antiquity* LVII: 88-94.

Kenoyer, J.M. and J.N. Pal (1983), 'Report on the Excavation and Analysis of an Upper Acheulean Assemblage from Sihawal-II', in G.R. Sharma and J.D. Clark (eds.), *Palaeoenvironments and Prehistory in the Middle Son Valley*. Allahabad: Abinash Prakashan, pp. 23-38.

Misra, V.D. (1977), *Some Aspects of Indian Archaeology*. Allahabad: Prabhat Prakashan.

—— (1997), 'Lower and Middle Palaeolithic Cultures of Northern Vindhyas', in V.D. Misra and J.N. Pal (eds.), *Indian Prehistory*: 1980. Allahabad: Department of Ancient History, Culture & Archaeology, University of Allahabad.

Misra, V.D., R.S. Rana, J.D. Clark and R.J. Blumenshine (1983), 'Preliminary Excavations at the Son River Section at Nakjhar Khurd', in G.R. Sharma and J.D. Clark (eds.), *Palaeoenvironments and Prehistory in the Middle Son Valley*. Allahabad: Abinash Prakashan, pp. 101-16.

Misra, V.D., B.B. Misra and J.N. Pal (1996-97), 'Recent Explorations in the Adwa Valley in the Districts of Mirzapur (U.P.) and Sidhi and Rewa (M.P.)', *Pragdhara* 7: 59-65.

Misra, V.D., B.B. Misra, U.C. Chattopadhyaya, D.K. Shukla and P. Sinha (1992-93), 'Excavations at the Primary Context Mesolithic Occupation Site of Banki, District Sidhi, M.P.: A Preliminary Report', *Pragdhara* 3: 5-11.

Pal, J.N. (1980-81), 'Upper Palaeolithic Cultures of the Mid-Son Valley', *Puratattva* 12: 23-30.

—— (1997), 'Environmental Change and Human Adaptation in the Quaternary Period in the Vindhyas, Central India', in B.M. Khanduri and Vinod Nautiyal (eds.), *Him-Kanti: Archaeology, Art and History (Prof. K.P. Nautiyal Felicitation Volume)*. Delhi: Book India Publishing Co., pp. 1-10.

—— (2002), 'Mesolithic Gangetic Plain', in V.D. Misra and J.N. Pal (eds.), *Mesolithic India*. Allahabad: Department of Ancient History, Culture and Archaeology, University of Allahabad, pp. 289-305.

Pal, J.N. and J.N. Pandey (1992-93), 'Palaeolithic Maihar, Satna District Madhya Pradesh: A Preliminary Report of Excavations', *Pragdhara* 3: 1-4.

Pal, J.N. and M.C. Gupta (2002–03), 'Archaeological Investigations at Baidha and Neighbouring Area in the Adwa Valley in Mirzapur District, Uttar Pradesh', *Pragdhara* 13: 227-30.

Pant, P.C. (1982), *Prehistoric Uttar Pradesh*. Delhi: Agam Kala Prakshan.

Sankalia, H.D. (1974), *The Prehistory and Protohistory of India and Pakistan*. Poona: Deccan College.

Sharma, G.R. and B.B. Misra (1980), *Excavations at Chopani Mando*. Allahabad: Department of Ancient History, Culture and Archaeology, University of Allahabad.

Smith, V.A. (1906), 'The Pygmy Flint', *Indian Antiquary* XXXV: 185-95.

Sussman, C., R. Blumenschine, J.D. Clark and B.B. Misra (1983), 'Preliminary Report on Excavations at the Mesolithic Occupation Site at Baghor II Locality', in G.R. Sharma and J.D. Clark (eds.), *Palaeoenvironments and Prehistory in the Middle Son Valley*. Allahabad: Abinash Prakashan, pp. 161-96.

Tewari, Rakesh (1990), *Rock Paintings of Mirzapur .U.P.* Lucknow: State Archaeological Organization.

Varma, R.K. (1964), 'The Stone Age Culture of Mirzapur', D. Phil dissertation, University of Allahabad, Allahabad.

—— (1965), 'Comments on Mesolithic Phase in Prehistory of India', in V.N. Misra and M.S. Mate (eds.), *Indian Prehistory: 1964*, pp. 73-76.

—— (1984), 'The Rock-Art of Southern Uttar Pradesh with Special Reference to Mirzapur', in K.K. Chakravarty (ed.), *Rock-Art of India*. New Delhi: Arnold-Heimann, pp. 206-12.

—— (1986), *The Mesolithic Age in Mirzapur*. Allahabad: Paramjyoti Prakashan.

—— (1996), 'Subsistence Economy of the Mesolithic Folk as Reflected in the Rock-Paintings of the Vindhyan Region', in Gennadi E. Afanasev, Serge Cleuziou, John R. Lukacs and Maurizio Tosi (eds.), *Colloquium XXXIII, Bioarchaeology of Mesolithic India: An Integrated Approach*. Forli, Italy: The Prehistory of Asia and Oceania, International Union of Prehistoric and Protohistoric Sciences Congress.

—— (2000), 'Hunting Strategy of the Mesolithic Folk as Revealed by Rock Paintings', in V.D. Misra and J.N. Pal (eds.), *Mesolithic India*. Allahabad: Department of Ancient History, Culture and Archaeology, University of Allahabad, pp. 401-20.

—— (2012), *Rock Art of Central India: North Vindhyan Region*. New Delhi: Aryan Books International.

Varma, R.K. and J.N. Pal (1997), 'The Upper Palaeolithic Culture of the Vindhyan Region', in V.D. Misra and J.N. Pal (eds.), *Indian Prehistory: 1980*. Allahabad: Department of Ancient History, Culture and Archaeology, University of Allahabad.

Williams, M.A.J. and Keith Royce (1983), 'Alluvial History of the Middle Son Valley, North Central India', in G.R. Sharma and J.D. Clark (eds.), *Palaeoenvironments and Prehistory in the Middle Son Valley*. Allahabad: Abinash Prakashan, pp. 161-96.

Williams, M.A.J. and M.F. Clarke (1995), 'Quaternary Geology and Prehistoric Environments in the Son and Belan Valleys, North Central India', in *Quaternary Environments and Geoarchaeology of India: Essays in Honour of Professor S.N. Rajaguru*. Bangalore: Geological Society of India, pp. 282-308.

Williams, M.A.J., J.N. Pal, M. Jaiswal and A.K. Singhvi (n.d.), *River Response to Quaternary Climatic Fluctuations: Evidence from the Son and Belan Valleys, North-Central India*.

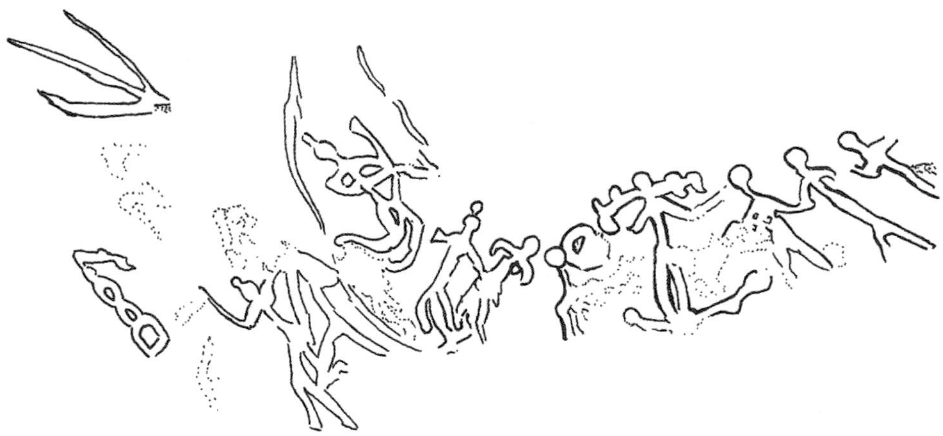

18

The Rock Art of Northern Vindhyan Region

Radha Kant Varma

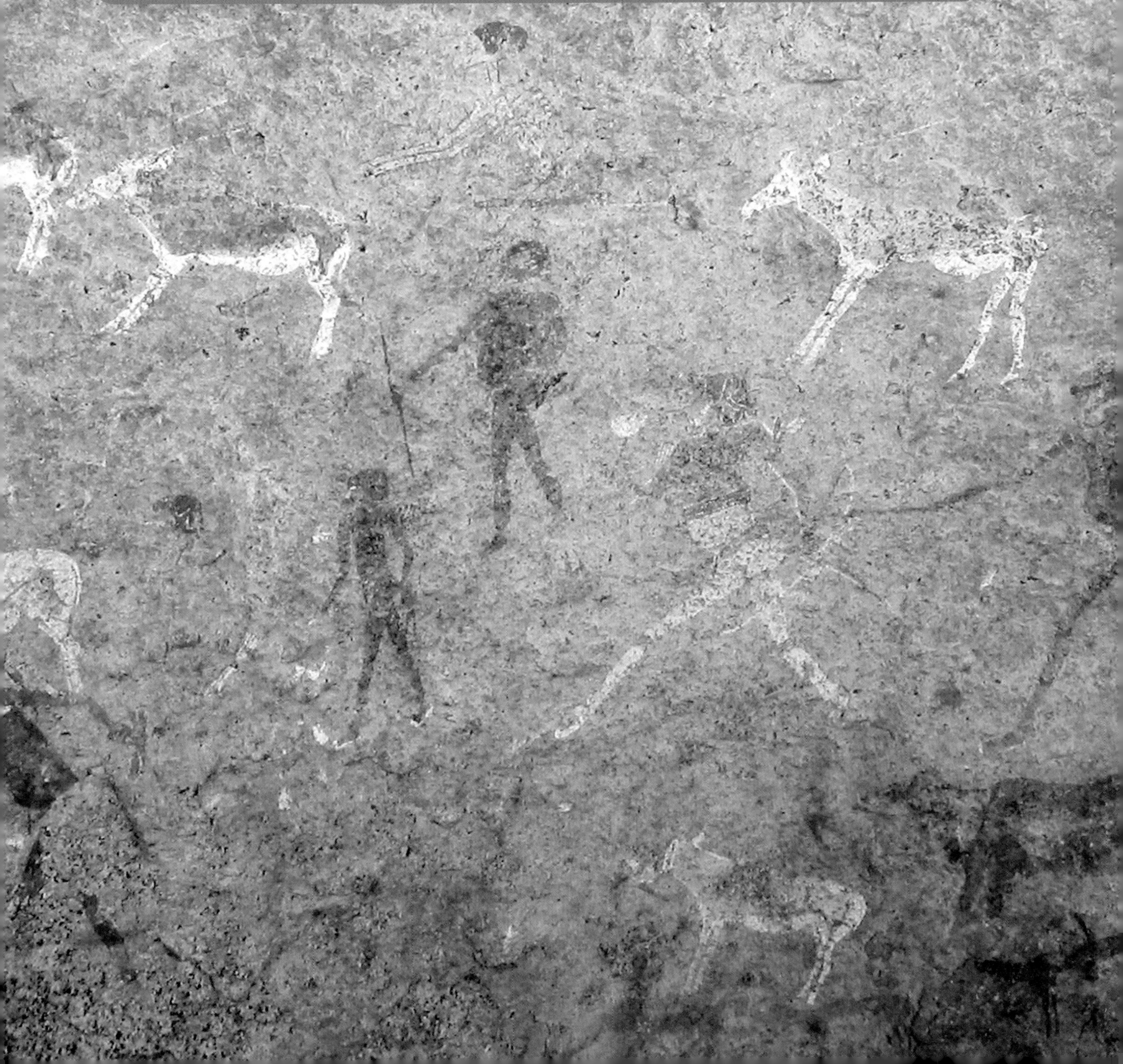

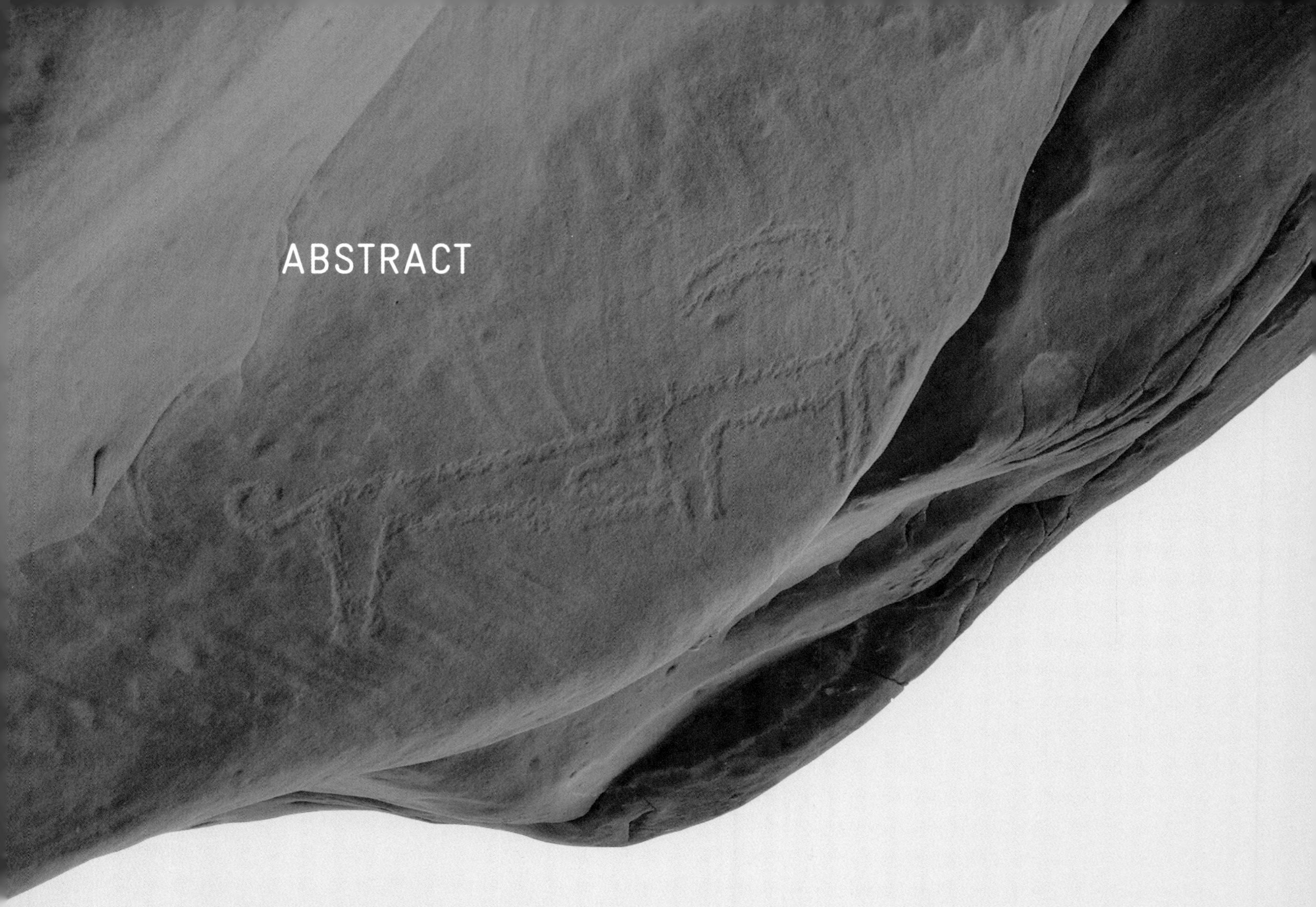

ABSTRACT

The term 'rock art' is generally used to denote paintings, petroglyphs and engravings made on rock surfaces generally found in rock shelters or in caves. In the present context, only rock paintings found in the northern Vindhyan region in Central India are discussed. Among all the rock art sites—painted shelters—of the northern Vindhyan region, especially those located in undivided Mirzapur in Uttar Pradesh (UP), in Central India hold a unique position. Actually, in a number of ways, they are more important than the much publicised Bhimbetka group of rock shelters in Madhya Pradesh.

The first group of painted rock shelters noticed in India in 1867-68—nearly a decade before the Altamira discovery—is located in the Robertsganj sub-division in Mirzapur near Rajpur (now in Sonbhadra) in the present-study area. The credit for this discovery goes to Carlleyle. It is a pity that this great discovery remained in obscurity for a long time. We find the first reference to this discovery in the 1883 issue of the 'Proceedings of the Asiatic Society of Bengal' and a detailed account appeared in *Indian Antiquary* in the article 'Pygmy Flints' by Smith.

Credit must be given to Carlleyle not only for the discovery of the shelters but also for placing them in their proper perspective. He wrote that 'some of these paintings appeared to illustrate in a very stiff and archaic manner scenes from the life of the ancient stone chippers; others represent animals or hunts of animals by men with bow and arrows, spear and hatchet'.

Among the other pioneers who worked in this area, mention may be made of Cockburn who was a late contemporary of Carlleyle. He made extensive surveys and published detailed accounts (Cockburn 1883a: 56-64, 1883b:123, 1883c: 125-6, 1888: 57-65, 1894: 21-37, 1899: 89-97). Cockburn was also of the opinion that the best of rock shelters and drawings are to be found on the southern scarp of the Kaimur, which overhangs the valley of the Son (J. Cockburn 1889). Regarding the antiquity of the paintings, Cockburn did not have the same views as those held by Carlleyle but he agreed that the rock paintings did not show any metallic weapons. He agreed that they were older than the oldest rock or copper inscriptions.

No appreciable discoveries were made in the area under study till the middle of the last century. A new era in Indian rock art studies started from the late 1950s, when the lead in prehistoric explorations passed into the hands of young Indian scholars and universities were given permission to excavate and undertake archaeological explorations. The universities of Allahabad, Ujjain and Sagar soon emerged as leading centres of rock art research in India.

The present author along with his colleagues and students explored the northern Vindhyan region consisting of the undivided districts of Varanasi, Mirzapur, Allahabad and Banda in Uttar Pradesh and Rewa, Satna, Sidhi and Shahadol in Madhya Pradesh. Almost at the same time, Wakanker from Ujjain University, who was later joined by S.K. Pandey, Yashodhar Mathpal and many others, explored and located a large number of painted shelters including the Bhimbetka group of shelters. Within two-and-a-half decades from 1955 (1955–80), thanks to the efforts of these pioneers, most of the rock art sites had been located, important excavations had been undertaken and important research projects/dissertations and publications completed.

NATURE AND CONCEPT OF ROCK ART

In the beginning, there were a lot of misgivings regarding the nature, antiquity, authorship, motive, etc. of rock art. But gradually the picture started getting clearer when archaeologists started taking an interest in the study of rock art. Some thought that this rock art belonged to the prehistoric period while others thought it to be of recent past.

Generally, each canvas is full of figures made by artists, sometimes separated from each other in time and belonging to different subsistence economies. The canvas thus looks extremely confusing. With the application of the archaeological method of stratification of lines of figures, the pictures become clearer. It has been seen that normally on a canvas all the figures cannot be placed within one time bracket and the painters too belonged to different subsistence economies. Hence, in order to understand and appreciate rock art, it is necessary to first understand the environment and the subsistence economy of the people who produced these works of art.

Some people try to analyse ancient art objects and paintings using principles of modern aesthetics. The general trend today is to classify non-utilitarian objects that attract attention, either positive or negative, as art objects. Beauty divorced from utility is the essence of modern aesthetics. According to author, this classification is not fair when we discuss the art of the ancient period. Modern principles of aesthetics cannot be applied to these artistic creations because they were not created as 'art for art's sake' simply to gratify the senses of the artists or to fill their leisure time. Prehistoric rock art was not the product of an individual's efforts. This is clear from the selection of shelters, the placement of paintings on the canvas and the subsistence economy of the painters who painted them. It is also clear that the painters had the support of the entire society. If this contention is correct then we have to admit that this rock art definitely fulfilled some social need. Coomaraswamy (1977: 93) is of the opinion that: 'The production of art is never an end in itself; it has a social value'. Art is an end product of the creative activity of imagination that springs from the give-and-take between an individual and society. It is possible that the need for creativity resulted in the emergence of art but it developed not because of aesthetic pleasure but because it served some social need. It is also possible that it was used as a vehicle of magic/sympathetic and magic/ritual/religion, etc. Whatever the reasons, its purpose must have been utilitarian. R.K. Mukherjee has rightly said that the artist is producing a utility. It is only in this sense that we can understand the value and importance of rock art. It fulfilled the social and economic aspirations of the then people.

One should also remember that rock art is actually 'conceptual' art and not 'perceptual' art. The artist was neither preparing photocopies of animals nor a particular 'bison' or a 'rhinoceros'. He was universalising the animal. In other words, the artists did not prepare a photocopy of the animals. They drew these animals as per their conceptualisation. This may also explain the variations in the forms of animals. The variations in forms may also be because they were drawn by persons with different levels of creative perfection. If we accept that this art had some relationship with magic/rituals then we will also have to accept that most of the hunters were performing the painting ritual without reference to their artistic abilities.

Besides, it should also be understood that Indian rock art covers a very long span of time and each painted canvas has been produced by generations of painters belonging to different stages of the subsistence economy right from the purely hunting-gathering stage to the beginning of agriculture and even till modern times. Thus, the entire rock art cannot be placed within the prehistoric period. Motive, subject matter and style of painting underwent changes with the passage of time. The motive during prehistoric times when man was completely dependent on nature and during the early historic period when he had learnt to tame and modify the natural agencies would not have been the same.

However, there are certain common features in rock paintings of different periods and different regions, such as the canvas, the technique and the use of pigments. Normally paintings are found in sandstone formations and engravings/bruisings on granite formations. The canvas remained natural rock surface that was never prepared. The technique of painting by and large remained the same. There does not seem to be any difference in the preparation of colours. The paintings are executed with haematite (*geru*) or other oxides of iron and natural colours.

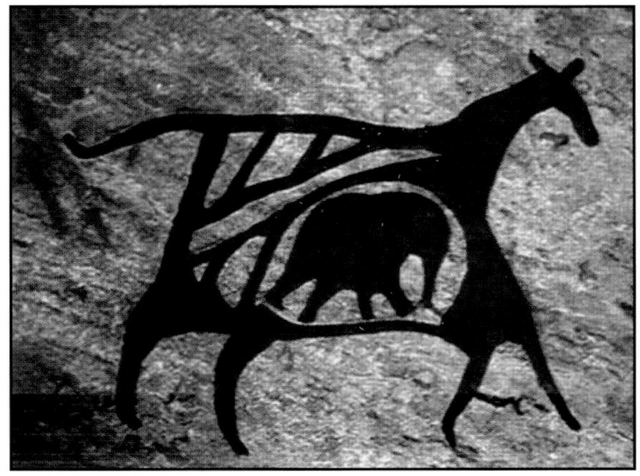

Fig. 18.1 Pregnant nilgai with a baby elephant in the stomach (after Drummond and Wakankar 1976).

The painters derived their motifs from the environment in which they lived. The animals are the ones that were found during that period. They have been painted again and again running, standing and grazing singly or in a group. The same canvas has been used by different generations of painters separated from each other in time. Thus, sometimes the lines are so mixed and jumbled that it becomes difficult to separate one figure from the other both horizontally and vertically.

While interpreting rock art, subjective elements play an important role and in order to avoid this subjectivity, it is necessary to examine the figures again and again in different lighting conditions. While making eye copies, a photocopy should also be prepared. Sometimes some figures escape the eye view but the camera catches them. For example, Wakankar and Brooks published (1976: 84) a photograph in which in the stomach of a pregnant *nilgai* a baby elephant has been shown (Fig. 18.1). Krishna Ramamurthy points out that 'a study of the painting itself and an un-reconstructed photograph reveals that this is not an elephant but a baby *nilgai'* (Rammurthy 1988: 80). Such mistakes are common in the absence of proper recordings or repeated observations. There are many such cases of perceptual mistakes in the reproduction of other scholars also (see Mathpal 1983). A large number of scholars like Wakankar, Mathpal and Neumayer have prepared excellent eye copies of rock paintings. But they are not true copies and sometimes they do not create the real impact of rock art. Moreover, a slight twist in the stroke changes the figure completely. For example, if the eye copy prepared by Neumayer (Fig. 18.2a) and the photocopy (Fig. 18.2b) are placed alongside, the differences between the two are obvious.

Again, see the eye copy of Lekhunia (RJP) prepared by Neumayer 1993Fig. 254 p.114 (Fig. 18.3) and photographs taken by me (Fig. 18.4a-b). In the eye copy, a number of details are missing. Eye copies can never be true copies. They put the early and late paintings in one level disregarding stratification. Neumayer has missed some important figures, such as the big bird in red which the author has identified as an ostrich (?)

(Fig. 18.5). But, here, I must say that my observations about making 'eye copies' do not in any way minimise the tremendous contributions that these scholars have made towards the study of rock art in India. Making eye copies is a big task. It requires an in-depth study of the lines superimposing each other both horizontally and vertically. To bring out the correct recording, eye copies should always be accompanied with photographs of the original.

The difference between the two becomes clear when both are placed side by side. The eye copy does not bring out the real impact of the canvas. All the paintings seem to belong to one period of painting activity. It brings out a false picture. Those who have not seen the actual canvas will never be able to understand the real nature of the rock paintings.

INDIAN AND EUROPEAN ROCK ART

Indian rock art has its own personality. There are considerable differences between Indian rock art and its European counterpart with respect to the canvas, mode of execution and cultural milieu. Hence, they should not be compared.

The first most important difference lies in the location of painted caves and the canvas on which the paintings were executed. In Europe, deep underground dark caves and grottoes were used exclusively for painting activity. Even the rays of the sun did not penetrate the hollows. Sometimes lamps were lighted to dispel darkness. These caves are like long galleries and the canvas too is fairly big. To the best of our knowledge they were never used for habitation, for burial purposes or as factory sites for making tools.

In India, walls and ceilings of rock shelters made by natural agencies, located on small hillocks or hollows in sections of escarpments were used as a canvas (Fig. 18.6).

The painted rock shelters are well lighted and comparatively much smaller in size. The excavations carried out in some of the rock shelters prove that they were used as living places, where people painted, buried their dead and also manufactured their tools.

European cave art is essentially animal art. It is always or nearly always inspired by the animal world. The depictions are fundamentally

Fig. 18.3 Eye copy of Lekhunia (RJP) by Neumayer (1993, Fig. 238). It does not show stratification of figures.

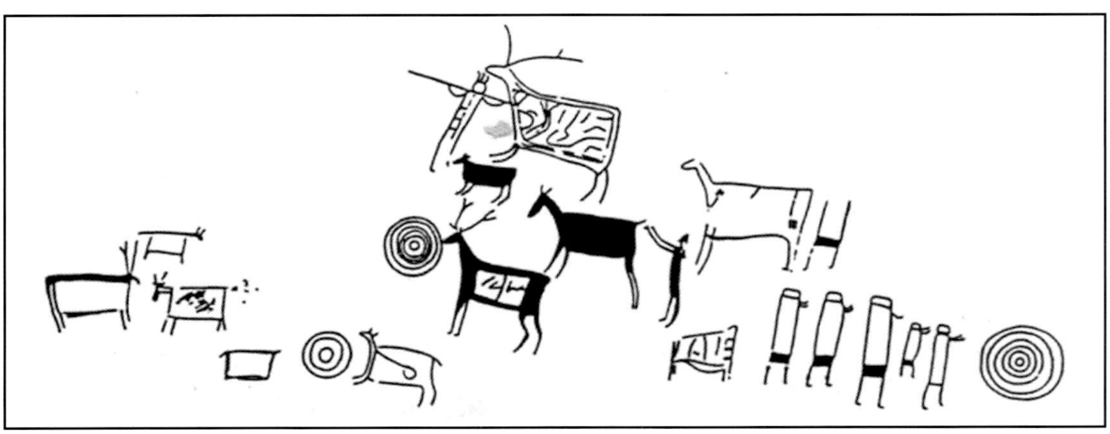

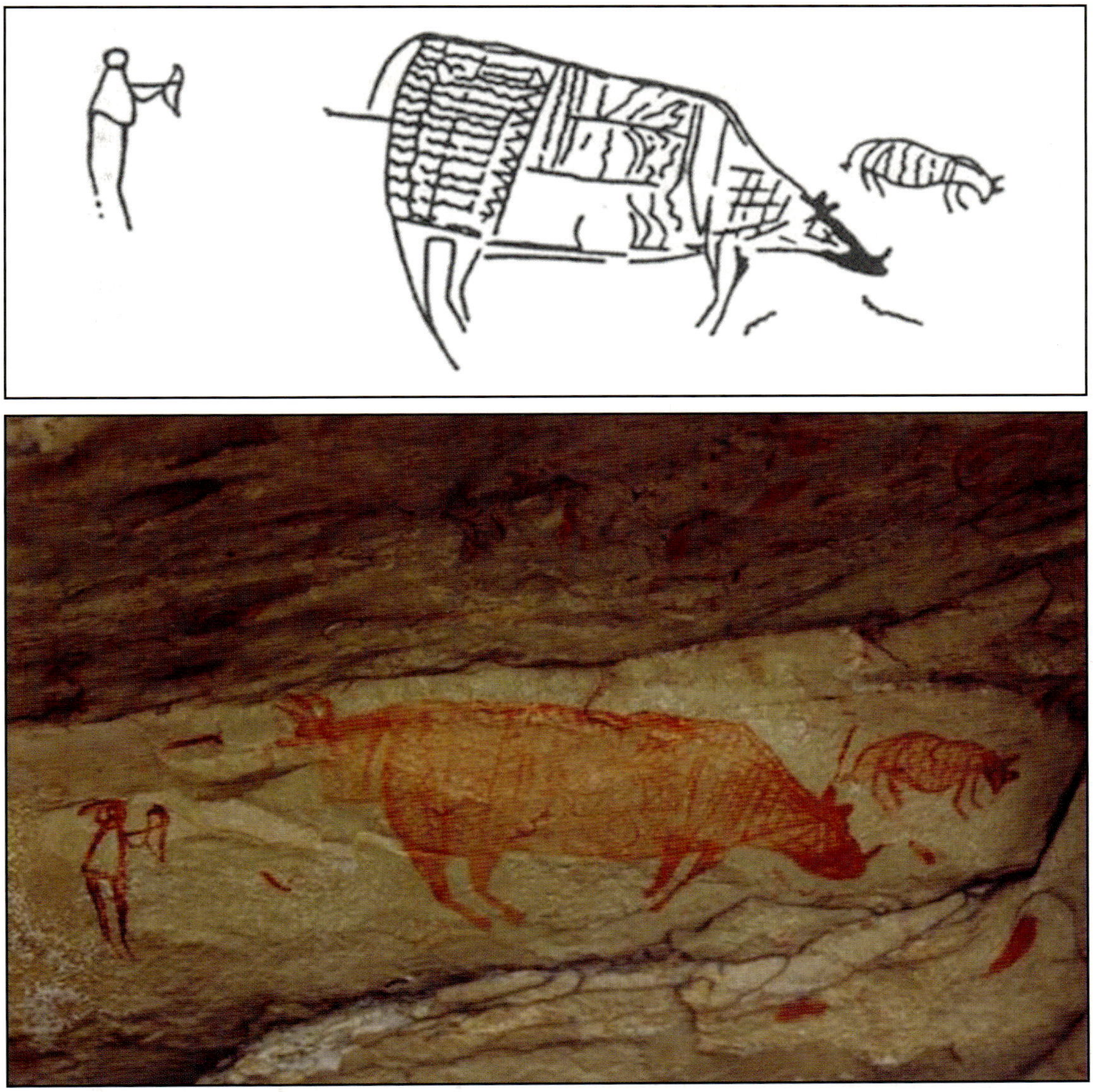

Figs. 18.2 (a-b) The eye copy prepared by Neumayer and photo of the original painting.

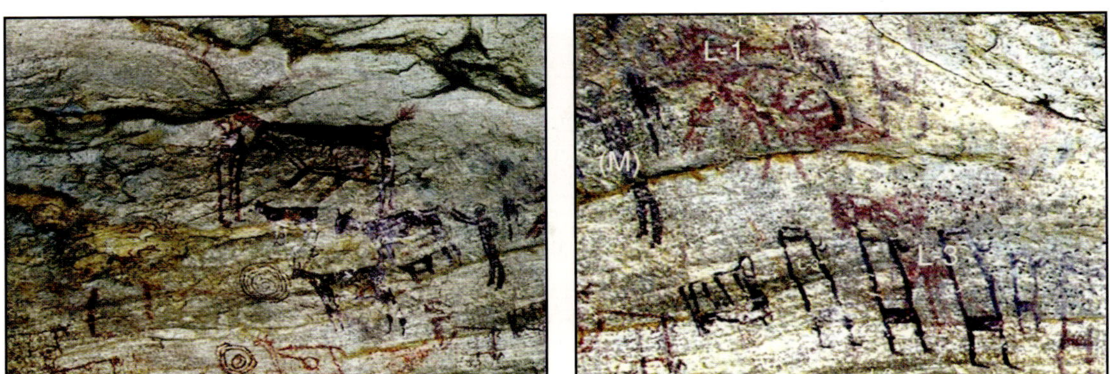

Fig. 18.4 (a-b) Photographs taken by the author. In Fig. 4 (a-b), at least three periods of painting activity on the basis of stratification of figures have been marked. They have been indicated by L1, L2 and L3.

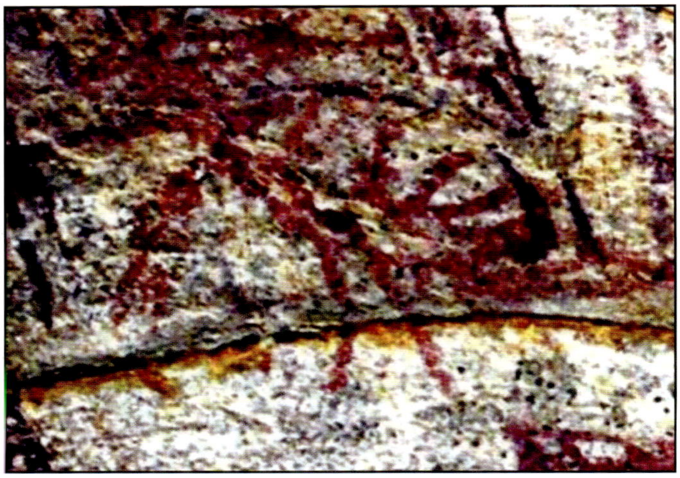

Fig. 18.5 (L-1 in Fig. 18.4b) An ostrich (?).

realistic and the animals are painted in their customary attitudes. The artist strove to represent the animals as they really were and rarely depicted them in a schematised or stylised manner.

European rock art is the product of the last Ice Age only—the upper Palaeolithic age, and with the end of the upper Palaeolithic period the art also vanishes. In India, painting activity has a very long history. According to some scholars, it starts from the upper Palaeolithic (?)/Mesolithic and continues till modern times.

VARIATION IN THE ROCK ART OF NORTHERN AND CENTRAL VINDHYAN REGIONS

The northern and the Central Vindhyan regions are the two most studied and documented regions in India so far as painted shelters are concerned. Both the regions have their own distinct personalities even though there is no difference with respect to the environment, the location of painted shelters, the canvas and the use of pigments and techniques of painting. The difference lies in the cultural milieu and the range of cultural activities, human occupation of the shelters and in the styles of depiction. Under the circumstances, it would be erroneous to make general comments regarding the paintings of the Vindhyan region as a whole.

Fig. 18.6 A view of an Indian rock shelter (Ronp rock shelter).

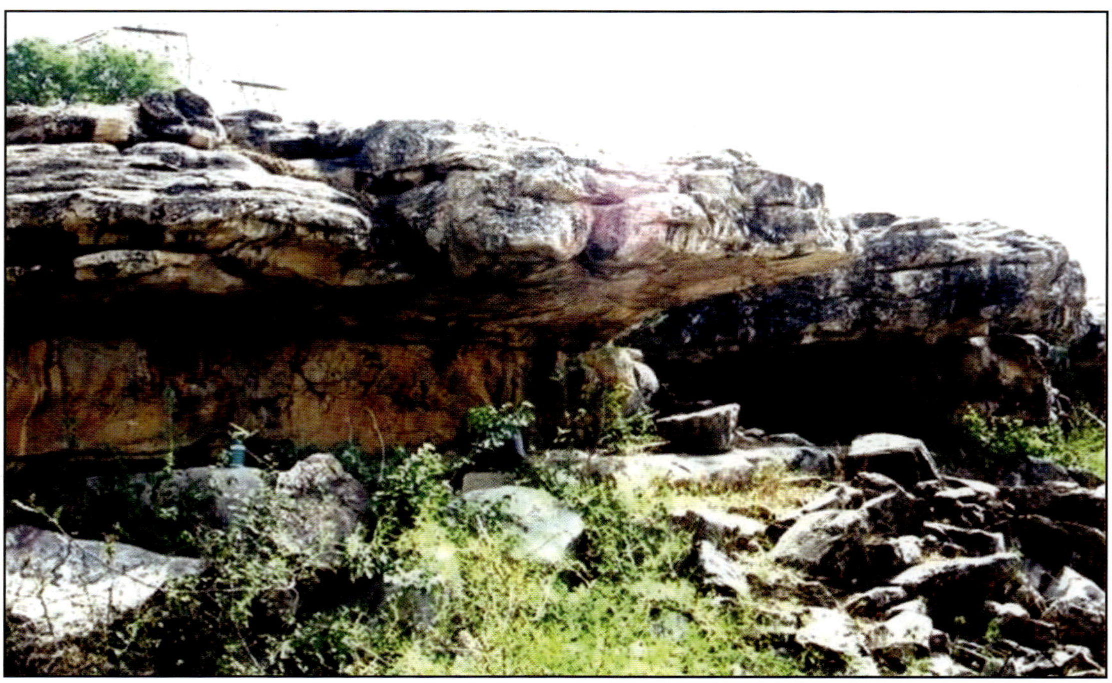

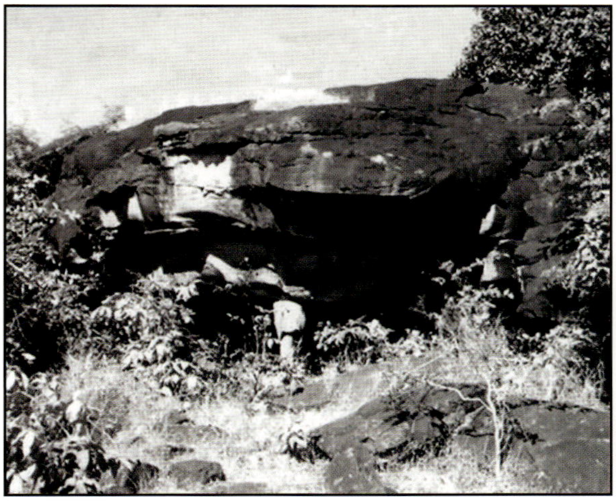

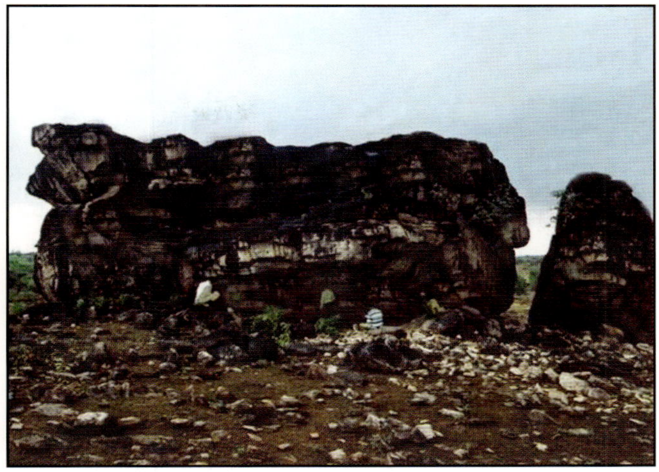

Left: **Fig. 18.7** Morahana Pahar R.S. No 4 in 1959.

Right: **Fig. 18.8** Baghahi-khor Shelter no.1.

Excavations carried out in the rock shelters in the northern Vindhyan region reveal that the shelters were first occupied in the Epi-palaeolithic period and were deserted soon after the Mesolithic. Excavations carried out in Morahana Pahar both inside and outside the shelter make this clear (Fig. 18.7). No excavated shelter has yielded any earlier or later material. The excavations carried out in Baghahi-khor (Figs. 18.8 & 18.9) and the Lekhahia rock shelter near Bhainsore village on the Great Deccan Road confirm this. They clearly show that the shelters were occupied during the Epi-palaeolithic period and were deserted at the end of the Mesolithic (Varma 1986). They remained deserted till the beginning of the historical period. This is also confirmed from observations made by Carlleyle, Cockburn and other scholars who have worked in that region; it is also attested by the paintings.

Paintings belonging to the Historical period form a separate group and consist of some *alpana* designs (Fig. 18.10), caparisoned horses in procession and *Shankha lipi* (Fig. 18.11). But these, too, are found only in some shelters like the Ronp gr.

Fig. 18.9 Cross section of the burial in Baghahi-khor Shelter no.1, Mirzapur.

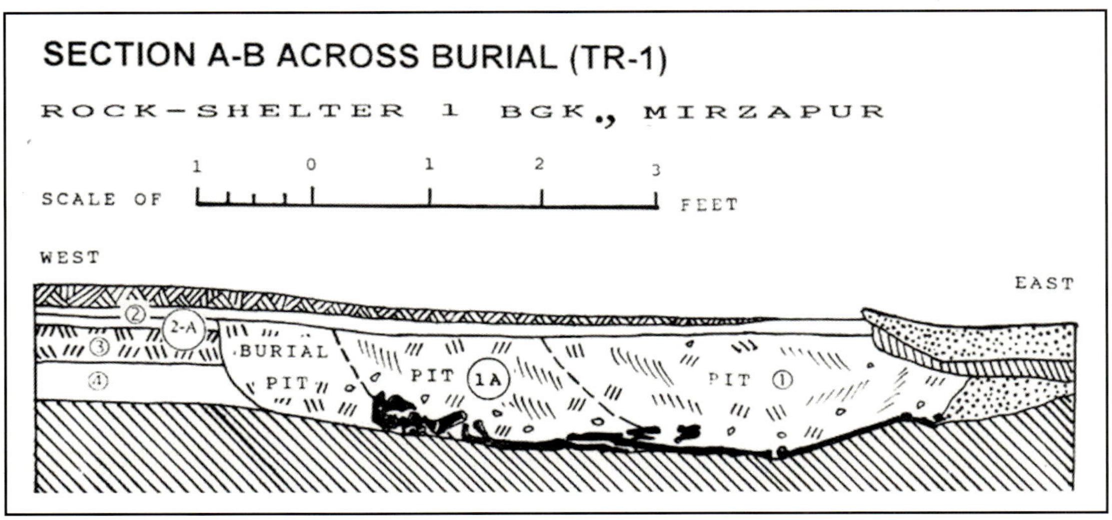

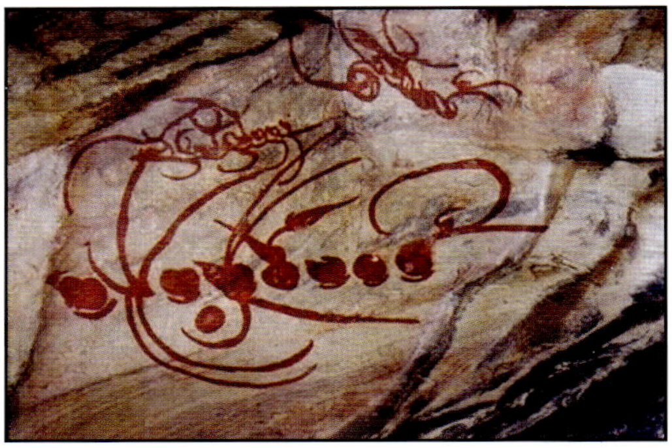

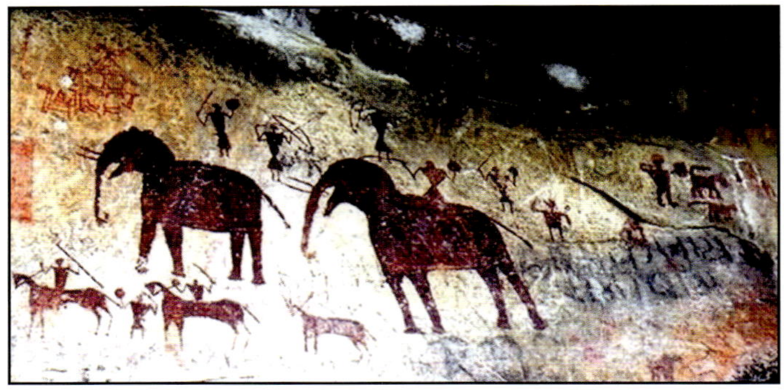

Left: **Fig. 18.10** Alpana designs Shankha Lipi (Ronp Shelter).

Right: **Fig. 18.11** War scenes, mounted horses and elephants, Lekhunia dari (Ahiraura).

Shelters adjoining Robertsganj—Ronp gr. (Panchmukhi gr.) Lekhunia (RJP) and near Bhainsore on the Great Deccan Road, Lekhahia gr., Morahana Pahar gr., Bedia gr. and Baghahi Khor, etc. form a separate group within the northern Vindhyan region. Painted shelters in Kerwaghat and Kauva Khoh seem to be different. Unfortunately, the author could not examine them personally but from whatever he has gathered from the published material (Tewari 1985), he is convinced that they do not go with the paintings of the group discussed above. Comparatively, they seem to be later in time.

Excavations in the Central Vindhyan region have revealed multi-cultural assemblages. Some of them were occupied during the lower Palaeolithic period and continued to be occupied till the historical period with breaks in between. The subject matter of the paintings is also varied. They belong to different cultural phases superimposing each other, making it difficult to either distinguish them or to identify them periodwise. The excavations have revealed pigment material from all the cultural deposits.

In the Central Vindhyan region, painting activity starts either with highly stylised dancing human figures or with intricate designs (Sonavane: *Purakala*, 1997. Vol. 8). Both show a very high degree of artistic perfection (Fig. 18.12a). The animal figures are also sometimes decorated with intricate designs (Fig. 18.12 a-c).

Left: **Fig. 18.12a** Stylised dancing human figures.

Right: **Fig. 18.12b** Animal figures with intricate designs.

Human figures are full of dynamic action and show perfection in figure sketches and compositions. They are distinguished by a high

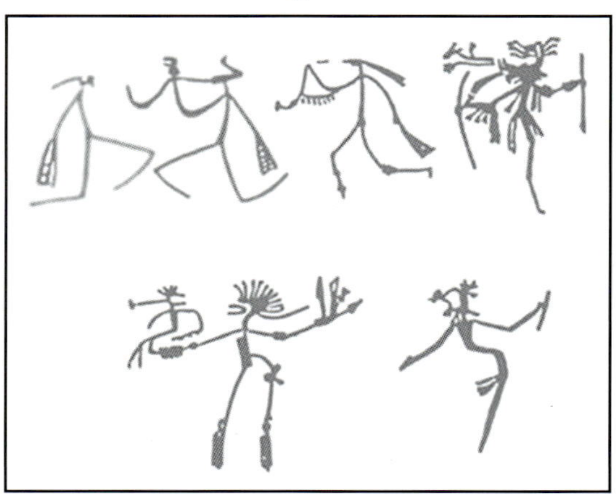

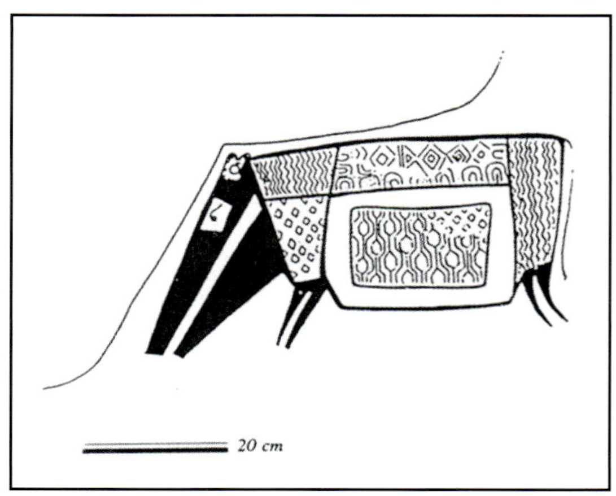

degree of craftsmanship and a uniformity of intricate design patterns. Neumayer thinks that 'this stylistic and formal uniformity was only possible through a long and continuous development, encompassing the ideological make-up of prehistoric hunting and gathering cultures on the Indian subcontinent' (Neumayer: 1993; p. 44). He further writes that 'No where at the known rock-art sites exists an indication of a "primitive stage" of art in the sense of non-proficiency in the act of application of pigments and lines' (Neumayer op. cit). How this excellence was obtained is difficult to comprehend.

Human figures form a part of the depictions from the earliest times. They have been shown participating in a variety of activities related to daily activities. They have been shown in narrative scenes (Fig. 18.13) that are perfectly drawn with all the details.

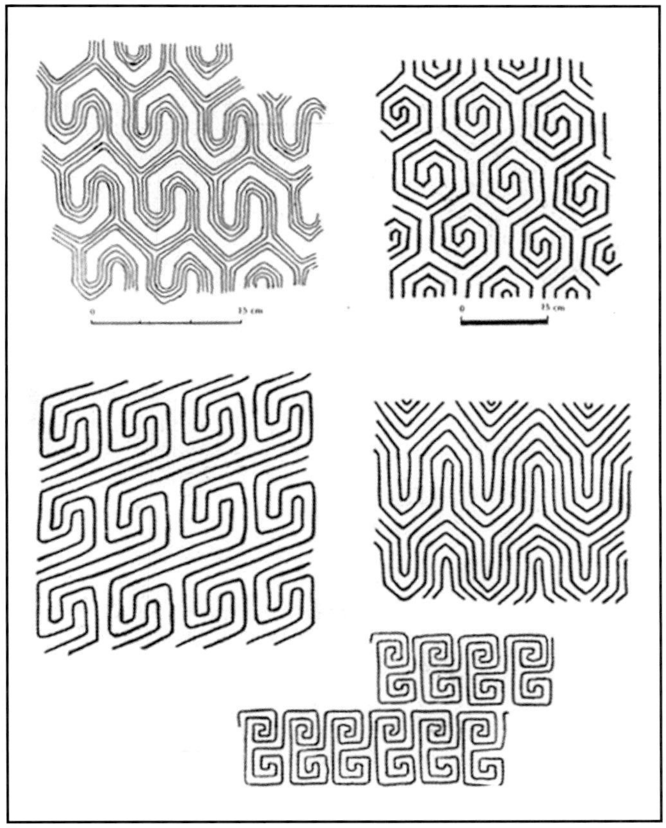

Fig. 18.12c Intricate design patterns used in rock art of Central Vindhyan region.

Effort has also been made to indicate environmental and ecological conditions in some of the paintings (Neumayer: 1993; Figure 133). Undergrowth or water has been depicted by wavy lines (Fig. 18.14). In some paintings (Neumayer: 1993; Figure 144, Jaora: 75), an effort has been made to depict a jungle before an elephant.

A painting in Lakhajoar (Neumayer: 1993; Figures 206-7) depicts activities being performed on an artificial platform like a modern circus group or by *nats* (Fig. 18.15).

There are some abstract paintings with deeper significance, such as Fig. 18.16 (Neumayer 1993: Fig. 120). According to Neumayer, the painting shows a square, divided into several stripes, of which each one is decorated with a variety of design patterns, while the centre of the space is indicated by a circle. On the upper periphery of the square are shown fish between reeds or lotus stems with buds (?). Along the other side are water birds. Besides the square are four flying birds. The whole composition looks as if the Mesolithic artist wanted to represent the cosmos with the square forming the earth, with water.

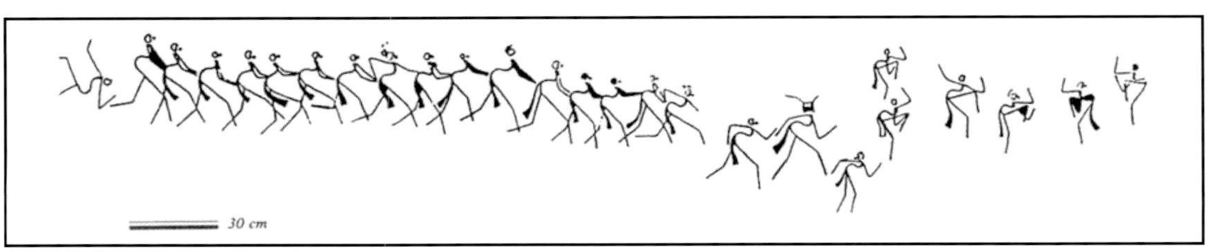

Fig. 18.13 Depiction of human figures ('S'type).

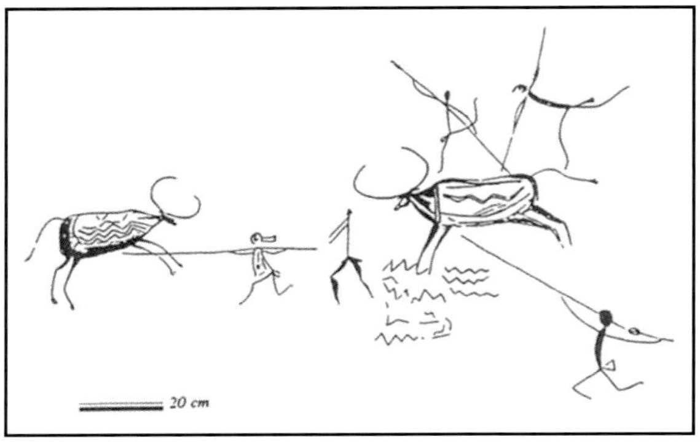

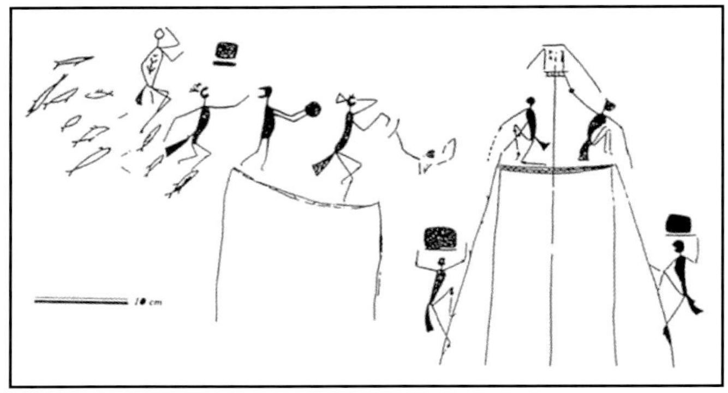

Left: **Fig. 18.14** Water has been depicted by wavy lines (Neumayer, 1993: Fig. 133, Bhopal, Dharampur, p. 70.).

Right: **Fig. 18.15** A painting in Lakhajoar (Neumayer, 1993: Figs. 206-7) depicting activities being performed on an artificial platform like a modern circus group of *nats.*

There are a number of paintings with excellent narrative themes, such as Fig. 18.17 & 18.18 (Neumayer, 1993: p.78, Fig. 153 Jaora; Fig. 147-149, p. 76, Kathotia), which depicts food collecting and processing activity by a group. Similarly, Fig. 18.19 (Neumayer, 1993: p. 77, Figure 152 from Lakhajoar) depicts 'a man, a woman and a child sitting at a well-laid table..... The meal laid out consists of some round-shaped food and two small fish. A vessel or container is in the hand of the man, while two more containers are placed nearby.'

In the rock art of the northern Vindhyan region, no such paintings are depicted. Neumayer correctly observes that '...the pictures of the Northern Vindhyas show a basically different development of stylistic evolution than what was observed at the much richer sites further west in the Vindhyan hills. The paintings of the Mirzapur region do not depict extensive narrative scenes with all those minute details in which the pictures of the food-gatherers excel' (Neumayer 1993: 114).

The sense of perspective is better in the paintings of Central Vindhyan region. In comparison to the human figures, the animal figures are painted in bigger size to empasise their bulky and well-built body.

In the earliest period, human figures are very rare or are absent in the Northern Vindhyan region. Wherever they form a part of hunting scenes, they are very clumsily painted. They look lifeless (Fig. 18.25). No attempt has been made to distinguish between a male and a female figure. Female figures are extremely rare if not completely absent.

Left: **Fig. 18.16** Abstract painting (Neumayer, 1993: Fig. 120).

Right: **Fig. 18.17** In this painting from Jaora, several women are shown cooperating in catching rats from their subterranean burrow (Neumayer, 1993: Fig. 153, p. 78).

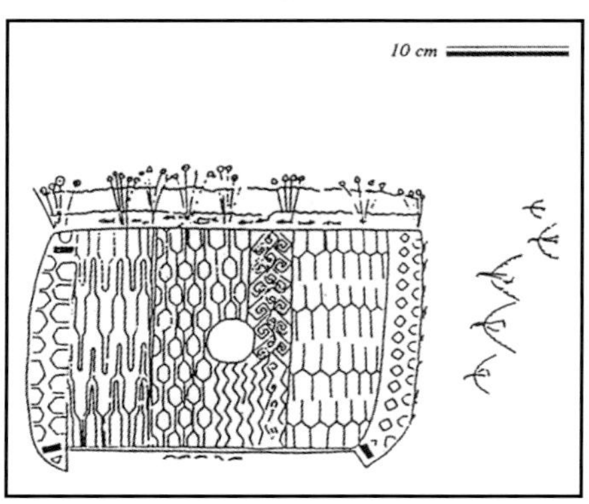

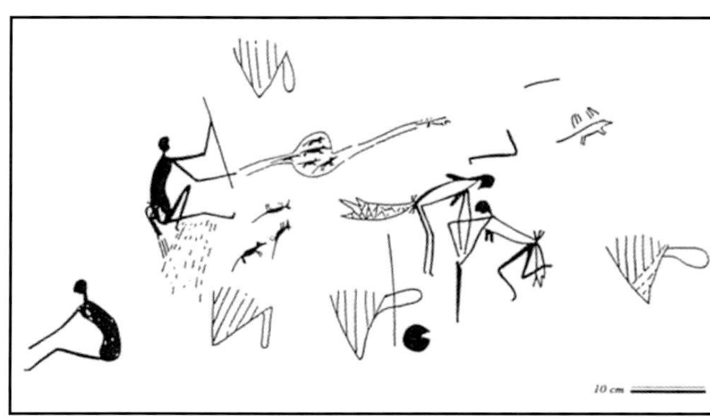

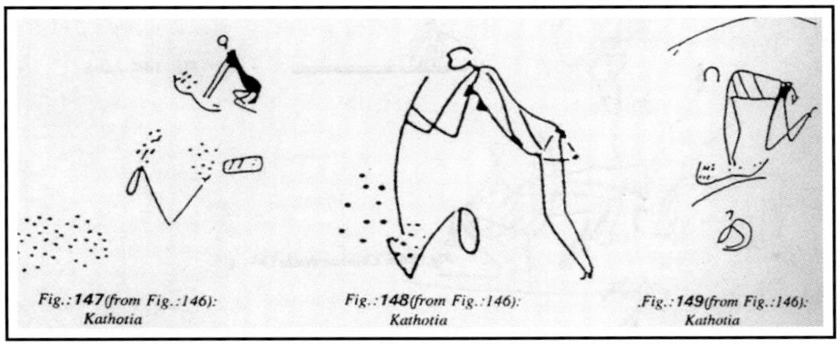

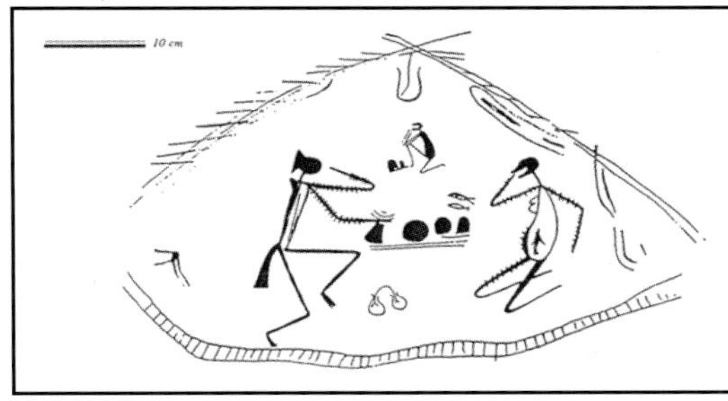

Left: **Fig. 18.18** Women processing vegetal food.

Right: **Fig. 18.19** A figure from Lakhajoar.

In the paintings of the Central Vindhyan region, the females have been clearly shown. They are depicted as being bulkier with heavier buttocks and pronounced breasts and waists (Figs. 18.20 & 18.21) (Neumayer: Figure 65, Bhimbetka).

In the northern Vindhyan region in the earliest paintings, single animals are depicted; they are larger in size (Fig. 18.22 a-b). Later they are shown in groups, and then come the hunting scenes. At this stage man appears. But the depiction is always lifeless. There are no depictions of intricate designs or 'S' type dancing figures such as those found in Central Indian rock art. The northern Vindhyan rock art revolves around animals. They have sometimes been painted very realistically. Human figures are only symbolic.

During the long period of the rock art tradition (especially in the rock art of Mirzapur), we find that there was a continuous growth of knowledge with each succeeding generation. We find that there is a gradual growth in the technique of depiction and composition of figures. It develops from single animal figures to a group of figures and then to a thematic depiction of figures (Figs. 18.23-18.25).

In a nutshell, the rock art of the northern Vindhyan region, especially of Mirzapur, is essentially animal art. It revolves around animals only. The paintings look more archaic. But Central Vindhyan rock art cannot be called a purely animal art. It has a mixed character.

PAINTED SHELTERS

The shelters are generally located on the steep side of hillocks, overlooking deep valleys, on one or both the banks of a river, nala, or rivulet flowing on the bedrock or in a deep canyon or gorge (Fig. 18.26). Besides, they are also found on the top and the slope of high hillocks (Fig. 18.27) overlooking undulating land slowly merging with the low-lying valley.

Left: **Fig. 18.20** A figure from Bhimbetka (Neumayer, 1993: Fig. 52, Gupha Masir, p. 49).

Right: **Fig. 18.21** Depiction of a female with heavier buttocks and pronounced breasts and waists (Neumayer, 1993: Fig. 65, Bhimbetka).

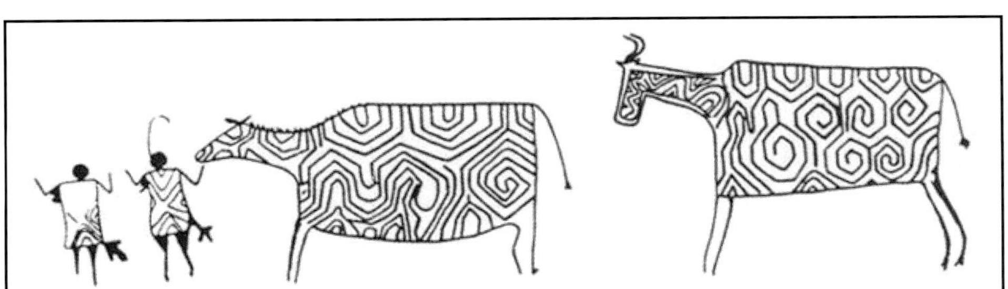

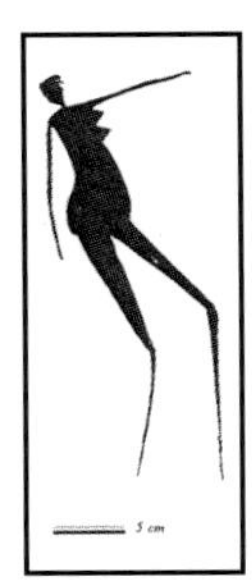

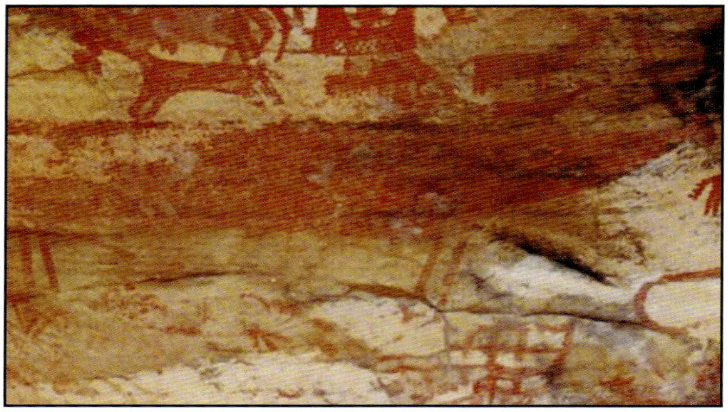

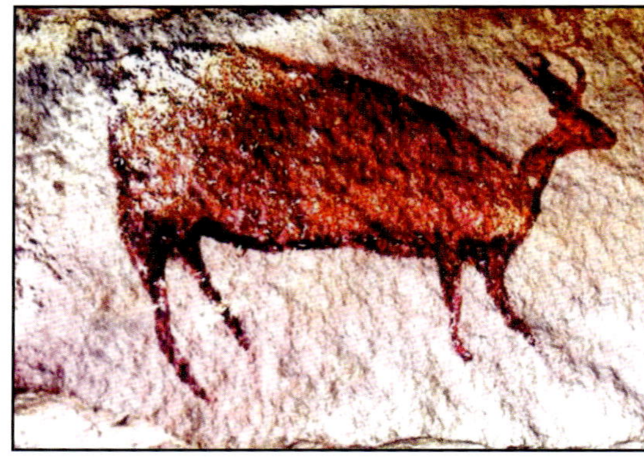

Left & Right: **Fig. 18.22** (a-b) Earliest paintings of animals are single and of larger sizes.

The shelters that are located on the steep side of a gorge in its section overlooking a valley are generally box-shaped with an opening towards the valley.

Shelters found on the top of hillocks are umbrella shaped (Fig. 18.27).

Shelters formed out of huge blocks of sandstone are hut-like (Fig. 18.28).

Some cave-like shelters have also been located (Fig. 18.29).

Only such rock shelters that are connected with some perennial source of water are painted.

The floor of the shelters is not always even. Sometimes it is rocky and without any accumulation. But within the natural (mud crack) cavities of the rocks of the Vindhyan formation sometimes a very large number of microliths and pieces of small bones are found imbedded (Morahana Pahar rock shelters). Some

Fig. 18.23 Single animals painted without any design.

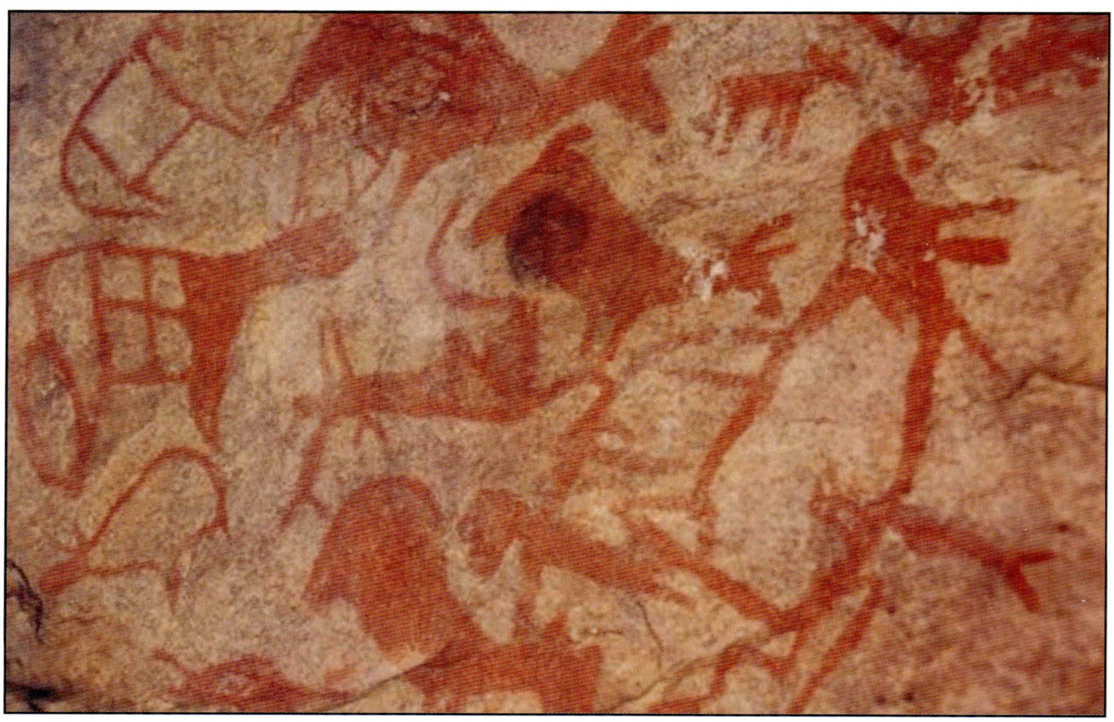

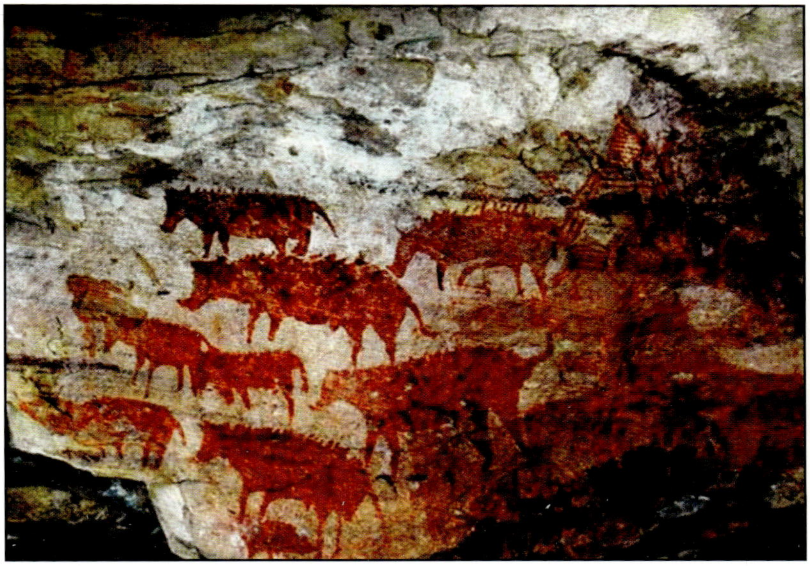

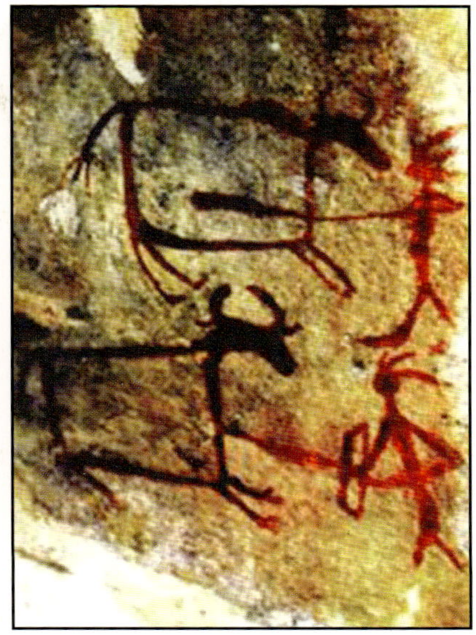

Left: **Fig. 18.24** Group of wild boars in clottish blood colour in Bedia shelter near Bhainsore village.

Right: **Fig. 18.25** Thematic depiction of figures where human figures are lifeless.

shelters contain habitation deposits or evidence of occupation in the form of burials, microlithic tools and debitage. Some of these shelters, especially the painted shelters of Baghel Khand and south Uttar Pradesh, were definitely used for living purposes during the Epi-palaeolithic/Mesolithic periods (on the basis of present evidence). The accumulation in the shelters varies from a few inches to nearly 15 to 24 inches.

Some shelters continued to be in use for thousands of years. The Lekhahia rock shelter near Bhainsore village on the Great Deccan Road is one such shelter which was used as a burial site for more than 5,000 years (Fig. 18.30 Lekhahia R.S. 1 (Bhainsore).

There are four consistent C-14 dates ranging from 3560±110 (TF-417) to 8370±75 (GX-20983-AMS). The entire burial activity has been divided on the basis of stratigraphy into 13 phases; 17 skeletons were discovered. There is still no date from the earliest levels. So far, no hearth (of the prehistoric period) has been located within the shelter. But in all likelihood some of these shelters were used for living purposes, especially those in which burials have been located.

Within the shelters the paintings are usually executed on the walls and on ceilings. At times they are found at such places in the shelter where one cannot reach easily without a ladder or, at very low places where one can reach only after lying down on one's back. Sometimes there is hardly a gap of more than 15 to 20 inches between the reclining ceiling and the ground floor. A good example of such a painted shelter can be seen on the top of LKH-shelter no 1, where there is another small shelter hardly 20 to 25 inches high. There, a large number of paintings of animals are drawn. These figures must have been drawn while lying on the back.

No system seems to have been followed in the arrangement of paintings (Fig. 18.31). The author is not agree with Wakankar and Brooks when they write, 'These paintings on

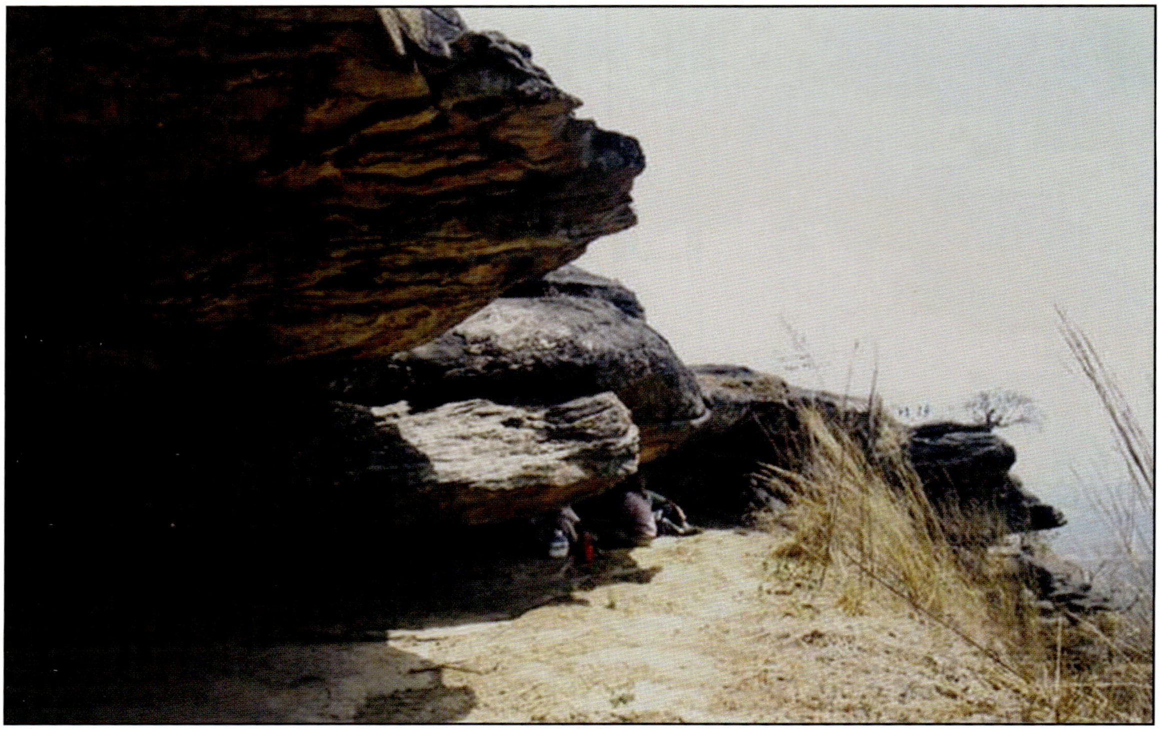

Fig. 18.26 Lekhahia R.S. (RJP).

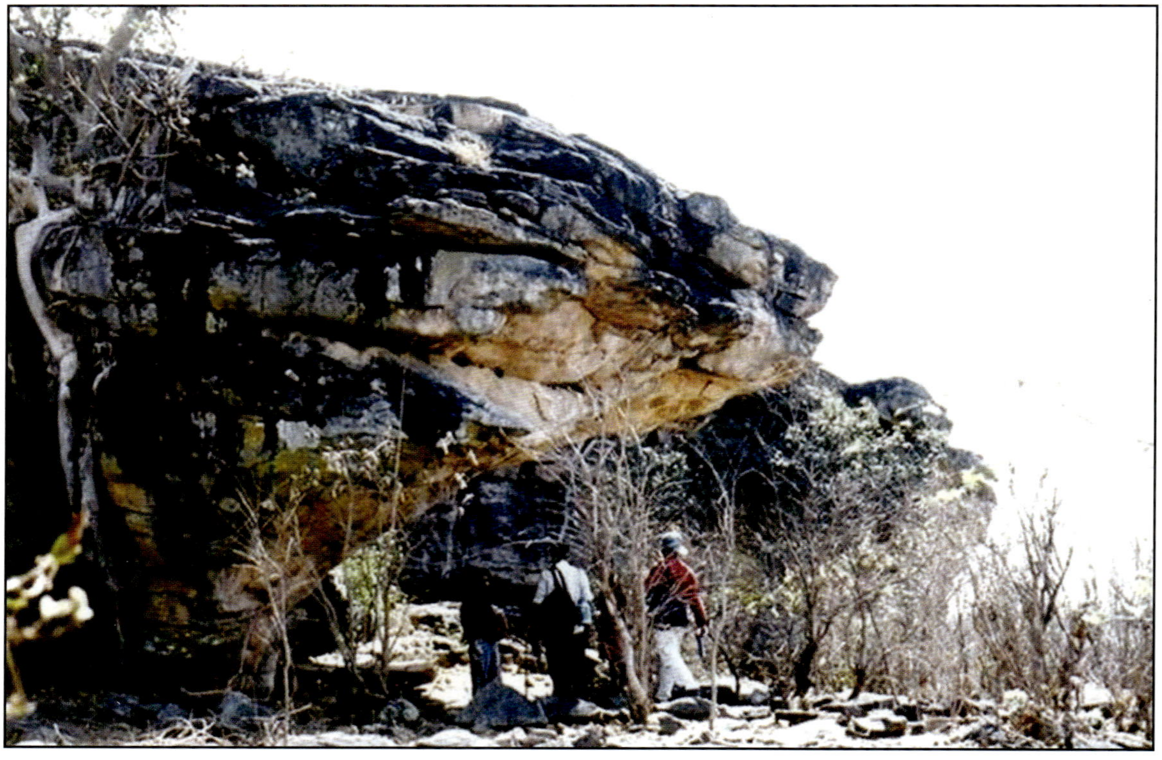

Fig. 18.27 Shelter no.1 of Morahana Pahar where an open-air trench was excavated.

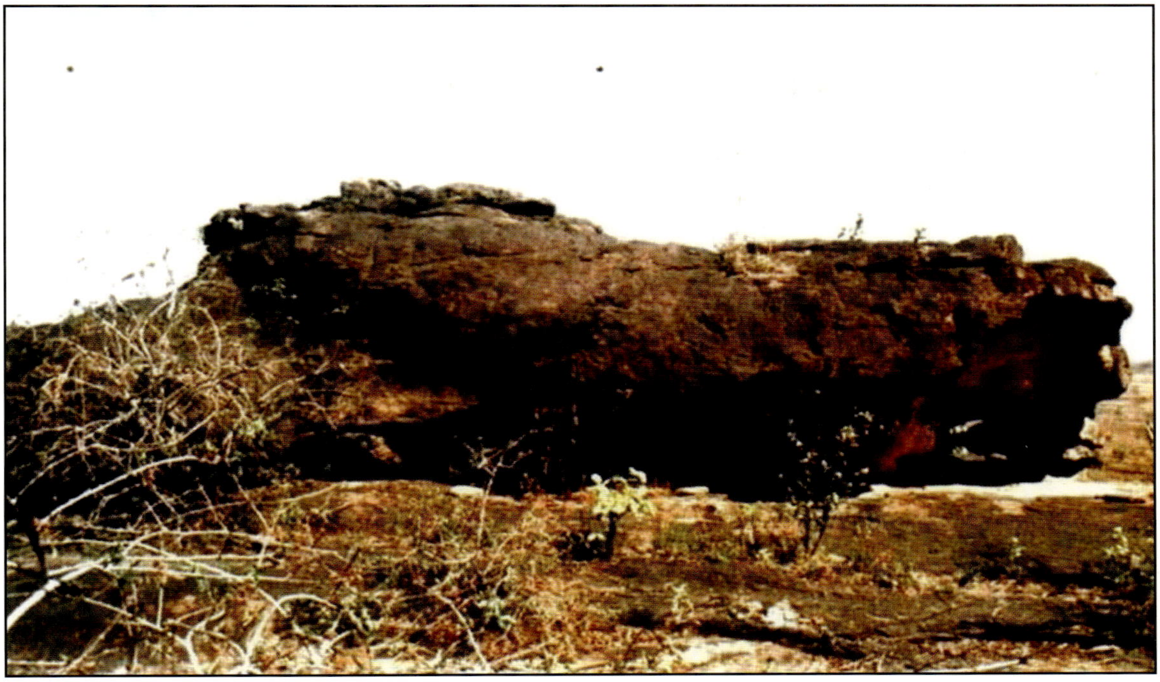

Fig. 18.28 Dhaunsara rock shelter in Satna Distt.

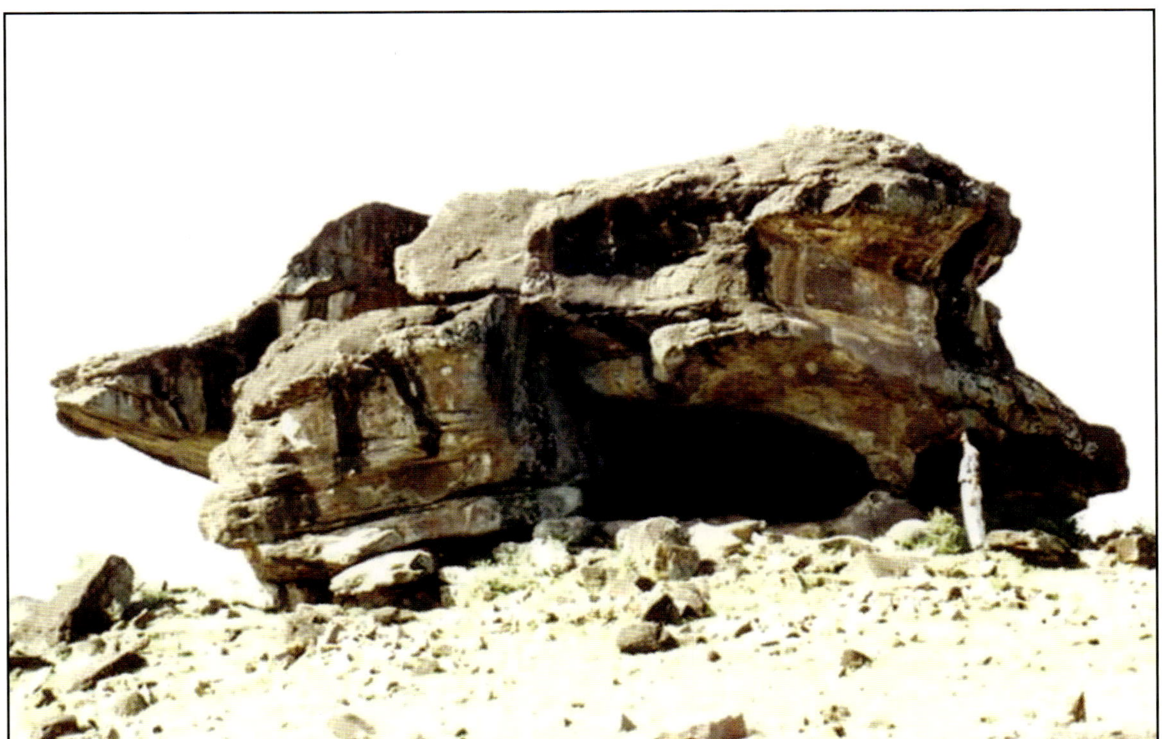

Fig. 18.29 Gaddi rock shelter (Rewa).

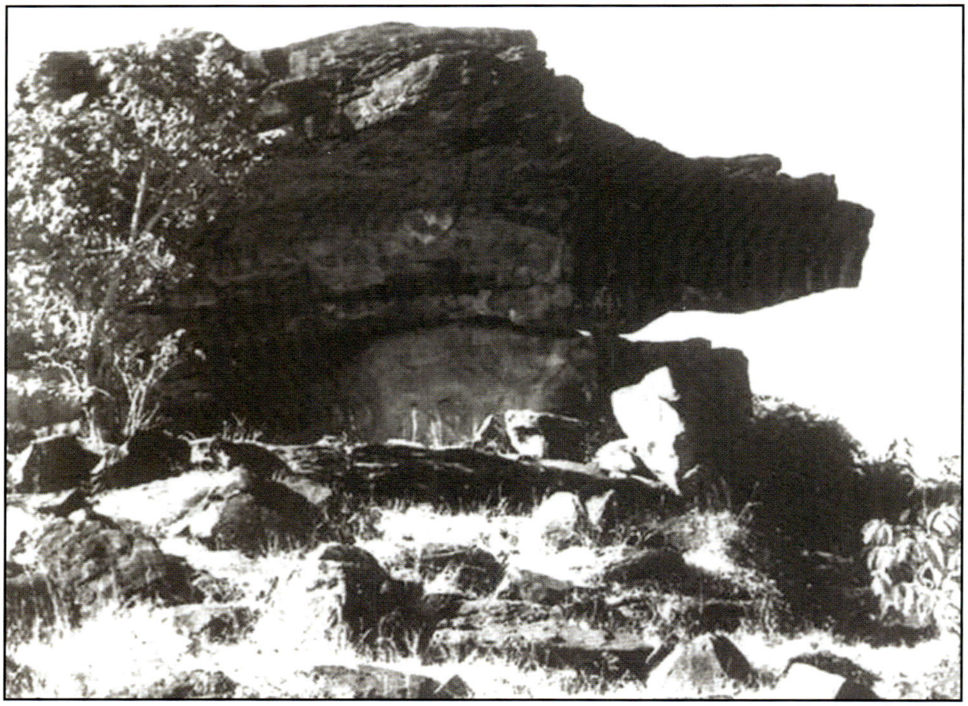

Fig. 18.30 Lekhahia R.S.1 (Bhainsore).

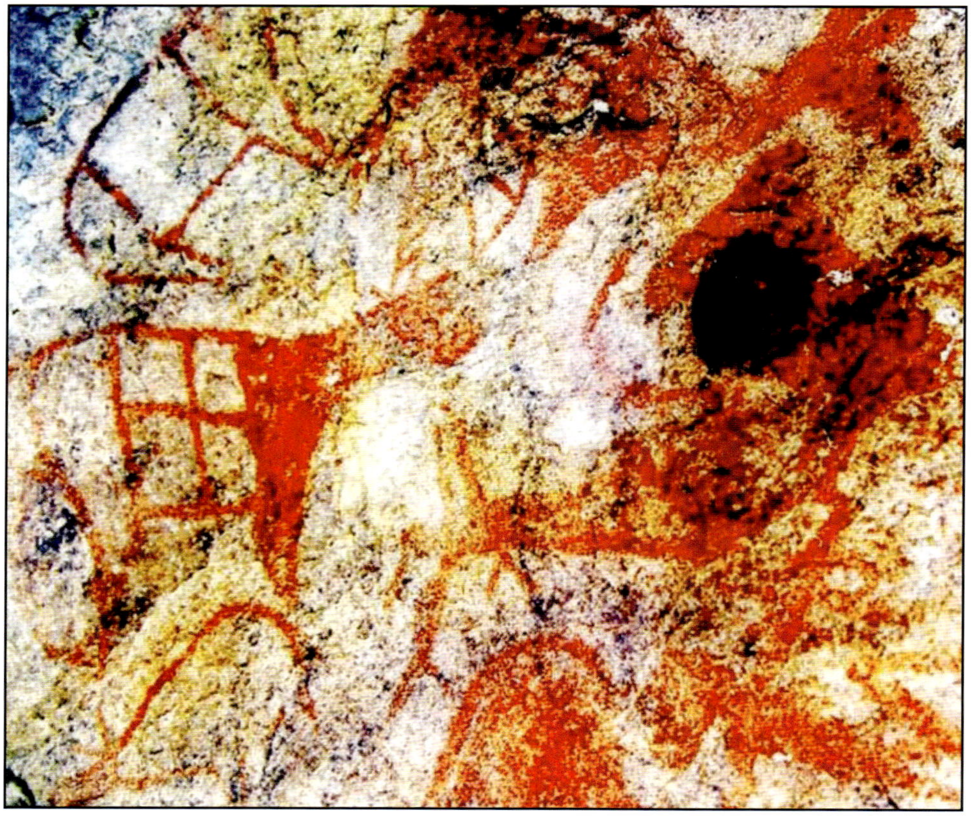

Fig. 18.31 There is no systematic placement/pattern of paintings on rock walls.

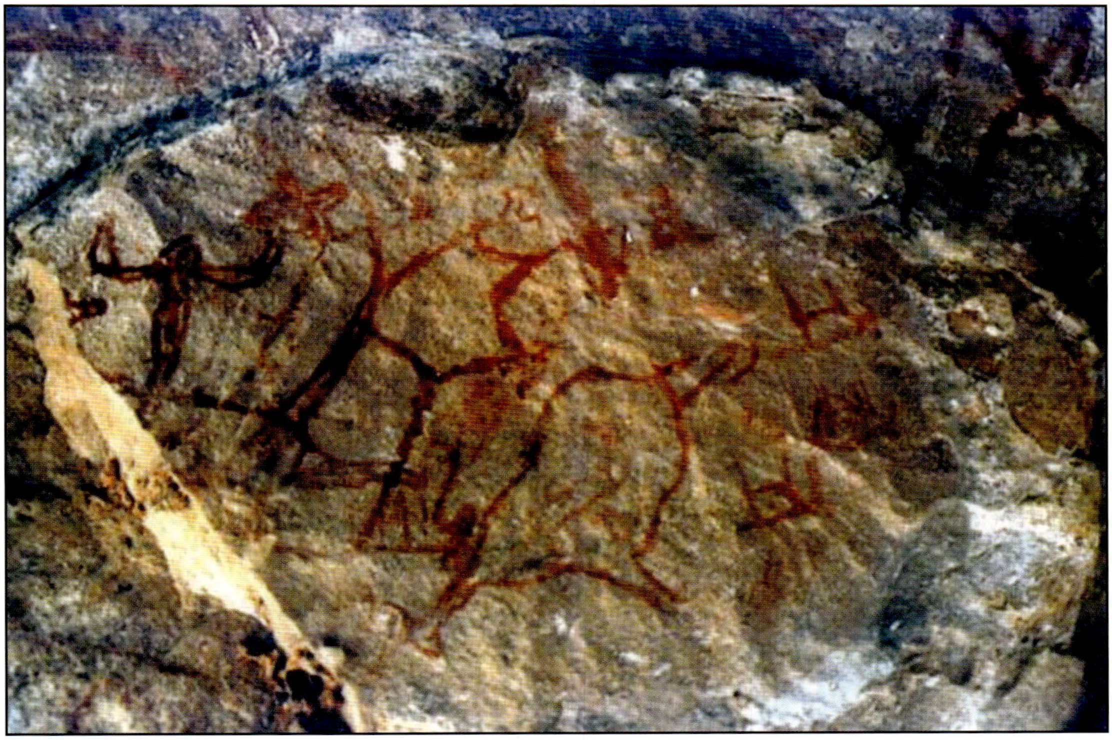

Fig. 18.32 Dhaunsara Shelter (Satna), painted ceiling.

the walls are usually arranged roughly horizontally.' Actually they were never arranged consciously. If they sometimes look like that then it is simply coincidental. Moreover, generally there is time gap between the paintings. Each painting forms a separate unit except those that narrate some episode.

The paintings on the ceilings are sometimes found in different orientations because they were painted in a lying down position (Fig. 18.32).

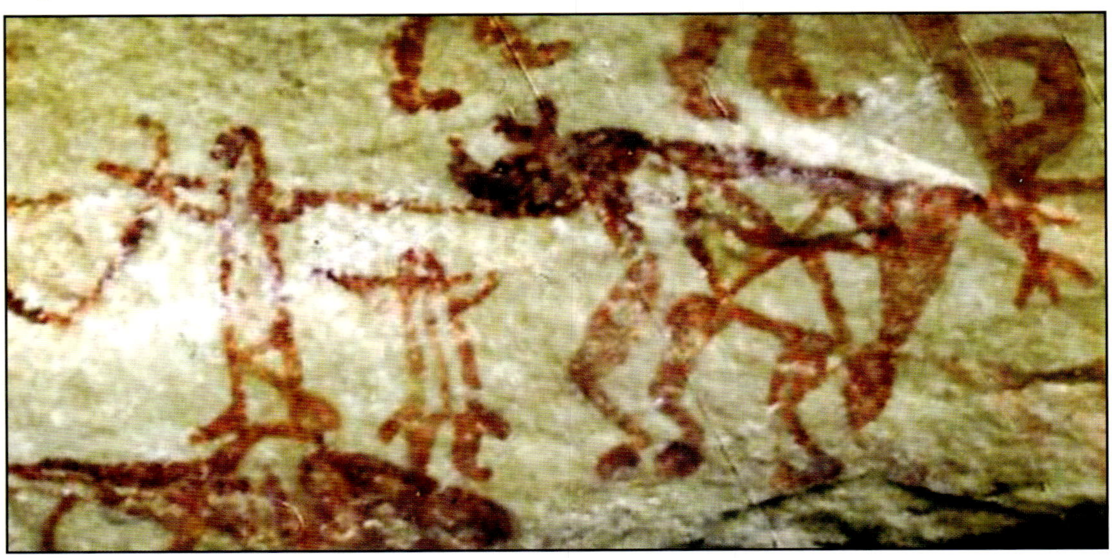

Fig. 18.33 Earlier paintings are generally of big animals.

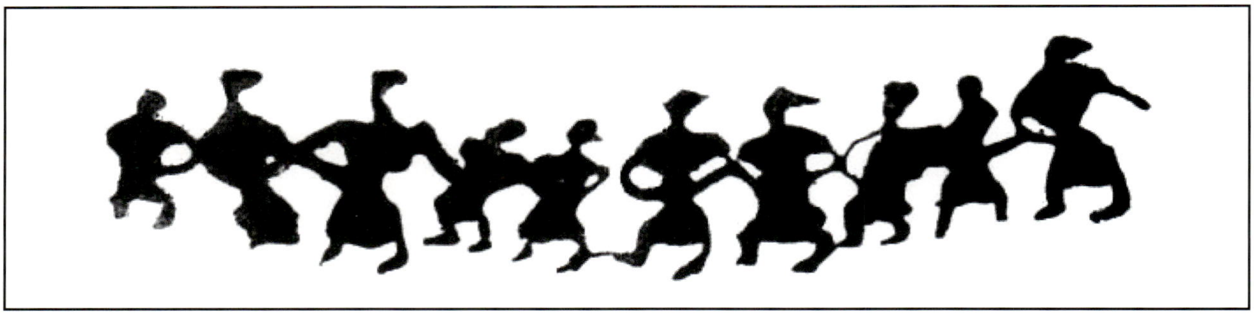

Fig. 18.34a Dancing human figures.

COMPOSITION

In the paintings of the earliest phase, only single animal figures are found. They are larger in size as compared to the later paintings. In the second or the next stage, more than one animal figure was painted together forming a group. It was only in the third stage that hunting or trap scenes appeared and the figures revolved round a theme.

Large animals like bison or rhinoceros have been depicted in a number of shelters being attacked by either one hunter or by a group of hunters (Figs. 18.2 & 18.33).

It is at this stage that man first makes an appearance. He is depicted as a hunter (Fig. 18.33) singly or in a group or is shown dancing in a group or going for a hunting spree (Fig. 18.34 a-b).

It is only rarely that man is depicted dancing solo. The Kandakot (Sonbhadra) painting is an exception where a figure with disheveled hair is shown dancing (Fig. 18.35).

Fig. 18.34b Going for hunting.

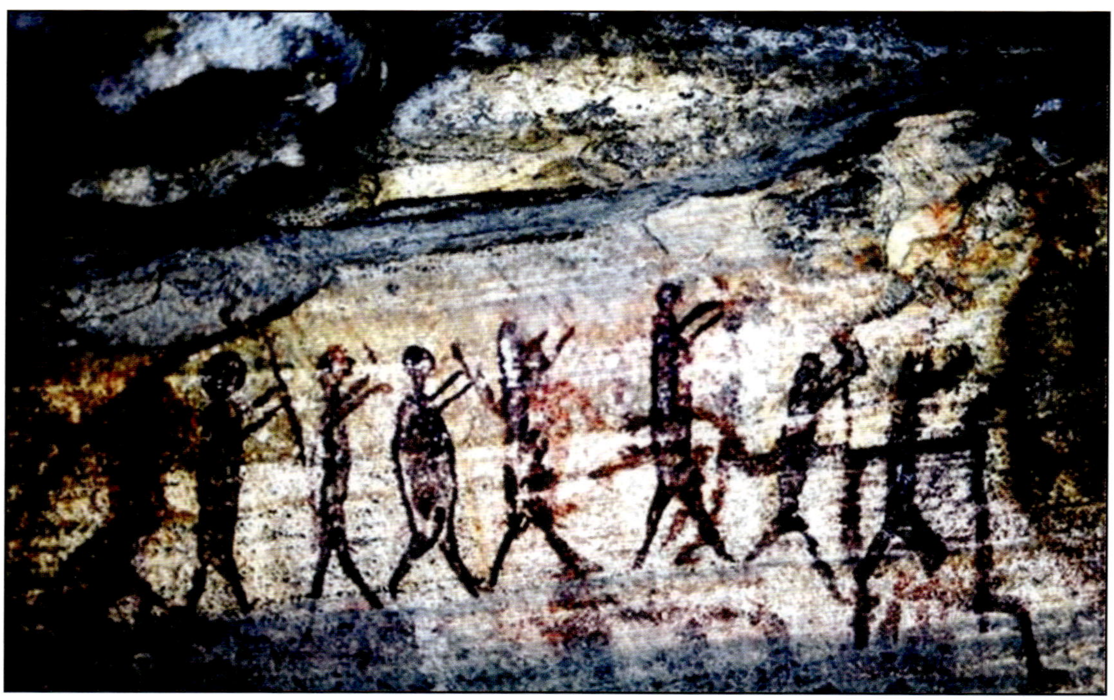

PIGMENT

The paintings are generally made from haematite pallets (*Geru*) or other oxides of iron. This is found in a range of yellows, browns, oranges, reds, etc. They are available in plenty in Vindhyan formations in the form of nodules or pallets.

For blacks and very dark browns, an oxide of manganese was also used and whites were obtained from kaolin (limestone). Sometimes white pigment was prepared from mineralised white chalcedony. A copper compound was used to obtain a bright shade of green. In the present study area, to the best of our knowledge, green has not been used.

SUPERIMPOSITION

It has been observed that sometimes a canvas was used by a large number of artists with utter disregard to earlier paintings. Hence, figures are found superimposed by figures of later periods.

Superimpositions are mainly of two types. In the first type, both the underlying and overlying figures are of the same colour and style. Such figures may belong to one period (Figs. 18.36 & 18.37).

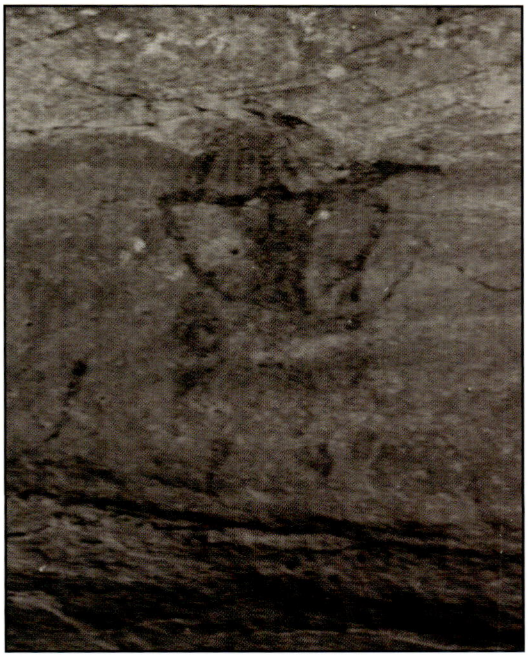

Fig. 18.35 Depiction of a solo dancer, Kandakot (Sonbhadra).

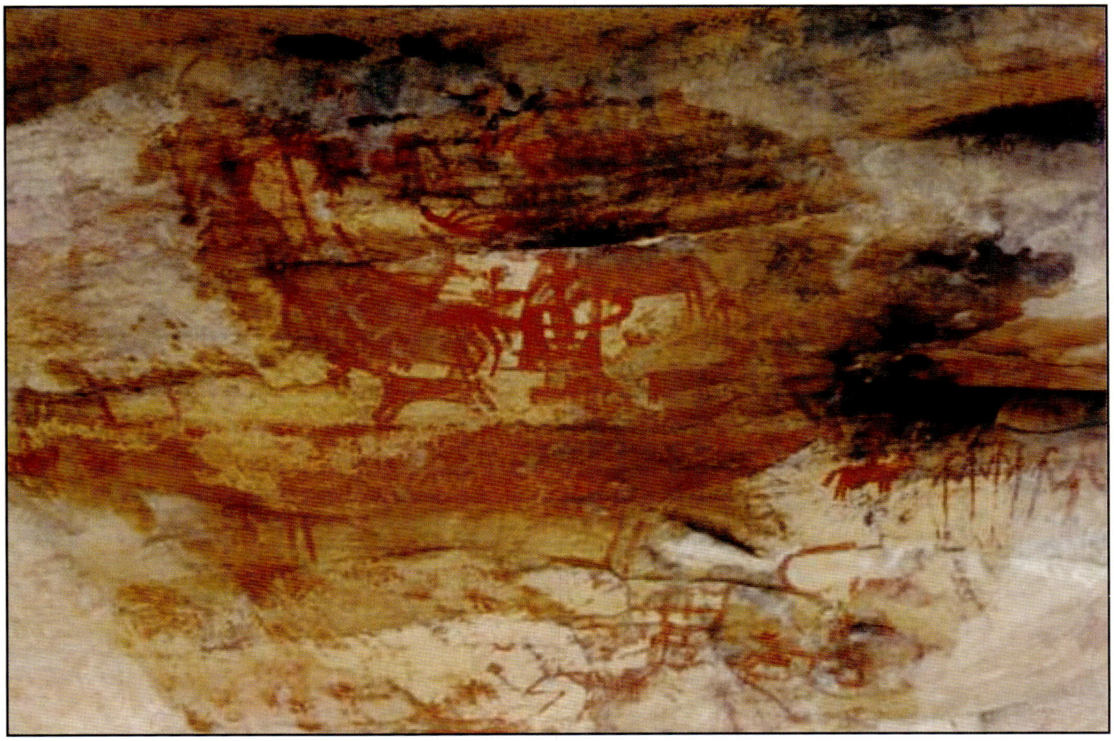

Fig. 18.36 Superimposition.

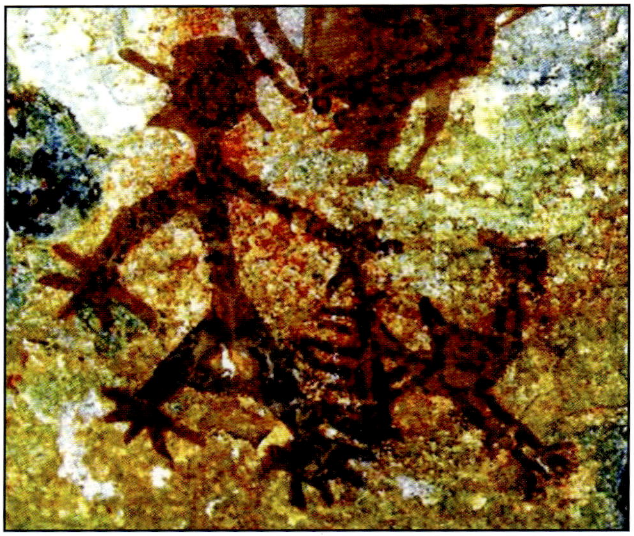

Fig. 18.37 Superimposition.

In the second category of superimposition, the underlying and overlying paintings can be distinguished either due to the difference in the shades of the colour or due to the style of the figures or due to both. The first type of superimposition has not been dealt with because it shows neither any evolution nor a separate period (Fig. 18.4b).

From the point of view of superimposition and style, at least four periods of painting activity can be marked in the northern Vindhyan region. In the first period, paintings in red ochre overlie paintings of the same colour. The difference between the two lies in the style or technique. This can be seen in the Lekhunia (RJP) rock shelter. In such cases of superimpositions, the underlying paintings are always more realistic than the overlying ones which have a tendency to become stylistic.

Another illustration can be cited from rock shelter no. 4 at (Morahana Pahar) Sahabahia Ki Pahari where over the big two-horned deer painted in flat wash in clottish-blood colour in naturalistic style are painted small animal figures, which are unidentifiable (Fig. 18.36).

In the second type of superimposition, stylistically painted figures underlie a number of symbols and diagrams. A representation of this type of superimposition can be cited from shelter no. 4 at Sahabahia in which unidentifiable figures of animals and spotted deer underlie a number of diagrams and symbols (Figs. 18.38 & 18.39).

In the third type of superimposition, paintings in red underlie those in off white. This is a common feature in every group of shelters; hence, it may indicate an entirely new phase in the rock art of the region under study. It heralds a new tradition of painting activity both in the sense of colour and style. It indicates a reversal in the cyclic evolution of the style of painting.

Left: **Fig. 18.38** A big two-horned deer in rock-shelter No. 4 at (Morahana Pahar) Sahabahia Ki Pahari. They are marked as L1, L2, L3 and L4.

Right: **Fig. 18.39** Superimpositions of paintings at shelter no. 4 at Sahabahia.

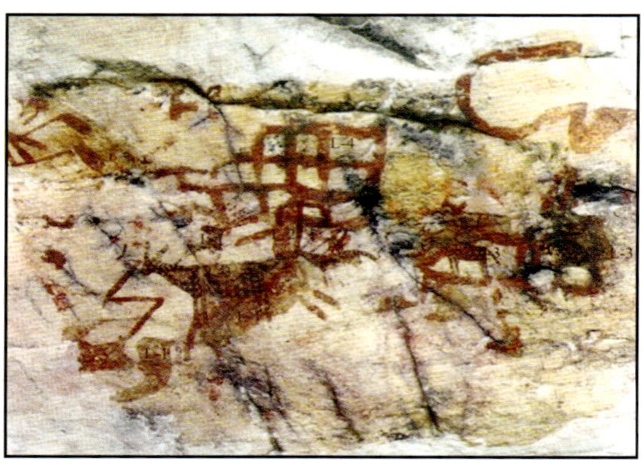

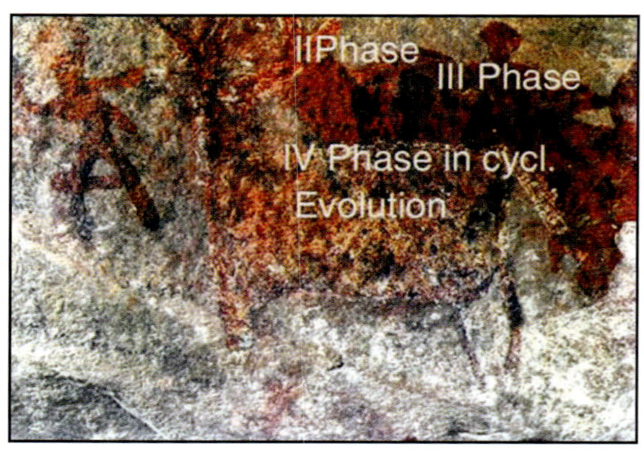

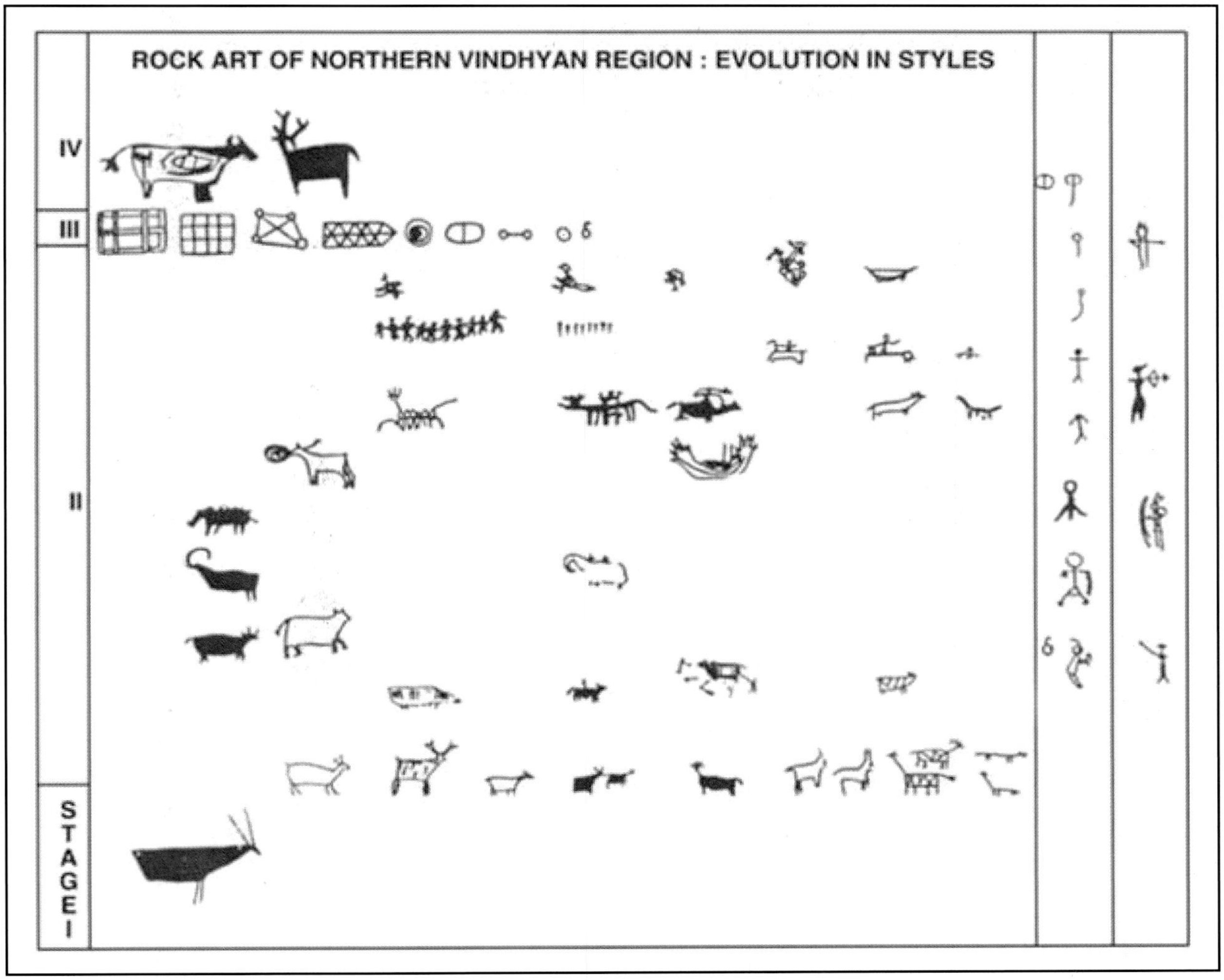

Fig. 18.40 Various stages of paintings.

On the basis of superimpositions, the following stages can be demarcated. An evolutionary sequence in the paintings can be observed in Fig. 18.40 which may be summed up as under:

STAGE I (NATURALISTIC)

The figures of the first stage are realistic and life-like. The paintings of this period may be described as imitative. Due care was taken to paint the animals as life-like figures. The figures are larger in size and the paint has been applied thickly, the shades being usually clotted blood or burnt red. In this stage, only animal figures were painted. There is no human figure in any of the shelters that can be assigned to this stage (Fig. 18.41).

STAGE II (STYLISTIC)

To this stage belongs the largest number of paintings of the northern Vindhyan region. They cover a very long duration of time; hence, they show a lot of minute variations in

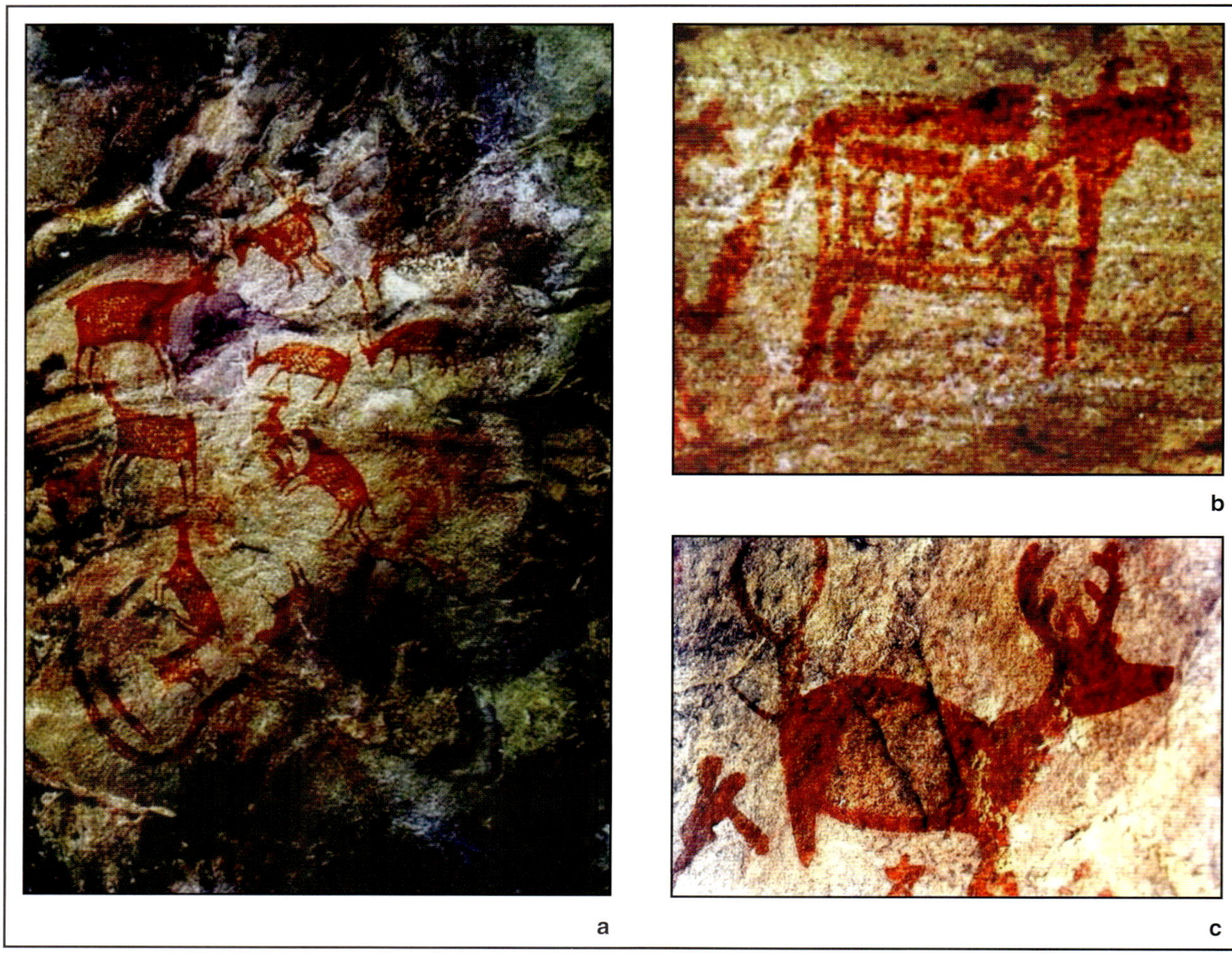

Fig. 18.41 (a-c) Single and somewhat realistic figures of animals of Stage I.

style. This stage includes all the paintings that are neither perfectly imitative nor are they completely symbolic. A careful study of the paintings of this group indicates how changes in style took place gradually.

On the basis of variations in style, the paintings of this stage may further be divided into a number of sub-stages:

(A) Paintings belonging to the first sub-stage look very life-like but they are not imitative. The figures are smaller in size and have usually been drawn in outline only (Fig. 18.42).

(B) Though the paintings of this sub-stage usually conform to the generally accepted outlines of figures of men and animals, yet they are not life-like. The different limbs on the body are not shown proportionately but the characteristic features are maintained (Figs. 18.43 & 18.44).

(C) Paintings that have been placed in the third sub-stage of this group include extremely simplified figures. The curves of the body vanish and the whole figure

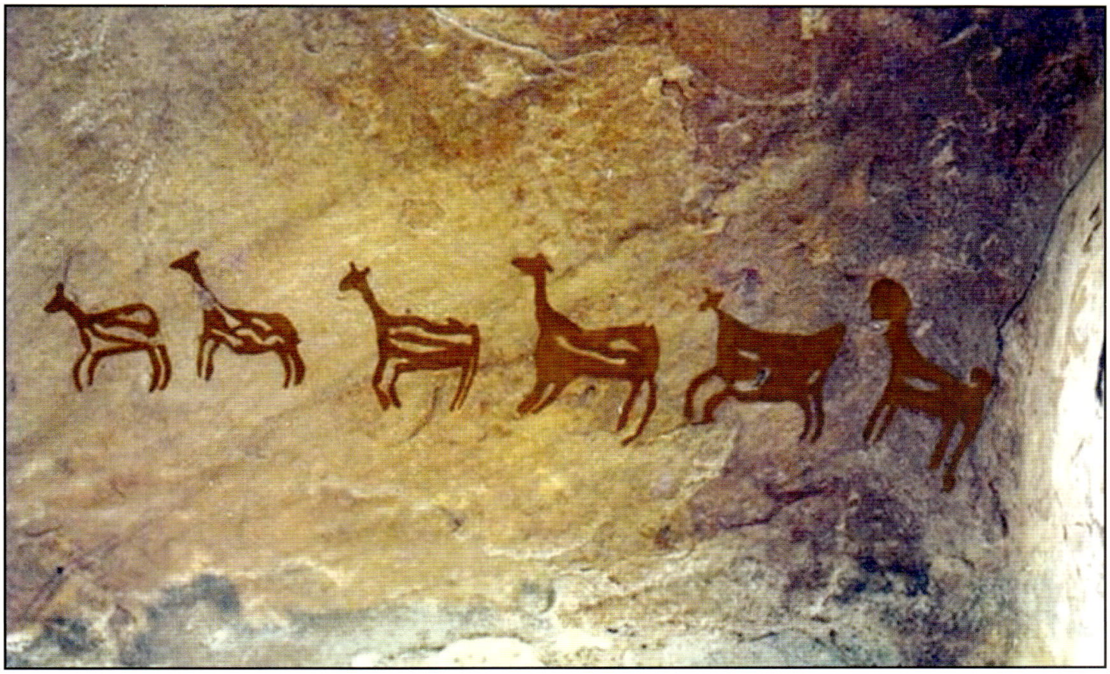

Fig. 18.42 The paintings belonging to the first sub-stage look very life-like but are of smaller size.

is reduced to a straight line with sharp angles. The important feature of this stage is that the characteristic features of the animal's anatomy have been emphasised (Figs. 18.43 & 18.44).

STAGE III (SYMBOLIC)

To the third stage belong the paintings that may be termed as symbolic. The pictures are sometimes reduced to a triangle, to just an angle, a circle or a dot, a spiral line or a loop and latticed designs. Such symbols are found in almost all the shelters. These always overlie the paintings belonging to the second group. The paintings in Ronp shelter no. 1 mainly belong

Fig. 18.43 The paintings belonging to the second sub-stage are of generally outlined figures.

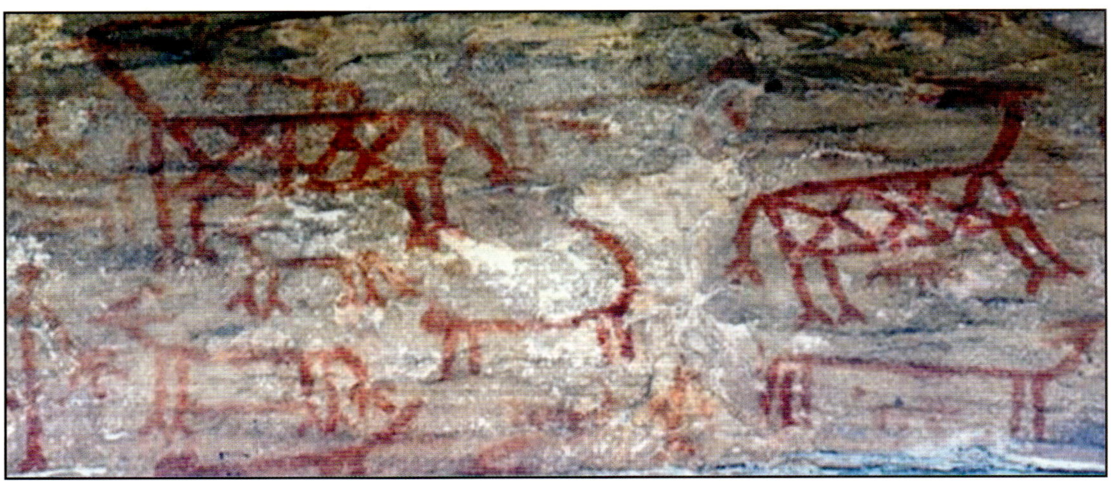

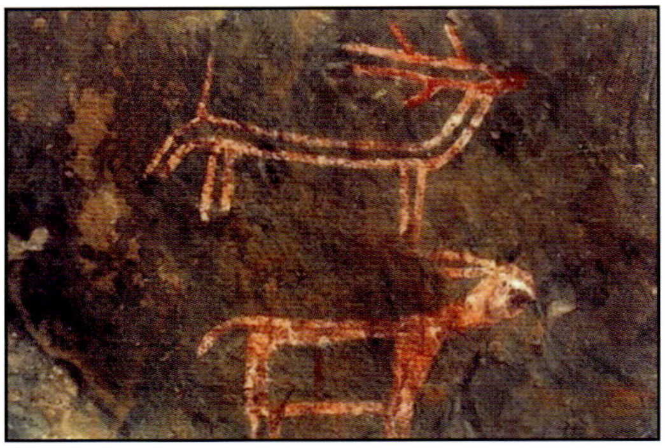

Fig. 18.44 The paintings belonging to the third sub-stage have extremely simplified and are reduced to straight lines and sharp angles.

to this group. What these symbols stand for is difficult to understand but it is certain that they do stand for particular things (Fig. 18.45).

STAGE IV (PAINTINGS IN WHITE)

The paintings of the fourth stage are in off white. As already indicated, these paintings show a reversal in the cyclic evolution of the style of paintings. Stylistically, these belong to Stage I and to the first few sub-stages of Stage II, but since these overlie the paintings of stages I to III in chronological order, they come later (Fig. 18.46).

RECENT

There is one more group of paintings which differs from the rest both in subject matter and in the mode of presentation. Paintings belonging to this group may be termed as recent in relation to the rest of the paintings. These paintings no longer deal with animals and hunting, etc. They usually depict big compositions dealing with royal processions and war scenes, etc. The other paintings include chariots drawn by horses (Figs. 18.47 & 18.48), caparisoned elephants, *alpanas*, mural designs and phallic symbols.

Usually orange wash has been thinly applied in such paintings. Moreover, paintings of this group are painted away from the rest of

Fig. 18.45 The paintings of different symbols in Ronp shelter no. 1.

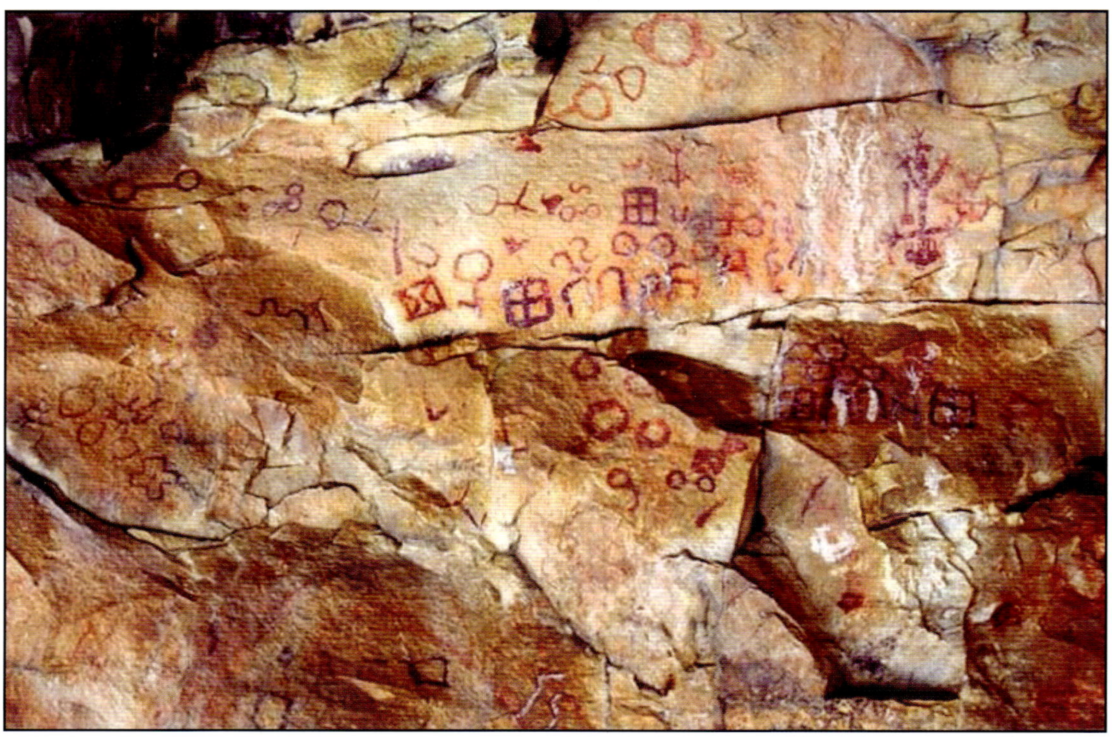

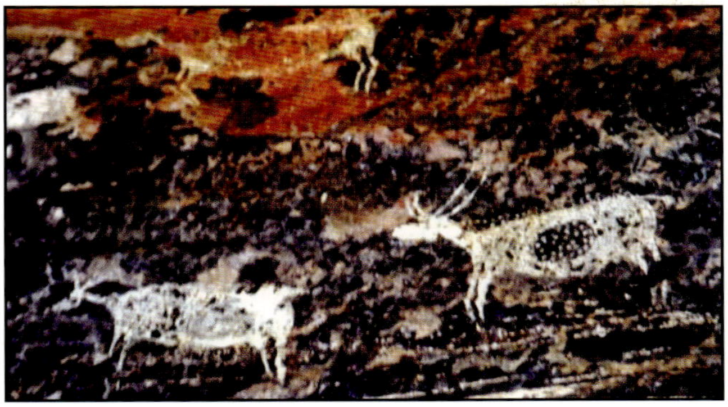

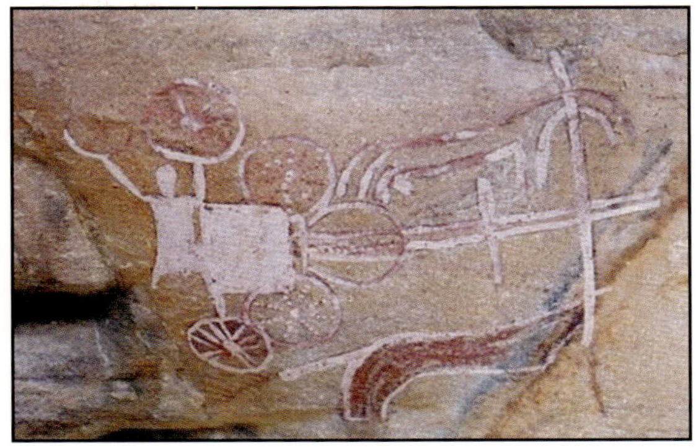

the paintings indicating indirectly that they do not have any connection with the other paintings. These form an entirely separate group.

Left: **Fig. 18.46** Paintings in off white colour.

Right: **Fig. 18.47** Painting of chariots drawn by horses.

SUBJECT MATTER OF PAINTINGS

The rock art of the northern Vindhyan region is mostly the product of a people who were primarily hunters and food-gatherers. Their entire existence—economic, social and spiritual—was dominated by hunting. Everything was focused on the quest for a game. Hence, the subject matter of the paintings also centres around animals. They have been shown in their natural attitudes standing, running, grazing singly or in a group or forming a part of hunting scenes.

Usually, animals that were eaten were painted again and again. Other animals like feline animals that did not form a part of their diet were very rarely painted. Deer seems to have been the favourite animal of these people. In almost every cave or rock shelter, figures of deer are found singly or in groups (Figs. 18.49-18.51). Among the different species of deer, sambhar, chital and chincara are more commonly painted. Rhinoceros also seems to have been a much liked animal (Figs. 18.2 & 18.33). In the rock shelters of Sonbhadra and Mirzapur, paintings of this animal are very common. They generally form part of hunting scenes.

They are either shown with a rider or depicted in a hunting scene being attacked by men with bows and arrows or spears. Besides these, the other animals depicted are elephants, bison (Fig. 18.52), nilgai or blue bull (Fig. 18.53), horses, feline animals (Fig. 18.54), horse

Left: **Fig. 18.48** Chariot without wheels.

Right: **Fig. 18.49** Gaddi shelter (Rewa).

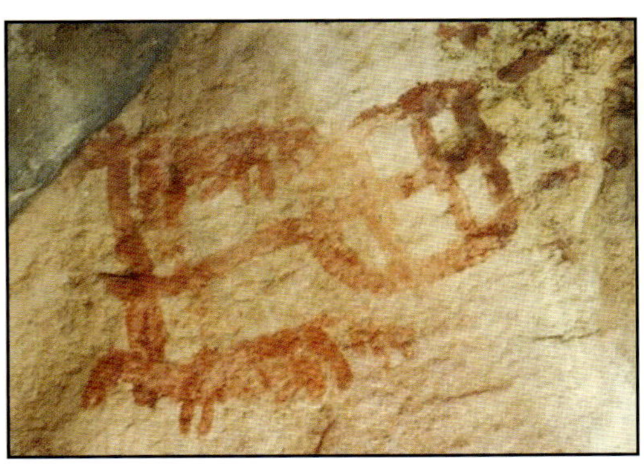

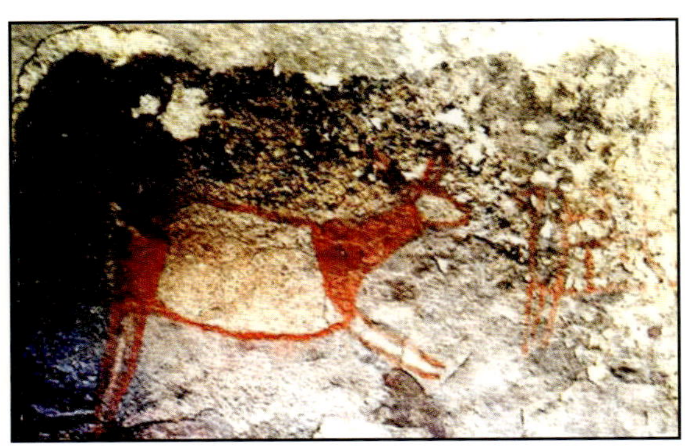

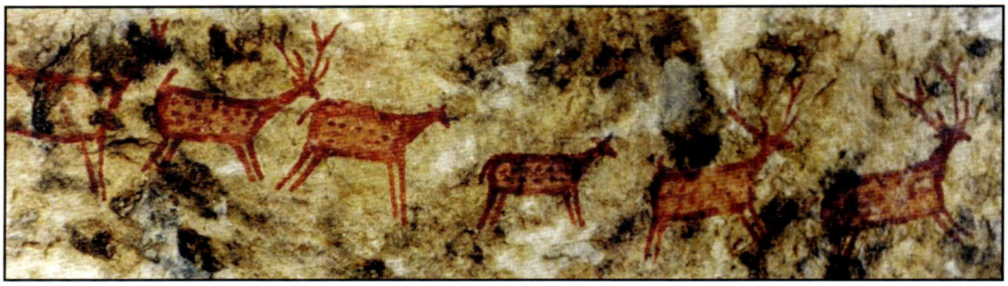

Fig. 18.50 Lekhahia (Bhainsore).

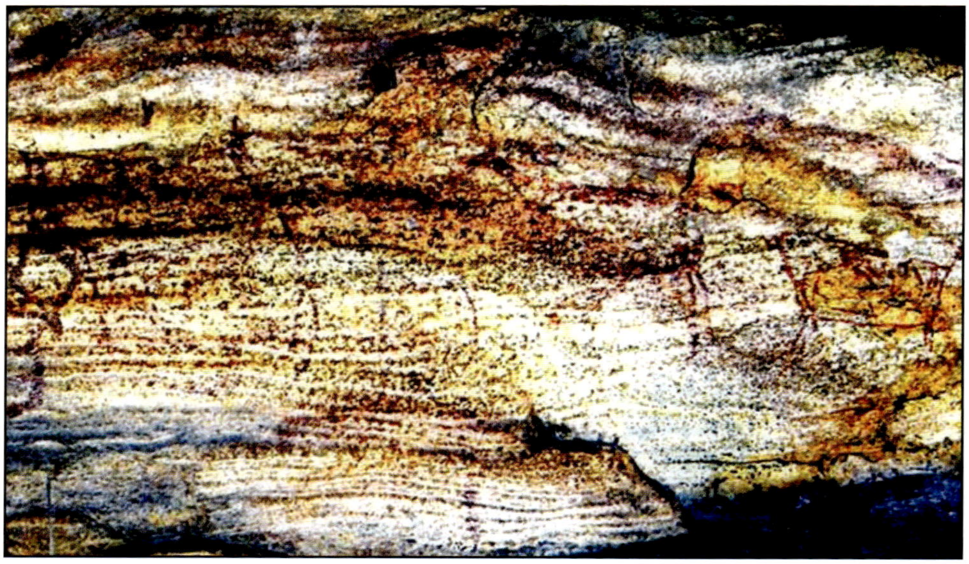

Fig. 18.51 Lekhunia (RJP): Barasingha marching in a file.

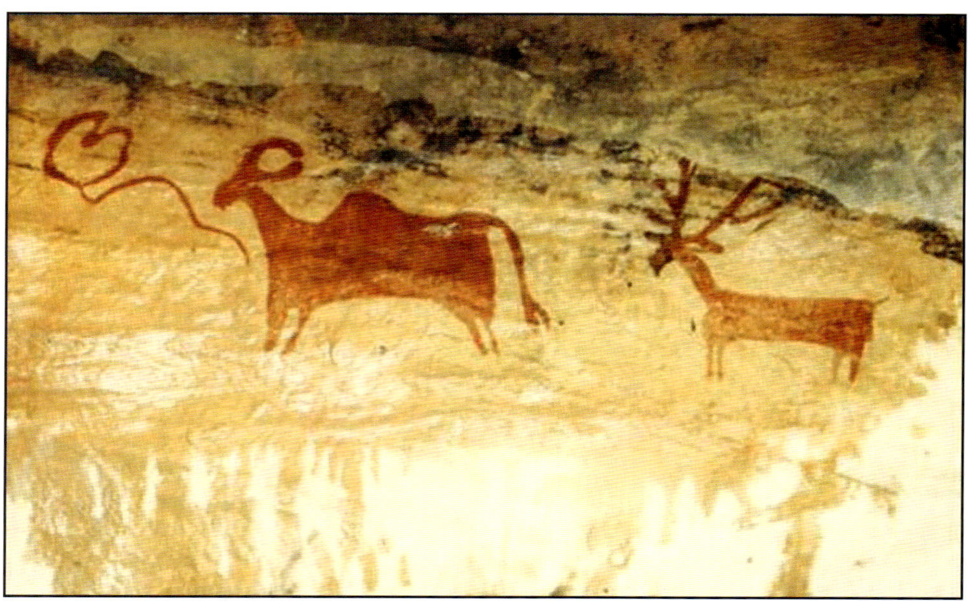

Fig. 18.52 Bison (Mirchahawa), Bhainsore.

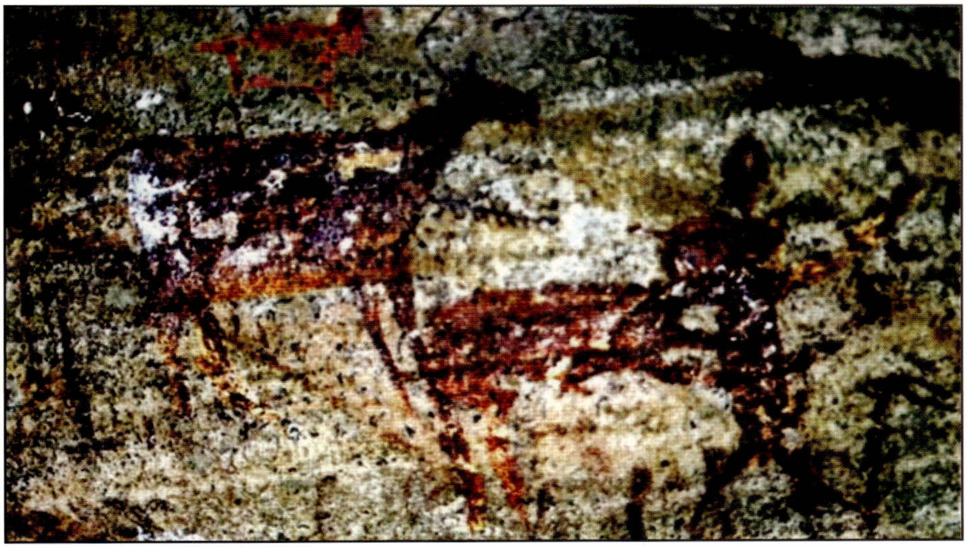

Fig. 18.53 Nilgai or blue bull, Lekhunia (RJP).

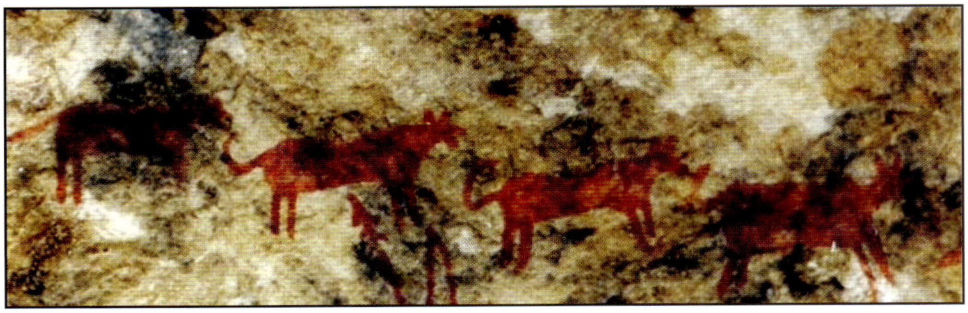

Fig. 18.54 Feline animals, Lekhunia R.S.3 (Bhainsore).

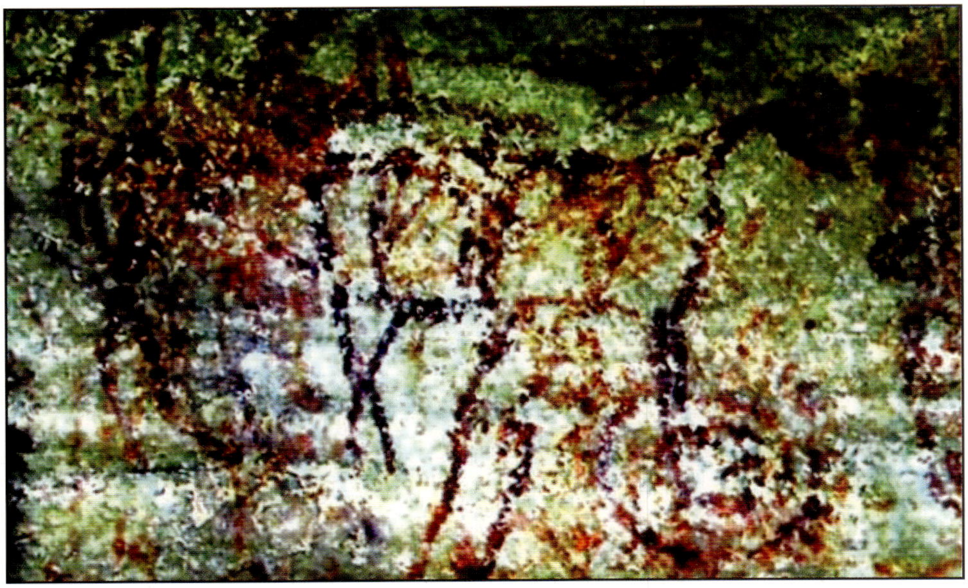

Fig. 18.55 Horse (Ronp).

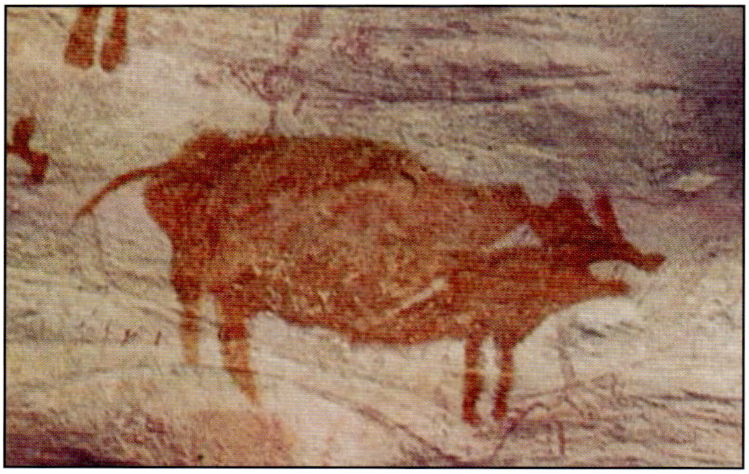

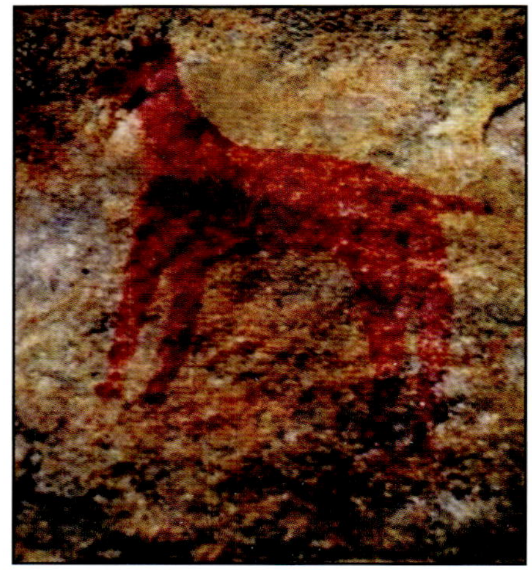

Left: **Fig. 18.56** A boar in agony, Bhaldaria.

Right: **Fig. 18.57** Wild dog Ronp.

(Fig. 18.55), boar (Fig. 18.56), wild dog (Fig. 18.57), serpents, etc. and there are a few animals that could not be identified.

Birds are also painted but their paintings are not common. A beautiful painting of a peacock (Fig. 18.58) in the Morahana Pahar shelter, a cock (Fig. 18.59) in the Ronp shelter and one figure of an ostrich has been identified in Lekhunia rock shelter (RJP) (Fig. 18.60)

Hunting scenes are also common but their depiction (barring a few) is clumsy and lifeless. In most of the cases, the tip of a spear only touches the lifeless standing animal. In some paintings, the animal is shown being attacked by a man or a group of men with arrows, spears or harpoons (Fig. 18.61).

Trap scenes are also not uncommon. In some cases traps have been symbolised by concentric circles (Fig. 18.63a) while in others elaborate arrangements have been shown with minute details (Fig. 18.63b).

In one painting on the ceiling of Lekhunia shelter (RJP), two hunters are depicted in the act of entrapping a doe.

Human figures form a very small percentage of the total number of paintings. Man appears in the third stage as a hunter. Sometimes they are shown with a mask (Figs. 18.64 a-b). No attention was paid

Left: **Fig. 18.58** Peacock, Morahana Pahar shelter.

Right: **Fig. 18.59** A cock, Ronp shelter.

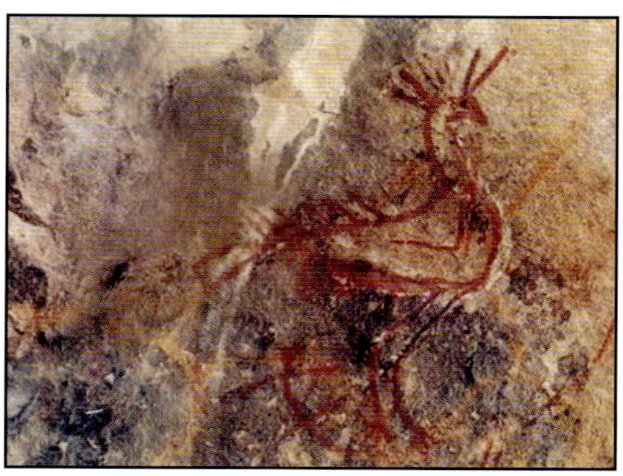

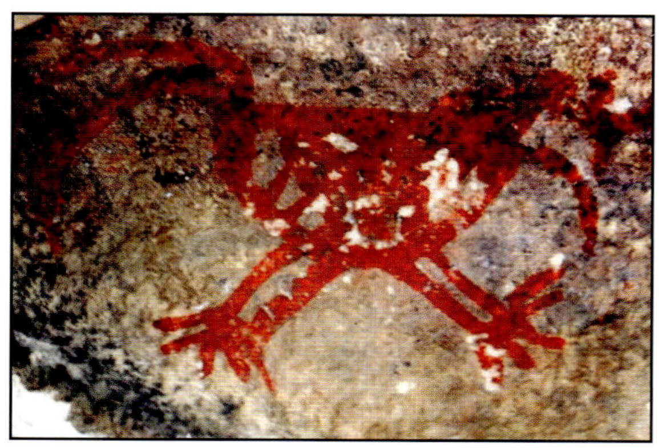

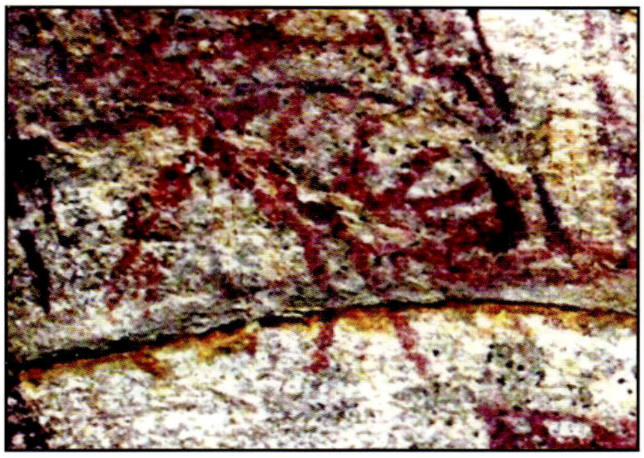

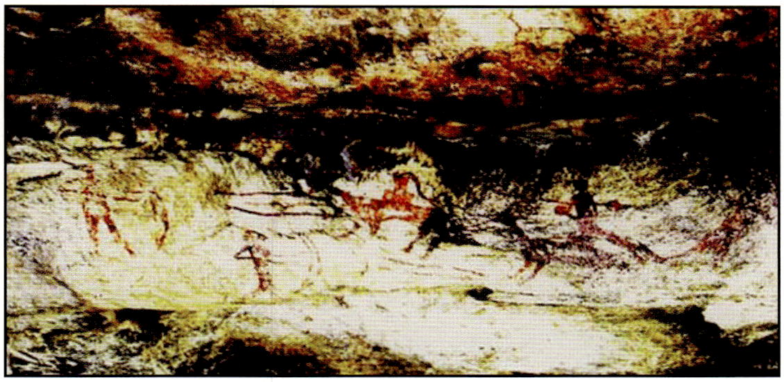

Left: **Fig. 18.60** Ostrich (?), LKH-RJP.

Right: **Fig. 18.61** Hunting scene, Lekhunia (RJP).

to paint him realistically. The figures are depicted more symbolically than realistically (Fig. 18.65). Single human figures are rare. Usually, the human figures are depicted in a group or in hunting scenes. In one case, a hunter with a monkey face (mask) has been painted (Fig. 18.66). They are shown shooting an arrow or spearing an animal. In some of the rock shelters, a number of human figures are shown enacting ritual dances. Narrative scenes are extremely rare in the northern Vindhyan region.

There are a number of non-figurative diagrams and symbols—dot and line, loop and circles, circles within circles, dot within a circle and a straight line with two circles on either end. What these symbols stand for is not easy to understand. An attempt has been made to understand the meaning of a few symbols.

CHRONOLOGY OF ROCK ART

The question of dating rock art is still unsettled. So far, there is no absolute date. All the dates suggested are based on circumstantial evidence, subject matter and archaeological material. The subject matter does not help much when we are dealing with prehistoric data on a multi-cultural site. The life pattern during the upper Palaeolithic, Mesolithic and early Neolithic was not very different. Subsistence was primarily based on hunting and gathering during the upper Palaeolithic and Mesolithic periods. Lithic hunting tools too cannot be distinguished easily. The bow and arrow, spears,

Left: **Fig. 18.62a** Hunting scenes: Rhino hunt (after Rakesh Tewari).

Right: **Fig. 18.62b** Gaur hunt, Lakhma shelter (MZP) (after Rakesh Tewari).

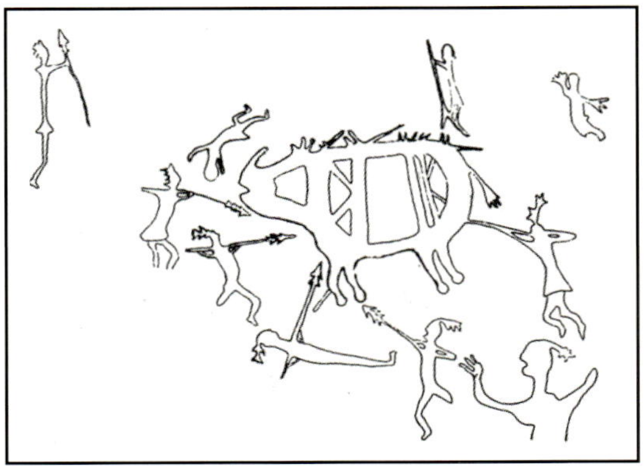

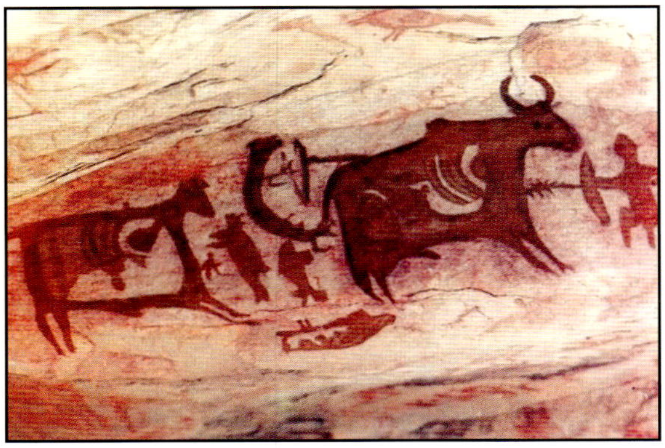

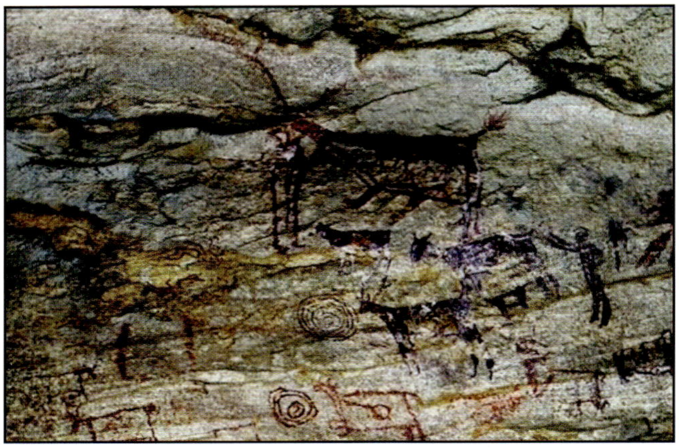

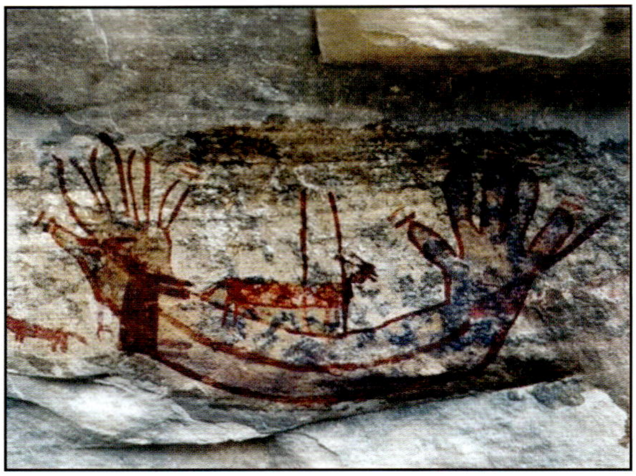

Left: **Fig. 18.63a** Trap scenes-concentric circles (LKH, RJP).

Right: **Fig. 18.63b** Trap scene, Morahana Pahar (RS4).

harpoons and catapult had evolved during the upper Palaeolithic period and were used in succeeding cultures also. Trapping methods like ambushing and pit traps also must have been in vogue during both the periods as some of these methods are still practiced. There was no difference in the fauna also. Distinguishable tools and life patterns start from the Neolithic period when domestication of animals and plants started. Domestication in its rudimentary form had started at some places during the Mesolithic period. It must, therefore, be emphasized that conclusions drawn on the basis of subject matter alone would be misleading.

Attempts to fix the antiquity of Indian rock art have been made by almost all leading rock art scholars. Wakankar divided the entire painting activity in five periods and 20 styles (Wakankar and Brooks 1976: 31).

Left & Right: **Fig. 18.64** (a-b) Close-up of archers with long bow and arrow.

He placed styles 1–6 in Mesolithic or earlier and provided a time bracket 8000 (?)–2500 BCE. He placed some green paintings at Bhimbetka in the upper Palaeolithic period. While excavating the

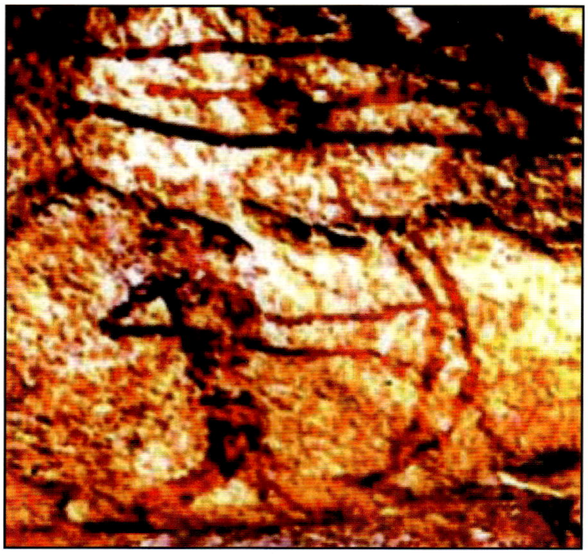

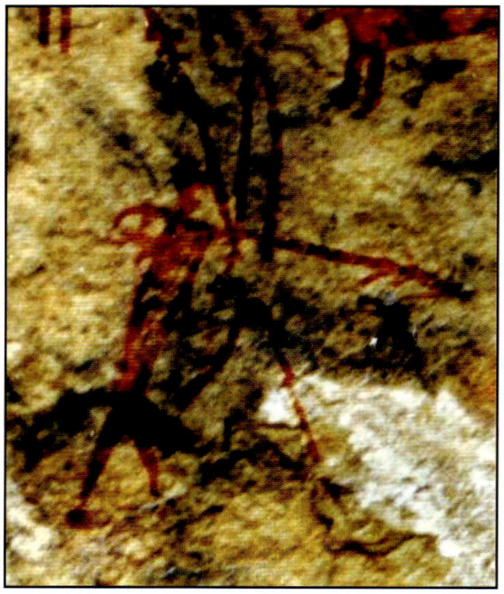

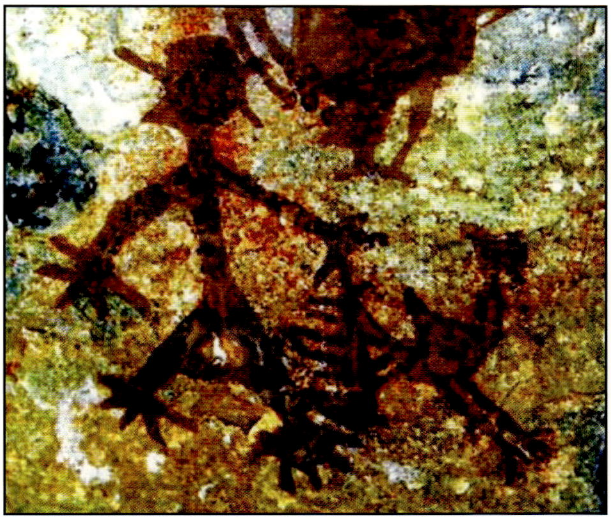 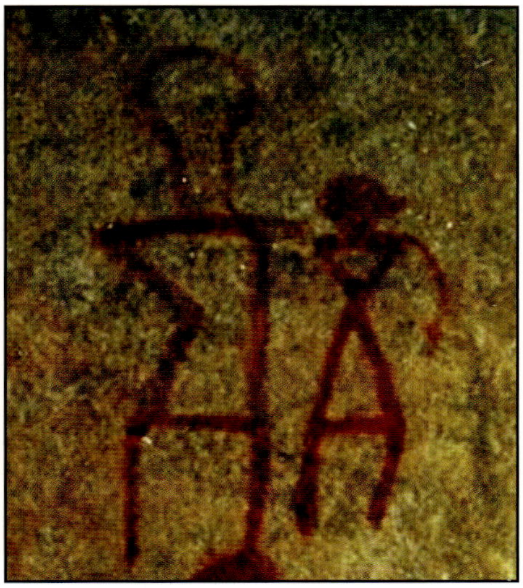

Left & Right: **Fig. 18.65** Different types of human figures.

Bhimbetka shelter III-A-28, Wakankar obtained green pigments from upper Palaeolithic levels and on this basis he assigned the upper Palaeolithic age to the green paintings. Thus, according to Wakankar, the green paintings ('S' type) are the earliest (Kumar 1981: 279 and 1984:123; Wakankar 1984: 50; Wakankar and Brooks 1976: 31, 81).

But Pande and Tyagi are of the view that these green paintings are not the earliest as there are paintings in red and intricate designs which precede them. Under the circumstances, it is difficult to come to any definite conclusion as this requires more investigation.

V.N. Misra and Mathpal have divided the entire painting activity into nine chronological phases. The first five phases (ABCD and E) belong to the prehistoric or Mesolithic period, the sixth (Phase F) to the transitional or Chalcolithic period and the last three (GH and I) to the historic period (Misra and Mathpal 1979: 27-33).

Subsequent work by Tyagi (1988) added a new dimension to this classification. According to him, intricate designs precede the green figures. Thus, according to Tyagi, painting activity in the Central Vindhyan region commences with non-figurative intricate designs.

S.K. Pandey has classified the paintings under five categories: (a) naturalistic, (b) stylised, (c) schematic, (d) conventionalised, and (e) eclectic. This is based on the same pattern as devised by R.K. Varma (1964). According to Pandey, painting activity started during the upper Palaeolithic period. The basis of assigning the paintings an upper Palaeolithic association has not been stated.

Erwin Neumayer has divided the entire painting activity into two very broad divisions: (1). Rock pictures of early hunters and gatherers and (2). Rock art of agriculturists and animal keepers. The first division has been put under the cultural division known as Mesolithic. According to Neumayer, 'the microlith technology shown in these paintings could be as old as 25,000 years or only 5,000 years... some of the earliest paintings might have been done during the Upper Palaeolithic period.'

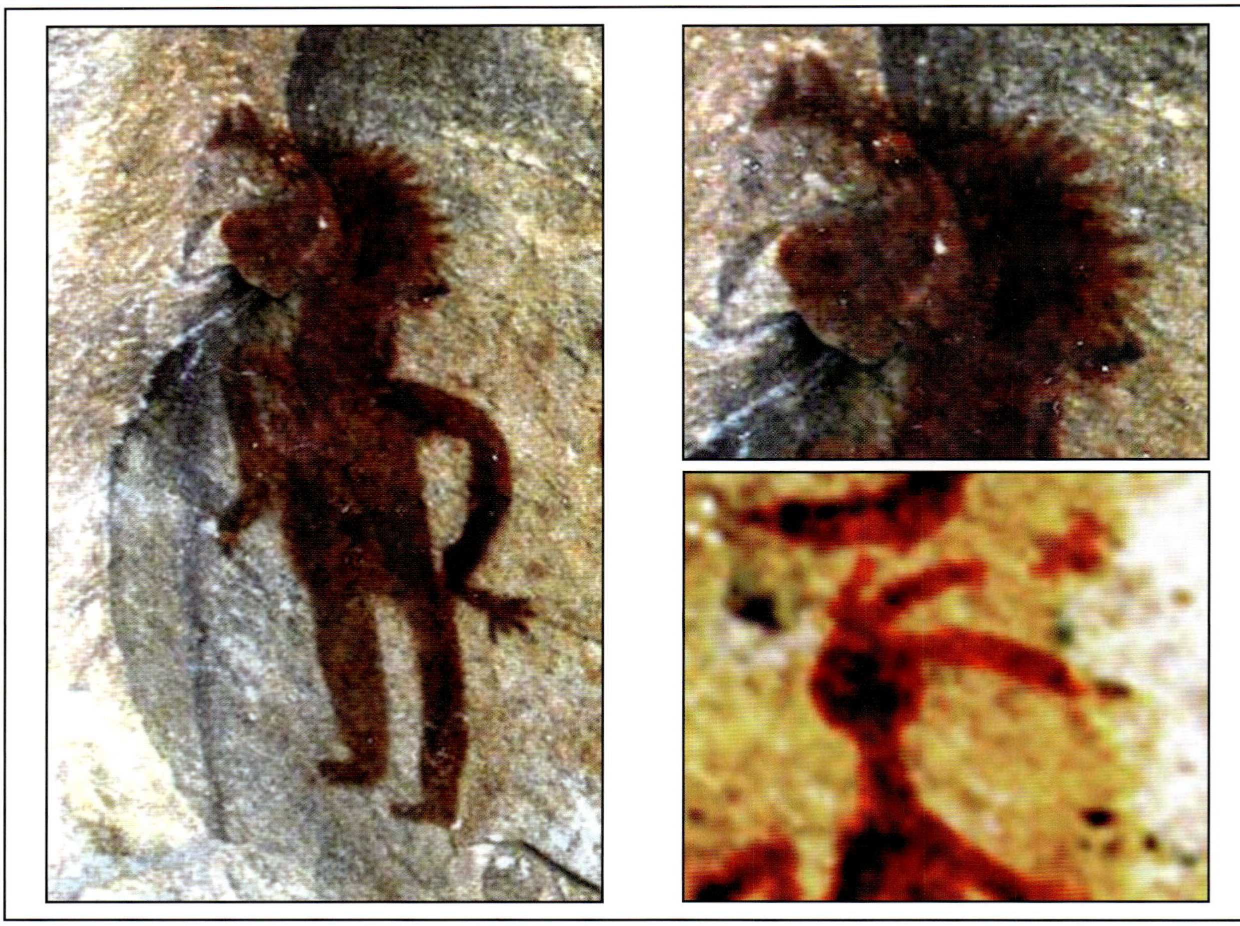

Fig. 18.66 Painting of a monkey face masked hunter.

But his classification is very subjective and many of the paintings assigned by him to the Mesolithic period cannot be placed within the Mesolithic cultural phase. They seem to belong to a much evolved cultural phase. On the face value, the classification cannot be accepted in toto.

On the basis of present evidence from excavations, painted shelters of the northern Vindhyan region were first occupied in the Epi-Palaeolithic period—a period of transition from upper Palaeolithic to Mesolithic. Mesolithic folk lived in the shelters, made their tools and buried their dead there. This makes the position of the rock shelters of the northern Vindhyan region unique. Since the shelters remained under the occupation of Mesolithic people only, it is reasonable to suppose that these were the people who were also responsible for the paintings.

There are a number of C14 dates now, which help us to arrive at certain conclusions regarding the antiquity of the Mesolithic of the northern Vindhyan region. By implication that would be the time bracket for the painting activity also.

From the Lekhahia rock shelter (Bhainsore group), we have four dates. Two C14 dates belonging to Phase III of the Vindhyan Mesolithic are: TF–417: 3560±110 BP (1710±110 BCE) and TF–419: 4240±115 BP (2410±115 BCE).

Two more C-14 dates, by accelerator mass spectrometry from human bone apatite, were also obtained. These dates are based on thorough pre-treatment and sample preparation methods and suggest that the skeletons from Lekhahia may have an antiquity two times greater than previously believed: Geochron 8370±75 BP (Skl.IV) and Geochron 8000±75 BP (Skl. XIII, XV).

These are not isolated dates. There are confirmatory dates from Belan, Son and Ganga Valley sites also.

The upper Palaeolithic horizon (Gravel III) in Belan valley has given two C-14 dates reading 23840 BCE (PRL 86) and 17765 BCE (TF 1245). Another date reading 18000 BP has been obtained from the Upper Palaeolithic horizon (Clark and Williams 1990: 13-24).

The Epi-Palaeolithic horizon (Gravel IV) in the Belan section has yielded five dates (Possehl and Rissman 1992; Varma 1981-83) reading 13740+400/-380 BP (PRL 603); 11550±180 BP (BS 130); 10980±190 BP (PRL602); 9830±160 BP (BS 131); and 9740±115 BP (SVA 1421).

Baghor II, a Mesolithic settlement (geometric microliths unassociated with pottery) in the Son valley, has yielded one C-14 date reading 6380±220 BCE (PRL 715) (Clark and Williams 1990).

Similar early dates have been obtained from the Mesolithic settlements of the Ganga Valley (Mesolithic Phase II of the Vindhyan region). There is one date from Sarai Nahar Rai TF 1104; 8365±110 BCE and one TL date 5000–7000 BCE and two AMS C-14 dates reading 6670±65 BCE and 6915±69 BCE.

On the basis of this discussion, the Epi-Palaeolithic may be placed roughly within a time bracket of 14000–13000 BCE to 10000–9000 BCE and the Mesolithic can be placed safely within 12000–11000 BCE to 2000–1500 BCE with the possibility of the beginning to be pushed back further by a couple of thousand years when the dates for the first phase of the Vindhyan Mesolithic comes to be known. At present, all the dates are from Phase II and III only. Hence, there is a possibility that the date of the beginning of Mesolithic will be pushed back considerably.

On the basis of this discussion, prehistoric rock paintings of the Bhainsore region can also be assigned the date of the Epi-Palaeolithic/Mesolithic of the region (14000–13000 BCE to 2000–1500 BCE). From the available evidence it is clear that the Mesolithic folk were the authors of prehistoric paintings. The historical paintings may be placed between 1000 and the recent past. These dates are subject to change with the discovery of new data.

REFERENCES

Cockburn, J. (1883), 'A Short Account of the Petographs in the Caves and Rock Shelters, the Kaimur Range in the Mirzapur District', *Proceeding of the Asiatic Society of Bengal*, pp. 125-26.

—— (1883), 'On the Recent Existence of Rhinoceros Indicus in the North Western Provinces, and a Description of A tracing of an Archaic Rock Painting from Mirzapore Representing the Hunting of This Animal', *Journal of the Asiatic Society of Bengal* v. 52(2): 56-64.

—— (1884), 'On the durability and Hemetite Drawings on Sandstone Rocks', *Proceedings of Asiatic Society of Bengal*, pp. 141-43.

—— (1899), 'Cave Drawing in the Camure Range North West Provinces', *JRAS:* 88-91.

Coomaraswamy, A.K. (1956), *Christian and Oriental Philosophy of Art*. New York: Dover Publications, Inc., p. 11.

—— (1977), 'Ornament', in Roger Lipsey (ed.), *Traditional Art and Symbolism*. Oxford University Press, pp. 93.

Kumar, G. (1981), 'Painted Rock Shelters from Rajasthan', in V.S. Srivastava (ed.), *Cultural Contours of India*. New Delhi: Abhinav Publications.

Kumar, Giriraj and Geeta Narvare (1984), 'Ostrich Egg Shells and Early Rock Painitng in India', in K.K. Chakravarty (ed.), *Rock Art of India*. New Delhi: Arnold-Heinemann, pp. 120-25.

Mathpal, Y. (1984), *Prehistoric Rock Paintings of Bhimbetka, Central India*. New Delhi: Abhinav Publications.

Misra, V.N. and Y. Mathpal (1979), 'Rock Art of Bhimbetka Region, Central India', *Man and Environment* 3: 27-33.

Neumayer, Erwin (1993), *Prehistoric Indian Rock Paintings*. Delhi: Manohar.

Rammurty, Krishna (1988), 'The Rock Paintings of Central India: An Approach through Myth', *Man and Environment* XII: 76.

Smith,V.A. (1906), 'Pygmy Flints', *The Indian Antiquary*—V(35): 185-95.

Tyagi, G.S. (1996), 'Conservation of Rock Art in India', in R.K. Sharma and K.K. Tripathi (eds.), *Recent Perspectives on Prehistoric Art in India and Allied Subjects*. New Delhi: Aryan Books International, pp. 105-18.

Varma, R.K. (1964), 'Stone Age Cultures of Mirzapur', D. Phil. thesis, Allahabad University.

—— (1981-83), 'The Mesolithic Culture of India', *Purattava:* 13-14.

—— (1984), 'The Rock Art of Southern Uttar Pradesh with Special Reference to Mirzapur', in K.K. Chakravarty (ed.), *Rock Art of India*. New Delhi: Arnold-Heinemann, pp. 206-13.

—— (1984), *The Mesolithic Age in Mirzapur*. Allahabad: Paramjyoti Prakashan.

—— (1994), 'The Rock Art of the Vindhyan Region', Paper presented in the 15th IPPA conference at Chiang Mai, Thailand.

—— (2002), 'Hunting Strategy of the Mesolithic Folk as Revealed by Rock Paintings', in V.D. Misra and J.N. Pal (eds.), *Mesolithic India*.

—— (2006) 'Keynote Address', to the Indo-French Joint Seminar on Prehistoric Cave Paintings, Bhopal.

—— (2012) *Rock Art of Central India, North Vindhyan Region*. New Delhi: Aryan Books International.

Wakankar, V.S. (1962), 'Painted Rock Shelters of India', *Rivista de Science Prehistoriche* 17(1-4): 237-53.

—— and R.R. Brooks (1976), *Stone Age Painting in India*. Bombay: D.B. Tarporewala & Sons.

—— (1973), 'Painted Rock Shelters of India', Ph.D. thesis, Poona University.

—— (1973) 'Bhimbetka Excavation', *Journal of Indian History:* 25-32.

—— (1975), 'Prehistoric Cave Paintings', *Marg* 28(4): 17-34.

—— (1984), 'Bhimbetka and Dating of Indian Rock-Paintings', in V.S. Wakankar and R.R.R. Brooks (eds.), *Stone Age Painting in India*. Bombay: D.B. Taraporevala & Sons.

—— (1984), 'Bhimbetka and Dating of Indian Rock-Paintings', in K.K. Chakravarty (ed.), *Rock Art of India*. New Delhi: Arnold-Heinemann: 44-56.

—— (1992), 'Rock Painting in India', in Michel Lorblanchet (ed.), *Rock Art in the Old World*. New Delhi: Indira Gandhi National Centre for the Arts, pp. 319-36.

19

Inventory of Indian Rock Art: A Multidisciplinary Approach

Bansi Lal Malla

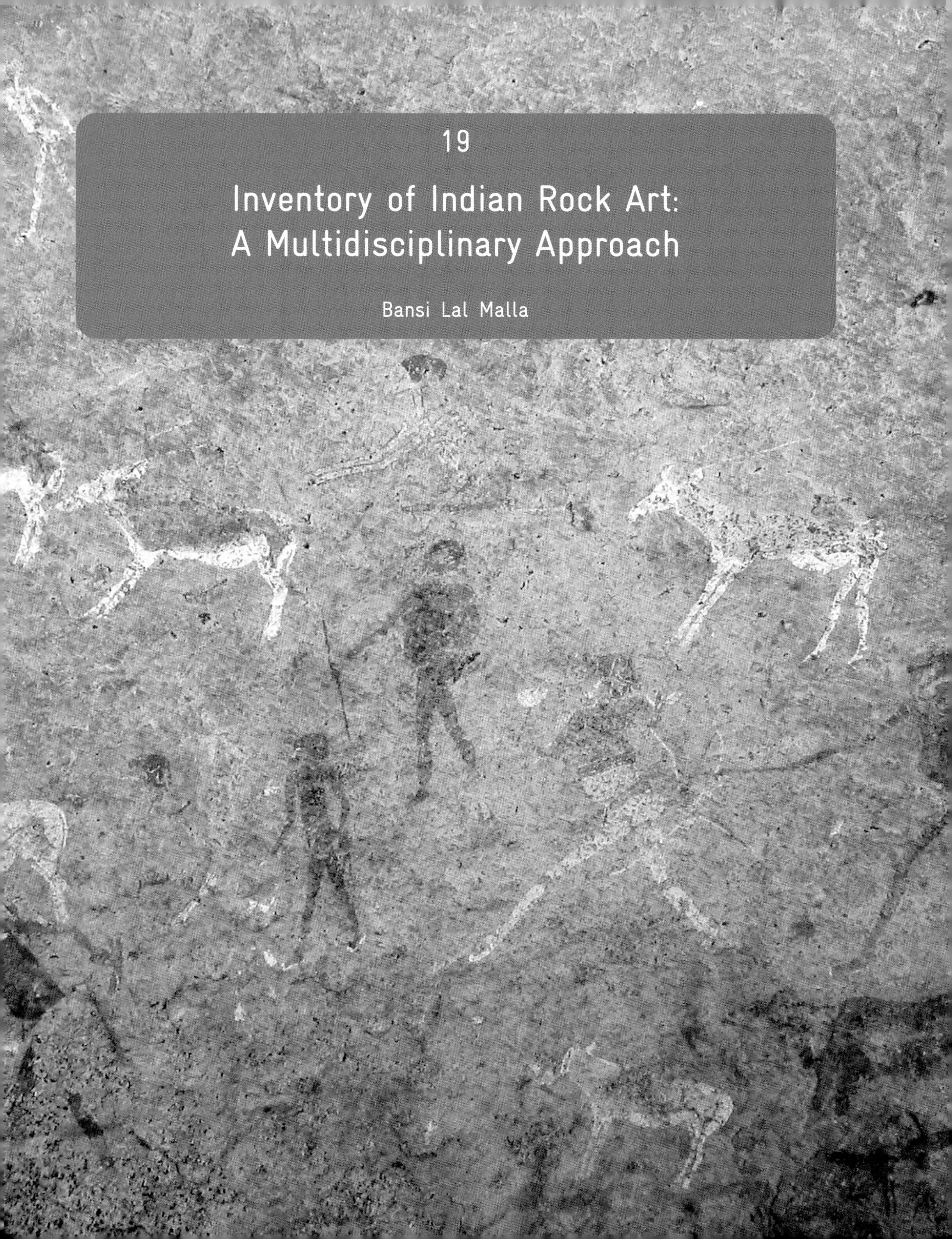

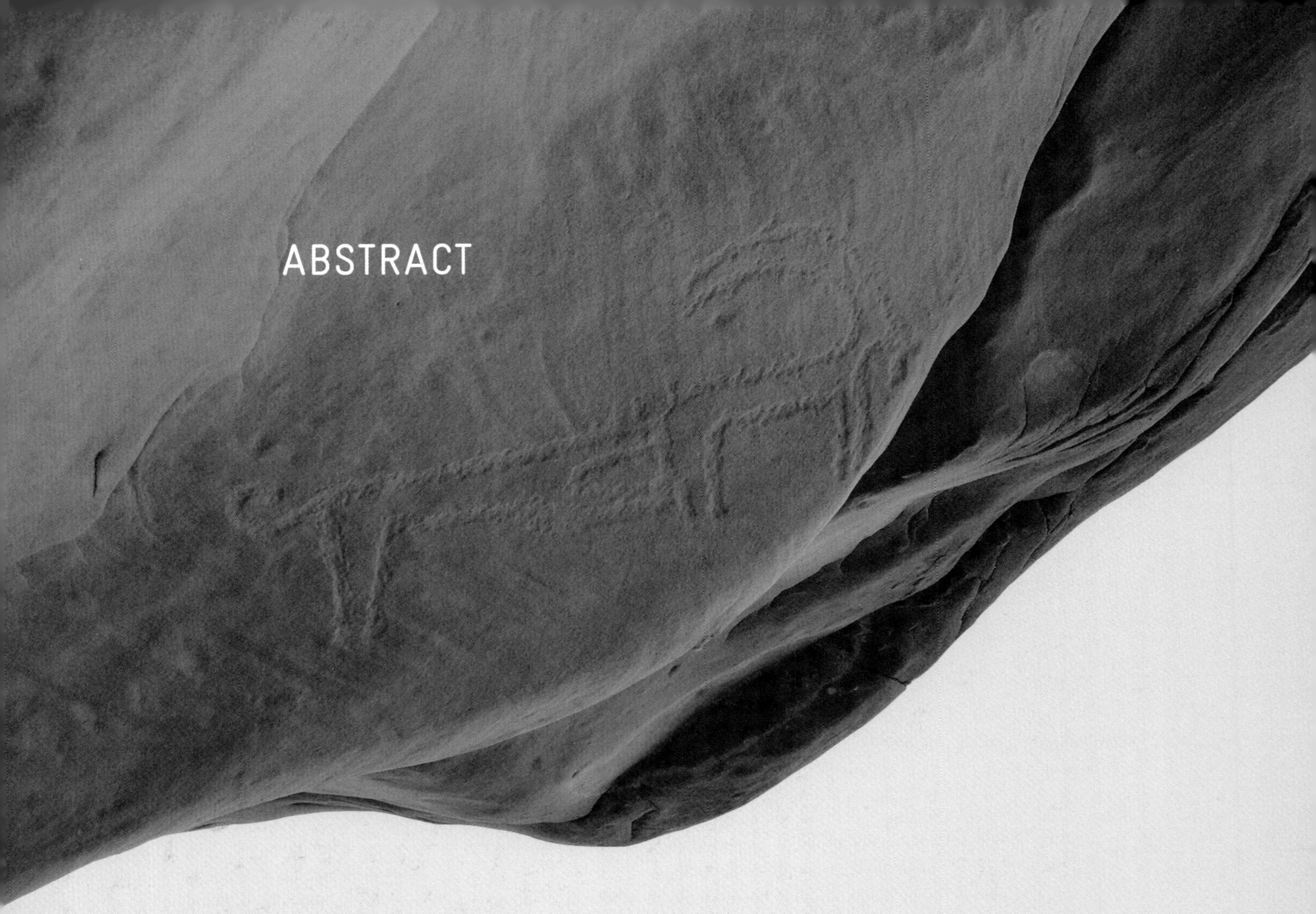

ABSTRACT

One of the major academic programmes of the Indira Gandhi National Centre for the Arts (IGNCA) relates to exploring artistic manifestations emanating from man's primary sense perceptions. Rock art forms a crucial component of the Adi Drishya programme. The Sanskrit term 'Adi Drishya' is an indicator of multiple levels of interpretations of the adi world (primeval world). Rock art is one of the richest cultural resources in the world, which depicts the earliest expressions of humankind. We should not ignore the fact that rock art sites are very vulnerable both to natural and human factors, as they are in open and attract attention. Human vandalism not only indicates lack of sensitivity and knowledge but also an alienation from the human family. Keeping in view these dangers to rock art, IGNCA has taken up a project for the survey, documentation and study of Indian rock art sites in a holistic perspective. The field documentation is being done with scientific means in collaboration with local experts and institutions in the areas/zones concerned. At the national level, the data is being collected in a uniform format developed by IGNCA. The documented rock and its allied subjects are then analysed according to their geographical and cultural settings.

BACKDROP

Rock art is one of the richest cultural resources in the world, which depicts the earliest expressions of humankind. This prehistoric art perhaps comes to signify the underlying philosophies and the worldview of the ancient people, and tells us about the soul of a community, its thoughts, beliefs and emotions. It is also associated with cultural values, particularly in countries like India and Australia, where this art is a part of the living cultural heritage of their native populations. Rock art images can be treated as a source for cultural communication with the past, present and the future. Fortunately, India has one of the world's six major prehistoric rock art concentrations of the Stone Age era. Other places in the world which have prehistoric rock art concentrations are—South-Western Europe, Russia, North Africa, South Africa and Australia.

The term 'rock art' is generally used for all types of artistic activities found on rocks and is classified into two main forms: pictographs and petroglyphs. Pictographs refer to painted figures and are also termed rock paintings. Petroglyphs include engravings, carvings, brushings, dotting and cup-markings. Pictographs are found on rock shelters, while petroglyphs are usually confined to open rocks and boulders.

One of the major academic programmes of the Indira Gandhi National Centre for the Arts (IGNCA) relates to exploring artistic manifestations emanating from man's primary sense perceptions. The classification of art in Indian tradition is based on different aesthetic senses—vision (*drishya*) and hearing (*shravya*). Architecture, sculpture and paintings originate from vision; music and poetry originate from hearing; and theatre from the two together. Hence, Indian aesthetics is a well-experimented psychoanalytical process of judgement. Man's first awareness of the world around him came through his primeval sense of sight and his ability to hear.

Rock art forms a crucial component of the *Adi Drishya* programme under which IGNCA records all rock art motifs by all possible means of documentation. These motifs are then analysed according to their geographical and cultural settings. It will not be an exaggeration to say that IGNCA is the only institution in the country where rock art is being studied as the earliest visual manifestation of mankind, a study which is necessary to understand human society holistically.

IGNCA's fundamental approach to all its works is multidisciplinary, multidimensional, multidirectional, multilayered and multi-meaning within the systematic cultural whole. Its conceptual plan aims to open the doors to the realisation that rock art is pure and absolute and hence capable of dispensing experiences beyond its original culture and time. IGNCA's concern with prehistoric rock art is not restricted to archaeologists' and prehistorians' concerns with establishing a linear chronological order of prehistoric rock art, nor is it restricted to the identification of styles and schools as criteria for establishing chronology. Instead, it is a concern for man's creativity across time, space, civilisations and cultures through the perception of sight.

The Sanskrit term *Adi Drishya* is an indicator of the multiple levels of interpretations of the *adi* (primeval) world. IGNCA has envisaged *Adi Drishya* display (s) which will create a degree of experiential contact with prehistoric art that is otherwise restricted to rock art shelters/caves. It will provide the basis for entering into the changing aspects of man's living art. It is believed that man's awareness of the world around him came through his primeval senses of sight and sound. These two stimulated artists' expressions, visual and aural, in the prehistoric past as also in contemporary cultures. Exploring, through the faculty of sight, we can construct the kind of worldviews that have nearly ceased to exist, and try to infer from them an articulation of the lifestyles that continue to the present in radically altered ways. Besides, emphasis is also given to creating both a perception of time as well as the unchanging material and non-material needs in the physical and environmental settings common to all humankind without linking the past and the present in an evolutionary framework.

While considering the diversity of form and manifold concepts of time, there is no good reason to restrict the understanding of rock art in terms of linear time, making it outfixed points of time in history. On the conceptual side, the display (s) that IGNCA proposes will attempt to bring out the universals among world cultures that existed in prehistoric times. It is intended that by placing cross-cultural products side by side, it can be demonstrated that they are universal in this system of visualisation holding great relevance today. In fact, the endeavour will be to create a greater appreciation of the global past among Indians. With a view to preparing for eventual display (s) of rock art, a lot of research and the gradual building up of permanent collections are very necessary.

CONSERVATION HAZARDS

We should not ignore the fact that rock art sites are very vulnerable to natural and human factors, as they are in open and attract attention. Ecological disturbances and problems of bio- deterioration are creating havoc in the preservation of rock art. With increasing population and relatively improved access to formerly remote areas, threats to these sites have increased immensely. Human vandalism not only indicates a lack of sensitivity and knowledge about rock art and its importance, but also an alienation from the human family. Increasing pressure from tourism as well as fundamental problems of weathering and of the impact of vegetation and stock, indicate that there is an urgent need for conservation and management of Indian rock art sites.

Here arises a question: Who will be entrusted with the direct protection and management of these rock art sites? This needs to be worked out urgently. Ideally, it should be—and it is—the responsibility of the central/state governments, but the involvement of local people should not be ignored. Government agencies still do not know the extent and locations of all rock art sites in the country and, therefore, are also not aware of the problems that confront each one of them. So far the prehistoric era has not been a priority area for art conservation in the country. Since most of the rock art sites are located in forestlands, the Ministry of Environment and Forests could play a vital role not only in conserving this precious art form, but also in facilitating the study of the hinterland where forest-based communities may yield useful clues for deciphering rock art. An attempt is being made to explore, document and conserve the intangible aspect of rock art among these communities. An appreciation of prehistoric rock art in India will improve greatly when these sites are made widely known, can be seen by the people and are protected for posterity as national treasures.

AIMS OF THE ROCK ART PROJECT

- Documenting rock art sites, their environment and communities living around the sites.
- Discussing extant theories of rock art and the intrinsic value of palaeo-art as a cultural heritage and not merely as the cultural property of a particular nation where it is found.
- Examining concrete cases for the conservation, preservation and management of rock art sites.
- Identifying common conservation hazards and practices.
- Evolving strategies for managing, conserving and computerised documentation of rock art sites.
- Suggesting national policies for management of rock art sites.
- Enriching children, common people and serious scholars.

AGENDA OF THE ROCK ART PROJECT

- To make inventory of rock art sites;
- To make contextual video and photo documentation;
- To communicate with people in the hinterland for archaeological research, and to build up a biocultural map, a mental and ecological atlas of the rock art landscape, on the basis of documentation of related folklore and natural and manmade features;
- To make documentaries on the basis of the video documentations in the field;
- To develop a digital archive of videos, photo and other electronic data;
- To make suggestions for structural, ecological, and, in rare cases, direct conservation, preferably using local materials and techniques;
- To prepare a Conservation Manual for rock art sites;
- To bring out publications, both in print and electronic media;
- To organise exhibitions (permanent, mobile, temporary).

MAIN COMPONENTS OF THE ROCK ART PROJECT

- National Rock Art Project: Documentation and study of rock art sites in India.
- International collaborative projects: to study/research, training of scholars and publications of international volumes and books.
- Organisation of conferences, seminars, lectures to promote and share researches of rock art at national and international level.
- Acquisition of objects and data related to rock art of India and establishment of archives (reprographic, photographic materials and tools, etc.)
- Cataloguing.
- Outreach/public awareness programmes.

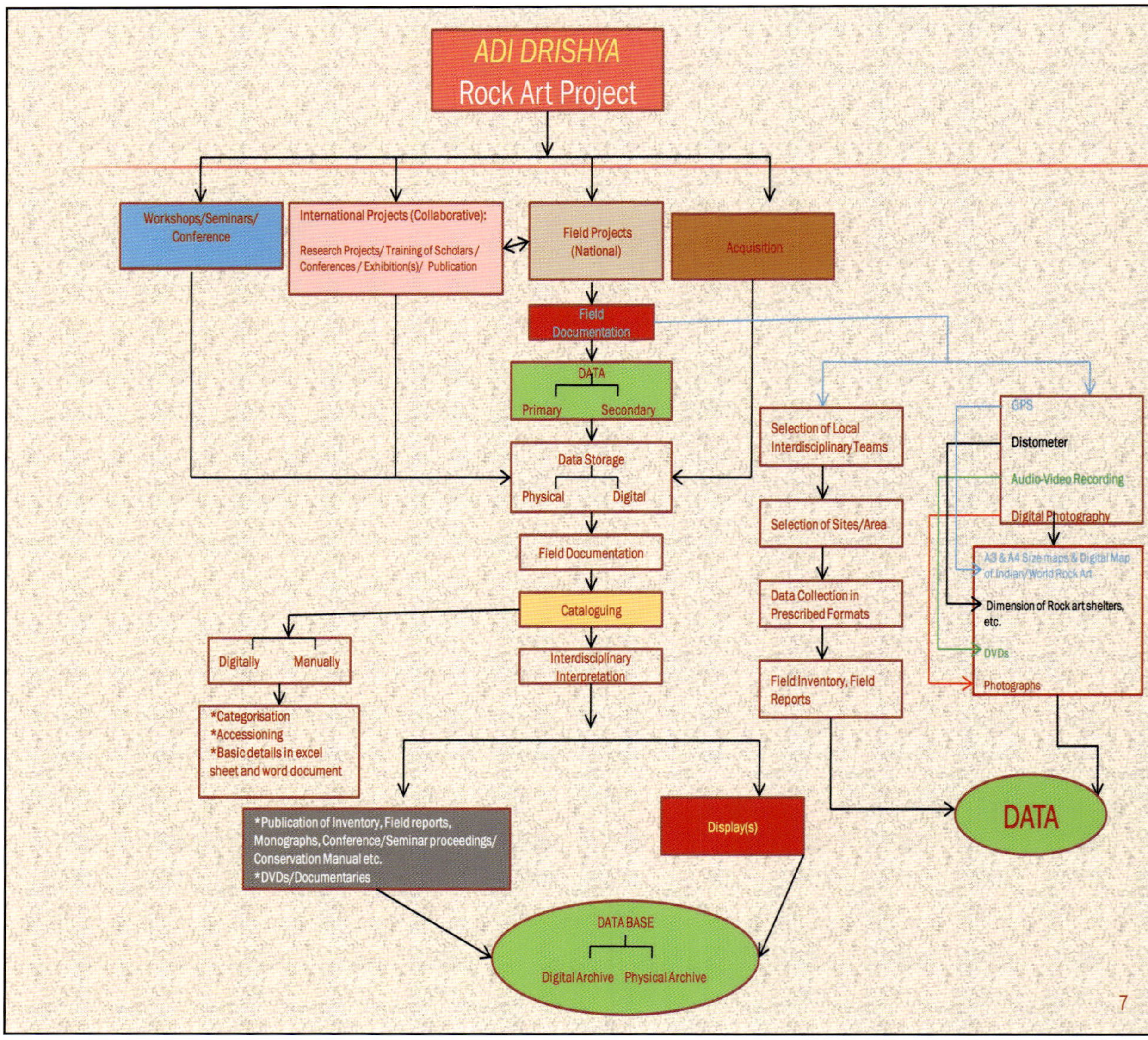

Fig. 19.1 *Adi Drishya* Rock Art Project.

LONG-TERM OBJECTIVES

- To create a comprehensive multimedia databank and establish a Resource Centre on the rock art of India and the world.
- To spread awareness about rock art sites and to ensure protection and preservation of this important cultural heritage. Also, to act (become) as a pressure group for rock art protection to ensure a separate law or amendment in existing laws for protection of rock art sites.
- Continuous exchange of rock art studies and researches with national and international organizations through collaborative projects.
- Publications would be an outcome of these projects and researches in form of proceedings of conferences and seminars, detailed field reports, inventories, conservation manuals, monographs, DVDs, documentaries, etc.

SHORT-TERM OBJECTIVES

- Identification of rock art sites under various threats and to ensure their protection and conservation.
- To document the endangered rock art sites of India on priority basis under the national project.
- Evolving site management strategies and conservation strategies to the site specific.
- To finalise work plans and intents for international collaborations.
- Documentation of living traditions of the communities living in proximity of these rock art sites.
- Organising exhibitions and work shops on rock art for dissemination and awareness.
- Training of young researchers.
- To bring out methodological and basic text on rock art.

Keeping in view these aims and objectives, IGNCA has taken up this ambitious project on rock art survey and documentation, and also an ethno-archaeological study of rock art. This rock art project was initiated in 1989-90. Major fieldwork/projects undertaken before 2005 were: a project on the rock art of Kumaon Hills in northern India, Kerala in south India and Jhiri in Central India. Multidisciplinary field- based studies and documentation started on a large scale in 2005-06. Field documentation is being done in collaboration with local experts and institutions in the areas/zones concerned. Data is being collected at the national level in a uniform format developed by IGNCA. A huge database has been compiled in this process. Thousands of images have already been digitised. Under the rock art publication series, nine volumes have been published so far. Four CD/DVDs have also been brought out. An international conference (1993) and three national seminars (1991, 1996 and 2004) have been conducted on the subject. An exhibition on 'Deer in Rock Art of India and Europe' was held in 1993. So far, documentation work has been initiated in the following regions/states:

In north India, documentation was initiated in the states of Uttarakhand and Jammu and Kashmir. In Central India, the work was initiated in Madhya Pradesh, Chhattisgarh and Jharkhand. In eastern India, work has been completed in Odisha. In western India, work was initiated in Rajasthan and in southern India, work was initiated in Andhra Pradesh, Karnataka and Tamil Nadu.

In Uttarakhand, documentation work was conducted in Almora and Nainital districts. Fifteen rock art sites and three villages were documented. In Jammu and Kashmir, documentation work was done in the two districts of Leh and Kargil in the Ladakh region. Thirty-three rock art sites and a village were documented. In Madhya Pradesh, documentation work was completed in the three districts of Bhopal, Raisen and Sehore. Eight rock art sites and three villages were documented. In Chhattisgarh, documentation work was done in Raigarh district. Ten rock art sites and three villages were documented. In Jharkhand, documentation work was done in Hazaribagh and Chatra districts. Eight rock art sites and two villages were documented. In Odisha, documentation work has been completed in the four districts of Bargarh, Jharsuguda, Sundargarh and Sambalpur.

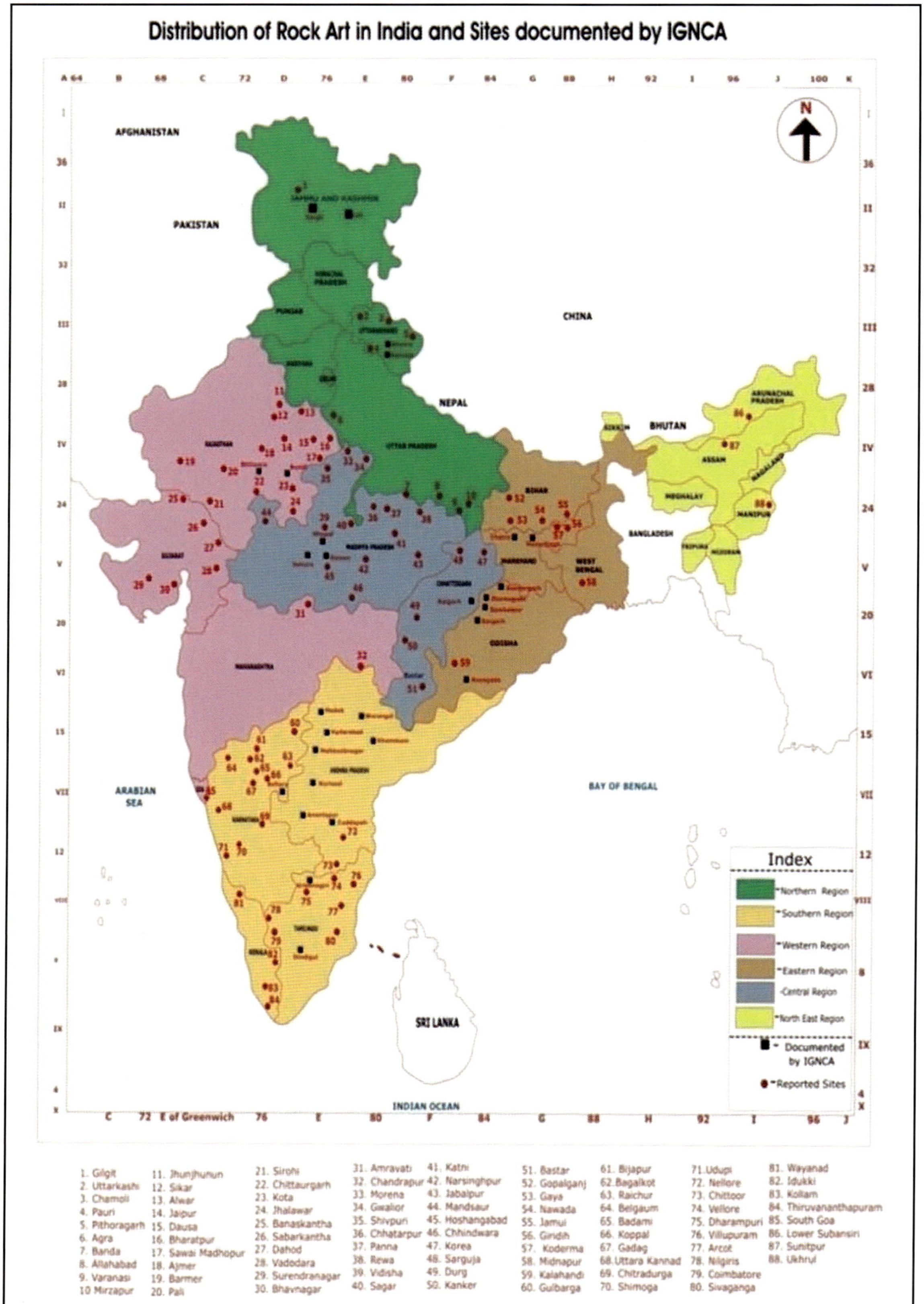

Map 19.1 Distribution of rock art sites in India and sites documented by IGNCA.

Seven rock art sites and five villages were documented in these four districts. In the Raigada district of Odisha, 15 villages were also documented for the study of tribal art. In Karnataka, documentation work has been completed in Bellary district. Thirteen rock art sites and five villages were documented. In Rajasthan, documentation work was completed in the Bundi district. Thirteen rock art sites and three villages were documented. In Andhra Pradesh, documentation work was initiated in the districts of Hyderabad, Medak, Mahaboobnagar, Warangal and Khammam. Seven rock art sites and four villages were documented. Documentation work in Tamil Nadu was conducted in Krishnagiri and Dharampuri districts. Thirteen rock art sites and five villages were documented. Since the documentation and research of rock art is an ongoing programme at IGNCA, we may take up documentation work in the remaining sites/states from next year. In India, about 1,100 rock art sites are known/reported so far (Table 19.1).

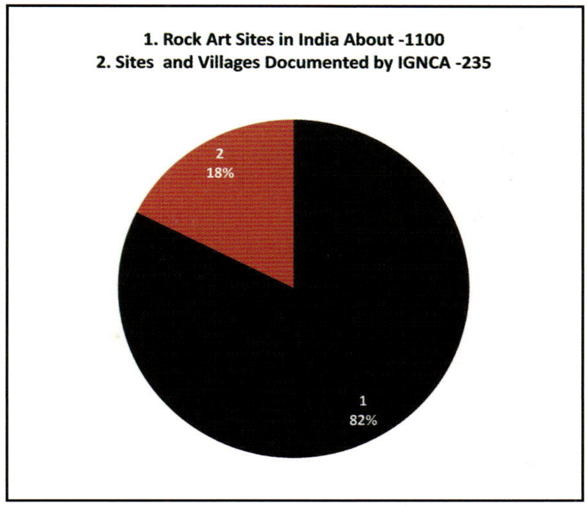

Fig. 19.2 Rock art sites documented by IGNCA.

Table 19.1 Concentration of Indian Rock Art (district/areawise).

North/ North-East	South	East	West	Central
JAMMU & KASHMIR: Leh, Zanshakar, Kargil, Gilgit (area), Burzahama, Bomai (52 sites) UTTARAKHAND Almora and Srinagar (42 sites) UTTAR PRADESH Agra, Allahabad, Almora, Banda, Chamoli, Mirzapur, Uttarakashi and	ANDHRA PRADESH Anantapupr, Chittoor, Cuddapah, Karimnagar, Kurnool, Mahboobnagar, Nellore, Ranga Reddy, Medak, Hyderabad, Warangal, Khammam (32 sites) KARNATAKA Bangalore, Bellary, Bijapur, Gulbarga,	BIHAR Nawada, Jamui and Giridih (86 sites) JHARKHAND Hazaribag, Chattra, Singhbhum (41 sites) WEST BENGAL Midnapur ODISHA Keonjhar, Sambalpur,	GUJARAT Bhavnagar, Sabarkantha (4 sites) RAJASTHAN Bhilwara, Chittorgarh, Jaipur, Kota, Bundi, Jhalawar, Sikar, Sirohi (52 sites)	CHHATTISGARH Bastar, Raigarh, Rajgarh, and Kanker (42 sites) MADHYA PRADESH Bhopal, Chhatarpur, Chhindwara, Damoh, Datia, Durga, Gwalior, Hoshangabad, Jabalpur, Mandsaur, Morena, Narsinghpur, Nimar, Panna,

North/ North-East	South	East	West	Central
Varanasi (155 sites) ASSAM Sonitpur (3 sites) MANIPUR Ukhrul ARUNACHAL PRADESH Lower Subansiri (Parsi Parlo)	Raichur, Sorapur (55 sites) KERALA Idukki, Kollam, Trivandrum, Wyand (10 sites) TAMIL NADU Dharmapuri, Dindigal, Krishnagiri, Madurai, Nilgiri, South Arcot (42 sites)	Sundargar, Bargarh, Jharsugud, Kalahandi, Mayurbhan, Nupara and Suvarnapur (106 sites)		Raisen, Rajgarh, Rewa, Sagar, **Sehore**, Shivpuri and Vidisha (310 sites) Note: Sites in

Briefly, the goal is not merely to develope a huge database or multimedia displays but also to establish *Adi Drishya* as a school of thought and research on alternate means of understanding prehistoric art. At the moment, there is not much available in India by way of an interpretive treatment of prehistoric art. For achieving all these goals, inventrisation and interpretive research of rock art is going hand in hand.

II

(A) IGNCA Inventory Format for Rock Art Site Documentation

Site: Mander (Jharkhand)
Present name: Mander (Satpahar).
Village: Mander (Shiruha Mander).
Block: Tandwa.
District: Chatra.
State: Jharkhand.

Physical setting: The site is located on the top of the easternmost end of the Satpahar range and the western-north Karanpura Valley in Chatra district of Jharkhand. The nearest villages are Mander and Khander.

Approach: Mander is located 58 km south of Hazaribagh town and 33 km from Badka gaon (on the road to Hazaribagh via Badka gaon).

Geo-coordinates: The site is located at a height of 575 m MSL on 23° 47' 11.8" North and 84° 59' 45.2" East.

Geo-cultural set-up:

a) Shelter: With painting.
b) Materials: Sandstone.

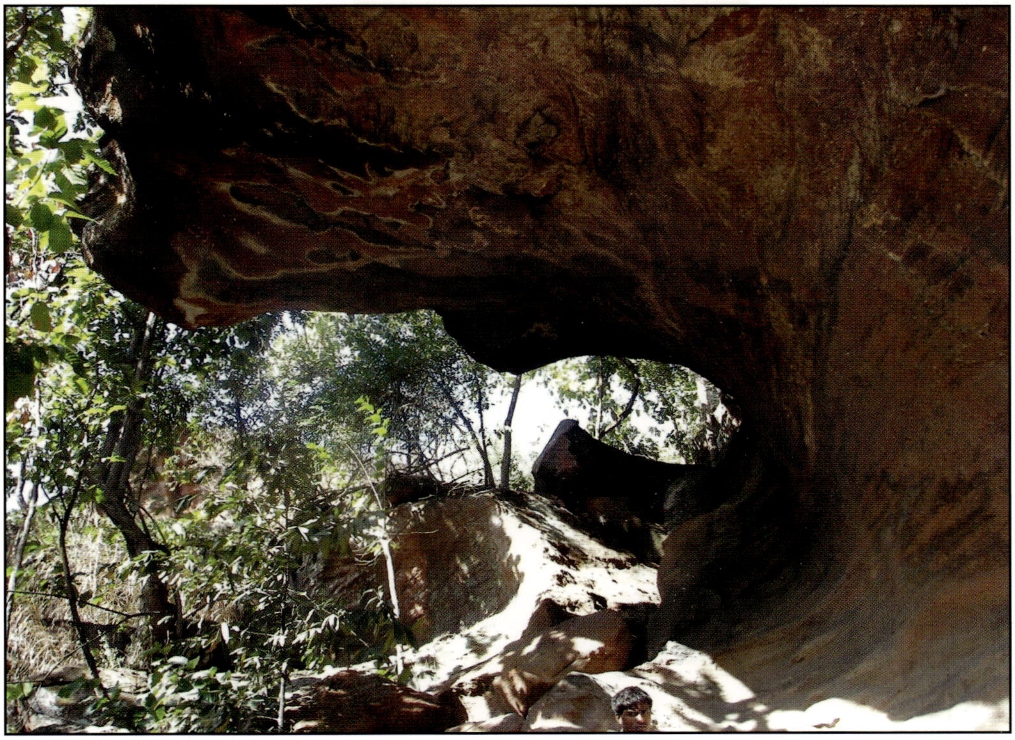

Fig. 19.3 General view of rock shelter.

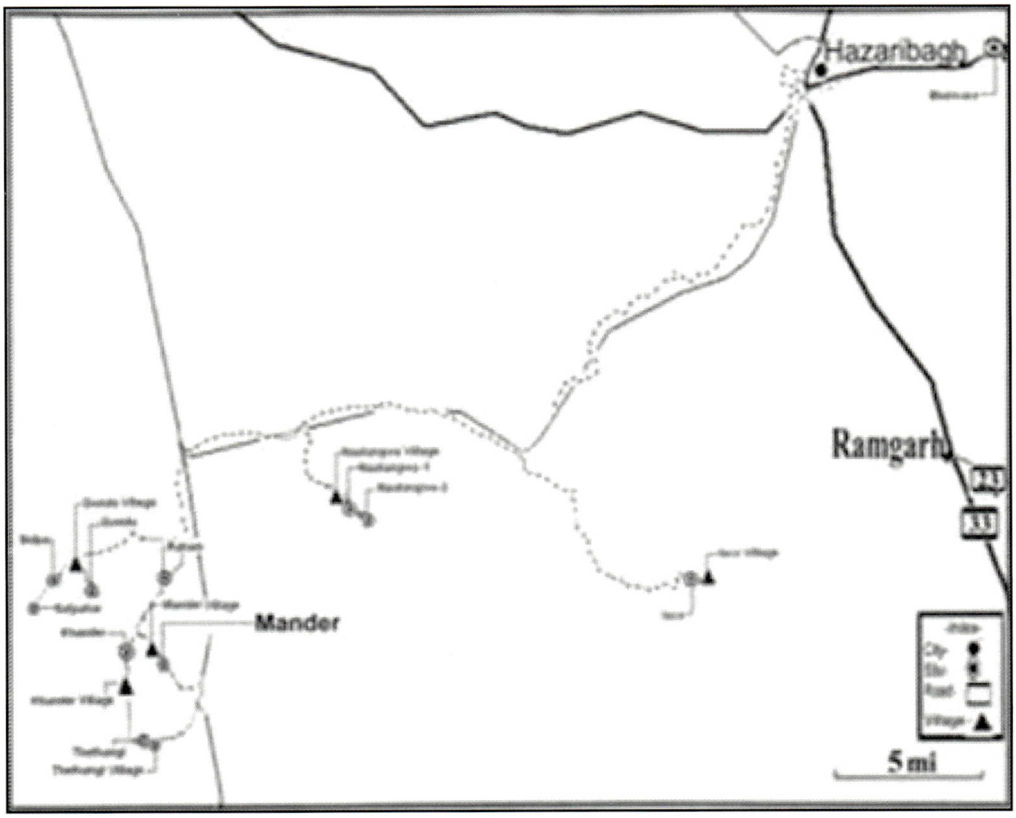

Fig. 19.4 Geo-coordinates of the site.

c) Ownership: State Department of Forests.

d) Use description:

Past: A habitational site?

Present: Not in use.

Type of rock art:

a) Pictograph and Petroglyph (cup-marks).

Colour: Painting in red ochre and white colour.

b) Superimposition: Some figures are superimposed.

Rock art motif:

a) Anthropomorphic.

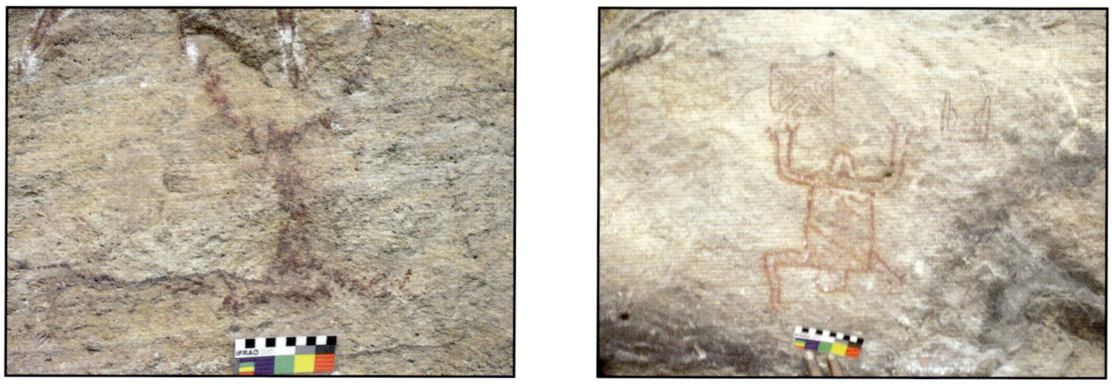

Fig. 19.5 (a-b) Depiction of anthropomorphic figures.

b) Zoomorphic.

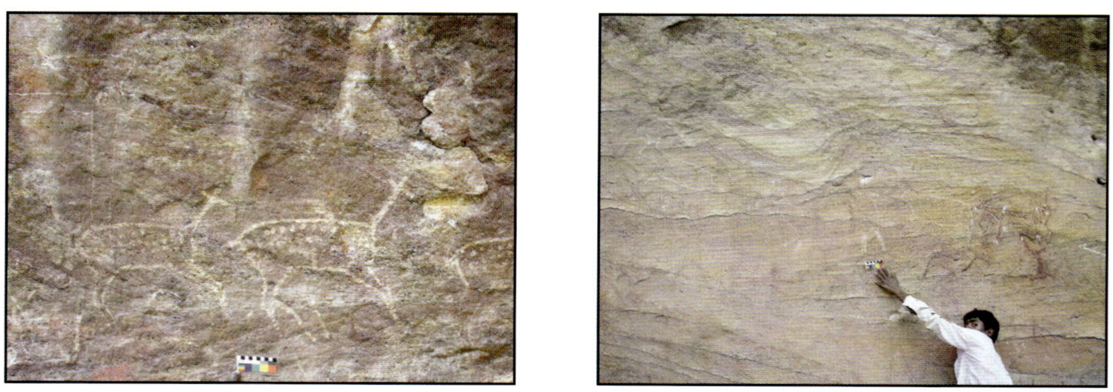

Fig. 19.6 (a-b) Depiction of animal figures.

c) Geometric.

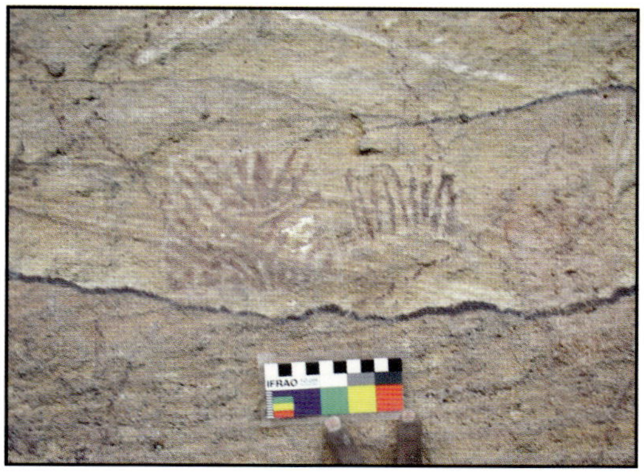

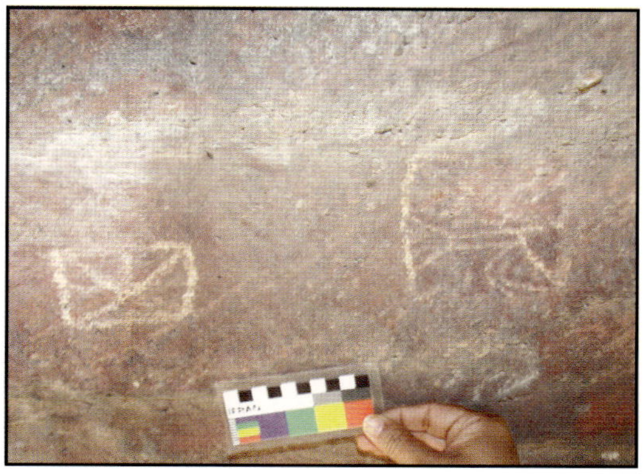

Fig. 19.7 (a-b) Depiction of geometric patterns.

d) Others

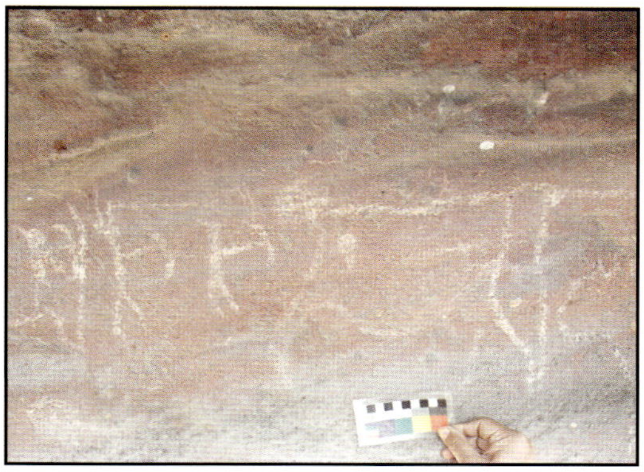

Fig. 19.8 Depiction of hunting.

There are four painted rock shelters in the Mander site in Chatra district:

Shelter 1: Geometric patterns, rectangular motifs, running animal figures and trees are the central subjects of this shelter.

Shelter II: It is the biggest shelter at this site. It has a number of animal figures like deer, bison, wild boar, tiger, tigress, cow and monkey. The scene of a monkey and tiger hunting a boar are the most attractive figures at this shelter. Besides this, there are also various geometric patterns; some grinding holes are also seen on the platform of the rock shelter.

Shelter III: The shelter has painted figures of spotted deer, wild boar, palm impression, etc.

Shelter IV: Presently, a majority of the paintings at this shelter have been washed away due to water seepage.

Age description: Prehistoric and Historical.

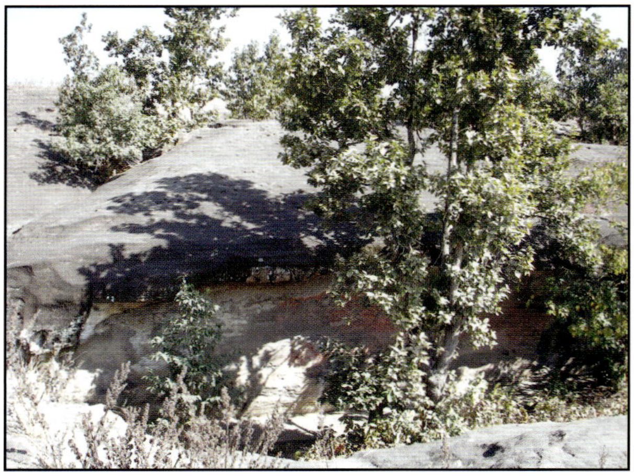

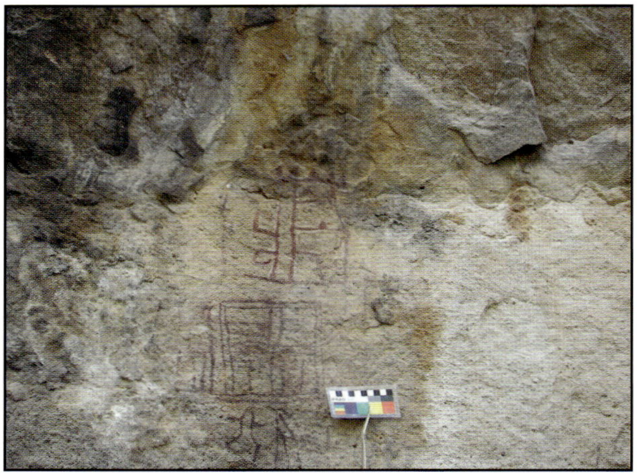

Left: **Fig. 19.9** General view of site.

Right: **Fig. 19.10** Showing signs of deterioration.

Area quantification:

a) Area/Site/Block L x B.
The length of Shelter I is 14.20 m.
The height of Shelter I at the highest point is 7.10 m.
The length of the painted panel at Shelter I is 5.80 m.
The depth of the painted panel at Shelter l is 1.75 m.
The length of Shelter II is 17.20 m.
The height of Shelter II at the highest point is 11.70 m.
The length of the painted panel at Shelter II is 6.30 m.
The depth of the painted panel at shelter II is 1.10 m.
The length of Shelter III is 9.80 m.
The height of Shelter III at the highest point is approximately 20 ft.
The length of the painted panel at Shelter III is 3.80 m.
The depth of the painted panel at Shelter III is 15 ft.
The length of Shelter IV is 10.80 m.
The height of Shelter IV at the highest point is 15 ft.
The length of the painted panel at Shelter IV is 1.80 m.
The depth of the painted panel at Shelter IV is 70 cm.

b) Orientation: Shelter I has north-south orientation and north-west face opening. Shelter II has two blocks; one has a west face and the other has a south face opening. The shelter has east-west orientation. Shelter III has an east-west orientation with south face opening. Shelter IV has north-south orientation with south-west face opening.

c) No. of blocks: Shelter II has two blocks.

Geology: The rock shelters of Mander belong to the Damuda series of the lower Gondwana group. The rock is sandstone in light red, red, white and yellow colours and the lithology of the stone contains red sandstone, iron stone shale, limestone, clay material and pebbles of different colours.

Status of conservation: Showing signs of deterioration (SSD).

Perceived threats: Both natural and human.

A) Natural: Exposure to direct sunlight, water seepage from the top of the rock and microbiological growth (algae and lichens) are the main threats.

B) Human: Increased mining activities for extracting minerals like coal and iron ore by the government department, deforestation and influx of local people are serious threats to this art.

General description, inter-aiia:

Flora and fauna: The forest has trees like *Sal, Sakhbi, Muhul, Karada, Harda, Ainal, Bahada* and *Domkurdu* and fauna like bear, leopard (*tendua*), boar, wild fox and leaf monkey (*langur*).

(B) Inventory of Ethno-Archaeological Study, Bhelwara Village (Jharkhand)

(I) Village Location and Extent

- Village Name: Bhelwara.
- Other Name:
- Physical Setting:
  - Geography, Geology and Environment:
  - Village Type: Revenue village.

House types: Mud houses, bamboo-thatched and tile roofs with mud flooring and mud walls. There is a courtyard in the middle of the house. Various vegetables are grown in kitchen gardens. The houses mainly have one door for entry and exit, usually in the front of the house. Now, brick and RCC structures are replacing these traditional houses in this village.

Social set-up: Basically, a tribal village dominated by the Kurmis. Male dominated society. The people of this village perform marriages in their own community and all the activities of the marriage are arranged locally. They have their own priest and own barber to carry out all the activities during the function.

Economic system/status: The people of the village cultivate paddy and some vegetables; they are mainly dependent on agricultural products and on the coal mine. Most of the people are engaged in

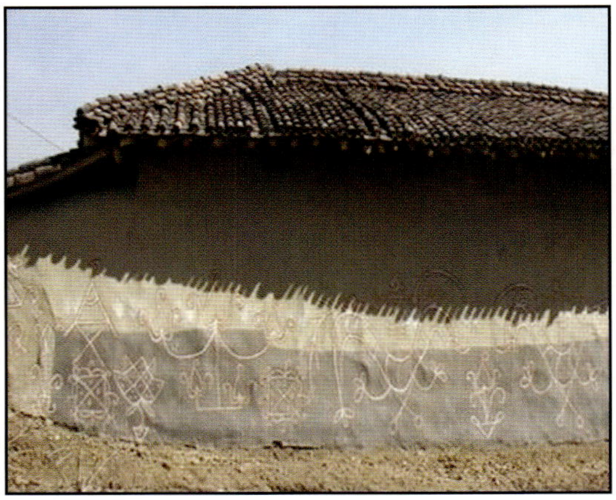

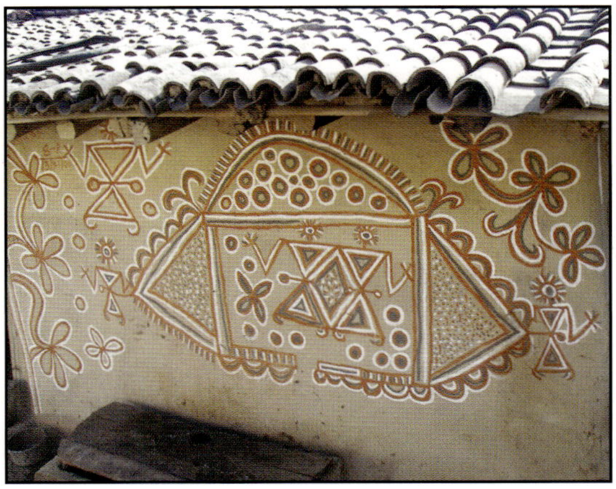

Fig. 19.11 (a-b) Traditional paintings on the walls of the village houses.

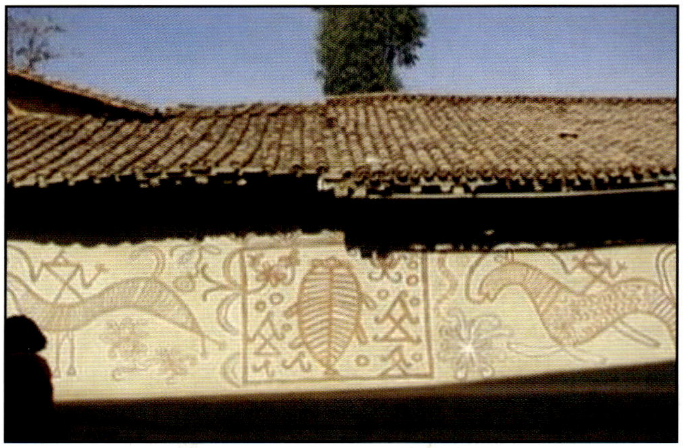

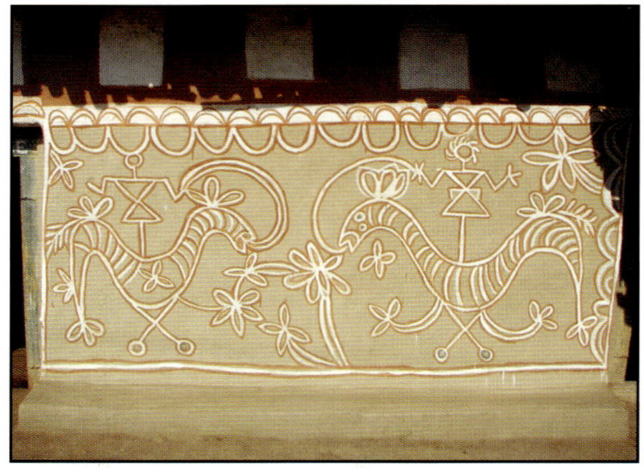

Left & Right: **Fig. 19.12** (a-b) Depiction of different motifs on the walls of the village houses.

daily labour. The village has one middle school. There is no medical facility like hospital or dispensary. A handpump and wells are the main source of water for drinking and other day-to-day activities.

Belief system: Shrines, deities and festivals—Hindu gods and goddesses.

Modes of transmission of knowledge: Both oral and written.

Approach: The village is located in the Hazaribagh district of Jharkhand and is about 37 km north of Hazaribagh town. It is located on NH 100 from Hazaribagh to Kolkata.

- District: Hazaribagh.
- State: Jharkhand.

(II) Forms of village creativity

- Paintings: The villagers make excellent paintings on their walls. Usually, the paintings are of trees, flowers, creepers, wildlife, birds, decorative horses, horses eating flowers, horse-riders, human figures, snakes, peacocks, fish, creepers, animals and various decorative motifs. Comb paintings are exclusive to the village and are drawn on the interior and exterior parts of the house.
- Embossing
- Carving
- Performing arts
- Any other form: *(including pottery, basketry, weaving, carpentry, smithy, etc.—tradition and innovation):* Village women make tattoos on their hands and legs.

(III) Classification of village art

- Theme
  — *Cosmic/human/symbolic*
- Artist/painter
  — *Social group, gender, specialists.*
- Associated myths and rituals:

They paint the walls during Dipawali for their betterment and prosperity.

- Associated dreams/trances.

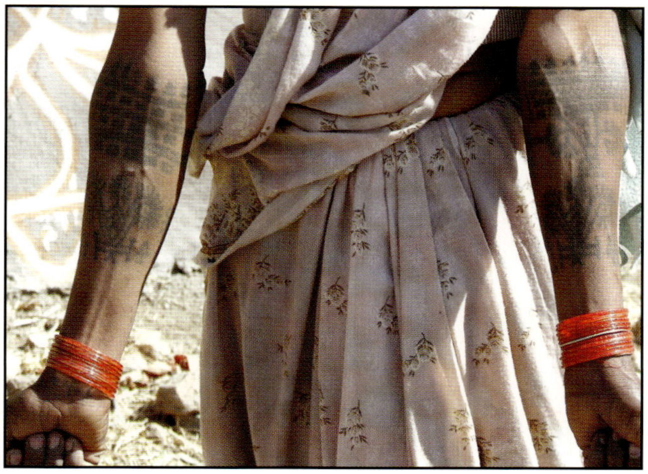

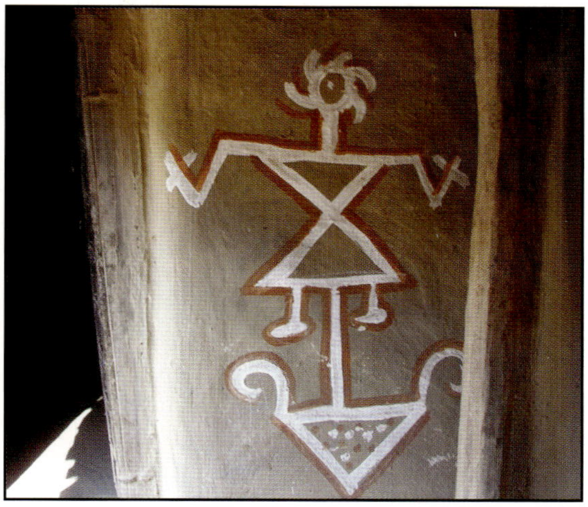

Left: **Fig. 19.13** Tattoos on the hands of a woman.

Right: **Fig. 19.14** Symbols of village art.

- Materials: Rice dust and natural mud and other natural colours.
- Colours: Pigment composition in case of paintings.
- Location: Mainly on the interior and exterior parts of the wall.

(IV) Geo-cultural set- up of the village:

- Name of rock art site nearby: Isco/Kohabar/Ambakargha.
- Site history: Ritual purpose/habitat (?)
- Use description:
  Past: Ritualistic (?)
  Present: Tourist attraction.
- Archaeological deposition in and around the site: The site has not been excavated as yet.
- Forms of rock art:
  — *Pictographs:* Painting.
  — *Petroglyphs:* Cup-marks (?)
- Superimposition: Many of the paintings are superimposed.
- Materials used: Haematite and kaolin.
- Age description: Prehistoric to historical.
- Preservation status: Showing signs of deterioration.
- Perceived threats: Both natural and man-made.

A) Natural: Exposed to direct sunlight, flaked off, cracked, blasting by winds, accretion of dust, dirt and soot, water seepage, flowing water, leaching by rainwater, growth of large plants and shrubs, microbiological growth (algae, fungi and lichens), mineral deposition and salt formation on the painted surface, mineral deposits and mineral accretion.

B) Man-made: Deforestation, influx of local people. Mining and blasting of stones and extractions of minerals (coal and iron ore) are the major threats to this site. Human vandalism in the form of improper development, creating a 35 cm deep concrete flooring on the floor of the rock shelter and building an RCC structure in front of the rock shelter as a rest house by the Department of Tourism. The Rautpara opencast project (opencast coal mine) will also be a big threat to this site.

- Ownership details:
  Under the State Department of Forest.

(V) Tracing similarities/variations in form and content of both rock and village art.

REFERENCES

Malla, B.L. (ed.) (1999), *Conservation of Rock Art*. New Delhi: IGNCA and Aryan Books International.

Malla, B.L. (2004), 'Rock Art and Ethnography—An Ethnographical Approach for Studying Rock Art in Indian Context', *Pre-proceedings of the XXI International Valcamonica Symposium*. Italy: CCSP and CAR.

Malla, B.L. (2012), 'New Approaches to Rock Art Research', in N. Chandramouli (ed.), *Twilight of the Past: Probing Indian History and Archaeology*. New Delhi: Aryan Books International.

(PS: I would like to acknowledge the help of Shri Ranbeer Singh, SRF, IGNCA Rock Art Project, for preparing the maps for this paper).

20

Conservation of Rock Art Sites: Problems and Issues

R.C. Agrawal

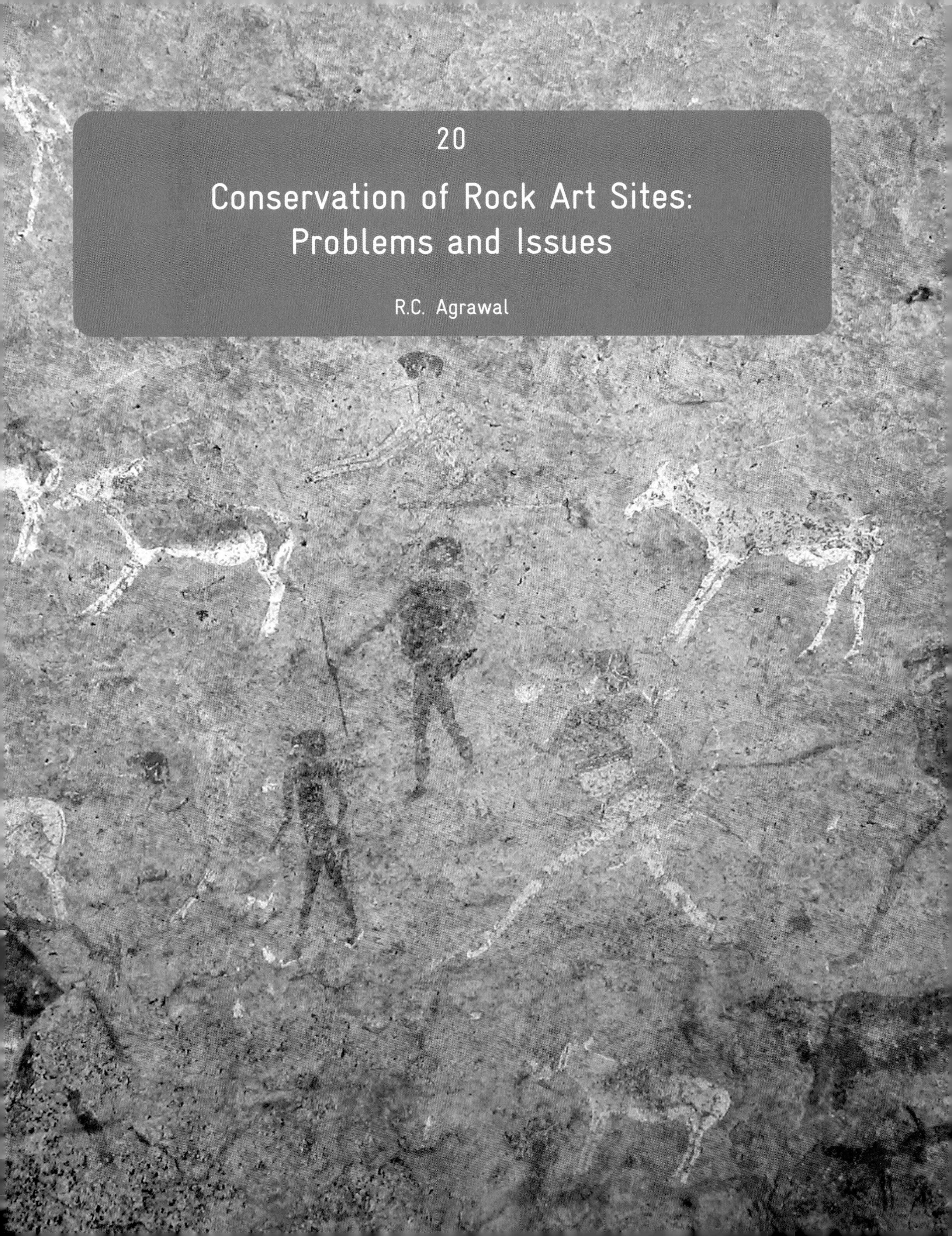

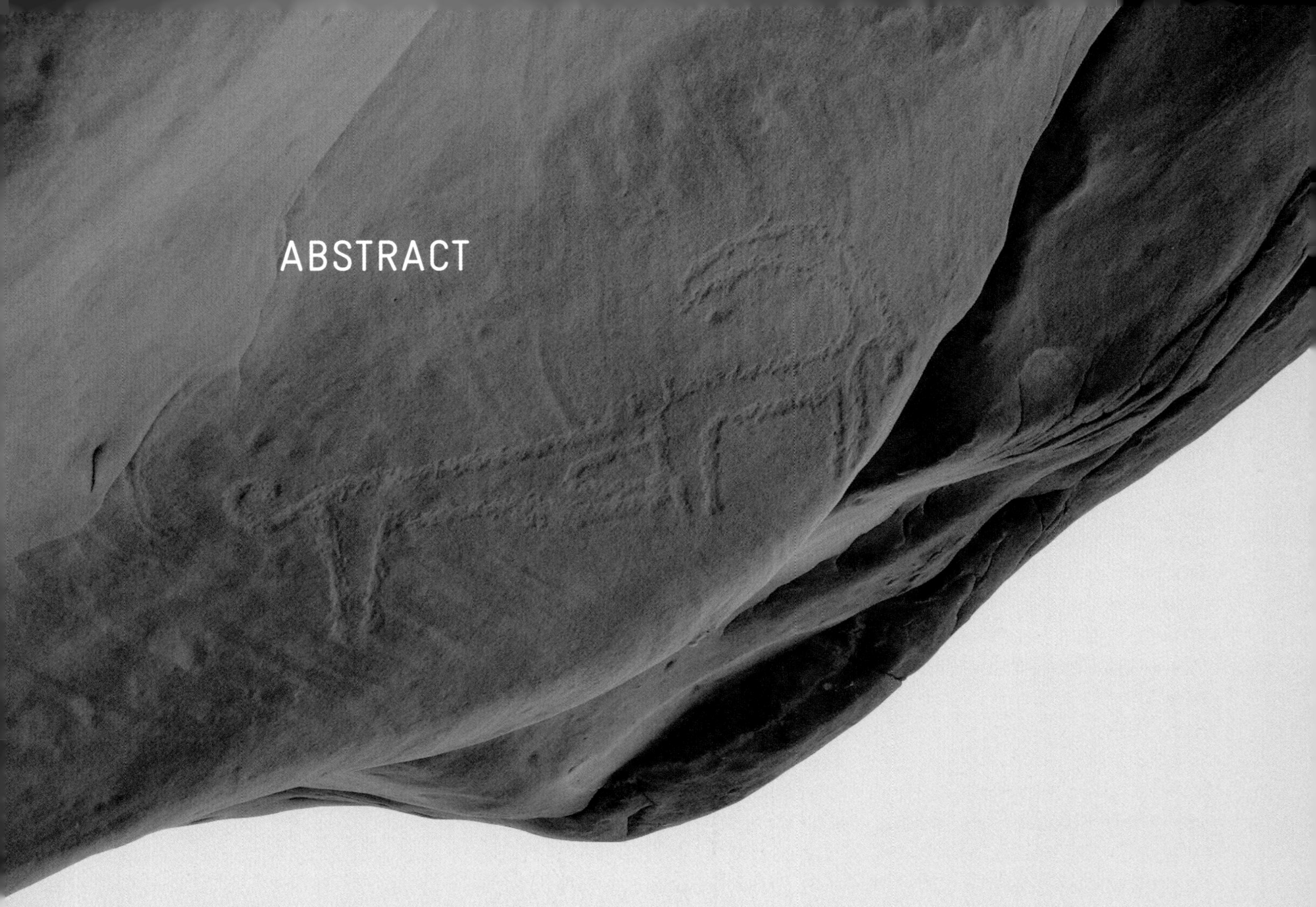

ABSTRACT

Paintings, engravings and bruisings on the walls and ceilings of natural caves like formations, often termed as rock shelters in archaeological parlance, were first noticed in 1880 by Archibald Carlleyle and John Cockburn. These discoveries were followed by a host of scholars in the late 19th and 20th centuries. To celebrate these discoveries and to assess the progress made by research in the last 100 years, a national-level seminar was organised in 1981 in Bhopal, largely keeping in view that the region has 157 groups of rock shelters scattered over 24 districts. The participants discussed various aspects of the discipline including the preservation of rock shelters and their ecosystems, which are an essential aspect of preservation of rock art sites across the world.

Paintings, engravings and bruisings on the walls and ceilings of natural cave-like formations, which in archaeological parlance are often termed 'rock shelters', were first noticed in 1880 by Archibald Carlleyle and John Cockburn. These discoveries were followed by a host of scholars in the late 19th and 20th centuries (C.W. Anderson, Panchanan Mitra, Manoranjan Ghosh, G.R. Hunter, Bridget and Raymond Allchin, Dr. Radhakant Varma, Dr. G.R. Sharma, Dr. S.K. Pandey, Dr. Jagdish Gupta, Dr. V.S. Wakankar, Dr. K.D. Banerjee, Dr. R.V. Joshi, Dr. K.V. Soundarajan, Dr. V.H. Sonawane, Dr. Giriraj Kumar and many others).

These celebrated scholars devoted much of their time and energy in understanding the nature of the rock art and its cultural significance. D.H. Gordan in 1934 realised the importance of rock art and bracketed the paintings between 700 BCE and 1000 CE. Excavations were taken up by G.R. Hunter in 1934-35 at Pachmarhi; by M.C. Dixit in 1957-58 in Modi (Mandasaur); by R.V. Joshi and M.D. Khare during 1960-61 in Adamgarh (Hoshangabad); by Professor K.D. Bajpai in 1971 in Bhimbetka (Raisen); by Dr. V.S. Wakankar and Dr. V.N. Mishra of Deccan College in 1973-76, established the importance of rock shelters and their cultural significance.

At the lowest levels, the Pachmarhi excavations yielded microliths whereas excavations conducted inside a rock shelter in Modi yielded a large number of lithic tools (triangles, lunates, flakes, blades, and haematites).

Excavations at Adamgarh (Hoshangabad) during 1960-61 by R.V. Joshi and M.D. Khare found Palaeolithic tools (handaxes, cleavers, scrapers, and cores showing predominantly Achulian characters) while excavations at Bhimbetka by K.D. Bajpai in 1971, Dr. V.S. Wakankar in 1972-77 and by V.N. Mishra in 1973-77 provided a cultural sequence going to lower Palaeolithic levels. Here, for the first time, a firm cultural sequence starting from lower Palaeolithic levels (Pd 1A lower Palaeolithic, Pd 1B Achulian culture, Pd 2 middle Palaeolithic, Pd IIIA upper Palaeolithic, Pd 3B Mesolithic, Pd4 Chalcolithic, Pd5 early historic, and Pd6 medieval and recent) to Medieval levels were noticed. Excavations were also conducted in rock shelters in Mirzapur by G.R. Sharma and R.K. Varma of Allahabad University and they also came across coloured stone pieces and microlithic tools establishing the antiquity of the rock shelters going up to lower Palaeolithic levels.

The survey and the studies conducted in the last decade of the 20th century by Bednarik, Neumayer (1995), Giriraj Kumar (1996), Chakravarty (1997), and the author of this article (1992-93, 1993-94) discovered and identified cupules which changed the overall antiquity of rock shelters in India. Excavations conducted at Daraki Chattan provided a new dimension to the antiquity of these rock shelters. Excavations conducted at Daraki Chattan for the first time established that there are lower Palaeolithic cupule remains in India.

Interest gradually developed in these valuable antiquities and it was thought appropriate to take concrete steps to preserve these rock shelters. Efforts were initiated in 1990-91 for protecting the deposits likely to be available in the opening of the rock shelter at Bhimbetka by providing stone pitching in mud mortar and diverting the rain water falling in front of the shelter. A comprehensive study was carried out at Daraki Chattan to find out the problems and issues involved in conserving rock art sites in India.

The Daraki Chattan shelter is a Palaeolithic cupule site. Facing west, the shelter is located in the quartzite buttresses of Indragarh hill, a reserve forest area in Mandsaur district in Central India. On the top of the hill are remains of a fort from the Medieval period. Excavations conducted in the vicinity of the fort revealed early historical remains. These discoveries established the antiquity of the site but the importance of the hill area could not be traced. The importance of this site was realised only during 1993-95 when it was studied.

Daraki Chattan is located in the upper strata of quartzite buttresses broken into big blocks with vertical fracturing. It faces almost to the west and overlooks a nearly 1.5-km wide fertile valley bound on both sides by the Vindhya hills. The valley opens on to the plains of fertile agricultural fields and *panvaries* (betel farms). Deccan trap escarpments with laterite capping in places join the hill on the north-western side of the valley. Through the valley flows the Rewa, a small perennial river.

Both the faces of the narrow cavern have cupules of different dimensions and different series. From the surface, the cupules appear to be shallow and narrow in depth. Over time, the surfaces of many cupules have developed growths of patina and many of these cup marks have developed exfoliation and indicate different stages of weathering. Within the narrow cavern, particularly on its southern face, dripping water was noticed whereas on the northern side in a different section, a heavy flow of water was observed largely on the eastern side.

An examination of all these details showed that the cup marks had suffered extensive damage due to the following reasons:

1. Patination
2. Encrustation
3. Exfoliation
4. Ultra violet rays
5. Wind velocity
6. Fracturing of the rock
7. Human vandalism

Prehistoric man had two necessities—food and sex. After satisfying these two biological needs, in his spare time he created non-iconic art, which has been given different names by various experts. This non-iconic art in the form of petroglyphs has been found in various parts of the world and has been associated with middle Palaeolithic and upper Palaeolithic cultures. But in India this has been found at the lower Palaeolithic levels. Typological and scientific dating and other evidence have provided ample information about the antiquity of these earliest traces of human activity on rock surfaces. These earliest traces of 'art' in the form of petroglyphs discovered at Bhimbetka (Bednarik 1993) have deteriorated extensively.

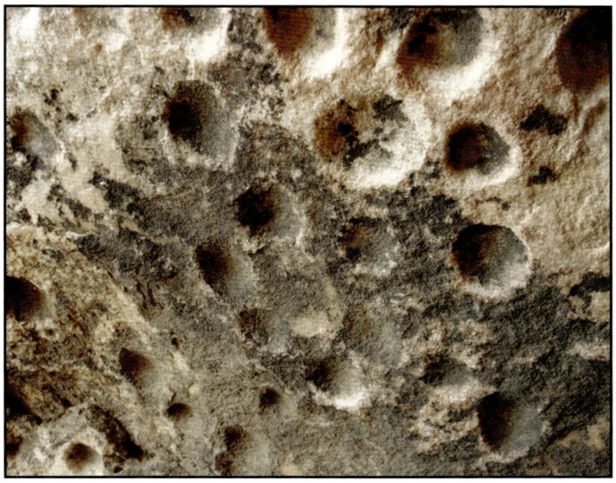 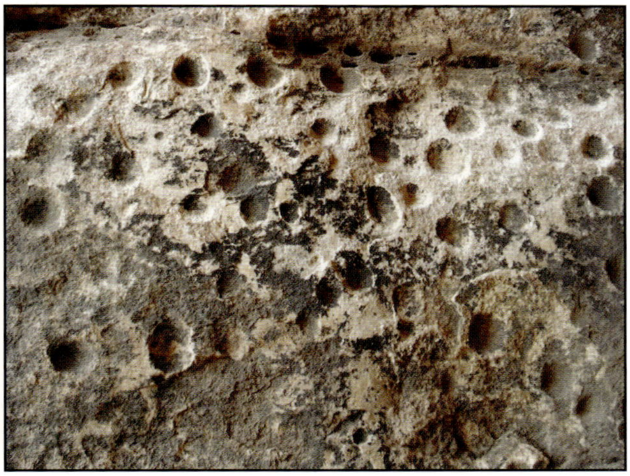

Left: **Fig. 20.1** Growth of patina on copules, Daraki Chattan.

Right: **Fig. 20.2** Exfoliation of cup marks, Daraki Chattan.

PATINATION

The growth of patination over an exposed surface is a natural phenomenon and rock art surfaces are not an exception to this. Patination is a very slow process and its examination reveals the age of the patination and the cause of its formation. Daraki Chattan cupules have also indicated patination not only on its mouth but also in close proximity and inside the body of the shelter (Fig. 20.1). This patination differs in thickness and formation. A close examination of the various cupules and the exposed surfaces indicates that the process of patination took place at a very slow pace and has disfigured the overall appearance of the cup marks. Extraction of samples and microscopic studies may reveal the time period of the formation of the patina; this process is underway at the moment. Patina over cup surfaces has discoloured the cupules and the deposition film has altered their overall appearance. To protect the cup marks, the crevices in the rock formation need to be plugged to avoid the formation of patina.

ENCRUSTATION

Encrustation is the process of deposition of external material over the surface and this was noticed in the cupules of Daraki Chattan. Micro-growth of vegetation was also noticed and in some places this has formed a crust inside the cup marks. This has largely happened on the outer surface or the faÁade of the cave and wherever seepage is noticed. To avoid encrustation around the cup marks or within the cups, the flow of water inside the rock has to be diverted.

EXFOLIATION

Exfoliation is a very common phenomenon in rock formation, which largely happens due to cooling and heating effects especially in the front and first half of a cave. The rock in which cupules have been carved is hard quartzite, but it is still susceptible to climatic changes (Fig. 20.2). The rock surface on the northern and southern side has suffered

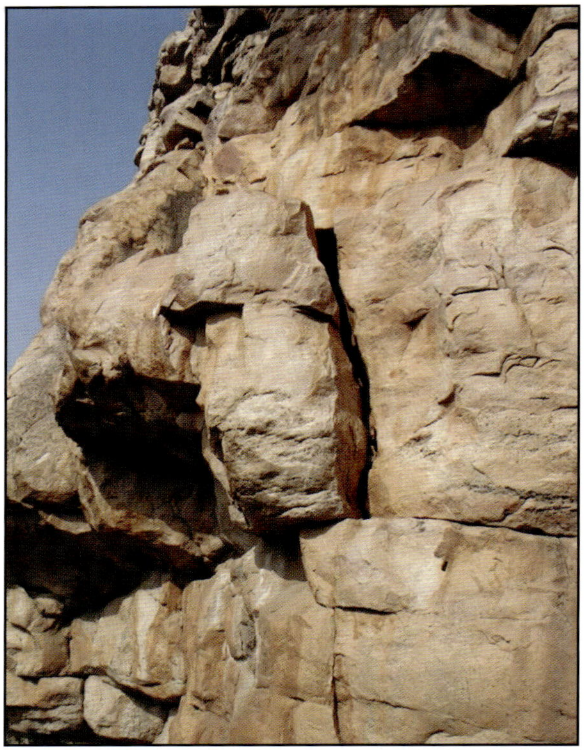

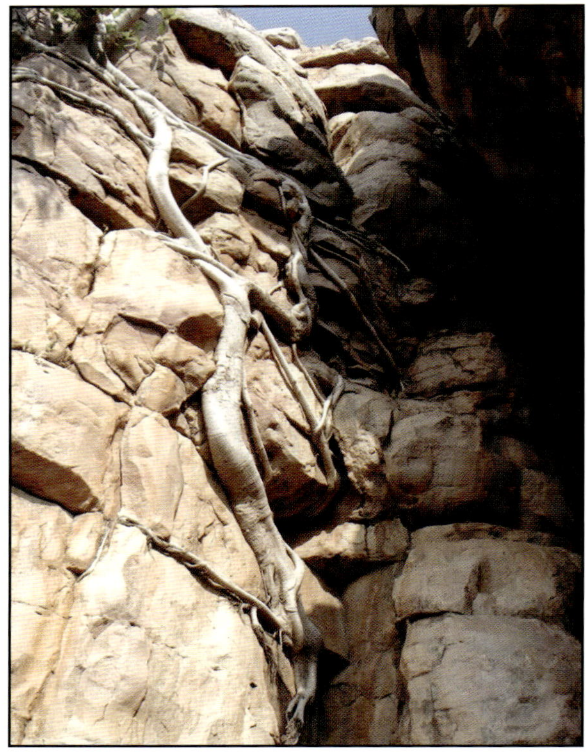

Left: **Fig. 20.3** Fracture in rock formation, Daraki Chattan.

Right: **Fig. 20.4** Growth of vegetation on rock formation, Daraki Chattan.

maximum exfoliation. Many cup marks have either deformed or are at the verge of extinction due to exfoliation. To avoid exfoliation of the rock surface, growing vegetation around the face of the rock is an essential remedial measure.

WIND

Wind has also affected the cupules inside the rock shelters and in many places abrasion marks were traced, which indicated that wind-borne sand grains have affected the circumference of the cupules to some extent. They have also damaged the uniform surface of the rock.

FRACTURING

A close examination of the rock surface revealed hairline cracks in many places; these fracture lines have travelled over a long distance. These hair cracks have become a source of water penetrating into the body of the rock and also work as a water trap. With the passage of time, these fractured crevices have developed and led to the disintegration of the rock ultimately causing serious damage to the old rock surface bearing cupules (Figs. 20.3 & 20.4). To arrest this phenomenon, cement grouting is required on the top of the rock surface and rainwater from the top also needs to be diverted. In the absence of these remedial measures, the rocks will continue to disintegrate.

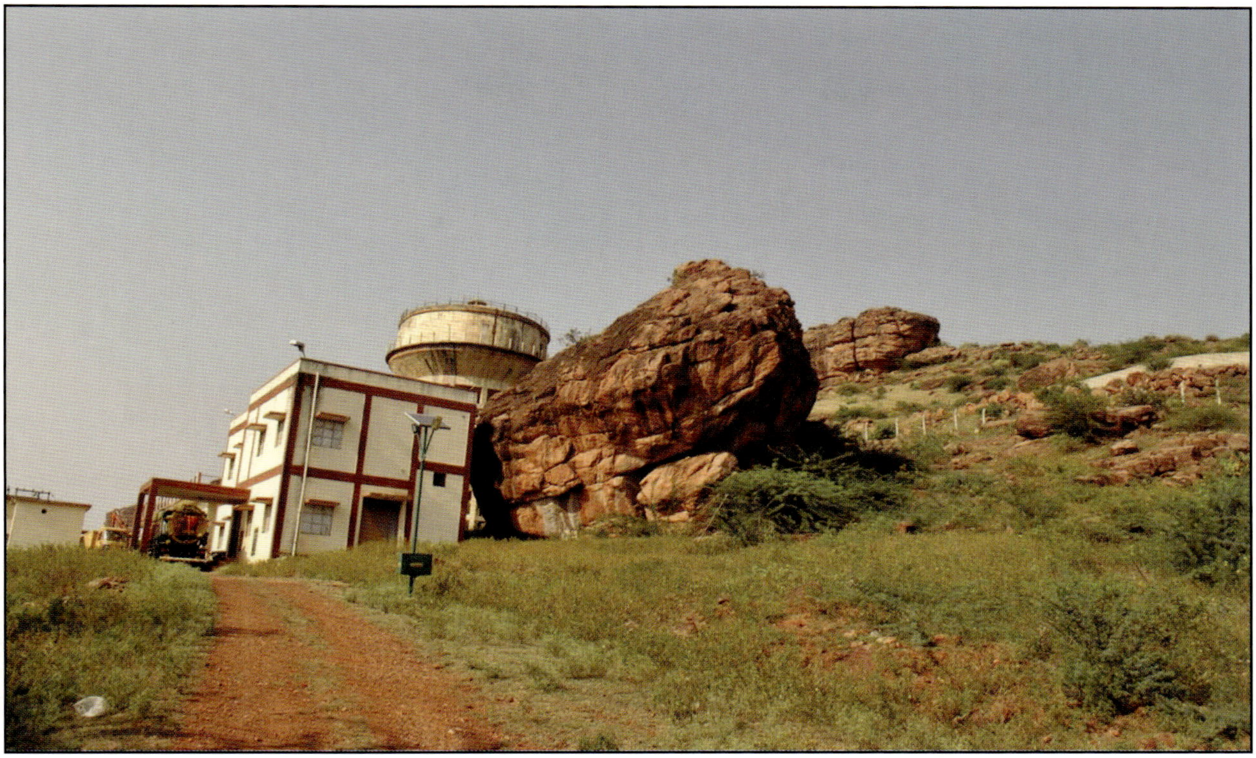

Fig. 20.5 Modern construction near the site of Badami Rock Shelter.

HUMAN VANDALISM

Human vandalism is a very serious problem all over the world. Out of excitement, many visitors cause serious threat to the existence of rock art. It is essential that public access to these rock formations be restricted and only scholars and researchers be allowed to enter the shelters. Restricted entry of the public will save the rock shelters from man-made disfigurements.

With the popularity of some sites, especially those at Bhimbetka, Pachmarhi, Adamgarh, and Daraki Chattan, the number of visitors has increased manifold. The shelters are very narrow and human tendencies to interfere with the monument, in whatever way, has/will pose serious threats to the very existence of the paintings and cupules in their pristine condition (Figs. 20.5 & 20.6). This will also seriously limit future scientific investigations of the world's earliest rock art going back to the lower Palaeolithic period. Hence, keeping in mind all these threats, we recommend that the sites should be opened only for scientific studies. For the general public, we recommend that a facsimile of the rock shelter be made on the ground close to the site (as has been done in the case of Ajanta caves, a World Heritage Site).

RECOMMENDATIONS

Daraki Chattan being the only site in the world which is so rich in petroglyphs and has cupules from lower Palaeolithic levels, needs to be protected and conserved for the posterity and also deserves world heritage status by UNESCO.

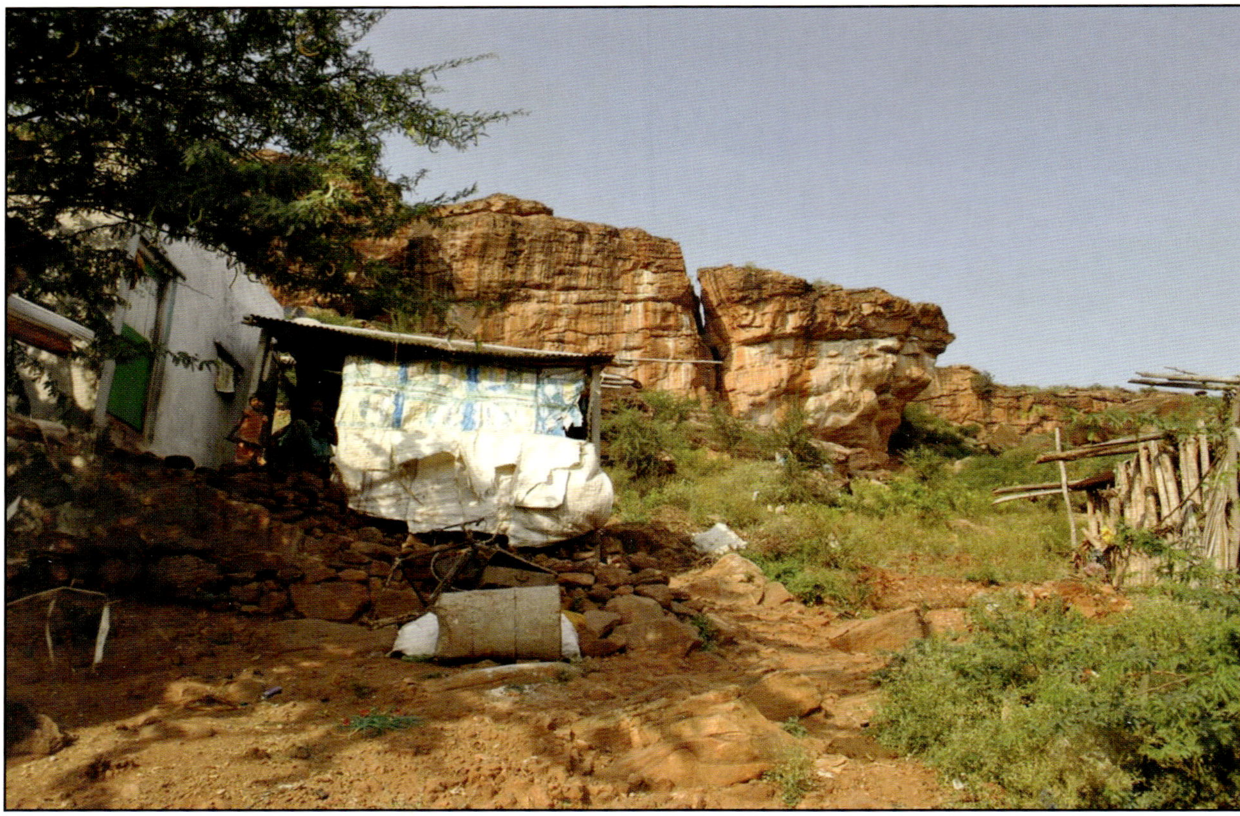

Fig. 20.6 Modern construction near the site of Badami Rock Shelter.

After observing and studying rock shelters/sites, the following recommendations are made for their scientific protection and conservation:

1. The Forest Department should plant and grow trees in front and around the cave. The trees will work as a windshield and will also prevent direct sunlight from entering the cave. This will control wind action and fluctuations in temperature particularly in the front and first half of the cave.
2. Controlling rainwater seeping into the cave and overflowing in the front area is the second major task which needs to be taken up immediately. Rainwater has to be controlled by diverting it in four or more directions starting from the slope on the top of the hill and gradually coming down up to the cave. Grouting of the crevices in the rock by cement concrete is necessary to check further weathering and exfoliation of the rock.
3. Daraki Chattan and other cupule sites on the Indragarh-Chanchalamata hill should be taken under protection by the Archaeological Survey of India at the earliest.
4. Action should be taken on these recommendations by concerned authorities.

REFERENCES

Badam, G.L. (2002), 'A Preliminary Note on the Fossils of Bhanpura Region', *Purakala* 13(1-2): 37-38.

Bednarik, R.G. (1993), 'About Cupules', *Rock Art Research* 10(2): 138-39.

—— (2001), 'Early Indian Petroglyphs and their Global Context', *Purakala* 11-12: 37-47.

Ganjoo, R.K. and S.B. Ota (2002), 'EIP Project–III, Preliminary Geo–archaeological Study on Quaternary Deposits of River Rewa near Indragarh, Madhya Pradesh', *Purakala* 13: 29-36.

Kumar, G. et al. (1992), 'Rock Art of Upper Chambal Valley, Part I; Rock Art and Rock Art Sites', *Purakala* 3 (1–2): 13-55.

Trivedi, H.V. and V.S. Wakankar (1959-60), 'Excavation at Indragarh', *MP Indian Archaeology: A Review 1959-60.*

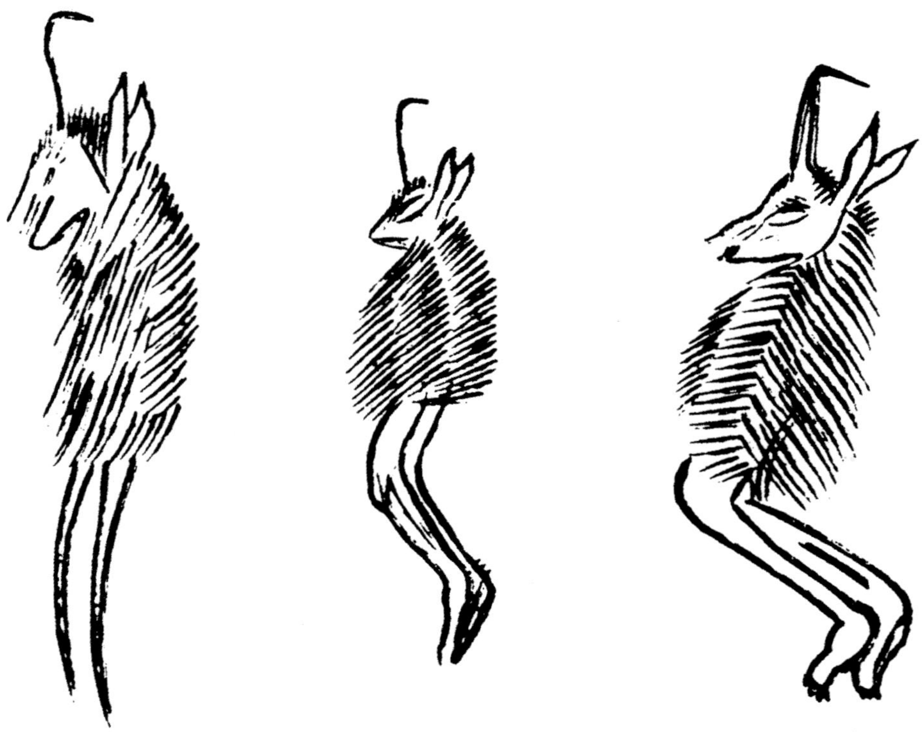

21

An Analysis of the Evaluation and Diagnosis of Environmental Impacts of Rock Art Sites of the Guaniguanico Mountain Range, Cuba

Racso Fernández Ortega, Dany Morales Valdés, Dialvys Rodríguez Hernández and Hilario Carmenate Rodríguez

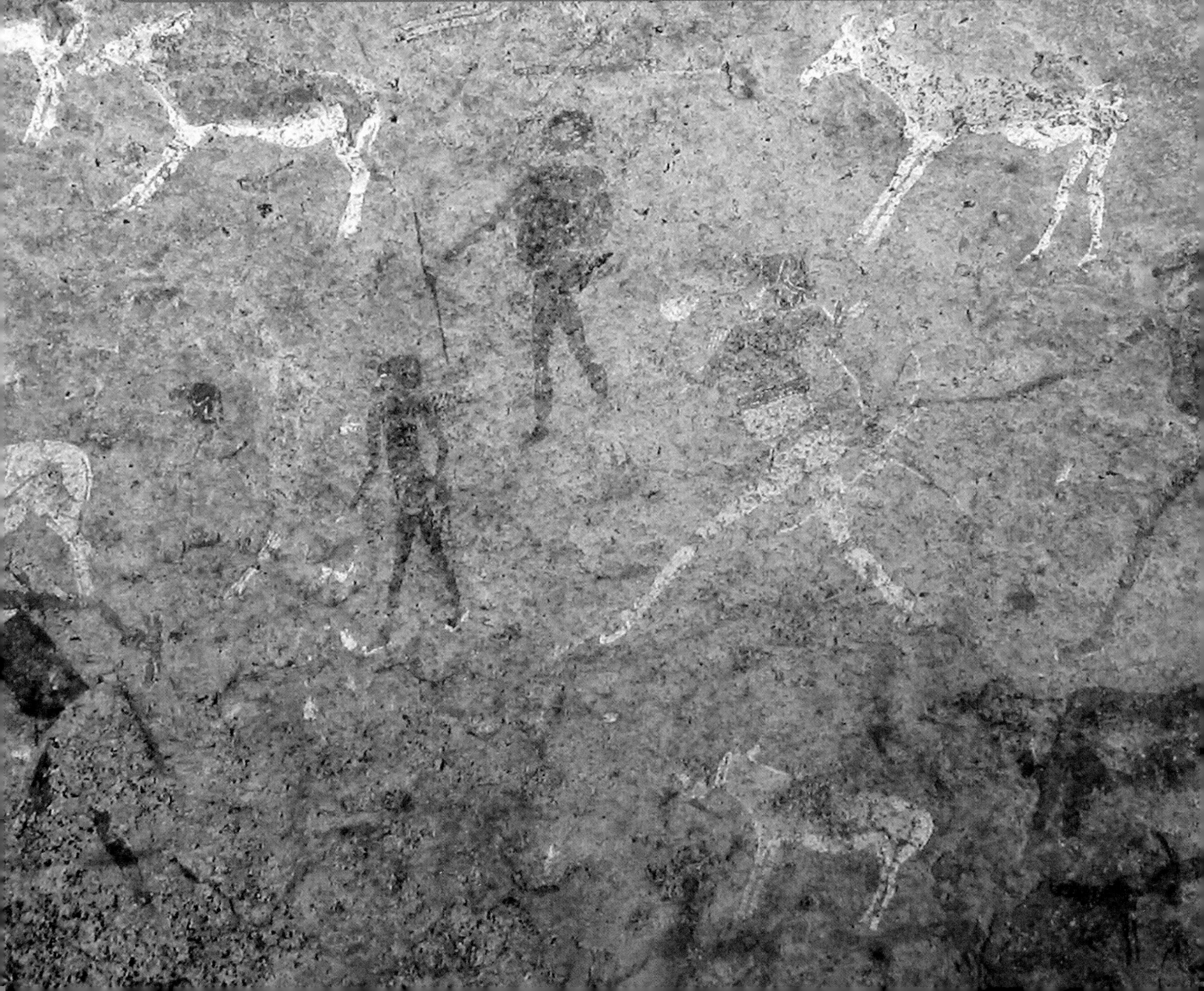

ABSTRACT

A group of people from the Cuban Rock Art Research Group undertook an expedition to evaluate the environmental impact on the rock drawings of the Pinar del Rio province. Fifteen of the 38 sites located in the area were randomly selected to evaluate and diagnose the environmental impact that had earlier been studied by a group from the Department of Archaeology of the Cuban Institute of Anthropology on the research project, 'Evaluation and diagnosis of the archaeological and socio-cultural patrimony of Cuba'. The methods used help in classifying natural and anthropic actions for best solutions to eliminate the damage, or the practice of palliative actions to stop, in some way, its deterioration. For that, the actions and impacts that affect the state of conservation of this Cuban important heritage are defined, enumerated and characterised in this paper.

INTRODUCTION

The problem of protecting and conserving rock art is a universal concern, linked to the fact that every year a great number of sites get lost because of diverse factors, but mainly because of uncontrollable and negative actions of human beings. Three examples in Cuba are the rock art sites of Cueva Mesa and Cueva La Jarra in the municipalities of Viñales, Pinar del Río and San Cristóbal in Artemisa province, or the Cueva de los Golondrinos in Baracoa, Guantínamo province. These sites were victims of adaptation because of their 'setting in value' or the habilitation of the archaeological places with different purposes and strategies, without a true impact study that analysed the consequences of such activities on the paintings. Harmful results on rock art began occurring and as a consequence they are deteriorating faster than the natural processes of deterioration.

As it is very well known, pictographs and petroglyphs are products of social conscience, and they regrettably remain joined to the natural aging of their support, pigments and agglutinants, which themselves become vulnerable and fragile resources over time.

Even so, this ancient heritage has remained for us—on many occasions with an antiquity of several thousands of years—something that provides evidence of its good invoice, resistance and adaptation to environmental changes that have taken place from the time of its creation. That is why on some occasions the opinions of some officials, that regrettably 'development' cannot depend on a manifestation that sooner or later will disappear, is not well accepted.[1]

However, the Cuban experience demonstrates that anthropic effects, whether voluntary or not, are the biggest source of irreversible damage (Ferníndez and Gonzílez 2001). This highlights the urgent necessity of protecting Cuban rock art registrations effectively in their environmental context. The present paper discusses and analyses various threats to the rock art sites in the Guaniguanico mountain range, on the western side of Cuba.

With this objective, the research project PNAP/0409 on 'Evaluation and diagnosis of the archaeological and socio-cultural patrimony of Cuba' was developed by a team in the Department of Archaeology, in the Cuban Institute of Anthropology (ICAN), during 2006-08. What triggered the project was the fast process of economic and social development of last decades, which led to damage and a threat to a number of sensitive archaeological places in the country.

Hence, it was decided in June 2007 that a study would be carried out along with members of the Cuban Group of Rock Art Researches, based on the approach accepted by international experience, that bad anthropic manipulation of ecosystems settled around rock art sites is the fundamental cause that leads to secondary effects, such as the presence of micro-organisms and of plants and zoological species that damage this heritage.

STUDY AREA

Two mountainous elevations are located on the western side of the Cuban island, which extend along an important area of Pinar del Río and Artemisa provinces. This mountain range is well known by its Aboriginal name Guaniguanico; it projects almost parallel to both the north and south coasts, and it has several physical-geographical divisions which are different from each other because of their peculiar natural characteristics. The superficial extension of the Guaniguanico mountain range is around 3,102 square km and it spreads from the west to the east for about 150 km approximately from Cerros de Guane till the elevations located in Cayajabos, in the central part of the current Artemisa. In the north and south sectors, surrounding the mountain range are located the Llanura Ondulada and the Llanura Deltaica, which extend for around 10 and 20 km from the coast and move till 20 and 30 km to the sea respectively.

The mountain range Sierra de los Órganos is located in the western part of Guaniguanico, and is very old in geological terms. It exhibits a characteristic flora, well known as the 'Vegetation Complex of Mogotes' growing on the typical carsic 'mogotes' of fertile valleys with floors of high quality.

In the east area of Guaniguanico is located the Sierra del Rosario, which is the youngest section in this orographic system with altitudes over the 500 MSL, and with a vegetation of evergreen forest. The Pan de Guajaibón (named with another Aboriginal term) is located among both the mountain ranges, and it is the highest elevation in western Cuba at 700 MSL, and has vegetation similar vegetation to that found in Sierra del Rosario.

The Guaniguanico mountain range is mainly constituted of calcareous rock concentrates and has some of the biggest caves in the country, with smaller caves and lapels inside. Ancient communities, or the first residents of the territory, were attracted to the area because they could exploit the fauna and vegetation on these elevations that guaranteed the development of survival activities. They used these caves as establishment towns, funeral and nature magic-nun sites. These underground places have important water resources that also slip as small and medium streams, which the Aboriginal residents found favourable for settling down. That is why it is common to find outstanding archaeological and rock art evidence in the caverns of this wide orographic system (Table 21.1, Fig. 21.1).

Table 21.1 Composition of rock art sites in the municipalities in the Guaniguanico mountain range

No.	Municipality	Kind of Site			Total
		Pictographic	Petrogliphic	Mixed	
1.	Guane	2	-	-	2
2.	Minas de Matahambre	10	1	-	11
3.	Viñales	5	2	2	9
4.	La Palma	6	-	-	6
5.	Pinar del Río	1	-	-	1
6.	Candelaria	-	1	-	1
7.	Bahía Honda	3	-	-	3
8.	San Cristóbal	1	3	-	4
	Total	28	7	2	37

CRONO-CULTURAL RELATIONSHIP

The territory referred to throughout this paper was in most parts inhabited by Aboriginal people belonging to fisher-gathering communities (Alonso 1995; Moreira 1999), and on the basis of these archaeological evidence, they occupied practically the whole geographical space of the current provinces of Pinar del Río and Artemisa.

The depictions of farming groups in this area are quite dispersed indicating that their arrival in this area was still in the exploration and recognition phase, and not at the conquest and occupation stages. This has been interpreted on the basis of a study of the archaeological pieces recovered in places and caves in the provinces of Pinar del Río, Artemisa, Havana and Mayabeque; and also by the pictographs registered and documented in caves such as Pluma, García Robiou and Solapa de la Perdiguera in the provinces of Matanzas, Mayabeque and Pinar del Río respectively. On the other hand, permanent and stable establishments of agricultural Aboriginal populations in the west of Cuba took place after a collision with the Europeans; these too can be interpreted through rock art manifestation like 'the bovine' found in cave system Guara in Mayabeque territory, or as can be demonstrated in the transculturation's ceramic sample in Guanabacoa, where the Europeans forced an Aboriginal establishment.

Because of what has been previously expressed, we should consider the fishing and hunting communities. Probably they executed the well-known rock art manifestation in the region, accepting that the inherited characteristics of these groups seem to be characterised by a tendency towards abstract forms and simple geometric representations, standing out of concentric circles.

Chaotic lines, without order or reason, is another characteristic of these human collectives as if the artist followed sinuosities with the instrument that the selected support capriciously imposed, and where stains are also common (Ferníndez et al. 2009a). What is also known is that they used red and black colours more frequently (Moreira 1999; Ferníndez et al. 2009a). Many of these elements are common in the studied sites, as well as the use of red and black pigments, which were used in 88 per cent of the places that were studied.

According to authors like Rosa (1996), Alonso et al. (2002) and Gonzílez (2008), several sites can be associated with the art of African origin, linked to graphic expressions of fugitive slaves on coffee and sugar plantations that were abundant in the area between the 16th and 19th centuries.

The radio-carbon dates available for this territory were unfortunately not carried out directly on the rock art, but in the archaeological findings rescued from archaeological locations, so they are associated with the base material found in the rock art sites.

In this sense, we should assume that the manifestation were carried out by fishing and hunting Aboriginal communities, in one period between 3320 BCE as the earlier limit and 1200 CE, as the later date, considering that the earlier dated ones belong to Cueva de la Lechuza in San Cristóbal municipality, with 5270+120 AP, and the latest belong to the Mogote de la Cueva in Pinar del Río municipality with 650+200 AP (Pine 1995: 2, 5). However, the authors consider that this proposal should be taken just for orienting the research, first because the experience has demonstrated that it is not always opportune to link the archaeological registration located in the rock art site directly with the depictions, and second due to the fact that there are not enough number of absolute dates to find an association between both the elements.

It can also be deduced that for the few sites that are considered as the fruit of the ideological and cultural activities of communities well-known as farmers (agroalfareros or Islander Taino), the author (Ferníndez 2012) has identified numerous designs characterised by their iconography and even some ideographic representations that remind one of the deities of the mythological vault of these groups common to Cuba and other Antilles islands. This allows the assumption that these graphic registrations were executed by members of the Arawak linguistic branch (with a producer economy and a social gentile organisation) (Tabío and King 1966: 202; Guarch 1978:108), Agroalfarero (Dacal and Rivero de la Calle 1986: 140; Tabío 1991: 23), nowadays denominated as farmers (Moreira 1999: 149). In their unavoidable advance toward the occident of the national territory, they started the marks that defined new landscapes that constituted unequivocal samples of the passing by of a socially different group from the territory to settle down with other patterns in the selection of sacred spaces.

In accordance with radio-carbon dates of the farming places in Cuba, it can be determined that this stage developed around 820 CE (1120+160 to AP), according to the older dated one in Residuario del Paraiso in Santiago de Cuba (Pino 1995: 10) and 1785 CE. (165+60 to AP), obtained for Aguas Gordas in the eastern Holguín province (Pino 1995: 11).

ENVIRONMENTAL IMPACT ON ROCK ART HERITAGE

Threats to rock art were explained in the article 'The Conservation of the Cuban Rock Art Patrimony. Current Situation and Perspectives' published in *Boletín del Gabinete de Arqueología* (Gutiérrez et al. 2007). However, for the research being discussed here and in trying to be more precise, a specific area of the Cuban territory was selected to deepen the study of the deterioration of rock art and the threats that this archaeological region faces.

This particular study of the environmental impact on graphic patrimony meant dividing the threats that it faces into four groups to facilitate a better analysis of the damage. The classifications followed the origin of the damage as a premise, and were differentiated in natural, industrial, anthropic and cultural sites.

NATURAL THREATS

Natural threats are those that appear as a result of the planetary processes of nature, in which man does not have a primary or direct role to play, such as geological, carsological, biological or climatic alterations. These can be sub-divided into the following categories (Fig. 21.2):

a. Geological: In this group is included the damage that takes place by the formation of deposits of carbonates on the area with graphic representations. It also includes damage caused by detachments or collapses of blocks or fragments of rocks as a

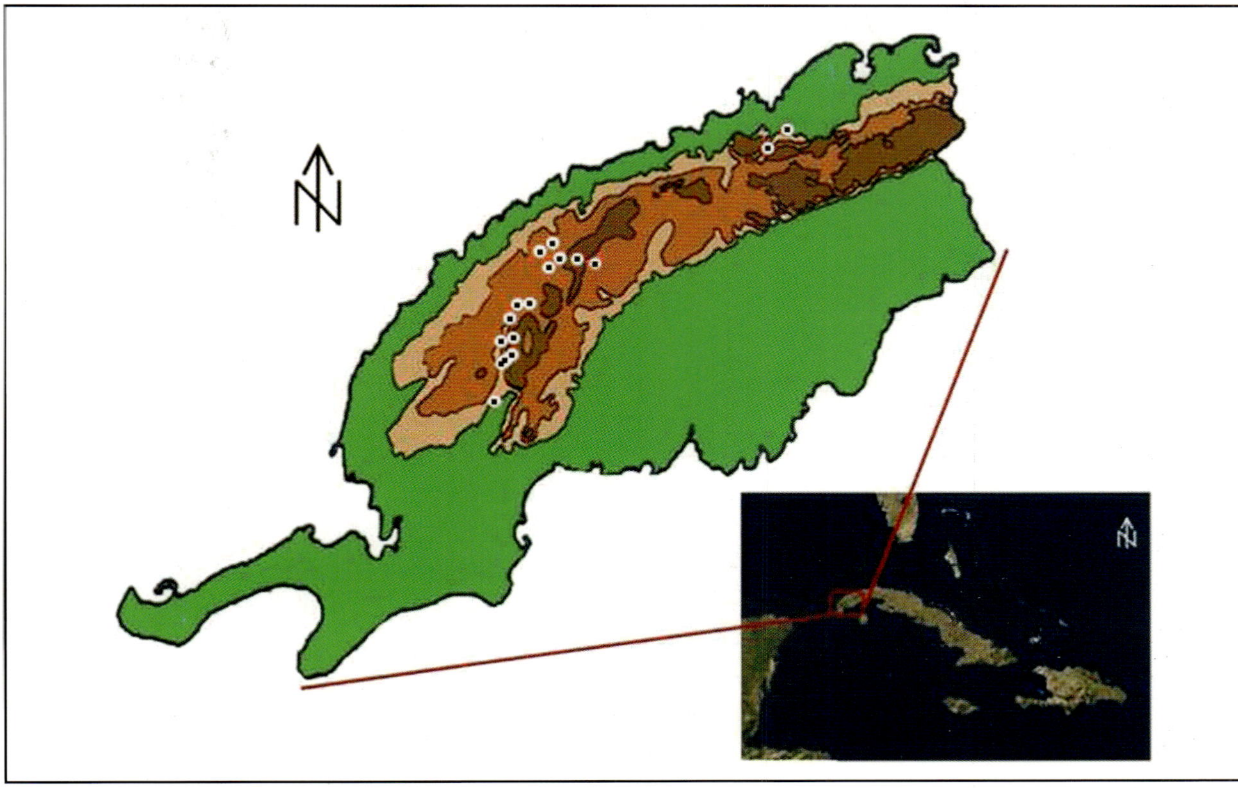

Fig. 21.1 Cartographic location of the rock art sites evaluated in the Guaniguanico mountain range.

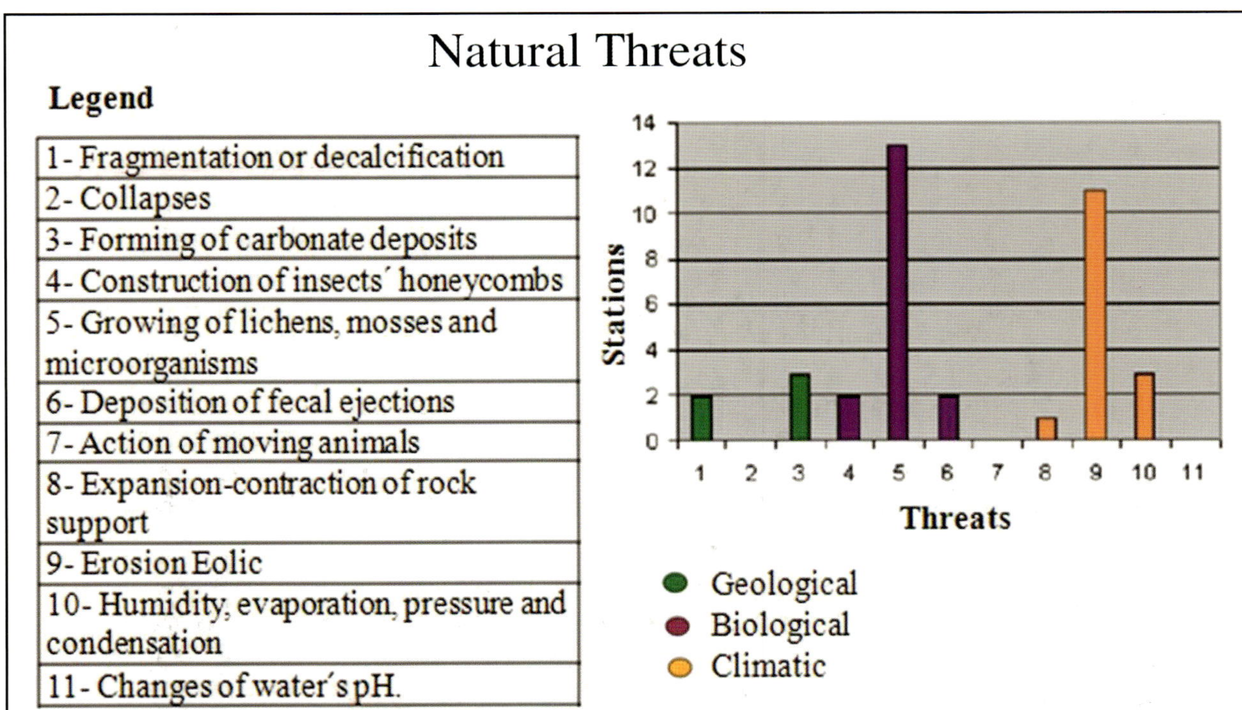

Fig. 21.2 Types of natural threats that affect rock art sites.

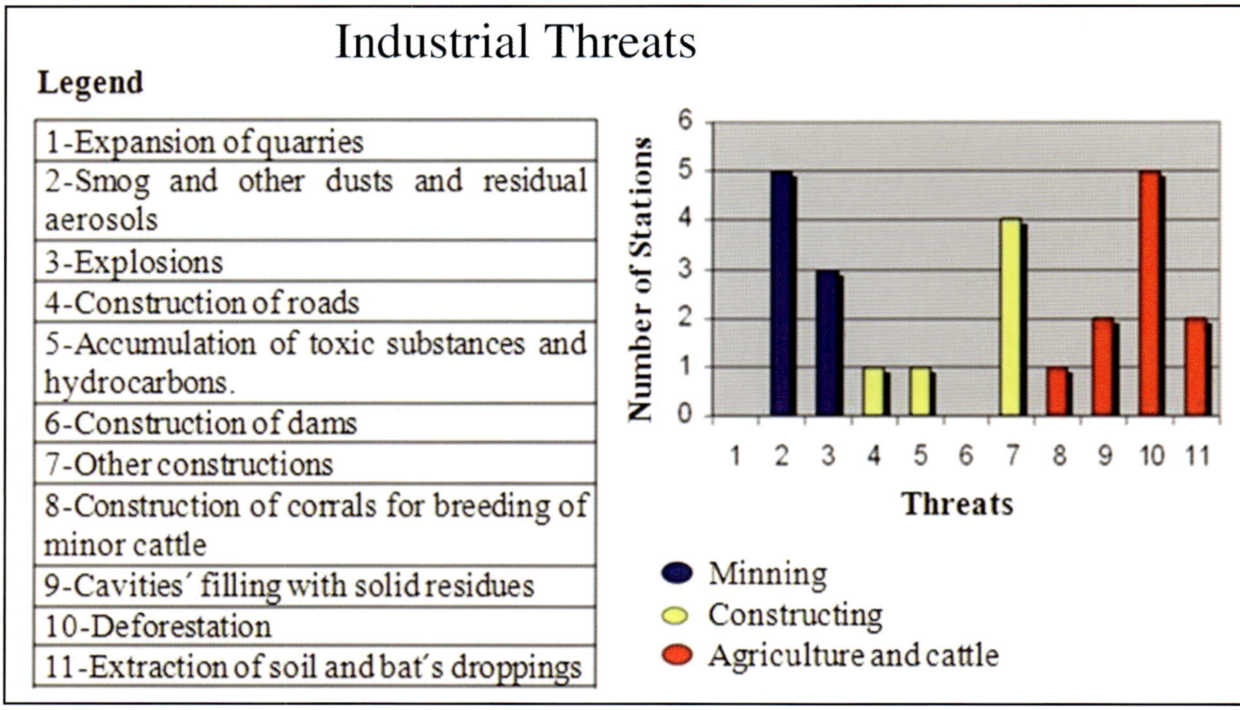

Fig. 21.3 Types of industrial threats that affect rock art sites.

result of structural adjustments in the localities. Cracking or scaling is also included; it happens when there is a crack or a jump in small parts in the support that contains the graph.

b. Biological: In this is included the damage caused by the natural growth of mushrooms, lichens, mosses, algae, ferns and other vegetable organisms on the support on which the graphs were carried out. Another common phenomenon is faecal ejections of bats, rodents, birds and other permanent or eventual inhabitants of the sites as well as those caused by the movement of some animals on the graphs, or because of the construction of honeycombs and nests by insects and birds.

c. Climatic: In this kind of threat are included eolic erosions, changes in humidity—relative and absolute—in the caves' environment, as well as the evaporation, condensation, pressure of carbon dioxide, oxidation and other microclimatic variables.

INDUSTRIAL THREATS

These include actions provoked by man as a secondary effect due to modification in the environment and the ecosystem that surround the sites, in the name of industrial development with the purpose of developing economy.

It has been observed that on occasion, when there is a reference to the environment of rock art sites, it is common to think of the space surrounding these rock sites. However, meticulous field studies have demonstrated, for example, that the effects of the emanation

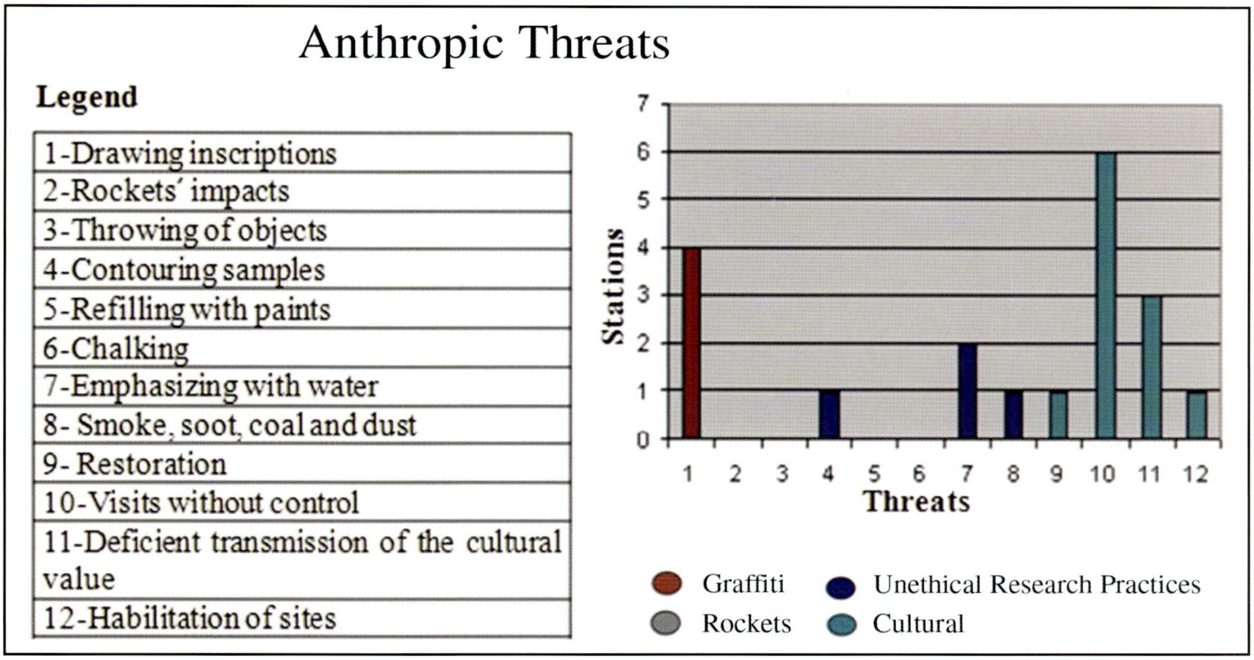

Fig. 21.4 Kinds of anthropic threats that affect rock art sites.

of hydrosulfuric gas from the petroleum wells in the north coast of Havana province, have led to the decalcification of the calcareous rock of the caves located in a 5-km radius. The pictographs of the Cinco Cuevas cave have been lost due to the scaling off of the rocky surface (Fig. 21.3).

Industrial damage can be divided into the following categories:

a. Mining: Linked fundamentally with the exploitation of quarries and the explosions that take place during the mining process. It also includes smog and other gases like residual aerosols characteristic of the extraction of petroleum, natural gas, etc.

b. Construction: These are associated with the construction of highways and the continuous vibrations that take place because of the circulation of heavy vehicles. It also includes the construction of dams and using the area for the storage of toxic substances, chemicals and hydrocarbons, as well as the creation of micro-urban towns near the sites.

c. Agricultural: These are related with agricultural, cattle raising and forest processes; as well as with deposition of stones, industrial and crops waste and domestic garbage in the cavities. Treatment of the ground for multiple agricultural activities that provoke micro-climatic changes as products of deforestation and/or reduction of the edaphic layer around caves or rocky lapels are also included here. Livestock breeding (bovine, porcine, etc.) that establishes room spaces in the caves which are protected from the sun and, where the animals rub their bodies against the walls which have pictographs or petroglyphs, provoking climatic and microbiological changes that in turn lead to the deterioration of the rock paintings both in the short and long term.

ANTHROPIC THREATS

Anthropic threats represent the actions carried out by modern man in rock art sites and their environment in a direct and intentional way. These constitute, without doubt, the most abundant and devastating damages that these ancient cultural manifestations continually receive in the whole world and Cuba too is included in this reality (Fig. 21.4).

a. Graffiti: This includes the damage that has impacted rock art sites in the country the most during the last three centuries. It consists of 'decorating' the walls of the caves with signs and dates and drawings on occasion, which are done with any material like pencils, crayons, spray or diverse varieties of pigments with acrylic and oil bases.

b. Rockets: Refer to two kinds of practices with similar consequences: the first, to shoot guns toward the drawings; and the second to throw all types of objects towards the walls or the secondary formations that support graphic manifestations.

c. Unethical Research Practices: Procedures like the use of water or chalk on the pictographs and/or petroglyphs with the intention of improving their visibility and perception. Also included in this are the contours of the pictographs or petroglyphs so that they are better defined and they stand out. All these actions are executed mainly by researchers to take pictures or the tracing of the registrations for documentation. The damage is also caused when someone blazes a light or burns tyres inside the caves and lapels.[2]

d. Cultural: The lack of awareness among the villagers and neighbours about an archaeological site's discovery leads to the destruction or deterioration of the site because of different reasons. Researchers are mainly responsible for creating false expectations and concerns around the sites, instead of facilitating their custody and protection.

EVALUATION AND DIAGNOSIS OF ROCK ART HERITAGE

From the beginning of archaeology as a science, the protection of archaeological heritage has been one of its special interests, although it has enjoyed both success and failure in its dependence on a scientific vision.

In our country, different institutions from the beginnings of the 20th century have dealt with—by means of important regulations—the handling and conservation of archaeological/historical places.[3] Also, during the revolutionary period many laws and ordinances for patrimonial protection were carried out, modified and applied. At the same time, institutions have been created for archaeological research and the management of heritage, which have organised and carried out campaigns to rescue and salvage some places and locations. However, lack of control and constant endeavours by the state about conservation, and even about the strategies to be followed for continued excavations, have led to a situation where the archaeological heritage has been damaged (Robaina 2003). Cuban rock art patrimony is not an exception in the destruction of its sites, which is why a strategy became necessary to discern the main damage and threats of deterioration, and the designing of instruments to preserve it. So, a methodology was implemented so as to be able to identify at least the main threats.

The 'Methodology for the evaluation of environmental impact in archaeological places', proposed by members of the Group of Auxiliary Sciences in the Department of Archaeology in the Cuban Institute of Anthropology, belonging to the Ministry of Science, Technology and Environment (CITMA), was used. In this methodology, the indicators are evaluated for each impact: sign, intensity, extension, moment, persistence, reversibility, recoverability, synergy, accumulation and rhythm or period.

Attention was directed to those indicators that expressed the level and the intensity of the affectation the best: the *accumulative effect*, in which the inductor agent's action is prolonged in time. This happens, for example, in sites when felling the surrounding vegetation provokes systematic loss of the colouration of drawings because of the daily incidence of solar rays.

Synergistic effect: When several combined impacts take place and it is verified by the simultaneous presence of several actions called Synergistic Effect. This threat includes environmental changes, impact of which is bigger than the effect of individual action contemplated in an isolated way. Enough examples of rock art sites exist where due to the felling of surrounding vegetation, they started facing major changes in temperature between day and night. That consequence in fractures and cracks development in the rocks further destruction of painting/rock art and contributed in beginning or creating opportunities of growth of micro-organism like lichens, mushrooms, etc. that caused or produced acids. This leads to weakening of structure and further weakening of pictographs.

Non-renewable Source: Many pictographs have been attacked by overwriting and graffiti that can be eliminated by expensive chemical processes but this operation is potentially risky due to the alteration or mutilation of the petroglyphs. This indicates the permanent loss of the patrimony as it is almost impossible to restore to its previous state.

The importance of being able to carry out the evaluation and the diagnosis of the environmental impacts on archaeological places was based on planning short trips to different areas in the national territory with or without risks of modifications, affectations or destruction. The objective of these trips was to make quick and reliable evaluations that allow—by a transverse study—to know the real situation in the study areas, or, in a random way, to select a proportional number of places that facilitate an analysis of the approximate state of the general total (Fernídez et al. 2009b).

The analysis was carried out to determine the best way to proceed and 17 rock art sites were randomly selected from the 37 sites to obtain a vision of a general approach of the impacts that are creating a large number of affects in the same ones, and to carry out pertinent recommendations to eliminate or mitigate the damage that has occurred.

Systematic monitoring and evaluation of the situation of rock art Sites at a national level carried out by GCIAR reveals that 17 per cent sites face industrial and 83 per cent sites face anthropic threats. Just 23 per cent sites out of the 274 sites reported in the country are protected under the 'monuments' category and only 15 per cent are included in national parks and natural reserves. Until now, historical-cultural values were not taken into account so that these sites could be included in protection areas inside the protected regions (Table 21.2)

Table 21.2 Status of legal protection of rock art sites in the Guaniguanico mountain range

Municipality	Rock Art Sites with Legal Protection			
	Local Monuments	National Monuments	In Protected Areas	Without Protection
Guane				2
Minas de Matahambre	1			10
Viñales	3	1	9	-
La Palma	1		1	4
Pinar del Río				1
Candelaria				1
Bahía Honda	1			2
San Cristóbal				4
Total	6	1	10	24

THE EXPERIENCE IN THE GUANIGUANICO MOUNTAIN RANGE: SELECTION OF THE SAMPLE

To apply the selected methodology, 17 caves and lapels with rock art manifestations were selected from the three municipalities of Minas de Matahambre, Viñales and Bahía Honda, and a cave in La Palma, which were considered to be the most representative.

It was decided to carry out research over several days with a chronogram that allowed carrying out visits with a minimum time of two to three hours being spent at each site, to evaluate satisfactorily the actions and their impact. During the inspections, each site was graphically and photographically documented with the impact detected to maintain a systematic log of their positive or negative evolution.

The Rock Sites

Topographically, the sites are located between an altitude of 0 m (Solapa de la Vaquería) and 253 m MSL (Cuevas del Garrafón).

In general, these manifestations of the cultural material can be found in caves—as those of Cueva del Cura and El Garrafón—that present a few longitudinal developments among 20 m in Cueva de las Manchas and more than 700 m in Cueva de los Petroglifos; but it reaches the maximum height of 2500 m in Cueva de Mesa; or in big lapels that on occasion reach between 2 and 10 m in depth like Solapa de la Vaquería and y la Cueva de Las Manchas.

Realisation Substrates

The selection of the realisation substrates in the group of sites that we analysed was determined by three categories: walls and roofs of the cavities, secondary formations (lytogenesis) and clastic morphology (blocks of collapses).

According to the established categories, the use of the walls and roofs as substrates represent 97 per cent, in opposition to 1 and 2 per cent in use of the secondary formations and clastic morphology respectively.

The use of cave support from the point of view of the composition allows us to conclude that pictographs are present in the three categories of the selection of realisation substrates, and that the petroglyphs were carried out on the walls and roofs of the shelters.

Selection of Spaces

Some researchers of Cuban Rock Art Studies are now taking a special interest regarding the study of 'selection of space and shelter' based on archaeological principals to reveal cultural and chronological elements (Fernídez and Gonzílez 2001; Fernídez 2005) (Table 21.3).

Table 21.3 Sites selected for the evaluation and diagnosis of the environmental impact study in the Guaniguanico mountain range

No.	Name	Location
1.	Solapa de La Sorpresa	Sierra del Pesquero
2.	Cueva de Camila	Sierra de Mesa
3.	Solapa de La Perdiguera	Sierra de Sumidero
4.	Cueva de Nicolás	Sierra de Sumidero
5.	Solapa de Los Círculos	Sierra de Cabeza
6.	Solapa de Los Pintores	Sierra de Cabeza
7.	Solapa de Quemado	Sierra de Quemados
8.	Cueva de Mesa	Sierra de Quemados
9.	Cueva de Los Petroglifos	Sierra de Galeras
10.	Cueva del Garrafón	Sierra de Viñales
11.	Cueva de Las Manchas	Sierra de San Vicente
12.	Solapa de La Vaquería	Sierra de San Vicente
13.	Cueva de Los Estratos	Sierra de San Vicente
14.	Cueva del Cura	Sierra de Guasasa
15.	Solapa María Antonia	Sierra de Gramales
16.	Cueva La Espiral	Macizo Pan de Guajaibón
17.	Cueva Canilla II	Macizo Pan de Guajaibón

One of the analysed approaches is related to the sunlight and its approach to the shelters. In the area studied: 11 places manifested their representations in areas where sun beams are directly reaching the walls (threshold areas), two sites show their exponents in areas where the solar rays infiltrate by reflection (sub-threshold areas), and in four sites art manifested in areas where there is no sunlight or absolute darkness.

With the use of these approaches, it could be observed in detail that the most used space was that in the sub-threshold areas (65 per cent of selectivity); so the presence of rock drawings in the threshold and sub-threshold areas was unequivocally related with pictographs.

Evaluation and Diagnosis of the Conservation

For the evaluation and the diagnosis of the conservation of rock paintings in the mountain range, the research used 28 types of actions proposed to begin with, but once the investigation got underway, it was proven that these categories were insufficient. Hence, some necessary modifications were introduced and they were expanded to 34 types, as we faced newer particularities of human activities.

The evaluation of the state of conservation of the paintings shows that lichens, mosses or micro-organisms affected the sites the most (84 per cent) (Figs. 21.5, 21.8 & 21.9); while deforestation was the second most important impact (70 per cent) (Table 21.4).

Table 21.4 Main threats to rock art in the Guaniguanico mountain range

Group	Category	Action	Affected Sites
Natural	Geological	Expansion-contraction of rock support	2
		Collapses	-
		Forming of carbonate deposits	3
	Biological	Construction of insects' honeycombs	2
		Growing of lichens, mosses and micro-organisms	13
		Deposition of fecal ejections	2
		Action of moving animals	1
	Climatic	Expansion-contraction of rock support	1
		Erosion eolic	11
		Humidity, evaporation, pressure and condensation	3
		Changes in water's pH.	-
Industrial	Mining	Expansion of quarries	-
		Smog and other dusts and residual aerosols	5
		Explosions	3
	Construction	Construction of roads	1
		Accumulation of toxic substances and hydrocarbons	1
		Construction of dams	-
		Other constructions	4

Group	Category	Action	Affected Sites
	Agriculture and Cattle	Construction of corrals for breeding of minor cattle	1
		Cavities filling with solid residues	2
		Deforestation	7
		Soil erosion and bat excreta	2
Anthropic	Graffiti	Drawing/writing	3
	Rockets	Impacts of rockets	-
		Throwing of objects	-
	Unethical Practices	Contouring samples	2
		Refilling with paints	-
		Chalking	-
		Emphasising with water	2
		Smoke, soot, coal and dust	1
		To enumerate	1
	Cultural	Uncontrolled tourism and tourists visit	5
		Deficient transmission of the cultural value	16
		Habilitation of sites	1
		Restoration	1
Total number of affected sites			16

Thanks to the fact that the sites in the mountain range are generally located in remote and distant places and far away from urban cities and towns, graffiti did not constitute one of the major human vandalisms, as has been demonstrated by studies carried out at the national level (Ferníndez and Gonzílez 2001; Gutiérrez et al. 2007) (Table 21.5).

Table 21.5 Actions that affect rock art sites evaluated in the Guaniguanico mountain range

Kind of Action	Impact
Deforestation	Provokes growing of micro-organisms and micro-flora on the paintings in the threshold zone due to the sun's rays
Eolic erosion	The pigment layers become loose in some paintings
Contouring of painting's borders	Contouring, may be with graphite, of a painting's borders, for better recognition
Growing of lichens, mosses and micro-organisms	Growing of stains that cover the paintings partially or totally

Kind of Action	**Impact**
Humidity, evaporation, pressure and condensation	Growing of calcite layers on the paintings
Uncontrolled visits	Construction of hearths and fires that spread smoke and ashes on the pictographs
	Direct action of visitors on walls and paintings
	Accumulation of solid waste
Expansion-contraction of rock support	Cracking and loss of the pigment layer in the paintings
Extraction of soil and bat droppings	Uncontrolled extraction and movement of archaeological evidence
Construction of corrals for breeding of minor cattle	Deposition of feacal ejections that modify soil's pH
	Movement of the soil
	Growing of micro-organisms and micro-flora
Deposition of feacal ejections	Increasing of acidity and degradation of walls and paintings
	Loss of colour of the paintings
Intention to restore	Contouring samples
	Retouching of affected areas with clay
Construction of insects' honey-combs	Formation of concrete on walls and paintings

Impact due to graffiti was detected in the evaluated sites of Cueva de los Estratos, Nicolás and Camila. These are coincidentally near more affluent areas and they are also frequently visited by outsiders, furtive hunters, occasional tourists and visitors. The places with more variety in impacts are Cueva de Camila (12), the Cueva de la Tabla (8), and Cueva de Nicolás (5) (Fig. 21.8), Solapa de la Vaquería (7) and Solapa de Las Manchas (6) (Gonzílez et al. 2007).

It can be proven that Los Estratos', Camila's and Nicolás' Caves, and Las Manchas' and La Vaquería's lapels are sites that present bigger risks because of the intensity of the impacts detected inside, the ones that were evaluated in the category of 'high risk'. The bigger impact was due to civil construction in a range of 2 and 30 m of the sites that generated harmful impacts because of the dust and residual aerosol aggravated by movement of the arid soil over long and intense periods, and the effect of explosions and actions linked to the partial or total deforestation of the areas that indirectly affected these sites (Fig. 21.6).

The Cueva de Nicolás site is located next to the highway that goes to Sumidero town. This is used as a public sanitary service, because it does not have any mark or sign that points out its patrimonial and cultural value.

There are also several rock art sites that have been protected as they have been included in areas belonging to national parks or biosphere reserves that have protection systems. The efforts that have allowed better protection of these sites have shown a decrease in the deterioration to pictographs and petroglyphs (Fernı́ndez et al. 2012).

In this sense, the cavity which is well known as Cueva de Mesa in Gran Caverna de Santo Tomís, is the only one that has a specialised guide service as it is located in the territory belonging to the Viñales National Park, and in the property of the former National School of Speleology that has obligatory access through a control post (Fig. 21.7).

Tourism at the Gran Caverna de Santo Tomís system began at the end of the 19th century and new entrances to the cavity were created to facilitate tourism. Unfortunately, during the study, possible impacts of tourism to these sites were not calculated properly and systematically monitoring of the same was not carried out. This led to many problems to the cavity and irreparable deterioration due to tourist and visitors' flow.

A community of investigators in the county tried to restore some of the engravings applying some splashes of carbonate sand, which they got from the area around the petroglyphs, by using dental brushes like a rustic aerosol and by using a sharp instrument to emphasise them.

This inadequate procedure did not have an impact and there is no documentation of the original petroglyphs, neither is there any documentation of the whole process with a description of the applied procedures. This action on the paintings and murals as well as the unimaginable number of microbiological and microclimatic dangers that cannot be valued today and also completely perceptible morphological modifications, have led to the deterioration of this site.

The institutions involved in the research, conservation and safeguarding of the cultural and natural patrimony are directly responsible for making the laws that protect our heritage worthwhile at every level. They should also bring together their efforts to achieve the execution of effective dispositions and correct or complete the corresponding documentation of the correct safeguards.

Hence, it can be confirmed that the state of conservation of rock drawings in sites in the Guaniguanico mountain range are classified as 'high risk' and that is why it is necessary for the municipal

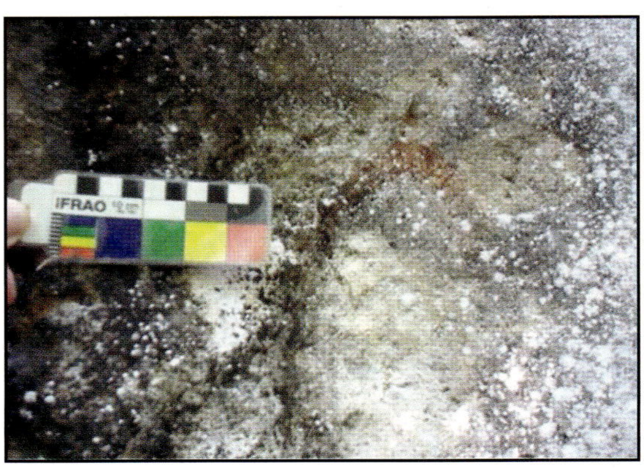

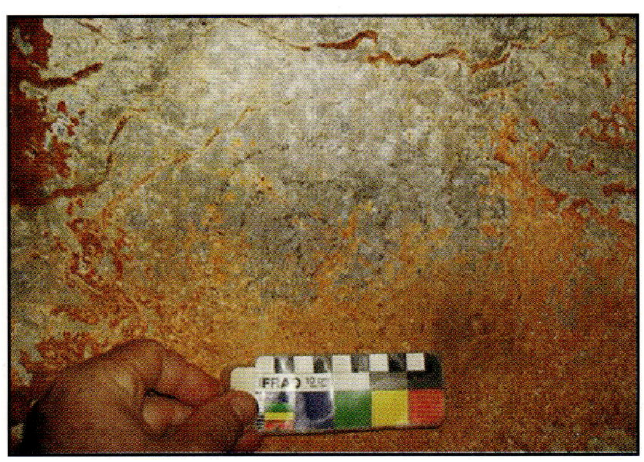

Left: **Fig. 21.5** Solapa de la Sorpresa in Sierra del Pesquero. Painting affected by the growth of micro-organisms on the wall.
Note: From GCIAR files.

Right: **Fig. 21.6** Cueva La Espiral in Macizo de Guajaibón. Formation of carbonate deposits.
Note: From the author's files.

governments in this region to consider this heritage as one of the most fragile cultural resources and make efforts to protect it.

Table 21.6 Grades for general affectation for sites

No.	Name	Affectation grade
1.	Solapa de La Sorpresa	3
2.	Cueva de Camila	1
3.	Solapa de La Perdiguera	2
4.	Solapa de Los Círculos	2
5.	Solapa María Antonia	4
6.	Solapa de Los Pintores	4
7.	Solapa del Quemado	3
8.	Cueva de Mesa	1
9.	Cueva de Los Petroglifos	4
10.	Cueva del Garrafón	3
11.	Cueva de Las Manchas	1
12.	Solapa de La Vaquería	1
13.	Cueva de Los Estratos	1
14.	Cueva del Cura	3
15.	Cueva de Nicolás	1
16.	Cueva Canilla II	2
17.	Cueva La Espiral	4

Note: Very high affectation (1), High affectation (2), Moderate (3), and Slight affectation (4).

CONCLUSIONS

The impact that a large number of problems are having on the visited sites is due to the wrong anthropic manipulations of the ecosystems around them that provoke secondary effects, such as the presence of micro-organisms, plants and zoological opportunist species that irreversibly damage this heritage.

Left: **Fig. 21.7** Cueva de Mesa in Gran Caverna de Santo Tomís. Contouring restoration by incised lines.
Note: From GCIAR files.

Right: **Fig. 21.8** Cueva de Nicolás in Sierra de Sumidero. Growth of micro-organisms on the rock support.
Note: From GCIAR files.

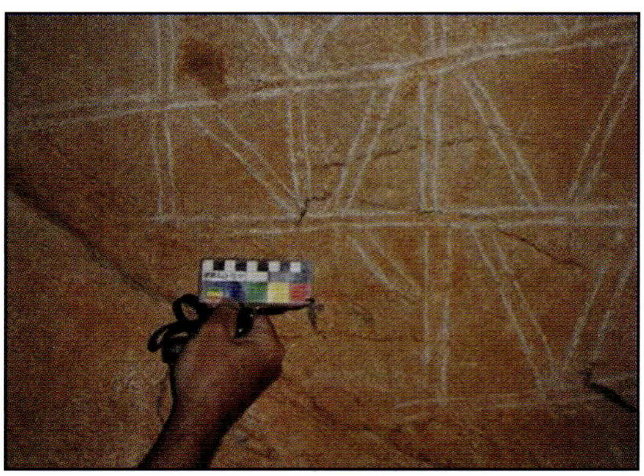

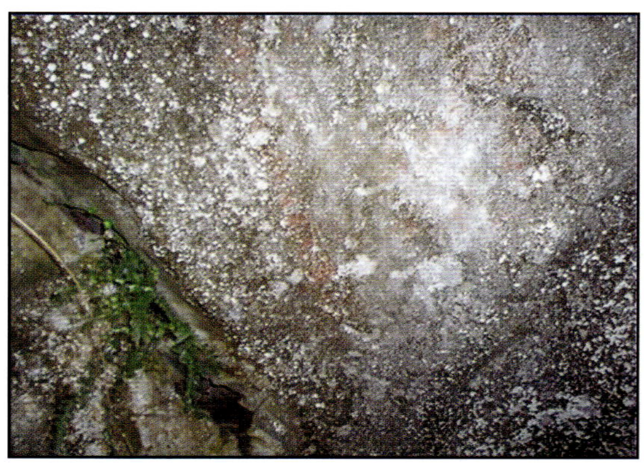

The country has legal machinery that should guarantee the protection and conservation of its cultural heritage, but regrettably it does not mention rock art in the specificities, such as architectural elements, among others. In this sense, and taking into account the proposals which resulted in the International Consultation of Specialists on the Study, Documentation and Conservation of Rock Art, celebrated in Valcamónica in 1981, we all agreed with the necessity of establishing a corpus of particular laws for protecting the heritage and for its conservation, administration, use and handling.

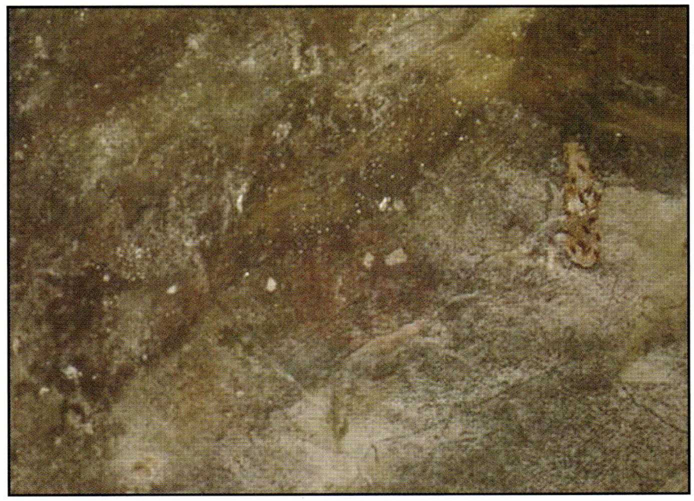

Fig. 21.9 Solapa de los Círculos in Sierra de Cabeza. Development of insects' honeycombs.
Note: From GCIAR files.

The institutions involved in the research, conservation and safeguarding of the cultural and natural heritage have the direct responsibility of using the laws that protect our heritage, and using the best methods for their preservation.

NOTES

1. Nowadays, a non-sustainable development that does not take advantage of the particularities of the surrounding ecosystem of each selected area, is unthinkable. The value of the historical-cultural heritage represents an important source of national identity and the residents can play the main/key role in its protection and conservation.
2. It is a habitual practice among the peasants, beaters, fishermen and campers, to mark the walls with smoke, soot, coal, powder and other toxic substances leading to the decalcification of the rock due to oxidation.
3. Magazine of Archaeology and Ethnology, Special Number on Legislation, year 1957; Protection of the Cultural Patrimony. Compilation of legislative texts, Ministry of Culture, Havana (1996).

REFERENCES

Alonso, E.M. (1995), *Fundamento para la historia del Guanahatabuey de Cuba.* La Habana: Editorial Academia.

Alonso, E.M. et al. (2004), 'Pinar del Río: Arte Rupestre', CD-ROM *II Taller Internacional de Arte Rupestre.* La Habana.

Comité Estatal de Estadísticas (1981), Estudio sobre la Cordillera de Guaniguanico. *Censo de población y vivienda.* Marzo de 1981. Instituto de Demografía y Censos. 36pp.

Corvea, J.L., R. Novo, Y. Martínez and I. de Bustamante y J.M. Sanz (2006), El Parque Nacional Viñales: un escenario de interés geológico, paleontológico y biológico del occidente de Cuba. En *Trabajos de Geología,* Univ. de Oviedo, 26: 121-29.

Dirección de Patrimonio Cultural (1996), *Protección del Patrimonio Cultural. Compilación de textos legislativos.* La Habana: Ministerio de Cultura.

Fernîndez, R. (2005), 'El registro grîfico rupestre como fuente de información Arqueológico-antropológica. La Caverna de La Patana, Maisí, Guantînamo, Cuba', Tesis en Opción al Título

Académico de Míster en Antropología Sociocultural. Facultad de Filosofía e Historia, Universidad de la Habana (inédito).

Ferníndez, R. and y J.B. Gonzílez (2001), Afectaciones antrópicas al arte rupestre aborigen en Cuba. *Rupestre* Revista de Arte Rupestre en Colombia, Año 4, No. 4, Bogotí.

Ferníndez, R. and J.B. Gonzílez y and D.A. Gutiérrez (2009a), 'History, Survey, Conservation, and Interpretation of Cuban Rock Art', (with translation by Michele H. Hayward), in Michele H. Hayward, Lesley-Gail Atkinson y Michael A. Cinquino (eds.), *Rock Art of the Caribbean*. Tuscaloosa: The University of Alabama Press, Colección Caribbean Archaeology and Ethnohistory Series, pp. 22-40.

Ferníndez, R.D. Morales et al. (2009b), La evaluación y el diagnóstico del estado de conservación del patrimonio arqueológico de Cuba.

Ferníndez, R., D. Morales and D. Rodríguez y V. Cué (2012), Arqueología y turismo en Cuba. Simbiosis para el desarrollo sostenible? *Boletim do Museu Paraense Emílio Goeldi "Ciencias Humanas"*, Belem, Brasil. (En prensa).

Gonzílez, J., B.R. Ferníndez, D. Gutiérrez, H. Carménate and Y. Chinique y D. Rodríguez (2007), *Reporte del trabajo realizado en 13 de las estaciones de arte rupestre de la provincia de Pinar del Río.* Proyecto de evaluación y diagnóstico del patrimonio sociocultural de Cuba. Archivos del Dpto. de Arqueología del Instituto Cubano de Antropología, La Habana.

Gutiérrez, D., R. Ferníndez and y J.B. Gonzílez (2007), La conservación del patrimonio rupestrológico cubano. Situación actual y perspectivas. En *Boletín del Gabinete de Arqueología*, Oficina del Historiador de la Ciudad, Año X, (X): 107-24.

Junta Nacional de Arqueología y Etnología (1957), Nómero Especial sobre Legislación, Revista de la Junta Nacional de Arqueología y Etnología, época 3[ra.], La Habana.

Robaina, J.R., M. Celaya, O. Pereira and R. Rodríguez (2003), *Gestión y manejo de recursos y valores arqueológicos patrimoniales de la Repóblica de Cuba.* Monografía (inédita). Fondos Documentales del Instituto Cubano de Antropología. Resultado de Investigación.

22

Geological Aspects and Management of Rock Art with Special Reference to Conservation

Devananda Beura

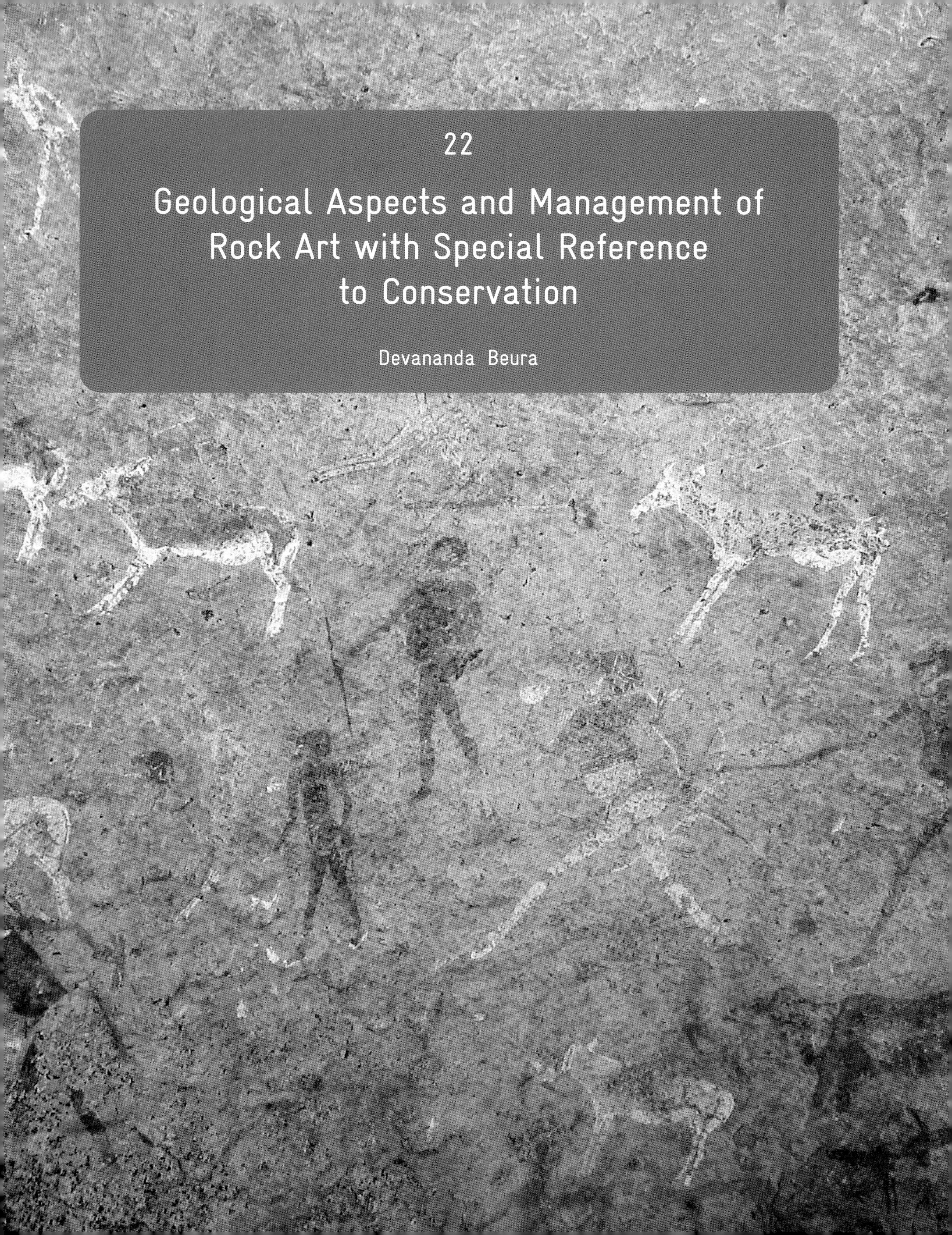

ABSTRACT

Ancient man could express art on the surface of a rock. Since he did not know about the various properties of a rock, he continued drawing and engraving. Pictograph and petroglyph art related to his socioeconomic and cultural life can be found in various rock art sites and in rock shelters. This art encompasses a lot of information about the ancient civilisation that enriches subjects like geo-archaeology, anthropology and ancient history. Rock art, created thousands of years ago, is now in a vulnerable condition as far as its longevity, resilience and stability are concerned. Both natural and manmade factors are contributing to its vulnerability. Conserving rock art, therefore, is an urgent need.

While preserving rock art, the natural settings of the rock surface containing the art, structural elements, composition, texture and matrix of the rock and geological hazards like earthquakes and land use patterns are to be kept in mind.

INTRODUCTION

Ancient man could express his instinct for art on the surface of a rock. Since he did not know the various properties of rocks, he drew and engraved pictures on rocks. Pictograph, geoglyph and petroglyph art are related to man's socio-economic and cultural life and are now present at various rock art sites and in rock shelters. This art encompasses a lot of information about ancient civilisations that enriches subjects like geoarchaeology, anthropology and ancient history.

Rock art created thousands of years ago is now in a vulnerable condition so far as its longevity, resilience and stability are concerned. The art on rocks was done with incipient and indigenous knowledge. Knowledge about rock art was silent about the type of rocks, compositions and impact of different geological agents like water, sun, rain, wind and chemicals. Also, ancient man did not know the ingredients and durability of colours. At present, when rock art has emerged as a valuable heritage, we have started giving serious thought to its preservation as it is being subjected to various degrading factors, both natural and man-made. Weathering and erosion are the two important processes which destroy rock art.

Rock art is found on various rock types like granite, dolerite, basalt, sandstone and quartzite. It is found that hard rocks were used for painting, while engravings were done on comparatively soft rocks. Rock art in varying forms like pictographs and petroglyphs might have been part of man's artistic evolution. Prehistoric man chose rock shelters for making art on the walls of rocks. Rock shelters used by man were natural features with high cliffs, tilted faces and vertical erections, which could partially protect man from rain, sun and wild animals. The geomorphology of the area thus becomes a path-finder for exploring rock shelters and rock art. The nature of rock art depends mostly on the properties of the rock on which it is made like compositions, textures, matrix, pore spaces and alterations.

The immense heritage of prehistoric art is vulnerable to natural processes of wear and tear, obliteration and destruction, which are further accelerated by human activities. Every day, bits and pieces of rock surfaces are falling apart. Development projects, construction of roads, building houses and agriculture can hardly be stopped, but steps need to be taken to document and record rock art in its current state to assure that its testimony remains for future generations.

STABILITY AND CONSERVATION OF ROCK ART

Rock art in the present context is given wide attention so far as its importance in studying ancient art and culture is concerned. It gives enormous information about the art and culture of the past and how they evolved. Studies and research on rock art have broadened and intensified today. Ancient art in different forms is preserved on rock surfaces and emerges as a major source of evidence to support academic endeavours. Rock art, the piece-work of ancient eminency, has sustained its existence for thousands of years under an open sky, in sun and rain, against wind, frost and natural disasters. Rock art is in different stages of vulnerability from natural as well as man-made threats. It, therefore, needs to be protected through cultural resource management (CRM). Archaeologists, geologists and others should adopt CRM as their professional and disciplinary responsibility to protect archaeological records.

Before taking up rock art for protection, what needs to be identified is whether the art is endangered by natural or human activities. Natural degradation and deterioration of panels is very slow and unmarkable within a short span of observation. Comparatively, human interference is very quick to damage art panels. In particular, newly explored rock art creates confusion about its degree of decay as past appearance in the art is lacking. Rock art sites which are open to visitors may follow a strategy of trying to restrict vandalism. Such measures can be taken up by archaeologists and the civil administration.

Geological studies of rock art areas bring the author to a discussion on stability and conservation factors. Normally natural hindrances to the sustainability of rock art are overlooked in many cases. Only some instant measures with regard to restricting human visits and human activities are taken up. Going through this system of protective measures, he has conceptualised the Integrated Rock Art Management System (IRAMS). The purpose of IRAMS is to take up strategies to maximise the sustainability of rock art. The scope of this system is more or less similar to the Rock Art Stability Index (RASI), but with the addition of applied geological and geotechnical measures to human-natural measures. Also, geoenvironmental issues get emphasised while considering protective measures.

THREATS TO ROCK ART

Rock surfaces with art that is exposed to the environment are acted upon by different natural agencies. So, they undergo weathering due to mechanical, chemical and biological actions associated with such agencies. Weathering and erosion are the main degrading factors of rock art, the intensity of which varies according to a number of natural factors like climate, topography, structure, texture, composition of the rock and vegetation cover. Time plays an important role, as the intensity and amount of weathering increases with time.

PHYSICAL THREATS

Physical threats to rock art are caused by the mechanical disintegration of rocks. Various forces, pressures and stress generated by natural agents like sun, rain, water, wind, varying temperatures, change in pressure, freezing and frost are responsible for the physical weathering of rock art.

CHEMICAL THREATS

These threats come from chemical weathering of rocks when they get decomposed because of various chemical reactions. Rock surfaces interact with a number of atmospheric constituents that are chemically active. Among them carbondioxide, oxygen and water are the prominent ones. The most common and widespread chemical threat comes from water through the processes of hydration and hydrolysis. The mineral constituents of rocks, in association with water, alter themselves to either a different composition or a different physical state like swelling. The nature of water in terms of alkalinity and acidity regulates the intensity of the chemical action. These qualities depend on the pH value of water. More the pH value, more is the alkalinity and stronger the dissociation. Similarly, carbonation and oxidation processes harm the rock surface and hence the art on it. Water dissolved with atmospheric carbon dioxide (CO_2) turns to carbonic acid. This affects rocks containing calcium, magnesium, sodium and potassium constituents more. Similarly, free oxygen mixed with water acts as an active oxidising agent. Iron minerals present in the rock are highly prone to oxidation.

BIOLOGICAL THREATS

These refer to damage caused by living beings, such as animals, plants and micro-organisms. As most of the rock shelters exist in jungles, plants play a major role in biological weathering. Plant roots enter minor joints and fracture planes, widen the openings, allow water and other agents to pass through and finally expose the rock body to cumulative actions caused by such elements. Frictional damage by plants because of rubbing the art surface is also not uncommon. Similarly, interactions of animals on rock bodies destroy the objects. Burrowing animals, termites, bacteria and algal, mosses and lichens, decay and disintegration of dead animals and plants and bird droppings cause harm to rock surfaces as well as to rock art. Invasion of these places by humans for various purposes is also responsible for damage to the art.

While discussing conservation issues, utmost care should be taken with respect to the following points:

1. Natural Setting of the Rock Surface Containing Art

It is essential to record the location of the rock art site with respect to its geomorphological setting and topographical configuration. There may be a possibility that it is situated on a hilltop, in a foothill, horizontal surface, high altitude, low land and inner or outer walls of caves. A rock art site may be situated near a stream, river or any isolated waterbody. Sometimes, art is drawn on a huge boulder, rock fragment or a fractured rock piece, which remains in an unstable zone with little assistance. Care should be taken to study the status of the rock art site with respect to its natural setting.

2. Weathering and Erosion Agents

The most active and effective natural agents for weathering and erosion are sun, rain, water, wind and frost. They change the chemical and physical structure of the rock significantly and lead to damage. Water washes away hydrate minerals, weakens the grains and matrix of the rock to destroy its colour as well as its engravings. Wind-blown water or sand scours the surface of the rock, gradually removing pictographs or sanding down petroglyphs. Temperature fluctuations can eventually flake small chips from the rock, damaging or obliterating rock art.

3. Structural Elements Present in Rock Art Sites

Rocks with geological structures like joints, fractures, cracks and fault planes are weak and unstable in nature. Art drawn earlier in that zone or rocks containing art undergo structural deformation—both are vulnerable to damage. They facilitate fragmentation, flaking, breaking and detachment of rock masses by allowing degrading agents to intrude.

4. Pattern of Disposition of Rocks Containing Art (Such as Horizontal, Vertical, Gentle Sloping or Light Sloping)

The spatial disposition of rock bodies that contain art is a key factor for receiving external forces from natural agents. The geometry of rock art sites determines the magnitude and effectiveness of eroding parameters.

5. Composition, Texture and Matrix of Rocks

The durability or weakness of a rock depends on its mineral composition, texture and matrix. Rocks of igneous origin like granite, basalt, gabbro and dolerite are hard and strong and can withstand the destroying impact for a long period. Metamorphic rocks like quartzite, khondalite, gneiss and schist and sedimentary rocks like sandstone, shale and limestone are comparatively weaker in their texture and matrix. The texture of a rock indicates the grain size and mutual relationship among the grains. Rock grains may be compact or loose, well- sorted or ill-sorted and equigranular or inequigranular. Rocks having equigranular, well- sorted and compact forms are prone to less degradation. Matrix is the fine particle material that keeps the constituent grains intact in the rock body. This is otherwise known as cementing material. It may be homogenous or heterogeneous in composition. In sedimentary rocks, the matrix is responsible for hydration, oxidation and absorption of fluids which bring about instability.

6. Physical Properties like Hard, Massive and Soft

Hardness of rock bodies keeps the drawings and engravings intact on their surface. A hard and massive rock cannot be easily endangered by degrading forces, while soft rocks are less stable against destructive agents.

7. Hydro-geological Properties like Porosity and Permeability

Porosity is interstitial pore spaces which are measured in percentages in a given volume of rock. The in-depth absorption of fluids in a rock body depends on its porosity. Also, permeability (interconnectivity of pores) regulates the transmission of liquid into the rock body. Loose and coarse-grained rocks have high porosity and permeability. Hard, compact and fine-grained rocks lack these and hence form suitable panels for rock art. Rock art on sandstone shows a deeper existence of liquid and therefore suffers from different episodes of weathering.

8. Eroding Facilitators

There are some materials or agents which do not cause appreciable damage to rock art but facilitate its erosion by their presence. Various organisms grow on rock surfaces as well as on rock art and modify their stability by different actions. For example, mosses hold moisture on the surface, some lichens make the surface more friable and the roots break the stones apart. Plant leaves hold moisture and water content, which softens the rock surface and facilitates erosion. Micro-organisms develop in large numbers and damage the paintings and engravings. Micro-climate, temperature fluctuations, rainfall patterns and pollution are also responsible for catalysing erosion in rock art panels.

9. Development of Sedimentological Features on Art

A number of sedimentary features develop on rock art panels due to erosion-transportation-deposition processes. Petroglyphs provide a suitable avenue for sedimentation. Fine bedding, banding, lamina, stalactites and stalagmite develop on the panels and overlap the art. The patina is an abundant feature which may be caused by non-biological mechanisms, such as the oxidation of various metals in the rock or by the leaching of metal carbonates, oxides and sulfates such as iron and manganese, from the interior rock with deposition on the surface.

10. Lithological Affinity to Erosion

Rock art done on different types of litho-units is very important in the sense that rocks respond differently to different erosion processes. Sedimentary rocks as compared to igneous and metamorphic ones are susceptible to erosion. Sandstone, limestone and shale are more easily eroded than basalt, granite, quartzite and dolerite.

11. Geological Hazards like Earthquakes, Volcanoes, Tremors, Mass Movements and Landslides

Geological hazards like earthquakes, volcanoes and landslides can severely affect rock art panels. Again, these hazards are unpredictable and cannot be stopped or properly tackled by human beings. Earthquakes can alter a site by breaking down a panel or sub-ducting the region. Volcanic eruptions can destroy rock art by lava flow on the panel or burying the art when the erupted material pours inside. Mass movements and landslides uproot art sites, displace and diminish the material.

12. Land-Use Pattern

Land-use pattern is changing fast to accommodate different needs of human beings. Mining, industries, crushers, river dams, rail, roads and townships are encroaching on forests and free land at a great pace. Forest land is converted to agricultural land where shifting and poddu cultivation are practiced. Rock art sites are subjected to risks and many of them are destroyed due to frequent interference by man and machines, pollution and flooding.

13. Mineral Coating

In due course of time, pictographs are covered with leached away minerals; this is known as mineral coating. This is one type of natural protection that comes about by the deposition of minerals on top of the pictographs. The common mineral coating contains calcium carbonate, aluminium silicate and other water soluble minerals. These minerals are leached out from rocks underlying the pictographs or washed on to the surface of the pictographs. When the water evaporates, the minerals harden into a thin film which protects the pictographs.

INTEGRATED ROCK ART MANAGEMENT SYSTEM (IRAMS)

In most of the cases, rock art sites or rock shelters containing art are located far away, in abandoned places and in the interiors. Whether they are present in remote areas or near human settlements, rock art sites have been existing in natural settings since their inception. They have encountered human intervention only in the later part of their existence. In both the cases, rock art sites are in danger with respect to their sustainability. Given the thinking about focusing on the importance of archaeological records and heritage, rock art needs to be protected so that it can survive for the future.

It does not come as a surprise that a number of rock art sites lack conservation measures. Even where rock art is being preserved, protection from natural threats is inadequately addressed. Only human vandalism is taken care of while illustrating a potential management approach. Workers and researchers from different disciplines study the stability and longevity of rock panels. An interdisciplinary approach (Dorn et al. 2008) provides appropriate action, which is already being followed in many instances (Fig. 22.1). In this domain, the Integrated Rock Art Management System (IRAMS) has been

Fig. 22.1 Interdisciplinary nature of studies of conservation of rock art resources; Source: Modified from Pope et al. (2002).

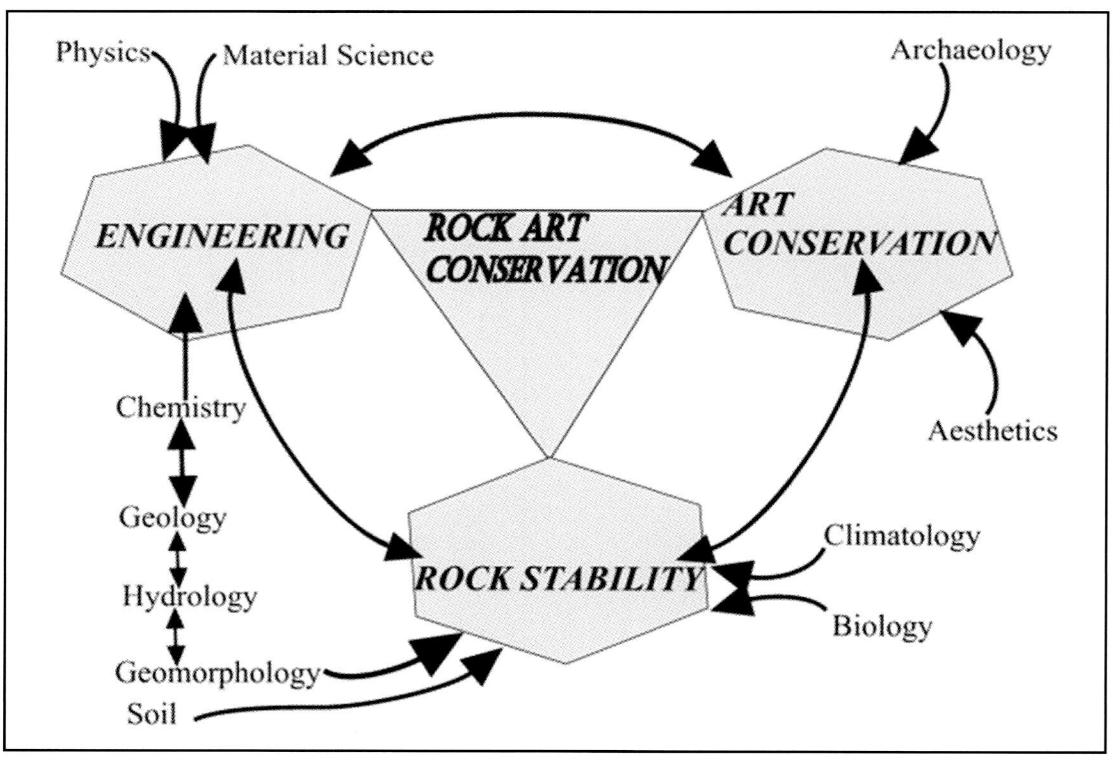

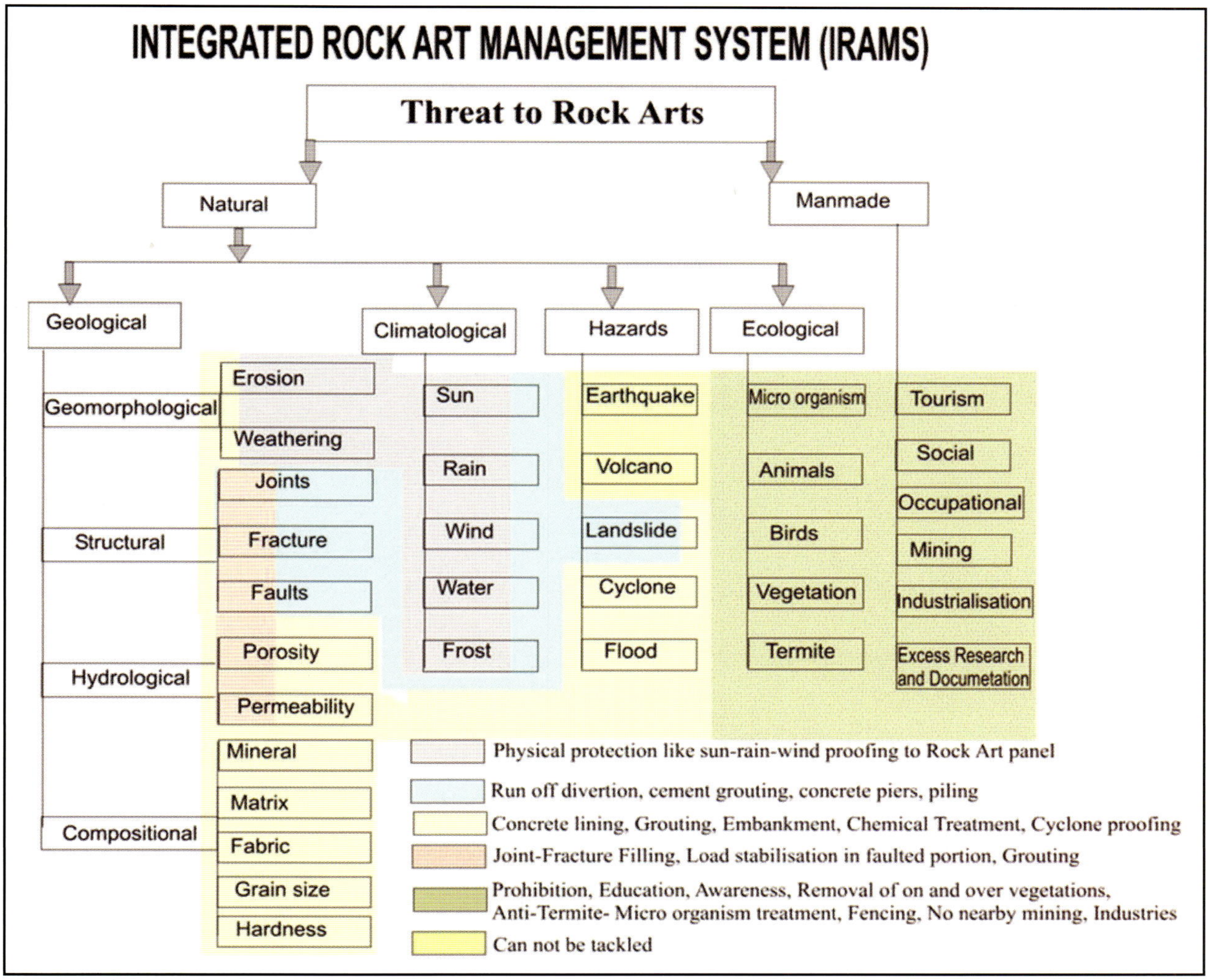

Fig. 22.2 Integrated Rock Art Management System (IRAMS) with natural and man-made threats and their management.

conceptualised with the main objective of addressing natural and man-made threats together (Fig. 22.2). IRAMS, in its scope, does not follow a large number of methods, which require many hardcore professionals, training and huge amounts of money. The polarisation of specialists with regard to academic research and training, attending conferences and publishing materials (Smith et al. 2005) is an augmented practice in rock art management. It recognises various threats which hamper the stability of the rock art and draws upon simple, suitable and strategic measures to combat the threats (Figs. 22.3-22.7). The state of vulnerability in terms of the degree of destruction can be studied with the help of the Rock Art Risk Index (RARI) which empowers IRAMS.

ROCK ART RISK INDEX (RARI)

The Rock Art Risk Index (RARI) can be defined as the pre-destruction state of rock art in which a situation of vulnerability is attained due to threatening agents. It is the degree of

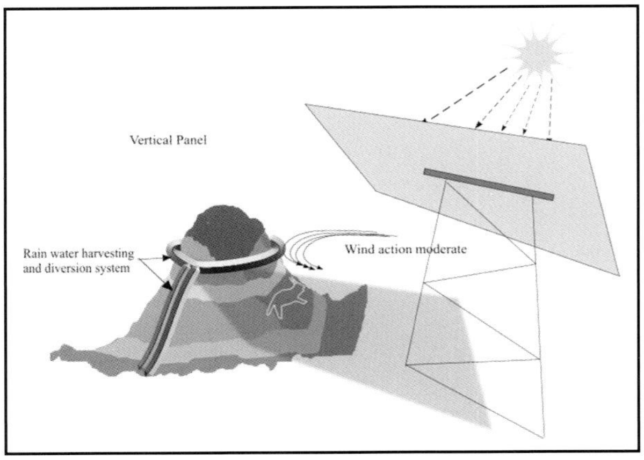

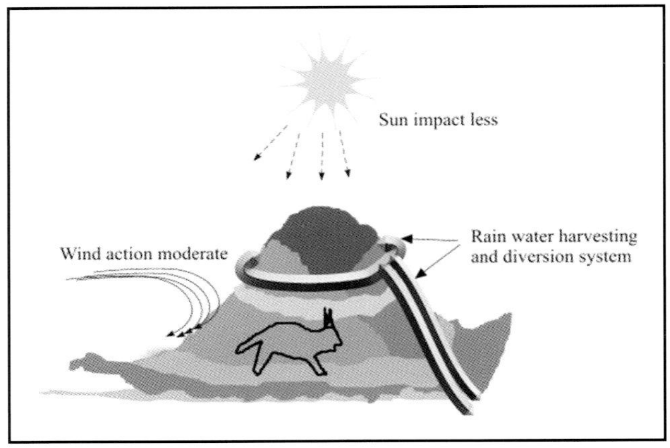

Left: **Fig. 22.3** Schematic diagram showing vertical geometry of panel with sun, rain and wind management.

Right: **Fig. 22.4** Schematic diagram showing vertical geometry of panel with position of art and impact of sun, rain and wind.

loss to the whole or a part of a rock art panel at risk resulting from natural or man-made phenomena of a given magnitude. In other words, risks can be defined as quantified and conditional probabilities that show that the consequence of vulnerability will be destructive.

RARI has three risk components:

1. Element at risk (R_E). This comprises rock art, rock shelter, rock mass, colour, culture and academic research which are under the threat of destructive agents in an area.
2. Specific risk (R_S). It is the degree of loss likely to be caused by a particular destructive force. It may be expressed as a product of destructive force F and time of vulnerability V.
3. RARI or total risk (R_T). The total risk (R_T) represents RARI. It consists of the number of art likely to be lost, damaged or destroyed at rock sites because of a particular destructive phenomenon. It is the product of a specific risk (R_S) and the element at risk (R_E).

$$\text{RARI} = R_S \times R_E = R_E \times (F.V)$$

For example:

Suppose rock art is under threat of destructive agent rainwater. Let the element of risk (R_E) be a deer (rock art).

Left: **Fig. 22.5** Schematic diagram showing vertical geometry of panel with art on the slope with impact of sun, rain and wind.

Right: **Fig. 22.6** Schematic diagram showing disposition of art at different locations with impact of natural agents.

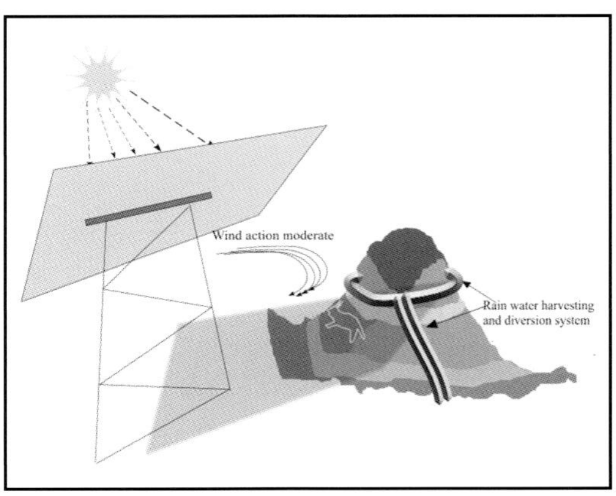

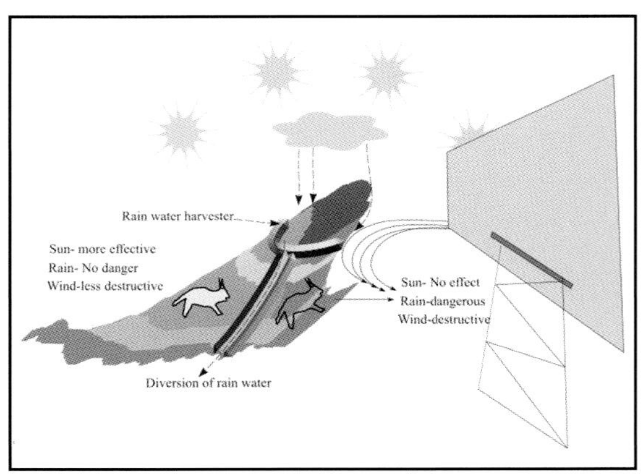

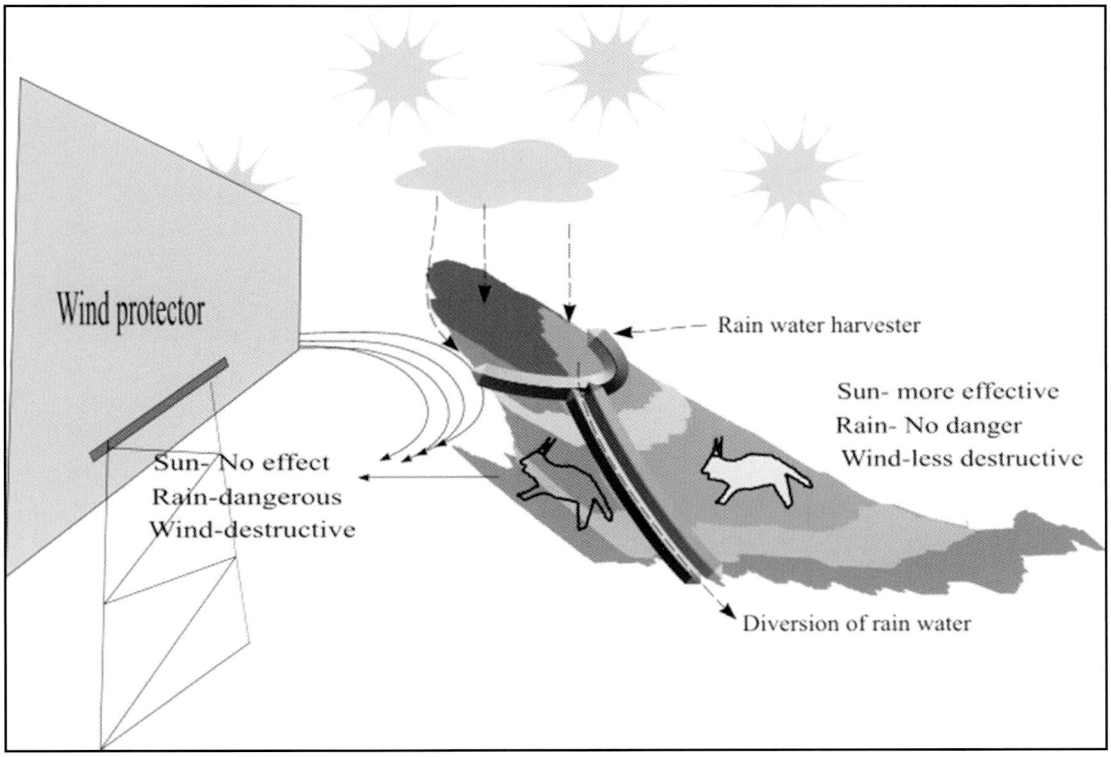

Fig. 22.7 Schematic diagram showing disposition of art at different locations with impact of natural agents.

Specific risk (R_s) will be the degree of loss (expressed in terms of whole or part in percentages) of the art in a specific period and in a range of periods.

Now let us consider deer art when subjected to rainwater action, which may damage the work of art in part or whole within a span starting from 10 years to 50 years. If we take 10 years as the point of time for damage:

R_s = destructive force X time of vulnerability = FV

= Rainwater X 10 years

where,

F = Rainwater

V = 10 years

Now RARI = Total risk (RT)

=RE X RS

= Art of deer (Rainwater X 10 years)

This equation explains that if the natural destructive agent rainwater acts upon the art of a deer for 10 years' RARI will be less.

RARI may change with respect to magnitude depending on:

1. Type of natural destructive agent (sun, rain, wind, frost, fog, snow, etc.)
2. The nature of destructive agent (scanty, heavy, torrential rain fall, cloudburst, etc.)

3. Continuity of action by the destructive agent (time to time, continuous, seasonal, throughout year)
4. Impact of the individual agent (only sun or rain or wind, etc.)
5. Impact of multiple destructive agents (sun, rain and wind, etc.)
6. Disposition of the element at risk
7. Composition of the element at risk
8. Architecture and dimension of the rock art
9. Anthropogenic interference
10. Biogenic activities

Based upon these characteristics and time of impact, a scale measuring RARI has been derived, which may be known as the Beura Scale of RARI (after the author). The scale ranges from number 1 to 5 with respective intensity ranges from less to destructive (Table 22.1).

Table 22.1 The Beura RARI scale

Magnitude	Intensity
1	Less
2	Moderate
3	High
4	Severe
5	Destruction

RARI with scale 1 indicates less damage to the rock art, which may be due to weak destructive agent/force acting on the art for less time of vulnerability. Keeping the impact of the agent same, if the time of vulnerability is increased, the scale will shift to the next higher level.

CONCLUSION

The emerging importance of rock art is because of its discovery in a wide spectrum. Wide appreciation of such art does not seek only exploration works but also demands long-term sustainability. Therefore, a strong and effective base of resource management is essential for protecting rock art. As part of the management system, the art requires documentation and recording. Emphasis should be given to establishing provincial databases. We have derived a number of ways and means to provide protection to rock art in nature's gallery. But most of the time these do not act effectively due to lack of coordination. In this paper, the author conceptualised IRAMS that speaks of a simple and coordinated way of managing the protection of rock art from natural and man-made threats. Similarly, for evaluating vulnerability which can assist in an effective application of IRAMS, he has developed a methodology termed RARI. In IRAMS, one finds that geological aspects overrule the management of natural threats. I hope that these concepts are accepted and adopted by researchers so that rock art conservation can be strengthened.

REFERENCES

Dorn, R.I. et al. (2008), 'The Rock Art Stability Index A New Strategy for Maximising the Sustainability of Rock Art', *Heritage Management* 1(1): 35-70.

Pope, G.A., T.C. Meierding and T.R. Paradise (2002), 'Geomorphology's Role in the Study of Weathering of Cultural Stone', *Geomorphology* 47: 211-25.

Smith, B.J., A.V. Turkington and J.M. Curran (2005), 'Urban Stone Decay: The Great Weathering Experiment?', *Geological Society of America Special Paper* 390: 1-9.

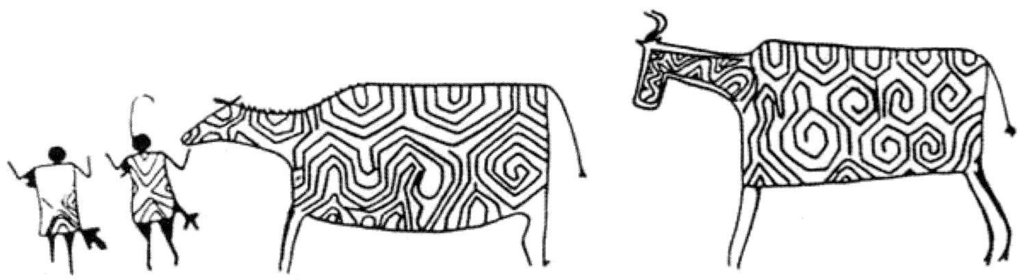

23

Study and Conservation of Rock Art Sites in Andhra Pradesh—A Botanical Perspective

M. Raghuram

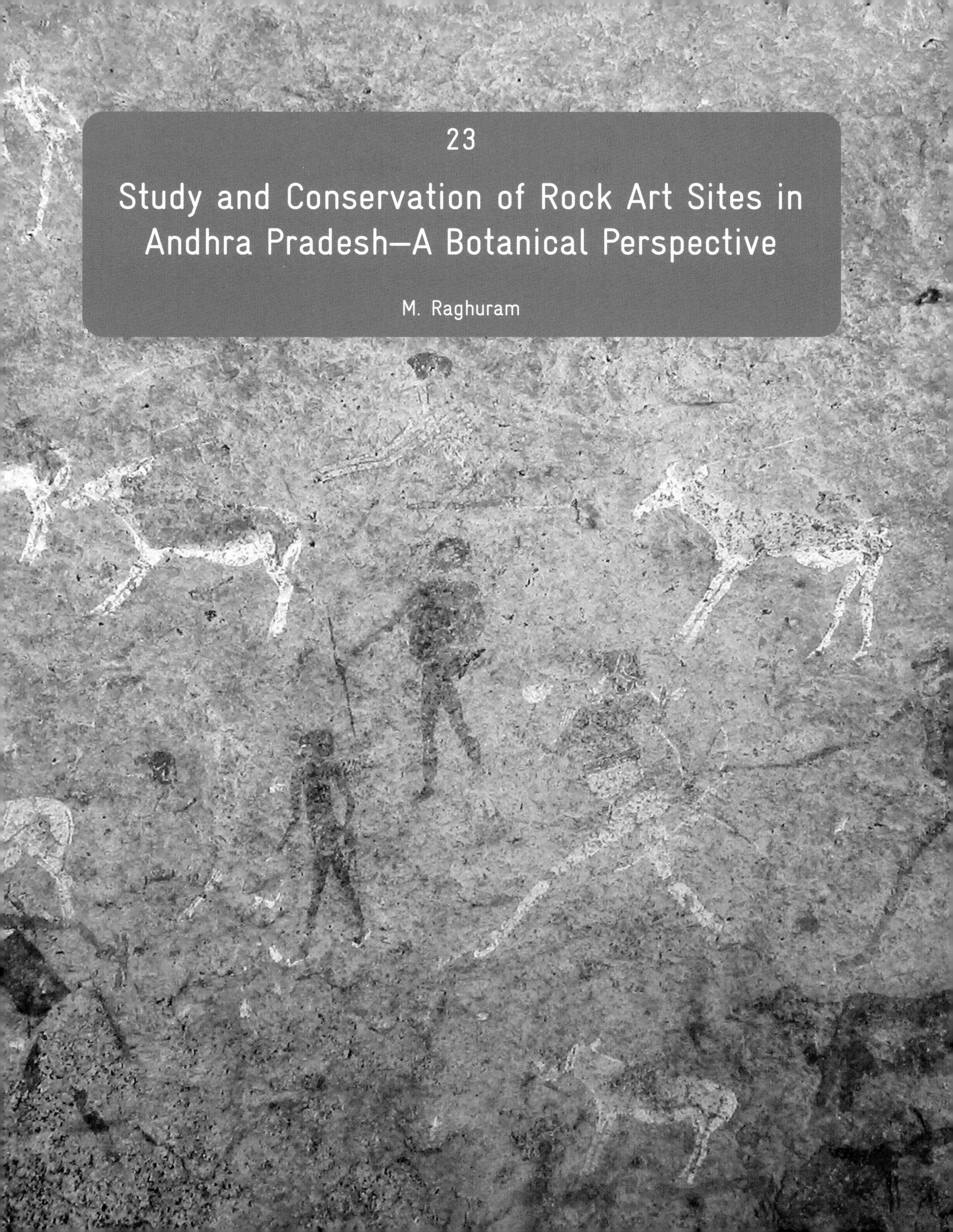

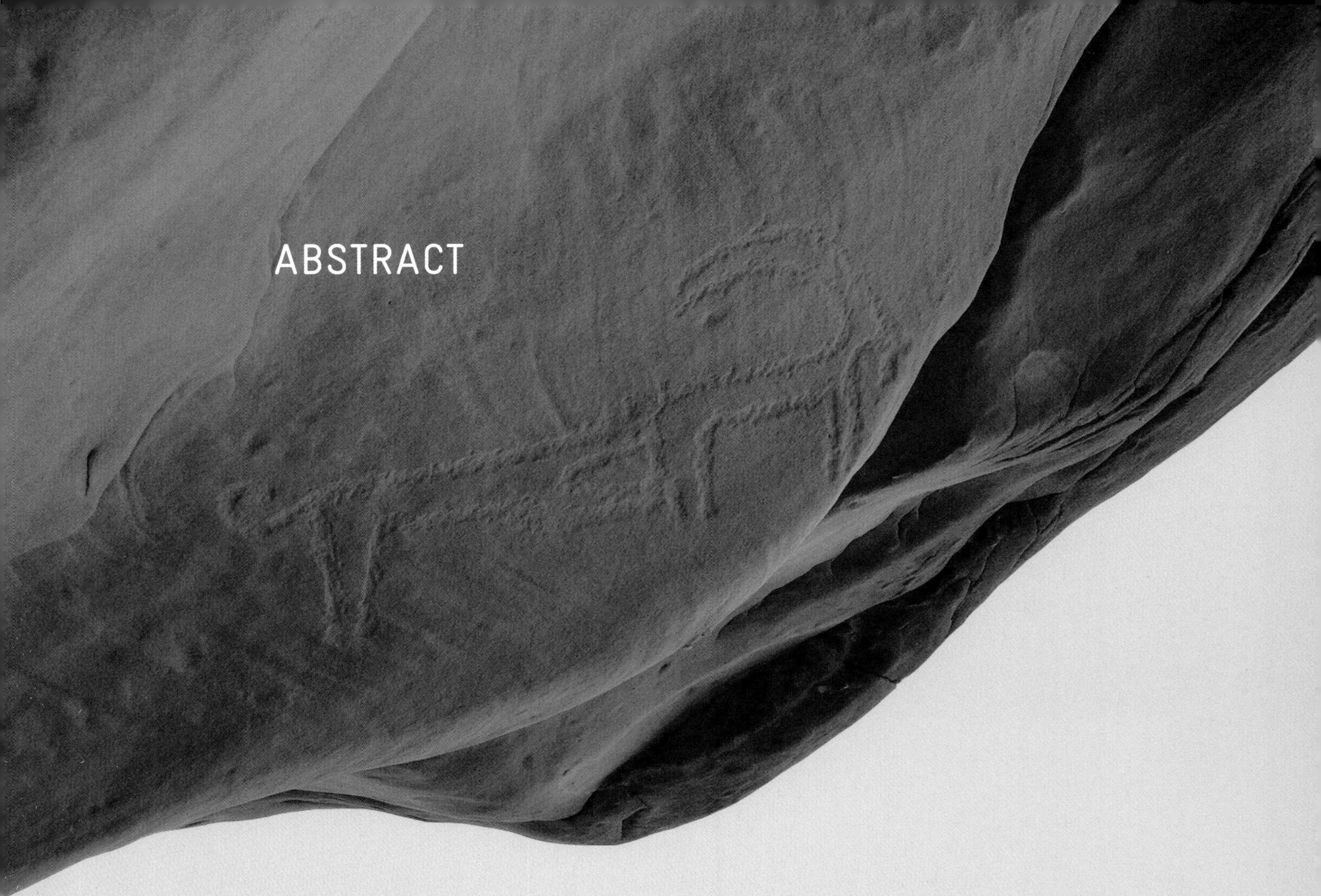

ABSTRACT

A botanical survey was conducted in 15 rock art sites distributed in six districts of Andhra Pradesh. The sites are mostly located on small hillocks, hilltops and in the middle of crop fields. Two sites at Mahaboobnagar and Medak are under severe threat due to quarrying. One site at Khammam and another at Warangal are under threat due to vandalism. The paintings found at these sites are mostly of animals such as deer, stag, antelope, hyena and fish; there are also some human figures. Dr. Ram's paper provides evidence about the material used for the drawings. The painting material was prepared by crushing flowers and fruits. To get the right thickness, the ancient man also used seeds (oil seeds—mustard, castor) along with honey. Direct evidence from paintings comes from figures of honeycombs and honeybees.

Rock art sites distributed in six districts of Andhra Pradesh were surveyed as a part of a national project on 'Documentation of the rock art sites and ethno-archeological studies', organized by the Indira Gandhi National Centre for the Arts (IGNCA), New Delhi. Most of the sites are located on small hillocks, while a few are on hilltops and some others are in the middle of crop fields. Out of the 15 sites, the Doopad Ghat is under severe threat of loss due to quarrying. One site in Khammam and another in Warangal too are under threat of loss due to vandalism. In a majority of the sites, the figures have faded due to exposure to sun and rain. The paintings are mostly of animals like deer, stag, antelope, hyena and fish; there are also some human figures. There were no figures of any plant parts. In addition to rock art, mural paintings were observed at one site—Pandavulagutta—in Warangal district. In this mural painting, a panel of figures on tree-like structures can be seen.

As a part of the botanical survey, the plants growing in and around the sites were observed and identified. Out of the 16 endangered plant species recorded in Andhra Pradesh (AP), nine were recorded near the rock art sites in Rayalaseema district. The major contribution of the present study is providing evidence of the material used for the drawings made by ancient man. In addition to the already reported material, ancient man might have used flowers and fruits along with nectar for preparing drawing material. The colourful petal and fruit walls contain natural pigments which are everlasting. This shows that flowering plants existed even before man; the land in and around the sites was suitable for plants to grow. In one of the rock art sites ancient man drew the figures of honeycomb and honey bees, but not the flowers from which the honeybees prepared the honey. Drawings of honeycombs and honeybees provide direct evidence of the presence of flowers in the vicinity of the sites, and that ancient man used them in preparing the paint.

Existence of plants is evident from the Paleozioc period (330,000,000 yrs). The first human beings set foot on the Indian subcontinent, including Peninsular India, somewhere between 200000 BCE and 40000 BCE presumably; agriculture began in the Mesolithic period (from 12000 to 6000 BCE). Prehistoric man lived in rock shelters and made several rock paintings. Rock art in India belongs to the Mesolithic to Megalithic periods (6000 BCE to 400 CE) and records from 12000 BCE are also available. Prehistoric man made drawings including those of figures of animals, skeletons and also some human figures. For these, he used natural colours including plant extracts. Though it is a fact that human life on earth is inseparable from plant life, from these rock art paintings, a direct link cannot be drawn between plants and the prehistoric man as there are no drawings of plants or any plant parts.

PREHISTORIC EVIDENCE OF RELATION BETWEEN MAN AND PLANTS

Though it is known that plants existed on earth in the Paleozoic period (330,000,000 yrs.), it was only in early 20th century that Walton demonstrated the existence of certain fossil plants and recognised them as the bryophyte species, *Hepaticites*.

The prehistoric period can roughly be calculated from 200000 BCE to about 3500–2500 BCE, when the first civilisations began to take shape. Somewhere between

200000 BCE and 40000 BCE, the first human beings set foot on the Indian subcontinent, including in Peninsular India. They mainly lived on hunting, fishing and gathering food like fruits, roots and berries. They used hand-axes, which were simple hand-held stone tools attached to thick branches from trees with ropes made from animal skin. Domestication of plants and growing of wild varieties of crops was at this time.

Since the beginning of civilisation, people have used plants as medicine. There is evidence of plants being used by ancient man for medicinal purposes. Plants have also been recovered from pyramids. Hence, looking at human life on this planet will not be complete without a look at the role of plants. There are voluminous records on the many thousands of plant species used for human functioning.

USE OF PLANTS FROM PREHISTORIC TIMES

There is evidence of the use of various plant substances for curing pain and sickness by prehistoric man in around 58000 BCE to 48000 BCE. Probably, man at this time used the plant *Ephedra*/woody horsetail as a stimulant. Around 6000 BCE, natives of southern South America actively started cultivating certain plants, including tobacco, and this practice eventually spread across all the Americas.

Mandrake and opium (source of both heroin and morphine), and marijuana were used as drugs during the late prehistoric times. Opium was farmed in the western Mediterranean region around 6000 BCE.

Opium seeds can be used in baking and its seed oil burned for cooking and lighting purposes. Its greatest use seems to have been for its psychoactive properties—pain relief. Cannabis/marijuana was widespread before 3500. BCE Cannabis was not only remarkable for its psychoactive elements, but was also used for its fiber strength (hemp). It was a primitive source of fibers for making ropes by prehistoric man.

In spite of this evidence, rock art made by ancient man depicts only pictures of animals and other figures related to man's lifestyle, but not of plants.

FINDINGS OF THE SURVEY

The survey by the author covered four districts of Telangana and three of Rayalaseema. In all, the Telangana sites, relatively poor vegetation was seen while in the sites in Rayalaseema very good vegetation was evident. In the Telangana region, the sites in Mahaboobnagar district were exposed to withering without any plants near the sites. However, fertile land with crops was seen surrounding the sites. In Pandavulagutta in Warangal district in addition to rock art, he also found one panel of mural painting near the site. The mural painting has been declared a tourist spot by the Andhra Pradesh Tourism Department. In Khammam district, the Neeladrigutta rock shelter was in the middle of a thick forest with many tall trees and shrubs around it. In Anatapuram district, the rock art shelters were exposed to withering without any thick vegetation in nearby areas. However, the rock art hill was surrounded on three sides by fertile agricultural land and on one side by a village. In Kadapa district, the rock art shelters near Chinthakunta village were covered with spiny bushes like *Prosopis sp.* and surrounded by fertile agricultural fields. The rock art shelter in Mylavaram dam was an island in the river with

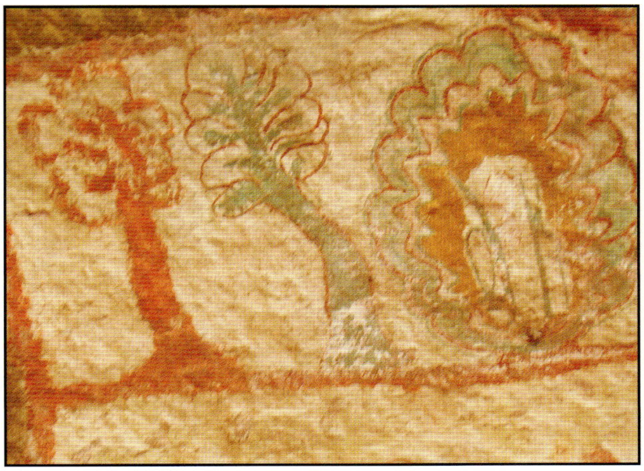

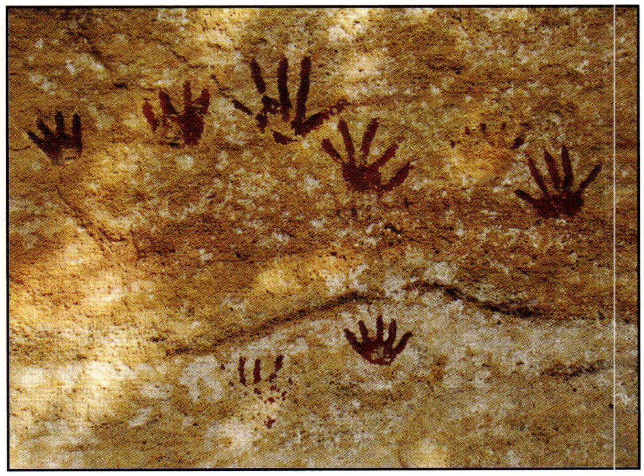

Left: **Fig. 23.1** Part of the panel in Pandavulagutta showing plant figures.

Right: **Fig. 23.3** Handprints at Neeladri Gutta.

a thick vegetation of bushy plants close to the art. In Kurnool district, Kethavaram on one side and Purcharla on the other side of a hill range had many rock art sites. At Kethavaram, the sites were covered by spiny bushes and with fertile agricultural fields nearby. One of the shelters was charred by smoke emanating from the preparation of country liquor by the local people. At Purcharla, two to three sites intermingled with agricultural fields while the remaining three were in *zyziphus* plantations.

FINDINGS AND CONCLUSIONS

i) Pandavulagutta near Warangal was the only site with mural paintings, depicting figures from the *Mahabharata*. On the same panel there were three plant figures. Green and brick red colour had been used for the paintings. The first figure appeared like a bush while the remaining two are like trees. Each tree is shown with a trunk, branches and a canopy of foliage. However, no idea about the correct species of the plant can be got from the paintings (Fig. 23.1).

Fig. 23.2 Honeycomb at Neeladrigutta in Khammam district.

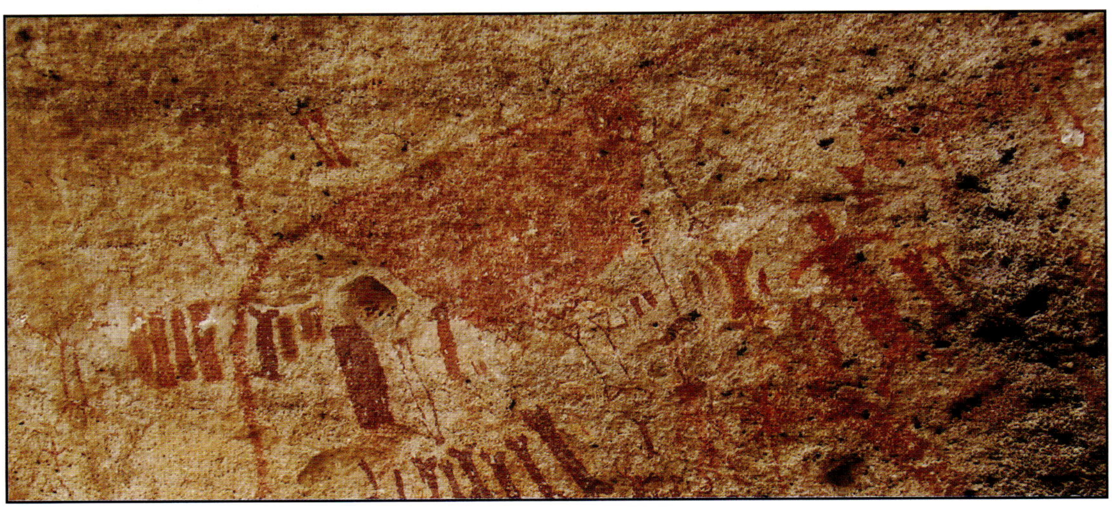

This rock art, thus, does not show any direct relationship between plants and prehistoric man.

ii) At Neeladrigutta in Khammam district, a figure of a honeycomb was observed, giving indirect evidence of the occurrence of flowering plants near the rock art shelters during prehistoric times (Fig. 23.2). Flowering plants were the sole source of nectar and honey. There are about 500 flowering plant species, both wild and cultivated, which are useful as major or minor sources of nectar and which are visited by honeybees. Prehistoric man might have used honey. Hence, it is clear that prehistoric man might have come across flowering plants in his lifetime and also used the flowers and fruits in preparing paint. Unfortunately, there is no single figure of a flower, fruit or any part of a plant. The important point of debate is why ancient man could not draw any figures related to plants even though he lived with them and used them for various purposes?

(iii) Possibly, plants were secondary sources of food after animals for prehistoric man and that is why there are no pictures of plants.

BOTANICAL PERSPECTIVE FOR THE CONSERVATION OF ROCK ART

By closely observing rock art at different sites, it became clear that pictures at most of the sites had faded due to natural weathering. Rock art at Neeladrigutta, Khammam was very good with dark colour without any weathering, as the site was totally covered by a thick canopy of forest trees. At this site, handprints had been protected from withering by the presence of tall deciduous trees very close to the art (Fig. 23.3).

As a measure of conservation of th rock art, it can be suggested that plantation of tree species with thick foliage like *Pterospermum acerarifolium Mimosops elengi, Madhuca indica, Terminalia chebula, Dalbergia latifolia, Butea monosperma, Anogeissus latifolia, Combretum sp., Muntingia calabura, Wrightia tinctoria, Tectona grandis, Gmelina arborea,* etc., in the vicinity of rock art is more beneficial. Similarly, plantation of spiny bushes like *Zyziphus sp., Prosopis julifera,* etc., nearer to the site relatively reduces vandalism and thereby gives protection to the rock art.

List of Contributors

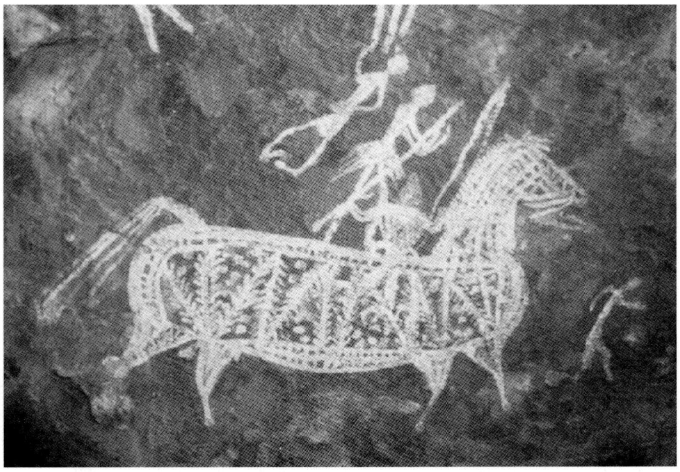

Ariela Fradkin
Centro Camuno Di Studi Preistorici
25044 Capo Di Ponte, Italy
E-mail: ccspreist@tin.it, emmanuel.anati@gmail.com

A.K. Prasad
Flat No. 695, Sector 28
Arun Vihar, NOIDA 201303 (UP)
E-mail: drakprasad@gmail.com

Bansi Lal Malla
Indira Gandhi National Centre for the Arts (IGNCA)
11, Mansingh Road
New Delhi - 110 001
E-mail: drblmalla@yahoo.com

B.R. Mani
Joint Director General
Archaeological Survey of India
Janpath, New Delhi - 110 001
E-mail: brmani@hotmail.com, adg2.asi@gmail.com

Dany Morales Valdés
Grupo Cubano de Investigaciones de Arte Rupestre (GCIAR)
Calle Amargura No. 203
entre Aguiar-y Habana
Habana Vieja, La Habana
Cuba
E-mail: itibacahubaba@yahoo.com.ar

Devananda Beura
Dept. of Geology
Utkal University
Vani Vihar, Bhubaneswar - 04 (Odisha)
E-mail: dbbaruah@rediffmail.com

Dialvys Rodríguez Hernández
Grupo Cubano de Investigaciones de Arte Rupestre (GCIAR)
Calle Amargura No. 203
entre Aguiar-y Habana
Habana Vieja, La Habana
Cuba
E-mail: itibacahubaba@yahoo.com.ar

Dwipen Bezbaruah
Department of Anthropology
Guwahati University
Jalukbari - 781 014
Guwahati, Assam
E-mail: dbbaruah@rediffmail.com

Emmanuel Anati
Centro Camuno Di Studi Preistorici
25044 Capo Di Ponte, Italy
E-mail: ccspreist@tin.it, emmanuel.anati@gmail.com

Hilario Carmenate Rodríguez
Grupo Cubano de Investigaciones de Arte Rupestre (GCIAR)
Calle Amargura No. 203
entre Aguiar-y Habana
Habana Vieja, La Habana
Cuba
E-mail: itibacahubaba@yahoo.com.ar

Hipólito Collado Giraldo
Asociación Cultural 'Colectivo Barbaón' (ACCB)
Míralrío, we 13, 3e E
10002 Cáceres
Spain
E-mail: hipolitocollado@gmail.com

José Julio García Arranz
Department of Art and Sciences
University of Extremadura, Spain
E-mail: jjturko@gmail.com

J.N. Pal
Department of Ancient History, Culture and Archaeology
University of Allahabad
Allahabad (UP)
E-mail: jnpal@hotmail.com

K. Rajan
Department of History
Pondicherry University
Puducherry - 605 014
E-mail: rajanarchy@gmail.com

M. Raghuram
Acharya Nagarjuna University
Guntur - 522 510 (India)
E-mail: mraghuram2002@yahoo.co.uk, mraghuram2002@gmail.com

N. Chandramouli
Block 1: School of Humanities and Social Sciences
Silver Jublee Campus
Pondicherry University
Puducherry - 600 014
E-mail: c.navuluri@gmail.com

Nandini Bhattacharya Sahu
Prehistory Branch
Archaeological Survey of India
Old High Court Building
Nagpur - 440 001
E-mail: Nandinibsahu@gmail.com

Patrick Paillet
Museum national d'Histoire naturelle
Département de Préhistoire
Bgtiment 140
43 rue Buffon
75005 Paris (France)
E-mail: paillet@mnhn.fr, patrick.paillet@mnhn.fr

Pindi Setiawan
Indonesian Association of Rock Art (IARA)
Sangkuriang R-2
Bandung 40135
Indonesia
E-mail: pindisp@yahoo.com

Prabash Sahu
Prehistory Branch
Archaeological Survey of India
Old High Court Building
Nagpur - 440 001
E-mail: Nandinibsahu@gmail.com

R.C. Agrawal
E-212, Sector IX
Vijay Nagar
Ghaziabad (UP)
E-mail: rcagrawal1947@gmail.com

Racso Fernández Ortega
Grupo Cubano de Investigaciones de Arte Rupestre (GCIAR)
Calle Amargura No. 203
entre Aguiar-y Habana
Habana Vieja, La Habana
Cuba
E-mail: itibacahubaba@yahoo.com.ar, racsof@sangeronimo.ohc.cu

Radha Kant Varma
Former Chairman
Allahabad Museum Society
Allahabad, Uttar Pradesh
E-mail: radhak37_kant@rediffmail.com

Ruman Banerjee
Hodgkin House, Clifton
BS8 1JG, Bristol
United Kingdom
E-mail: deccanruman@gmail.com, arxrb@bristol.ac.uk

S.C. Malik
185, Mandakini Enclave
Near Alaknanda
New Delhi
E-mail: subhash.bhashi@gmail.com

Shanker Sharma
Asst. Archaeologist
Archaeological Survey of India
Patna Circle
Patna, Bihar

Somnath Chakraverty
5/1 Suri Lane
Kolkata - 700 014
E-mail: somraja2008@gmail.com

Tashi Ldawa Thsangspa
Post Box No-185
EJMC Leh
Leh, Ladakh 194101
E-mail: ldawalay123@yahoo.co.in

Zhang Yasha
Rock Art Research Association of China
School of Ethnology & Sociology
Minzu University of China
27 Zhongguancun South Avenue
Haidian District

Beijing, 10008, China
E-mail: yqlljx@gmail.com

Zhu Lifeng
Art School
China Women's University
No.1 Yuhui East Road
Chaoyang District
Beijing, 100101 (China)
E-mail: yqlljx@gmail.com

Zulfiqar Ali Kalhoro
Pakistan Institute of Development Economics (PIDE)
Quaid-I Azam University Campus
P.O. Box 1091
Islamabad (Pakistan)
E-mail: zulfi04@hotmail.com